THE RIGHT TO LEAVE AND RETURN AND CHINESE MIGRATION LAW

The Right to Leave and Return and Chinese Migration Law

BY

GUOFU LIU

MARTINUS NIJHOFF PUBLISHERS
LEIDEN / BOSTON

A C.I.P. record for this book is available from the Library of Congress.

Printed on acid-free paper.

ISBN-13: 978-90-04-15614-2
ISBN-10: 90-04-15614-3

Koninklijke Brill NV incorporates the imprints Brill, Hotei Publishers, IDC Publishers, Martinus Nijhoff Publishers and VSP.

<http://www.brill.nl>

Printed and bound in The Netherlands.

Contents

List of Graphs

Preface

The Right to leave and return (RLR) has been affirmed as a fundamental human right in several international instruments. While being a fundamental human right, each State has the sovereign right to regulate RLR in accordance with its own laws. The regulation of RLR, however, is not only an attribute of sovereignty but an issue with important political, economic and security implications for the State. Given its significance, it is understandable and desirable that States regulate RLR. The regulation must however take account of both the interests of the State and the human rights dimension of the right. This is an issue of balance.

In the case of China, the country's communist political system has significantly affected the development of RLR and the country's approach to it. As a rule China's approach is restrictive. As part of its reform and 'opening up' policies, China has embarked on a range of reforms to liberalise RLR, but the reforms lack cohesion and focus, and remain restrictive. Given its peculiar past and complex social and economic conditions, China may have some justifications for its approach, but on balance, has more to gain from adopting a more liberal approach. The issue of RLR in China is crucial both for the future of China, and for development of RLR in the world.

China's current policy's on RLR still reflects a closed culture. A more open policy is not only consistent with international human rights norms, but also a useful infrastructure for the country's place in the global economy. Great achievements over the last 25 years and encouraging developmental trends demand acceleration of reforms to protect RLR in China. A careful and well-coordinated migration strategy with a well-defined RLR focus could enhance China's economic progress as well as its international human rights image. When designing the reform strategy, the balance of the Western experience and Chinese realities needs to be finely kept.

This book explored the Chinese regulatory regime governing RLR to determine its consistency with international standards. The book is divided into 13 chapters. It investigated RLR in international migration law and practice; analysed RLR in the context of China, and identified its driving factors; investigated the conditions and practical concerns relevant to the protection of RLR; and concluded with recommendations on how the Chinese regulatory regime governing RLR can be improved.

The aim of this book is to explore the Chinese regulatory framework governing the right to leave and return (RLR), to determine its consistency by reference to international human rights ethics. The intention of this research is not only to criticise and expose the deficiencies of RLR in China, but to investigate the possibility, necessity and solution of adequately addressing these problems.

Lists of Acronyms

Chinese institutions

BBSCA	Bureau of Border Security Check and Administration
BEEA	Bureau of Exit and Entry Administration
CCTV	China Central Television
Central Bank	The People's Bank of China
CEPA	The Closer Economic Partnership Arrangement
CNTA	Chinese National Tourism Administration
CPC	Communist Party of China
HKSAR	Hong Kong Special Administration Region
MFA	Ministry of Foreign Affairs, China
MFERT	Ministry of Foreign Economic Relations and Trade, China
MLSS	Ministry of Labour and Social Security, China
MOC	Ministry of Commerce, China
MOE	Ministry of Education, China
MOP	Ministry of Personnel, China
MPS	Ministry of Public Security, China
MSAR	Macao Special Administration Region
NPC	National People's Congress, China
SAFE	State Administration of Foreign Exchange, China
SAFEA	State Administration of Foreign Experts Affairs, China
SAIC	State Administration of Industry and Commerce, China
SBS	State Bureau of the Statistics, China
SHMO	State Council Hong Kong and Macao Affairs Office, China
SOCO	State Council for Overseas Chinese Affairs Office, China
STO	State Council Taiwan Affairs Office, China

International institutions

CPDPM	UN Sub-Commission on Prevention of Discrimination and Protection of Minorities
HRC	UN Human Rights Committee
ICHR	International Court of Human Rights
ICJ	International Court of Justice
IMF	The International Monetary Fund
IOM	The International Organization for Migration

NGO	Non-Governmental Organizations
OECD	Organization of Economic and Cooperation Development
WTO	The World Trade Organisation

Regional and other countries' institutions

AFCM	African Commission on Human and People's Rights
AMCM	Inter-American Human Rights Commission
AMCT	Inter-American Court of Human Rights
CPV	Communist Party of Vietnam
ECJ	European Court of Justice
EU	European Union
EUCM	European Human Rights Commission
EUCT	European Court of Human Rights
MLWS	Ministry of Labour, War Invalids and Social Affairs, Vietnam
OAS	The Organization of American States
SBV	State Bank of Vietnam
USCR	US Committee for Refugees

Others

1963 Ingles' Study

on RLR	*Study of Discrimination in Respect of the Right of Everyone to Leave any country, including His Own, and to Return to His Country: Special Repporteur of the Subcommission on Prevention of Discrimination and Protection of Minorities*
OAED	*Oxford Advanced Learner's English-Chinese Dictionary*
PRC	The People's Republic of China
RLR	The right to leave and return
ROC	The Republic of China
SARS	Severe Acute Respiratory Syndrome
USVISIT	USA Visitor and Immigration Status Indication Technology System

Chapter One
Introduction

1.1 Research Objectives and Significance

The aim of this book is to explore the Chinese regulatory framework governing the right to leave and return (RLR), to determine its consistency by reference to international human rights ethics. In more specific terms, the book focuses on four main objectives: (i) an investigation of RLR in international migration law; (ii) an analysis of RLR in the context of China and an identification of the factors that drive it; (iii) an investigation of the favourable conditions and practical concerns relevant to the protection of RLR in China; and (iv) identification of the policy implications for the protection of RLR in China.

Although considerable research has been devoted to human rights in the world and in China,[1] less attention has been paid to RLR in China, especially from the

[1] Ingles, Jose D., *Study of Discrimination in Respect of The Right of Everyone to Leave Any Country, Including His Own, and to Return to His Country: Special Repporteur of the CPDPM,* United Nations Publication Sales No.: 61.4. XIV. 2 New York, 1963; Freedman, Warren, *The Right to Travel: A Right or A Privilege? Work Paper of Sao Paulo Conference on the Law of the World* (Washington, the USA: the World Peace Through Law Centre, 1981); Hannum, Hurst, *The Right to Leave and Return in International Law and Practice* (Dordrecht, the Netherlands: Martinus Nijhoff Publishers, 1987); Plender, Richard, *International Migration Law*, Revised 2nd ed, (Dordrecht, the Netherlands: Martinus

perspectives of universal principles and Chinese realities.[2] The limited research about RLR in China has tended to focus on a few limited aspects of economics, social science, demography and history, such as Chinese coolie (unskilled labourer) migration and Chinese life and integration in host countries, rather than law.[3] The limited research regarding Chinese migration law has been descriptive rather than analytical.[4] Chinese researchers have thus in the past considered that

---

Nijhoff Publishers, 1988); Vasak, Karel etc. (ed.), *TheRight to Leave and Return: Papers and Recommendations of the International Colloquium Held in the Uppsala, Sweden, 19–21 June 1972*, The American Jewish Committee, Ann Arbour, the USA, 1976.

[2] Baehr, Peter R. et al. (ed.), *Human Rights: Chinese and Dutch Perspectives* (The Hague, the Netherlands: Kluwer Law International, 1996); Bradley, Catherine, *What Do We Mean by Human Rights: Freedom of Movement* (London: Franklin Watts, 2002); Cranston, Maurice, *What are Human Rights?* (New York: Taplinger Publishing Co., Inc., 1973); Edwards, R. Randle, Henkin, Louis and Nathan, Andrew J., *Human Rights in Contemporary China* (New York: Columbia University Press, 1986); Friedmann, Daniel and Barak-Erez, Daphne (ed), *Human Rights in Private Law*, (Oregon, the USA: Hart Publishing c/o, 2001); Hegarty, Angela and Leonard, Siobhan (ed.), *A Human Rights: An Agenda for the 21st Century,* (London: Cavendish Publishing Limited, 1999); Kent, Ann, *Human Rights in PRC*, Discussion Paper No. 3, 1989–90, Legislative Research Service, the Parliamentary of the Commonwealth of Australia, 1990; Ness, Peter Van, *Human Rights and Democracy in China: Four Theories on Why the World Need Care*, working paper No. 167, Peace Research Centre, Research School of Pacific Studies, Canberra, The Australian National University 1996; Wu, Yuanli et al., *Human Rights in PRC*, (Boulder, Colorado, the USA: Westview Press, 1988); and Human Rights White Papers of The Chinese Government, Reports of Human Rights in China, and IOM reports, and UN reports.

[3] Campbell, Persia Crawford, *Chinese Coolie Emigration to Countries within the British Empire China* (London: Frank Cass and Company Ltd., 1923), Etienne Dennery, *Asia's Teeming Millions: and Its Problems for the West* (Port Washington, Kennikat Press, 1931); Irick, Robert L., *Ch'ing Policy Toward the Coolie Trade 1847–1878*, Chinese Materials Centre Asian Library Series No. 18, 1982; Judith M. Brown & Rosemary Foot, *Migration: The Asian Experience*, (London: The Macmillan Press Ltd. 1994); Sun, Wangning, *Leaving China: Media, Migration, and Transnational Imagination*, (Maryland, the USA: Rowman & Littlefield Publishers, Inc., 2001), Buggy, T. P. *Chinese Immigration and the Emergence of an Australian Image of China 1848–1861* (M.A. diss., Macquarie University, 1978); Wang, Gungwu, *Don't Leave Home: Migration and The Chinese* (Singapore: Times Academic Press, 2001); Wang, Sing-wu *The Organization of Chinese Emigration 1848–1888 with Special Reference to Chinese Emigration to Australia*, Chinese Materials Centre Inc. San Francisco, 1978.

[4] Committee of Exit and Entry Administration under Chinese Association of Police, (ed), *The Collection of Papers on the Control of Exit and Entry (III) (Churujing Guanli Lunwenxuan (san))*, Interior Published within Public Security Organs (*Gongan Jiguan Neibu Faxing*) (Beijing: the Publishing House of Qunzhong, 2001); Committee of Exit and Entry Administration under Chinese Association of Police, (ed), *The Collection of Papers on the Control of Exit and Entry (II)*, (*Churujing Guanli Lunwenxuan (er)*), Interior

there are no gaps and deficiencies in the protection of RLR in China, or that any gaps and deficiencies are not serious enough to require urgent reform of relevant laws. The reason for this is that the most-used research methodology is that of vertical, rather than horizontal, comparison.[5] With vertical comparison, the main conclusions focus on achievements in the protection of RLR in China – and tend to unrealistic optimism in regard to the protection of RLR. An inclination towards vertical comparison may stem from a lack of full understanding of the protection of RLR in international migration law.

This underdeveloped research becomes particularly relevant as the importance of the "the partnership with the countries of origin" is increasingly acknowledged by receiving countries when devising their migration policies.[6] It is time to accelerate research on the current status of RLR, the issues that affect it, and possible solutions in the Chinese context. It is hoped that this book will fill the research gaps in the area of RLR and Chinese migration law by conducting a comprehensive and critical legal analysis.

This research is significant in several respects. It will help to lay the legal groundwork for reform of Chinese regulatory framework governing RLR, enhancing the effective protection of RLR in China. Establishing this legal groundwork is an essential precondition for further reform of Chinese regulatory framework governing RLR. Advancing a legislative reform strategy may turn a theoretically possible RLR into a RLR that is real in practice. The Chinese government, in pursuing policies of openness and reform, needs a more comprehensive legal framework as a reference to then support the reform and improve the effective protection of RLR.

Published within Public Security Organs (*Gongan Jiguan Neibu Faxing*), (Beijing: the Publishing House of Qunzhong, 1999); Department of Exit and Entry Administration, Beijing Public Security Bureau, *the Kit of Exit and Entry* (*Churujing Xuzhi*) (Beijing: the Publishing House of Renshi, 2000); Ministry of Public Security of the PRC, *The Textbook Control of Country Board and Administration of Exit and Entry* (*Bianfang Yu Churujing Guanli*) (Beijing: the Publishing House of the University of People's Public Security, 1999); Wong, Li, *International Immigration Law and the Practices* (*Guoji Yimin Fa Lilun Yu Shijian*) (Beijing: the Publishing House of Law, 2001); Xiang, Dang, *The Guide to the Law of Exit and Entry in China and Foreign Countries*, (*Zhongwai Churujing Falv Zhinan*) (Beijing: the Publishing House of China University of People's Public Security, 1998).

[5] See "Simplified Exit-entry Rules Seen as Vital to China", 23/11/2001, *The China Daily,* http://www.chinadaily.com.cn/en/doc/2001–11/23/content_94971.htm (accessed 12/09/2006); "China to Give Its Citizens More Freedom in Foreign Currency Purchase", *The China Daily,* 04 Sep. 2003, http://www.chinadaily.com.cn/en/doc/2003–09/04/content_261171.htm (accessed 12/09/2006) and Information office of the State Council of The People's Republic of China, "Fifty Years of Progress in China's Human Rights (June 2000)", http://www.fmprc.gov.cn/ce/celt/eng/xwdt/t125479.htm (accessed 12/09/2006).

[6] Biao, Xiang, "Emigration from China: A Sending Country Perspective", *International Migration*, vol. 41, no. 3 September 2003, 21–48 (28).

It is hoped that this research will contribute to the development of a more effective regulatory framework, by advocating a regulatory model, and by making practical recommendations to afford effective protection of RLR in China. It provides a more comprehensive series of recommendations to protect RLR in China than undertaken to date. It is also hoped this research will assist the international community to better understand RLR in China, and promote a better understanding within China of RLR as it operates internationally. The detailed discussions of the foundations of RLR in international migration law may offer the Chinese government and academics an objective basis for understanding how RLR can be legislatively implemented. No research of this kind has been previously undertaken by Chinese government or academics. This discussion also partially fills research gaps in the area in international migration law.

1.2 Research Context

The inevitable trend of globalisation cannot be divorced from orderly international migration, which is, in turn, founded on RLR. According to the International Organisation of Migration (IOM), "At the start of the 21st century, one out of every 35 persons worldwide was an international migrant. Over the last 35 years, the number of international migrants has more than doubled."[7] The late 20th century has been described as both the age of migration and the age of rights. In 1948, the *Universal Declaration of Human Rights* (UDHR) was proclaimed, followed by the *International Covenant on Civil and Political Rights* (ICCPR) in 1966, in which RLR was affirmed as a fundamental human right that entitles everyone to freely leave any country, including one's own, and to freely return to one's country. Without doubt, RLR has an important role in human rights because one of the most essential and general forms of human freedom can only be realised through it – namely that people are free to choose where to go, where to stay, and where to live.[8] From a legal perspective, current debate regarding RLR is mainly concentrated on the precise interpretation of RLR and its practical enforcement.

In 2000, 513,000 people, 0.04 percent of the Chinese population, or one out of every 2,500 Chinese people was an international migrant. Chinese international migration has increased exponentially, especially since the reforms of exit and entry administration at the end of 2001.[9] Yet Chinese international migration is a

[7] The total number of international migrants is estimated 175 millions persons in 2002, 2.9 percent of the world population, in "Facts and Figures on International Migration", *Migrations Policy Issues*, No. 2 (2003): 1.

[8] Foldesi, Tamas, "The Right to Move and Its Achilles Hell: the Right to Asylum", *Connecticut Journal of International Law* Spring (1993): 289.

[9] According to 2001–2002 Exit and Entry Data published by the Bureau of Entry and Exit Administration, China, Beijing, 2003; in 2002, 121,330,000 Chinese citizens travelled

level of migration considerably lower than the rest of the world.[10] With further integration into the world, China presents a huge potential for human resources with significant implications for international migration and for the protection of RLR.

The relatively slow pace in the development of international migration in China is mainly due to strict control policies over RLR. The strict visa policy of destination countries, such as the USA, is the main obstacle for the entrance into other countries of Chinese people. However, it is beyond the research scope of this book. With the ratification of the ICCPR by 152 countries in June 2004, concern over RLR has now passed its global peak, but it is still a problem for China. China is actually one of the few countries, such as Vietnam and North Korean worldwide that exercises restrictive policies in relation to RLR of its nationals. Nevertheless, the protection of RLR in China is no longer as hopeless as it was before 1978. The most important cause for this change of attitude is the relaxation of strict control policies over RLR in China, which began in 1978 alongside economic reforms. Reforms aimed at the simplification of exit and entry procedures began in December 2001. However, the discrepancy between RLR protection in China and the rest of the world remains significant.

The universality of RLR conditions in 21st century cannot be divorced from the experience of China's 1.3 billion people that make up 21 percent of the human population. Increasing RLR protection is desperately needed to stop restrictions that are inconsistent with international norms and which encumber effective interchange and cooperation between China and the rest of the world. The issue of RLR in China is crucial both for the future of China, and the development of RLR in the world.

---

to 240 foreign countries and areas, an increase of 11.485 percent from the same figure in 2001. 118,000 Chinese citizens were approved to permanently immigrate to other countries, 4,017,000 Chinese were approved to go abroad firstly. In 2002, 112,263,000 aliens entered China from 239 countries and areas, an increase of 10.49 percent from the same figure in 2001.

[10] According to *International Migration*, October 2002, Department of Economic and Social Affairs, Population Division, the United Nations, different countries and regions migration stock rates have been calculated by the author as following: Egypt (0.29 percent), India (0.62 percent), Indonesia (0.19 percent), Romania (1.4.19 percent), Russian Federation (9.11 percent), Hungary (2.97 percent), Cuba (0.73 percent), Brazil (0.32 percent), Japan (1.27 percent), Republic of Korea (1.27 percent), Singapore (33.65 percent), United Kingdom (6.78 percent), France (10.59 percent), the USA (12.35 percent), Australia (21.4.58 percent) and New Zealand (22.50 percent). Migration stock rate in China is just a little higher than that in Vietnam (0.028 percent). 0.04 percent is also significantly lower than the average rate in more developed regions, less developed regions and least developed countries, which are 8.739 percent, 1.452 percent and 1.566 percent correspondingly.

RLR theory is the cornerstone of Chinese migration law. It forms the basis of entry and exit control, passport administration, and other key mechanisms or systems in Chinese migration law. Chinese migration law is the central safeguard and reflection of RLR in China. Based on the above considerations, accelerating Chinese migration law reform may improve the protection of RLR in China.

1.3 Research Scope, Methodology and Sources

Research scope

The Chinese regulatory framework governing RLR includes Chinese migration law (*Zhongguo Yimin Fa*), the Constitution, administrative law, and administrative procedural law and foreign exchange law. The Chinese government has not yet promulgated statutes that use the terms 'migration', 'immigration' or 'emigration'. The contents of migration laws are contained in laws governing exit and entry. Chinese migration law here means Chinese existing laws governing exit and entry, which is also called Chinese exit and entry administration law (*Zhongguo Churujing Guanli Fa*).

Chinese migration law is confined to migration laws on the Mainland of the People's Republic of China (PRC). The regulations of Hong Kong Special Administrative Region (HKSAR), Macao Special Administrative Region (MSAR) and Taiwan, concerning the control over Chinese citizens including residents in Hong Kong, Macao or Taiwan travelling between those regions and the Mainland, will not be included in Chinese migration law. This is due to the particular administrative status of special administrative regions, as in the cases of Hong Kong and Macao, or as an independent region, in the case of Taiwan. In view of the aim of endeavouring to provide some legal reform recommendations based on RLR, apart from migration laws, other pertinent regulations including constitution and administrative law will be scrutinised from the perspective of RLR.

Given the explicit distinctions between RLR and the right to freedom of movement within the territory, the latter will not be discussed in this study. RLR for public affairs or official duties constitutes one part of RLR. Unless noted otherwise, RLR in China in this book merely implies RLR for private affairs in China. If there are statistical contradictions between international organisations and the Chinese authorities regarding the same fact, this research will favour the former. As a consequence of the lack of freedom of information legislation, or an effective monitoring system in China, Chinese data is less reliable than that from international organisations.

Research methodology

The multi-disciplinary nature of this book has required adopting a number of approaches for evaluating the Chinese regulatory framework governing RLR, including an analysis of migration law, of international law, of substantive and procedural administrative law, and of public policy and economics. The overall approach is based on traditional legal methods, such as the analysis of the legal provisions, combined with insights from other disciplines including a comparative methodology, historical methodology and critical theory. The overall approach for this study allows a suitable method to be applied to a specific area of the analysis where that technique is the most relevant. Each research strategy has its limitations and no single strategy is adequate for the complete analysis undertaken. It is only by adopting a multi-disciplinary approach that the constraints of individual disciplines are overcome.

Reference sources

The reference sources used for this book include primary legal sources, policies and formal reports; as well as secondary sources such as texts, journal articles, research theses, news reports and governmental speeches. Data, ministerial provisions and reports about exit and entry and RLR in China, are not totally open to the public, as they can be in Western countries, due to the political sensitivity of RLR and the lack of freedom of information legislation in China. Textbooks and academic papers regarding RLR and exit and entry are only published within public security departments. Because it is so difficult to access to Chinese materials from Australia, I returned to Beijing in August 2003 and May 2004 to collect materials. To better understand Chinese statutes, besides the English and Chinese title of Chinese statutes, I also give the promulgation bodies, promulgation date and effective date in the List of Chinese Statutes.

Three more points must be noted. Firstly, no Chinese legal cases are quoted to support the book because China has a civil law system. Earlier higher Courts' verdicts are not legal sources for the purpose of making later determinations by the lower Courts. Secondly, I have had to personally translate some materials from Chinese into English because only some Chinese texts have been officially translated into English. Thirdly, the changing nature of existing Chinese laws governing exit from and entry into China requires updated materials to be included in the book. Limited by the fact that some provisions are not open to the public, the analyses of the updated provisions are mainly based on official news and speeches, usually found on the Chinese official websites.

Governmental dynamics continue to operate and many aspects of RLR remain in transition. Thus, it is necessary to establish a cut-off date after which no further legal information would be sought or included. The currency of this research is limited to January 1st, 2005.

1.4 Organisation of the Book

The first three chapters of this book will explore RLR in international migration law. The remaining chapters identify factors driving RLR in China, analyse the historical development, present status and issues of RLR in China, then argue as to the favourable conditions and practical concerns for protection of RLR, to then identify the policy implications for its protection.

The introductory chapter briefly sets out the research objectives, context and scope, organisation of the book, research methodology, sources and research significance. It gives a general picture of this book. In developing the analytical rationale, it is necessary to decide at the outset what the foundations of RLR are, and what States' responsibility for the protection of RLR might entail. In other words, it is necessary to benchmark the measurement of RLR in China. Chapter two is concerned with identifying the foundations of RLR from three angles: philosophy, history, globalisation and international migration.

Critical research of RLR in China and Chinese migration law requires knowledge of the rules and practice in international migration law. Chapter three summaries and describes RLR in international migration law. It aims to provide an objective criterion to which China could make reference and comparison from five perspectives, namely general considerations on RLR, State acceptance of RLR, permissible limits on RLR, the right to leave the country, and the right to return to one's own country.

Chapter four identifies the factors that drive RLR in China from the perspectives of the politics, economics, culture and law. The political and legal factors are the foremost and most direct factors affecting RLR in China. The analysis of above factors argues that the development of RLR in China and the emergence of the issues of RLR, explored from chapters five to eleven, is a corollary of these driving factors. In order to better appreciate the issues associated with RLR in China, it is necessary to trace the historical development of the Chinese regulatory framework governing RLR. A brief historical sketch starting from the Qing dynasty, yet focused on the period from 1979 to 2001, is included in Chapter five. Chapter five also explores planned reform strategies and measures of exit and entry administration from 2001 to 2005, to predict which issues of RLR in China could be solved with their implementation, what situation might result if no more reform measures were taken, and what influences the reform strategies and measures have had.

Do serious issues of RLR exist in China? If so, are they serious enough to demand the close attention of the Chinese government and foreign States? Building on reference to RLR in international migration law and selected States in chapters three, chapters six to eleven attempt to answer these questions based on an analysis of the Chinese regulatory framework governing RLR. These chapters form the centre of the book – that many serious issues demand prompt resolution in order to protect RLR in China.

Chapter six argues that there are bureaucratic barriers to RLR posed by the formalities of passport application and passport administration. Chapter seven argues that there are many unacceptable prohibitions and limits on the right to leave in China. Chapter eight discusses regulatory measures that limit the right to return of Chinese citizens. Chapter nine questions and critiques the control over the travel of Mainland Chinese to and from the HKSAR, MSAR and Taiwan. In particular, to question the principles of processing applications, which are questions overlooked by past researchers and officials, as a consequence to their being too accustomed to them. Chapter ten considers the unique institution of the emigration intermediary agencies. Chinese emigration intermediary agency laws are an indispensable part of the regulatory framework governing RLR. An advanced agency can help realise RLR. Chapter eleven argues that Chinese exit and entry administrative system faces serious issues.

It is worth noting that many of the limits on RLR identified in chapters from six to eleven have been ignored or have received little attention in China because research into RLR in China is a politically sensitive topic, which brings big risks and little economic benefit to researchers. Further, research into the exit and entry administration in China is underdeveloped, which has the effect of weakening RLR. Most of the arguments regarding the limits on RLR in China presented in this book have not been previously raised in the academic literature.

Chapter twelve investigates why it is necessary and feasible to protect RLR, and explodes the myths which justify opposing protection of RLR in China. Chapter thirteen, by a series of recommendations, seeks to find a possible solution to the issues addressed from chapters six to twelve.

Chapter Two

Foundations of the Right to Leave and Return (RLR)

INTRODUCTION

Although RLR has been affirmed as a fundamental human right in the UDHR, the ICCPR and other international and regional conventions, violations of RLR are common. By its very nature, RLR has implications for neighbouring States; violations of RLR may therefore have important implications for the security and order of neighbouring States. The issue of RLR thus easily transcends the borders of the State of origin.

It is therefore necessary to analyse both China-related factors and international-related factors when discussing RLR in China. An analysis from an international perspective provides the international criteria and a point of reference for China when evaluating the actual situation and issues of the existing Chinese law governing exit and entry. It also provides experiences to consider when designing any reform plan to deal with RLR in China.

To appreciate RLR and its special role as a fundamental national and international human right and to appreciate the particular factors that drive it in China, one must first understand the foundations of RLR. This Chapter seeks to explore the foundations of RLR from the three aspects of philosophy, history, globalisation and international migration.

2.1 Philosophical Foundations

All legal theories must contain elements of philosophy.[1] The legal theory of RLR is no exception. The nature of RLR cannot be understood effectively without understanding the nature of migration. The analysis of the nature of RLR to follow focuses on natural rights rooted in natural law, which have evolved into positive rights. This section ends by discussing the consequences of violating RLR and justifications of the limits on RLR.

2.1.1 *The definition of RLR*

In basic terms, RLR is the right of a person to be able to freely leave and return to a nation-State. In fact, RLR has been integrated into international instruments. Before the ICCPR came into force, RLR was most clearly proclaimed in the UDHR. Article 13 (2) of the UDHR provides that "Everyone has the right to leave any country, including his own, and to return to his country." RLR is most clearly contained in the ICCPR provisions on the right to freedom of movement. This is the most comprehensive and well-established UN treaty on civil and political rights, and has yielded the lion's share of UN jurisprudence in this area. The ICCPR also provides for applicable limits on RLR that are not stated in the UDHR. Article 12 (2) (3) (4) of the ICCPR state that:

> (2) Everyone shall be free to leave any country, including his own.
> (3) The above-mentioned rights shall not be subject to any restrictions except those which are provided by law, are necessary to protect national security, public order (*ordre public*), public health or morals or the rights and freedoms of others, and are consistent with the other recognized in the present Covenant.
> (4) No one shall be arbitrarily deprived of the right to enter his own country.

Article 5 (d) of the *International Convention on the Elimination of All Forms of Racial Discrimination* 1965 (CERD) stresses that States parties are duty-bound to prohibit and eliminate racial discrimination in all its forms and to guarantee the rights of everyone without distinction as to race, colour, or national or ethic origin, to equality before the law, notably in the enjoyment of RLR.

---

[1] Friedmann thought "all systematic thinking about legal theory is linked at one end with philosophy and, at the other end, with political theory." See Friedmann, W., *Legal Theory* (London: Law Publishers, 1944), 3.

Jose Ingles,[2] Hurst Hannum,[3] Richard Plender[4] and Warren Freedman[5] regarded the above-mentioned provisions as a statement of RLR. Later attempts of the international community to codify RLR have been unsuccessful. While *Draft Principles on Freedom and Non-Discrimination in Respect of the Rights of Everyone to Leave Any Country, Including His Own, and to Return to His Country* 1963 (1963 UN Draft Principles on RLR), *Declaration on the Right to Leave and the Right to Return* 1972 (1972 Uppsala Declaration on RLR) and *Strasbourg Declaration on the Right to Leave and Return* 1986 (1986 Strasbourg Declaration on RLR) have been accepted as the most known specific international instruments in this area, these regulations have not developed into a unified codification of RLR. The following statement regarding RLR, from Article 1 of the 1986 Strasbourg Declaration on RLR, must be borne in mind.

> Everyone has the right to leave any country, including one's own, temporarily or permanently, and to enter one's own country, without distinction as to race, colour, sex, language, religion, political or other opinion, national or social origin, property, birth, marriage, age (except for unemancipated minors independently of their parents), or other status.

With the development of evolving jurisprudence of RLR, RLR may be defined as the right of the person to leave any country and return to one's country without the discrimination and according to one's own will.

RLR can be variously classified by different criteria. According to general purpose, RLR can be classified as the right to leave and right to return. In relation to the right to leave, RLR can also be classified as the right to seek asylum, the right not to be expelled, the right to travel abroad, the right to leave to study, the right to leave to unite with family members and the right to leave to do business. The right to return can be translated into the right to be admitted to one's own country. Based on the general purpose and the subject RLR may be classified into the right of a national to leave one's country, the right of a national to return to

---

[2] Ingles, Jose D, *Study of Discrimination in Respect of the Right of Everyone to Leave any country, Including His Own, and to Return to His Country: Special Repporteur of the Sub-commission on Prevention of Discrimination and Protection of Minorities,* United Nations Publication Sales No.: 64. XIV. 2, New York, 1963, 9–12.

[3] Hannum, Hurst, *The RLR in International Law and Practice* (Dordrecht, the Netherlands: Martinus Nijhoff Publishers, 1987), 20.

[4] Plender, Richard, *International Migration Law*, Revised. 2nd ed. (Dordrecht, the Netherlands: Martinus Nijhoff Publishers, 1988), 133 and 96.

[5] Freedman, Warren, *The Right to Travel: A Right or A Privilege? Work Paper of Sao Paulo Conference on the Law of the World*, Washington, the USA: the World Peace Through Law Centre, 1981, 1.

one's country and the right of a foreigner (including a stateless person) to leave the country. Pursuant to the period of leaving and returning, RLR can be classified into RLR permanently and RLR temporarily.

2.1.2 *The nature of the migration*

The basis of migration is found in the nature of humanity. The focus of migration has gone from seeking a better natural environment in ancient times, into the pursuit of better economic, social, cultural and political environments in modern times. John Hosack contended in 1882 that, "the enterprising nature of man and his migratory habits would lead him frequently to wander beyond the limits of birthplace."[6] A similar view was expressed by the Organisation of Economic and Cooperation Development (OECD) in 1990, that:

> Man is naturally mobile. In every epoch, in every part of the world and in every civilization, there has been migration. Migration must not therefore be regarded as abnormal phenomenon disturbing the natural order of things. The migrants are no exception because migration is a normal part of people's individual and collective lives. This is an essential truth that is little appreciated nowadays and of which we should all become more fully aware.[7]

The United Nations (UN) declared in 2002, that "a fundamental characteristic of people is their movement from place to place."[8]

RLR is originally derived from people's migratory nature. As with all living beings on earth, human's respond when they face an unbeneficial environment is to escape or quickly move. All people strive for longevity and better living conditions. One of the most important means to realise this basic purpose is to move from an unbeneficial environment to a beneficial one. All detailed causes, such as war, political pressure, employment, education and family union for migration stem from this basic need or purpose.

By nature each human person evaluates the costs and benefits of 'escaping' one environment for another. Different conditions and environments produce different demands and perceptions of escape. In 'pure' theory, it is unnecessary for the government or community to affect or intervene in a person's decision to migrate. Migration is wholly natural phenomenon and needs to be fully recognised

---

[6] Hosack, John, *on the Rise and Growth of the Law of Nations, as Established. by General Usage and by Treaties, From the Earliest Time to the Treaty of Utrecht* (Covent Garden, the UK: Jas. Wade, 1882), 1.

[7] Laroque, Pierre, *The Future of Migration*, the OECD, 1990, 27.

[8] Population Division Department of Economic and Social Affairs, United Nations Secretariat, *International Migration Report 2002*, ST/ESA/SER.A/220, the United Nations, New York, 2002, 62 pages, 1.

as such – the human urge to migrate, where it exists, can be neither ignored nor oppressed. It is my own belief that humans will always have the orientation of migration, when a need presents itself, unless they are psychologically or physically incapable.

Human instinct, however, does not demand that migration should be allowed unconditionally or uncontrolled – people must live together peaceably to pursue their largest interests in the face of sustained challenges from an imperfect world. Peaceably cohabitation requires that migrants must follow rules of migration designed by the State on the basis of sovereignty.

2.1.3 *RLR is a natural right rooted in natural law*

RLR has evolved from a natural right to a positive right. The notable legal philosopher Maurice Cranston asserted that RLR was the first and most fundamental of human rights,[9] because it is from human nature or instinct and is the basis of other human rights. Depriving people of RLR is to oppress human nature or instinct and inhibit human development. Hurst Hannum observed that RLR gave meaning to other fundamental rights of speech, expression and communications.[10] Warren Freedman summarized that the right to travel as a right as solemn and imperative as the right to breathe. It is indivisible from such other human rights as justice, equality, liberty and peace.[11]

The ancient Greeks most commonly contrasted their freedom to being bound or tied, and being, from this cause, unable to move.[12] The freedom of human action based on the will and activity of the individual is the starting point of Samuel Pufendorf's natural law theory.[13] Samuel Pufendorf's natural law obliges and entitles man to protect one's life, body, migration and all that belongs to him or her to

---

[9] Cranston, Maurice, *What are Human Rights?* (New York: Taplinger Publishing Co., Inc., 1973), 31.

[10] Hannum, Hurst, *The Right to Leave and Return in international Law and Practice* (Dordrecht, the Netherlands: Martinus Nijhoff Publishers, 1987), 4.

[11] Freedman, Warren, *The Right to Travel: A Right or A Privilege?* Work Paper of Sao Paulo Conference on the Law of the World (Washington, the USA: the World Peace Through Law Centre, 1981), 1; See also Bradley, Catherine, *What Do We Mean by Human Rights: Freedom of Movement* (London: Franklin Watts, 2002), 7. Bradley though that RLR was an important human right. Restricting people's ability to move around was a loss of freedom.

[12] Pohlenz, Max, *Freed.om in Greek Life and Thought* (Reidel: Dordecht, 1966), 181.

[13] Pufenddorf, Samuel, ed., *Of the Law of Nature and Nations* (Oxford: C. H. and W. A. Oldfather, 1934), 1, 1, 8; The concept of natural law was firstly elabourated by Cicero, the foremost scholar of the Stoics of the Hellenistic period, who contended that "there is true law, right cause, in accordance with nature; it is unalterable and eternal."

the utmost within his or her power (self-preservation). Thomas Aquinas emphasised self-migration in the theory of natural law – that:

> Man is said to be made to God's image, in so far as the image implies an intelligent being endowed with free-will and self-migration: now that we have treated of the exemplar, i.e., God, and of those things which come forth from the power of God in accordance with his will; it remains for us to treat of his image, i.e., man inasmuch as he too is the principle of his actions, as having free-will and control of his actions.[14]

To, John Stuart Mill, rights are "grounded on the permanent interests of a man as a progressive being."[15] John Locke meticulously explored the motives for the formation of the social contract to protect individual liberty.[16] Rousseau made the surrender of all natural rights of the individual to the State dependent on the fulfilment of two conditions: a political one and a social one, to fulfil the two conditions, the individual will may and must be made powerless as against the will of the State.[17] Immanuel Kant transformed the social contract, which Rousseau regards as an ideal to be realised in history, into a transcendental idea; that is to say, into a rational principle for the judgment of all compulsions. In Kant's theory nothing is left but the postulate that the State ought to realise the idea of right. He envisaged that freedom of thought, feeling and migration was the one sole, original, inborn right, belonging to every man by virtue of his humanity.[18] As Margaret Ng commented, the concept of rights was quite clear in classical liberalism, and its strength lay in that clarity and in its nature. These rights may not be all that is needed to bring about an ideal society, but they are fundamental, axiomatic and inviolate.[19]

Emmer de Vattel wrote, "every man has a right to quit his country, in order to settle in any other, when by that step he does not expose the welfare of his

---

[14] Aquinas, Thomas, *Summa Theologiae*, Prologue, Benzinger 1947, 1–2.

[15] Mill, John Stuart, "On Liberty", in Warnack, May, editor, *Mill, John Stuart, Utilitarianism, "On Liberty," Essay on Bentham* (London: Fontana Press, 1962), 17th Impression, 1985, 138.

[16] Neumann, Franz, *The Rule of Law: Political Theory and the Legal System in Modern Society* (Warwickshire, the UK: Berg Publishers Ltd, 1986), 117 and 118. Locke used the notion of the social contract to demonstrate the transfer of all natural rights to authority, but on the contrary, to justify government by majority and to show that governments hold their power in trust, with the duty to preserve the individual rights whose protection the individuals have entrusted to them. See Friedmann, W., *Legal Theory* (London: Law Publishers, 1944), 123.

[17] Rousseau, Jean-Jacques, *The Social Contract*, Translated and introduced by Cranston, Maurice (Harmondsworth, Middlesex, England: Penguin Books Ltd., 1968), 33.

[18] Quoted in Neumann, Franz, *The Rule of Law: Political Theory and the Legal System in Modern Society* (Warwickshire, the UK: Berg Publishers Ltd, 1986), 144.

[19] Ng, Margaret, "Are rights Culture-bound?" in Davis, Michael C. editor,, *Human Rights and Chinese Values: Legal, Philosophical, and Political Perspectives* (New York: Oxford University Press, 1995), 60.

country."[20] William Blackstone stated it as the right "to go out of the realm for whatever cause he pleaseth, without obtaining the King's leave, providing he is under no injunction of staying home."[21]

The feature of RLR as a natural right derived from nature law reveals the moral aspect of RLR. Legal positivists mainly claim that law and morality are strictly separable. They assert that although legality and morality are of course combinable, they are likewise disjoinable.[22] The theory of legal positivism is usually taken to be analytical, descriptive and explanatory. The point of legal positivism, on this view, is to provide an accurate account of law as it actually is, rather than, as it ought to be.[23] By the very inclination of their argument, legal positivists opposed RLR as a natural right.

John Austin asserted, "There are no laws merely creating rights. There are laws, it is true, which merely create duties: duties not correlating with correlating rights, and which, therefore may be styled absolute."[24] Jeremy Bentham believed that the State existed for the greatest good of the greatest number. Bentham insisted that from real laws came real rights, but from imaginary laws, from laws of nature came imaginary rights; that natural right was simple nonsense.[25] He also believed that talking about natural rights was mischievous. Governments issuing declarations of the rights of man were merely making rhetorical utterances costing them nothing, instead of getting on with the real work of reform. Certain critics of natural rights, such as David Hume and Edmund Burke, shared his attitude. Both of them were conservatives who disliked talking about the rights of man because it inflamed the common people to revolutionary action. It led men to think they were entitled to have things, which they could not possibly have. In the words of Burke, the rights of man were mere "abstractions": the rights of Englishmen were realities – a "positive recorded hereditary title to all that can be dear to the

---

[20] Emmer De Vattel, *The Law of Nations or Principles of the Law of Nature Applied to the Conduct and Affairs of Nations and Sovereigns*, bk. 1, Ch. 19, para. 220.

[21] William Blackstone, *Commentaries on the Laws of England I*, bk. 1, ch. 1, 2, ch. 7.

[22] Kramer, Matthew H., *In Defence of Legal Positivism: Law without Trimmings* (New York: Oxford University Press, 1999), 1.

[23] Campbell, Tom, "The Point of Legal Positivism", in Campbell, Tom D., editor, *The International Library of Essays in Law and Legal Theory Second Series: Legal Positivism* (Aldershot Hants England: Dartmouth Publishing Company Ltd., Brookfield Vermont the USA: Ashgate Publishing Limited 1999), 323.

[24] Austin, John, "A Positivist Conception of Law", Feinberg, Joel and Gross, Hyman, editor, *Philosophy of Law*, 3rd, (Belmont, the USA: Wadsworth Publishing Company, 1986), 33.

[25] Quoted in Cranston, Maurice, "The Political and Philosophical Aspects of the Right to Leave and Return", Vasak, Karel and Liskofsky, Sidney, editor, *the Right to Leave and Return: Papers and Recommendations of the International Colloquium Held in Uppsala, Sweden, 19–21 June 1972* (Arbour, the USA: The American Jewish Committee, 1976).

man and citizen."[26] Natural law from Grotius to Kant is a scientific foundation for revolution.[27]

The question becomes, what is wrong with common people thinking of rights progress and revolution? The *Bill of Rights* enacted by the English Parliament after the Glorious Revolution in 1689 raised the curtain of capitalist revolution.[28] Another the *Bill of Rights* which was adopted by a representative convention in Virginia, the United States of America (USA) in 1776, proclaimed "all men are by nature equally free and independent, and have certain inherent rights."[29] Similar words recur in the *Declaration of Independence* in 1776 and the *United States Constitution 1787*. Following the English and USA models closely, the French National Assembly adopted the *Declaration of the Rights of Man and Citizen* after the great revolution in 1789. It can be argued that the above revolutions exerted a plenarily positive influence on civilised society.

Conversely, Germany did not follow English and American models. The later legal theory of national socialist Germany appears to have concentrated on the justification of absolute State supremacy and racial conception of law. In order to attain this end, it was necessary to abolish all systems of checks and balances in all spheres. The result was absolute obedience to the positive law imposed by the State, tempered by an expression of respects for the idea of right or natural law.[30] Germany under Hitler promulgated numerous laws on the basis of Neo-Hegelian theories and Duguit positive legal theory. Unfortunately, most Westerners, including millions of deluded Germans, accepted the belief, and therefore required obedience. The consequence, it may be argued, was that it contributed to German provocation of two World Wars which wrought such havoc on the rights of millions during the course of those conflicts over a period of 30 years.[31]

Another example can be found in communist regimes that accepted Marxist-influenced legal theory. In contrast to a natural rights view, in which law is seen as a constraint on the power of the State, law in the Union of Soviet Socialist

[26] Quoted in Cranston, Maurice, "The Political and Philosophical Aspects of the Right to Leave and to Return", Vasak, Karel and Liskofsky, Sidney, editor, *the Right to Leave and Return: Papers and Recommendations of the Internation Colloquium Held in Uppsala, Sweden, 19–21 June 1972* (Arbour, the USA: The American Jewish Committee, 1976), 23.

[27] Stahl, F. J., *Uber die gegenwartigen Parterien in State und Kirche*, Berlin, 1883, 23.

[28] Stipp, John L., Dirrim, Allen, W. and Hollister, C. Warren, *The Rise and Development of Western Civilization: 1660 to the Present* (New York, London and Sydney: John Wiley & Sons, Inc. 1967), 43.

[29] Quoted in Cranston, Maurice, *What are Human Rights?* (New York: Taplinger Publishing Co., Inc., 1973), 1.

[30] Friedmann, W., *Legal Theory* (London: Law Publishers, 1944), 235–239.

[31] Stipp, John L., Dirrim, Allen, W. and Hollister, C. Warren, *The Rise and Development of Western Civilization: 1660 to the Present* (New York, London and Sydney: John Wiley & Sons, Inc., 1967), 449, 450 and 608.

Republics (USSR) was regarded as a means of enforcing and strengthening government authority. The underlying principle of law was that it should regulate society, rather than the actions of the government; it was designed to impose duties on the people rather than to protect their rights. This situation is greatly changing since 1990s. The rise of communist regimes eventually led to strict emigration controls that lasted up until the early of 1990s. The reunification of Soviet Jews with their families in Israel, for instance, was not permitted before mid-1960s.[32]

2.1.4 *RLR translation from natural right to positive right*

Right comes necessarily into existence as soon as people live together.[33] In its broad sense, the right is a formation of relationships of life, with a view to the attachment of freedom, which is realised and developed as the destination of the individual. In its narrowest sense, the right is used as the correlative of duty; and, to convey this meaning, the synonym 'claim' seems best.[34] RLR is more than the aspiration or assertion of the good – it is essentially a claim of entitlement founded on a moral order under natural law. Hugo Grotius characterised the right to depart as the "most specific and unimpeachable axiom of the law of nations".[35] RLR creates the corresponding obligations not only from the State itself but from anyone that might try to stop the person from exercising their rights. Anyone endowed with RLR may apply for the remedies when his or her RLR is violated.

We additionally need to admit that the positive law is the creation of people, and natural law, however, is not. The creation of law logically has a moral purpose, usually for the sake of the common good.[36] The natural law itself requires that people exercise authority in political communities and that the authority fulfils one's moral functions by translating certain principles of natural law into positive law

[32] Population Division, Department of Economic and Social Affairs, United Nations Secretariat, *International Migration from Countries with Economies in Transition: 1980–1999*, ESA/P/WP.176 , New York, 2002, 123 pages, 12.

[33] Hastie, W., *Outlines of the Science of Jurisprudence: an Introduction to the Systematic Study of Law*, (Holmes Beach, the USA: Gaunt, Inc., 2000), 150.

[34] Wellman, Carl, *A Theory of Rights: Persons Under Laws, Institutions, and Morals* (Totowa, New Jersey, the USA: Rowman & Allanheld Publishers, 1985), 54.

[35] Quoted in Plender, Richard, *International Migration Law*, Revised. 2nd ed., (Dordrecht, the Netherlands: Martinus Nijhoff Publishers, 1988), 96.

[36] According to Aquinas, "we can only accept the saying that the ruler's will is law, on the proviso that the ruler's will is ruled by cause; otherwise a ruler's will is more like lawlessness." See Aquinas, Summa, 1a2ae, 90.1, Quoted in Hunter, Ian, and Saunders David, "Introduction", in Hunter, Ian, and Saunders, David, editor, *Natural Law and Civil Sovereignty: Moral Right and State Authority in Early Modern Political Thought* (New York: Palgrave Macmillan, 2002), 2.

and reinforcing and backing up these principles with the threat of punishment for law breaking. A morally valid authority, in a sense, thus derives positive law from natural law; or translates natural principles of justice and political morality into rules and principles of positive law.[37]

Among the achievements of recent analytical jurisprudence is its virtual elimination of false opposition between natural law theory and legal positivism. Theorists of natural law such as John Finnis and legal positivists such as Neil MacCormick have developed refined understandings of relationships between law and morality, in the light of which it no longer makes sense to suppose that a commitment to legal positivism logically excludes belief in natural law.[38]

H. L. A. Hart argued that statutes might be a mere legal shell and demand by their express terms to be filled out with the aid of moral principles. No positivist could deny that the stability of legal systems depends in part upon such types of correspondence with morals.[39] Philosophically and historically RLR was thus conceived to exist before the State, and the State developed as the means to its realisation. Given the widely accepted influence of morality on law, modern civilisation translated RLR from natural rights to positive rights, serving as a limit of the power of the State.

Human society develops well if positive rights are more consistent with natural rights, and if they are otherwise, society lacks both stability and order. As far as RLR is concerned, it is the fact that RLR is a right provided in positive way only late in the evolution of States. The State has an obligation to preserve itself and its resources including human resources, therefore the State has a duty to develop the regulatory regime of RLR, as it deems necessary. The more effectively realised RLR, the more developed human society might be in the area of the reallocation of natural and human resources, and the more positive the change of attitudes to and quality of life, thus affecting human and social evolution.

Human rights are a 20th century name for what has been traditional known as natural rights or, in a more exhilarating phrase, the rights of man. Human rights are not rights which derive from a particular status. They are rights which belong to individuals simply because they are human. In Kent Ann's opinion, human rights embrace three generations of rights, which are civil and political rights as the first generation of human rights, economic and social rights, as the second generation of human rights, and the third generation being group rights.[40] As one right reaffirmed in the ICCPR, RLR is usually regarded as one of the civil and political

---

[37] George, Robert P., *In Defence of Natural Law* (London: Clarendon Press, 1999), 107.

[38] George, Robert P., *In Defence of Natural Law* (London: Clarendon Press, 1999), 108.

[39] Hart, H. L. A., *The Concept of Law* (London: Oxford University Press, 1961), 199 and 200.

[40] Kent, Ann, *Human Rights in the People's Republic of China, Discussion Paper No. 3, 1989–90*, Legislative Research Service, the Parliament of the Commonwealth of Australia.

rights. Civil and political rights may be understood as conferring "rights of immunity upon the individual, as requiring non-interference from others and as not normally dependent upon general social conditions."[41] Lester B. Orfield thought in 1965 that the *Charter of the United Nations*, the UDHR and the proposed Covenant on Human Rights showed the recent trend had been to extend the scope of international law to cover matters of interest to the individual.[42]

In practice 152 countries had ratified the ICCPR up until to June 2004, and therefore recognised RLR as a fundamental human right. Most ratifying States have translated 'paper' RLR into real RLR, few have yet to do so.[43] Hurst Hannum has reminded us that:

> Whatever theory one adopts to explain the original source of RLR, they now have acquired the status of positive law through the widespread acceptance of the international covenants and numerous other international agreements.[44]

This international practice and acceptance has consolidated RLR as part of customary international law. The party States to the ICCPR thus accepted the international obligations under the ICCPR to respect RLR in domestic law. The non-party States to the ICCPR must salute the university of RLR in domestic law. In this context, we call RLR a positive right. Admitting RLR as a positive right is mainly to describe the wide legal recognition in the world, rather than to implicitly accept the utilitarian, or to deny the nature of RLR as a natural right.

2.1.5 *Consequences of violating RLR*

It may be that the effect of barring RLR can have consequences far more serious than the actual restrictions on RLR. Restricting emigrants, even when their numbers are only few, creates the general feeling for people of being shut within their own territories. A country seems smaller as soon as individuals are forbidden to leave it, and the desire to leave becomes more urgent. The feeling in the breasts

---

[41] Kamenka, Eugene, "Human Rights, Peoples' Rights", in *Bulletin of the Australian Society of Legal Philosophy*, Vol. 9, No. 33, June 1985, 157.

[42] Orfield, Lester B. and Re, Edward D., *Cases and Materials on International Law*, Revised Edition (Indianapolis, Kansas City and New York: The Bobbs-Merrill Company, Inc., 1965), 178.

[43] Being a member of the ICCPR, Egypt however provided an illustration of the restrictions on RLR of resident of Palestinians. See Human Rights Watch, *Human Rights Watch Policy on the Right to Return: Relevant Background: Treatment and Rights in Arab Host States*, http://hrw.org/campaigns/israel/return/arab-rtr.htm (accessed 16/09/2006).

[44] Hannum, Hurst, *The Right to Leave and Return in International Law and Practice* (Dordrecht, the Netherlands: Martinus Nijhoff Publishers, 1987), 5.

of a whole nation that they are being pent in is perhaps a greater source of danger than the strictures of the lands in which they dwell. Restricting people's ability to move around is a loss of freedom. Someone who is prevented from travelling or is unable to choose where to live, for no good cause, is being denied his or her human rights.[45]

Without freedom of human migration, or the freedom of movement of knowledge and goods, other inherent freedoms and human rights cannot be realised completely. In the words of one international instrument, the denial of RLR is "the cause of widespread human suffering, a source of international tensions, and an object of international concern."[46] The protection of RLR is said elsewhere to be essential for "the effective enjoyment of other human rights and fundamental freedoms, and promotes mutual understanding and co-operation among the peoples of the world."[47]

2.1.6 *Justification of the limits on RLR*

If the freedom of individuals may truly exist, it has to be rational, and that means it must maintain itself within the limits of human nature. In practice, there are certain fundamental rights, which cannot be alienated even the Constitution permits amendment.[48] The idea of fundamental rights including RLR contains the demand for justice on the one hand, and the demand for the satisfaction of vital human and State needs in the various spheres of social life on the other. In response to the above spirit, almost all current international instruments and national laws recognise the principle of freedom and equity in everyone's dignity and rights. These international instruments meanwhile recognise the limits on RLR to harmonise the possible conflict of every individual's interests.

2.2 Historical Foundations

Given the legal basis of RLR, the history of RLR is inextricably linked with the history of the laws governing it. The basis of those laws will be dealt with first. The historical development of the laws governing RLR will be then described in an

---

45 Bradley, Catherine, *What Do We Mean by Human Rights: Freedom of Movement* (London: Franklin Watts, 2002), 7.

46 Preamble paragraph 5, *Strasbourg Declaration on the Right to Leave and Return*, adopted by Experts on the Right to Leave and Return on 26 November 1986.

47 Preamble paragraph 3, *Declaration on the Right to Leave and the Right to Return*, adopted by the Uppsala Colloquium, Uppsala, Sweden, on 21 June 1972.

48 Haines, C. Groves, *The Revival of Natural Law Concepts*, Harvard, 1930, 336; and Willoughby, W. W., *The Constitution Law of the USA*, 2nd edition, Vol. I, 598.

annalistic style. As passport laws and international instruments related to RLR play an important role in the historical development of the laws governing RLR, they will also be described. The factors driving RLR will be finally analysed from the perspective of the economics and politics.

2.2.1 *The basis of the laws governing RLR*

The sovereignty of States forms the basis of the laws governing RLR. While retaining the character of RLR as a fundamental human right, each State also has the sovereign right to regulate RLR in accordance with its own laws. Each State establishes its own legal system to distinguish citizens from foreigners, for border controls to inspect people who wish to enter, and to implement policies that affect the settlement and integration of non-citizens.

The sovereignty of the State is derived from the allegiance of its subjects to the State. In feudal terms it existed in that all persons born within the power or protection of the Crown owed natural allegiance to the King, and were natural-born subjects of the realm, while all who were born out of the allegiance or protection of the King, were aliens born, and remain aliens unless they are subsequently made denizens or naturalised.[49] Blackstone described the natural allegiance in these terms:

> A debt of gratitude which cannot be forfeited, cancelled or altered by any change of time, place or circumstance, nor by anything but the united concurrence of the legislature. An Englishman who removes to France or to China owes the same allegiance to the King of England there as at home, and twenty years hence as well as now [. . .] Natural allegiance was intrinsic and primitive and antecedent to the other. [. . .] indeed, the natural-born subject of one prince, to whom he owes allegiance, may be entangled by subjecting himself absolutely to another; but it is his own act that brings him into these straits and difficulties, of owing service to two masters; and it is uncauseable that, by such voluntary act of his own, he should be able at pleasure to unloose those bonds of by which he is connected to his natural prince.[50]

The term 'subject' was brushed aside as a feudal term, and replaced with the term 'citizen' in countries with democratic constitutions.[51] He who before was a 'subject of King' is now a 'citizen of the State'. Citizenship is conceived of as a territorially determined relationship between subjects and sovereign, by which the subject is tied to one's sovereign. There are no essential distinctions between

[49] Henriques, H. S. Q., *The Law of Aliens and Naturalization including the Text of the Aliens Act, 1905* (London: Butterworth & Co., 1906), 29.

[50] Blackstone, Volume 1, 369 and 370.

[51] Koessler, "Subject, Citizen, National and Permanent Allegiance", 56 *Yale Law Journal* 58. (1946), 58–76, 59.

nationality and citizenship, the former is a norm of international law, and the latter is a norm of domestic law. Since the 18th century, the concept of human rights has become an important argument in the campaign to obtain freedom for the individual in relation to the State. The Nottebohm case [1955] ICJ Reports 4 supports it as well.

The regulation of international law since the end of Second World War has expanded to include individuals and non-governmental organisations. The idea of membership of a national community, subject to a specific sovereign authority, has begun to lose force. In the sphere of international relations at least a partial limit of the sovereign rights was imposed on each State. People have become more independent and free from the State than ever. The regulation of RLR is therefore not only an attribute of the sovereignty, but also an issue with important international implications for States. While this is the case links of allegiance between individuals and States still exist, because allegiance continues to be intrinsic and primitive and one is antecedent to the other. The independence and freedom gained are not enough to be divorced from the sovereignty. The sovereignty of States remains a dominant theme in the relationship between the citizen and the State.

2.2.2 *The historical development of the laws governing RLR*

It was only in the early 20th century that the system of passports and visas developed to regulate RLR. Practical prohibitions and limits on RLR existed and were serious prior to that time and were gradually relaxed in the 20th century. Since the emergence of the modern idea of the passport it has become the major instrument governing RLR. With the establishment of international and regional organisations such as the UN and European Union (EU), RLR has become universally recognised at a regional and world level. During the process of universal recognition, international and regional instruments governing RLR play an increasingly important role.

2.2.2.1 Laws governing RLR in ancient times

Ancient societies did not impose prohibitions and limits on the leaving and returning of subjects by law, while the slaves, bondmen, serfs and peasants of those societies were not considered subjects or complete subjects. In other words, the nobility and free townspeople were given the exclusive privilege of leaving and returning, subject to the will of the King.[52]

---

[52] The privilege is the foundation of slave and feudal societies and its chief curse. See Stipp, John L., Dirrim, Allen, W. and Hollister, C. Warren, *The Rise and Development of*

People in remote regions, such as nomads, often moved from deserts and steppes of Asia and Africa to the vast reaches of the Pacific and Indian Oceans. The extent of migration depended on the spirit of adventure and ability of the relevant population, alongside the practical requirements of trade and agriculture. Some examples of decisive mass movement include the Hebrew exodus from Egypt, the settlement of Eastern Europe, and colonisation of the Americas. Vinogradoff has pointed out that the country now called Hellas was not regularly settled before. The people were migratory, and readily left their homes whenever numbers overpowered them. They could obtain a bare subsistence anywhere and they were always ready to emigrate.[53] From the very earliest times foreigners in large numbers have entered England.

Something akin to RLR was legally recognised as early as 1215 in the *Magna Carta*, a worthy climax of the first stage of growth of English law. Article 41 guaranteed to merchants "safe and secure exit". Article 42 proclaimed:

> It shall be lawful to any person, for the future, to go out of our Kingdom, and to return, safely and securely, by land or water, saving his allegiance to us, unless it be in time of war, for some short space, for the common good of the Kingdom: excepting prisoners and outlaws, according to the law of the land, and of the people of the nation at war against us, and Merchants who shall be treated as it is said above.

These regulations developed in succeeding centuries a common law writ of *ne exeat regno*. Chao JU-KUA, Ibn Batuta and Marco Polo enjoyed the comparative freedom to leave and return to their respective countries, as well as in entering and leaving the many kingdoms of Asia and the outlying islands through which they travelled in the Middle Ages. Francisco de Victoria said at the start of 16th century: "It was permissible from the beginning of the world for anyone to set forth and travel wheresoever he would."[54]

The right to return to one's country was popularly recognised in ancient times. This can be partly proved by the record of perpetual exile being the only means of avoiding capital punishment in ancient Athens.[55]

Mercantile and military considerations led most States to view their slave populations as valuable commodities to be retained rather than permitted to leave, whereupon they could increase the prosperity of other States. They were bound

Western Civilization: 1660 to the Present (New York, London and Sydney: John Wiley & Sons, Inc., 1967), 119.

[53] Vinogradoff, Paul, *Outlines of Historical Jurisprudence, Volume Two, The Jurisprudence of the Greek City* (Oxford, the UK: Oxford University Press, 1922), 1–2.

[54] Quoted in Ingles, Jose D., *Study of Discrimination in Respect of The Right of Everyone to Leave any Country, Including His Own, and to Return to His Country: Special Repporteur of the Sub-commission on Prevention of Discrimination and Protection of Minorities*, United Nations Publication Sales No.: 64. XIV. 2 New York, 1963, 2.

[55] Vinogradoff, Paul, *Outlines of Historical Jurisprudence, Volume Two, The Jurisprudence of the Greek City*, (Oxford, the UK: Oxford University Press, 1922), 179.

to the cultivating land in ancient Europe, ancient Asia and America of the 19th century. According to the law of colonial Virginia (1705), Kentucky (1798), and the Louisiana Territory (1806), the slaves were regarded part of the land.[56] In ancient Europe, the nobility and free townspeople could move between regions as they pleased.[57] In ancient China, only merchants could be permitted to go abroad, and if people who went abroad were not merchants, they would be given a flogging.[58] Given the fact that slaves, bondmen, serfs and peasants were the overwhelming majority of the population in ancient times,[59] it could be accepted that most people were not entitled to RLR.

2.2.2.2 Laws governing RLR in modern and contemporary times

RLR in modern times, especially in contemporary times has become an entitlement for everyone, without distinction as to one's social status. Recognition of RLR by States increased following the Second World War; and international instruments have also evinced that the recognition of RLR is being gradually moved beyond the national borders.

Settlement Laws 1691 (UK) was refined to ease the labour mobility in Britain.[60] Blackstone has pointed out that English citizens enjoyed an absolute RLR in the second half of 18th century.[61] Title I of *French Constitution of 1791* guaranteed

---

[56] Friedman, Lawrence M., *A History of American Law* (New York: Simon and Schuster, 1973), 197.

[57] Quoted in Cranston, Maurice, "The Political and Philosophy Aspects of the Rights to Leave and Return", in Vasak, Karel and Liskofsky, Sidney, editor, *the Right to Leave and Return: Papers and Recommendations of the International Colloquium Held in Uppsala, Sweden, 19–21 June 1972* (Arbour, the USA: The American Jewish Committee, 1976), 29.

[58] Merchants' freedom to travel abroad was protected by *Commentaries of Law Codes* the Tang Dynasty (618–907), *Uniform Penal Code*, the Song Dynasty (960–1279). The control of exit and entry in ancient China had been regulated in some special regulations such as *Guangzhou Regulations Governing Exit and Entry* (*Amendment*) 1080 of Song Dynasty, and the *Regulations of Further Governing Exit and Entry* 1293 of Yuan Dynasty and the *Rules of Exit and Entry* 1314 of Yuan Dynasty (1206–1368). See Wong, Li, *International Immigration Law and the Practices* (*Guoji Yiminfa Lilun Yu Shijian*) (Beijing: the Publishing House of Law, 2001), 13.

[59] Serfs under private landlords were about half of the population in Russian in 1767. See Stipp, John L., Dirrim, Allen, W. and Hollister, C. Warren, *The Rise and Development of Western Civilization: 1660 to the Present* (New York, London and Sydney: John Wiley & Sons, Inc., 1967), 118.

[60] Yu, Shutong and Wen, Jia, editor, *A New Chinese-English Law Dictionary* (*Xin Hanying Faxue Cidian*) (Beijing: Publishing House of Law, 1998), 1263.

[61] Blackstone, *The Great Charter and Charter of the Forest*, 3rd edition, 1771, Quoted in Ingles, Jose D., *Study of Discrimination in Respect of The Right of Everyone to Leave any Country, including His Own, and to Return to His Country: Special Rapporteur of the*

"the freedom of everyone to go, to stay, or to leave, without being halted or arrested unless in accordance with procedures established by the Constitution." The 1830s helped to establish the future shape of Australian society, during which time it was possible to freely immigrate.[62]

The US Supreme Court has given constitutional protection to the right to travel since 1823.[63] The right to travel abroad is protected under the Fifth Amendment of *The Constitution of the USA* as an aspect of the 'liberty' of which an individual cannot be deprived save by due to process of law. The Indian Supreme Court has held that the right to travel abroad, though not specially provided for, is implied in the right to personal liberty of which a person may not be deprived according to a procedure established by law.[64] Twenty-four countries have formally recognised RLR in constitutional texts or laws and in 1961 12 countries recognised RLR through judicial interpretation. According to the statistics of Richard Plender, up to 1988 the right to depart from a State's territory was recognised expressly in the constitutions of 44 States.[65]

The international community recognised that RLR as an equal and inalienable right of all members of the human family, and is based upon attributes of human personality, and not derived from one being a national of a particular State, in Article 13(2) of the UDHR, Article 12(2)(3)(4) of the ICCPR, Article 2 of the *Protocol No. 4 of European Convention for the Protection of Human Rights and Fundamental Freedoms* 1950 (EHR P4), Article 22 (3), (4) of *American Convention on Human Rights* 1969 (AMR), Article 12 (2) of *African Charter on Human and People's Rights* 1981 (AFR), and *Arab Charter on Human Rights* 1994 and other international or regional human rights conventions. The number of States that had ratified the ICCPR was 35 in 1976, 85 in 1985 and increased to 148 in 2002 and 152 in 2004. The States parties to above international conventions owe an international duty to give effect to relevant provisions of international conventions by protecting RLR through domestic law and international cooperation.

Sub-commission on Prevention of Discrimination and Protection of Minorities, United Nations Publication Sales No.: 64. XIV. 2, New York, 1963.

[62] Molony, John, *History of Australia* (Ringwood, Australia: Penguin Books Australia Ltd, 1987), 61.

[63] Freedman, Warren, *The Right to Travel: A Right or A Privilege? Work Paper of Sao Paulo Conference on the Law of the World* (Washington, the USA: the World Peace Through Law Centre, 1981), 6.

[64] *Maneka Gandhi v. Union of India and another [1978] SCR 312*; *Satwant Singh Sawhney v. Ramarthnam et al. [1967] 3 SCR 525.*

[65] Plender, Richard, *International Migration Law*, Revised 2nd edition (Dordrecht, the Netherlands: Martinus Nijhoff Publishers, 1988), 95–96.

2.2.2.3 Historical development of laws governing passport

A national must possess a passport or other travel documents if he or she wishes to leave or return to one's country. Without being entitled to the right to be issued with travel document, especially a passport, RLR cannot be realised.

Historically, RLR did not involve the modern document of a passport, for the simple reason that that there was no international traffic of travellers, so no need for laws to govern traffic. Possession of a passport was not generally a requirement for the crossing of national borders in Europe prior to 20th century.[66] The growth of the Roman Empire and improvement in means of communication meant that international travel was more easily achieved, and occasionally a traveller could cover hundreds of miles for commercial purposes.[67] In 1548, the term 'passport' was first used in by English statute, where it referred to a license given by a military authority to a soldier to go on furlough.[68] In the 18th and early 19th centuries, the passport was mainly issued to aliens by the territory in which the documents were effective. In the course of 19th century the practice of issuing passports to aliens for travel in the issuing country seems to have fallen into disuse.

The people in ancient China who intended to go abroad had to apply for a letter of approval from the local government. In the Han dynasty (206 B.C.–A.D. 220), the approval letter for businessmen was called '*Chuan*', for government officers it was '*Jie*'. It was then named '*Guosuo*' in the Tang dynasty (618–907), '*Gongju*' in the Song dynasty (960–1279), '*Gongyan*' in the Yuan dynasty (1206–1368) and '*Wenyin*' in the Ming dynasty (1368–1644).[69]

In 1905, Lord Alverstone CJ , in *Rex* v. *Brailsford* defined a passport as:

> A document issued in the name of the Sovereign on the responsibility of a Minister of the Crown to a named individual, intended to be presented to the Governments of foreign nations and to be used for that individual's protection as a British subject in a foreign country, and it depends for its validity upon the fact that the Foreign office in an official document vouches the respectability of the person named.[70]

---

[66] Weis, P., *Nationality and Statelessness in International Law*, 2nd revised edition (B. V., Alphen aan den Rijn, the Netherlands: Sijthoff & Noordhodd International Publishers, 1979), 222–223.

[67] Freedman, Warren, *The Right to Travel: A Right or A Privilege? Work Paper of Sao Paulo Conference on the Law of the World* (Washington, the USA: the World Peace Through Law Centre, 1981), 7.

[68] Sibley, N. W., "The Passport System", *Journal of the Society of Comparative Legislation*, new series Volume vii (1906), 26–33, 32.

[69] "Above laws contain the provisions about the establishment of administrative organs, application for approval letter, inspection of exit and entry, restrictions on the people going abroad and staying period abroad, and punishment." Wong, Li, *International Immigration Law and the Practices* (Beijing: the Publishing House of Law, 2001), 13–15.

[70] [1905] 2 K. B. 730 at 745, Quoted in Turack, Daniel C., *The Passport in International Law* (Toronto, Canada: Lexington Books, D. C. Health and Company, 1972), 16.

This definition illuminates the significance of the modern passport. Since the end of the First World War, it has been almost universally recognised that a passport is largely issued to the State's own nationals as an identity and travel document. The League of Nations Passport Conference of 1926 reiterated the recommendation of 1920 Passport Conference for the abolition of exit visas. That recommendation has been accepted by a large number of States, however the process of achieving uniform international rules governing passports is a long way off. Daniel Turack has reminded us that:

> Although the UN has convened an international meeting of experts on passport and a conference on international travel and tourism during which passports were widely discussed and concrete recommendations adopted, is has not yet prepared a compilation of the passport laws of its members and the member States of specialised agencies similar to the works produced on nationality. The fruit of such an undertaking would stimulate greater activity in an area deserving of independent research.[71]

2.2.2.4 Historical development of international instruments related to RLR

Numerous conventions dealing with RLR entered into force after the Second World War. The UN and regional organisations have made efforts to arrive at uniform rules governing RLR, to avoid repeating the tragedy of the persecution and murder of six millions Jews' during the 1930s and 1940s.

In the words of a UN General Assembly representative from France, the UDHR represented "a world milestone in the long struggle for human rights",[72] Article 13 (2) of the UDHR affirmed that RLR should be enjoyed fully and without discrimination. RLR may in no case be exercised contrary to the purposes and principles of the UN.

The *Convention Relating to the Status of Refugees* 1951 (CSR) is the most important international instrument protecting refugees, Article 28 of which obligates States parties to issue travel documents to refugees in their territory, especially those unable to secure such documents from the country of their lawful residence, and to issue travel documents to Stateless persons lawfully staying in their territory.

Article 7 (3) of The *Convention on the Reduction of Statelessness* 1961 proclaimed that, "a national of a contracting State shall not lose his nationality, so as to become Stateless, on the ground of departure, residence abroad, and failure to register or on any similar ground." Article 9 further regulated that "a contracting

---

[71] Turack, Daniel C., *The Passport in International Law* (Toronto, Canada: Lexington Books, D.C. Health and Company, 1972), 33.

[72] The Office of the High Commissioner for Human Rights, "The Universal Declaration of Human Rights: A Magna Carta for All Humanity", www. Unhchr.ch/udhr/miscinfo/carta.htm (accessed 18/05/2003).

State may not deprive any person or group of persons of their nationality on racial ethnic, religious or political grounds."

RLR was formally protected in the ICCPR, which is the most important international covenant in this regard. Article 12 (2) provides the general circumstance of RLR as being that "everyone shall be free to leave any country, including his own." Article 12 (3) detailed general restrictions on RLR:

> The above-mentioned rights shall not be subject to any restrictions except those which are provided by law, are necessary to protect national security, public order (*ordre public*), public health or morals or the rights and freedoms of others, and are consistent with the other recognized in the present Covenant.

These restrictions were reaffirmed and cited in the conventions about RLR to follow. Article 12 (4) stressed the right to return, as being that "No one shall be arbitrarily deprived of the right to enter his own country." Article 13 provides procedural rights against expulsion. Article 5 d (ii) of the CERD regulated that in the enjoyment of RLR, States parties undertake to prohibit and to eliminate racial discrimination in all its forms and to guarantee the right of everyone, without distinction as to race, colour, or national or ethnic origin, to equality before the law. The *Convention on the Rights of the Child* 1989 (CRC) entered into force in 1990. It is an elaboration of human rights standards in respect of the child. It contains several provisions respecting and safeguarding RLR of the child and one's parents.[73] *Guiding Principles on Internal Displacement* 1997 were "noted" by the Commission on Human Rights and have been referred to in various General Assembly resolutions. Principle 15 provides that:

> . . . internally displaced persons have (a) the right to seek safely in another part of the country; (b) the right to leave their country; (c) the right to seek asylum in another country; and (d) the right to be protected against forcible return to or resettlement in any place where their life, safety, liberty and/or heath would be at risk.

The 1963 UN Draft Principles on RLR were adopted by UN Sub-Commission on Prevention of Discrimination and Protection of Minorities (CPDPM) in 1963. The

---

[73] Article 10 of the *Convention on the Rights of the Child* 1989 provides "1. In accordance with the obligation of States Parties under Article 9, paragraph 1, applications by a child or his or her parents to enter or leave a State Party for the purpose of family reunification shall be dealt with by States Parties in a positive, humane and expeditious manner. States Parties shall further ensure that the submission of such a request shall entail no adverse consequences for the applicants and for the members of their family. 2. . . . States Parties shall respect the right of the child and his or her parents to leave any country, including their own, and to enter their own country. The right to leave any country shall be subject only to such restrictions as are prescribed by law and which are necessary to protect the national security, public order (ordre public), public health or morals or the rights and freedoms of others and are consistent with the other rights recognized in the present Convention."

1972 Uppsala Declaration on RLR was adopted by the Uppsala Colloquium in 1972, and which contains the right to leave, the right to return, and addresses travel documents and general procedures for responding to violations. The 1986 Strasbourg Declaration on RLR was adopted by the Meeting of Experts on RLR in 1986 and developed procedural safeguards of RLR. The above instruments are only three international instruments focused on RLR. They offer the most comprehensive and detailed regulations up to now in this regard. Despite their non-binding character they are of significant importance in the development of laws governing RLR.

In 1980s and 1990s some international instruments reaffirmed RLR. They are the *Declaration on the Human Rights of Individuals Who are not Nationals of the Country in Which They Live* 1985, the *International Convention on the Protection of the Rights of All Migrant Workers and Member of Their Family* 1990, the *Declaration on the Protection of All Persons from Enforced Disappearance* 1992, the *Draft United Nations Declaration on the Rights of Indigenous Peoples* 1994, the *Declaration on the Right and Responsibility of Individuals, Groups and Organs of Society to Promote and Protect Universally Recognised Human Rights and Fundamental Freedoms* 1998, and *Nationality of Natural Persons in Relation to Succession States* 2000. The above international instruments are not effective yet.

As of June 2004, 104 of the 152 States parties to the ICCPR were also parties to the First Optional Protocol to the ICCPR. Under the optional protocol, individuals of ratified States parties can claim any of the rights enumerated in the ICCPR, including RLR. They can submit communications to the Human Rights Committee (HRC) when all domestic remedies have been exhausted. The HRC has made some notable comments regarding RLR, such as *Vidal Martins v. Uruguay*, *Stewart v. Canada*, and *Peltonen v. Finland.*

Since 1948, Europe has made the most significant inroads into advancing human rights. Doubtless, the achievements are linked with the origin of the human rights including RLR in Europe. RLR is emphasised in Article 2 (2) (3), 3 and 4 of Protocol No. 4 of the EHR, the Part 1. d of *Final Act of the Helsinki Conference* 1975, Article 9.5 of the *Document of the Copenhagen Meeting of the Second Conference on The Human Dimension of the CSCE* 1990, Article 19 (6) of the *European Social Charter (Revised)* 1996, and Article 45 of the *Charter of Fundamental Rights of the European Union* 2000.

America has generally followed the European model, and made encouraging achievements. Article VIII of the *American Declaration of the Rights and Duties of Man* 1948 States that "every person has the right [. . .] not to leave the State of which he is a national, except by his own will". RLR is formally guaranteed under Article 22 of *American Convention on Human Rights* 1969 (AMR) that provides for a Commission and a Court, and bears a general resemblance to the European Convention.

Taking into account the evolution in the understanding and content of regional instruments related to RLR, African countries and the Arab world have made great efforts to effectively protect RLR. RLR was recognised separately in Article 12 (2), (3), (4) and (5) of the *African Charter on Human and People's Rights* 1981 (AFR), the Preface of *Cairo Declaration on Human Rights in Islam* 1990, Article 1 and 2 of the *Declaration on the Protection of Refugees and Displaced Persons in the Arab World* 1992 and Article 21, 22 and 23 of the *Arab Charter on Human Rights* 1994.

It should also be noted that at present there are no Asian conventions pertinent to RLR, and no regional intergovernmental institution created to protect RLR. The gist of the Asian countries' rejection of developing a regional convention is that "human rights, as propounded in the West, are founded on individualism and therefore have no relevance to Asia, which is based on the primacy of the community."[74] Asian countries adopted the *Bangkok Declaration* in April 1993. It contains the aspirations and commitments of the Asian regions on human rights, including RLR.

RLR norms is crystallising into customary international law, and commanding universal observance, binding even those States that are not parties to the conventions setting forth RLR norms will thus become the trend. Efforts to promote the universality of RLR by attempts to assure concordant behaviour, both by non-parties to the pertinent instruments and by those States that have dissented from their adoptions, will and must continue, despite the tension, which these efforts generate between the important values embodied in the relevant norms and the sovereignty of non-parties.

The credibility of the norms requires that attempts to extend their universality and further to reduce the already contracting domain of domestic jurisdiction. The fabric of international law need not be torn to establish the legitimate place of RLR in general international law. Unlike most other fields of international law, the observance of RLR is not based on reciprocal interests of States, but on the broader goal of States to establish orderly and enlightened international and national legal regimes. By the creative adaptation of the traditional and classical concepts and methods, it is possible to build the customary law of RLR and humanitarian norms in a process that will enhance their credibility and effectiveness.

2.2.3 *The factors driving the historical development of the laws governing RLR*

There are many factors that drive the historical development of the laws governing RLR. They include politics, economics, culture and law which have different

[74] Ghal, Yash, "Human Rights and Governance: the Asia Debate" in Steiner, Henry J. and Alston, Philip, *International Human Rights in Context*, 2nd edition (New York: Oxford University Press, 2000), 550.

features in different States. Among these factors politics and economics are foremost. The former decides the grant of RLR by governments. The latter decides the practical demands of RLR by people. The influence of politics on RLR is more significant than the influence of economics. An advanced economic system demands RLR more, since the realisation of RLR can benefit economic development. The greater the economic development, and the less economic differences between States, the fewer limits imposed on RLR.

This correlation can be seen in history. An agrarian society requires a dense and stable labour force to be bound to the land. Although the absence of the systems of ports and customs further increased the need of travel in some senses, the travellers of agrarian societies were mainly youth seeking knowledge, artists, foreign spectators, traders, those seeking cures for bad health, and wealthy people travelling for distraction and recreation.[75] The slave in Rome Empire was a man who could not go where he wished, and the free man was a man who could. If the Roman or Greek slave, or European serf could freely leave the castle or manor, the Mediterranean ancient civilisations and European feudal society would not have developed as they did.

Demographic theories assert that economic development involves evolution from a predominantly agrarian, peasant economy to an industrialised, market-oriented economy, characterised by a greater division of labour, urbanisation and weakening of traditional migratory customs.[76] An industrial technology demands inventiveness and depends upon a labour force that is skilled or capable of being trained. The population must be induced to undergo the social dislocations of a mobile labour force and often also undergo a shift of social, economic, and political power. The institutions and policies focused on the liberalisation of RLR may enhance the social dislocations of a mobile labour force. One of the changes industrialisation underwent has been the conversion of the majority of the labouring population from peasants to an urban proletariat, and the increase of international migrants.[77]

According to the *International Migration Report 2002* published by the UN, with the great progress of the world's economy the number of international migrants stood at 175 million in 2000, up from 75 million in 1965. International

---

[75] Cantor, Norman F. and Werthman, Michaels, editor, *The History of Popular Culture to 1815* (London: The Macmillan Company, New York and Collier-Macmillan Ltd., 1968), 40.

[76] Coale, A. J. and Hoover, E. M., "The Effects of Economic Development on Population Growth and the Effects of Population Growth on Economic Development" in Drake, Michael, editor, *Population in Industrialization* (London: Methuen & Co. Ltd., 1969), 12–14.

[77] Willis, F. Roy, *Western Civilization an Urban Perspective: Volume II from the 17th Century to the Contemporary Age* (Lexington, the USA: D. C. Heath and Company, 1973), 659.

migrants are not distributed evenly across countries or regions. Sixty percent of the world's migrants currently reside in the more developed regions and 40 percent in the less developed regions. In 2000, international migrants made up 8.7 percent of the population in developed countries, while they accounted for only 1.5 percent of the population in developing countries.[78]

Politics has then simultaneously driven the development of the laws governing RLR, along with economic imperatives. Civilised political systems can improve the recognition of RLR and the effectiveness of its protection. By contrast, the centralisation of State power or autocracy has the inclination to deny RLR.

This correlation can also be seen historically. It is widely accepted that slave-owner and feudal King had autocratic powers in slave societies and feudal societies. Feudal monarchy could be interpreted as a lord-subject relationship without reciprocal rights and obligations of the lord-vassal concept. Absolute monarchs built royal supremacy into the machinery of their governments and subjects. Therefore, the slave and bondsman who were numerous could not move freely unless they were liberalised. The word 'iberal' in Latin has it origin in the idea of being unimpeded in the exercise of movement.[79] David Potter regarded communist rule as the opposite of democracy.[80] The communist States present the most consistent policy, generally very restrictive in the areas of travel and emigration, despite their geo-political differences. None of the countries in this group recognise RLR by constitutional provision or statute, although Mongolia, North Korea, and Vietnam are parties to the ICCPR.

The post-Cold War era has seen the creation of a number of new States, particularly in the former USSR and Eastern Europe. They have changed their political systems from communist systems to Western-style democracies. Most of these States have liberalised RLR.[81] The rate of economic increase in China is greater than that of the former USSR and eastern European countries, however Chinese

---

[78] Population Division, Department of Economic and Social Affairs, *International Migration Report 2002*, United Nations Secretariat, 2002, ST/ESA/SER.A/220 (New York: the United Nations, 2002), 62 pages, 2 and 11.

[79] Maurice Cranston, "the Political and Philosophical Aspects of the Right to Leave and to Return", in Vasak, Karel and Liskofsky, Sidney, editor, *the Right to Leave and Return: Papers and Recommendations of the International Colloquium Held in Uppsala, Sweden, 19–21 June 1972* (Arbour, the USA: The American Jewish Committee, 1976), 29.

[80] "As a result of result of the end of communist rule many democracies were established, although a definition of the precise form of democracy that came into existence was often hazardous and – at the end of 1995 – could only be tentative on the basis of just six years of systemic change." See Potter, David, Goldblatt, David, Kiloh, Margaret and Lewis, Paul, editor, *Democratization* (Malden MA, the USA: Blackwell Publishers Inc. 1997), 394.

[81] Joseph, Sarah and Sehultz, Jenny et al., *The National Covenant on Civil and Political Rights: Cases, Materials, and Commentary* (New York: Oxford University Press, 2000), 5.

laws governing RLR have not yet fundamentally changed as they have in those countries. This is largely because a dramatic change in the political system has not occurred in China. In other words the advent of socialism in China along with one party rule has as yet brought no strong commitment to human rights which would include RLR.[82]

The influence of the political system on RLR is ultimately more significant than the influence of economics. The ability to exploit a right and the demand to a right are not the precondition to the rights necessity. As far as RLR is concerned, the ability to financially afford the leaving and returning, and the demand to leave and return, are not the premise of upholding RLR. It is thus possible for States to entitle people to RLR in paper only under law. Upholding RLR plays a catalytic role in helping people to realise RLR in practice. Some developing States, such as Burundi and Cambodia, the members of the ICCPR grant people RLR, even though their nationals are unable in practice to exercise those rights. In contrast, some developed States, such as Saudi Arabia and Singapore, non-members of the ICCPR, do not officially grant people RLR, even though their nationals more often have the financial ability to exit and re-enter their countries.

2.3 Globalisation and International Migration

2.3.1 *Globalisation*

Globalisation is an inevitable international trend. According to McGrew, globalisation is the multiplicity of linkages and interconnections that transcend the nation-State (and by implication the societies) which make up the modern world order. It defines a process through which events, decisions and activities in one part of the world significantly effect distant individuals and communities. Capitalism relies upon the market-oriented system, which underlines competition and free-flow of human resources among States. Of the 100 largest economies in the world, 51 are global corporations, whereas only 49 are States.[83] Yet the contemporary age is not the first global epoch. In the words of D. Held:

> Globalisation, as an historic process, cannot be characterised by revolutionary logic. Historical patterns of globalisation have been punctuated by great shifts and reversals, while the temporal rhythms of globalisation differ between domains.[84]

---

[82] Edwards, R. Randle, Henkin, Louis and Nathan, Andrew J., *Human Rights in Contemporary China* (New York: Columbia University Press, 1986), 22.

[83] Quoted in Amnesty International, "AI on human Rights and Labour Rights" at Lechner, Frank J. and Boli John editor, *Globalisation Reader* (Malden, the USA: Blackwell Publishers, 2000), 187.

[84] Held, D., McGrew, A., Goldblatt, D., and Perraton, J., *Global Transformations: Politics, Economics, and Culture* (Malden, the USA: Blackwell Publishers, 2000), 414.

Although the Roman, Germanic and Mongol people were known to have engaged in large scale migration during times of ancient imperialist expansion, and similarly significant movement from 1500 to 1900, contemporary patterns of migration can be distinguished from historical examples on the basis of their extent and intensity.

Globalisation significantly influences international migration. It has made more people aware of conditions and opportunities abroad to study, work and live. Global restructuring generates or amplifies international migration and, in turn, that movement of people across borders is an indication of the globalisation of societies, and of the obsolescence of national boundaries.[85] New development in information and transportation technology increases the volume of temporary, repeat and circulatory migration. Globalisation – as the increased international flow of trade, capital, information and people – has delivered undeniable wealth and opportunity and created millions of jobs. Positively speaking, some countries have grown through entering the global economy. In 2003, the International Organization of Migration (IOM) observed that like other flows, whether financial, commercial, or flows of information or ideas, the rising tide of people crossing frontiers is among the reliable indicators of the intensity of globalisation.[86] Kofman even suggested that international migration is central to the study of globalisation.[87]

Globalisation has underpinned the interdependence of markets, production, culture and languages by the exchange of goods, services, capital, information, skills and people. The process has inextricably tied trade, competition and employment to international migration more than ever. The effect on private companies is that their employees, in the course of their employment, need to become 'international' citizens in accessing foreign countries. Managing their international mobility is inherent to their human resource value. In relation to multilateral agreements between States, the General Agreement on Trade and Services (GATS) clearly articulates the relationship between trade barriers and immigration controls. The use of immigration laws to restrict the movement of services providers is a non-tariff barrier to the trade of services.

---

[85] Pellerin, Helene, "Global Restructuring and International Migration: Consequences for the globalisation of Politics', in Kofman, Eleonore and Youngs, editor Gillian, *Globalisation: Theory and Practice* (New York: Pinter, 1996), 6.

[86] "Facts and Figures on International Migration", *Migration Policy Issues*, No. 2, March 2003, IOM (Geneva, Switzerland: International Organization for Migration, 2003), 1.

[87] Kofman, Eleonore and Youngs, Gillian, editor, *Globalisation: Theory and Practice* (New York: Pinter, 1996), 6.

2.3.2 *International migration*

Some introductory facts are that:

- The rate or the distribution of international migration has not dramatically changed over the last 40 years. International migrants increased 1.9 percent per year since 1965; it is only slightly ahead of the annual world population growth rate of about 1.8 percent.[88]
- Furthermore, there has not been an even distribution of migrants between countries, but a steady increase in the number of immigrants travelling to developed countries. International migrants live in Europe (56 million), Northern America (41 million), Oceania (6 million), Asia (50 million) and Africa (16 million) in 2000. It increased by 15.8%, 48%, 22.8%, –0.4% and 0.3% from 1990.[89]
- The official number of migrants accounts for a small percentage of estimated actual migration.[90]
- The effect of international migration on population growth and distribution rates for some receiving States is significant. This is in large part due to the fact that these countries exhibit persistently low rates of natural population growth.
- Migrants' remittances continue to be a major source of some developing countries' national income. For example, as a proportion of total financial inflows, remittances amounted to 66% and 51% of the Moroccan and Egyptian national incomes respectively.[91]

With globalisation, new patterns of international migration are emerging, which are closely linked and interdependent with pre-existing patterns. It can be observed that permanent and temporary migration stimulate one another. Some examples of these newer forms of migration include circular migration, the 'astronaut phenomenon', and the migration of retired people, women, students and parents.

---

[88] Population Division, Department of Economic and Social Affairs, United Nations Secretariat, *Measuring International Migration: Many Questions, Few Answers*, UN/POP/MIG/2002/BP/1 (New York: United Nations, 2002), 10 pages, 4.

[89] Calculated according to the data at Population Division Department of Economic and Social Affairs, *International Migration Report 2002,* United Nations Secretariat, *2002,* ST/ESA/SER.A/220 (New York: United Nations, 2002), 62 pages, 2.

[90] Martin, Philip and Widgren, Jonas, "International Migration: Facing the Challenge", in *Population Bulletin*, March 2002 issue (Population Reference Bureau, Washington, the USA: 2002), 39 pages, 4.

[91] "Facts and Figures on International Migration", *Migration Policy Issues*, No. 2 (2003) (Geneva, Switzerland: International Organization for Migration), 1.

Causes of international migration

The most fundamental cause of international migration is the quest for personal security and economic improvement, or rather, the attempt to defend oneself against personal insecurity or economic deterioration or underdevelopment.[92] In terms of family migratory patterns, the cause is generally related to family reunion, the hope for a better future, political stability and marriage.[93] Emigrants in the humanitarian stream prefer to move in order to escape war or the political situation in their homeland, and to seek better employment opportunities.[94] Skilled migratory patterns prove that immigration may yield economic benefits to the host country.

Circular migrants mainly prefer to temporally return to their home country because they find it very hard to realise their initial hopes, such as finding a better job and having a better future for their family in the host country. Other causes for circular migration can also be due to policies in the country of origin and host country that encourage temporary migration. Some of the essential characteristics of circular migrants are that they retain their original citizenship, consider themselves to be expatriates, maintain important links with their home country, may intend to return to it, and are often highly paid and skilled.[95]

The frequency of international migration is more likely to increase because of the above causes. The result may be a strong set of 'pull and push' factors, from changing circumstances, which may encourage a growing number of people to migrate in the near future. Other macro motivations will also trigger a future increase of international migration, such as that:

- Western countries regard international migration as one of important measures to relax the ageing of the overall population.[96]
- The income gap between different countries is sufficient cause to make a rational choice to migrate. Growing disparities lead to increased migration in the near future.

---

[92] Papademetrious, Demetrios, G., *Reflections on International Migration and its Future* (Geneva, Switzerland: International Organization for Migration, 2002), 58 pages, 25.

[93] Hugo, Graeme, Rudd, Dianne and Harris, Kevin, *Emigration from Australia: Economic Implications*, Second report on an ARC SPIRT grant CEDA Information Paper No. 77, Adelaide University Australia, June 2001, 72.

[94] Hugo, Graeme, Rudd, Dianne and Harris, Kevin, *Emigration from Australia: Economic Implications*, Second report on an ARC SPIRT grant CEDA Information Paper No. 77, Adelaide University Australia, June 2001, 74.

[95] Newland, Kathleen, "Migration as Factor in Development and Poverty Reduction," http://www.migrationinformation.org/USFocus/display.cfm?ID=136 (accessed 16/09/2006).

[96] Hugo, G., "The Demographic Underpinning of Current and Future International Migration in Asia", *Asian and Pacific Migration Journal*, 7 (1) 1998, 1–25.

- The labour migratory movement, once started, develops its own dynamics and cannot easily be stopped. This can be explained by competition between interest groups in receiving countries.[97]
- It is well known that most migrants follow 'beaten paths' and go where their compatriots have established a bridgehead, making it easier to find a job and integrate into the host country. This may be called 'chain migration' or 'networks migration'.
- Migration for the purpose of seeking asylum, or undocumented migration, is likely to increase, with little hope that global conflicts will be resolved in the foreseeable future.
- More free trade treaties will eliminate the many barriers of all kinds erected between States and parties within States over centuries, bringing freedom of movement in free trade regions for persons pursuing economic activities, and for goods, services and capital.

Management of international migration

The management of international migration is likely to become more controversial, difficult and urgent in the 21st century. It will bring into play many sensitive issues of national security and identity, of social change and cultural adaptation, and of economic vitality and development. Properly managed, immigration may provide important answers to some of the world's more developed countries' most intractable current and long-term dilemmas, and it might give some balance and foundation for a more mature international dialogue. The key to dealing with the patterns of international migration is not to prevent or obstruct movement, but to make the order of movement effective. If all actors in the migration process are to gain the maximum benefit from migration, the policy effort must focus on some of the grossly under-explored topics in the public discourse on international migration. Policies at a local level play a considerable role in the management of migration.

2.3.3 *International migration policy*

An increased number of countries have formulated new immigration policies to face the trend of globalisation and the reality of international migration. Firstly, a diverse group of countries, including Italy, Portugal, South Korea and Germany, have boosted the numbers of immigrants. Secondly, since the 1980s,

---

[97] Castles, Stephen, "Migration and Community Formation under Conditions of Globalisation", in *International Migration Review,* Winter (2002) v36 i4, page 1143 (26) http://www.blackwell-synergy.com/doi/abs/10.1111/j.1747–7379.2002.tb00121.x#search=%22Migration%20and%Community%20Formation%20under%20Conditions%20of%20 Globalization%22 (accessed 16/09/2006)

many immigrant-receiving countries, including the USA, Canada, Australia, and New Zealand have implemented immigration policies that are designed to attract economic migrants such as entrepreneurs, executives, scientists, professionals and technical specialists.

Thirdly, receiving countries have tightened the management of immigration services. The immigration service industry is already regulated in Australia and the UK. Canada and New Zealand are developing a system that aims to provide a dependable mechanism to prevent unscrupulous immigration consultants from using their fiduciary position for their own profit, or mismanaging their clients' immigration affairs.[98] Similar policies can be found in emigration services in those countries. In China, regulations introduced in 1999, 2001 and 2002 paved the way for comprehensive regulation of several of emigration intermediary agencies through the Ministry of Public Security (MPS), the Ministry of Labour and Social Security (MLSS), the Ministry of Education (MOE) and China National Tourism Administration (CNTA), etc.

Fourthly, asylum seeking and other forms of migration have long been viewed as separate issues by some governments. Asylum policies are now at the core of the discussion of migration in many parts of the world. The international asylum regime prevailed from the early 1950s through the late 1990s, and eventually challenged the States' prerogative to decide on the recognition of asylum seekers. Extensive media coverage of the plight of refugees has contributed to the politicisation of international migration. Restrictions on asylum have become quite common in both developed and developing countries.[99] However, some analysts think that regardless of whether migration has a positive or negative effect, more developed countries will be unable to stop the arrival of desperate migrants, and that only military intervention will prevent large numbers of poor migrants attempting to enter affluent countries, threatening their security.[100]

Finally, countries increasingly view flexible citizenship as an important and practical tool of integration. Recent North American and European research indicates that immigrants quickly adopt many conventional norms and values of the receiving society, while still maintaining a strong positive valuation of their own culture and language.[101] Acknowledging the realities of permanent residence

---

[98] The National Citizenship and Immigration Law Section of the Canadian Bar Association, *Submission on Immigration Consulting Industry*, 2000, 16 pages, 1; and Hon Dalziel, Lianne, the Minister of Immigration. *Options for Setting Enforceable Standards for Immigration Consultants*, 2001, 8 pages, 1.

[99] Population Division Department of Economic and Social Affairs, United Nations Secretariat, *International Migration: Explicit Policies, Uncertain Consequences,* UN/POP/MIG/2002/BP/2, New York, 2002, 15 pages, 10.

[100] Martin, Philip and Widgren, Jonas, *International Migration: Facing the Challenge* (Washington, the USA: Population Reference Bureau, 2002), 39 pages, 5.

[101] Newland, Kathleen, "Migration as Factor in Development and Poverty Reduction",

abroad, and the process of accessing citizens' rights in receiving countries, many sending countries tend to stress the importance of legal regulations that permit emigrants to qualify for foreign naturalisation without surrendering their original citizenship. Sending countries wish to maintain close contacts with their citizens abroad and tend to encourage emigrants to retain their citizenship and transfer it to their children. The complex situation created by dual citizenship can be limited by bilateral and international conventions.[102]

As globalisation creates multi-ethnic societies, and traditional notions of citizenship become increasingly inadequate, some States are considering multiple citizenship, which is occurring both within existing nation-States and in new regional entities such as the European Union (EU).[103] The facts outlined below support the finding that regional free trade agreements usually precede the free flow of people, which simultaneously enhances free trade.

- Following *Schengen Agreement* in 1995 and *Treaty of Amsterdam* in 1999, the EU became a zone of free movement for EU nationals. The EU established a common asylum and immigration policy after May 2004.
- The *North America Free Trade Agreement* permits the temporary entry of highly qualified workers in 64 professions. It allowed open borders for professionals among three countries after 2003.[104]
- The *Managua Agreement*, which was adopted by the El Salvador, Guatemala, Honduras and Nicaragua in 1993, provided for the creation of a system to facilitate the movement of people without requiring a passport or visa, the functions of which are instead supplied by a valid identity card from the respective country, and an application form as provided for in the Agreement. Travellers are authorized to a 90-day, non-extendable stay in the region, without any territorial limits.[105]

The *Closer Economic Partnership Arrangement* (CEPA) was signed between the HKSAR and Mainland China in June 2003, creating a unique free trade zone. Under the arrangement, many HKSAR products will enjoy a zero tariff rate in the

http://www.migrationinformation.org/USFocus/display.cfm?ID=136 (accessed 16/09/2006).

[102] Icduygu, Ahmet, "Citizenship at the Crossroads: Immigration and the Nation-State", at Kofman, Eleonore and Youngs, Gillian, editor, *Globalisation: Theory and Practice* (New York: Pinter, 1996), 157.

[103] Davidson, Alastair, "Globalisation and Citizenship", in *ARENA Journal*, No. 12 (1998), pp. 83–105, 83.

[104] Martin, Philip and Widgren, Jonas, *International Migration: Facing the Challenge* (Washington, the USA: Population Reference Bureau, 2002), 39 pages, 11.

[105] International Organization for Migration, *The State of Migration Management in Central America: an Applied Research, Final Report* (Geneva, Switzerland: International Organization for Migration, 2002), 89 pages, 13.

Mainland market.[106] Both the Mainland and the HKSAR have been taking measures to simplify passport and visa application procedures. Since May 2002, it is easier for Mainland Chinese to obtain a visa for Hong Kong.[107] Since August 2003, residents in South China's Guangdong Province have been able to commute to Hong Kong with only an identification card rather than a passport.[108] It is predicted that further increases in the number of people moving between the regions will occur.

2.4 Conclusions

Migration stems from human nature or instinct. It provides the basis for a 'natural right' to leave and return. With a progression from agrarian to industrial societies, RLR has correspondingly progressed and crystallised into a recognised legal right. Admitting RLR as a positive right is mainly to describe the wide legal recognition in the world, rather than to accept the utilitarian aspect or deny the nature of RLR as a natural right. In actuality, the more RLR in the sense of positive law conforms to RLR in the sense of natural law, the more the relevant laws are efficient and violations lessen. Meanwhile, RLR needs be rational; to maintain itself within the limits of human nature.

The history of laws governing RLR reveals that the right developed from the privilege of people with special status, to the right of all people. Following the Second World War, recognition of RLR by States has increased and international instruments have also evinced that the recognition of RLR is moving gradually beyond the national borders. While the formal recognition of RLR is not enough to ensure its enjoyment, it is undoubtedly a significant starting point for its effective protection. Since the emergence of the modern concept of the passport, the passport has become the major instrument governing RLR. The trend is toward simplification and easing of passport application procedures and the standardisation of forms. Among the factors driving the development of the laws governing RLR, political imperatives decide the grant of rights and economic imperatives set the practical demands of RLR by people. The influences of politics on RLR are more significant than the influences of economics.

---

[106] "Guangdong Could Win big from the CEPA" in *The China Daily*, 4 August 2003, http://www.getgd.net/cepa/cepa_e/GD%20win%20big.htm (accessed 16/09/2006); Wong, Alan, *Hong Kong: Stronger than Ever* at dinner talks at Four Seasons Hotel, Sydney, Thursday 10 July 2003.

[107] Jiang, Zhuqing, "Mainland SAR Visa Procedures Simplified" in *The China Daily,* 30 May 2002, http://www.chinadaily.com.cn/en/doc/2002–05/30/content_121768.htm (accessed 16/09/2006).

[108] Duan, Ruolan, "ID to be travel passport" in *The China Daily,* 18 March 2003, http://www.chinadaily.com.cn/en/doc/2003–03/18/content_158340.htm (accessed 16/09/2006).

Global restructuring generates or amplifies international migration and, in turn, the movement of people across borders is an indication of the globalisation of societies. An increased number of countries have formulated new immigration policies to face the trend of globalisation and the reality of international migration, for example, to attract more economic migrants and be inclined to accept flexible multi-citizenship policies. Although the causes of international migration do not change much, the management of international migration is likely to become more controversial, difficult and urgent in the 21st century, because it brings into play many sensitive issues of national security and identity, of social change and cultural adaptation, and of economic vitality and development.

Chapter Three
RLR in International Migration Law

INTRODUCTION

Few rights are more generally proclaimed or more widely abridged than RLR.[1] This chapter will define the current legal status of RLR in international migration law, to identify important issues that determine criteria by which RLR may be reasonably restricted.

The analysis begins with the recognition and standards of RLR, and sources of evolving jurisprudence of RLR. Given that an individual's RLR is bound with the possession of a passport and enough foreign exchange, this chapter will then analyse rights related to those possessions. Permissible limits on RLR have always emerged as the most contentious issue in this area and are therefore a focus of attention here. A necessary extended analysis of the right to leave and the right to return then follows in two sections. The analysis in Chapter three may provide an objective criterion and reference by which China could compare its laws.

---

[1] Plender, Richard, *International Migration Law*, Revised 2nd ed. (Dordrecht, the Netherland: Martinus Nijhoff Publishers, 1988), 95.

3.1 General Considerations on RLR

This section examines the recognition of RLR in international migration law, to clarify the standards of RLR internationally and domestically, to then consider disputes with respect to standards and review the sources of evolving jurisprudence of RLR.

3.1.1 *The recognition of RLR*

By whichever criterion it is classified, RLR has considerable international recognition as a human right. Its wide recognition is one of the most important reasons for its significance. Where RLR is concerned, countries can generally be placed in two groups. The first comprises 152 countries that have ratified the ICCPR before June 2004, and recognised RLR as a fundamental human right, with an international obligation to effectively protect it. Most of these countries fulfill their international obligations by incorporating the terms of the international instruments into the detail of their domestic laws, including their Constitutions. The second group of about 40 countries including Indonesia, Malaysia, Pakistan, Turkey, Saudi Arabia, China and Cuba that have not yet ratified the ICCPR. While they ratified the *Charter of the United Nations* and the UDHR, and accordingly might recognize RLR as a human right, they usually do not regard RLR as a real right in practice – it remains an aspirational right, on paper.

The recognition of RLR and the recognition of the freedom of movement within a territory do not necessarily follow one another. In China, for example, the fact that people do not enjoy freedom of movement within the territory is not the key cause for preventing them from leaving China.[2] This is contrary to the idea that "when he is confined to a particular locality or reservation, he is in effect prevented from leaving the State itself."[3] Freedom of movement and RLR are not always indivisible.

---

[2] Though millions of Chinese people might move around mainland China, their households, personal dossiers, medical treatments, employment, education, housing could not be moved together. There are much differences in these fields between the original resident areas and migration areas. From this angle, Chinese people have not truly enjoyed the freedom of movement. Most Chinese scholars, for example Liu Wujun, Zeng Wenhong, Peng Xiuzhi, Zhang fan etc. accepted this point.

[3] Ingles, Jose D., *Study of Discrimination in Respect of the Right of Everyone to Leave any Country, Including his Own, and to Return to His Country,* the UN Publication Sales No.: 64. XIV. 2 New York: 1963, 9.

3.1.2 *Standards of RLR*

There is a widely accepted common standard of human right in international migration law, while a particular standard of human rights simultaneously exists in some countries. The Preamble of the UDHR established that:

> A common standard of achievement for all peoples and all nations, . . . to secure their universal and effective recognition and observance, both among the peoples of Member States themselves and among the peoples of territories under their jurisdiction.

As far as RLR is concerned, the common standard is stated in Article 13 (2) of the UDHR and the ICCPR. The UN Human Rights Committee (HRC) considers that RLR contained in the ICCPR is the universal minimum standard. The ICCPR is not merely the codification of our highest values. It is elsewhere considered that it is also a formula for the effective defence of democratic societies from terrorism. Preamble, Paragraph 5 of the ICCPR set out that States have the obligations under the *Charter of the United Nations* to promote universal respect for, and observance of, human rights and freedoms, which certainly include RLR. The efforts of the international community on human rights have drawn upon earlier notions from religion and natural law that implied the existence of a common humanity.

It is not surprising that the universal minimum standard mentioned above reflects Western, particularly American values and institutions. This is due to American dominance after the Second World War in the very period that contemporary concepts of international human rights have taken shape. Therefore, some countries do not accept it. The standard and model preferred by Asian countries, for instance, places a heavy emphasis on economic development. Asian States have recognised in Article 8 of the *Bangkok Declaration* 1993 that:

> While human rights are universal in nature, they must be considered in the context of dynamic and evolving process of international norm-setting, bearing in mind the significance of national and regional particularities and various historical, cultural and religious background.

The Chinese government contends that the core of exit and entry administration is in the examination and approval of applications. Chinese citizens cannot go abroad without justification.[4] This is quite different from the international standard

[4] Mao, Fengping, editor, *The Explanation of the Law and Regulations Governing exit and entry and the Collections of Related Regulations* (*Chujing Rujing Falv Fagui Sijie Yu Xiangying Fagui Zhaibian*) (Changchun, China: the Publishing House of Jilin Renmin, 1994), 75. Also see Department of Politics under the Ministry of Public Security, *Frontier Defence and Exit and Entry Administration, the Series of Basic Textbook of People's Police Operation*: (*Bianfang Yu Churu Jing Guanli, Renmin Jingcha Gongan Yewu Jichu*

that regards the protection and realisation of RLR as the core of exit and entry administration, and therefore that it is unnecessary for the authorities of a State to require reasons for going abroad.

The international community respects the various national standards of human rights. The same legal logic can be used in regard to RLR. The UN has declared, in the Second World Conference on Human Rights that "the significance of national and regional particularities and various historical, cultural and religious backgrounds must be borne in mind."[5] In other words, the Second World Conference on Human Rights did not effectivelu negate the notion of cultual relativism espoused by the earlier Bankok Declaration. Scholars have also asserted that Western countries should not and cannot regard their own human rights standards as the only proper ones to which all other countries must conform.[6] Meanwhile, countries and regions preferring particular standards need also to accept and respect the universal minimum standard – particularity does not justify the denial of a common standard or its substitution with another. Fortunately, Asian countries have reaffirmed their commitment to principles contained in the *Charter of the United Nations* and the UDHR. The Chinese have officially accepted that it will perform its international obligations with respect to RLR in the light of the *Charter of the United Nations*, the UDHR and the ICCPR.[7]

It is a difficult but necessary task to find a way to resolve the differences between national and international standards, because unlike other human rights, usually limited to one country's territory, RLR is distinguished by its transnational character. The violation of RLR in one country may lead to the abuse of other fundamental human rights in other countries. The acceptance of the same common standard of RLR internationally and within all countries will not occur without a joint effort of particular countries, the international community and the West. RLR in the South can only be empty paper promise without the cooperation and assistance of the North.

Jiaochai), examined by Committee of Textbook Editing and Examination of the Ministry of Public Security, Internal Publication in Public Security Organs (Gongan Jiguan Neibu Faxing) (Beijing: the Publishing House of Qunzhong, 1999), 318.

[5] The United Nations General Assembly, *Report of the World Conferences on Human Rights Vienna, 14–25 June 1993 Report of the Secretary-General*, Distr. General A/CONF.157/24 (Part I), 13 October 1993, 18.

[6] Liu, Shengping, Xia, Yong, editor, *Human Rights and the World* (*Renquan Yu Shijie*) (Beijing: the Publishing House of People's Courts, 1996), 126–130.

[7] Committee of Textbook Editing and Examination of the Ministry of Public Security, *Frontier Defence and Exit and Entry Administration, the Series of Basic Textbook of People's Police Operation* (*Renmin Jingcha Gongan Yewu Jichu Jiaocai: Bianfang Yu Churu Jing Guanli*), Internal Publication in Public Security Organs (*Gongan Jiguan Neibu Faxing*) (Beijing: the Publishing House of Qunzhong,1999), 279.

The West in this regard is faced with a dilemma. If it requires certain countries to reform the national standard of RLR, they may receive a mammoth flow of immigration in the short term. If the West ignores the violation of RLR in certain countries who do not perform their international obligations, their national interest in those countries will be damaged in the long term. In practice, the West has been trying to balance national interests and human rights idealism. As the US Secretary of the State commented in 2003, the "combination of idealism and practical policy implementation has become a hallmark of our foreign policy in the area of international human rights."[8]

3.1.3 *Sources of evolving jurisprudence of RLR*

As discussed earlier, RLR has been widely recognised in numerous international conventions, international declarations and domestic laws. The HRC was established under Part IV of the ICCPR in 1977.[9] The European Human Rights Commission (EUCM), the inter-American Human Rights Commission (AMCM) and the African Commission on Human and People's Rights (AFCM) have become far more active in recent years. As Hurst Hannum has pointed out, an increasingly large corpus of jurisprudence of RLR has emerged since the 1972 Uppsala Declaration on RLR.[10] Although the evolving jurisprudence of RLR does not possess formal institutions responsible for law creation, there are recognised and accepted methods by which legal rules come into existence and several ways in which the precise content of legal rules can be identified. These are the sources of evolving jurisprudence of RLR.

The first source is international conventions or treaties. Article 38(1)(a) of the *Statute of the International Court of Justice* (Statute of ICJ) speaks of "international conventions, whether general or particular, establishing rules expressly recognised by the contesting States." Treaty means formal agreement between two or more countries.[11] Treaties range from those generally defining RLR, such as the

---

[8] Powell, Colin L. Preface to *Supporting Human Rights and Democracy: The U.S. Record 2002–2003* by the Bureau of Democracy, Human Rights, and Labour, the State Council, the USA, http://www.state.gov/r/pa/prs/ps/2003/21820.htm (accessed 16/09 2006).

[9] The HRC has the competence to receive complaints from other States, and mediate in order to achieve a settlement. See part IV of the ICCPR.

[10] Hannum, Hurst, *The Right to Leave and Return in International Law and Practice* (Dordrecht, the Netherlands: Martinus Nijhoff Publishers, 1987), 46.

[11] Hornby, A. S., *Oxford Advanced Learner's English-Chinese Dictionary* (*Niujin Gaojie Yinghan Shuangjie Cidian*), 4th editon (Hong Kong and Beijing: The Commercial Press and Oxford University Press, 1997), 1625.

ICCPR and the 1975 Helsinki Final Act, to those specially dealing with one part of RLR, such as the CERD and the CRC and those focusing on RLR in regional area such as the EHR, AMR, AFR and *Benelux Agreement* 1960. Given the character of consciousness and deliberation, international conventions are the most important source of evolving jurisprudence of RLR.

The second source is international custom. Article 38(1)(b) of the Statute of ICJ refers to "international custom, as evidence of a general practice accepted as law".[12] Article 102(2) of *The Third Restatement of the Foreign Relations Law of the United States* 1987 provides that more specifically, customary international law "results from a general and consistent practices of States which is followed by them from a sense of legal obligation." Although there has been a tendency to codify customary international law,[13] and codification brings with it divergences between the opinions of different States and a certain amount of compromise and slow process, international custom has a definite advantage in enabling international law to develop in line with the needs of the time.

The evidence of international custom may be found in the actual practice of States. A rough idea of a State's practice can be gathered from a State's statutes, as for instance with the *Norwegian Immigration Act* 1988,[14] and from reports of actions taken by States. For instance here, the Chinese Xinhua News Agency reports that the Foreign Affairs Committee of the USA agreed to cancel the restrictions on travelling to Cuba.[15] It can also be gathered from statements made by government representatives to Parliament, to the press, at the international conferences and meetings of international organisations, as for instance in China when spokesperson Zhang Qiyue of the Ministry of Foreign Affairs, China (MFA) told the press that the Chinese government has always committed itself to protecting human rights and fundamental freedoms of the Chinese people.[16]

The third source is general principles of law. Article 38(1)(b) of the Statute of ICJ mentions "the general principles of law recognised by civilised nations." It is

---

[12] Brierly remarks "what is sought for is a general recognition among States of a certain practice as obligatory." See Judge Read in the *Fisheries* case, ICJ Reports (1951), I9I: "Customary international law is the generation of the practice of States."

[13] Akehurst, Michael, *A Modern Introduction to International Law*, 6th edition (London: Harper Collins Academic, 1987 and New York: Routledge, 1987), 33.

[14] Section 17 of the *Norwegian Immigration Act* 1988 regulate "Any refugee who is in the realm or at the Norwegian border has on application the right to asylum (refuge) in the realm."

[15] Chinese Xinhua News Agency, "The Foreign Affairs Committee Agree to Cancel the Restrictions on Travelling to Cuba" (*Mei Canyiyuan Waiweihui Tongyi Jiechu Dui Guba Lvxing Xianzhi*), *Australian Chinese Daily*, 8, 9 November 2003, International News section.

[16] "Spokesperson Zhang Qiyue's Remarks on the Country Report on Human Rights Issued by the US (26/02/2004)", http://www.fmprc.gov.cn/eng/xwfw/2510/t69782.htm (accessed 02/03/2004).

designed to provide a solution in cases where treaties and custom provided no guidance, and to ensure that there is always some rule to fall back on.[17] It means the general principles of both international law and national law. In a decision of the European Court of Justice in 1975, it was said that it was a principle of international law, which the (at that time) European Economic Community (EEC) Treaty could not be assumed to disregard in the relations between Member States, that a State is precluded from refusing to its own nationals the right of entry or residence.[18]

The fourth source can be found in judicial decisions, which are described in Article 38(1)(d) of the Statute of ICJ as a subsidiary means for the determination of law. This direction is made subject to the provisions of Article 59 of Statute of ICJ, which states, "the decision of the court has no binding force except between the parties and in respect of that particular case". However it is widely agreed that judges can also create new law. Many of its decisions introduced innovations into international law, which have subsequently won general acceptance to avoid accusations of bias. The International Court of Justice, European Court of Human Rights (EUCT) and inter-American Court of Human Rights (AMCT) play a key important role in this regard.

The case law of some quasi-judicial international and domestic bodies like the HRC, Ombudsman's offices, administrative human rights commissions, and/or legislative human rights committees, cannot be ignored. For example, the prevailing majority interpretation of 'one's own country' in *Stewart v Canada* (538/93) seems quite harsh to a State's long-term alien residents. States parties have raised limits to justify restrictions on RLR in *Peltonen v Finland*. They often provide a progressive interpretive approach – albeit not always legally binding, however at times more creative than those found in judicial decisions.

The fifth source is 'the teachings of the most highly qualified publicists of the various nations' which is also set forth as subsidiary means for the determination of rules of law in Article 38(1)(d) of the Statute of ICJ. The *Study of Discrimination in Respect of the Right of Everyone to Leave any Country, including his Own, and to Return to His Country* (1963 Ingles Study on RLR), including *1963 Ingles Draft Principles on RLR* (1963 Ingles Draft Principles on RLR) made by Jose D. Ingles[19] has had some formative influence on the jurisprudence of RLR.

[17] Dixon, Martin, *Textbook on International Law* (London: Blackstone Press Ltd., 1990), 30.

[18] *Van Duyn v. Home office* [1975] I C.M.L.R. I, I8. See also Weis, *Nationality and Statelessness in International Law* (1956), 49–50, Quoted in Goodwin-gill, Guy S., *International Law and the Movement of Persons Between States* (Oxford: Oxford University Press, 1978), 137.

[19] Mr. Jose D. Ingles is one Philiphine Judge. He, as the Special Rapporteur, drafted *The Study of Discrimination in Respect of the Right of Everyone to Leave Any Country, Including His Own, and to Return to His Country*. The study was finally submitted to the

They are many other sources analogous to the 'publicists', and at least as authoritative. As far as RLR is concerned, it is mainly the reports and declarations accepted by the UN, the HRC and other international experts conferences. For example, the 1963 UN Draft Principles on RLR adopted by the CPDPM, the 1972 Uppsala Declaration on RLR adopted by the Uppsala Colloquium, the 1986 Strasbourg Declaration on RLR adopted by the Meeting of Experts on RLR, and 1999 General Comment No.27 on Freedom of Movement (Article 12) adopted by the HRC.

3.2 State Acceptance of RLR

RLR is generally conceptualised as a right, or the freedom from arbitrary State interference with an individuals' rights. It requires States to accept citizens leaving and returning to the territory. The minimum expected of a State, by way of positive activity, are the guarantee of a passport[20] and the ability to exchange foreign currency. In this section, the right to obtain necessary travel documents, particularly a passport, will be outlined, followed by a discussion of passport administration, and the effect on RLR of not having a passport. Finally, the right to access foreign exchange will be analysed.

3.2.1 *The right to obtain necessary travel document, particularly a passport*

An individual's RLR, in the overwhelming majority of cases, is inextricably linked to one's possession of a passport. In order to enable an individual to enjoy RLR, obligations are imposed both on the State of residence and on the State of nationality. The State of residence is primarily obliged to avoid interfering with an individual's freedom to leave. The State of nationality owes a positive duty to ensure that it is effectively possible to leave by issuing the necessary travel documents, usually a passport.

Sub-Commission on Prevention of Discrimination and Protection of Minorities at its fifteenth session in 1963. The principles respecting this right, drafted the study was adopted by the Sub-Commission at the same session. The study is the first comprehensive work focused on RLR. Both of them exerted great influence on future research on this field.

[20] Foldesi, Tamas, "The Right to Move and Its Achilles' Heel, The Right to Asylum", in *Connell Journal of International Law*, Spring 1993 (8) 289, 12.

A passport is intended to distinguish between those who may and may not enter or leave.[21] It is primarily an expression of the attempt by modern nation-States to assert exclusive control over the legal means of international movement. The passport has developed into serving as both a travel and identity document for the nationals of the issuing State, stateless persons, and aliens who are unable or unwilling to obtain passports from the authorities of their countries of nationalities.[22] The passport cannot be reduced to an instrument of State control, even if that is its principal function today.

Possession of a passport equates with having permission to leave one's State. With respect to the right to be admitted into a State, the passport provides a certificate of identification. Passports have come to be universally required for admission to foreign territory, but they may not, in themselves, be sufficient to gain admission.[23] In the case of the right to return, the passport is evidence that the bearer has an incontestable right to enter the territory controlled by its issuing State, if the bearer is denied entry into or expelled from other States.

3.2.2 *Passport administration*

As analysed in last sub-section, States are obliged to grant their nationals the right to obtain the necessary travel documents, particularly a passport. Although the issuance of a passport to a citizen is clearly a matter within the jurisdiction of State authorities, the following rules for the administration of passports need to be followed.

(1) No State shall refuse to issue a passport on the ground of the applicant's inability to present authorisation to enter another country, such as a letter of invitation, detailed route schedule, or financial evidence.
(2) Procedures for the issuance of passports shall be expedient, not be uncauseably lengthy or burdensome. In the environment of information technology, online or telephone applications play a vital role of facilitating efficiency. It is unacceptable to fail to reply to an application.
(3) Every applicant shall be entitled to promptly obtain a certified receipt for the application. The receipt must clearly state the date of application.

[21] Torpey, John, *The Invention of The Passport: Surveillance, Citizenship and the State* (Cambridge, the UK: Cambridge University Press, 2 000), 1.

[22] Weis, P., *Nationality and Statelessness in International Law,* 2nd revised editions (B. V., Alphen aan den Rijn, the Netherlands: Sijthoff & Noordhodd International Publishers 1979), 223.

[23] Torpey, John, *The Invention of The Passport: Surveillance, Citizenship and the State* (Cambridge, the UK: Cambridge University Press, 2 000), 163.

(4) Where a passport is denied, withdrawn, cancelled or postponed, the applicant shall be informed officially in writing of the decision, with the facts upon which the decision is based and the available avenues to appeal against the decision.[24] Rejection of the application without providing detailed causes is inconsistent with international law and practice.
(5) No one shall be arbitrarily denied passport under domestic law.[25]

Further, "The formalities for the issuance of any travel document, including the conditions for its denial, withdrawal or cancellation, shall be provided by law or regulations which shall be made public."[26] The applicant shall access to all laws and regulations. In countries which have freedom of information laws, such as Australia, people have the right to "see documents (including those containing information about the applicant) held by Commonwealth Ministers, their Departments and some statutory authorities" and to "see rules and practices which are used in making decisions", and to "look at and buy copies of manuals and guidelines which agencies use in making decisions".[27] In contrast, in countries without freedom of information laws, such as China, numerous unpublicised administrative measures and policies are inaccessible, reflecting a closed legal culture and presenting a bureaucratic barrier to information concerning the cause for administrative decisions.

3.2.3 *The effect on RLR of not having a passport*

The lack of a passport significantly influences RLR. In *Vidal Martins v Uruguay*, the HRC commented that:

---

[24] Mr. Mamdouh Habib, the Australian who spent three years in Guantanamo Bay prison. Habib returned to Australia without being charged with an offence in January 2005. Upon arrival, his passport was seized by the Federal Government, amid claims that he remains a security threat. He Mamdouh Habib is appealing that decision to Australian Appeal Tribunal (AAT). See Hassan, Toni, "Habib fights for his Australian passport" (4 February, 2005), http://www.abc.net.au/worldtoday/content/2005/s1296064.htm (accessed 2005–7–7)

[25] These five rules of the administration of passport are draw from Article IV of 1963 Ingles Draft Principles on RLR, Article IV of 1963 UN Draft Principles on RLR, Article 13 to 16 of the 1972 Uppsala Declaration on RLR, and Article 4 (g), Article 9 and Article 10(c) to (e) of the 1986 Strasbourg Declaration on RLR

[26] Article II (d) of *1963 Ingles Draft Principles on RLR,* adopted by the UN Sub-Commission on the Prevention of Discrimination and Protection of Minorities, Res. 2B (XV), UN Doc. E/CN. 41846 (1963).

[27] Window on the Law Home Page, http://www.law.gov.au, quoted in Healey, Justin editor, *Human Rights and Civil Rights, Issues in Society, Volume 139*, The Spinney Press, Independent Educational Publisher, Balmain, Australia, 2000, 33.

> The refusal by a State to issue a passport or prolong its validity for a national residing abroad may deprive this person of the right to leave the country of residence and travel elsewhere.[28]

Additionally, the effect of not having a passport on the right to return are less than on the right to leave. The UN Sub-Commission on Prevention of Discrimination and Protection of Minorities (CPDPM) determined that "[n]o one shall be denied the right to return to his own country on the ground that he has no passport or other travel document."[29] It is presumed that the effect of not having a passport on the right to return might be greatly reduced if this is accepted and exercised in practice.

Refusal to issue a passport, so restricting the right to leave, must be justified pursuant to Article 12(3) of the ICCPR. The issuance of other identity and travel documents is not an acceptable cause. This point was enunciated by the HRC in the Liechtenstein Case, where it was stated that the issuance of identity and travel documents by the State of residence in no way releases the State of nationality from its obligation to issue or renew a passport.[30]

States that deny their citizens a passport violate Article 12(2) of the ICCPR, insofar as this denial is not justified pursuant to Article 12(3) of the ICCPR. Even if refusal of a passport did not prevent the applicant from moving to another State, it would still interfere with the freedom of movement. The freedom to leave a country implies that there is freedom to leave any country into which a person has been admitted.

3.2.4 *The right to access foreign exchange*

The right to access foreign exchange is not an issue in States that have a freely convertible foreign exchange market. It is a significant issue for RLR in States that have a managed foreign exchange system. Deprivation of the right to access foreign exchange could result in financial difficulties when travelling abroad. Thus, despite being issued with a passport, RLR cannot be realised without access to foreign exchange.

---

[28] The HRC, "Freedom of movement (Art.12): 02/11/99. CCPR/C/21/Rev.1/Add.9, the ICCPR General comment 27. (General Comments)", http://www.unhchr.ch/tbs/doc.nsf/(symbol)/CCPR.C.21.Rev.1.Add.9,+CCPR+General+comment+27.En?OpenDocument (accessed 30–05–2003).

[29] Article II (d) of the 1963 Ingles Draft Principles on RLR, adopted by the UN Sub-Commission on the Prevention of Discrimination and Protection of Minorities, Res. 2B (XV), UN Doc. E/CN. 41846 (1963).

[30] Nowak, Manfred, *U.N. Covenant on Civil and Political Rights: the ICCPR Commentary*, Kehl am Rhein, Strasbourg, Arlington, Germany, 1993, 206.

Incontrovertibly, States owe a positive obligation to allow access to a minimum amount of foreign currency.[31] 'A minimal amount foreign currency' means the amount to meet one's financial requirements while abroad, consistent with the living standards of the destination State, rather the living standards of the home country. The CPDPM has accepted "economic controls or currency restrictions imposed with a view to safeguarding the national economy shall not be abused to deny any national the right to leave his country."[32]

Three matters need to be addressed in order to aid the realisation of RLR. Firstly, the applicant is entitled to exchange enough currency before leaving the country. Obviously, the applicant cannot plan into the future without adequate funds. Secondly, the applicant must be able to carry outwards enough foreign exchange, as preferred by the applicant, whether in cash or non-cash forms. The capping of carrying foreign exchange sums need to accommodate the sum needed by the emigrant or traveller. Thirdly, applicants need to be entitled to freely remit foreign exchange from their home countries to deal with ordinary and unexpected costs. Otherwise, the right to leave, especially the right to leave for business or investment, will be adversely affected.

3.3 Permissible limits on RLR

Although RLR and limits on RLR have been widely accepted and acknowledged in the international community, permissibility of the limits on RLR are disputed. This section will clarify the universally permissible limits on RLR, or reasonable restrictions, to provide a reference point for the assessment of other issues regarding RLR in international and Chinese migration law.

3.3.1 *General permissible limits*

Clearly, limiting RLR can be justified. No reasonable person would wish to assert that RLR is absolute. States must refrain from violations of RLR, and any limits on any of those rights must be permissible. The question is, what limits are acceptable? Article 29 (2) of the UDHR applies to RLR, which provides:

> In the exercise of [one's] rights and freedoms, everyone shall be subject only to such limits as are determined by law solely for the purpose of securing due recognition and respect for the rights and freedoms of others and of meeting the just requirements of morality, public order and the general welfare in a democratic society.

[31] Foldesi, Tamas, "The Right to Move and Its Achilles" Hell, The Right to Asylum", *Connell Journal of International Law*, Spring 1993, 289, 12.

[32] Article I (f) of the 1963 Ingles Draft Principles on RLR, adopted by the UN Sub-Commission on the Prevention of Discrimination and Protection of Minorities, Res. 2B (XV), UN Doc. E/CN. 41846 (1963), 40.

In specifically addressing RLR, Article 12(3) of the ICCPR adds three new terms, beyond those contained in Article 29(2), namely: national security, *ordre public* and public health; and omits the expression "the general welfare in a democratic society". According to Article 12 (3) of the ICCPR, States may limit RLR in order to protect the kinds of interests enumerated in the ICCPR, provides that the limits:

- are provided by law;
- are consistent with the other rights recognized in the Covenant;
- to protect national security, public order (*ordre public*), public health or morals or the rights and freedoms of others; and
- are necessary for achieving this purpose.[33]

The limits permitted by Article 12(3) of the ICCPR are more extensive than those permitted by Article 29(2) of the ICCPR. However, given the relatively limited cases law of the HRC on RLR, it can be surmised that the above limits may be interpreted in a similar manner to the way they have been in the context of other ICCPR rights. Similar limits are found in Article 2(3) of the EHR P4, Articles 18 and 19 of *European Social Charter* 1961 (ESC), Article 22(3) and (4) of the AMR, Article 12(2) of the AFR, and other international human rights conventions.

Permissible limits are statements of duties, rather than rights, because RLR is framed in negative terms.[34] That is, States must not prohibit or obstruct a person's attempt to leave and return.[35] The permissible limits on RLR are of a general nature. Individual States are free to enact specific rules regulating RLR within their jurisdiction. In many cases, permissible limits relating to RLR apply to other human rights. Although the words used by international instruments should be uniformly interpreted, their practical significance may vary according to character of the right to which they relate.

If States correctly interpret permissible limits, abuse of RLR is less likely. Examples of permissible limits include road rules, access to nature reserves or animal sanctuaries, earthquake, avalanche or quarantine zones, areas of civil unrest and private property. Specific individuals may be subjected to legitimate limits on their RLR, such as convicted criminals[36] and those performing military service.[37]

---

[33] Henkin, Louis, editor, *The International Bill of Rights: the Covenant on Civil and Political Rights* (New York: Columbia University Press, 1981), 178.

[34] Copenhagen Conference on the Human Dimension of the CSCE, June 1990, Article 9.5.

[35] Baubock, Rainer, *Transnational Citizenship: Membership and Rights in International Migration* (Cheltenham, the UK: Edward Elgar, 1994), 325.

[36] Joseph, Sarah and Sehultz, Jenny et al., *The International Covenant on Civil and Political Rights: Cases, Materials, and Commentary: Cases, Materials, and Commentary* (New York: Oxford University Press, 2000), 259.

[37] The HRC "acknowledges that it is normal for individual performing military service to be subjected to restrictions in their freedom of movement." Quoted in Joseph, Sarah and

3.3.2 *State practice*

Almost all States impose various limits on RLR. Generally speaking, they are similar to the terms used in international instruments. However terms concerned vary in the laws of different countries. It is necessary to judge these limits from international migration law rather than only from domestic law.

In the USA:

> In the case of comparable magnitude, *Koremastu v. United States*, 323 US 214, 218, the court allowed the Government in time of war to exclude citizens from their homes and restrict their freedom of movement only on a showing of "the gravest imminent danger to the public safety".[38]

In the case of Egypt:

> Egyptian males who have not competed compulsory military service, may not travel abroad or emigrate, although this restriction can be circumvented. Unmarried women under the age of 21 must have permission from their fathers to apply for passports; unmarried women over 21 have their applications for passports checked by the police; married women require permission from their husbands.[39]

For Fiji, Section 34 (7) of the *Constitution of the Republic of the Fiji Islands* provides:

> A law may limit, or may authorize the limit of, the right of a person to freedom of movement:
>
> (a) in the interests of national security, public safety, public order, public morality or public health; or
> (b) for the purpose of protecting the economy of a particular area or the ecology or distinctive culture of the area;
> (c) for the purpose of imposing a restriction on the person that is caused by required to secure the fulfilment of an obligation imposed on the person by law; or
> (d) for the purpose of imposing causable restrictions on the holders of public offices as part of the terms and conditions of their employment; but only to the extent that the limit is causable and justifiable in a free and democratic society.

In Sri Lanka, Article 12(2)(3) and 13 of the *Constitution of the Republic of Sri Lanka* stipulate restriction on RLR as following:

Sehultz, Jenny et al., *The International Covenant on Civil and Political Rights: Cases, Materials, and Commentary: Cases, Materials, and Commentary* (New York: Oxford University Press, 2000), 237.

[38] "Right to Travel: the constitutional Case", http://www.ibike.org/cuba/ofac/law.htm (accessed 15/11/2004), 16 pages, 2.

[39] Baehr, Peter, Sadiwa, Lalaine and Smith Jacqueline, editor, *Human Right in Developing Countries 1996 Yearbook* (the Hague, the Netherlands: Kluwer Law International, 1996), 145.

Article 12 Freedom of movement.

12. [. . .]

(2) Every person shall be free to leave the Republic.

(3) Any restrictions shall not be placed on the exercise of the rights declared and recognized by this Article other than such restrictions prescribed by law as are necessary in a democratic society in the interests of national security or public order or national economy or the protection of public health or morality or for the purpose of securing due recognition and respect for the rights and freedoms of others or for the extradition of persons from the Republic.

Article 13 Freedom to return to Sri Lanka.

13. Every citizen shall be entitled to return to the Republic.

3.3.3 *Interpretation of permissible limits*

Diversity of experience, background, language, and culture of the ICCPR parties ensure that the interpretation of RLR is not based on one system of law or set of values. The HRC, the authoritative UN body for interpreting the ICCPR, considers that RLR should have a universal common meaning.[40] The interpretation of Article 12(3) of the ICCPR is based on customary international law and related international conventions. Article 31 (1) of the *Vienna Convention on the Law of Treaties* 1980 provides:

> A treaty shall be interpreted in good faith in accordance with the ordinary meaning to be given to the terms of the treaty in their context and in the light of its object and purpose.

The 'context' refers to the text itself, including its preamble and annexes, any agreements relating to the treaty, and instruments connected with the treaty. Other relevant agreements between States parties that are governed by international law should also be taken into account.[41] As a central rule of interpretation, an instrument should be construed in accordance with its dominant purpose. In the case of the ICCPR, the purpose is to protect individuals against government excesses.

Further, 'limit clauses' permitting derogations from and limit of rights, should be strictly and narrowly construed.[42] This point is widely supported. In 1999, the HRC produced a thorough commentary on Article 12 of the ICCPR (General Comment No. 27 of the HRC on Freedom of Movement). This represents the most

---

[40] Joseph, Sarah and Sehultz, Jenny et al., *The International Covenant on Civil and Political Rights: Cases, Materials, and Commentary: Cases, Materials, and Commentary* (New York: Oxford University Press, 2000), viii.

[41] Henkin, Louis, editor, *The International Bill of Rights: the Covenant on Civil and Political Rights* (New York: Columbia University Press, 1981), 293.

[42] Quoted in Hannum, Hurst, *The right to Leave and Return in International Law and Practice* (Dordrecht, the Netherlands: Martinus Nijhoff Publishers, 1987), 22.

authoritative interpretation of the ICCPR available. According to Article 5(1) of the ICCPR, any limit must be strictly construed. It provides:

> Nothing . . . may be interpreted as implying for any State, group or person any right to engage in any activity or perform any act aimed at the destruction of any of the rights and freedoms recognised herein or at their limits to a greater extent than is provided for in the present Covenant.

The EUCM concluded that restrictions of rights might not be applied so as to completely suppress the freedom, but are only necessary for preserving the values which the provision enumerates and protects. Accordingly, the Commission considered whether or not there had been an interference with the right protected and, whether or not this interference was justified in the light of the prescribed restrictions.[43] Article 29(c) of the AMR has more detailed provisions in this regard:

> No provisions of this Convention shall be interpreted as: (a) permitting any State Party, group, or person to suppress the enjoyment or exercise of the rights and freedoms recognised in this Convention or to restrict them to a greater extent than is provided for herein; (b) restricting the enjoyment or exercise of any right or freedom recognized by virtue of the laws of any State Party or by virtue of another convention to which one of the said State is a party; (c) precluding rights or guarantees which are inherent in the human personality or derived from representative democracy as a form of government; (d) excluding or limiting the effect that the *American Declaration of the Rights and Duties of Man* and other international acts of the same nature may have.

This is consistent with the objective of the limits, which is to ensure the effective enforcement of RLR, rather than to permit an increase in State power.

3.3.4 *The meaning of the terms used in the limit clauses*

This subsection will consider the interpretation of limits to RLR, according to the rules of construction discussed above. These are 'provided by law', 'national security', 'public order (*ordre public*)', 'public health', 'public morals', 'the rights and freedoms of others' and the 'test of necessity', and 'consistent with the other rights recognised in the present Covenant'.

3.3.4.1 'Provided by law'

'Provided by law'[44] suggests that an act must be authorised by specific legal provisions. It presumes that an act illegally authorised can never be justified,

---

[43] *Hanydside v. UK*, App. No. 5493/72, European Court of Human Rights, Judgment of 7 December 1976, Ser. A No. 24. Quoted in Sieghart, Paul, *The International Law of Human Rights* (New York: Oxford University Press, 1983), 91.

[44] The term of "provided by law" was used in Article 12 (2) of the ICCPR and Article 12 (2) of the AFR.

regardless of whether it is consistent with other rights. The terms 'prescribed by law',[45] 'in accordance with law'[46] and, 'pursuant to law'[47] are found in other international instruments. The former has the same meaning with 'provided by law' expressed in the ICCPR. The two latter connote that the action must be satisfied by reference to general legal principles, common law, the rule of law, or accepted government authority[48] as to provide a rational legal basis to a decision.

'Provided by law' is designed to ensure that citizens are plainly advised of any restrictions on RLR.[49] In contrast to Article 13, limits under Article 12(3) must be set down in law or by the judiciary.[50] As such, the law must be accessible to the public and formulated with sufficiently certain as to enable a person to regulate their conduct and foresee the legal consequences of their action.[51] General Comment No.27 of the HRC on Freedom of Movement stated that laws should adopt precise criteria for the application of restrictions of freedom, and may not confer unfettered administrative discretion.

'Law' means the domestic law of a State. Importantly, legal limits may either relate to the limit of the substantive right to leave and return or to administrative procedure. It is possible to detract from RLR protection by erecting bureaucratic barriers that deny access to appeals against administrative decisions. The EUCT asserted that the word 'law' covers not only statute law, but also unwritten law, subordinate legislation and Royal the Decrees.[52] In *Silver v United Kingdom*, the Court held that:

---

[45] Article 10 (2) of the CRC; and Article 5 (2) (a) of the *Declaration on the Human Rights of Individuals Who are not Nationals of the Country in Which They Live*, 1985.

[46] Article 2 (3) of the EHR P4.

[47] Article 22 (3) of the AMR.

[48] 10 GAOR Annexes, UN Doc. A/2929 1955 pages 58–59.

[49] De, Sous La Direction, editor, *The Limit of Human Rights in Comparative constitutional Law*, Les Edition Yvon Blais Inc. Canada, 1986. Also see opposite opinion, the term of "provided by law" could be satisfied only by a statute by either national congress or provincial congress." Pages 11–12.

[50] Nowak, Manfred, *U.N. Covenant on Civil and Political Rights: CCPR Commentary*, Kehl am Rhein, Strasbourg, Arlington, Germany, 1993, 209.

[51] *Malone v. the UK*, App. No. 8691/79, European Court of Human Rights, Judgment of 2 August 1984, Ser. A No. 82, 30; *Silver et al. v. the UK*, App. No. 5947/72, European Court of Human Rights, Judgment of 25 March 1983, Ser. A No. 61; Handyside *v.* the UK, App. No. 5493/72, European Court of Human Rights, Judgment of 7 December 1976, Ser. A No. 24; *Pinkney v. Canada*, Communication No. 27/1978, Human Rights Committee, Annual Report, 37 UN GAOR, Supp. No. 40, 1982 page 10.

[52] *Sunday Times v. the UK, X. v. Switzerland,* (7055/75) Report: DR 19.5; and *De Wilde, Ooms and Versyp v. Belgium* (2832/66; 2835/66; 2899/66) Judgment: 1 EHRR 373; Quoted in Sieghart, Paul, *The International Law of Human Rights,* (New York: Oxford University Press, 1983), 91–92.

> A norm cannot be regarded as a 'law' unless it is formulated with sufficient precision to enable the citizen to regulate his conduct: he must be able – if need be with appropriate advice – to foresee, to a degree that is causable in the circumstances, the consequences which a given action may entail.[53]

Mere administrative provisions are insufficient. Unfettered administrative discretion, without clear legislative directives and adequate notice to an applicant of the grounds on which a request is to be granted or denied, would not be sufficient to meet the requirement that limits be 'provided by law'.[54] Limiting the right to leave by way of administrative act, directive or plan is only permissible when the grounds upon which the right is interfered with are sufficiently certain. It is noted that the HRC is not qualified to evaluate whether the responsible departments of a State have correctly interpreted and applied its domestic law, unless it is established that they acted in bad faith or committed an abuse of power.[55]

As a final point, one must be careful to assess what is lawful in the context of RLR because of the complex relationship between international and domestic law. I am mindful of the words of Sam Blay and Ryszard Piotrowicz about lawfulness in the context of human rights. Their words can be cited to argue for a way to judge the lawfulness of domestic provisions related to RLR:

> It is difficult to maintain the argument, as Australia did in *A V Australia*, that the municipal law is in itself sufficient to provide the standard to assess the lawfulness of State conduct where international law seeks to reply on municipal standards and oversight, on the one hand, and national sovereignty and responsibility, on the other hand. Nevertheless, the point still remains that international obligations, particularly in the domain of human rights, if they are to be implemented in municipal law, would have little meaning if the eventual standard for compliance is the municipal law regime alone.[56]

3.3.4.2 'National security'

The 'nation' is a political entity constituted by a large group of people having a common origin, language and tradition. Nationhood does not contemplate the sur-

---

[53] *Silver et al. v. the UK*, App. No. 5947/72, European Court of Human Rights, Judgment of 25 March 1983, Ser. A No. 61; and *Sunday Times v. the UK*, (7055/75) Report: DR 19.5.

[54] Response of the representative of the Ukrainian S.S.R. to questions by members of the Human Rights Committee, UN Doc. the ICCPR/CSR. 612, 1985, 9.

[55] *Maroufidou v. Sweden* (R. 13/58) the HRC 36, 160, Quoted in Sieghart, Paul, *The International Law of Human Rights* (New York: Oxford University Press, 1983), 92.

[56] Blay, Sam and Piotrowicz, Ryszard, "the Awfulness of Lawfulness: Some Reflections on the Tension between International and Domestic Law", in Charlesworth, Hilary, McCorquodale, Robert etc., editor, *The Australian Year Book of International Law* Volume 21, the Centre of International and Public Law, Faculty of Law, Australian National University, 2001, 19.

vival of any particular government or ruling elite, whether that government has been democratically elected or imposed upon the population.[57] In the context of international law, 'security' should be consistently interpreted with the *Charter of the United Nations*, in which means political independence and territorial integrity, including the ongoing existence of a State.

National security is generally understood to mean protection of a State from espionage, sabotage, politically motivated violence, the promotion of communal violence, attacks on its defence installations, and from acts of foreign interference.[58] National security could be invoked as a justification for limiting human rights.[59] Article 4 of the 1986 Strasbourg Declaration on RLR provides that:

> A restriction based on 'national security' may be invoked only in situations where the exercise of the right poses a clear, imminent and serious danger to the State. When this restriction is invoked on the ground that an individual acquired military secrets, the restriction shall be applicable only for a limited time, appropriate to the specific circumstances, which should not be more than five years after the individual acquired such secrets.

The EUCT does not require the declaration of a state of war or national emergency as a precondition to the imposition on limiting RLR. Limits can be imposed in peacetime to prevent activities such as espionage or to protect military secrets.[60] Under the ICCPR, an individual cannot be prevented from leaving a country merely on the grounds that he or she holds of State secrets,[61] other than in times of war or national emergency.[62]

---

[57] Hannum, Hurst, *The right to Leave and Return in International Law and Practice* (Dordrecht, the Netherlands: Martinus Nijhoff Publishers, 1987), 28.

[58] Nygh, Peter E. and Butt, Peter, editor, *Butterworths Australian Legal Dictionary* (Sydney, Australia: Butterworths 1997) 774.

[59] Hannum, Hurst, *The Right to Leave and Return in International Law and Practice* (Dordrecht, the Netherlands: Martinus Nijhoff Publishers, 1987), 38; and Human Rights Committee, cited in Joseph, Sarah and Sehultz, Jenny et al., *The International Covenant on Civil and Political Rights: Cases, Materials, and Commentary: Cases, Materials, and Commentary,* (New York: Oxford University Press, 2000), 400; However, Kiss, Alexandre Charles opposed this opinion. "A threat to territorial integrity or economic well-being is not in itself sufficient to constitute a threat to national security." Henkin, Louis, editor, *The International Bill of Rights: the Covenant on Civil and Political Rights* (New York: Columbia University Press, 1981), 296.

[60] Henkin, Louis, editor, *The International Bill of Rights: the Covenant on Civil and Political Rights* (New York: Columbia University Press, 1981), 292.

[61] Paragraph 5 of General Comment No. 27 of the HRC on Freedom of Movement (Article 12)

[62] Ingles, Jose D, *1963 Ingles' Study on RLR,* the UN Publication Sales No.: 64. XIV. 2 New York: 1963, 40.

According to Ingles view, a person's activities should only be deemed prejudicial to national security if such activities are criminal, and criminal prosecution would be the best safeguard against the arbitrary denial of the right to leave any country on the grounds of national security. A threat to national security is not established on the grounds of political opinion, religious belief, or if the person is specially trained.[63] Terrorist activities are widely accepted as providing a threat to national security.

Acts constituting threats to national security have been enumerated in Article 4 of the *Law of State Security* 1993 (PRC) as follows:

> An act committed by institutions, organizations or individuals outside the territory of the People's Republic of China, or by other persons under the instigation or financial support of the afore-mentioned institutions, organisations or individuals, or by organisations or individuals within the territory in collusion with institutions, organisations or individuals outside the territory:
>
> (1) plotting to subvert the government, dismember the State or overthrow the socialist system;
> (2) joining an espionage organisation or accepting a mission assigned by espionage organisation or by its agent;
> (3) stealing, secretly gathering, buying, or unlawfully providing State secrets;
> (4) instigating, luring or bribing a State functionary to turn traitor; and,
> (5) committing any other act of sabotage endangering State security."

National security assessments are often made by the executive government, with minimal judicial review. Joseph and Schultz observe that:

> If executive governments are unprepared to reveal evidence grounding national security decisions to their own judiciary, they are extremely unlikely to reveal such evidence to an international body such as [the HRC].[64]

3.3.4.3 'Public order (*ordre public*)'

Public order is an ambiguous term that lacks a uniform meaning across jurisdictions. The term generally relates to orderly or peaceful behaviour in public places. 'Public order (*ordre public*)' provides a basis for restricting RLR in order to promote the efficient functioning of the public institutions. Article 4(e) of the 1986 Strasbourg Declaration on RLR explains:

---

[63] *Kent v. Dulles*, 357 the USA 116 (1958); *Aptheker v. Secretary of State*, 378 the USA 500 (1964); *Zemel v. Rusk*, 381 the USA 1 (1965); Henkin, Louis, editor, *The International Bill of Rights: the Covenant on Civil and Political Rights* (New York: Columbia University Press, 1981), 178.

[64] Joseph, Sarah and Sehultz, Jenny et al., *The International Covenant on Civil and Political Rights: Cases, Materials, and Commentary: Cases, Materials, and Commentary,* Oxford University Press, New York: 2000, 274.

> A restriction based on 'public order (*order public*)' shall be directly related to the specific interest which is sought to be protected. 'Public order (*order public*)' means the universally accepted fundamental principles, consistent with respect for human rights, on which a democratic society is based.

Loss of public order could cause instability or administrative confusion, affecting society as a whole. Criminal laws provide for a number of public order offences, such as riot and affray, offensive, indecent or obscene conduct, and damage of property. Public law also regulates activities such as change of name.

The addition of the French concept of *ordre public* may broaden the concept of 'public order'. *Ordre public* applies to the sphere of private law, whereas the common law notion of 'public order' relates to the public arena.[65] The concepts of public order and *ordre public* form an overarching principle designed to protect a minimum level of public interest and social organisation, consistent not only with the values of the individual society but with universal social norms.

Nowak has questioned, in respect of civil law obligations, whether an individual's freedom to leave the country might be restricted on account of private legal obligations, or to secure payment of a tax liability where there is no accompanying criminal allegation. Article 11 of the ICCPR prohibits imprisonment for private contractual breaches or financial obligations owed to the State or to private entities. Unpaid tax has recently been acknowledged as an acceptable limit on the right to leave. In the Peltonen Case, the HRC concluded that non-performance of a national obligation justifies deprivation of RLR.[66] This principle applies to States that require the performance of military service.

3.3.4.4 'Public health'

Limiting RLR on the grounds of public health, especially through the imposition of quarantine laws, can be regarded as a measure to preserve public order. Henkin points out that psychiatric evaluations cannot be used to deny RLR.[67] However, the quarantining of geographic areas following an outbreak of disease or other acute health risks, such as in the vicinity of a nuclear power plant, is permissible. Temporary restrictions on movement to prevent the breakdown of sanitation

---

[65] Lockwood, B. Jr., Finn, J. and Jubinsky, G., *Working Paper for the Committee of Experts on Limit Provisions,* 7 HRQ 35, 1985. Order public may be used to negate private law contacts 'in the interest of higher imperatives'; 'public order' is not used in the same way in common law jurisdictions.

[66] Joseph, Sarah and Sehultz, Jenny et al., *The International Covenant on Civil and Political Rights: Cases, Materials, and Commentary* (New York: Oxford University Press, 2000), 252.

[67] Henkin, Louis, editor, *The International Bill of Rights: the Covenant on Civil and Political Rights* (New York: Columbia University Press, 1981), 179.

services are also acceptable.[68] Support for limiting RLR on the basis of public health can be adduced from Article 12 of the *International Covenant on Economic, Social and Cultural Rights* 1966 (ICESCR), which provides that:

1. The States Parties to the present Covenant recognise the right of everyone to the enjoyment of the highest attainable standard of physical and mental health.
2. The steps to be taken by the States Parties to the present Covenant to achieve the full realisation of this right shall include those necessary for:

   (a) The provision for the reduction of the stillbirth-rate and of infant mortality and for the healthy development of the child;
   (b) The improvement of all aspects of environmental and industrial hygiene;
   (c) The prevention, treatment and control of epidemic, endemic, occupational and other diseases;
   (d) The creation of conditions which would assure to all medical service and medical attention in the event of sickness.

In addition, public health is expressly protected in Article 11 of the ESC and the ESC (Revised) 1996. Under these instruments, such measures can be taken to remove of the causes of ill health and prevention of epidemic, endemic and other disease. The Additional Protocol to the *American Convention on Human Rights in the Area of Economic, Social and Cultural Rights* 1988, recognises health as a public good and broadens it terms to include "the enjoyment of the highest level of physical, mental and social well-being". States Parties are obliged to adopt measures to provide universal immunisation against the principal infectious diseases and, prevent and treat endemic, occupational and other diseases.[69]

During the Severe Acute Respiratory Syndrome (SARS) epidemic, unaffected countries adopted temporary measures including limiting the freedom of movement and imposing quarantine restrictions, to prevent its proliferation, in April 2003, 94 countries had imposed travel restrictions on Chinese nationals. For example, Australia enacted laws to permit the cancellation of a visa where its holder was suspected of SARS infection. SARS affected countries, such as China, adopted temporary measures to limit persons leaving the territory, whether the person was a national or an alien. The Entry and Exit Inspection Service and Quarantine Bureau, China, advised people within the territory to postpone overseas travel if SARS symptoms appeared, and to seek diagnosis and treatment.[70]

---

[68] Jagerskiold, *The Freedom of Movement*, in Nowak, Manfred, *U.N. Covenant on Civil and Political Rights: ICCPR Commentary* (Kehl am Rhein Strasbourg-Arlington, the USA: N. P. Engel Publisher, 1993), 215.

[69] Article 10 of *Additional Protocol to the AMR in the Area of Economic, Social and Cultural Rights, 1988,* Ermacora, Felix, Nowak, Manfred and Tretter, Hannes editor, *International Human Rights: Documents and Introductory Notes*, (Vienna, Austria: Law Books in Europe, 1993), 320.

[70] Xinhua News Agency, "Proclamation: Strengthen Medical Examination for Exit and

It is uncertain whether a State must prohibit an individual who presents a health risk from travelling abroad, or may only recommend an individual not travel abroad. If a person must be prohibited from leaving on public health grounds, given that the permissible limits are not applicable to the right to return to one's own country, there is a potential for inconsistency between the right to exercise the permissible limits and the right to return. The situation demonstrates that the right to leave and the right to return can never be entirely separated, despite assertions to the contrary. To overcome this possibility, international co-operation during times of disease outbreak is important.

3.3.4.5 'Public morals'

Public morality is derived from social, philosophical and religious traditions. Limits on RLR on the grounds of protecting public morals should reflect a pluralist view of society rather than the dominant culture. The HRC has acknowledged, in *Hertzberg et al. v. Finland*, that public morals differ widely. There is no universally applicable common standard. Consequently, a margin of discretion must be accorded to the responsible national authorities.[71] The 'margin' seems to mirror the 'margin of appreciation' conferred on States Parties to the EHR P4. The margin of appreciation confers the benefit of the doubt with respect to a State compliance with the provisions of the EHR P4. The European Court of Justice (ECJ), in *Handyside v. UK*, indicated that it was not possible to find a uniform European conception of morals in the domestic law of the various European States.[72]

3.3.4.6 'The rights and freedoms of others'

The permissible limits on RLR to protect the rights and freedoms of others are potentially somewhat of a catchall. The HRC has never commented on its outer limits. It is hoped that 'rights' refers to other human rights, though unnecessarily in the ICCPR.[73] Others are certainly obliged not to interfere with RLR. Paragraph 6 of General Comment No. 27 of the HRC on Freedom of Movement regulates

---

Entry, Prevent SARS from Spreading worldwide" (*Gonggao: Jiaqiang Churujing Tijian Fangzhi Feidian Guoji Chuanbo*) (15–04–2003)", http://news.21cn.com/domestic/guoshi/2003–04–15/1008114.html (accessed 23–07–2003).

[71] Joseph, Sarah and Sehultz, Jenny et al., *The International Covenant on Civil and Political Rights: Cases, Materials, and Commentary* (New York: Oxford University Press, 2000), 393.

[72] *Handyside v. the UK*, App. No. 5493/72, European Court of Human Rights, Judgment of 7 December 1976, Ser. A No. 24.

[73] Joseph, Sarah and Sehultz, Jenny et al., *The International Covenant on Civil and Political Rights: Cases, Materials, and Commentary: Cases, Materials, and Commentary* (New York: Oxford University Press, 2000), 407.

that the State must ensure that RLR is protected from public and private interference. Family members (other than parents of minors), employers or other persons may not prevent the departure of any persons from the State.[74] RLR should not be inhibited by a husband in relation to one's legal or de facto wife, by parents of adult daughters, or by the State in relation to the movement of women generally.[75] Restrictions may be imposed to avert avoidance of an individual's duty to support their children; but it is otherwise difficult to deny RLR unless the right of another will be adversely affected.[76]

3.3.4.7 'The test of necessity'

RLR can be limited if it is 'necessary' to do so. The ICCPR refers only to 'necessary', Article 22(3) of the AMR and Article 2 of the EHR P4 qualify the term with the expression 'in a democratic society'. Neither term is used in Article 12 (2) of the AFR or Articles 18 and 19 of the ESC.

The absence of the words 'in a democratic society' in the ICCPR seems to stem from the understanding that the concept of democracy might be interpreted differently in various countries. However, a democratic society could be characterised by its respect for the principles of numerous human rights conventions. Paragraph 16 of General Comment No. 27 of the HRC on Freedom of Movement plainly requires a restriction of RLR on the grounds of necessity to be based on clear legal grounds and be proportionate to the circumstances of the case. Finally, paragraph 12 of General Comment No. 27 of the HRC on Freedom of Movement accepts that permissible restrictions must be necessary in a democratic society.

The term 'necessary' infers that the act is essential or unavoidable.[77] P. K. McWilliams argues that an act is necessary if performed in 'an emergency to causeably protect health, life or property' and 'there is no alternative'. Where an act 'interferes with the interests of another for the purpose of preventing harm to self or others', 'imminent peril must exist'.[78] Paul Sieghart argues that the notion 'necessary' implies the existence of a 'pressing social need' which may include a 'clear and present danger' determined by the circumstances of a given case.[79]

---

[74] Article 4 (f) of *Strasbourg Declaration on the Right to Leave and Return,* adopted by Experts on the Right to Leave and Return on 26 November 1986.

[75] Paragraph 16 of General Comment No. 27 of the HRC on Freedom of Movement (Article 12)

[76] Hannum, Hurst, *The right to Leave and Return in International Law and Practice* (Dordrecht, the Netherlands: Martinus Nijhoff Publishers, 1987), 43.

[77] Hornby, A. S., *Oxford Advanced Learner's English- Chinese Dictionary,* 4th edition (Hong Kong and Beijing: The Commercial Press and Oxford University Press, 1997), 983.

[78] McWilliams, P. K., *Canadian Criminal Evidence*, 3rd edition (Aurora, Canada: Canada Law Book, 1988), 4–11.

[79] *Arrowsmith v. the UK* (7050/75) Report : DR 19.5; *Golder v. the UK* (4451/70)

The application of the justification of necessity involves balancing the rights of the individual and the utilitarian 'greater good'. The State should attach priority to the rights of individuals when restricting RLR. The HRC has indicated that the mere assertion by a State that an individual was engaged in 'subversive activities' is not sufficient to discharge the burden of showing that detention of that individual was "necessary" within the meaning of Article 19 (3) of the ICCPR. Article 4(c) of the 1986 Strasbourg Declaration on RLR defines a restriction as 'necessary', "only if it responds to a pressing public and social need, pursues a legitimate aim and is proportionate to that aim." The requirement of necessity underscores the principle that restrictions on RLR are always the exception, not the rule.

3.3.4.8 'Consistent with the other rights recognised in the present Covenant'

The phrase 'consistent with the other rights recognised in the present Covenant' concedes that a person's RLR may be inconsistent with other rights or freedoms recognised in international conventions. RLR cannot be used to interfere with other rights or freedoms. To overcome an inconsistency under international law, domestic laws must be 'consistent with the other rights recognised' in the ICCPR. Whether States are to conform to the permissible scope of limits on human rights is a question of international law. It is questionable that States are capable of determining the permissible limits of RLR. It is therefore vital to create an appropriate international supervisory body to supervise State acts, and determine whether international standards have been complied with.

3.3.5 *The principle of proportionality*

The principle of proportionality is used to clarify the requirement of necessity. A limitation will only be proportionate to the circumstances that gives rise to the necessity if (i) the measures are carefully designed and rationally connected to achieve the objective; (ii) the right or freedom at issue is minimally impaired; (iii) a proportion exists between the effect of the measures which limit the right and the objective.[80] The HRC has endorsed the need for proportionality between the restriction of individual rights and the objective.[81] Thus, the severity, duration and,

---

Judgment: 1 EHRR 524; James, Young and *Webster v. the UK; Sunday Times v. the UK*, (7055/75) Report: DR 19.5; *Handyside v. the UK*, App. No. 5493/72, EUCT, Judgment of 7 December 1976, Ser. A No. 24. Quoted in Sieghart, Paul, *The International Law of Human Rights* (New York: Oxford University Press, 1983), 93.

[80] Dukelow, Daphne A. *The Dictionary of Canadian Law* (Barrie, Ontario, Canada: A. Carswell Publication, 1991), 835.

[81] Paragraphs 14–15 of General Comment No. 27 of the HRC on Freedom of Movement

geographic scope of any limits on RLR are justified only to the extent that they are strictly necessary and proportionate to achieve the objects of protecting national security, public order, public health and morals, and the rights and freedoms of others.

3.4 The Right to Leave the Country

Grotius characterised the right to leave as the most specific and unimpeachable axiom of the law of nations.[82] According to Article 12(2) of the ICCPR, the right to leave implies the right to leave a country at one's own will, whether the country of nationality, residence or any other country in which an individual finds oneself.

The right to leave is expressly recognised in the Constitutions of numerous States, diverse in their geographical locations, legal traditions and political inspirations.[83] Some of the more rigorous rules have operated in France, which once required exit visas and China, which has required various forms of exit passes or certificates for its nationals[84] and aliens.[85] In practice, a State might violate the right to leave. The most extreme example is that of Cuba, which is party to the *Inter-American Convention on Asylum* 1928 and the ICCPR. Nevertheless, Cuban nationals have been imprisoned or executed for attempting to leave the territory. This was graphically illustrated in October 1994, when over 40 men, women and children were killed for attempting to flee the island.[86]

(Article 12). Also see paragraph 6 of *General Comment No. 31 [80]: the Nature of the General Legal Obligations Imposed on the States Parties to the Covenant*, "Where such restrictions are made, States must demonstrate their necessity and only take such measures as are proportionate to the pursuance of legitimate aims in order to ensure continuous and effective protection of Covenant right."

[82] Plender, Richard, *International Migration Law*, Revised 2nd edition, 1988 (Dordrecht, the Netherlands: Martinus Nijhoff Publishers), 96.

[83] Plender, Richard, *International Migration Law*, Revised 2nd edition, 1988 (Dordrecht, the Netherlands: Martinus Nijhoff Publishers), 95.

[84] Article 2, the *Provisional Measures on the Exit and Entry National Border of Overseas Chinese* 1951 (PRC), promulgated by the Ministry of Public Security.

[85] Exit certificates for aliens required under Article 4, the *Provisional Measures on Exit of Aliens in China* 1954 (PRC), promulgated by the Ministry of Public Security; Exit visas for aliens required under Article 7, *Regulations on the Administration of Entry, Exit, Transit, Residence and Travel of Aliens in China* 1964 (PRC), promulgated by the State Council; Exit registration cards for aliens, see: Mao, Fengping, editor, *Chujing Rujing Falv Fagui Sijie Yu Xiangying Fagui Zhaibian* (*The Explanation of the Law and Regulations Governing exit and entry and the Collections of Related Regulations*) (Changchun, China the Publishing House of Jilin Renmin, 1994), 77.

[86] Section 2 (18) of the *Act of Cuban Liberated and Democratic Solidarity,* 1996 (the

This section will firstly analyse who may exercise the right to leave. Recognised grounds for limiting the right to leave and bureaucratic barriers of the right to leave will then be discussed in detail. Finally, this section explores the loss of technical expertise from the State through emigration.

3.4.1 *Who may exercise the right to leave?*

International human rights instruments attribute the right to leave to 'everyone',[87] 'every person'[88] and 'every individual'.[89] The right to leave is based on citizenship.[90] Citizens' right to leave cannot be discriminated against on the grounds of social status, occupation, age, gender, religion, ownership of property, race or colour, or political opinion. An example of impermissible discrimination can be found in North Korea, where ordinary people are not allowed to travel abroad, unlike diplomats or members of the department of Foreign Affairs.[91] The status of a dual national's right to leave is determined by the law of their country of residence, rather than by the law of their State of nationality. For the purpose of establishing the right to leave of dual nationals, the test of effective nationality is applied.[92]

The right to leave is available to aliens in the territory of a State,[93] even those unlawfully in the country.[94] Stateless persons within a State are thus entitled to leave the territory. No provisions in international migration law deny the right of stateless person to leave the country. 'Everyone', 'every person' or 'every individual' implies the inclusion of stateless person. It can also be supported by

USA), H.R.927, One Hundred Fourth Congress of the United States of America, http://usinfo.State.gov/usa/infousa/laws/majorlaw/h927_enr.htm (accessed 4/09/2003)

[87] Article 13 (2) of the UDHR; Article 12 (2) of the ICCPR; Article 2 (2) the EHR P4.

[88] Article VIII of *American Declaration of the Rights and Duties of Man*, Article 22 (1) the AMR.

[89] Article 12 (2) of the AFR.

[90] Rubenstein, Kim, *Australian Citizenship Law in Context*, Pyrmont (Australia: Lawbook Co., 2002), 285.

[91] Young, Song Ji, "The Invisible Refugees: North Korean Asylum Seekers in China", http://iso.hrichina.org/iso/article.adp?article_id=4248&subcategory_id=287 (accessed 18/05/2003), 8 pages, 2.

[92] Weis, P., *Nationality and Statelessness in International Law*, 2nd revised editions (B. V., Alphen aan den Rijn, the Netherlands Sijthoff & Noordhodd International Publishers, 1979), 202.

[93] Article 13 of the ICCPR; Article 22 (6) of the AMR; Article 12(4) the AFR.

[94] Joseph, Sarah and Sehultz, Jenny et al., *The International Covenant on Civil and Political Rights: Cases, Materials, and Commentary* (New York: Oxford University Press, 2000), 250; and also see paragraph 8 of General Comment No. 27 of the HRC on Freedom of Movement (Article 12).

the principle of non-discrimination on the grounds of race, religion or country of origin.

3.4.2 *Recognised grounds for limiting the right to leave*

States should give effect to the right to leave by enacting legislation or by other means. Conditions cannot be imposed on the right, such as insisting that the right is used for a prescribed purpose, limiting the destination of individuals, or limiting the period of time that a person may remain overseas.[95] However, the right to leave one country does not mean that a person has the right to enter another, nor does it guarantee the right of return to a country other than the national State. The right to leave can only be limited under the recognised grounds.

Criminal cases

According to the AMCM, the right to leave is deniable if the individual is accused or has been convicted of a crime. The restriction may also apply to RLR.[96] The extent to which the right is denied varies between States. For instance, German law permits the denial of a passport to a person who is accused of any offence.[97] In China, people who are suspected of any crime by the public security department, 'persons undergoing rehabilitation through labour,' and people who have been convicted of a crime and are serving a sentence are denied the right to leave.[98] By contrast, Japanese legislation imposes fewer limits. A Japanese national will only have their passport confiscated if they are subject to prosecution for criminal offences that are punishable by a term of imprisonment of not less than two years, or if a warrant for the persons arrest has been issued.[99]

---

[95] Paragraph 8 of *General Comment No. 27 of the HRC on Freedom of Movement* (Article 12).

[96] Inter-American Commission on Human Rights, *Sixth Report on the Situation of Political Prisoners in Cuba*, 1979, O.A.S Doc. No. OEA/Ser. L/V/II 48; doc. 7, 9.

[97] Section 7 (1) *Passport Law of Germany* 1952, Quoted in Plender, Richard, *International Migration Law*, Revised 2nd ed. (Dordrecht, the Netherlands: Martinus Nijhoff Publishers, 1988), 114.

[98] Article 6 Paragraph 2 of the *Suggestions of the Ministry of Public Security on Some Issues Concerning the Execution of Law on the Control of Exit and Entry of Citizens 1985 (PRC) and its Detailed Rules of the Implementation 1987 (PRC)*.

[99] Kenkyusho, Buraku Kaiho, *Human Rights in Japan, 1984,* Quoted in Plender, Richard, *International Migration Law*, Revised 2nd ed. (Dordrecht, the Netherlands: Martinus Nijhoff Publishers, 1988), 113.

Civil cases

It is unclear whether a pending civil suit justifies denial of the right to leave. In Australia, Belgium, Brazil, Ghana, the Netherlands, Poland and the USA,[100] the right can be denied if the person is liable for an outstanding debt. In China, permission to leave is denied if the person is party to an unresolved civil dispute.[101] Under German law, an alien may be prevented from leaving if the person is liable to provide maintenance.[102] However, denial of the right on the grounds of debt is strongly opposed by the international community. At its most extreme, debt bondage, such as that found in India, [103] can result in the forcible return of a person to their creditor, effectively resulting in a form of constructive imprisonment.

Performance of public service

The right to leave can be limited in order to ensure that a person performs a compulsory public service, such as national military service.[104] The restrictions of the right to leave of individuals who have not yet performed their military service are in principle to be considered necessary for the protection of national security and public order.[105] The people having the obligation to perform public service can be extended to the people who conduct scientific experiments on specific sites.[106] If an individual was prevented from leaving a country merely on the grounds that he or she is the holder of 'state secrets', or if an individual was prevented from travelling internationally within a specific permit, the basic grounds do not meet the test of necessity and requirements of proportionality.[107] Despite this, some countries, such as China, restrict people leaving the country who hold national secrets, or have been discharged from active service related to secrets before the known secrets expire.

---

[100] Tiburcio, Carmen, *The Human Rights of Aliens under International and Comparative Law* (The Hague, the Netherlands: Kluwer Law International, 2001), 233.

[101] Article 8(2) the *Law on the Control of Exit and Entry of Citizens* 1985 (PRC).

[102] s 19(2) of German *Aliens Law* 1965.

[103] Bradley, Catherine, *What Do We Mean by Human Rights: Freedom of Movement* (London: Franklin Watts, 2002), 39.

[104] Reid, Karen, *A Practitioner's Guide to the European Convention on Human Rights* (London: Sweet & Maxwell, 1998), 246; see German *Aliens Law* 1965 s 19(2).

[105] Joseph, Sarah and Sehultz, Jenny et al., *The International Covenant on Civil and Political Rights: Cases, Materials, and Commentary* (New York: Oxford University Press, 2000), 255.

[106] Bradley, Catherine, *What Do We Mean by Human Rights: Freedom of Movement* (London: Franklin Watts, 2002), 21.

[107] Paragraph 16 of General Comment No. 27 of the HRC on Freedom of Movement (Article 12).

Aliens

If aliens violate the law of their residence State, limits may be imposed on their right to leave that are different to those affecting nationals. Each State may determine the extent of those limits. In China, aliens are unable to leave if he or she is (i) a criminal defendant or suspect; (ii) is party to an unresolved civil dispute; (iii) is awaiting decision for any violation of Chinese law and whose case, in the opinion of the responsible department, calls for investigation.[108]

In comparison, Japanese law will only refuse to allow an alien to leave (i) if the person is subject to criminal proceedings for an offence punishable by imprisonment for a minimum of two years, or if a warrant has been issued for their arrest; (ii) if the person has been sentenced to a term of penal servitude and the person has not yet served the sentence; (iii) if a warrant for the provisional confinement of the person has been issued for the purpose of extradition.

3.4.3 *Bureaucratic barriers*

According to *Oxford Advanced Learner's English-Chinese Dictionary* (OAED), 'bureaucracy' means "excessive or complicated official routine, esp. because of too many departments and offices".[109] The bureaucratic barrier to exercising the right to leave usually occurs when procedures are complex, difficult to obtain information about, when the responsible department cannot be readily accessed, or when there is a delay in processing applications. Procedures for issuing passports should be expeditious, and the applicant should be informed in writing of the cause for a refusal or revocation of the document. In *Gonzalez del Rio v. Peru*, the HRC accepted that pending judicial proceedings justified delaying the issue of a passport. However, if the proceedings are unduly delayed, the right to leave the territory cannot be denied. In that case, the applicant had not been permitted to leave Peru for seven years, pending trial. His right to leave had been unjustifiably denied by cause of an undue administrative delay.

The imposition of high administrative costs may adversely affect the right to leave. The cost of applying to leave must be causable.[110] 'Cost' refers both to

---

[108] Article 23 of the *Detailed Rules for the Implementation of the Law on the Control of Exit and Entry of Aliens* 1985 (PRC).

[109] Hornby, A. S., *Oxford Advanced Learner's English-Chinese Dictionary* (*Niujin Gaoji Yinghan Shuangjie Cidian*), 4th edition (Hong Kong and Beijing: The Commercial Press and Oxford University Press, 1997), 181.

[110] Henkin, Louis, editor, *The International Bill of Rights: the Covenant on Civil and Political Rights* (New York: Columbia University Press, 1981), 380; Article IV (a) of the 1963 Ingles Draft Principles on RLR, adopted by the UN Sub-Commission on the Prevention of Discrimination and Protection of Minorities, Res. 2B (XV), UN Doc. E/CN. 41846 (1963), 40.

administrative service fees and taxes.[111] 'Causable cost' has been narrowly construed to mean 'nominal fees' by Article 13 of the 1972 Uppsala Declaration on RLR, [112] and Article 4(g) of the 1986 Strasbourg Declaration on RLR sets the inspirational target that travel documents should be issued free of charge, or subject only to nominal fees. In 1997, the UN criticised the former Iraqi government for the high administrative costs associated with the issuing of passports to its nationals.[113]

A further bureaucratic barrier to the right to leave is imposed by the requirement of a deposit or return ticket. Chinese residents cannot travel abroad in a group unless a bond is paid. The bond ranges from US$4,000 to $6,000. This represents a significant sum of money for an ordinary person, in a country where per capita GDP was US$1,058 in 2003.[114] Further, according to Article I (e) of the 1963 UN Draft Principles on RLR, a national should not be required to pay a deposit or provide any other form of guarantee of their return to the State.

According to customary international law, a person should not be denied the right to leave on the grounds that they lack authority to enter another State,[115] or cannot provide a letter of invitation from a foreigner, letter of approval from an employer or family member, or detailed travel route. Were it necessary to obtain the approval of an employer or family member, the individual's right to leave could be subverted by the interests of a third party. Restrictions on families travelling as a group, harassment of applicants by administrators, or refusing an application to leave on the basis that the applicant may damage the reputation of the State present impermissible limits on the right to leave.

3.4.4 *Loss of technical expertise from the State through emigration: the 'brain drain'*

The loss of technical expertise from a State through emigration is one of most important issues connected with the right to leave. The three aspects for discussion here are (i) the development of skilled emigration; (ii) the impacts of this type of emigration on original and host countries; and (iii) the debates about depriving the right to leave based on the 'brain drain' or loss of intellectual talent; and (iv) resolving issues related to skilled emigration in migration law.

---

[111] Article IV (c), the 1963 UN Draft Principles on RLR.

[112] ". . . Such documents or permits shall be subjected only to nominal fees." See Article 13 of the 1972 Uppsala Declaration on RLR.

[113] *Concluding Comments on Iraq* (*1997*), the UN Doc. the ICCPR/C/79/Add. 84, paragraph. 14.

[114] Market Information and Analysis Section, Department of Foreign Affairs and Trade, Australia, *China: the Fact Sheet*, using the latest data from the ABS, the IMF and various international sources, October 2003.

[115] Article 10 (c) of the 1986 Strasbourg Declaration on RLR.

3.4.4.1 The development of skilled emigration

The term 'brain drain' was coined in the UK in the 1960s to describe the loss of skilled workers and their technical expertise through emigration to States seeking technological development, especially the USA and the former USSR.[116] This pattern of migration was regarded as a very serious problem by OECD countries during this period,[117] on the grounds that, in relation to the UK, the loss of its 'most talented and highly trained citizens' would cause 'incalculable damage' to the British economy.[118]

The notion of the 'brain drain' of skilled emigration has since acquired a connotation of people moving from developing countries to the industrialised West, especially the USA.[119] The international Monetary Fund (IMF) has estimated that Iran loses 25% of its professionals through emigration, South Korea loses 15%, the Philippines lose 10%, and India and China lose 3%.[120] In order to avoid the possible loss caused by the 'brain drain', the GDR and Czechoslovakia, the former Warsaw Pact countries require that emigrating citizens of working age pay back to the State the costs of their education.

The causes of skilled emigration include more career opportunities and higher incomes in destination counties, and concerns about political and economic stability in the national State. In the 1960's Quinton Hogg first rejected the idea of 'levelling down' – the pursuit of a crude form of egalitarianism, as a way of promoting talent at home and dissuading skilled people from emigrating.[121]

Skilled emigration has been promoted by the immigration policies of developed countries, which are keen to attract qualified immigrants and students. Globalisation is, in part, a product of this pattern of migration. The USA, Canada, Australia, and New Zealand have implemented 'skill selective' and 'wealth

---

[116] Simanovsky, et al., 1996, Quoted in Iredale, Robyn, "The need to Import Skilled Personnel: Factors Favouring and Hindering its International Mobility", *International Migration* Vol. 37(1) 1999, 89–114, 92.

[117] Fabian, Y. Muzart, G. and Young, A., "International Movements of Scientists and Engineers in the 1960s as An Aspect of the Mobility of Highly Qualified Manpower" in Friborg, Coran, editor, *Brain Drain Statistics: Empirical Evidence and Guidelines, Report on International Expert Meeting in Stockholm 1973 and Guidelines for Future Studies*, offset originals i Sundt offset, Stockholm, 1975, 107.

[118] Hogg, Quinton, *The Brain Drain*, CPC Outline Series No. 1 (London: the Conservative Political Centre, 1967), 3.

[119] Hannum, Hurst, *The right to Leave and Return in International Law and Practice* (Dordrecht, the Netherlands: Martinus Nijhoff Publishers 1987), 35.

[120] Stalker, Peter, *The No-Nonsense Guild to International Migration* (Oxford, the UK: New Internationalist Publications Ltd., 2 001), 104.

[121] Hogg, Quinton, *The Brain Drain*, CPC Outline Series No. 1 (London: the Conservative Political Centre, 1967) at 7.

selective' immigration policies to help highly skilled or professional people relocate.[122]

3.4.4.2 The effects of skilled emigration on original and host countries

Original country

Peter Stalker has mindfully identified five principle effects of skilled emigration, namely:

(i) a reduction in the country's capacity for long-term economic growth and human development; (ii) deprivation of many urgently needed skills; (iii) the loss of investment dollars for higher education, as university graduates and skilled workers take their qualifications elsewhere; (iv) the social cost borne of family separation as one spouse emigrates, generally a young man, as to place extra burdens on the shoulders of women who have to maintain the household; and (v) the cultural cost of emigration, as young men, who have few opportunities at home have come to regard emigration as a rite of passage.[123]

However, skilled emigration is not necessarily detrimental to the country of origin. Many developing countries have more graduates than they need; and as Graeme Hugo has identified, highly skilled graduates can contribute more to the development of their home country by working abroad than by staying home.[124] This emigration pattern means that emigration States need to regard overseas remittance from ex-patriots as a source of national income. On balance, the effect of skilled emigration is negative, despite long-term economic benefits.

Host country

Both Rachel Freidberg and Jennifer Hunt comment that the effect of immigration on the labour market of host countries is small, and that the impact of immigration on the earnings of the local population depends upon the quality of the immigrants in terms of representing 'human capital'.[125] Host countries need to balance

---

[122] Findlay, A. M., Li, F. L., et al., "Doctors diagnose their destination: an analysis of the length of employment abroad for Hong Kong doctors', *Environment and Planning*, Vol. 26 1994, 1605–1624

[123] Stalker, Peter, *The No-Nonsense Guild to International Migration* (Oxford, the UK: New Internationalist Publications Ltd., 2 001), 106–107.

[124] Hugo, Graeme, Rudd, Dianne and Harris, Kevin, *Emigration from Australia: Economic Implications*, Second report on an ARC SPIRT grant CEDA Information Paper No. 77, June 2001, Adelaide University Australia, 39.

[125] Friedberg, Rachel M. and Hunt, Jennifer, "The Impact of Immigrants on Host Country Wages, Employment and Growth", *Journal of Economical Perspectives*, Volume 9, Number 2, Spring 1995, pages 23–44, 42.

the benefit of receiving skilled immigrants who can supplement local shortages, while finding a way to maximise the gain from skilled immigration, without creating additional domestic pressures. They need to maintain a balance between permanent and temporary skilled immigration, facilitate the entry of skilled immigrants, and ensure that the immigrants satisfactorily integrate into the labour market.

3.4.4.3 The debates about depriving the right to leave based on the 'brain drain'

Whether the 'brain drain' caused by skilled emigration is an acceptable cause of depriving an individual of the right to leave is controversial. Jose D. Ingles,[126] J. Bhagwati[127] and Richard Plender[128] independently contend that it is acceptable to impose limits on skilled emigration from developing countries, because the community has some legal claim on the skills and talents developed by its members at the community's expense. They have also argued that it is justified for those States to impose a 'return of service' obligation on people who have been trained at public expense.

Louis Henkin asserts that many countries have more skilled professionals than they can use and can afford to have them to emigrate. Even if there were a shortage of skilled labour, he concludes that States should not prohibit emigration, because to do so would violate the ICCPR.[129] Carmen Tiburcio agrees with Henkin on the point that deprivation of the right to emigrate would unjustifiably contravene the ICCPR. Moreover, she suggests that the skills of an individual belong to that individual, "not to the community where he or she was educated" and as such, the person cannot be denied the right to leave on the grounds of 'owing' their community for their education.[130] Henkin and Tiburcio's arguments seem more persuasive.

---

[126] "Such restrictions are understandable in the case of developing countries which find it necessary to prohibit the departure of persons having specified skills in order to prevent their limited supply of skilled manpower from being drained away by the better conditions offered in industrialized countries", Ingles, Jose D., *1963 Ingles' Study on RLR*, the UN Publication Sales No.: 64. XIV. 2, New York: 1963, pages 44–45.

[127] "Developing countries should levy a tax on the earnings of professional, technical and kindred persons who emigrate from less developed countries to developed countries." Bhagwati, J., editor, in *Taxing the Brain Drain: A Proposal* (Vol. I) and *The Brain Drain and Taxation,* (Vol. II), Quoted in Plender, Richard, *International Migration Law*, Revised 2nd edition (Dordrecht, the Netherlands: Martinus Nijhoff Publishers, 1988), 301.

[128] Plender, Richard, *International Migration Law*, Revised 2nd edition (Dordrecht, the Netherlands: Martinus Nijhoff Publishers, 1988), 101.

[129] Henkin, Louis, editor, *The International Bill of Rights: the Covenant on Civil and Political Rights* (New York: Columbia University Press, 1981), 378–179.

[130] Tiburcio, Carmen, *The Human Rights of Aliens under International and Comparative Law* (The Hague, the Netherlands: Kluwer Law International, 2001), 319–320.

3.4.4.4 Solving skilled emigration in migration law

Although the most direct way of stemming the loss of skilled nationals is by prohibiting their emigration, there are less drastic means of discouraging skilled emigration, or encouraging skilled repatriation. The UN has found that family connections heavily effect a person's decision to repatriate.[131] The imposition of income tax on the income of an ex-patriot could be used as a restraint on the right to leave. However, RLR experts agree that citizenship is not a proper foundation for the imposition of taxes, and such taxes would be difficult to enforce without the co-operation of the immigration States.[132]

Robyn Iredale has addressed the need for a co-ordinated international response to deal with the effects of skilled migration.[133] A global strategy founded on co-operation, which includes the payment of compensation by immigration States to the original States, through a series of bi-lateral agreements, is needed. Compensatory measures could include the provision of increased training within, and technology transfer to, developing emigration States.

On the domestic plane, governments need to encourage skilled workers to stay at home, and implement migration policies designed to encourage the return of skilled nationals. In the 1960's Quinton Hogg, during the run-up to a general election in the UK asserted that the government should:

> Provide an environment in which the pursuit of excellence in every department could flourish. Talent would be encouraged and hard work and distinguished qualifications, unlike virtue, would not have to be their own reward.[134]

India encourages professionals to return home by offering five years of tax-free employment and providing incentives to set up a business. The HKSAR has developed home ownership projects and has mooted the idea of double passport provisions.

---

[131] Glaser, William A., *The Brain Drain: Emigration and Return, Findings of a UNITAR Multinational Comparative Survey of Professional Personnel of Developing Countries who Study Abroad* (London: Pergamon Press, 1978), XXV.

[132] Hufbauer, Gary Clyde, "The State, the individual, and the Taxation of Economic Migration", in Bhagwati, Jagdish N. and Wilson editor, John Douglas, *Income Taxation and International Mobility* (Massachusetts, the USA: the Massachusetts Institute of Technology, 1989), 93.

[133] Iredale, Robyn, "The need to Import Skilled Personnel: Factors Favouring and Hindering its International Mobility", *International Migration* Vol. 37(1) 1999, 89–114, 310.

[134] Hogg, Quinton, *The Brain Drain*, CPC Outline Series No. 1, the Conservative Political Centre, London: 1967, 7.

3.4.5 *The right to enter another State*

In order to enjoy the right to leave, there must be another country to which a person can enter.[135] However the right to enter does not form part of RLR under international conventions. According to Article 1 of *Havana Convention on the Status of Aliens* 1928, States are free to determine, through legislation, the conditions of entry and residence of aliens in their territory.

Historically, aliens have never been entitled to enter another country. Blackstone has asserted, 'No member of one society has a right to intrude into another.'[136] The right to enter, similar to the right to leave, touches on the self-interest of States, and it is common to find the view expressed that these are matters pre-eminently within the reserved domain of domestic jurisdiction. It is thus understandable that the State enjoys an absolute and uncontrolled discretion, or sovereign power, to determine whether, and on what conditions, it will permit the entry of aliens

States generally require aliens to possess identity documents, such as a passport and a visa. In 2000, approximately 190 States required aliens to obtain an entry visa.[137] Some States discriminate in their treatment of visa applicants, pursuant to the States national interest. Following September 11, the USA amended its immigration regulations such as to require applicants from Arab States to meet additional requirements. An alien should be admitted once they have been issued with a visa. Justifications for refusal need be on the grounds of upholding public security, public order, public health or morality, or the rights and freedoms of others.

3.4.6 *Procedural right against expulsion*

Nobody can be forced to leave any country, including one's own, without justified causes.[138] Article 9 of the UDHR provides "no one shall be subjected to arbitrary exile". Article 13 of the ICCPR further provides that:

---

[135] Baubock, Rainer, *Transnational Citizenship: Membership and Rights in International Migration* (Cheltenham, the UK: Edward Elgar, 1994), 326.

[136] Henriques, H. S. Q., *The Law of Aliens and Naturalisation including the Text of the Aliens Act, 1905* (London: Butterworth & Co., 1906), 9.

[137] Martin, Philip and Widgren, Jonas, *International Migration: Facing the Challenge* (Washington, the USA: Population Reference Bureau, 2002), 39 pages, at 4.

[138] There are three different expressions, 'free' or 'freely' or 'has the right' relating to the act of the right to leave in international instruments. What they claim in nature is the way in which everyone is entitled to the right to leave in the line with one's own will, rather than government or others' will. Based on the right to leave, nobody can be forced to leave any country including one's own, without justified causes.

> An alien lawfully in the territory of a State Party to the present Covenant may be expelled therefrom only in pursuance of a decision reached in accordance with law and shall, except where compelling causes of national security otherwise require, be allowed to submit the causes against his expulsion and to have his case reviewed by, and be represented for the purpose before, the competent authority or a person or persons especially designated by the competent authority.

Article 13 regulates only the procedure and not the substantive grounds for or against expulsion.[139] It thus does not strictly protect an alien from expulsion, so long as procedural guarantees to expulsion are available. Adherence to procedural safeguards helps ensure that the State Party's substantive law regarding expulsion is not being administered in an arbitrary manner.[140]

'Lawful aliens'

RLR protected by Article 12 of the ICCPR is subject to the condition that everyone is 'lawfully within the territory of a State'.[141] Without the words 'an alien lawfully within the territory of a State' the national authorities would be prohibited from expelling an alien who has managed to enter the country legally. The words not only express non-interference with the admission policy of national authorities in regards to aliens, but confine the eligibility of aliens under the procedural right against expulsion. In this context, an alien includes stateless persons.

The provisions do not cover illegal entrants and aliens who have stayed longer than the law or their permits allow. An alien is only lawfully within the territory if they comply with the conditions of their admission and hold a valid visa. The domestic law of the State concerned determines 'lawfulness'. This means that national law regarding the requirements for entry and stay must be considered in determining the scope of the procedural right against expulsion. If the legality of an alien's entry or presence in the territory is in dispute, any decision on this point leading to expulsion or deportation ought to be taken in accordance with Article 13 of the ICCPR. Article 13 protects lawful aliens against being arbitrarily expelled, regardless of the content of the domestic law of a State party. Causes for the expulsion of an unlawful alien must be given if the decision is based on public interest.

---

[139] Paragraph 10 of General Comment No. 15 of the HRC on the Rights of Aliens.

[140] Joseph, Sarah and Sehultz, Jenny et al., *The International Covenant on Civil and Political Rights: Cases, Materials, and Commentary* (New York: Oxford University Press, 2000), 268.

[141] *Celepli v. Sweden* (456/91) 18/07/1994, Human Rights Committee, cited in Joseph, Sarah and Sehultz, Jenny et al., *The International Covenant on Civil and Political Rights: Cases, Materials, and Commentary* (New York: Oxford University Press, 2000), 247.

'In pursuance of a decision reached in accordance with law'[142]

The phrase 'in pursuance of a decision reached in accordance with law' means that a decision must be made lawfully and in a manner that is procedurally fair and free from discrimination.[143] The HRC has comprehensively explained the meaning of the term in *Maroufidou v. Sweden*, which is worth reproducing:

> The reference to 'law' is to the domestic law of the State party concerned, though of course the relevant provisions of domestic law must in themselves be compatible with the provisions of the ICCPR. . . . The interpretation of domestic law in the context of protecting aliens against arbitrary expulsion is essentially a matter for the courts and authorities of the State party concerned. It is not within the powers or functions of the Committee to evaluate whether the competent authorities of the State party in question have interpreted and applied the domestic law correctly in the case before it under the Optional Protocol, unless it is established that they have not interpreted and applied it in good faith or that it is evident that there has been an abuse of power.[144]

Generally, the HRC will not overturn a State's decision in the absence of clear procedural defects.

Procedural guarantees

Article 13 of the ICCPR establishes certain procedural guarantees to protect aliens against arbitrary expulsion. Domestic law determines the nature and content of procedural rights against expulsion. However, for review of the grounds upon which the person is to be expelled, a decision by a competent tribunal is the minimum requirement. As a feature of procedural fairness, an alien must be allowed to make submissions and be represented to resist expulsion.

The phrase 'to have his case reviewed' supports this interpretation. Paragraph 10 of General Comment No.15 of the HRC on the Rights of Aliens, provides that the principle of Article 13 is related to not only the entitlement to review, but to appeal against expulsion. Article 13 also introduces the requirement of a hearing, although less settled is the question of whether a hearing must be permitted to the alien.[145] In general, the alien should be afforded an oral hearing, although written submissions may suffice. In the cases of *Hammel v. Madagascar, Giry v. the Dominican Republic* and *Canon Garcia v. Ecuador*, the HRC found that the right against expulsion had been violated because the affected person had been denied an opportunity to appeal against the decision.

---

[142] For more details of the word of the term 'law', see part 3.3.4.1 'provided by law' of this book.

[143] Article 26 of the ICCPR.

[144] No. 58/1979, § 10.1 Cf. also de Zayas & Moller, 1986 NJIL page 387 f.

[145] Goodwin-gill, Guy S., *International Law and the Movement of Persons Between States* (Oxford: Oxford University Press, 1978), pages 263–265.

The term 'be represented' means the right to represent oneself, or to appoint suitably qualified counsel. In *Chahal v. United Kingdom*, the EUCT found a decision made by an advisory panel was invalid because there were insufficient procedural safeguards. In that case, the details of the case against the applicant had not been disclosed, and legal representation had not been allowed. The HRC noted with concern, "that adequate legal representation is not available for asylum-seekers effectively to challenge administrative decisions".[146]

'Compelling causes of national security'

An alien must be given an effective opportunity to pursue a remedy against expulsion. Those opportunities cannot be granted in a discriminatory manner. The right against expulsion can only be departed from where there are 'compelling causes of national security'. The HRC held the view in *V.M.R.B. v Canada* that the term 'compelling' contained in Article 13 of the ICCPR means that States must provide persuasive evidence of serious national security threats if the person remains in the territory.[147] Based on the word 'compelling' in Article 13 of the ICCPR, States Parties are required to furnish persuasive evidence of serious national security danger.[148]

Obviously, the above widely accepted interpretation of 'compelling' is still too ambiguous to fundamentally reduce the possibility for the State to consider not applying the procedural guarantees against expulsion. A similar issue occurs in the words 'competent authority', which might well be the same body that has taken the original decision, and there could, therefore, be no right of impartiality. Both of the above weakness may severely reduce the effectiveness of the procedural right against expulsion.

The practice in Europe needs to be noted because Europe rejected the proposal of inserting certain procedural rights against expulsion to the HER P4 in favour of aliens about to be expelled.

> The grounds were that to limit rights to those of a procedural nature, was insufficient – it was better to have no provision at all. Firstly, the guarantees would not apply where the State 'considers' compelling reasons other required. Secondly, the 'competent authority' might well be the same body which had taken the original decision, and there could, therefore, be no guarantee of impartiality.[149]

---

[146] The UN doc. the ICCPR/C/79/Add. 55 (1995), paragraph. 16.

[147] *V.M.R.B. v Canada* (236/87), See Joseph, Sarah and Sehultz, Jenny et al., *The International Covenant on Civil and Political Rights: Cases, Materials, and Commentary* (New York: Oxford University Press, 2000), 274.

[148] Jagerskiold, S., 'Freedom of Movement' Henkin, L. editor, *The International Bill of Rights: The Covenant on Civil and Political Rights* (New York: Columbia University Press, 1981), 184.

[149] Goodwin-gill, Guy S., *International Law and the Movement of Persons Between States* (Oxford, Oxford University Press, 1978), 291.

3.5 The Right to Return to one's Country

3.5.1 *The general considerations of the right to return to one's country*

The right to return to one's country includes the right to remain in one's own country, the right to return after having left one's own country, and the right to enter the country for the first time if he or she was born outside the country. It also includes the right of return for refugees, and the prohibitions enforced population transfers to other countries.

The right to return is expressly recognised in Article 13 (2) of the UDHR and Article 12 (4) of the ICCPR, which provides that 'No one shall be arbitrarily deprived of the right to enter his own country'. It is also recognised in Article 3 (2) of the EHR P4, Article 22 (5) of the AMR, Article 12 (2) of the AFR, and other international and regional human rights instruments. These instruments place no restrictions on the right to return, and is guaranteed to nationals in the Constitutions of many countries. Paragraph 13 of the Schedule to the CSR entitles a stateless person to whom a travel document has been issued according to Article 28 to re-enter the territory of the issuing State at any time during the period of passport validity. Thus the right to return is accepted so widely that its existence as a rule of law is virtually beyond dispute.

Without being admitted to return freely, exiled nationals have to continually move around – nobody obviously would like to be subjected to that. Without the right to return, an individual may be subject to political repression, prevented from observing their religion, from obtaining an education or a job of their choice, or may be frustrated in efforts to enjoy family life. If a person cannot return to his or her State of nationality, the person will be stateless.

Different opinions about the meaning of the terms 'one's own country' and 'arbitrarily' hamper the complete enforcement of the right to return in the world. Violations of the right to return emerge from time to time, especially not to accept expelled nationals and to exile nationals. Considering the above issues, this section will analyse (i) consequences of violating the right to return; (ii) the term 'one's own country'; (iii) the meaning of 'arbitrarily'; (iv) the duty to accept expelled nationals and the duty not to expel nationals.

The right to return is fundamental because exile is a fundamental deprivation of one's homeland, a deprivation that goes to the heart of those immutable characteristics that comprise our personal and collective identities.[150] It is unacceptable to deprive any person of close contact with one's family, friends, or the series of

[150] Rosand, Eric, "The right to Return under International Law following Mass Dislocation: the Bosnia Precedent?" in *Michigan Journal of International Law*, Summer (1998), 1091, 11.

relationships that form one's social environment. As Van P. Panhuys has contended, "the duty to admit nationals is considered so important a consequence of nationality that it is almost equated with it."[151]

3.5.2 *'One's own country'*

Customary international law provides that an individual outside his/her country cannot be arbitrarily denied the right to return to it.[152] Nevertheless, the precise meanings of 'one's own country' and 'arbitrarily' are disputed and in some respects obscure. An individual must prove that the State in which they wish to enter is their 'own country' before being entitled to the right to return to that country. Article 12 (4) of the ICCPR promulgated that 'no one shall be arbitrarily deprived of the right to enter his own country', it does not distinguish between nationals, stateless persons and aliens. Thus, it is only possible to identify the persons who are entitled to exercise this right by interpreting 'one's own country'.

Compared with 'the right to enter his own country' in the ICCPR, 'the right to enter the State of which he is a national' was used in the EHR and the AMR, 'the right to return to his country' was used in 13 (2) of the UDHR and Article 12 (2) of the AFR Obviously, the meaning of the former term is more narrow than 'the State of which he is a national' and to 'his country'.

This term of 'one's own country' was initially chosen in favour of 'country of nationality' and 'country of one's permanent home'. This means that individuals who have never lived in their country of citizenship can 'enter' the State, although, since they have never resided there, cannot 'return'.[153] The intention of having a broader and more precise meaning can be supported by the preparatory work on Article 12 (4) of the ICCPR. Marc J. Bossuyt summarised the preparatory work as following after an overview of the three important international sessions regarding the draft of the ICCPR, Commission on Human Rights, 5th Session (1949), 6th Session (1950) and 8th Session (1952).

> Difficulties arose in connection with this provision connecting the right to enter one's own country for States in which the right to return to one's country was governed, not by rules of nationality or citizens, but by the idea of a permanent home. The early drafts dealt only with the right of nationals to 'enter' their country. It is intended to

---

[151] Panhuys, P. Van, *The Roles of Nationality in International Law: An Outline*, 1959 (Leyden, the Netherlands, A. W. Sythoff), 56.

[152] Rosand, Eric, "The right to Return under International Law following Mass Dislocation: the Bosnia Precedent?", *Michigan Journal of International Law*, Summer (1998) 1091, 11. Also see 1974] ECR 11337, 1351.

[153] Hannum, Hurst, *The Right to Leave and Return in International Law and Practice* (Dordrecht, the Netherlands: Martinus Nijhoff Publishers, 1987), 56.

> cover cases such as those of persons born abroad who have never been to the country of their nationality. Such a formula was not satisfactory for a State which granted the right of "return" to persons who were not nationals but who had established their home in the country. A compromise was reached, based on Article 13, paragraph 2, of the UDHR, by replacing the reference to 'country of which he is a national' by the words: 'his own country'. The right to 'enter' the country was retained.[154]

However, Jose Ingles and Richard Plender supported the narrow interpretation. Ingles referred to '[t] he right of a national to return' throughout his study and incorporated the expression in his draft principles. The Ingles Draft Principles on RLR II (b) provides that "[n] o one shall be arbitrarily deprived of [their] nationality, or forced to renounce [their] nationality, as a means of divesting [them] of the right to return to country."[155] This was adopted by the CPDPM in 1971. Plender asserted that "every State must admit its own nationals to its territory' and that 'each State has the right to deny admission to aliens."[156]

Above interpretation was then broadened to include permanent residents by the 1972 Uppsala Declaration on RLR and the 1986 Strasbourg Declaration on RLR. Articles 9 and 10 of the 1972 Uppsala Declaration on RLR affirm that "every person is entitled to return to the country of which [they are] a national" and that "no person shall be deprived of [their] nationality for the purpose of divesting [them] of the right to return to [their] country." Article 12 of the 1972 Uppsala Declaration on RLR affirms "the re-entry of long-term residents who are not nationals, including stateless persons, maybe refused only in the most exceptional circumstances." Articles 6(b) and 7 of the 1986 Strasbourg Declaration on RLR expanded the interpretation of 'one's own country' which provided:

> Article 6(b): No person shall be deprived of nationality or citizenship in order to exile or to prevent that person from exercising the right to enter his or her country.
> Article 7: Permanent legal residents who temporarily leave their country of residence shall not be arbitrarily denied the right to return to that country.

Hurst Hannum, Jagerskiold, Knisbacher, and Mazzawi are supporters of the broadened interpretation. Hannum noted "a newly independent State might create a right of entry for large numbers of previously stateless persons or even those who held another nationality at one time."[157]

---

[154] Bossuyt, Marc J., *Guide to the Travaux Preparatoires' of the International Covenant on Civil and Political Rights* (Dordrecht, the Netherlands: Martinus Nijhoff Publishers, 1987), 261.

[155] Ingles, Jose D., *1963 Ingles' Study on RLR*, the UN Publication Sales No.: 64. XIV. 2 New York: 1963.

[156] Plender, Richard, International Migration Law, Revised 2nd ed. (Dordrecht, the Netherland: Martinus Nijhoff Publishers, 1988), 133.

[157] Hannum, Hurst, *The right to Leave and Return in International Law and Practice* (Dordrecht, the Netherlands: Martinus Nijhoff Publishers, 1987), 59–60.

In 1999, the HRC ruled that the scope of 'one's own country' is broader than the concept 'country of one's nationality'. It is not limited to nationality in a formal sense, that is, nationality acquired at birth or by conferral; it embraces, at the very least, an individual who because of his or her 'special' ties to or claims in relation to a given country, cannot be considered to be a mere alien. This would be the case, for example, for nationals of a country who have been stripped of their nationality in violation of international law, and of individuals whose country of nationality has been incorporated into or transferred to another national entity, whose nationality is being denied them.

In order to claim rights under Article 12(4) of the ICCPR, the person must either be a national of the relevant State, or has been stripped of his or her nationality by that State, or denied nationality by that State in violation of international law, where the country of nationality has been incorporated into or transferred to another State whose nationality has being denied to them.[158] Individuals who do not claim rights under Article 12(4) of the ICCPR are deemed to have elected to remain as aliens in the country of residence.

Sarah Joseph, Jenny Schultz and Castan envisaged that it was open to an alien to show that there are well-established links with a State, and that he or she is entitled to claim the protection of Article 12 (4) of the ICCPR. However, this broad interpretation does not appear to be widely accepted or easily implemented. Article 12 (4) of the ICCPR permits an interpretation that might embrace other categories of long-term residents, including stateless persons arbitrarily deprived of the right to acquire the nationality of the country of residence.[159] The HRC stated that 'his own country' as a concept applies to individuals who are nationals and to certain categories of individuals who, while not nationals in a formal sense, are also not 'aliens' within the meaning of Article 13, although they may be considered as aliens for other purposes.[160] This inclusive interpretation provides protection for those who have a special connection with a country. If a person, after entering a foreign country, loses his citizenship in one country, without acquiring citizenship in another, then the State of earlier citizenship is bound to readmit the person at the request of the State in which the person is residing.[161]

---

[158] Stewart *v* Canada (538/93) 1/11/1996, Quoted in Joseph, Sarah and Sehultz, Jenny et al., *The International Covenant on Civil and Political Rights: Cases, Materials, and Commentary* (New York: Oxford University Press, 2000), 264.

[159] Paragraph 20 of General Comment No. 27 of the HRC on Freedom of Movement (Article 12).

[160] Stewart *v* Canada (538/93) 1/11/1996, Quoted in Joseph, Sarah and Sehultz, Jenny et al., *The International Covenant on Civil and Political Rights: Cases, Materials, and Commentary* (New York: Oxford University Press, 2000), 262.

[161] Weis, P., *Nationality and Statelessness in International Law,* 2nd revised editions (B. V., Alphen aan den Rijn, the Netherlands: Sijthoff & Noordhodd International Publishers 1979), 55.

Lawrence M. Freidman has observed that the *Scott Act* 1888 (USA) prohibited 20,000 Chinese immigrants, who had temporarily left the USA, from returning.[162] Current international instruments endeavour to prohibit similar violations of RLR in the future. Under the ICCPR, the right to return does not depend on a person's refugee status. Human Rights Watch contended that every individual who has maintained 'genuine and effective links' with a territory in question should enjoy the right to return to their own country, regardless of whether he or she is a refugee.[163]

'A genuine and effective link' was defined in the *Nottebohm* decision of the ICJ. According to the ICJ, 'a genuine and effective link to one's own country' can be constituted from various factors, including language, long-term residence, cultural identity, participation in public life, and family ties. The relative importance of each factor depends on the circumstances of the case.[164] On this basis, a genuine and effective link could diminish over time. However, this would be rare in the case of those who fled from persecution. A determination should not be made in respect of people who have fled until they have had the opportunity to exercise the right to return over a reasonable period of time, have chosen not to exercise the right, or have taken steps to cut the link.[165] The right to return is not restricted to nationality or permanent residency status.

In other words, the right to return to the country of one's habituated residence is acceptable. Principle 22 of *Concluding Document of the Vienna Meeting* of January 15, 1989 provides that, "[the States parties] will allow all refugees who so desire to return in safety to their homes." However, the meeting failed to clarify the conditions under which the refugees would be admitted. This has resulted in some practical problems.

Many Palestinian refugees were born in Egypt, Lebanon and other Middle East countries, where they have lived for more than 50 years. However, these countries have not afforded them the right to return, despite the international obligation to 'take the necessary measures' to guarantee Palestinians full freedom of movement between Arab countries in accordance with *Protocol for the Treatment*

---

162 Friedman, Lawrence M., *A History of American Law* (New York: Simon and Schuster, 1973), 444.

163 Human Rights Watch, "Human Rights Watch Policy on the Right to Return: Relevant Background, the International Covenant on Civil and Political Rights 1966", http://www.globalpolicy.org/security/issues/israel-palestine/return/2001/hrw.htm (accessed 16/09/2006).

164 *Liechtenstein v. Guatemala* (Nottebohm Case) Second Phase, Judgement, *International Court Journal Reports* 1955, Rep 4.

165 Human Rights Watch, "Human Rights Watch Policy on the Right to Return: Relevant Background: The Human Rights Committee General Comment on Article 12 of the International Covenant on Civil and Political Rights, 1966" http://www.globalpolicy.org/security/issues/israel-palestine/return/2001/hrw.htm (accessed 16/09/2006).

of Palestinians in Arab States 1965. In 1960, Palestinians were entitled to receive Egyptian travel documents. However, these documents did not grant the bearer the right to enter Egypt unless a visa is obtained from the Egyptian consulates abroad. Thus, holders of such documents who were born in Egypt or who had lived there for most of their lives had no right to re-enter Egypt. Egyptian consulates have reportedly refused to grant a re-entry visa to Palestinians born in Egypt, without providing reasons.

In relation to the problems facing Palestinian refugees, 'one's own country' should mean a country with which the person has a causable connection through a combination of race, religion, language, ancestry, birth and prolonged domicile. Governments come and go, but political fluctuation should not affect the right to return to one's own country and to have a homeland.

3.5.3 *'Arbitrarily'*

During the drafting the ICCPR, a provision prohibiting arbitrary exile was inserted into Article 12 (4), based on two grounds. The first is Article 9 of the UDHR, which affirms, "no one shall be subjected to arbitrary arrest, detention or exile". The second was the fact that, while in most countries exile no longer existed as a penalty, in some circumstances it might be more humane to exile a person than to inflict on him or her more severe punishment.[166] Some delegations submitted that the term 'arbitrary' was equivalent to 'unlawful', but it is clear that this narrow definition is not appropriate – despite the possible preference of the drafters for 'deliberate ambiguity' in this area.[167]

According to *Black's Law Dictionary*, an arbitrary decision is one that "depend[s] on individual discretion; specifically determined by a judge rather than fixed rules, or law; found on prejudice or preference rather than on cause or fact."[168] Paragraph 21 of General Comment No.27 of the HRC on Freedom of Movement (Article 12) provides that:

> The reference to the concept of arbitrariness in this context is intended to emphasise that it applies to all State actions, legislative, administrative and judicial. It guarantees that interference provided for by law should be in accordance with the provisions, aims and objectives of the Covenant and should be, in any event, causable in the particular circumstances.

---

166 Bossuyt, Marc J., *Guide to the "Travaux Preparatoires" of the International Covenant on Civil and Political Rights*, (Dordrecht, the Netherlands: Martinus Nijhoff Publishers, 1987), 260.

167 Pechota, *The Development of the Convention on Civil and Political Rights*, in Henkin, L. editor, *The International Bill of Rights: the Covenant of Civil and Political Rights* (New York: Columbia University Press, 1981), 32 and 57.

168 Garner, Bryan A., (Editor in Chief), *Black's Law Dictionary,* 7th edition (St. Paul, Minn., the USA: West Group, 1999), 100.

According to the HRC, there are few, if any, circumstances in which deprivation of the right to enter one's own country could be causable. A State party must not arbitrarily prevent a person from returning to his or her own country, by stripping that person of nationality or by expelling an individual to a third country.[169] A country can only derogate from their responsibilities under Article 12(4) of the ICCPR during the extreme circumstances described in Article 4. Article 4 refers to time of national emergency, such as a state of war or a threat of war,[170] a terrorist emergency, internal political instability, or natural disaster. Paragraph 2 of *General Comment 29, States of Emergency (article 4)* provides that before a State moves to invoke article 4, two fundamental conditions must be met: the situation must amount to a public emergency which threatens the life of the nation, and the State party must have officially proclaimed a state of emergency. The latter requirement is essential for the maintenance of the principles of legality and rule of law at times when they are most needed.[171] Even in these situations, States should ensure that their actions are not inconsistent with their other duties under international law, and that they do not involve discrimination on the ground of race, language, religion or ethnicity.[172]

For Article 12(4) to apply, the whole population must be affected by a public emergency.[173] Paris Standard 1(b) provides that 'public emergency' means an exceptional situation of crisis or public change, actual or imminent, which affects the whole population, or the whole population of the area to which the declaration applies, and constitutes a threat to the organisation of the community life of the State. The declaration of a State of emergency may cover the entire territory of the State or any part thereof, depending upon the areas actually affected by the circumstances motivating the declaration. This will not prevent the extension of emergency measures to other parts of the country whenever necessary, nor the exclusion of those parts where such circumstances no longer prevail.[174] The Paris

[169] Paragraph 21 of General Comment No. 27 of the HRC on Freedom of Movement (Article 12).

[170] According to *Canada War Measures Act*, civil liberties were severely restricted by regulations during the First World War, the Second World War and the 'October crisis' of 1970. See Hogg, P. W., *Constitution Law of Canada*, 2nd edition (Toronto: Carswell, 1985), 324–325.

[171] Human Rights Committee, General Comment 29, States of Emergency (article 4), U.N. Doc. CCPR/C/21/Rev.1/Add.11 (2001), http://wwwserver.law.wits.ac.za/humanrts/gencomm/hrc29.html (accessed 07/07/2005)

[172] Human Rights Watch, "Human Rights Watch Policy on the Right to Return: Relevant Background", https://nadaily.com/cgi-bin/nph-proxyb.cgi/010000A/http/www.hrw.org – (accessed 05–07–2003), 1.

[173] Ghandhi, P. R., "The Human Rights Committee and Derogation in Public Emergencies' in *German Yearbook of International Law* 1989, 323, 326.

[174] Quoted in Joseph, Sarah and Sehultz, Jenny et al., *The International Covenant on Civil and Political Rights: Cases, Materials, and Commentary* (New York: Oxford University Press, 2000), 625.

Standards considered that States with large territorial areas such as Canada, China or the USA, should be allowed to derogate from the terms of Article 12(4) in proportion to the geographical area that is affected by the public emergency, rather than requiring the whole population to be affected.

While exercising emergency powers, States need ensure that the fundamental functions of the legislature remain intact, despite the relative expansion of the authority of the executive. Thus, the legislature should provide general guidelines to regulate executive discretion; and legislative prerogatives, immunities and privileges should remain intact.

A State could prohibit its citizens from returning by refusing to issue a passport or refusing to prolong its validity, or by depriving the person of their nationality. In either event, procedural fairness should be guaranteed so that the decision is not arbitrary. Article II (b) of the 1963 UN Draft Principles on RLR provide "No one shall be arbitrarily deprived of [their] nationality or forced to renounce [their] nationality as a means of divesting [them] of the right to return to [their] countries." Similar provisions are found in Article 15 (2) of the UDHR, Article 9 of the 1972 Uppsala Declaration on RLR and Article 6 (b) of the 1986 Strasbourg Declaration on RLR.

In *Marcos v. Manglapus,* former President Marcos, his family and supporters were in Hawaii and requested travel documents to return to the Philippines. President Aquino refused the application. The Supreme Court found that the President had not acted arbitrarily because the return of the ousted president threatened the national interest.[175] If an applicant who has been refused permission to enter the territory attempts to do so, the person may be detained, investigated, and possibly deported to the country from which they have departed.

3.5.4 *The duty not to exile nationals and to accept expelled nationals*

The corollary of requiring a State to permit the entry of a national is that it may not expel a national. In Concluding Comments on the Dominican Republic, the HRC has noted that punishment by exile is inconsistent with the terms of the ICCPR.[176] Withdrawal of nationality for the purpose of expulsion would be considered arbitrary in light of the UDHR.[177] The AMR guarantees a right to nationality and prohibits any arbitrary deprivation of that right.[178] The EHR provides

[175] *Marcos et al. v. Manglapus et al.*, 177 SCRA (1989), reproduced in 4 *Asian Yearbook of International Law* pages 298–299 (1994), 225.

[176] (1993) UN doc. CCPR/C/790/Add. 18, paragraph 6. See Joseph, Sarah and Sehultz, Jenny et al., *The International Covenant on Civil and Political Rights: Cases, Materials, and Commentary* (New York: Oxford University Press, 2000), 259.

[177] Article 15 of UDHR provides "Everyone has the right to a nationality. No one shall be arbitrarily deprived of his nationality nor deprived the right to change his nationality."

[178] Article 20 (3) of the AMR provides "No one shall be arbitrarily deprived of his nationality or of the right to change it."

that arbitrary expulsion would occur if a State refused to confer nationality for the purpose of expulsion from the territory.

In ancient Athens, perpetual exile was the only means of avoiding capital punishment.[179] In some countries, it may be regarded as an alternative to other forms of punishment, such as lifetime imprisonment. There is a reluctance to sanction exile as a form of punishment.[180] In socialist countries, the issue of expelling nationals mainly concerns the expulsion of political dissidents. Expulsion was used by the former Eastern European socialist regimes as a way of removing political opposition, where imprisonment within the State was undesirable.[181] Socialist States are also reluctant to allow expelled nationals to return to the territory. For example, Chinese authorities granted many political prisoners passports or exit permits to allow them to leave the State in response to sustained diplomatic pressure by the USA in relation to China's most favoured nation status. However, these people were placed on a black list and barred from re-entry.

It should be emphasised that the right to return is – apart from the exception of punishment provided by law – guaranteed without restriction to all nationals, and to stateless persons and aliens who have established a permanent home in the territory of the State into which they wish to enter. It is permissible for States to require proof of nationality or a 'genuine and effective link' with the territory. The reduction of statelessness by international agreement may positively moderate the possibility if being exiled. Article 7 1 (a) of *Convention on the Reduction of Statelessness 1961* prescribes that if the law of a Contracting State entails loss or renunciation of nationality, such renunciation shall not result in loss of nationality unless the person concerned possesses or acquires another nationality. Article 7 1 (a) further regulates that the provisions of subparagraph (a) of this paragraph shall not apply where their application would be inconsistent with the principles stated in articles 13 (RLR) of the UDHR.

By contrast, a host country may expel aliens from the territory. This right produces a duty of the country of origin to permit the re-entry of those people. An individual, who is the national of one State, but who resides and is ultimately expelled from another State, has the guaranteed right to return to the State of nationality. This is important because if an individual becomes stateless, the State of nationality is obliged to receive him or her.

---

[179] Vinogradoff, Paul, *Outlines of Historical Jurisprudence, Volume Two, The Jurisprudence of the Greek City* (Oxford, the UK Oxford University Press, 1922), 179.

[180] Henkin, Louis, editor, *The International Bill of Rights: the Covenant on Civil and Political Rights* (New York: 1981Columbia University Press), 181.

[181] Foldesi, Tamas, "The Right to Move and Its Achilles' Heel, The Right to Asylum" in *Connell Journal of International Law*, Spring 1993 (8) 289, 6.

An alien may be returned to their country of origin if no other country is prepared to accept them.[182] States cannot deprive a person of their citizenship in order to prevent that person from exercising the right to return. Currently, States do not directly denaturalise citizens (as was the case in the 1920s and 1930s). Indirect methods are adopted to deprive citizens of the right to return, such as rejecting an application to return on the grounds of an infringement of the host countries' laws or a national law. The cause that implicitly supports this decision is that there will be an unacceptable financial burden placed on the State in relation to dealing with the offence, if the person returns.

3.6 Conclusions

RLR has been affirmed as a fundamental human right in several international instruments and the Constitutions of many States. While retaining its character as a fundamental human right, each State also has the sovereign right to regulate RLR in accordance with its own laws. The regulation of RLR however is not only an attribute of sovereignty but an issue with important political, economic and security implications for the State. Limits are thus imposed on RLR. Given its significance it is understandable and indeed desirable that States regulate or limit RLR. The regulation or limitation of RLR must however take account of both the interests of the State and the human rights dimension of RLR. In other words, only permissible limits are acceptable. The analysis in this chapter will basically correspond to the analysis, from chapters eight to thirteen, dealing with the current issues of RLR in China.

---

[182] Nowak, Manfred, *U.N. Covenant on Civil and Political Rights: ICCPR Commentary*, Kehl am Rhein, Strasbourg, Arlington, Germany, 1993, 228.

Chapter Four
Driving factors of RLR in China

INTRODUCTION

To systematically explain RLR, as it exists in China, it is necessary to first analyse the motivations, or driving factors, behind RLR in China. This chapter concentrates on the common factors of politics, economics, culture and law. The political and legal factors are the foremost and most direct factors affecting RLR in China. The four perspectives are further divided into a host of subsidiary aspects. These include the one party system, it being one member of former communist bloc, basic economic facts, public ownership, interaction between economic development and laws governing exit and entry, the community orientated culture, loyalty (*Zhong*) and filial piety (*Xiao*), the duty orientated culture, sublating (*Yangqi*), agrarian society and geographical isolation, absence of the Constitutional foundation of the protection of RLR, thc naturc of law, the aim of law, and the research on RLR in China. The analysis here will lay a basis for understanding the development and specific issues of RLR to be explored in the next seven chapters.

4.1 POLITICS

While migration can provide wide-ranging benefits, it also imposes costs. One major problem with evaluating the costs of migration in China is the way in which it affects different groups in different ways; some gain significantly, others marginally, while yet others lose. The different groups have different degrees of solidarity and political power. Thus, it needs to be remembered that it is often political power that shapes migration policy. Migration policy is related to the perceptions of those with the power to dictate policy. For example, the absence of the remedies for RLR in public affairs is consonant with the interests of government and the CPC who might control the movement of subordinates and solidify their privileges.

The Chinese political system is the communist system. Simply speaking, it determines what power and rights people can enjoy, and how they can be enjoyed. The communist political system has operated in China since 1949, when the People's Republic of China was established. This provides theoretical and political basis of the transitional market economy and Marxist legal theory and significantly affects the changing of traditional Confucian culture. Accordingly, the communist political system decides issues of RLR in China. This first section will be divided into two parts to first consider one party reign and then consider China as one member of the former communist bloc.

4.1.1 *The system of the multi-party cooperation and political consultation led by the Communist Party of China*

The most marked feature of the Chinese communist political system is the system of the multi-party cooperation and political consultation led by the Communist Party of China (Chinese party system). China is ruled and controlled by the CPC. The system has been legalised in Preamble Paragraph 7 of the Constitution and reiterated in important national documents including the report of the 16th CPC National Congress issued in November 2002. The State organ and armed forces[1] are subordinate to the CPC; whose role is to implement the party's policies.[2] The

---

[1] State organ in China means the organ that carries out State power and runs State affairs, including organ of State power, organ of administration, judicial organ, procuratorial organ, military armies, etc., e.g. National People's Congress (NPC), the Chinese People's Political Consultative Conference (CPPCC), the State Council, the people's congresses at all levels, the people's governments at all levels, the people's Courts at all levels, the people's Procuratorates at all levels, the public security organs at all levels. See Dictionary Department, Institute of Linguistics, Chinese Academy of Social Sciences, *The Contemporary Chinese Dictionary* (*Chinese-English edition*) (Beijing: Foreign Language Teaching and Research Press, 2002), 741. According to Article of 93 and 94 of the *Constitution of the PRC* (*Amendment*) 2004, the President of the PRC is also a part of the State organ.

[2] Political 'redness' has been used as the chief criterion for appointing cadres into the leading positions of judicial authority. See "Judiciary in Line With International Norms', in *Beijing Review*, No. 49 (5–11 December 1994), 5–6, Quoted in Teather, David C. B. and Yee, Herbert S., editor, *China in Transition* (London: Macmillan Press Ltd. and New York: St. Martin's Press Inc., 1999), 76.

CPC's constitutionally-mandated leadership and of its having almost all top positions of the State organ or apparatus and armed forces occupied by party members, ensures the primacy of Party Politburo guidelines and has enabled the CPC to set the broad parameters of national policy.[3] The structure of Chinese State organisations is listed in Appendix 1 of this book.

The situation of the system of the multi-party cooperation and political consultation led by the Communist Party of China discussed above results in the established fact that CPC vests most of interests in China, which are shared with the whole Chinese residents in theory. Although Article 33 Clause 2 of the *Constitution of the PRC (Amendment)* 2004 set forth "all citizens of the People's Republic of China are equal before the law", the absolute leadership of the CPC means that, in practice, citizens' social and political status is not complete independent and equal. Because the CPC is fully integrated into the State organ and important enterprises and institutions, the status of party member becomes the basic qualification to be one of ruling elite. High status within the CPC translates as having high social and political status. The Secretary-General of CPC's Central Committee is the highest-ranking person in the central State organ, and can also be, as for example with Jiang Zemin or Hu Jingtao, the President of the People's Republic of China and chairman of the Central Military Committee. The secretary of the CPC's provincial branch is the highest-ranking individual in the provincial State organ. It is logically accepted that the members of the CPC, especially the cadres of the CPC will further vest economic interests in China.

Chinese party system was established and operated in 1949 in which the People's Republic of China was found. In general, it is a successive system, which could be suitable to Chinese realities, and played a very important role in developing economy and civilizing politics. However, with the leap of the economy since 1978 and the fully integration to the world symbolized by the entrance of the WTO in 2000, the deficiencies of Chinese party system commences to become a barrier of further enhancing the development of economy. Following discussed deficiencies need to be sincerely considered. It is thus necessary to undertake relevant reforms to enrich the notion of Chinese party system, and advance the regulations of Chinese party system. In turn more efficiency and effectiveness might be equipped with Chinese party system.

While too little reform creates social change and instability that might challenge those interests, too much reform can do the same. In regard to the reform relevant to RLR, compared with the relaxtion of the restriction on the non-member of the CPC, it is acceptable that the limits over exit and entry of all party members, especial cadres of the CPC are much strict. Up to the end of 2003, the amount of

---

[3] US Department of State, "China (Including Hong Kong and Macao): Country Reports on Human Rights Practices 2002", http://www.state.gov/g/drl/rls/hrrpt/2002/18239.htm (accessed 16/09/2006).

members of CPC accounts 5.2% of the whole population in China. Given 68.2 million party members and their relatively high social status,[4] the limits on their exit and entry equates to limits on exit and entry of the elite of Chinese society. The strict control over exit and entry of all party members is thus the foremost reason or basis for a number of issues to be discussed in later chapters of this book. Issues of exit and entry within public affairs will be discussed in part 6.2; prerequisite certificates from the departments in which the applicants are employed in parts 7.3, 9.1.3 and 9.2.2 of this book; retention of passports by designed departments in part 6.3.3; and the right of nationals not to be exiled in part 8.4. These issues have not been subject to the reform of laws governing exit and entry, which will be discussed in next chapter.

Secondly, the system of the multi-party cooperation and political consultation led by the Communist Party of China can effectively undermine the independence of the State organ and armed forces. The absolute leadership of the CPC means that the acts of the CPC can be almost seen as synonymous with acts of the State organ. This may lead departments of the State organ applying CPC policy as the criteria for the practical exercise of discretionary power, and to enact regulations and rules based on CPC policy. Some relevant issues from this, to be discussed in part 7.1.2 of this book, concern the legitimacy of acts of the CPC in cases when public security departments are instructed to prevent individuals with knowledge of important political, military, technological, or economic secrets from exiting China.

A further influence of the system of the multi-party cooperation and political consultation led by the Communist Party of China is that, by conformity to CPC norms, and aspirations to social status, it can reduce an individual's urge or motivation to acquire RLR. It follows that the acquisition of a high position within the CPC is an important life goal. As a result, few efforts will be spared by the individual in dealing with CPC affairs in a manner that will please more senior members, even when this means that an individuals' potential to have personal rights and freedoms is greatly reduced.

Moreover, there are no independent political powers opposing the Communist Party in China. Article 35 of the *Constitution of the PRC (Amendment)* 2004 provides that the citizens enjoy freedom of association. However, the government restricts the right to establish political association in practice. According to 2001 *Human Rights Report of China* released by the US State Department, the formation of truly autonomous politics, human rights, religious, environment, labour, and youth organisations that directly challenge government authority is prevented.[5] The opposition party is illegal.[6] In this circumstance, no social and

---

[4] "Number of CPC members in China Exceeds 68 Million", http://english.peopledaily.com.cn/200407/01/eng20040701_148214.html (accessed 02/07/2004).

[5] US Department of State, "China (Including Hong Kong and Macao) Country Report on Human Rights Practices for 2001", http://www.State.gov/g/frl/rls/hrrpt/2001/eap/8289.htm (accessed 2/02/2004), 18.

[6] The Chinese People's Political Consultation Committee (CPPCC) is a key institution

political association may legally strive for RLR on behalf of Chinese citizens. Without the support and assistance of truly autonomous social and political associations, it is very hard to produce satisfactory results in the pursuit of RLR for citizens. The absence of independent political powers may reliably explain why the government, rather than other sources, initiate all changes of RLR in China.

The system of the multi-party cooperation and political consultation led by the Communist Party of China makes the research of RLR from a non-Marxist perspective a sensitive topic. It is difficult, therefore, to objectively, fairly or comprehensively understand the realities of RLR in China. Many of the issues concerning RLR, argued in chapters six to eleven, have had very little attention from academics and have been almost ignored by government. For that reason, the materials to support the arguments made in this book are in general derived from legislative provisions, reports and news items, rather than from the works of academics.

In recent years, the CPC has gradually reduced its formal involvement in government operations. This has allowed the government to exercise significant discretion in implementing policy. The CPC has continued to strengthen the capacity of members of the National People's Congress (NPC) and to reform the bureaucracy. The congresses at all levels play an increasingly independent role as a forum for local and provincial concerns, particularly as critics of local and national corruption and inefficiency.[7] Rural and village people have been learning about the practice of local elections.[8]

These reforms touch on an important and sensitive issue in China, political democracy. All democratic reforms are based on the system that, on the one hand can help reformers to popularize limited reform measures, so to safeguard the long-term interests of the CPC but, on the other hand, do not allow comprehensive reform from the perspective of the State rather than the Party which could undermine the status of the CPC. Under Chinese present realities, it is crucial to keep the leadership of the CPC to stabilize the society. When assessing the driving factor of Chinese party system, both the deficiencies and strong points of Chinese party system need to be carefully and completely considered.

---

for multi-party cooperation and political consultations under the leadership of the CPC, a Chinese people's patriotic united front organization, and a major channel for promoting socialist democracy. See "CPPCC Annual Session Opens (03/03/2002)", http://www.fmprc.gov.cn/eng/topics/3701/3703/t18937.htm (accessed 16/09/2006).

[7] "Chinese President Calls For Developing Socialist Democracy", http://english.people.com.cn/200409/21/eng20040921_157751.html (accessed 16/09/2006).

[8] "China to Further Promote Grass-roots Democracy", http://www.china-embassy.org/eng/gyzg/t122877.htm (accessed 16/09/2006).

4.1.2 *China as a member of the former communist bloc*

Despite of the collapse of the USSR and Eastern European communist countries in 1989, and China's commencement of the transition from a planned economy to a free market economy, we still find that the former socialist bloc casts dark shadows over Chinese exit and entry laws. C. P. Fitzgerald has suggested that the impression the USSR made on China was immense.[9] Some exploration of the former socialist bloc may help to understand why the starting point and theme of exit and entry administration are designed to control, rather than to ensure that citizens enjoy RLR.

Historically, all newly established communist regimes imposed strict emigration controls, which were kept in place until drastic political and economic changes occurred. Migration from communist countries to countries with established market economies was practically forbidden. Migration between communist countries occurred on a very limited scale and was usually not described as migration, but as temporary transfers of manpower for the coordinated use of the productive resources of friendly countries.[10] Although the former USSR recognised RLR in its Constitution and ratified the ICCPR and the CERD in 1973 and 1979, it actually imposed numerous superfluous requirements on those applying for exit and entry.

After the civil war from 1946 to 1949, which destroyed the Republic of China on the Mainland, and as a new socialist system was being built, China faced enormous economic problems and sought foreign help. The former USSR, Bulgaria, Romania, Hungary, North Korea and Poland successively established diplomatic relationships with and offered assistance to the new People's Republic of China (PRC), all within just six days of its establishment[11] The Western countries that had imposed sanctions on the PRC during the 1950s and 1960s.[12] Chinese people were called upon to follow in the footsteps of established communist countries, especially the former USSR. Mao Zedong exhorted that, "the Communists of the USSR are our best teachers, so we must learn from them".[13] Although China tried

---

[9] Fitzgerald, C.P., *The Chinese View of their Place in the World* (Amen House, London, E.C.4: Oxford University Press, 1964), 44.

[10] The United Nations, *International Migration Policies and Programs: A World Survey*. Sales No. E.82 XIII.4, 35.

[11] "The Lists of the Countries having Diplomatic Relationship with the PRC" (*Yu Zhongguo Jianjiao Guojia Yilanbiao*), http://www.fmprc.gov.cn/chn/lbfw/jjbiao/t9650.htm (accessed 16/09/2006).

[12] The USA Congressional – Executive Commission on China, "The People's Republic of China", http://www.cecc.gov/pages/virtual/Acad/his/prc.php (accessed 04/01/2005)

[13] Shen, Chen, "Language and Culture: Two Goals of Foreign Language Teaching in China, Lessons from History and Perspectives for the future", *Australia Review of Applied Linguistic* 12 / 2, 1989, 51.

to relax its hostile relationships with Western nations during this period, diplomatic ties were not improved until the 1970s, when Italy, the UK, Japan, Germany, Australia and the USA recognised the PRC.[14]

For a time, Soviet culture was the only foreign culture that impacted on China. In the 1950s laws of the former USSR governing exit and entry were followed when the PRC devised its own laws. Enemies of the State were allegedly so pervasive and menacing that security could only be achieved through State-enforced unity, order, solidarity, and discipline. The collective imperatives of internal order and national defence took precedence over individual freedom. Hence, RLR is practically denied in China, which imposed repressive migration policies similar to all communist countries. By 1958, diplomatic relations between the PRC and the USSR had cooled. Even though Chinese jurists at that time tried to break away from Soviet influences, no essential changes were made.

By the late 1980s and early 1990s, the Cold War had ended, drastic political and economic changes occurred in Eastern Europe and the former USSR, and the communist bloc had disintegrated. The hostile relationship between communist and Western countries had greatly eased. Some former Eastern European communist States have become members of the European Union (EU) and North Atlantic Treaty Organisation (NATO). Since the late 1980s, some communist countries began to soften their grip on the foreign travel of their citizens, or became more lenient to the demands of members of certain ethnic groups to emigrate. The UN summarised in *International Migration from Countries with Economies in Transition: 1980–1999*, that in the late 1980s and early 1990s, "most legal restrictions to migration were lifted and became practically non-existent."[15]

However, with no drastic political change in China having occurred, improvements of RLR in China have been considerably less effective than those in former communist countries. After the death of Deng Xiaoping in 1997, Jiang Zemin announced that he would continue with Deng's reforms, including the reform of the political structure. However, as the Australian Department of Foreign Affairs and Trade stated in 2003, "there was little evidence of political liberalisation."[16] Compared with the historical development of former communist countries' laws governing exit and entry of citizens, there is a long way to go before RLR in China moves from the strict repression of the past to full liberalisation.

---

[14] "The Lists of the Countries having Diplomatic Relationship with the PRC" (*Yu Zhongguo Jianjiao Guojia Yilanbiao*), http://www.fmprc.gov.cn/chn/lbfw/jjbiao/t9650.htm (accessed 16/09/2006).

[15] Population Division, Department of Economic and Social Affairs, United Nations Secretariat, *International Migration from Countries with Economies in Transition: 1980–1999*, ESA/P/WP.176 , New York, 2002, 123 pages, 5.

[16] Australian Foreign Affairs and Foreign Trade Ministry, "the People's Republic of China: Country Information," http://www.dfat.gov.au/geo/china/index.html (accessed 16/09/2006).

4.2 Economics

4.2.1 *Basic economic factors*

The Chinese economy is complex, unique and difficult for foreigners to understand. The largest population, economic underdevelopment and regional economic disparities are basic economic factors that China must face. In 2002, the Chinese population was approximately 1.3 billion, or 21 percent of the world's population.[17] Premier Wen Jiabao explained that problems caused by China's vast population as being that:

> Any small individual shortage, if multiplied by 1.3 billion, becomes a big, big problem. Any considerable amount of financial and material resources, if divided by 1.3 billion, becomes a very low per capital level.[18]

China's per capital GDP stood at a mere US$911 in 2001, a far cry from developed countries, such as Japan, where the per capita GDP was US$32,534.[19] Of the 129 countries covered by the World Development Report, China ranked 76th on per capital GDP.[20] According to official Chinese statistics:

> There are still 30 million farmers lacking food and clothing, 23 million city-dwellers living on a subsistence allowance, and 60 million disabled and handicapped people in need of social security aid.[21]

---

[17] "Population Density", http://www.unescap.org/stat/data/statind/pdf/t5_dec05.pdf (accessed 16/09/2006).

[18] "The Premier of Wen, Jiabao Accepted the Interview of the Chief-editor of *Washington Post*" (*Wenjiabao Zongli Jieshou Huashendun Youbao Zhubian Caifang*), 23 November 2003, http://www.fmprc.gov.cn/chn/zxxx/t44934.htm (accessed 04/12/2003).

[19] World Bank calculations based on purchasing power parity reckon that China's per capital GDP in 2004 equals Japan's level in 1950. See "Analysis: Will China's Growth Sustain 30 More Years?" http://english.people.com.cn/200411/08/eng20041108_163104.html (accessed 15/11/2004).

[20] Quoted in Kwan, Chi Hung, "China in Transition: How Far is Coastal Behind the Industrialized Countries? An Analysis Based on Purchasing Power Parity (August 2002)", http://www.rieti.go.jp/en/china/02080901.html (accessed 2/02/2004).

[21] Wen, Jiaobao, the Premier of the State Council, "Turning Yours Eyes to China", Speech at Harvard University on 11th December 2003, http://www.fmprc.gov.cn/eng/zxxx/t56076.htm (accessed 19/12/2003).

At the same time, economic growth differs from region to region.[22] In 2000, the per capita GDP for China was US$849,[23] whereas in Shanghai it was US$4,180,[24] and urban per capita income was 2.7 times that of rural per capita income.[25] In 2001 the US State Department reported that the economic disparity between coastal and inland regions, and between urban and rural areas continued to widen.[26] Premier Wen Jiabao predicted that China's economy would deteriorate unless this disparity could be resolved.[27]

In the light of these three basic economic factors, the Chinese government has been concerned with instability caused by extensive reform. Jiang Zemin has pointed out that "stability is a prerequisite for reform and development," and that reform and development should occur 'amidst social stability".[28] In order to avoid or reduce the possibility of instability, the government has seldom embarked on sweeping reforms over a short period. The gradual nature of reform is also obvious in relation to the reform of exit and entry laws and administration. The biggest overhaul will be gradually implemented between 2002 and 2004. Pilot reform projects were initially carried out in relatively developed areas, such as Guangdong, where some limits on RLR were eased for the purpose of a trial. The introduction of this process into all medium and large cities will be discussed in part 5.2.2 of this book.

Regional economic disparities relate especially to exit and entry administration of the HKSAR and MSAR, and to the emigration intermediary agencies. Only residents in Guangdong, Shanghai and Beijing, of all 33 provincial administrative areas, can freely travel to and from the HKSAR and MSAR. In various provincial

[22] "Foreign Ministry Spokesman's Press Conference on September 3 2002", http://www.china-un.ch/eng/xwdt/t88304.htm (accessed 16/09/2006).

[23] "Shanghai to Become Int'l Shopping Destination in 5 Years", http://english.enorth.com.cn/system/2001/11/29/000203168.shtml (accessed 16/09/2006).

[24] "China's GDP Predicted to Top US$1 Trillion: SIC, 2 November 2000", *The People's Daily*, http://english.peopledaily.com.cn/english/200011/02/eng20001102_54181.html (accessed 16/09/2006).

[25] US Department of State, "China: Country Report on Human Rights Practices 2001", http://www.State.gov/g/frl/rls/hrrpt/2001/eap/684.html (accessed 2/02/2004).

[26] US Department of State, "China: Country Report on Human Rights Practices 2001", http://www.State.gov/g/frl/rls/hrrpt/2001/eap/684.html (accessed 2/02/2004).

[27] "The Premier of Wen, Jiabao Accepted the Interview of the Chief-editor of *Washington Post*" (*Wenjiabao Zongli Jieshou Huashendun Youbao Zhubian Caifang*), 23 November 2003, http://www.fmprc.gov.cn/chn/zxxx/t44934.htm (accessed 04/12/2003).

[28] Jiang, Zemin, the President of the PRC, "Build a Well-off Society in an All-Round Way and Create a New Situation in Building Socialism with Chinese Characteristics: Report page 16th China Communist Party Congress (accessed 8/11/2002)", http://www.news.xinhuanet.com/english/2002–11/18/content_633685.htm (accessed 16/09/2006).

administrative areas, the requirements for the application for exit can vary, which will be discussed in part 5.2.3 of this book. The establishment and operation of the emigration intermediary agencies is explained and analysed in part 10.3.2 of this book.

The size of China's population also affects the administration of permanent residency. According to an OECD report in 2001, when compared to other countries where foreigners are granted permanent residency to fill labour shortfalls, China has a large labour force and low labour costs.[29] China, in protecting its own workforce, has therefore not sought to attract external labourers. China's policies with respect to the return of overseas Chinese citizens are addressed in parts 8.1, 8.2 and 8.3 of this book, in which it is noted that financial independence, rather than nationality is the key determinant in granting permission to resettle.

4.2.2 *Socialist public ownership of the means of production and a transitional economy*

Article 6 of the *Constitution of the PRC (Amendment)* 2004 stipulates:

> The basis of the socialist economic system of the People's Republic of China is socialist public ownership of the means of production, namely, ownership by the whole people and collective ownership by the working people.

Socialist public ownership of the means of production is also called State ownership. In theory, everyone is the owner of social resources. The task of China's parliamentarians is not to decide what resources the government should own, but how the government utilises those resources effectively. Under this system, individuals and private businesses are not completely independent participants in the economic interests of China.

Before reform and opening up, the 'binding net' between individuals and working units (*gongzuo danwei*) was the most important channel through which individuals could participate and co-operate in social activities. Individuals did not have the right to own or deal with resources. Every working urban resident belonged to a public working unit, since the State owned all working units. These working units provided their employee's with cradle-to-grave welfare guarantees and pensions. In turn, the working units approved almost all acts of their employees, including their employees' applications to go abroad. These 'binding nets' effectively turned employees into *de facto* appendages to their working unit. The approval requirements constituted a general violation of individual rights by the State, and controlled personal mobility. There was little ground to challenge the extensive exercise of public power by working units during this period, in rela-

[29] Chapter 4. China, the OECD, *Migration and the Labour Market in Asia: Recent Trends and Policies*, Paris: the OECD, 2001.

tion to private affairs. Consequently, it is not meaningful to discuss RLR or other rights during this period. Because exit and entry policies were those of the working units, this partially explains why there were so few laws governing the processing of the applications for exit and entry between 1949 and 1985, which will be discussed in parts 5.3 of this book.

China officially embraced market economics and abandoned the planned economy after the constitutional amendment of 1993. Foreign industries were legal in 1979 when the *Law on Chinese and Foreign Equity Joint Ventures* was promulgated, and private industries were legal after the constitutional amendments of 1988.[30] After that time private industries and the extent of foreign investment greatly developed. In 2002, "the non-State sector accounted for more than 70 percent of China's gross industrial output".[31] As of December 2003, 80 million persons were employed in private industry. Private firms contributed 23 percent of yearly GDP growth, and 65 percent of exported products were made by enterprises supported by foreign investment.[32]

The flourishing non-State sector has cultivated a new workforce beyond the working unit framework. Restructuring of the State sectors, including the streamlining of government offices and mass lay-offs from State enterprises, has left a great number of people without a working unit. Working units no longer form a binding net that covers all working people. The development of non-State industry provides an economic basis upon which to cancel the requirement of working unit approval for an application to leave China, which will be discussed from different angles in parts 7.3, 8.1.2, 9.1.3 and 9.2.2 of this book. A goal of the reform strategy is to enable a person to access a passport on demand. This will become more feasible if the structure of the working unit is further weakened.

Extensive development of private industry has fostered awareness among employees of their rights and interests. More Chinese people are growing rich, and are no longer dependent on the State. They will have increasing control over their own lives, particularly as they can enjoy private ownership. Increasing public awareness of individual legal rights and interests will cause people to doubt the legitimacy of their working units' control over intrinsically personal affairs which in effect limit RLR, which will be discussed in part 7.3 of this book.

---

[30] "Citizens' legal private property is inviolable" was inserted as Article 13 Clause 1 when the Constitution was further amended in 2004.

[31] Australian Foreign Affairs and Foreign Trade Ministry, *The People's Republic of China: Country Information*, http://www.dfat.gov.au/geo/china/cb_background.html (accessed 22/10/2003).

[32] "The Premier of Wen, Jiabao Accepted the Interview of the Chief-editor of *Washington Post*" (*Wenjiabao Zongli Jieshou Huashendun Youbao Zhubian Caifang*), 23 November 2003, http://www.fmprc.gov.cn/chn/zxxx/t44934.htm (accessed 04/12/2003).

4.2.3 *Interaction between economic development and laws governing exit and entry*

Three key events have made China increasingly open to the world: the 1978 new policy of reform; the establishment of a socialist market economy as the goal of reform in 1992; and China's entry into the World Trade Organisation (WTO) in 2001. China achieved an average annual GDP growth of above 9 percent from 1978 to 2003, a stunning record worldwide.[33] These economic achievements have created suitable conditions for the advancement of RLR in China, and had a profound effect on the extent to which the right operates.

1978 reform policy

The economic boom in China started with the implementation of Deng Xiaoping's economic reform policy in 1978. The demand for international integration has followed from the pattern of sustained economic development since then. The *Law on the Control of Exit and Entry of Citizens* (PRC), the *Law on the control of Exit and Entry of Aliens* (PRC) and their detailed rules of the implementation, were introduced in 1985 and 1986 to aid in the assessment of the numerous applications to leave China. Article 1 of the *Law on the Control of Exit and Entry of Citizens* 1985 (PRC) provides that "this law is formulated with a view . . . to promote international exchange." Article 1 of the *Law on the Control of Exit and Entry of Aliens* 1985 (PRC) sought to "facilitate international exchange" as one of its three legislative purposes.

The establishment of a socialist market economy as the goal of reform in 1992

Learning from the lessons of the drastic political and economic changes in Eastern Europe and the former USSR, in 1992 the CPC opted to establish a socialist market economy. Its establishment consolidated close links between China and the rest of the world and resulted in a doubling of the number of Chinese people leaving China. The number of emigration intermediary agencies mushroomed in response to demand. At the same time, the dramatic growth in the number of people wishing to exit and exit the territory raised a great number of issues. The laws governing exit and entry and RLR began to be improved after 1994, "In order to be suitable for reform and opening up and the development of [the] socialist market economy."[34] Laws governing intermediary agencies were hastily enacted.

---

[33] "Analysis: Will China's Growth Sustain 30 More Years?" http://english.people.com.cn/200411/08/eng20041108_163104.html (accessed 15/11/2004).

[34] Article 1 Clause 1 of the *Explanation of the Enforcement of the Amendment of Two Detailed Rules of the Implementation* 1995 (PRC) (*Zhixing Liangge Shishi Xize Xiuding Neirong De Shuoming*), promulgated by the Ministry of Public Affairs on 13th February

The entry to the WTO in 2001

With membership of the WTO in 2001, China reached a new phase in its embrace of the global economy.[35] It now needed both talented people from overseas to enter, and its own citizens to go abroad – the reforms of exit and entry served this purpose exactly. In November 2001, ten days after China joined the WTO, the biggest overhaul in the history of Chinese migration law was announced, which will be discussed in part 5.4 of this book. The reforms, just as China promised to open its market to the outside world, helped China to open its door for its own people.

4.2.4 *Impacts of the limits of the movement within the territory on RLR*

Under the household registration system established in 1958, to be discussed in part 5.3 of this book, free movement within China is prohibited. It has been accepted that if an individual could not freely move within China, he or she seldom considered overseas travel. This was particularly true for residents in remote areas in China who may have had feelings of trepidation about leaving China.[36] Undoubtedly, the outdated household registration system became a barrier to the free-flow of human resources needed by a market economy and globalisation. As Cai Fang, director of the Population institute of the Chinese Academy of Social Sciences, has argued, the outdated household registration system had long been blamed for the inefficient distribution of human resources, resulting in an excessive concentration of people in urban areas and a 'brain drain' from developing areas.[37]

For this reason, a new household registration system was implemented in 2001 under the *Circular of the State Council on Transmitting the Opinions of*

1995 and effective on the same day. See also the *Detailed Rules of the Implementation of Law on the Control of Exit and Entry of Citizens* 1985 (PRC) and the *Detailed Rules of the Implementation of Law on the Control of Exit and Entry of Aliens* 1985 (PRC) which were separately revised in 1994.

[35] Zhu, Rongji, the Former Premier of the State Council, "Report on the Work of the Government 2002" (16/03/2002), http://english.gov.cn/official/2005–07/29/content_18337.htm (accessed 16/09/2006).

[36] The household registration system led to the prohibition of non-registered resident area applications, which will be discussed in part 6.3.1 of this book. The requirements of household registration after returning to China, will be discussed in part 8.1.3, and the requirements of household deregistration before leaving China, will be discussed in part 7.4 of this book.

[37] Quoted in "Residence System Reform Speeds up Human Resources Flow," 31 October 2001, *The People's Daily*, http://www.china.org.cn/english/2001/Nov/21457.htm (accessed 16/09/2006).

the Ministry of Public Security Concerning the Expedition of the Small Town Registered Residence Management System Reform. This allowed all rural residents and non-natives (who have a legal and static dwelling place, a stable occupation and source of income), and their families, to apply for permanent residence in urban area towns where they work and live. By the end of 2001, several provinces, such as Jilin, Hunan, Guangdong, Fujian and Liaoning, had abolished the division between agricultural and non-agricultural household categories.[38]

The right to freely move within China will create the conditions for the individual awareness and enjoyment of RLR. The relaxation of the prohibition of non-registered resident area applications is discussed in part 5.4 of this book, alongside the cancellation of the deregistration of individuals who have been abroad for more than one year,[39] and the establishment of a mutual information network that combines exit and entry information and household registration management during 2004.[40] However, as Bao Suixian, deputy director of the Public Security Bureau of the MPS, emphasised in 2002, the registered residence management system will continue to exist for a long time, as it is an important component of China's administrative management.[41] Restrictions on RLR related to household registration can be predicted to remain in the near future.

4.3 Culture

Apart from political and economic factors, RLR in China is widely influenced by culture. Without doubt, the very heart of Chinese culture is Confucianism. Confucianism has existed for more than 2,500 years.[42] Although countless dynasties and governments have changed hands, the reverence paid to Confucianism has never waned. In Confucianism, the position of the individual in the society is relative independent in comparison with the in Christianity. A man in Confucianism

---

[38] "China to Cut Limits on Population Mobility," 26 February 2002, *The People's Daily*, http://english.peopledaily.com.cn/200202/26/eng20020226_90987.shtml (accessed 16/09/2006).

[39] "Reforms Make Life and Travel Much Easier", 8 August 2003, *The China Daily,* http://www1.chinadaily.com.cn/en/doc/2003–08/08/content_252954.htm (accessed 16/09/2006).

[40] "State to Simplify Entry-exit Rules", 11/22/2002, *The China Daily*, http://www.chinadaily.com.cn/en/doc/2001–11–22/content_94711.htm (accessed 16/09/2006).

[41] "MPS: China's Registered Residence Management System Will Not Be Abolished", 26 February 2002, *The People's Daily*, http://english.people.com.cn/200202/26/eng20020226_91010.shtml (accessed 16/09/2006).

[42] "In China, Confucius started in about 520. B.C. to disseminate knowledge of benevolence (*ren*) and decency (*Li*), and persists for decades." Yu, Shutong and Wen, Jia editor, *A New Chinese-English Law Dictionary* (*Xin Hanying Faxue Cidian*) (Beijing: Publishing House of Law, 1998), 1250.

must pay more loyalty to the State and his/her family than in Christianity. Confucianism pays more attention to the duty than right. Confucianism's attitude to the foreign cultures is sublating (from Hegelian philosophy, to put aside but not wholly dispense with). The existence and influences cannot be divorced from Chinese agricultural civilisations, its geographical environment. An analysis of the influences of Confucianism on RLR in China might be achieved by above main elements.

4.3.1 *The community-orientated culture*

Western democratic systems stress individuality, privacy, diversity, and protection of the individual from undue outside interference. A person should have freedom of movement, and then ask under what circumstances this freedom may be restricted. The traditional Chinese approach has been quite different.

Chinese traditional social mores have revolved around Confucian philosophical norms and ideals. Confucianism advocates the rule of rites and traditional ethics. Everyone forms part of a patriarchal social network, and has a node in the broader homogeneous structure. All nodes, which consist of the three cardinal rules (*Sangang*) and the five cardinal virtues (*Wuchang*), are inextricably interrelated by a number of threads. The three cardinal rules are that a monarch rules over the subjects (*Junjun chenchen*), a father rules over his child (*Fufu zizi*), and a husband rules over his wife (*Fufu qiqi*). The five cardinal virtues are benevolence (*Ren*), dutifulness (*Yi*), decency (*Li*), knowledge (*Zhi*), and faithfulness (*Xin*). Everyone must obey their fixed social position within the three cardinal rules and the five cardinal virtues. This position cannot be altered. Individuals, who are closely intertwined in this structure, are taught that it is their duty to suffer their treatments.

Chinese culture appreciates the importance of individuals but places greater emphasis on how a person functions within the context of a larger group. In the Chinese language, the term for 'individuals' (*Geren*) has the same meaning as 'oneself' (*Ziwuo*).[43] The term for 'oneself' often connotes selfishness (*Zisi*), and is frequently used as a contrast to the term 'public' (*Gong*) and 'collective' (*Jiti*), which implies the 'common' (*Gonggong*).[44] Preference for the larger collective unit over the individual continues into the present day, although there are certainly groups in China who are defined by loyalties other than kinship and hold to Communist rather than Confucian ideology. As Sun Changjiang has stated:

---

[43] Dictionary Department, Institute of Linguistics, Chinese Academy of Social Sciences, *The Contemporary Chinese Dictionary* (*Chinese-English edition*) (Beijing: Foreign Language Teaching and Research Press, 2002), 656.

[44] Dictionary Department, Institute of Linguistics, Chinese Academy of Social Sciences, *The Contemporary Chinese Dictionary* (*Chinese-English edition*) (Beijing: Foreign Language Teaching and Research Press, 2002), 667 and 668.

> In this social order, neither man nor one's personality is free. There is no true respect towards people, since one cannot speak of man's independence when there is no independent individual.[45]

The Australian Human Rights Centre has observed that the core of Confucianism puts the emphasis on community. Within such an environment, a code of ethics has evolved which places a duty on the individual to uphold group harmony, even if this necessitates suppression or subordination of individual claims and grievances.[46] In this context, RLR based on the independence of individual, is hardly to be completely recognised by Chinese society.

4.3.2 *Loyalty* (Zhong) *and filial piety* (Xiao)

Loyalty and filial piety, which link the principle of benevolence and the action, are the two most important concepts of traditional Confucian ethics. Loyalty is the root of social morality, and usually interpreted as meaning sincerity, conscientiousness, or the exhaustion of one's self in the performance of one's moral duties. Those who ignored the country's interests but instead keenly pursued individual wealth and blindly obeyed the orders of the monarch were considered 'traitors'.[47] Travel might expose Chinese inhabitants to other ideas and wider horizons, which may challenge the established social and ideological structures. Chinese leaders routinely punish political dissidents by imprisonment or exile on the grounds that dissent and disloyalty are indistinguishable.

Filial piety is the foundation of familial ethics, and should be a desire of one's innermost heart and practiced with respect and sincerity to one's parents. According to *Analects*, the bible of Confucianism, a child should keep oneself at one's parents' side at all possible times and try one's best to refrain from distant travels, in order to relieve their anxiety. Confucius said, "While his parents are alive, the son may not go abroad to a distance. If he does go abroad, he must have a fixed place to which he goes."[48]

---

[45] Sun, Changjiang "Chinese Society, Chinese Confucianism, and the Modernisation of China", at Krieger, Silke and Trauzettel, Rolf editor, *Confucianism and the Modernization of China* (Mainz, Eschwege, Germany: V. Hase & Koehler Verlag, 1991), 393 pages.

[46] Australian Human Rights Centre, "Human Rights in Taiwan: Issues for the 21st Century", http://search2.austlii.edu.au/au/journals/HRD/2002/21.html (accessed 16/09/2006).

[47] Lee, Cheuk-yin, "the Dichotomy of loyalty and Filial Piety in Confucianism: Historical Development and Modern Significance", at Krieger, Silke and Trauzettel, Rolf editor, *Confucianism and the Modernization of China* (Mainz, Eschwege, Germany: V. Hase & Koehler Verlag, 1991), 99.

[48] *Analects*, Chapter XIX, quoted at Chen, Lifu, *The Confucian Way: A New and Systematic Study of "the Four Books"*, translated from the Chinese by Liu, Shih Shun (London: KPI Limited, 1986), 382.

The doctrines of loyalty and filial piety have been important factors in maintaining the stability of Chinese government and family. These doctrines provided good reasons to persuade people never to move away from the State or one's ancestral home, in other words to deny RLR. Seeking settlement elsewhere was unwelcome. The act of an individual leaving home voluntarily was one of disloyalty (*Buzhong*) to the monarch and one of filial non-piety (*Buxiao*) to the parents. Any voluntary departure amounted to rejection of the family; and life as an exile from home was a serious form of punishment. Migration was simply not an option, only sojourning on official duty, or as a trader, was permissible.

As a consequence, "China is a country without a tradition of voluntary migration."[49] *Yimin* which today translates to 'migrant' and literally means 'moving people' comes from two phrases, 'moving' (*Yi*) and 'people' (*Min*), which imply an official decision to have people moved – either to strengthen defences on the border or to respond to changing economic demands. Chinese regarded their emigration as a temporary sojourn (*Qiao*),[50] or as the beginning of the idea of 'overseas Chinese' (*Huaqiao*), and would generally leave his wife and children at home to reaffirm his links with the village.[51] Chinese people believe that people residing elsewhere will finally return to their ancestral home (*Yeluo Guigen*).[52] If they did not, officials and even members of the family would treat them as vagabonds, outlaws, or a threat to social order. The term 'overseas Chinese' become politically loaded in order to encourage the Chinese so described to be loyal and patriotic to China.[53]

4.3.3 *The duty orientated culture*

Western culture has nurtured the concept of inherent and sacred individual rights. The Confucian code of ethics, which places emphasis on duty, does not mean that there is no the conception of right in China. However, the concept of a 'right' in China is different to the Western notion. The Chinese term that corresponds to the

---

[49] Wang, Gungwu, *Don't Leave Home: Migration and The Chinese*, Times Academic Press, Singapore, 2001, pages 8–9.

[50] Dictionary Department, Institute of Linguistics, Chinese Academy of Social Sciences, *The Contemporary Chinese Dictionary* (*Chinese-English edition*) (Beijing: Foreign Language Teaching and Research Press, 2002), 1549.

[51] Buggy, T. P., *Chinese Immigration and the Emergence of an Australian Image of China 1848–1861*, the thesis of M.A., Sydney: Macquarie University, 1978, pages 19–20.

[52] Dictionary Department, Institute of Linguistics, Chinese Academy of Social Sciences, *The Contemporary Chinese Dictionary* (*Chinese-English edition*) (Beijing: Foreign Language Teaching and Research Press, 2002), 2239.

[53] Wang, Gungwu, *Don't Leave Home: Migration and The Chinese* (Singapore: Times Academic Press, 2001), pages 38 and 144.

concept of a right is *quanli*. The Chinese character '*quan*' seems to have the meaning 'just', when it is used as a standard for the measurement of affairs and things. The traditional use of the term *quanli* relates to authority, power and profit, rather than the modern sense of 'rights'.[54] The modern term *quanli*, by which the modern concept of rights is expressed,[55] seems to be relatively recent creation.

Rights and obligations in Confucianism are reciprocally preconditioned, yet arise from a different relation to both culture and the natural world. Confucian culture focused on obligation (*Quanli Yiwuhua*). Confucianism gives rise to the assumption that man is born with the virtue (*Renzhichu*, *Xingbenshan*). Virtue obliges one to respect fellow members of the human race and all other living things in the natural world. Rights are relative and conditioned by circumstances. The Confucian concept of rights and obligations can only be seen by examining how, when, where and with what presupposed conditions they function in relation to social relationships as a whole. Dr. Sun Longji, an Amreican professor in history has a quite brilliant exposition regarding the relationship between the parents and the kids in Western culture. He found that the Western people focused on the independence of the kids, the relationship between the parents and the kids is a equal friend reltionship. Granting special consideration to one's parents is from one's love rather than one's obligations.[56] Instead the Confucian focused on the duty of the son to grant his father special consideration. Article 21 (1) of Marriage Law 2001 (PRC) expressly regulates that children shall have the duty to support and assist their parents.

The emphasis of Chinese tradition was duty. Kim Hyung discussed this in *Fundamental Legal Concepts of China and the West: A Comparative Study*, concluding that:

> While the Western tradition in the modern period emphasised the sphere of "rights' possessed by a person, traditional Chinese thought transposed the sphere of "rights' to the sphere of "duty", that is, the right act for one to do in virtue of the right of the other person. This is the reason why the Chinese tradition appears to be without a definite concept of rights and only with an emphasis on duty. The relationship between "right" and "duty" is so intimately related in Chinese tradition that one may often be puzzled and left without a clear concept of right in the area of the rights of persons.[57]

---

[54] Dictionary Department, Institute of Linguistics, Chinese Academy of Social Sciences, *The Contemporary Chinese Dictionary* (*Chinese-English edition*) (Beijing: Foreign Language Teaching and Research Press, 2002), 1595.

[55] Dictionary Department, Institute of Linguistics, Chinese Academy of Social Sciences, *The Contemporary Chinese Dictionary* (*Chinese-English edition*) (Beijing: Foreign Language Teaching and Research Press, 2002), 1596.

[56] Sun, Longji, *The Deep Structure of Chinese Culture* (Guiling, China: The Publishing House of Guangxi Normal University), 2004

[57] Kim, Hyung I, *Fundamental Legal Concepts of China and the West: A Comparative Study*, (Port Washington, the USA: Kennikat Press Corp. 1981), 121.

The idea that rights and obligations are reciprocally preconditioned still dominates philosophical thinking in contemporary China. According to the *Contemporary Chinese Dictionary (Chinese-English Edition), quanli* is defined as a "right to be performed by a citizen or juristic person and the interests he enjoys, opposed to 'obligation'".[58] At the 58th Session of the UN Commission of Human Rights, Wang Guangya, then Vice Foreign Minister, stated that China was not in favour of the Western approach to human rights or its processes in realising human rights. He said, "While protecting individual rights, we also advocate fulfilment of social responsibilities."[59] Under such circumstance, individuals seldom question the reasonableness of the exhortation not to leave home and do not have the incentive to struggle for RLR.

4.3.4 *Sublating* (Yangqi)

It is widely accepted that there are big differences between existing Chinese law governing exit and entry, the migration laws of the Western countries, and international norms, which are duly discussed in this book. The attitude of Chinese culture toward the migration laws of the Western countries and international norms helps to understand the motivation for, and pattern of Chinese legislative reform in this area.

The philosophy of sublating (*Yangqi*) dominates any investigation of foreign culture in contemporary China. According to the authoritative Chinese dictionary, 'sublating' means to, "(in metabolism *(Xinchen Daixie)*) develop what is positive and discard what is negative."[60] Western scholars refer to 'sublating' as 'critical inheritance'.[61] 'Sublating' or 'critical inheritance' stresses the doctrine of using the foreign to serve China (*Yangwei Zhongyong*).

In modern society, the nature of migration has undergone profound changes.[62] The migration laws have been changed accordingly. For instance, there has been

---

[58] Dictionary Department, Institute of Linguistics, Chinese Academy of Social Sciences, *The Contemporary Chinese Dictionary* (*Chinese-English Edition*) (Beijing: Foreign Language Teaching and Research Press, 2002), 1596.

[59] Wang, Guangya, "Statement by H. E. Vice Foreign Minister WANG Guangya at the 58th Session of the United Nations Commission on Human Rights, Geneva, 2 April 2002, United Nations High Commissioner For Human Rights", http://www.china-un.ch/eng/gjhyfy/hy2002/t85149.htm (accessed 16/09/2006)

[60] Dictionary Department, Institute of Linguistics, Chinese Academy of Social Sciences, *The Contemporary Chinese Dictionary* (*Chinese-English Edition*) (Beijing: Foreign Language Teaching and Research Press, 2002), 2218.

[61] Chang, King-yuh, "Confucianism in the Republic of China and its Role in Mainland China's Reform", at Krieger, Silke and Trauzettel, Rolf editor, *Confucianism and the Modernization of China* (Mainz, Eschwege, Germany: V. Hase & Koehler Verlag) 1991, 237.

[62] OECD *the Future of Migration* The secretary-general of the OECD 1986, pages 28, 33 and 34.

a recent shift in emphasis from migrants with rare skills to those who are trained and educated in interchangeable skills. Although the existing legislation has been reformed to take the requirements of a modern legal system into account, it is apparent that political and administrative factors still shape the interpretation and application of existing entry and exit legislation. Without doubt, it is necessary to accept a new Western doctrine to replace the inadequate Confucian teachings and Marxist legal theory, in order to meet the need of migration law reform.

Guided by the doctrine of sublating, China selects from foreign migration laws and international norms for its own purposes. Local Chinese legal cultures, which concentrate on instrumentalism, determine the selection and influences of international norms. Chinese governments generally selects laws that facilitate the control over exit and entry, rather than protect RLR. Accordingly, although China has ratified some international conventions concerning RLR such as the UDHR, ICESCR, CERD, CEDAW, CSR, and CRC, and acceded to the ICCPR, these conventions and foreign migration laws have had little effect on the basic normative premise underlying China's migration law system. Existing entry and exit law remains an instrument of the CPC-led model of governance, the typical example is the denial of Western skilled migration in 1995, which will be discussed in part 10.2.2 of this book.

A changing tide in social attitudes has not fundamentally negated the cultural norms engrained in China from centuries of Confucianism. In spite of increased public awareness of RLR, the cultural bias has manifested a general lack of real understanding of the right in everyday life.

4.3.5 *Agrarian civilisation and geographical isolation*

To exhort agricultural workers not to leave home was probably common to all agricultural civilisations, as mentioned in part 2.2.3 of this book, because of the labour loss caused to the family and the community in rural societies. It is also not generally necessary to make contact outside in a self-sufficient society.

The discouragement from leaving home in Chinese agricultural society permeates much more deeply than in the West, because China has four millennia of agrarian history,[63] much longer than the history of Western agriculture societies. The agricultural population and output in China still accounts for a large proportion of overall population and national economy. According to the data released by the State Bureau of Statistics, China (SBS) in 2002, there were 782 million rural residents, accounting for 60.9% of the overall population, agriculture contributed US$180 billion to the economy and accounted for in 14.5% of

[63] The first dynasty, Xia Dynasty started in 2070 B.C. See Dictionary Department, Institute of Linguistics, Chinese Academy of Social Sciences, *The Contemporary Chinese Dictionary* (*Chinese-English edition*) (Beijing: Foreign Language Teaching and Research Press, 2002), 2069.

GDP.[64] China is at the stage of industrialisation rather than post-industrialisation.[65] In this context, the recognition and improvement of RLR cannot be high on the Chinese government's agenda.

China's geography has favoured the development of a civilisation with little or no foreign contacts. The term 'China' (*Zhongguo*), which derives from two phrases, 'centre' (*Zhong*) and 'Kingdom' (*Guo*), means the central kingdom in the world. The traditional view was that China was the centre of the world, the sole upholder of true civilisation, and the lawgiver to the barbarians. This worldview facilitated the notion that China neither needed foreign allies, nor that any neighbour was worthy of being an ally. This view has been adjusted to take account of the modern world, but China retains its central importance in relation to other countries.[66] In light of all these cultural and demographic factors, it has been difficult to raise awareness of leaving China and settling abroad.

4.4 Law

Compared to political, economic and cultural factors, law has the most direct impact on RLR in China. In this section, the impact of law on RLR will be considered by considering (i) the absence of a constitutional foundation to protect RLR; (ii) the nature of law governing exit and entry as the 'ruling tool' to control exit and entry; and (iii) the aim of law governing exit and entry: to control exit and entry (iv) the conflicts of laws regarding exit and entry; and (v) legal research of RLR in China.[67]

4.4.1 *Absence of a constitutional foundation to protect RLR*

A Constitution is a good starting point for studying the extent to which international human rights standards have been implemented by a State, because it represent a negotiated consensus of at least some dominant groups in a society

---

[64] State Bureau of the Statistics, "Statistics Gazette of the People's Republic of China on 2002 National Economy and Social Development" (*Zhonghua Renmin Gongheguo 2002 Guomin Jingji he Shehui Tongji Gongbao*), 28 February 2003, http://www.rctj.gov.cn/2003rctjnj/wzl.htm (accessed 16/09/2006).

[65] "Analysis: Will China's Growth Sustain 30 More Years?" http://english.people.com.cn/200411/08/eng20041108_163104.html (accessed 16/09/2006).

[66] Fitzgerald, C. P., *The Chinese View of their Place in the World* (Amen House, London, E.C.4: Oxford University Press, 1964), pages 2 and 52.

[67] Lack of advanced legislative technique and lax law enforcement are two important issues in Chinese migration law. However they are also common issues in other Chinese branch law. The studies on these will not the centre of RLR study. Giving the length, this book excludes these two topics.

on basic political questions. There are no regulations relevant to RLR in the *Constitution of the PRC* 1982 and its four amendments.

Although Article 33 Clause 4 of the *Constitution of the PRC (Amendment)* 2004 stipulates "the State respects and safeguards human rights", it is doubtful that the reference to "human rights" includes RLR. The Chinese government's understanding of human rights will be discussed in part 12.1.1 of this book, is generally different from understandings in the West. In Western society, RLR is part of an individual's political rights. By contrast, the Chinese government has appealed to the international community to put more emphasis on economic, social and cultural rights and the right to development.[68]

If the Chinese government is inclined to recognise RLR as an indispensable aspect of human rights, Article 33 (4) of the Constitution then raises the issue of how to interpret "respect and safeguard." In Western societies, restrictions on RLR must be provided by law, must be necessary for the protection of a democratic society, and must be consistent with all other rights recognised in the ICCPR, which was discussed in part 3.3 of this book. The Chinese government has stressed the indivisibility of rights and duties and the special characteristics of measures used to protect Chinese society.[69] In March 2000, Tang Jiaxuan, the then Foreign Minister said, that "the international community should respect the measures countries take to promote and protect human rights according to their particular situation and reality".[70] The lack of constitutional recognition and protection of RLR clearly hinders the reform of the Chinese regulatory regime governing RLR.

4.4.2 *The nature of law governing exit and entry as the 'ruling tool'* (Tongzhi Gongju) *to control exit and entry*

The Chinese communist regime rejected the legal codes along Western lines drawn up after the fall of imperial rule and, after a brief hesitation, repudiated the Soviet communist model. The Chinese communist model has afforded a very narrow place for the law.[71] From the official and popular Chinese perspective, law or juristic method is:

---

[68] Sha, Zukang, Chinese Ambassador of the United Nations, "China Calls for Cooperation in Human Rights Field" (03/04/2003), http://www.english.people.com.cn/200203/20/eng20020320_92419.shtml (accessed 16/09/2006).

[69] Under Article 33 Clause 3 of *Constitution of the PRC* (*Amendment*) *2004*, "every citizen is entitled to the rights, and at the same time must perform the duties, prescribed by the Constitution and the law."

[70] "Chinese FM Meets Russian Human Rights Representative (16/03/2000)", http://english.people.com.cn/english/200003/16/eng20000316N108.html (accessed 16/09/2006).

[71] David, Rene and Brierley, John E. C., *Major Legal System in the World Today: An Introduction to the Comparative Study of Law*, 3rd edition (London: Stevens & Sons, 1985), 30.

> [A] code of conduct formulated by a legislative body, whose enforcement is guaranteed by State power, which embodies the will of the ruling class, and serves as one of the ruling tools.[72]

Laws are intended to be instruments of policy enforcement to achieve the immediate policy objectives of the regime. According to Pittman B. Potter:

> [Chinese] law is not a limit on State power; rather, its is a mechanism by which State power is exercised, as the legal forms and institutions that comprise the Chinese legal system are established and operate to protect the CPC and State's political power.[73]

Chinese constitutional and legal arrangements must conform to China's special circumstances, which in turn sets the conditions for policy enforcement and the justification for China's departure from international or Western legal norms.[74]

Based on above analysis, the existing exit and entry laws serve as the principle instrument of the CPC and the government to control exit and entry in China (*Xianxing Churujing Guanli Fa Shi Dang He Zhengfu Guanli Churujing De Gongju*). The discretionary powers of the exit and entry administration are hence overly broad, which will be discussed in part 11.2.1 of this book. Yet more seriously, the enforcement and reforms of existing laws are confined to the discourse of 'politico-legal work', in which the CPC leadership continues as a dominant player. Chen Yaotao underlined the notion that "public security organisations shall control exit and entry of aliens in accordance with the way and policy of the CPC".[75] Without CPC consent, some applications for exiting China are not granted, which will be discussed in part 7.1.2 of this book. In analysing the relationship between research of the exit and entry administration and the CPC, Wang Guoliang has observed that "research of the exit and entry administration [. . .] provides [. . .] constructive suggestions [for] reform of [the] administration of exit and entry with the CPC and the State".[76]

---

[72] Dictionary Department, Institute of Linguistics, Chinese Academy of Social Sciences, *The Contemporary Chinese Dictionary* (*Chinese-English Edition*) (Beijing: Foreign Language Teaching and Research Press, 2002), 527.

[73] Potter, Pitman B., *The Chinese Legal System: Globalisation and Local Legal Culture* (London and New York: Routledge, 2001), 10.

[74] Zhang, Youyu, "A Constitution that Reflects the Special Characteristics of China in the Present Stage" (*Yibu Juyou Xianjieduan Zhongguo Tese De Xianfa*), in *Chinese Jurisprudence* (*Zhongguo Faxue*), 1988, No. 2, pages 36–40, Quoted in Potter, Pitman B., *The Chinese Legal System: Globalisation and Local Legal Culture* (London and New York: Routledge, 2001), 10.

[75] Chen, Yuetao, *The Writing on the Documents of the Exit and Entry Administration of Public Security Organs* (*Gongan Churujing Guanli Wenshu Xiezuo*), *Series of the Applicable Writing of Public Security Organs* (*Gongan Yingyong Xiezuo Congshu*), Interior Published within Public Security Organs (*Gongan Jiguan Neibu Faxing*) (Beijing: the Publishing House of China University of People's Public Security, 1999), 7.

[76] Wang, Guoliang and Zhu, Lin, *The Administration on Exit and Entry, one of Planning*

4.4.3 *The aim of law governing exit and entry: to control exit and entry*

The emphasis of laws regarding exit and entry administration is control, rather than the protection of RLR. The legal theory, together with the traditional culture, make the theme of the development of RLR in China, discussed in chapter five, inclined towards easing restrictions on RLR rather than to protect those rights.

The *Law on the Control of Exit and Entry of Citizens* 1985 (PRC) is the most important of laws germane to RLR in China. Article 1 of the Law provides that "this law is formulated with a view to safeguarding the legitimate rights and interests of Chinese citizens with respect to their exit from and entry into China's territory. . . ." There are distinctions between RLR and 'legitimate' rights and interests. Article 1 permits the government to interpret the scope of RLR in the context of "legitimate". The opinion of Mao Fengping is representative; he has proposed that 'legitimate rights and interests' implies that Chinese citizens have the right to apply to exit China, provided that there is a good reason for doing so and that there are no circumstances prohibiting their exit.[77] Thus, the purpose of this law is not to recognise and protect RLR – at most, the *Law on the Control of Exit and Entry of Citizens* 1985 (PRC) could be construed as affording partial recognition and protection of RLR.

The aims of other three most important laws regarding exit and entry, the *Law on the Control of Exit and Entry of Aliens* 1985 (PRC), the *Provisional Measures on the Control over Chinese Citizens Travelling for Private Affairs to or from the Regions of Hong Kong or Macao* 1986 (PRC), and the *Measures on the Control over Chinese Citizens Travelling to or from the Region of Taiwan* 1992 (PRC) have neglected RLR.[78] Eight Articles of the *Law on the Control exit and entry of*

Textbooks of Higher Education of People's Police (*Renmin Jingcha Gaodeng Jiaoyu Guihua Jiaocha: Churujing Guanlixue*), Interior Published within Public Security Organs (*Gongan Jiguan Neibu Faxing*) (Beijing: the Publishing House of China University of People's Public Security, 2002), 10.

[77] Mao, Fengping, editor, *The Explanation of the Law and Regulations Governing exit and entry and the Collections of Related Regulations* (*Chujing Rujing Falv Fagui Sijie Yu Xiangying Fagui Zhaibian*) (Changchun, China: the Publishing House of Jilin Renmin, 1994), pages 76–77.

[78] Article 1 of the *Law on the Control of Exit and Entry of Aliens* 1985 (PRC) provides "the present law is enacted for the purpose of safeguarding the sovereignty and maintaining the security and public order of the PRC and facilitating international exchanges." Article 1 of the *Measures on the Control over Chinese Citizens Travelling for Private Affairs to or from the Regions of Taiwan* 1992 (PRC) regulates "the present measures is enacted for the purposes of safeguarding the communication of the people in the two sides of the Taiwan Straits and facilitating various sides exchanges and maintaining the social order." There are not the provisions of legislative aim in the *Interim Measures on the Control over Chinese Citizens Travelling for Private Affairs to or from the Regions of Hong Kong or Macao* 1986 (PRC).

citizens 1985 (PRC), which accounts for 40% of all Articles of the statute and 61.5% of its substantive content, effectively limit RLR, by using terms such as 'apply to', 'approve' 'certificate' or 'complete the relevant procedures'. Fourteen Articles of the *Detailed Rules of the Implementation of the Law on the Control of Exit and Entry of Citizens (Amendment)* 1994 (PRC), which accounts for 57% of all Articles, and 63.6% of substantive content, limit RLR as well. Limiting RLR is the most simple and direct means to control the exit form and entry into China.

4.4.4 *The conflict of laws regarding exit and entry*

4.4.4.1 The Chinese exit and entry legislative system

It is necessary to explain the legislative system before discussing the conflict of exit and entry laws. As a first principle of difference, the sources of RLR are multiple in China, which is inconsistent with Western norms that there is usually only one source of RLR and administrative discretion. For example, in Australia, s 4(2) *Migration Act* 1958 (Commonwealth) "provides for visas permitting non-citizens to enter or remain in Australia and the Parliament intends that this Act be the only source of the right of non-citizens to so enter or remain."

The supreme legislative authority in China is the National People's Congress (NPC). Article 7 and 8 of the *Law of Legislation* 2000 (PRC), the NPC enacts legislation, called '*Fa Lv*' (law), in much the same manner as other legislatures in modern bureaucratic States. RLR is referred to by ordinary statute. These include the *Law on the Control of Exit and Entry of Citizens* 1985 (PRC) and the *Law on the Control of Exit and Entry of Aliens* 1985 (PRC) which are *Fa Lv*, promulgated by the Standing Committee of the NPC.

The highest executive authority in China is the State Council. The State Council has the power to make rules, which are also regarded as a form of legislation. They are called '*Xingzheng Fagu*'" (administrative provisions) as opposed to the *Fa Lv* of the People's Congress.[79] The Bureau of Legislative Affairs drafts some *Fa Gui*. Other *Fa Gui* are drafted by the individual ministries that are under the State Council's jurisdiction, and then submitted to the Council for enactment. The *Provisional Measures on the Control over Chinese Citizens Travelling for Private Affairs to or from the Regions of Hong Kong or Macao* 1986 (PRC), and the *Measures on the Control over Chinese Citizens Travelling to or from the Region of Taiwan* 1992 (PRC) are *Xingzheng Fagui*.

Individual ministries have the power to issue various orders, directives, notifications, circulars, measures, detailed implementation rules and subsidiary rules, which are called '*Xingzheng Guizhang*' (administrative rules or regulations). The matters governed by rules are related to the enforcement of laws or the

[79] Article 56 of the *Law of Legislation* 2000 (PRC).

administrative regulations, decisions or orders of the State Council.[80] RLR is mainly realised and improved through ministerial-level implementing of provisions, discussed in part 11.1 of this book, such as the *Detailed Rules for the Implementation of Law on the Control of Exit and Entry of Citizens (Amendment) 1994 (PRC)*, the *Detailed Rules for the Implementation of Law on the Control of Exit and Entry of Aliens (Amendment) 1994 (PRC)* and the *Measures for the Implementation on Preventing Defaulting Taxpayer from Exiting Abroad* 1997 (PRC).

The People's Congresses, their standing committees and the governments of provinces, autonomous regions and municipalities directly under the Central Government may, according to the specific situations and needs of their administrative regions, enact '*Difang Fagui*' (local regulations) which do not contravene the Constitution, laws and administrative regulations,[81] for example *Implementation Opinion of Shanghai Municipality on Provisional Regulations of the Establishment and Administration of Sino-Foreign Equity or Cooperative Joint Venture Employment Agency* 2002 (Shanghai).

The above mentioned two *Fa Lv* should take precedence over hundreds of *Xingzheng Guizhang*; but in practice, *Xingzheng Guizhang* and *Difang Fagui* form the basis of assessing entry and exit applications and may take precedence over *Fa Lv* and *Fa Gui*. The policy contained in *Fa Lv* and *Fa Gui* only operates superficially and is therefore doomed to failure, because it can be overridden and made obsolete by implementing *Guizhang*.

Moreover, frequent updating is a distinctive feature of migration laws, while the two *Fa Lv* have not been amended since their enactment in 1984. Conflict within China's exit and entry laws is a major problem bewildering the exit and entry law community, and which creates an opportunity for government officials to become corrupt, or degenerate or abuse power for personal gain.

4.4.4.2 The conflict of laws regarding exit and entry

The conflicts of laws regarding exit and entry are serious and obvious. One example of a conflict between exit and entry laws and other Chinese laws is in the laws regarding the limits on emigration intermediary agencies. Article 14 (2) of the *Law on Administrative License* 2003 (PRC) provides that:

> When necessary the State Council may establish administrative license by issuing decisions. After implementation of administrative license (excluding temporary administrative license items), the State Council shall timely ask the National People's Congress and its standing committee to enact relevant laws or formulate administrative laws and regulations by itself.

---

[80] Article 71 of the *Law of Legislation* 2000 (PRC).

[81] Article 63 (1) and 73 (1) of the *Law of Legislation* 2000 (PRC).

Article 15 (2) the *Law on Administrative License* 2003 (PRC) further provides that:

> Local regulations and provincial governments' regulations shall create the administrative license of the qualification of citizens, legal persons or other organisations that should be determined by the State, or administrative license or proposed administrative license of the registration of establishment of the enterprises or other organisations. The administrative license established thereby shall neither prevent the individuals or enterprises of other areas from carrying out production and operation and providing services in the local area nor prevent the commodities of other areas from entering local market.

Under the above provisions of the *Law on Administrative License* 2003 (PRC), the legal validity of the legislations governing administrative license for the establishment of emigration intermediary agencies which were promulgated by ministerial or local government regulations, will be analysed in details in Chapter 10 of this book, is doubtful. Nonetheless, administrative license for the establishment of emigration intermediary agencies still remain.

The other example relates to laws placing limits on the exit of individuals from China on the grounds of public order. Under *Regulations on Conscription* 2002 (Beijing), which was promulgated by the Standing Committee of the Beijing Municipal People's Congress, individuals who avoid compulsory military service shall be prohibited from exiting China for two years. Surely, the question of avoidance of military service would be a national nor a local matter. According to Article 19 of the *Law on the Control of Exit and Entry of Citizens* 1985 (PRC) and Article 27 of the *Detailed Rules of the Implementation Law on the Control of Exit and Entry of Citizens (Amendment)* 1994 (PRC), local congress is not empowered to promulgate interpretative law prohibiting the right to leave. The legal validity of the *Regulations on Conscription* 2002 (Beijing) is therefore questionable, although it plays a conspicuous role in protecting public order, and would be regarded as permissible by international standards.

The conflicts of laws regarding merits review of exit and entry administrative decisions and external remedies of violating RLR are considerable. The legislation referred to in Appendix 2 of this book post dates the provisions in appendices 11 and 12, and by contrast is more sophisticated because certain elements are derived from Western States. The external remedies listed in Appendix 2 hence complement internal remedies listed in appendices 11 and 12. Article 13 and 14 of the *Law on the Control of Exit and Entry of Citizens* 1985 (PRC), for example, provides that the passport and travel certificate could be cancelled by the original issuing authority or their authorised agencies, or declared invalid, and any person who violates that law may be given a disciplinary warning, however, under Article 15 of the same law the affected person cannot appeal against the cancellation, invalidation or disciplinary warning in either an administrative or judicial forum. Instead, Article 6 Clause 1 (1) of the *Law on Administrative Review* 1999 (PRC) and Article 6 of the *Law of Administrative Penalty* 1996 (PRC) entitles penalised persons to appeal in either an administrative or judicial forum.

Although the legislation referred to in Appendix 2 partially resolves issues, which will be discussed in parts 11.3.1 to 11.3.3 below, as regards merits review of administrative decisions and external remedies, there is a measure of inconsistency between the two forms of relief for violations of RLR. The inconsistency is serious enough to affect the remedies for RLR. The provisions regarding the restriction of personal freedom and an order of deportation are two typical examples.

Article 9(2) of the *Law of Administrative Review* 1999 (PRC) provides "administrative penalties involving the restriction of personal freedom shall only be created by law," however there are many exit and entry administrative provisions restricting personal freedom, such as Articles 48 and 49 of the *Detailed Rules for the Implementation of the Law on the Control of Entry and Exit of Aliens (Amendment)* 1994 (PRC), Articles 24 and 25 of the *Detailed Rules for the Implementation of the Law on the Control of Entry and Exit of Chinese Citizens (Amendment)* 1994 (PRC), Article 26 to 28 of the *Interim Measures on the Control over Chinese Citizens Travelling for Private Affairs to or from the Regions of Hong Kong or Macao* 1986 (PRC), and Article 35 of the *Measures on the Control over Chinese Citizens Travelling to or from the Region of Taiwan* 1992 (PRC). These have been enacted by the MPS, or jointly promulgated by the MPS and MFA, or the MPS, MFA and Ministry of Communication.

According to Article 42 of the *Law of Administrative Review* 1999 (PRC), this law prevails over any other earlier inconsistent legislation. As a result, the law referred to in the preceding paragraph should be invalid. Despite this, individual departments sometimes apply the earlier inconsistent law. According to *The People's Daily*, Chinese police detained a Japanese national, who allegedly assisted two North Koreans and Chinese national to leave China illegally, under Article 49 of the *Detailed Rules for the Implementation of the Law on the Control of Entry and Exit of Aliens (Amendment)* 1994 (PRC).[82] The practice of giving priority to earlier inconsistent legislation was also officially reaffirmed in 2002.[83] This apparent disregard for valid and current law can affect the extent to which RLR is realised in China.

4.4.4.3 Resolving conflicts of exit and entry laws

The issues mentioned above can be partially attributed to the inefficient resolution of conflicts between exit and entry laws. Article 5(2) and (3) of the *Constitution*

---

[82] "Japanese Detained for Helping Koreans to Flee", 14 January 2004, *People's Daily Online*, http://english.peopledaily.com.cn/200401/14/eng20040114_132570.shtml (accessed 15/01/2004).

[83] Wang, Guoliang and Zhu, Lin, *The Administration on Exit and Entry, one of Planning Textbooks of Higher education of People's Police* (*Renmin Jingcha Gaodeng Jiaoyu Guihua Jiaocha: Churujing Guanlixue*), Interior Published within Public Security Organs (*Gongan Jiguan Neibu Faxing*) (Beijing: the Publishing House of China University of People's Public Security, 2002), 299.

of the PRC (Amendment) 2004 provides that, "the State upholds the uniformity and dignity of the socialist legal system. No laws, administrative or local rules, or regulations may contravene the Constitution". This provision is too obscure to be practically enforced because there is a lack of attached detailed legislation.

This situation was improved by the *Law of Administrative Review* 1999 (PRC), of which Article 7 provides:

> If citizens, legal persons or other organisations consider the following provisions (which the administrative departments take as the basis for their specific administrative acts) to be illegal, they may apply for examination of these provisions when applying for administrative review:
>
> (1) provisions formulated by departments under the State Council;
> (2) provisions formulated by local people's governments at or above the county level and the department under them; and
> (3) provisions formulated by a township or town people's governments.
>
> The provisions listed in the preceding paragraph do not include rules and regulations formulated by the ministries and commissions under the State Council, and by local people's governments. The examination of rules and regulations shall be carried out in accordance with laws and administrative regulations.

On the one hand, it is questionable as to whether these provisions could ensure the independence of the examination, because administrative review is conducted by legal departments within the relevant departments, as will be discussed in part 11.3.3 below. On the other hand, the right to apply for administrative review of subordinate legislation is greatly limited. Rules and regulations formulated by the ministries and commissions under the State Council, and by local governments – which are the most commonly used provisions in China – are excluded from the *Law of Administrative review* 1999 (PRC). Approximately 90% of the provisions quoted in this book fit into those categories. Consequently, these provisions and policies promulgated by the CPC and other ministerial level authorities cannot be reconsidered.

Responding to a number of issues raised by legislative conflicts, the *Law of Legislation* 2000 (PRC), the *Regulations on the Procedure for Formulation of Rules* 2001 (PRC), the *Regulations on the Record-keeping for Regulations and Rules* 2001 (PRC), the *Measures of Beijing Municipal People's Government on Formulation of Rules and Regulations* 2002 (Beijing), and the *Measures of Taiyuan Municipal People's Government on Legislation* 2002 (Taiyuan), were enacted to clarify the national legislative system. Articles 78 to 84 of the *Law of Legislation* 2000 (PRC) provide the principal means to reconcile conflicts between inconsistent laws. Despite of all theses resolutions, conflicting laws in China are still a major problem, because there is neither an independent responsible authority nor due process to make the necessary changes.

According to Articles 85 to 89 of the *Law of Legislation* 2000 (PRC), the responsible authorities include the NPC, the Standing Committee of the NPC, the State Council, the people's congress of provinces, autonomous regions and municipalities directly under the Central Government, the standing committees of the local people's congresses, the people's governments of provinces and autonomous regions, the enacting authority, and the delegating authority. The subject and procedure of submitting a written suggestion to review the laws are regulated in Articles 90 and 91 of the *Law of Legislation* 2000 (PRC).[84]

Besides the issues discussed earlier, the *Law of Administrative Review* 1999 (PRC) does not fully entitle persons affected by an administrative decision to seek judicial review of the subordinate legislation upon which the determination was based. The recent enactment of new exit and entry laws, which fail to include remedies for violations of RLR, provide more scope for individuals' RLR to be violated by administrative authorities. As a consequence, disputed regulations that adversely affect RLR, continue to be unlawfully applied. Conflicting laws continue to be an obstacle for Courts when they apply laws in specific cases.

The scope of the right to appeal against the contravention of laws is greatly narrowed. According to Article 90 of the *Law of Legislation* 2000 (PRC), Article 35 of the *Regulations on the Procedure for Formulation of Rules* 2001 (PRC), Article 9 of the *Regulations on the Record-keeping for Regulations and Rules* 2001 (PRC), and Article 39 of the *Measures of Beijing Municipal People's Government on Formulation of Rules and Regulations* 2002 (Beijing), government bodies or social organisations, enterprises, institutions and citizens is entitled to 'make a

[84] Article 90 of the *Law of Legislation* 2000 (PRC) provides "The State Council, the Central Military Commission, the Supreme Peoples' Court, the Supreme Peoples' Procuratorate and the standing committees of peoples' congresses of provinces, autonomous regions and municipalities directly under the Central Government which are of the opinion that certain administrative regulations, local regulations, autonomous regulations or separate regulations contravene the Constitution or the laws, may make a written suggestion (*Jianyi*) to the Standing Committee of the NPC for review. The working organ of the Standing Committee shall examine the matter and, when necessary, forward the matter to the special committees concerned for examination and comment. Other government bodies or social organizations, enterprises, institutions and citizens not mentioned in the previous paragraph who are of the opinion that certain administrative regulations, local regulations, autonomous regulations or separate regulations contravene the Constitution or the laws may make a written suggestion to the Standing Committee of the NPC for review. The working organ of the Standing Committee shall examine the matter and shall, when necessary, forward the matter to the special committees concerned for examination and comment." Article 91 prescribes that "Where the special committees of the NPC are, after examination, of the opinion that the administrative regulations, local regulations, autonomous regulations or separate regulations contravene the Constitution or the laws, they may give a written opinion to the enacting authority; the Law Committee and the relevant special committees may convene a joint examination and ask the enacting authority to explain the situation at the examination before giving a written opinion of the examination to the enacting authority. The enacting authority shall within two months decide whether to make any amendment and report to the Law Committee and the special committees concerned . . ."

written suggestion' rather than to initiate an 'appeal' and 'review'. That means the relevant authorities are not legally bound to process this application, or initiate the examination. Meanwhile, there are no detailed rules to regulate the procedure how to 'make a written suggestion'.

The terms of 'when necessary' of Article 90 of the *Law of Legislation* 2000 (PRC), 'study and handle' of Article 39 of the *Measures of Beijing Municipal People's Government on Formulation of Rules and Regulations* 2002 (Beijing), and 'handle this suggestions after investigation' of Article 35 of the *Regulations on the Record-keeping for Regulations and Rules* 2001 (PRC), further narrow the scope of the right to appeal against the contravention of laws, because the meaning of 'necessary', 'study', 'handle' and 'investigation' are not clear enough. It is thus possible for relevant authorities to abuse their discretion so to deny the suggestions of other government bodies or social organisations, enterprises, institutions and citizens. It will therefore fall to the person in power's discretion to decide when they should or should not be applied.[85] It is perhaps not unsurprising to find that it has not yet been relied upon.

According to international norms, the supervisory mechanism of subordinate legislation plays an irreplaceable role in remedying violations of RLR. The establishment of a supervisory mechanism in China must account for and define the relationship between the subject matter of the law, the administration and the community. How to establish such a mechanism is mainly a topic in legislative science and beyond the scope of this book.

4.4.5 *Legal research on RLR in China*

Almost all the literature on RLR is focused on the West, especially traditional immigration nations. Very little has been written about RLR in China. This subsection is to explore the reasons why the sum and depth of legal research on RLR in China is unusually low.

The Chinese official view, cited in instances below, is that RLR, like many other human rights, is too sensitive to be studied in China. The Chinese government thinks that the theory of human rights overriding sovereignty should be adamantly rejected,[86] China should be allowed to establish its own human rights models, in line with their own circumstances, and the so-called 'Country Report' on human rights issued by the USA, has made groundless accusations against China's human rights situation. The Chinese side expresses its strong indignation and firm

[85] Cheng, Jie Catherine, "Conflict of Laws in China", http://www.enstar.co.uk/china/law/vm_articles/items/item13.htm (accessed 16/09/2006).

[86] "Chinese FM Meets Russian Human Rights Representative (16/03/2000)", www.fmprc.gov.cn/eng/4020.html (accessed 1/07/2003).

opposition.[87] Beijing has stressed that the 'rampant' practice of political confrontation in the name of human rights, is the biggest problem in the area of human rights.[88] Any research undertaking research on RLR from a Western perspective risks raise questions as to the politics and patriotism. Consequently, RLR in China are usually discussed from the perspective of administrative law,[89] international law[90] or the exit and entry administration.[91]

Legal education and research institutions in China shed little light on RLR. It is sometimes not even discussed in works on exit and entry administration. Law schools teach nationality law as part of their international law curriculum and exit and entry administration is offered as an elective course in police higher education institutions, while the limited research on exit and entry administration is mainly focused on practical issues rather than theory.[92] Very few legal education and research institutions in China provided a degree course with a major in migration law, and there is no special body for the study of migration law.[93]

---

[87] "Spokesperson Zhang Qiyue's Remarks on the Country Report on Human Rights Issued by the US (26/02/2004)", http://www.fmprc.gov.cn/eng/xwfw/2510/t69782.htm (accessed 02/03/2004).

[88] Sha, Zukang, Chinese Ambassador of the United Nations, "China Call for Co-operation in Human Rights Field" (03–04–2003), http://english.people.com.cn/200203/20/eng20020320_92419.shtml (accessed 16/09/2006).

[89] Chen, Yuetao, *The Writing on the Documents of the Exit and Entry Administration of Public Security Organs* (*Gongan Churujing Guanli Wenshu Xiezuo*), *Series of the Applicable Writing of Public Security Organs* (*Gongan Yingyong Xiezuo Congshu*), Interior Published within Public Security Organs (*Gongan Jiguan Neibu Faxing*) (Beijing: the Publishing House of China University of People's Public Security, 1999), 9.

[90] Wong, Li, *International Immigration Law and the Practices* (*Guoji Yiminfa Lilun Yu Shijian*) (Beijing: the Publishing House of Law, 2001), 25.

[91] Wang, Guoliang and Zhu, Lin, *The Administration on Exit and Entry, one of Planning Textbooks of Higher Education of People's Police* (*Renmin Jingcha Gaodeng Jiaoyu Guihua Jiaocha: Churujing Guanlixue*), Interior Published within Public Security Organs (*Gongan Jiguan Neibu Faxing*) (Beijing: the Publishing House of China University of People's Public Security, 2002), 93; also see Department of Politics under the Ministry of Public Security, *Frontier Defense and Exit and Entry Administration, the Series of Basic Textbook of People's Police Operation: (Bianfang Yu Churu Jing Guanli, Renmin Jingcha Gongan Yewu Jichu Jiaocai*), examined by Committee of Textbook Editing and Examination of the Ministry of Public Security, Internal Publication within Public Security Organs (*Gongan Jiguan Neibu Faxing*) (Beijing: the Publishing House of Qunzhong, 1999), 276.

[92] Yu, Huaying and Gong, Yu, *The Legal Study on Exit, Entry and International Trade* (*Churu Jing Yu Guoji Jingmao Falv Wenti Yanjiu*), the Publishing House of Xinan Normal University, Chongqing, China 1997, pages 7–8.

[93] Yu, Shutong and Wen, Jia, Chief editors, *A New Chinese-English Law Dictionary* (*Xin Hanying Faxue Cidian*) (Beijing: Publishing House of Law, 1998), pages 1164–1174. The situation was improved recently. Zejiang University offered the course of LLM with the direction of international migration in 2004.

From a commercial perspective, Chinese legal scholars are not very interested in the research of migration law, but pay more attention to business law and other branches of law more closely aligned to daily life and the economy. As China establishes a socialist market-oriented economic system, there is financial support available to academics involved with the drafting and amendment of laws related to this field. The Legal Papers Database of *China Persecution Daily* demonstrates that between 1993 and 2001, only one academic legal paper focused on RLR was published in a national legal journal in Mainland China.[94] Meanwhile, Chinese migration consultants spare little effort to study the existing exit and entry legislation. The foremost business of the emigration intermediary agencies is to assist in visa applications. As such, agencies are inclined to spend their time becoming familiar with foreign immigration laws and ensuring that they maintain a high success rate for visa applications.

In practice, police higher education institutions and public security authorities rather than law schools are mainly responsible for the research into exit and entry legislation. The main collections of papers related to RLR in China are the *Collection of Papers on the Control of Exit and Entry (III)*,[95] the *Collection of Papers on the Control of Exit and Entry (II)*,[96] which were edited in 1999 and 2001, and the *Review of the control of exit and entry: the Collection of Papers on the Control of Exit and Entry of Shanghai Public Security Organisations*, edited by Li Wenyan, the Director of Shanghai Exit and Entry Administration in 1999. Unfortunately, none of the 120 papers forming these collections were footnoted,[97] which means that the quality of the research is compromised because their primary and secondary sources cannot be traced.[98]

---

[94] Legal Papers Database of *Prosecution Daily* (*Jiancha Ribao*), "The Search of Keyword of Immigration", http://review.jcrb.com.cn/ournews/asp/index.htm (accessed 16/09/2006)

[95] Committee of Exit and Entry Administration under Chinese Association of Police, (edit), *The Collection of Papers on the Control of Exit and Entry* (*III*) (*Churujing Guanli Lunwenxuan* (*san*)), Interior Published within Public Security Organs (*Gongan Jiguan Neibu Faxing*) (Beijing: the Publishing House of Qunzhong, 2001).

[96] Committee of Exit and Entry Administration under Chinese Association of Police, (edit), *The Collection of Papers on the Control of Exit and Entry* (*II*), (*Churujing Guanli Lunwenxuan* (*er*)), Interior Published within Public Security Organs (*Gongan Jiguan Neibu Faxing*), the Publishing House of Qunzhong, Beijing China, 1999.

[97] Li, Wenyan, *Review of the Control of Exit and Entry: the Collection of Papers on the Control of Exit and Entry of Shanghai Public Security Organs* (*Churujing Guanli Zongheng: Shanghai Gongan Churujing Guanli Lunwenji*), Internal publication (*Neibu Faxing*) (Beijing: the Publishing House of Police Education, 1998).

[98] "Guide to Essay Writing 2006 Edition", the Faculty of Law of the University of Technology, Sydney, Australia, http://www.law.uts.edu.au/students/assessment/2006 essayguide.pdf (accessed 16/09/2006).

4.5 Conclusions

The factors driving RLR in China exposes what is certainly the complex situation of China. For politics, the system of the multi-party cooperation and political consultation led by the Communist Party of China colours RLR with the protection of vested interests of the CPC, which dominates society in China. The origin of restrictions on exit and entry are easily traced to China's experience as a member of the former communist bloc.

Given the largest population, underdevelopment and considerable regional economic disparities, it is understandable for China to gradually reform exit and entry administration, to avoid the possible instability. A further depth of reform is however inevitable with economic development – past interactions between the development of the economy and laws governing exit and entry also prove this point. Meanwhile, it is hard to break through the restriction on persons employed in State-owned industry, because the public ownership of the means of production is still the basis of the economic system. The adverse impacts on RLR of limits on the right to move within China must also not be underestimated.

An analysis of the culture of Confucianism reveals that there is a long way to go before an awareness of RLR in China is fully fostered. Individuals, under Confucianism, are inclined to integration into the society, innately obliged to respect fellow members of the human race, and pay loyalty to China and filial piety to one's parents. Chinese culture is therefore a culture orientated toward duty, in which RLR is not easily recognised and the exhortation not to leave home is embraced. The philosophy of sublating, namely the subjective selection of foreign cultural aspects, isolates Chinese culture from other rights-oriented cultures. Agrarian society, from which Confucianism was born, is still an important part of the cultural fabric of China, with a proportionately large agrarian population and output.

Compared with politics, economics and culture, legal factors most directly affect RLR in China. If the laws governing exit and entry are accepted as one of the ruling tools of a ruling elite, it is not surprising to find that the law mainly facilitates the *control* of exit from and entry into China, rather than to protect RLR. The bias is to the community and not to the individual. Meanwhile, conflict within China's exit and entry laws is a major problem, bewildering exit and entry law community, and which creates opportunities for government officials to act degenerately or abuse exit and entry discretion for personal gain. The dispute of the constitutional foundation of RLR has produced ambiguity in regard to the protection of RLR.

Resolving conflicts of laws regarding exit and entry is important because it relates to the internal functioning of the administrative arms of government, their interpretation of the rights and obligations and penalties in primary legislation, and perhaps more deeply, the ethical and social foundation of the whole field of law. Neither the Constitution nor relevant laws provide practicable remedies for violations of RLR by legislative acts. The mechanism for resolution of conflicts of laws regarding the administration of exit and entry is far from efficient.

Chapter Five

Historical Development of Chinese Regulatory Framework Governing RLR

INTRODUCTION

With ratification of the ICCPR by 152 countries, international concern on RLR appears to have passed its peak,[1] and yet remains problematic for China. In the *Handbook of Citizenship Studies* on the right to emigrate, for instance, China scored zero out of a possible 100 points.[2] A careful and well-coordinated immigration strategy with a well-defined RLR focus has the potential to enhance China's economic progress and to improve its international human rights image. Such a strategy would demand careful evaluation of China's RLR policies, with the view to making them consistent with international law and practice. There are many issues pertaining to the protection of RLR in China that demand prompt solutions. A critical analysis of the realities and issues of RLR in China in the context of international norms has never been undertaken.

---

1 International Services for Human Rights, "The Ratification Status of the Main Human Rights Treaties", ishr-06–2004, http://ww.ishr.ch/About%20UN/Ratification/Ratification%20–%20Human%20Rights%20treaties.htm (accessed 18/05/2003).

2 Janoski, Thomas and Gran, Brain "Political Citizenship: Foundations of Rights", in Isin, Engin F. and Turner, Bryan S. editor, *Handbook of Citizenship Studies* (London: Sage Publications, 2002), 31–33.

The notions of 'RLR' and 'Chinese migration law' have only a very short history in China; the terms are mainly used by Chinese scholars.[3] There are no recorded attempts to precisely stipulate RLR and draw up a distinct code governing migration matters. Reforms (2001–2005) of the exit and entry administration do not introduce the specific notions of 'RLR' and 'Chinese migration law'. The substance of RLR and Chinese migration law are mainly regulated in statutes governing exit and entry.[4]

To better understand the issues, and appreciate the political, social and legal complexities of RLR in China, it is important to first trace its historical development and make valid observations about current reforms and future trends. The greatest emigration in Chinese history occurred in the Qing dynasty (1611–1911). The ancestry of many current overseas Chinese can be traced to these emigrants. The Qing government's exit and entry policies are therefore a logical starting point for analysis, to be followed by an analysis of the policies of the Republic of China (ROC) on the Mainland (1911–1949). This section will focus primarily on development since 1978, but will briefly consider the period between 1949 and 1958 to provide an essential backdrop against which the reform strategy can be viewed. The reform strategy and measures will be carefully analyzed from the perspectives of the context, goals, content, effects, deficiencies, nature and features to understand the possible future of RLR in China.

5.1 The Qing Dynasty (1616–1910): From Complete Prohibition to Practical Relaxation

The Qing government for most of its reign did not accept that their subjects had RLR. Decrees to forbid overseas trade and emigration were passed in 1712 and 1724.[5] The decrees were primarily meant to prevent any remaining forces of the

[3] Xiang, Dang, the *Guide to the Law of Exit and Entry in China and Foreign Countries* (*Zhongwai Churujing Falv Zhinan*) (Beijing: the Publishing House of China University of People's Public Security, 1998), 1; Wong, Li, *International Immigration Law and the Practices* (*Guoji Yiminfa Lilun Yu Shijian*) (Beijing: the Publishing House of Law, 2001), 28; also see Wang, Leiming, "Citizens May Exit Abroad for Private Purpose Easier and Faster" (*Woguo Gongmin Yinsi Chuguo Gengjia Bianjie*), http://www.news.xinhuanet.com/newscenter/2002–08/29/content_543014.htm (accessed 16/09/2006), quoted in Xinhua News Agency, 18/04/2003; and "Exiting Abroad is Becoming the Individual Needs of Chinese Citizens", (*Chuguo Kaishi Chengwei Zhongguo Gongmin Chuncui Geren De Xuyao*) Xunahuanet, 28 December 2003, http://news.sdinfo.net/72350064130916352/20031228/1233069.shtml (accessed 30/12/2003).

[4] Yu, Huaying and Gong, Yu, the *Legal Study on Exit, Entry and International Trade* (*Churu Jing Yu Guoji Jingmao Falv Wenti Yanjiu*) (Chongqing, China: the Publishing House of Xinan Normal University, 1997), 3–8.

[5] Buggy, T. P., *Chinese Immigration and the Emergence of an Australian Image of China, 1848–1861*, the thesis of M.A., Sydney, Australia: Macquarie University, 1978, 128.

Ming dynasty (1368–1644) from emigrating and establishing a financial and political base overseas that could threaten the stability of the incumbent government. Local officials and citizens, in the interests of trade, frequently disregarded the prohibition, and many Chinese, particularly those from Guangdong and Fujian provinces, established themselves as merchants throughout South Eastern Asia during the 17th and 18th centuries.[6]

After the first Opium War (1840–1842), the prohibition on emigration was partially broken down and coolie emigration began. The *Treaty of Nanking 1842* gave Britain extraterritorial rights in five treaty ports including shanghai and Guangzhou, but gave nothing to China in return. This provided Britain with the infrastructure and opportunity to develop the trade in unskilled labourers, or Coolies.[7] After the second Opium War in 1860, the restrictions on emigration were virtually lifted. The *Peking Convention 1860* and the Burlinghame Treaty with the USA in 1868 included clauses allowing Chinese to live abroad. Some Coolies left China as free migrants and paid their own way. Many more left as indentured or contracted labourers, enlisted directly by governments or labour recruiters. Others left on the "credit-ticket" system where their travel expenses were payed by employer and they were expected to repay the sum after working in the destination States.[8] Additionally, emigration agencies operated by Western States were established in Guangdong, Shantou and other coastal cities, with the approval of the Chinese authorities. Chinese who wished to obtain employment in foreign countries were invited to register at these agencies and sign a labour contract.[9]

The following years saw migration increase. According to UK statistics, before the destruction of the Qing government in 1911, 4.2 million Chinese people had emigrated, the majority of whom went to Southeast Asia.[10] Chinese

---

[6] Purcell, Victor, the *Chinese in South East Asia* (London: Oxford University Press, 1965), 24 and 29.

[7] According to the *Treaty of Nanking*, Chinese citizens had the right to settle in any part of the British Empire and were free to enter into arrangements with British subjects for that purpose, as well as being allowed to board any British vessel in one of the Treaty ports. Chinese people were able to emigrate opportunistically with the arrival of some European powers. However, Chinese people knew almost nothing about the British Empire and the outside world after about 200 years of closed policy. Thus in practice, they were usually sold as commodities.

[8] Sinn, Elizabeth, "Emigration from Hong Kong Before 1941: Organisation and Impact" in Skeldon, Ronald, editor, *Emigration from Hong Kong: Tendencies and Impacts* (Hong Kong: the Chinese University Press, 1995), 37.

[9] Wang, Sing-wu, the *Organisation of Chinese Emigration 1848–1888 with Special Reference to Chinese Emigration to Australia* (San Francisco: Chinese Materials Centre Inc., 1978), 47–58.

[10] The *Collection of the Branch Committee of Royal Asian Arts Committee* (*Huangjia Yazhou Wenhui Beihua Fenhui Jikan*), in Chen, Haoshen editor, *the Collection of Historical Materials on Overseas Labour Exiting Abroad* (*Huagong Chuguo Siliao Hvbian*) (Beijing: the Publishing House of China, 1985), 5.

emigrants established large and fairly stable communities in Spanish America, the Caribbean, the Pacific Islands, South Africa, North America and Australasia. This migration pattern and the establishment of trans-national community ties would greatly affect future migration policies.

With the increase of emigration, protection of Coolies and migrants formed a significant part of late Qing policy towards its overseas subjects. Reports of abuses in the coolie trade in Cuba led to the dispatch of a Commission headed by Chen Lan-ping, who later negotiated an immigration treaty with Spain in 1877, to improve the circumstances of Chinese coolies in Cuba.[11] In trying to come terms with the Coolie issue, the Qing government was compelled to question its traditional policy towards overseas subjects and the issue of emigration in general. It began to establish Chinese embassies and consulates in the places of overseas Chinese residence, to protect it subjects against discrimination.[12]

However, in this the government was constrained by the old prohibitive edicts that considered free emigrants undeserving to be protected because they were not within the government-sponsored program. In the late 19th century, the Qing government began to look upon overseas Chinese as assets to China. There had long been an awareness of the importance of their remittances to the economies of Fujian and Guangdong. In 1893, the Imperial Court finally repealed prohibitive edicts that criminalised those who ventured abroad. In other words, this liberalisation of going abroad was finally legalised.

5.2 The Republic of China (1912 to 1949): Limits and Encouragement

The second significant period is in the 38 years from the foundation of the Republic of China in 1912 and its movement into Taiwan in 1949. This period was marked by continual civil and foreign wars. The substitution of a monarchy with a republic provided many opportunities for the realisation of RLR. The nationalist government enacted a series of laws governing passports, overseas study, overseas employment and administrative structures, as well as adopting measures to promote communication with the outside world. Unfortunately, due to the economic depression in the capitalist world and the disruption caused by continuous wars, these laws were not completely implemented.

The first set of measures to protect RLR in China was the system of exit visas and exit registration. Citizens did not need to apply for an exit visa if they were

---

[11] Buggy, T. P., *Chinese Immigration and the Emergence of an Australian Image of China, 1848–1861*, the thesis of M. A., Sydney, Australia: Macquarie University, 1978, 128–129.

[12] Wichberg, Wdgar, "The Chinese as Overseas Migrants' in Brown, Judith M. & Foot, Rosemary *Migration: the Asian Experience* (London: the Macmillan Press Ltd., 1994), 32.

going abroad for the first time. An exit visa and a valid passport were only required for subsequent overseas travel. After 1935, citizens were banned from exiting without an exit registration certificate (*Chuguo Dengji Zheng*). They could either personally apply for an exit registration certificate or appoint an agent.

The second set of measures was to encourage and welcome the return of overseas Chinese. The Committee of Overseas Chinese Affairs was established to be responsible for the exit and entry administration. Overseas Chinese could apply for an overseas Chinese registration certificate to affirm their overseas Chinese status. This allowed them to apply for a passport and diplomatic protection. The nationalist government also encouraged the founding of overseas Chinese schools and provided financial and curriculum aid, especially during the 1920s and 1930s.[13]

The third set of measures regulated the emigration of the labour force. In order to cover the serious scarcity of human resources caused by World War One, the UK, France, Russia and other Western countries between 1916 and 1918 recruited approximately 230,000 labourers from China. The *Regulations on Chinese Labour Exiting China* 1918 (*Qiaogong Cuyang Tiaoli*), the *Outline of Chinese Labour Contract* 1918 (*Qiaogong Hetong Gangyao*) and the *Regulations on Labour Exiting China* 1935 (*Gongren Chuguo Tiaoli*) were promulgated soon after. Under their provisions, labour needed to apply for exit permission, accompanied by a signed labour contract with one's employers and a guarantee from the Chinese embassy or general consulate at the destination country.

Fourthly, the selection and administration of overseas students were improved. The nationalist government, in its quest for modernisation and appropriate skilled individuals, sent substantial numbers of students to Japan and the West for higher education. Many families in China saw overseas education as a new kind of migration opportunity and family strategy.[14] The government enacted the *Rules of Administration of Overseas Students in the USA* 1914 (*Guanli Liumei Xuesheng Shiwu Guicheng*) and the *Measures on Dispatching Overseas Students at One's Own Expense* 1943 (*Zifei Liuxuesheng Paiqian Banfa*) during this period.

Because of the shortage of foreign exchange after continuous wars, the number of students sent overseas during this period was small.[15] Chinese migration

---

[13] Wichberg, Wdgar, "The Chinese as Overseas Migrants in Brown", in Brown, Judith M. & Foot, Rosemary editor, *Migration: the Asian Experience* (London: the Macmillan Press Ltd., 1994), 32.

[14] Wichberg, Wdgar, "The Chinese as Overseas Migrants in Brown", in Brown, Judith M. & Foot, Rosemary editor, *Migration: the Asian Experience* (London: the Macmillan Press Ltd., 1994), 15.

[15] In the harsh environment of the 1937–1945 War of Resistance against Japan, 1,566 students were sent abroad. These students were mainly enrolled in engineering and science, in order to enable China to develop the skill base for the period of post-war State reconstruction; according to the statistic of Ministry of Education of ROC files, which were

was also limited by the immigration policies of destination countries. America and Canada attempted to limit Chinese immigration by legislation and practice. Sometimes discrimination uniquely targeted the Chinese. In Canada, between 1903 and 1923, only Chinese immigrants were required to pay a $500 tax to be admitted to the country. From 1923 to 1947, Chinese people were the only people prohibited by law from immigrating to Canada.[16]

The nationalist Republican government adopted many active measures to promote communication with the outside world. Restricted by an unstable political climate, poorly developed economy and unwillingness to afford individual human rights, RLR was severely limited in practice. Nonetheless, migration law made great progress and was objectively beneficial to the improvement of RLR in China.

5.3 The People's Republic of China (1949 to 2001): From the Prohibition Policy to Relaxation Policy

5.3.1 *1949 to 1978: the return of the prohibition policy of the Qing Dynasty*

The period from 1949 to 1978 marks the start of the People's Republic of China (PRC), through to the introduction of significant reforms and the 'opening up' of China in 1978. During this period, as discussed and analysed elsewhere in this book, going abroad was subject to strict scrutiny. Even though its population swelled in the same period from 400 million in 1949 to 1 billion in 1978, China only approved about 7,000 annual exits abroad for private affairs in that time.[17]

5.3.1.1 1949 to 1958: the establishment of the restrictive framework governing RLR

In the period from 1949 to 1958 China's door to the outside world was basically closed because the consolidation of the new government was deemed the most important priority of State reconstruction, however RLR was respected, and the

---

stored in the Second History Archive of China. The number of overseas students between 1937 and 1945 did not include 246 persons who were invited to lecture abroad.

[16] Wichberg, Wdgar, "The Chinese as Overseas Migrants in Brown", Judith, M. & Foot, Rosemary editor, *Migration: the Asian Experience* (London: the Macmillan Press Ltd., 1994), 24.

[17] Wang, Leiming, Xinhua News Agency, "Citizens May Exit Abroad for Private Purpose Easier and Faster" (*Woguo Gongmin Yinsi Chuguo Gengjia Bianjie*), (19/09/2002), http://news.xinhuanet.com/newscenter/2002–08/29/content_543014.htm (accessed 16/09/2006).

legal system governing exit and entry was gradually established. Most notably, freedom of movement was recognised in the *Constitution of PRC* 1954. The legalisation of freedom of movement stimulated the exit and entry. According to the Ministry of Public Security (MPS) statistics, 379,505 persons exited or entered China in 1951, approximately 7.7 times that of 1950.[18]

The policy to encourage overseas Chinese to return

Encouraging overseas Chinese to return to China to assist in the State's reconstruction was a foremost legislative purpose during this period. Under Article 2 and 3 of the *Provisional Measures on Exit and Entry National Border of Overseas Chinese* 1951 (PRC);

> Overseas Chinese may exit and enter with a valid passport and visa. Where they do not hold a valid passport and visa, as they are from the countries without a diplomatic relationship with the PRC, [they] must apply for an Overseas Chinese certificate (*Guiguo Huaqiao Zhengmingshu*) to ensure their overseas status when arriving in China. The government will look after them if necessary.

In addition, where a destination country hindered an overseas Chinese person from returning, they could indirectly return to China through Hong Kong or Macao. Simultaneously, unyielding efforts were made to negotiate with the West, especially with the USA, to permit overseas Chinese return to China. The *Treaty on the Issues Regarding to Civilian Returning to China between the PRC and the USA* was reached in 1955.

The control of return from Hong Kong or Macao was more extensive. Article 2 Clause 2 of the *Proclamation of the Ministry of Public Security, the Central People's Government Concerning the Control over Passengers Travelling to and from the Regions of Hong Kong and Macao* 1951 (PRC) provided that "the passengers who leave for the Mainland from Hong Kong or Macao must apply for the exit and entry pass (*Churu Tongxingzheng*) to the Public Security authority [in their] ancestral hometown or destination county or city". Given the physical distance and the underdeveloped state of communications, this process was lengthy and difficult.

The right to leave

Chinese citizens needed to apply for exit permission. Under Article 4 of *Provisional Measures on the Exit and Entry National Border of Overseas Chinese*

---

[18] Department of Exit and Entry under the Ministry of Public Security & Department of Border Security Checking and Administration, *Great Change over the Last 50 years: the Analysis of the Data of Exit and Entry of Individuals* (*Fenyun Bianhuan Wushi Nian: Cong Churujing Renyuan Tongji Shuju Kan Jianguo Yilai De Jubian*), No. 22 (1999) of *People's Public Security* (*Renmin Gongan*).

1951, "overseas Chinese exiting the country must apply for an overseas Chinese exit permit (*Huaqiao Chujing Tongxingzheng*) upon the authority of the document of proof prescribed by township government". Passengers exiting to Hong Kong or Macao, in accordance with Article 2 Clause 1 of the *Proclamation on the Ministry of Public Security, the Central People's Government Concerning the Control over Passengers Travelling to and from the Regions of Hong Kong and Macao* 1951 (PRC), needed to "apply for an exit and entry pass from the Public Security authorities of resident county or city upon the authority of a household certificate or written certificate prescribed by the township government".

More detailed restrictions were adapted to control aliens leaving China. According to Articles 2 and 4 of the *Provisional Measures on Exit of Aliens in China* 1954 (PRC), "aliens exiting the country must lodge an exit application in person to the public security departments of the municipality or county in which their residence is registered". After examining the prescribed document of proof, the provincial public security departments would issue an exit visa (*Chujing Qianzheng*) to aliens whose country had a diplomatic relationship with China, and exit permission (*Chujingzheng*) to aliens whose country had no diplomatic relationship with China. Article 3 of the *Provisional Measures on the Exit of Aliens in China* 1954 (PRC) further sets forth, "where an alien is party of a civil or criminal case, he or she has the duty to pay debt or tax, and will therefore be banned from exiting".

Administrative system

From 1957, the MPS and various public security departments were wholly responsible for the administration of exit and entry. In accordance with the Preface and Article 1 of the *Circular of the State Council on the Unified Responsibility of Ministry of Public Security Regarding the Administration of the Exit and Entry for Private Affairs of Citizens* 1956 (PRC), the administration on citizens' exit and entry, passports and visas, previously the responsibility of the Ministry of Foreign Affairs (MFA) and local foreign offices, were devolved to the MPS and local public security authorities. Specifically, the Bureau of Public Order within the MPS was responsible. Article 3 of the above Circular prescribed that Guangdong and Fujian Provinces were permitted to establish a special team in each provincial-, municipal-, or county-level public security department, to be responsible for the administration of exit and entry of citizens for private affairs. By contrast, other provinces could only appoint a full or part-time cadre for the same function. A national exit and entry administrative authority based around provincial departments was established.

Events that influenced RLR

Events, such as the land reform, after the establishment of the PRC had a far greater influence on Chinese migration than those of the period 1911–1949. The influence is best summed up by C. Y. Choi who has asserted that:

> . . . [A]mong these events, the Land Reform of 1950–1953 probably had the most far reaching effect because it greatly weakened the binding strength of the community due to the elimination of the ownership of large land holdings, especially clan land, and confiscation of land owned by overseas families. As the lineages began to disintegrate, loyalty among Chinese emigrants towards their families and lineages started to lose its basic foundation.[19]

Persecution, harassment and discrimination also encouraged emigration. Many Chinese left the Mainland once the Communists assumed power in 1949.[20] Against an unfavourable backdrop at home, Chinese migrants began to settle permanently abroad, and tried to bring their family to join them overseas. There began a mushrooming outflow of wealthy Chinese people seeking to avoid being persecuted as landlords and capitalists. This partially accounts for the imposition of stricter controls on migration.

Household registration

Household registration (*Hukou*) is closely linked to RLR. The initial goal of establishing household registration system in 1951 was to maintain public security and freedom of residence and movement.[21] Only persons residing in urban areas were subject to control.[22] It was intended to be temporary and imposed no limits on the movement within the territory. However, in 1955, the scope of registration was extended to the whole country including rural areas, and the system made permanent. Chinese still enjoyed the freedom of movement within territory at that time.[23]

Driven by rapid industrial development and the establishment of a planned central economy, the legislative goal of "safeguard[ing] people's freedom of movement" was repealed by the *Regulations on Household Registration* 1958 (PRC). This regulation essentially set out the limits of freedom of movement. Article 10, Clauses 2 and 3 prohibited citizens from permanently moving from rural areas to urban areas unless formally varying their household registration. In order to register elsewhere, the applicant needed to produce an employment certificate issued by an urban labour department, or a letter of offer from a higher education institution, or proof document of movement permission issued by an urban household

[19] Choi, C. Y., *Chinese Migration and Settlement in Australia* (Sydney: Sydney University Press, 1975), 57–58.

[20] Brown, Judith M. & Foot, Rosemary *Migration: the Asian Experience* (London: the Macmillan Press Ltd., 1994), 5.

[21] Article 1 of the *Provisional Regulations on Administration of Urban Household* 1951 (PRC) (*Chengshi Hukou Guanli Zanxing Tiaoli*).

[22] Article 2 of the *Provisional Regulations on Administration of Urban Household* 1951 (PRC) (*Chengshi Hukou Guanli Zanxing Tiaoli*).

[23] The *Directive of the State Council on Establishing Regular Household Registration System* 1955 (*Guowuyuan Guanyu Jianli Jingchang Huikou Dengji Zhidu De Zhishi*).

registration organ. Temporary movement for over three months was also prohibited under Article 16 of the *Regulations on Household Registration* 1958 (PRC). From the perspective of RLR, Chinese could not apply for exit permission or a passport at the public security departments in which their residence was not registered.

Simplistic style of regulations

Statutes promulgated during this period were very general and simple in form. One regulation was usually no longer that 100 to 200 Chinese characters. From the legal point of view, these might be regarded as directions rather than laws.

In conclusion, the development of the exit and entry legal system during this period was encouraging, because freedom of movement was recognised in the statutes, though exit permission was the prerequisite of leaving. Limits and general regulations on entry and exit were primarily established to facilitate the entry and exit of overseas Chinese, to control travel to or from Hong Kong and Macao, and strictly manage aliens exiting China. The effect of restricting limits, household registration and a simplistic form of regulations on RLR remains to date. The regime established in this period laid the foundation and direction for later exit and entry administration.

5.3.1.2 1958 and 1978: the development of the restrictive framework governing RLR

Regretfully, China's communist policies, poor economic conditions, political instability and hostility towards foreign countries brought an end to the encouraging trends in the development of regulatory framework governing RLR. From 1958, the Chinese government introduced policies to suppress right-wing political opposition. Many of the opponents were Chinese people who had been educated abroad and may have had family members overseas. They were sent to labour camps in remote rural areas and seriously restricted from leaving China. Anyone who wanted to leave China generally remained silent, out of fear of being regarded as right wing.

China adopted a highly concentrated emigration system, which adversely affected RLR. In April 1959, the MPS announced further restrictions on exit and entry. The *Rules for the Administration on Citizens Exit and Entry for Private Affairs* 1958 (PRC) were repealed. In 1964, the State Council promulgated the *Regulations on the Administration of Entry, Exit, Transit, Residence and Travel of Aliens in China* 1964 (PRC), Article 7 required all aliens to apply for a visa for the purposes of entry, internal travel and exit.

During the Cultural Revolution between 1966 and 1976, RLR was seriously abused. The provisions regarding the freedom of movement were deleted from the Constitution in 1974. Any person who applied to leave China was regarded as being dissatisfied with the Chinese socialist system, and suspected of having colluded with a foreign country to carry out illicit activities against China. This meant that many citizens and overseas Chinese refrained from applying to enter or exit the State.[24] In 1974, 1.6 million people exited and entered China for private affairs and public affairs, 26% less than in 1965.[25]

Hostility towards China by many countries initially motivated China's restrictive migration policy. This was especially true of the Western countries, such as the USA and Australia, where the governments of the time were suspicious of communist sympathisers; in Malaya after the 1948–1960 'emergency'; and in India after the 1962 Sino-Indian War. China was still sanctioned under the decree of the UN.[26] A 'one nationality' policy was introduced during this period. It was designed to encourage overseas Chinese to assimilate into their local foreign community and to abandon their Chinese nationality. This policy remains in force.

The draconian exit restrictions were politically indefensible then and still are. China was probably concerned that the disgruntled element within the emigrant population would form foreign counterpart groups for subversive movements within China. In such circumstances, there was almost no demand for the exit and entry for private affairs. For the others, political instability and danger in Mainland China during the Cultural Revolution of 1966–1976 encouraged irregular emigration, mostly in the form of refugees.

5.3.2 *1979 to 1985: the start of the reform of the restrictive framework governing RLR*

Since 1978, China has adhered to the policy of reform and opening-up, with the focus on economic reconstruction and the establishment of a socialist market economy. This has resulted in great economic achievements. Nevertheless, special laws regarding exit and entry were not promulgated until 1985. During this period, the Chinese government began to reform the exit and entry administration and started to relax restrictions on RLR.

---

[24] Wong, Li the *Theory and Practice of International Immigration Law,* (Beijing: the Publishing House of Law, 2001), 77.

[25] Department of Exit and Entry under Ministry of Public Security & Department of Border Security Checking and Administration, *Great Change over the Last 50 years: the Analysis of the Data of Exit and Entry of Individuals* (*Fenyun Bianhuan Wushi Nian: Cong Churujing Renyuan Tongji Shuju Kan Jianguo Yilai De jubian*), No. 22 (1999) of *People's Public Security* (*Renmin Gongan*).

[26] The USA Congressional – Executive-Commission on China, "The People's Republic of China", http://www.cecc.gov/pages/virtualAcad/his/prc.php (accessed 04/01/2005).

Recognition of the right to leave: a very advanced form of legislative thinking

Limits were primarily eased on the right to leave of overseas Chinese and their families who had re-entered the country. Encouragement of overseas Chinese to return is a traditional Chinese custom, and stood to attract overseas investment. In June 1978, the State Council approved and transmitted the *Suggestions of the Ministry of Public Security, the Ministry of Foreign Affairs and Overseas Chinese Office of the State Council on Relaxing and Improving Exit abroad Examining and Approving for Returned Overseas Chinese and Their Family Members* 1978 (PRC).

Most significantly, exiting was firstly recognised as a legitimate right of citizens in China, even though the prerequisite of 'legitimate' may offer opportunities to demolish the legal recognition.[27] Additionally, the government commenced the first overhaul of the exit and entry administration in 35 years with the publication of the *Suggestions of the Ministry of Public Security on Relaxing the Conditions of Examination and Approval of Exiting China for Private Affairs* 1984 (PRC). Unfortunately, influenced by leftist policy, many local administrative authorities ignored the reforms and legal recognition of RLR.[28] In order to redress the problem, the *Circular of the Ministry of Public Security on Seriously Carrying out the File of Gongfa (Jing) [84] 59 and Further Relaxing Exiting China for Private Affairs (Abstract)* 1984 (PRC) was published. Both instruments dramatically relaxed the limits on exit and entry of Chinese citizens and relatively relaxed limits applied to aliens.

---

[27] Article 1 of the *Suggestions of the Ministry of Public Security on Relaxing the Conditions of Examination and Approval of Exiting from China for Private Affairs* 1984 (PRC); and the *Circular of the Ministry of Public Security on Seriously Carrying out the File of Gongfa (Jing) [84] 59 and Further Relaxing Exiting from China for Private Affairs (Abstract)* 1984 (PRC) creatively provided that "application for exiting from China is a legitimate right and interests of Chinese Citizens." and that [E]xcepting Chinese citizens prohibited from exiting from China, the application for self funded exit from China for permanent residence, visiting relatives and friends, marriage, inheriting property, medical treatment, employment and tourism, without distinction to social class or origin, political thinking or family situation, should be granted if the visa of destination countries is possibly granted.

[28] As Hu Yaobang, the then General Secretary of the Central Committee of Communist Party of China (CPC) of that time pointed out, Some of our comrades have a very serious left leaning thinking in this regard, the strict limits on exiting from China have not been relaxed from the bottom despite the reiteration of the Central Committee. These issues must be solved quickly. See Preface of the *Circular of the Ministry of Public Security on Seriously Carrying out the File of Gongfa (Jing) [84] 59 and Further Relaxing Exiting Abroad for Private Affairs (Abstract)* 1984 (PRC) (*Gonganbu Guanyu Renzhen Guance Zhixing Gongfa (Jing) 59 Hao Wenjian Jinyibu Fangkuang Yisi Chuguo De Tongzhi*), promulgated by the Ministry of Public Security on 22 November 1984.

Article 1 of the later instrument underlined that administrative authorities had to respect and safeguard the lawful rights and interests of Chinese citizens wanting to exit China, to encourage and assist them to travel abroad, and to better consider the perspective of the applicant when processing their application. This was a very advanced form of legislative thinking, even in comparison to later reforms. Unfortunately, these advanced ideas were not enforced in practice, demonstrating that the communist ideology is deeply ingrained in administrative processes.

Passport application and passport administration

Article 8 of the *Regulations on Passport and Visa* 1980 (PRC) confers a right on Chinese citizens with specific qualifications to obtain a passport. Individuals exiting China for public affairs had to submit documents alongside the application form, undertake strict examination and hand in their passport for unified administration.[29] In fact, these limits on exit for public affairs had the effect of limiting almost all individuals likely to exit the State, given that only people employed by the government or a State owned enterprise could afford to travel abroad.[30] Additionally, lack of provisions for the processing of passport applications, resulted in the exercise of unfettered administrative discretion and arbitrary decision-making.

Notably, it was more difficult to obtain a passport if the applicant was a member of the Communist Party of China (CPC). Under Article 1 of the *Rules of Personal Department of Central Committee of Chinese Communist Party on Some Issues Regarding Party Members Exiting China, Hong Kong or Macao Areas for Private Affairs* 1981, a "member of Chinese Communist Party exiting abroad for private affairs must lodge the application [with the] work unit's Party Committee and local public security authority". After approval was obtained from both of these 'authorities', the "application [was] reported to senior Party Committee". An ordinary passport could then be granted. Given that Party members occupied all senior government positions and most positions in State-owned

---

[29] Article 3 clauses 1 and 2 the *Circular of Application for Passport and Visa for Individuals Exiting from China Temporarily for Public Affairs* 1983 (PRC) required individuals to be provided with an exit abroad task document and political examination document with a leader's instruction. Article 6 Clause 2 and 4 required that individuals exiting from China immediately hand in their passport (whether diplomatic, business or ordinary) to public affairs [meaning unclear here] to work unit upon return to China. If the person needed to exit China again, they would need to apply for a certificate issued by bureau-level work unit.

[30] According to official Chinese statistics, in 1985 the average annual per capita income for a rural person was C¥574.31 (US$66.18), whereas the average annual per capita income in urban areas was C¥748.92 (US$90.56). See "Per Capita GDP from 1952 to 2002" (*1952 Nian – 2002 Nian Renjun Guomin Shengchan Zongzhi*), http://www.menet.com.cn/shuju/gmjj/gmjj-rjgdp.htm (accessed 15/04/2004).

enterprises and institutions, these limits effectively restricted the exit of China's elite.

Exit visa

In 1980, the exit visa system was established. Under Article 2 of the *Regulations on Passport and Visa* 1980 (PRC) the exit visa is a permission document that would permit Chinese citizens and aliens to exit the Chinese border. Article 9 required Chinese citizens, overseas returnees and aliens must apply for a visa if they exit China.[31] Multiple entry and exit visas could be obtained if the applicant was involved in setting up a factory or other investments, or had bought a house and lived in the province for extended periods. This system was obviously outdated by international standards.

Single nationality

Also in 1980, the *Law of Nationality* (PRC) was enacted. It summarised the nationality policy that had operated since 1949. In particular, Article 3 expressly refused to recognise dual nationality. This policy had been introduced to avoid diplomatic issues with countries in which a Chinese national was resident and also a citizen. However, the policy significantly undermined the ability of overseas Chinese to maintain close links with China, as they needed to apply for a visa to enter, transit, settle or exit the country. This adversely affected their living, employment and educational opportunities in China.

The Bureau of Administration of Exit and Entry of Aliens under the MPS was established in 1983, creating a dedicated exit and entry administrative body. Furthermore, limits on overseas Chinese exiting China were eased. Economic development and reform measures outlined saw a marked increase in the number of people entering and exiting China.[32] China approved approximately 50,000

---

[31] The exit visa system was also contained in other regulations such as Article 3 Clause 1 of the *Interim Provisions of the Special Economic Zones in Guangdong Province for the Control of Personnel Entering and Leaving China*, 1981 (Guangdong, the PRC). That provision required foreigners and overseas Chinese to comply with entry and exit procedures and to obtain a visa.

[32] In 1978, 1.88 million people passed across China's borders, compared to 12.8 million by 1984 of this, the number of aliens travelling into and out of China in 1978 was 450,000, compared to 3 million in 1984. Committee of Textbook Editing and Examination of the Ministry of Public Security, *Renmin Jingcha Gongan Yewu Jichu Jiaocai: Bianfang Yu Churu Jing Guanli* (*Frontier Defence and Exit and Entry Administration, the Series of Basic Textbook of People's Police Operation*), Internal Publication within Public Security Organs (*Gongan Jiguan Neibu Faxing*) (Beijing: the Publishing House of Qunzhong, 1999), 281.

individual applications to exit for private affairs each year between 1979 and 1985.[33]

Looking back, the liberalisation of exit and entry during this period was very limited, while some improvements were made to exit and entry administration. The advanced legislative thinking in the regard of exit and entry administration was not carefully executed. Outdated passport administration and nationality administration continue to be a dominant theme.

5.3.3 *1985 and 2001: the development of the reform of the restrictive framework governing RLR*

From 1985 to 2001, over 400 statutes paved the way for comprehensive governance of exit and entry, mainly through the MPS. These laws gradually lifted the restrictions placed on Chinese citizens exiting China, encouraged the return of overseas Chinese, eased the restrictions on the entry and permanent residence of aliens, and established emigration intermediary agencies. Although the development did not extend to constitutional protection of RLR, or the liberalisation of exit and entry contained in ordinary statutes, it further improved RLR in China.

The return of legal recognition of citizen's RLR

Legal recognition of citizens' RLR was resumed in February 1986, when the *Law on the Control of Exit and Entry of Citizens* 1985 (PRC) came into force. Article 1 was:

> . . . formulated with a view to safeguarding the legitimate rights and interests of Chinese citizens with respect to their exit from and entry into China's territory and to promoting international exchange.

RLR was respected in qualified terms. The right was precondition upon being 'legitimate'. This excluded the possibility of full or unqualified protection of RLR and suggested that in-depth issues regarding RLR and Chinese migration law could not be resolved through non-essential migration law reform. But the lack of express recognition of alien's RLR was not changed. According to Article 1 of the *Law on the Control of Entry and Exit of Aliens* 1985 (PRC) "for the purpose of safeguarding the sovereignty and maintaining the security and public order of the PRC and facilitating international exchanges."

---

[33] Wang, Leiming, Xinhua News Agency, "Citizens May Exit Abroad for Private Purpose Easier and Faster" (*Woguo Gongmin Yinsi Chuguo Gengjia Bianjie*), (19/09/2002), http://news.xinhuanet.com/newscenter/2002–08/29/content_543014.htm (accessed 16/09/2006).

Legislation of the exit and entry

Although the provisions of these two laws provide for the formulation of later relevant laws, their contents were generalised and ambiguous. The enactment of the *Detailed Rules for the Implementation of the Law on the Control of Entry and Exit of Citizens* 1986 (PRC) and the *Detailed Rules for the Implementation of the Law on the Control of Entry and Exit of Aliens* 1986 (PRC) did not resolve the issue of ambiguity. The degree of ambiguity fostered the enactment of a large number of subsidiary orders, directives, rules and circulars.[34] Based on the incomplete collection of the Bureau of Party and Government Foreign Affairs Cadre, under the Organisation Department of the Central Committee of the CPC, 42 ministries, committees, State bureaus, Courts and banks promulgated 235 orders, directives, subsidiary rules and official documents and letters during the period between May 1980 and July 1994.[35]

These subsidiary regulations suggest that during this period, the legislative process was not unified. This model can be attributed to the influence of a planned central economy, in which individual ministries were separately responsible for managing different sections of the national economy and national development, in which competition did not play a key role. Each ministry had the power to enact regulations in a relatively autocratic manner, which led to the inconsistencies and disputes that arose within the body of legislation. The *Regulations on the Administrative Legislation Procedure* (PRC) 1989 that governed the rule-making activities of the State Council and its ministries was widely regarded by Chinese authorities as unsatisfactory.[36]

[34] The major regulations include the *Provisional Measures Concerning the Control over Chinese Citizens Travelling on Private Affairs to or from the Regions of Hong Kong or Macao* 1986 (PRC), the *Circular of the General office of the State Council on the Measures for Receiving Compatriots from Taiwan Coming to the Mainland to Visit Their Relatives or as Tourists* 1987 (PRC), the *Circular of the General office of the State Council on Students Studying Abroad* 1992 (PRC), the *Provisional Measures on Procedures for Contract Workers Sent Abroad Leaving the Country* 1996 (PRC), the *Provisional Measures on the Administration of Chinese Citizens' Tours Abroad at Their Own Expense* 1997 (PRC) and the *Law of the Rights and Interests of Returned Overseas Chinese and the Family Members of Overseas Chinese (Amendment)* 2001 (PRC).

[35] Calculated according to the Bureau of Party, Government Foreign Affairs Carder under Department of Personal of Central Committee of Chinese Communist Party, the table of content of the *Collection of Popular official Documents and Letters, Regulations and Laws Governing Examination and Administration of Exiting Abroad* (*Chuguojing Shenpi Ji Guanli Gongzuo Changyong Wenjian Fagui Xuanbian*), Interior Publication (*Neibu Faxing*) (Beijing: the Publishing House of Danjian Duwu, 1994), 1–33.

[36] Rubin, Edward L. "Administrative Law and the Complexity of Culture", in Seidman, Ann, Seidman, Robert B. and Payne, Janiceeditor, *Legislative Drafting for Market Reform: Some Lessons from China*, (London: Macmillan Press Ltd., 1997 and New York: St. Martin's Press, Inc. 1997), 91.

The public had little access to government policies and rules because there was no freedom of information legislation. The Bureau of Party and Government Foreign Affairs Cadre, under the Organisation Department of the Central Committee of the CPC, stated in the *Collection of Popular Official Documents, Regulations and Laws Governing Examination and Administration of Exiting China* that:

> Most of the collections in this book are internal official documents and must be safely kept. They are banned from being copied, publicly released, or cited unless publicly released.[37]

Consequently, a large number of unpublished official documents formed a bureaucratic barrier to RLR.

Formalities associated with passport applications and obtaining permission to exit China

A Chinese citizen needed to go through complicated formalities when applying for a passport, including approval from one's work unit, producing household registration documents, an invitation letter from overseas, as well as the financial guarantee for the duration of the visit. Having close relatives abroad was almost a prerequisite for obtaining permission to travel abroad. RLR was further restricted by the controls placed on access to foreign exchange. As Bard-Anders Andreassen and Theresa Swinehart observed in *Human Right in Developing Countries Yearbook 1990,* "foreign travel for private affairs is severely restricted [in China]."[38] In 1994, Mary Shi noted in *Human Right in Developing Countries Yearbook 1994* that:

> Freedom to leave and enter [China] remains under government control. Citizens who have not shown any sign of improper political attitude, however, will more easily be granted permission to study abroad than before. The time needed to obtain a passport will rather depend on the amount of contacts (*Guanxi*) one has within the bureaucracy of local authorities, the work unit or the neighbourhood committee, than on the relevant Ministry.[39]

---

[37] The Bureau of Party, Government Foreign Affairs Carder under the Department of Personal of Central Committee of Chinese Communist Party, "the Introduction of the editor" in the *Collection of Popular official Documents and Letters, Regulations and Laws Governing Examination and Administration of Exiting Abroad* (*Chuguojing Shenpi Ji Guanli Gongzuo Changyong Wenjian Fagui Xuanbian*), Internal Publication (*Neibu Faxing*) (Beijing: the Publishing House of Danjian Duwu, 1994).

[38] "China" at Andreassen, Bard-Anders and Swinehart, Theresa editor, Human Rights Institutes in Norway, Denmark, the Netherlands, Finland and Sweden (Compilation), *Human Right in Developing Countries Yearbook 1990*, (Kehl, Strasbourg and Arlington: N. P. Engel, Publisher, 1991, 125.

[39] Shi, Mary, "China" at Baehr, Peter, Hey, Hilde, Smith Jacqueline and Swinehart,

No one knows how many Chinese wanting to go abroad were discouraged from applying because they are aware of the complications and, more importantly, because they may have feared reprisals against themselves and their families. Fortunately, the restrictive framework governing RLR was experiencing further reform. In 1986, the first round of reforms characterised the effectiveness of the *Law on the Control of Exit and Entry of Citizens* 1985 (PRC) and the *Law on the Control of Entry and Exit of Aliens* 1985 (PRC). The system of entry-exit visas for citizens[40] was accordingly replaced with an exit registration card,[41] and aliens exit visa was abolished.[42]

The second round of reforms took place in 1992. After 1991, China set up the goal of establishing a socialist market economy. The demand for RLR was more pressing than ever. At this time, the registration card for exiting a second or subsequent time was abolished. In addition, the MPS simplified the procedure for exiting China for private affairs for intermediate and senior science and technology personnel. This group no longer needed to provide a certificate of approval from a provincial, regional and municipal level of government with their application.[43]

The third and fourth round of reforms occurred in 1996 and 2000. At the third, partial Chinese and overseas Chinese who had returned to China; as well as their families, no longer needed to submit a foreign letter of invitation with their application to leave.[44] The fourth permitted citizens to apply for a passport upon evidence of a foreign exchange deposit, rather than a certificate from the work unit.

Theresa editor, *Human Right in Developing Countries 1994 Yearbook* (Kehl, Strasbourg and Arlington, N. P. Engel, Publisher, 1995), 180.

[40] "Chinese citizens may leave or enter the country with valid passports or other valid certificates issued by the competent department of the State Council or other departments authorised by them. They shall not be required to apply for visas." Article 2 of the *Law on the Control of Exit and Entry of Citizens* 1985 (PRC).

[41] "The Chinese passport, together with the exit registration card, shall be issued by the entry-exit control department of the public security organ to the citizens residing in China whose exit applications have been approved." Article 6 of the *Detailed Rules for Implementing the Law of Exit and Entry of Citizens* 1985 (PRC) made pursuant to the *Law of Exit and Entry of Citizens* 1985 (PRC).

[42] "For exit from China, aliens shall present their valid passports or any other valid certificates." Article 22 of the *Law on the Control of Exit and Entry of Aliens* 1985 (PRC).

[43] The exit application of a research assistant, lecturer, engineer, medical practitioner and other intermediate and senior scientific and technical personnel will be processed pursuant to the *Law on the Control of Exit and Entry of Citizens* 1985 (PRC). Article 1 of the *Circular of the Ministry of Public Security on Simplifying the Formality of Intermediate and Senior Science and Technology Personals Exiting Abroad for Private Affairs* 1992 (PRC) (*Gonganbu Guanyu Jianhua Zhongji Gaoji Keji Renyuan Yinsi Chujing Shouxu De Tongzhi*).

[44] *Operational Norms of Application, Examination and Approval of Exiting from China and Passport For Private Affairs of Citizens* 1996 (PRC).

Occurrence of political and economic exile from 1980

After 1980, especially the Tiananmen crackdown in 1989, the number of Mainland Chinese students in Western universities who became political or economic exiles swelled.[45] It represented the biggest wave of Chinese migration since the gold rush of nineteenth century.[46] The expansion of the overseas Chinese network ensures the feasibility of further development of RLR in China in the near future.

The above graph dramatically shows average annual exit numbers in three different legislative stages. From 1949 to 1978, China had operated under a planned central economic system. The average number of exits each year was 7,000. From 1979 to 1986, China initiated its policy of reform and opening up but did not enact entry and exit laws. The average number of exits was 50,000 per year. From 1987 to 2001, the legal system of exit and entry was established and China began to integrate into the rest of the world. Limits on external travel were gradually lifted. The annual average increased to 1.1 million.

Effect of reforms of legislation governing exit and entry exit and entry

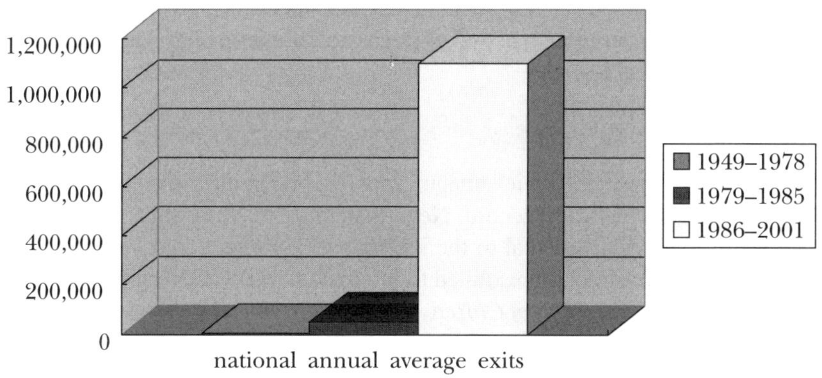

Graph 1: Average National Annual Exits in Three Migration Legislative Stages. Source: the Ministry of Public Security (MPS), China 2002

[45] Wichberg, Wdgar, "The Chinese as Overseas Migrants in Brown", Judith, M. & Foot, Rosemary, editor, *Migration: the Asian Experience* (London: the Macmillan Press Ltd., 1994), 16.

[46] For example, more than 42,000 Chinese students were granted permanent visas in Australia following the 1989 events in Beijing. This number grew to 100,000 when the students were allowed to bring their families to Australia to be reunited. That number accounts for 70.42% of all Chinese mainlanders who now live in Australia. See Banham, Cynthia, "Children of the revolution", in the *Sydney Morning Herald*, Australia, Christmas Weekend Edition, pages 26–28, December 2003.

At present, more than 10,000 passports are issued daily by the MPS, the daily number is more than the yearly total issued during the 1950s through to the 1970s.[47] Dating from 1989, when the first national conference on exit and entry administration was held, 1.334 billion entries and exits have been recorded by China's exit and entry administration, an annual growth of 27.91%.[48] In 1990, Chinese migration stock was 380,000, and 513,000 in 2000.[49] The above graph and figures demonstrate that legal reform played a positive role of promoting the realisation of RLR.

Emigration intermediary services

The rapid growth in the number of people exiting China has resulted in the development of an emigration intermediary service market, the formation of which, as a result of complex economic and socio-ideological causes, has been chaotic. The *Provisions on the Administration for Overseas Employment Intermediary Agencies* 1992 (PRC), the *Regulations on the Administration for Travel Agencies* 1996 (PRC) and the *Regulations for the Administrative on Intermediary Agencies for Self-funded Studying Abroad* 1999 (PRC) were enacted to regulate the industry. The new regulations developed a system of reserve funds related to overseas employment and overseas study intermediary agencies, and overseas travel agencies.

Final remarks

By 2001, some important achievements were reached in the protection of RLR, despite its motley historical record. Nevertheless, restrictions on RLR are still severe, and issues fundamental to the system of migration control remain. For example, most reform measures failed to integrate new policies into the *Law on the Control of Exit and Entry of Citizens* 1985 (PRC), and the *Law on the Control of Entry and Exit of Aliens* 1985 (PRC) and its detailed rules of implementation. Consequently, the achievements are perhaps unstable in the sense that their legal validity is in dispute.

---

[47] Wang, Chuyan, "Passport Gain Wider Currency in China", China Central Television, 18 October 2002, http://www.cctv.com/english/news/TVNews/MorningNews/20021018/100241/html (accessed 19/06/2003).

[48] "China to Reform Exit-Entry Administration", http;//www.chinadaily.com.cn/en/doc/2001–12/21/content_99065.htm (accessed 16/09/2006).

[49] Population Division, Department of Economic and Social Affairs, attached table of *International Migration Report 2002*, United Nations Secretariat, *2002*, ST/ESA/SER.A/220, New York: the United Nations, 2002, 62 pages.

5.4 THE CONTEXT AND CONTENT OF 2001–2005 REFORM STRATEGY AND MEASURES

In principle, China has acknowledged the importance of protecting RLR, and has taken steps to have its practices conform to international norms. Restrictions on RLR in China were gradually relaxed from 2002 to 2005. Procedures were greatly simplified.[50] According to the official media, this round of reforms will be the biggest overhaul of Chinese exit and entry administration in history.[51]

5.4.1 *The context of the reforms*

The fundamental reason for reforming exit and entry administration is that strict controls are incompatible with China's economic and social development. The then President Jiang Zemin argued in 2002 that, "reform and opening up have yielded substantial results. The socialist market economy has taken shape initially."[52] Meanwhile, an absence of corresponding reform of exit and entry administration has diluted China's ability to develop and integrate into the world. By international standards, since 1949 the Chinese government has exercised too much power over migration and RLR, yet this has received less attention than other aspects of the reform.

China's accession to membership of the World Trade Organisation (WTO) sparked exit and entry administration reform. The government widely recognised the need to simplify procedures. The then Prime Minister Zhu Rongji said in 2002 "China's accession to the WTO benefits its reform and opening up and its economic development as a whole."[53] Further, that "We need to actively participate in international economic cooperation and competition on a broader scale and in greater depth."[54] The then minister of the MPS Jia Chunwang, said in 2001:

---

[50] "Simplifying Exit-entry Procedures, a Vital Step for China", 23/11/2001, *The People's Daily*, http://english.people.com.cn/200111/23///eng20011123_85161.shtml (accessed 16/09/2006).

[51] "State to Simplify Entry-exit Rules", 11/22/2002, *The China Daily,* http://www.chinadaily.com.cn/en/doc/2001–11/22/content_94711.htm (accessed 16/09/2006).

[52] Jiang, Zemin, the President of the People's Republic of China, Part I Par 4 of "Build a Well-off Society in an All-Round Way and Create a New Situation in Building Socialism with Chinese Characteristics: Report at 16th China Communist Party Congress (8/11/2002)", http://www.fmprc.gov.cn/eng/37815.html (accessed 19/07/2003).

[53] Zhu, Rongji, the Premier of the State Council, Part 1 of Part II of "the Report on the Work of the Government (16/03/2002)", http://english.gov.cn/official/2005–07/29/content_18346.htm (accessed 16/09/2006).

[54] Zhu, Rongji, the Premier of the State Council, Part 1 of Part IV of "the Report on the Work of the Government (16/03/2002)", http://english.gov.cn/official/2005–07/29/content_18346.htm (accessed 16/09/2006).

> China's entry into the WTO will ensure the country participates in international cooperation in a more comprehensive manner, while these measures will deepen the reforms and serve the economic construction.[55]

Chinese society was in favour of these opinions. China Radio International, the most authoritative multi-languages State-owned radio station, announced that a flood of tourists and businessmen were expected to enter and exit the country after China's entry into the WTO.[56] *The China Daily*, the leading authoritative English newspaper owned by the State said "a far-reaching overhaul of border administration is to be kick started following China's entry to the WTO to cope with the expected deluge of tourists and businessmen".[57] Ten days after accession, the 2002 national annual meeting on exit-entry administration was held in Beijing in which the reform strategy was announced.

5.4.2 *Reform goals*

Six reform goals were announced at the annual national meeting on exit-entry administration in November 2001. With the exception of two goals related to the simplification of Chinese tourist group visas and permanent resident visa applications, the four remaining reform goals announced were pertinent to RLR. The 'passport on demand' policy is the centre of the reforms. By 2005, Chinese citizens in large and medium-sized cities will be able to obtain a passport merely by presenting their identity cards and household registration documents to the appropriate authorities.[58] Jia Chunwang, in 2001, explained that the reform was aimed at gradually supplying passports to those who required them.[59] The key to this measure is that applicants are no longer needed present written permission from work units; thereby better protecting individual privacy. Clearly, the policy of passport on demand advantages the urban population rather than people living in

[55] Quoted in "Simplifying Exit-Entry Procedures, A Vital Step for China", 23/11/2001, *The People's Daily*, http://english.people.com.cn/200111/23/eng20011123_85161.shtml (accessed 16/09/2006).

[56] Wang, Ling, "China Simplifies Entry-exit Rules", November 2001, China Radio International, http://english.cri.com.cn/english/2001/Nov/36826.htm (accessed 18/04/2003).

[57] "State to Simplify Entry-exit Rules", 11/22/2002, *The China Daily*, http://www.chinadaily.com.cn/en/doc/2001–11/22/content_94711.htm (accessed 16/09/2006).

[58] 'Simplifying Exit-Entry Procedures, A Vital Step for China", 23/11/2001, *The People's Daily* 23–11–2001 http://english.people.com.cn/200111/23/eng20011123_85161.shtml (accessed 16/09/2006).

[59] Quoted in *China Simplifies Entry-exit Rules*, November 2001, China Radio International, http://english.cri.com.cn/english/2001/Nov/36826.htm (accessed 18/04/2003).

small towns and rural areas. It was adopted after the experience of Zhongshan in Guangdong Province, where a passport on demand policy was initiated in April 2001.[60] The other three reform goals are:

- The cancellation of the requirement of providing invitation letters when applying for passport;
- The establishment of special channels at the airports for Chinese citizens; and
- The relaxation of restriction on travelling to the HKSAR or MSAR.

By the end of 2002, Chinese citizens no longer needed to provide invitation letters from the foreign country of destination when applying for a passport; and authorities no longer issued the exit registration card attached to the passports of citizens residing in China whose exit application had been approved.[61] During 2002, special channels for Chinese citizens were set up at ten airports in Nanjing, Kunming, Shenyang and other parts of China, as is currently being practiced in the Capital Airport and Shanghai-based Pudong Airport.[62] From September 2002, Mainland Chinese residents have been allowed to travel to the HKSAR and MSAR on business for up to three years before their visas expire. Those who stay for less than three months are now able to obtain a visa without the need to fulfil extra requirements on taxation or foreign exchange; and the number of travellers to these places is no longer limited. These measures were to accommodate increasing business travel to or from the HKSAR and MSAR.[63]

5.4.3 *Reform measures*

To reduce the social disruption that may have been caused by the reforms, the measures were gradually introduced in three rounds in 2002, 2003 and 2004. The 2002 reform measures focused on the pilot programs and trial implementation of reform

[60] "Guangdong Residents May Apply for Passport with ID and Resident Cards within 2003", (*Guangdong Niannei Shixian Ping Shenfenzheng Hukoubu Shenling HUzhao*), 06/03/2003 Southern Net, http://travel.21cn.com/news/focus/2003–03–06/958982.html (accessed 23/07/2003).

[61] "China Simplifies Entry-exit Rules", November 2001, China Radio International, http://english.cri.com.cn/english/2001/Nov/36826.htm (accessed 18/04/2003).

[62] "Simplifying Exit-Entry Procedures, A Vital Step for China", 23/11/2001, *The People's Daily*, http://english.people.com.cn/200111/23/eng20011123_85161.shtml (accessed 16/09/2006).

[63] MPS's Bureau of Exit and Entry Administration revealed that, in 2001, more than 2.46 million Mainland citizens entered and left the HKSAR and MSAR, three times the number in 1997. Quoted in Jiang, Zhuqing, "Mainland SAR Visa Procedures Simplified", 30/05/2002, *The China Daily*, http://www.chinadaily.com.cn/en/doc/2002–05/30/content_121768.htm (accessed 16/09/2006).

strategy. The 2003 and 2004 reform measures aimed to deepen and extend the 2002 reform. Provincial reforms are an indispensable part of the efforts to reform exit and entry administration. Under the MPS reform strategy, provincial governments may implement different reform measures according to individual needs. The provincial reforms are intended to compliment the national strategy and may not be inconsistent with it.

2002: the pilot programs and trial implementation of reform strategy

In 2002 measures emphasising pilot programs and trial implementation were adopted. The first was related to passport on demand. Twelve cities were selected for this pilot of program in the first half of 2002[64] and passport applications in these cities increased by over 40%.[65] By the end of 2002, the policy had been introduced into 24 large and medium-sized cities including, Shanghai, Nanjing, Qindao and Xiamen, whereupon passport applications increased by 30 to 50%.[66]

According to the *Circular of the Ministry of Public Security on Simplifying the Formalities of Mainlanders Short-term Exiting and Entry the Areas of HKSAR and MSAR* 2002 (PRC), the MPS adopted seven reforms for Mainland citizens' short-term visits to the HKSAR and MSAR from June 2002:

1. The types of visas available to entry into the HKSAR and MSAR were extended from family visits and tourist visas (as at 1997) to include visas for business, training, work and study.
2. The scope of visiting relatives was extended.[67]
3. The terms of business visas were expanded and their formalities simplified.[68]

[64] The 12 cities are Zhongshan, Shunde, Jiangmen, Fushan, Huizhou, Shantou, Shenzhen, Zhuhai, Guangzhou, Fushun, Qionghai and Zibo. See "Trial of New Passport Application Procedure Goes Smoothly: Shanghai will become China's Thirteen City to Try Out a Simplified Procedure for Passport Applications", August 2002, http://english.cri.com.cn/eglish/2002/Aug/69224.htm (accessed 18/04/2003).

[65] "Trial of New Passport Application Procedure Goes Smoothly: Shanghai will become China's Thirteen City to Try out a Simplified Procedure for Passport Applications", August 2002, http://english.cri.com.cn/eglish/2002/Aug/69224.htm (accessed 18/04/2003).

[66] Wang, Leiming, Xinhua News Agency, "Citizens May Exit Abroad for Private Purpose Easier and Faster" (*Woguo Gongmin Yinsi Chuguo Gengjia Bianjie*) (19/09/2002), http://news.xinhuanet.com/newscenter/2002–08/29/content_543014.htm (accessed 16/09/2006).

[67] A visa is available to visit a relative who is living, studying or working in the HKSAR or MSAR. The definition of "relative" has been extended to include a spouse, parents or parents in law, children, grandparents, grandchildren, siblings, aunts and uncles, and nieces and nephews and their spouses. Visas can be issued to allow entry once a month, once in three months, or three-month multi-entry visa. A visa to visit a spouse will generally be a three-month multi-entry visa.

[68] A business visa may be granted on the basis of being used once a fortnight, as a three months multiple-entry, a one-year multi-entry visa, or three-year multi-entry visa. The first

4. Tourist visas were given to people aged over 60 or under 14. Applications could be made at the local exit-entry administration bureau even if applicants were members of transient households.
5. Other visas will be issued to those who need to deal with property, attend court or be present at a migration interview.
6. Overseas Chinese who have returned to the Mainland can apply for passes or visas for the HKSAR and MSAR at exit-entry authorities of the city or county in which their residence is registered, or where they are employed.[69]
7. A certificate from the applicant's work unit or a police station is not required under certain circumstances.[70]

Lastly, the Chinese government has attempted to improve ordinary passports for public affairs. Part 8.1 and 8.2 will analyse ordinary passport for public affairs in details. According to Article 1 and 2 of the *Circular of Ministries of Education, Public Security and Foreign Affairs on Some Affairs Regarding Fulltime Students Exit China Short-term with Ordinary Passport for Private Affairs* 2002 (PRC), since February 2002, fulltime students have, in principle, been allowed to exit China with an ordinary passport for private affairs.[71] A representative of the MOE stated that the student-related reforms, "will play a proactive role for China to foster talent and enhance China's reputation in the educational fields".[72] However, in an objective sense, the improvements outlined above concerning ordinary passports for public affairs still fall short of international norms, such as in the

two categories are issued on demand. Prior tax and foreign exchange requirements have been cancelled. It is no longer necessary to provide documentary evidence when applying for a one-year multi-entry visa. Further, if two different public security administrations operate on the applicant's permanent resident area and work unit, the applicant may apply to the public security authorities of the city or county in which their residence is registered.

[69] Jiang, Zhuqing, "Mainland SAR Visa Procedures Simplified", 30 May 2002, *The China Daily*, http://www.chinadaily.com.cn/en/doc/2002–05/30/content_121768.htm (accessed 16/09/2006).

[70] Where Mainlanders holding valid passports are applying for subsequent exit and entry to HKSAR and MSAR, or overseas Chinese who have returned to the Mainland are applying for exit and entry to HKSAR and MSAR.

[71] According to the *Circular of Ministries of Education, Public Security and Foreign Affairs on Some Affairs Regarding Fulltime Students Exit China Short-term with Ordinary Passport for Private Affairs* 2002 (PRC), students need to provide documentary evidence from their school or institution with their passport application. The student, or the school acting on the student's behalf, can make applications to the relevant foreign embassy or consulate in China. Previously, an application had to be made for a public affairs passport to attend short-time governmental exchanges, international conferences, undertake cooperative research, attend study tours, training, international competitions, or other exchange activities.

[72] Quoted in "Student Can Go Abroad with Private Passport February 1 on, 4 March 2002", Xinhuanet, http://www.edu.cn/20020304/3021674.shtml (accessed 19/12/2003).

continued requirement of documentary evidence from a school or educational institution.

2003: extension of 2002 reforms

Based on the experience of 2002, with emphasis on the results of the pilot program in Guangdong province, the MPS introduced three new rulings in August 2003 designed to facilitate the daily life of ordinary people in regard to exit and entry.[73] These rulings were intended to enhance the 2002 reforms. With respect to passport applications, residents in 100 designated large- and medium-sized cities, accounting for one third of all Chinese cities, were allowed to directly apply for a passport on demand, using their identity card and residence booklets.[74] Since September 2003, working citizens no longer require approval of their work unit in order to apply for a passport, unless they are serving government officials, intermediate or senior management in State-owned enterprises or a member of the CPC.

Furthermore, from 2003, residents from Guangzhou, Shenzhen and Zhuhai, Shanghai and Beijing may apply for travel permission to the HKSAR and MSAR on an individual basis by showing their identity card and resident's booklets. These visitors are not allowed to stay for more than seven days, but can apply an unlimited number of times. Residents in the 100 designated cities can travel to the HKSAR and MSAR and Taiwan and do not have to present a letter of approval from the employers or from their public security offices. Lastly, for Chinese who have gone abroad and who have lived overseas for more than one year, the stipulation that their household registration be cancelled, was rescinded.[75]

2004: further deepening of the reforms

2004 was a crucial year for the conclusions of the reform goals.[76] Four measures were undertaken to further deepen the reforms. First, the passport on demand policy was expanded to 80% of large and medium sized cities, mainly in the central area. The remaining 20% of the country's large and medium sized cities will adopt this measure in 2005. Next, a long awaited 'green card' system was

---

[73] "New Rulings to Bring a Freer Life", 1208//2003, *China Business Weekly*, http://www.chinadaily.com.cn/en/doc/2003–08/12/content_255194.htm (accessed 16/09/2006).

[74] "Reforms Make Life and Travel Much Easier", 8 August 2003, *The China Daily*, http://www.chinadaily.com.cn/en/doc/2003–08/08/content_252954.htm (accessed 16/09/2006).

[75] "New Rulings to Bring a Freer Life", /1208//2003 *China Business Weekly*, http://www.chinadaily.com.cn/en/doc/2003–08/12/content_255194.htm (accessed 16/09/2006).

[76] Quoted in "China to Further Relax Entry and Exit Control", 25 December 2003, Xinahuanet, http://news.xinhuanet.com/english/2003–12/25/content_1247315.htm (accessed 30/12/2003).

introduced to grant aliens with permanent residence permits in August 2004.[77] Thirdly, the issuance and management of credentials for Mainlanders to conduct short-term travel to the HKSAR and MSAR was further improved. Researchers at the MPS are identifying technologies for automatic passage systems at some Chinese ports.[78] Lastly, procedures for travelling to and from Taiwan were further simplified.[79]

5.5 EFFECTS, DEFICIENCIES AND NATURE OF THE REFORMS

5.5.1 *Effects of the reforms*

Reform measures have recorded improvement of exit abroad applications in China. Before examining the effects of current reforms, it is useful to re-examine the impact of prior reforms on average national exits between 1949 and 2001.

Graph 2 depicts the number of registered exits and entries per one million Chinese citizens over five typical years.

- In 1978, at the start of China's reform and reintegration with the world, there were 14 per million exits and entries.
- In 1988, two years after the enactment of exit and entry laws, there were 62 per million.
- In 1996, the figure stood at 11,321 per million. This was the time at which the first regulations associated with applications, examination and approvals for exits were formulated, and passports for private affairs were made available to all citizens.
- In 2003, the second year of the reforms, the number of exits and entries was 30,538 per million, despite the SARS outbreak in the first half of that year. This figure represented a 20% increase on the number of citizens crossing China's borders in 2002.

---

77 "China Begins to Implement its own 'Green Card' System", http://english.people.com.cn/200408/20/eng20040820_153939.html (accessed 16/09/2006). Also see the provisions of *Regulations on Examination and Approval of Permanent Residence of Aliens in China, 2004*.

78 "Exit and Entry of Citizens Will be More Easier Next Year, Four Measures will be Implemented" (*Mingnian Gongmin Churujing Jiang Geng Bianli Gonganbu Zai Tui Sixiang Xin Jucuo*), 24/12/2002, CRI net, http://www.cnradio.com.cn/news/200312240292.html (accessed 30/12/2004).

79 Zhang, Tao, "Relax the Restrictions Travelling to and from Taiwan, Chongqing Publish Series of Measures to Facilitate Exit and Entry of Resident" (*Wanglai Taiwan Fangkuan Xianzhi Congqing Tuichu Xilie Churujing Bianmin Cuoshi*), 17/03/2004, http://www.cq.xinhuanet/news/2004–03/17/content_1797126.htm (accessed 16/09/2006).

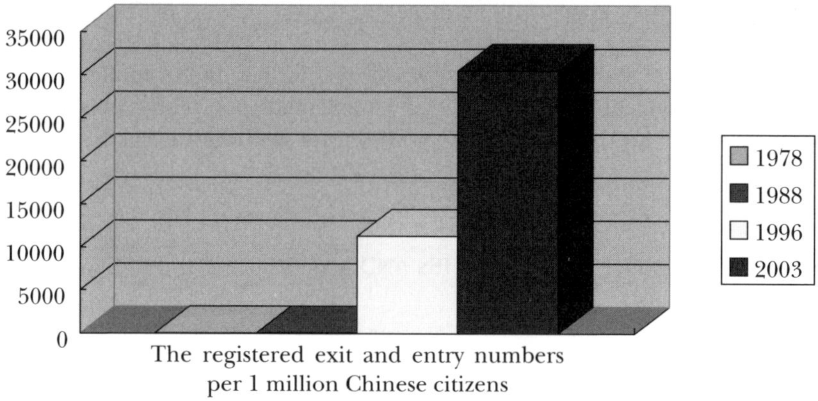

Graph 2: Registered Exit and Entry Numbers Per One Million Chinese Citizens in 1978, 1988, 1996, and 2003. Source: the Research on Population Issues in the Period of Reform and Opening-up[80] and the MPS[81]

The next figures illustrate the effects of the current reform measures on international migration flow. One is from national perspective; the other two are from provincial perspectives. At the end of 2001, the Chinese government instituted the biggest process of exit and entry reform. One year later, the number of exits increased from 3,080,000 of 2001 to 4,010,000 of 2002. This suggests that the reforms were integral to promoting overseas travel of Chinese nationals.

The number of passports issued to Guangdong residents increased from 376,923 in 2001 to 490,000 in 2002. These figures are more significant in light of the fact that only 30 million people (34.71%) of Guangdong's total population[82] can take advantage of the passport on demand policy. Since August 2003, Shanghai residents have been able to apply for the travel permission on an individual basis to the HKSAR and MSAR. Dao Shuming, Vice-Director of the Shanghai Travel Administration Committee, forecast that the number of people to travel to the HKSAR would exceed 300,000 after one year of the policy's imple-

[80] Sa, Jicai and Cao, Jingcun, the *Research on Population Issues in the Period of Reform and Opening-up*, (Beijing: the Publishing House of Beijing University, 1994), pages 229–232, Quoted in Huang, Ruilong, Bao, Sidun, Liu, Ling, "Overseas New Migrants over Last One Decade (*Jin Shinian Woguo Dalu Haiwai Xin Yimin*)", *the Journal of Population & Economics* (*Renkou Yu Jingji*) No.1 [1998].

[81] Calculated according to the date quoted in "China Sees Unusual Fall in Exit-entry Numbers in 2003", 12 January 2004 *People Daily Online*, http://english.people.com.cn/200401/12/print20040112_132362.html (accessed 16/09/2006).

[82] The population of Guangdong Province is 86.42 million in March 2001. "Guangdong Province", *The People's Daily,* http://english.peopledaily.com.cn/data/province/guangdong.html (accessed 30/12/2003).

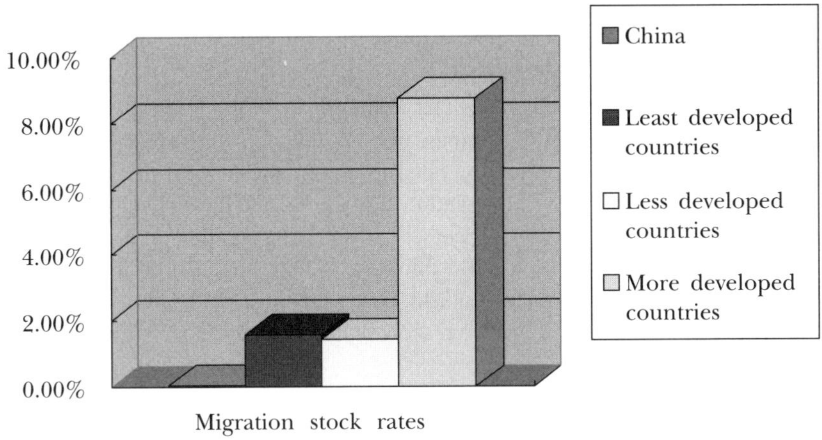

Graph 3: Comparison of international migration stock rates Source: *International Migration 2002*, the IOM

mentation. According to statistics from the Shanghai Travel Administration Committee, the number of exits to the HKSAR was 136,000 in 2002. 89,000 of this number were tourists. It demonstrates that the policy to permit individual travel to the HKSAR and MSAR stimulated applications to travel to the HKSAR.[83]

As discussed in part 1.2 of this book, international migrants in China are still considerably lower than that in the rest of the world.[84] In 2000, 0.04 percent of the Chinese population were international migrants. The average rates in more developed regions, less developed regions and least developed countries are 8.739 percent, 1.452 percent and 1.566 percent respectively. This shows that with the development of China, international migrants will be further increased, and that issues in the protection of RLR in China follow.

---

[83] "Shanghai Residents May Apply for the Travel Permission on an Individual Basis to SARS very easily, It Only Take 5 Minutes" (*Shanghairen Qingsong Ban Geren Gangao You, Quanguocheng Hua 5 Fengzhong*), Xinhuanet, 2 September 2003, http://news.21cn.com/dushi/csts/2003/09/02/1252195.shtml (accessed 02/09/2003).

[84] According to *International Migration 2002*, the Department of Economic and Social Affairs, Population Division, the United Nations, October 2002, some countries and regions migration stock rates have been calculated by the author as following: Egypt (0.29 percent), India (0.62 percent), Indonesia (0.19 percent), Romania (1.4.19 percent), Russian Federation (9.11 percent), Hungary (2.97 percent), Cuba (0.73 percent), Brazil (0.32 percent), Japan (1.27 percent), Republic of Korea (1.27 percent), Singapore (33.65 percent), United Kingdom (6.78 percent), France (10.59 percent), USA (11.35 percent), Australia (21.4.58 percent) and New Zealand (22.50 percent). Migration stock rate is just a little higher in China than the same rate in Vietnam (0.028 percent).

Generally speaking, the future effects of the reform of exit and entry procedure on the Chinese economy and society, and on Chinese global integration, are subtle and lasting rather than instantaneous and short-term. The reforms may foster an awareness of, and desire to protect RLR, among individuals and governments. The impressive response of the Chinese people to the opening up of the country in 1978 demonstrates a compelling need to communicate with the world. The reforms have triggered a high demand to exit China, and have changed the way in which applications to exit are processed. Simplifying passport applications and processing may challenge some old thinking. It may begin to be thought that applying to exit China is exerting a right, rather than just performing a duty, and that the process itself is designed to protect that right, rather than simply to control exit and entry.

The reforms have revealed shortcomings in exit and entry administration and the underdevelopment of migration laws. Residents outside Guangdong, Shanghai and Beijing are aware that the administrative practices governing their applications are relatively more restrictive, and may question this. The exit and entry administration in the pilot program cities are perhaps faced with mounting paperwork in light of the rising number exit applications and number of people entering China. This has created a pressing demand to perfect relevant legislation and reduce the bureaucracy. Arguably, China must relax exit and entry restrictions further and give effect to essential reform measures, before it can achieve the goal of realising RLR.

It must be accepted that the reforms only benefit a small number of Chinese people, because public officials, or those involved in public affairs, as discussed earlier in this book, are not subject to the reforms. Among the people covered by the reforms, only those who can or will travel abroad will be practically affected. Given China's vast population and the notion that lives on of a central empire, the rate of people who actually can or will keep in touch with people in other nations is very small. In the absence of RLR and with low incomes of many Chinese people, these reforms are not relevant to many ordinary citizens.

5.5.2 *Deficiencies in the reforms*

Although the reform strategy and measures have stimulated the remarkable increase of passport applications, four key deficiencies must be kept in mind. In the first place, as above, reforms are limited to private individuals not involved in public affairs. The reforms relate only to applications for ordinary passports for private affairs. Other passport categories, especially ordinary passports for public affairs, have been excluded. This means that about 653 million people are unable to take advantage of the reforms. The scope and adverse influence of reforms to applying to the application for ordinary passports for public affairs will be discussed in part 6.2 of this book.

Secondly, the reform strategy does not apply to the whole system of application for ordinary passports for private affairs, not all private affairs passports are included. People with special status, such as some government officials and managers of large and medium-sized State-owned enterprises and institutions, must still obtain permission from their work units when applying for passports.[85] According to statistics from the Exit and Entry Administration of Hainan Public Security Department, 1% of the population, or 13 million people, fall into this category.[86] Not only does that account for a large number of people, but the people affected make up China's elite. It is well known that the Chinese people residning in rural areas are usually poor and lower educated. According to *Chinese Industry and Business Times*, the income of the rural residents, which comprise 60% of the whole population, is 20% of the national income. So, the influences of residents of rural areas are less than the influences of residents of urban areas. Limits on these individuals are more significant than on residents of rural areas.

Moreover, the laws and the reforms do not correspond the reform policies. Prior laws and regulations were not amended upon announcement of the reform measures. As such, there are many vital contradictions between valid laws and statutes and the effective reform measures. For example, in pursuance of the reform strategy and measures, exit registration cards are no longer attached to passports. However, under Article 5 of the *Detailed Rules of the Implementation of the Law on the Control of Exit and Entry of Citizens (Amendment)* 1994 (PRC), the entry and exit administration of the public security organ shall attach a registration card. The 1994 rules were approved by the State Council and jointly promulgated by the MPS, MOE and Ministry of Communication. Within the Chinese legal system, the 1994 rules prevail over the 2001/2002 policies. The later policy is invalid in theory, but is executed in practice.

Only retrospective amendment of the 1994 rules could overcome the problem. The MPS has stressed that the legal system of exit and entry administration needs to be improved.[87] In November 2001, Jia Chunwang acknowledged this problem and announced that the MPS would speed up the legal process of entry-exit management to ensure that it is fair, open, and conforms to relevant laws and regulations.[88] However, the relevant amendments were not adopted for another three

---

[85] "Passport More Accessible for Beijingers", 01/09/2003, http://www.chinadaily.com.cn/en/doc/2003–09/01/content_260238.htm (accessed 16/09/2006).

[86] "Extension: Residents in Four Districts of Hainan Province May Apply for Passport Simpler" (*Fanwei Kuoda: Hainan Si Diqu Ke Jianhua Shenling Chuguo Huzhao Shouxu*), Xinhuanet, 21 October 2003, http://www.hiholiday.com/cgi-bin/feature/view.asp?id=4350&First_item=1&Second_item= (accessed 16/09/2006).

[87] Zhu, Daqiang, "Summarisation: China Ensure the Direction of Exit and Entry Administration after Access to the WTO, 23 November 2001", China News Agency, http://review.jcrb.com.cn/ournews/asp/readNews.asp?id=63921 (accessed 18/04/2003).

[88] Quoted in Wang, Ling, "China Simplifies Entry-exit Rules, November 2001", China

years. The inconsistency between laws and reform policy will undermine the authority of the law, and undermine public confidence that the administration will act in accordance with the law. The inconsistency also violates Article 5 Clause 2 of the *Constitution of the PRC (Amendment)* 2004, which require the State to uphold the uniformity and dignity of the socialist legal system.

Finally, these reform arrangements have affected the relationship between the central authority and local authorities, undermining central authority. The Central government is vested with the power to control the exit and entry by the Constitution. Article 89 Clause 1(9) of the *Constitution of the PRC (Amendment)* 2004 provides that the State Council exercises the functions and powers to conduct foreign affairs. Exit and entry administration is one of foreign affairs.[89] Even so, provincial governments often promulgate local regulations and reform measures which actually amend national laws and regulations. As Lin Yicong, an officer of Guangdong Public Security Bureau argued in 2001:

> The infringement by provincial governments upon the central government powers became a way of meeting regional or individual interests. It invades the applicants' rights and interests as well as violates the central government's power.[90]

With the development of Guangdong, Shanghai and Beijing local legislation and implementation of local reform measures, central government power is further eroded.

5.5.3 *The nature of the reforms*

It is vital that the nature of current reforms be seen more clearly so that we can better understand the future evolution of RLR in China. The official media has accepted that the reform strategy aims to simplify exit and entry procedures. More precisely, it is the simplification of procedures governing the exit of citizens, and the permanent residence of aliens. According to *The People's Daily*, the newspaper of the Central Committee of the CPC, the reforms will "greatly simplify

---

Radio International, http://english.cri.com.cn/english/2001/Nov/36826.htm (accessed 18/04/2003).

[89] The website of the Chinese police states that foreign affairs policemen are responsible for supervising the exit, settlement, residence, tour and entry of Chinese citizens and aliens. See "The People's Republic of China Department of Public Safety Police Specific Set-up", http://www.chinesecop.com/CNPO1.html (accessed 19/12/2003).

[90] Lin, Yicong, "The Review on the Amendment Principle of Amending Current Exit and Entry Laws", in Committee of Exit and Entry Administration, Chinese Association of Police editor, the *Collection of Papers on the Control of Exit and Entry (III)* Interior Published within Public Security Organs (*Gongan Jiguan Neibu Faxing*) (Beijing: the Publishing House of Qunzhong, 2001), 20–21.

procedures and are viewed as an important step for the Chinese people to further join the international community".[91] *The China Daily* reported that the core of the new reform drive is the simplification of entry and exit procedures for people seeking to invest or travel in the country.[92] In May 2003, the Ministry's Bureau of Exit and Entry Administration (BEEA), with respect to the reforms for travelling to the HKSAR or MSAR, stated that:

> The reason for the change in procedure is to meet the needs resulting from the increasing demand for economic, cultural and personnel exchanges between the Mainland and the HKSAR and MSAR.[93]

In addition to the simplification of procedures, some scholars have asserted that the reform strategy could play a catalytic role on the realisation of RLR. Meng Yanhong, a leading Chinese historian, contended that the simplification of exit and entry rules was an irreversible trend. He argued that if China's entry into the WTO was considered as a milestone, for its reform and opening up, such measures could be viewed as "natural outcomes" of the drive.[94] A Shanghai analyst has said, "the change in issuing passports was dramatic. I have a strong feeling that Chinese people are enjoying more freedom and China is becoming more open to the outside world."[95] Professor Xu Xianming, the President of China University of Politics and Law, has argued, "Freely leaving and returning on demand is a vital symbol of the realisation of more citizens' freedom."[96]

It is accepted that simplifying exit and entry procedure helps to protect RLR. However the simplification should merely be the means by which reform is achieved, not the nature of it. The current approach – which regards administrative simplification as the nature of reform – attends to trifles and neglects the

---

[91] "Simplifying Exit-Entry Procedures, A Vital Step for China", *The People's Daily*, 23–11–2001 http://english.peopledaily.com.cn/200111/23/eng20011123_85161.shtml (accessed 18/04/2003).

[92] "State to Simplify Entry-exit Rules", *The China Daily*, 11/22/2002, http://www.chinadaily.com.cn/en/doc/2001–11/22/content_94711.htm (accessed 16/09/2006).

[93] Quoted in Jiang, Zhuqing, "Mainland SAR Visa Procedures Simplified", 30/05/2002, *The China Daily*, http://www.chinadaily.com.cn/en/doc/2002–05/30/content_121768.htm (accessed 16/09/2006).

[94] Quoted in "Simplified Exit-entry Rules Seen as Vital to China", 23/11/2001, *The China Daily*, http://www.chinadaily.com.cn/en/doc/2001–11/23/content_94971.htm (accessed 12/09/2006).

[95] Quoted in "Shanghai Simplifies Passport Application Procedure", 3 September 2002, *The China Daily,* http://www.english.people.com.cn/200209/03/print20020903_102522.html (accessed 12/09/2006).

[96] "Exiting Abroad is Becoming the Individual Needs of Chinese Citizens", (*Chujing Kaishi Chengwei Zongguo Gongmin Chuncui Geren De Xuyao*), 28/11/2003, Xinhuanet, http://news.sdinfo.net/7235006413091635 2/20031228/1233069.shtml (accessed 12/09/2006).

essential needs of citizens. With the deepening of the reform measures, the awareness of the passport as a symbol of prestige may dilute, and the awareness of RLR will increase. More limitations will be seen in the reforms orientated towards simplifying exit and entry procedure.

5.6 Conclusions

Rich and complex experiences of historical development are two sides of a coin for China today. China can play a catalytic role in helping protect RLR, or place a heavy burden on and hamper the improvement of RLR. The Chinese government needs thus to objectively discriminate its position in relation to RLR by reference to international human rights ethics, rather than exclusively to Chinese national experience or tradition.

Given the long years of war and abnormal relations with Western countries, it is understandable that a relaxation of limits has only been intermittent; restriction has been a dominant theme. Issues of RLR in China are not only the issues of today but also those accumulated over time. That history cannot be cited as an excuse not to solve the current issues of RLR. As a rule, inertia of historical development can be affected and overcome by outside force, though such change is often reactionary and overly sudden. With RLR in China, the dominant theme of restriction will remain until the legislation governing exit and entry is reformed. In respect of the complexity underlying a history of accumulated issues in China, a well-designed reform strategy focused on RLR needs to be gradual.

A more liberalised RLR meets the need to enhance economic progress and integration into the world. China's accession to the WTO sparked the biggest overhaul of Chinese migration law in history. The reforms are characterised by the simplification of the procedures for exit and entry, with a focus on passports on demand. They have not brought the country's administrative procedures for exit and entry into line with international standards. The reforms are superficial, and it is not surprising to find serious deficiencies in them. The scope of reform is too limited to cover the right to return and the right to leave for public affairs, the right to leave of citizens employed by governments, State-owned enterprises and institutions and members of the CPC for private affairs and RLR of aliens. As such, the nature and content of the reforms benefit only some of the population. The issues of the infringement by provincial governments upon central government powers regarding exit and entry administration remain untouched. Even the integration between prior laws and new policies has been technically ignored.

The deficiencies do not completely undermine the significance of the reforms. The reforms will exert subtle and lasting positive impacts on the social and economic development of China and the country's integration into the world. Encouragingly, the reforms foster the awareness of RLR among individuals and governments. Given the fact that Chinese international migration stock rate is only

0.46% of average international migration stock in the world,[97] it is understandable that the number of entries and exits increased considerably due to the relaxation of severe restrictions.

In the development of rights in China, RLR is a very new issue, the discussion and conception of which is mainly provided by contemporary scholars. Government authorities have not yet completely accepted the idea of RLR. In Chinese society all electronic and print media are controlled by the CPC, hence there is little ground for building awareness of the existence and the need to improve upon RLR of individuals. This lack of awareness of RLR in the public domain hinders the complete execution of laws to enhance exit and entry and may also, if overlooked, hinder the design of an advanced reform strategy to solve the issues of RLR in China.

97 Calculated according to data quoted in Population Division, Department of Economic and Social Affairs, attached table of *International Migration Report 2002,* United Nations Secretariat, *2002,* ST/ESA/SER.A/220 (New York: the United Nations, 2002), 62 pages.

Chapter Six
The Right to be Granted a Passport in China

INTRODUCTION

As discussed in part 3.2, State acceptance of RLR internationally means nationals are entitled to travel documents, such as a passport or other certificates needed to leave and return. Any formalities related to the issuing of passports, as well as powers to deny, withdraw or cancel a passport should be appropriate, provided by law and publicly accessible. This chapter examines (i) the categories of passports, the scope of passports, passport issuing authorities and passport legislation; (ii) ordinary passports for public affairs; and (iii) ordinary passports for private affairs.

6.1 GENERAL CONSIDERATIONS OF THE PASSPORT

6.1.1 *Categories of the passport*

The Chinese system of passport categories is more complex than anywhere else in the world with the exceptions of North Korea and Vietnam.[1] According to Article 1 Clause 2 of the *Regulations on Passport and Visa* 1980 (PRC):

[1] Wan, Zhenshan, editor, *the General Updated Guide of the Exit and Entry of Individuals*

> Passports of the People's Republic of China are classified into diplomatic passports, service passports and ordinary passports. Ordinary passports are further composed of ordinary passports for public affairs and ordinary passports for private affairs.

After China reoccupied the HKSAR in 1997 and the MSAR in 1999, the HKSAR and MSAR passports become part of the Chinese system. In addition to passports, there are travel permits, seafarer's passports, the HKSAR document of identity, the HKSAR seaman's identity book, and the travel permits of the HKSAR and MSAR. While more complex, the scope of diplomatic passports, service passports and ordinary passports for public affairs (public affairs passports), while having been expanded in recent times, remains narrower than in other countries, opposed to the shrinking scope of the ordinary passport for private affairs (private passport).

In theory, the Chinese passport is a certificate to prove Chinese nationality for the purpose of travelling or residing in foreign countries.[2] In practice, it is revered as a symbol of social status, and a product of the influence of China's old feudal history. Diplomatic passports, service passports and public affairs passport are regarded as the passports of officials, whereas the private passport is regarded as the passport of common people. Applicants generally prefer to apply for the former rather than the latter. The preference for an official passport may hinder reforms of the passport system.

6.1.2 *The Scope of various kinds of passports*

The scope of three official passports has been expanded under the communist political system and socialist public ownership of the economy. The scope of the diplomatic passport in China is broader than in other countries.[3] In order to avoid the abuse of diplomatic passports, Paragraph 2 of the *Circular of State Council on the Amendment of Article 6 of Regulations on Passport and Visa* 1984 (PRC)

(Zuixin Renyuan Churu Jing Quanshu) (Beijing, the Publishing House of Renshi, 2002), 94.

[2] Article 1 Clause 1 of *the Regulations on Passport and Visa* 1980 (PRC), the "passport of the People's Republic of China is issued to Chinese citizens as the certificate to prove their identity abroad for the purpose of entering or exiting Chinese border."

[3] The Diplomatic Passport is principally issued to senior officials who currently hold the position of vice-minister or over of the governments, senior officials who currently hold the position corresponding to vice-minister or over of the Communist Party and its attached organs and institutions, and the People's Liberation Army, principle leaders who currently hold the position corresponding to vice-minister or over of the National People's Congress, the Chinese People's Political Consultative Conference, and all democratic parties, people's organs, diplomats, consular officers and their accompanying spouses, underage children, diplomatic couriers, and etc. See the Amendment of Article 6 of *Regulations on Passport and Visa* 1984 (PRC).

stresses "there is no relationship between the diplomatic passport and the holder's official level and [they are] irrelevant to interior political treatment."

In the case of service passport, according to Article 7 Clause 1 and 2 of the *Regulations on Passport and Visa* 1980 (PRC),

> A service passport is issued to individuals who are permanently working overseas in Chinese foreign departments, and their accompanying spouses and underage children, and individuals temporarily Exiting China excluding diplomatic passport holders.

However, according to the MFA in 2003, the scope of service passports is yet broader. The MFA has stated that:

> [a] service passport is principally issued to officials with the rank of Division Chief and above of governmental offices, staff members of diplomatic and consular missions in foreign countries, the United Nations' Organizations and its specialised agencies, and their accompanying spouses and underage children.[4]

The scope of public affairs passports has also been expanded. According to Article 8(1) of the *Regulations on Passport and Visa* 1980 (PRC), an ordinary passport for public affairs is "issued to postgraduates, individuals attending in an advanced study, overseas students, labours and seamen employed foreign companies." In 2003, the MFA explained it in a broad sense, that; "ordinary passports for public affairs are principally issued to staff in the governmental departments at all levels, and to employees of State-owned enterprises or institutions."[5]

Although the *Regulations on Passport and Visa* 1980 (PRC) and the MFA expressively provide the scope of private passports,[6] the narrowing of its scope is the corollary of the expansion of the scope of three official passports. The shrinking scope of private passports implies that more applications will be restricted, and RLR will in turn be limited.

---

[4] The MFA, "Chinese Passport and Other Travel Documents", 03/08/2004, http://gr.china-embassy.org/eng/lsqw/hz/t146143.htm (accessed 12/09/2006).

[5] The MFA, "Chinese Passport and Other Travel Documents", 03/08/2004, http://gr.china-embassy.org/eng/lsqw/hz/t146143.htm (accessed 12/09/2006).

[6] Under Article 8(2) of *the Regulations on Passports and Visas* 1980 (PRC) an ordinary passport for private affairs is issued to Chinese citizens exiting China for private affairs, citizens residing overseas, and other citizens for whom the passport authorities regard the granting of a private passport appropriate. Also according to the MFA, a private passport is issued to people who are travelling for personal affairs, emigrating, visiting friends or relatives, inheriting property, studying, working or sightseeing. The MFA, "Chinese Passport and Other Travel Documents", 03/08/2004, http://gr.china-embassy.org/eng/lsqw/hz/t146143.htm (accessed 12/09/2006).

6.1.3 *Passport issuing authorities*

The authority to issue passport in China is exercised by a variety of governmental authorities, including the MFA, MPS and Chinese diplomatic missions in foreign countries. Under Article 3 Clause 2 of the *Regulations on Passport and Visa* 1980 (PRC) and Article 12 of the *Law on the Control of Exit and Entry of Citizens* 1985 (PRC), the MFA and 55 foreign affairs offices of local governments (authorised by the MFA) are responsible for issuing, renewal, page adding and endorsement of passports. The Bureau of Harbor Superintendence and its delegates are authorised to issue seafarers passports. Diplomatic missions can issue passports and travel documents to Chinese people who are abroad.

The central Chinese government has authorised the HKSAR and MSAR governments to issue passports in accordance with Chinese law.[7] Specifically, this refers to the Immigration Departments of the HKSAR and MSAR. These departments are also authorised to issue alternative travel documents in lieu of a passport, or to cancel or withdraw the passport and alternative travel documents.

As one effect of this, the diversity of passport issuing authorities undermines the unity of passport administration. Different authorities apply different criteria and processing formalities and advance different departmental interests. The separation of issuing authorities increases administrative costs associated with passports. As another effect, the separation provides applicants with an opportunity to exploit the loophole of being able to apply for a passport many times. If an individual is not successful in applying for a public affairs passport from one authority, he or she may be successful in exiting China by applying for a private passport from another authority, and vice versa. This loophole can only be closed by the use of advanced information technology and the introduction of a more advanced administrative system.

6.1.4 *Passport laws*

Passport law is inconsistent and outdated. The *Regulations on Passport and Visa* 1980 (PRC) is currently the most important law regarding passports. It was promulgated by the State Council in 1980, and most recently amended in 1984 by the *Amendment of Article 6 of Regulations on Passport and Visa* 1984 (PRC). The great development in China over last 25 years has considerably changed the legislative background of the 1980 laws. It is imperative to enact new laws.

The current laws governing passports are also inconsistent. A large number of regulations, rules, measures and circulars have been promulgated to give detailed

---

[7] Article 154 Clause 1 of *Basic Law of the Hong Kong Special Administration Region of the PRC* 1990 (PRC) and Article 139 Clause 1 of *Basic Law of the Macao Special Administration Region of the PRC* 1993 (PRC).

effect to laws. Most of the legislative and regulatory provisions are simultaneously effective. As an example of inconsistency between laws, both *Supplementary Opinions of State Education Commission, the Ministry of Foreign Affairs and Ministry of Public Security on Issuing Ordinary Passport for Private Affairs for Citizens Studying Abroad Sent by the State* 1993 (PRC) and the *Circular of State Education Commission, the Ministry of Public Security and Ministry of Foreign Affairs on Holding Ordinary Passport for Private Affairs of Citizens Studying Abroad* 1993 (PRC), provide that citizens studying abroad use private passports; even those sent by the State under some circumstances. On the other hand, Article 8(1) of the *Regulations on Passport and Visa* 1980 (PRC) stipulates that overseas students shall apply for and hold ordinary passport for private affairs.

In theory, the *Regulations on Passport and Visa* 1980 (PRC) should prevail over later inconsistent subordinate legislation, policies and rules like the above the Supplementary Opinions and the Circular. In practice, this is not the case. Departments usually process passports in accordance with their own policies and rules. This results in chaotic legislation and policy making, which in turn undermines the integrity of the national passport laws.

6. 2 Ordinary Passport for Public Affairs

Serious issues pertaining to ordinary passport for public affairs, of which Chinese scholars are aware, adversely affect RLR in China. Wang Zhenshan has contended from a macro-level that:

> The issues existing in relation to [. . .] public affairs [passports] consist of two aspects. One is the system issue, for example, the integration of government functions and enterprises management, multi-level examination and overly-elaborate formalities that contribute to lower efficiency and miss business opportunities; the other is the management issue, mainly the absence of a [. . .] jurisdictional criteria between public security departments and foreign affairs departments that results in the phenomenon of "one person, two passports".[8]

In what follows we consider: (i) the scope of public affairs passport; (ii) the application procedure and examination criteria; (iii) the management of public affairs passport; and (iv) the causes of the issues associated with (i), (ii) and (iii).

6.2.1 *The scope of the public affairs passport*

The public affairs passport category is so wide that it encompasses a significant number of people who would otherwise apply for a private passport. In addition

---

[8] Wan, Zhenshan editor, *the General Updated Guide of the Exit and Entry of Individuals (Zuixin Renyuan Churu Jing Quanshu)*, the Publishing House of Renshi, Beijing, 2002, 94.

to applicants mentioned in part 6.1.2 of this book, the following individuals are required to participate in the complicated procedures to apply for this type of passport:

1. Fulltime students who are participating in a group exit of China which has been organised by a government department;[9]
2. Individuals undertaking advanced studies, overseas students, labours and seamen employed in foreign companies, officials in Party Committees and governments, officers and soldiers in armed forces, employees in people's Organizations, State-owned enterprises and institutions, [. . .] for all affairs related to work units.[10]
3. All students studying religion (who must also be State-funded);[11]
4. Individuals participating in sports, education and cultural exchange, and seamen, crews of trains and planes, staff of the international postal union, individuals exiting China temporarily for enterprise's affairs, individuals exiting China under project contracts.[12]
5. Employees in experimental enterprise groups as which have been approved by the State Council who are travelling for economic purposes or to attend a trade fair;[13]

---

[9] Article 5 of *the Circular of Ministries of Education, Public Security and Foreign Affairs on Some Affairs Regarding Fulltime Students Exit Abroad Short-term with Ordinary Passport for Private Affairs* 2002 (PRC) (*Jiaoyubu, Gonganbu, Waijiaobu Guanyu Zaixiao Xuesheng Duanqi Chuguo Chiyong Yinsi Huzhao Youguan Shixiang De Tongzhi*), promulgated by the MOE, MPS and MFA on 25 January 2002.

[10] Article 3 Clause 1 of *the Circular of the General office of the Central Committee of Chinese Communist Party and the General office of the State Council on Refraining of Excessively Sending Group, Team and Individuals Exit China*, 1986 (PRC) and the Preface of Some Rules of the General office of the Central Committee of Chinese Communist Party and the General office of the State Council on Serious Restriction Cadres in the Departments of Party Committees and Governments Exit China, 1987 (PRC).

[11] Article 3 of *the Circular of State Education Commission, State Council Bureau for Religions Affairs, the MPS and MFA on Dealing with Some Issues of Recruiting Students Studying Abroad in China without Allowance by Certain Organizations in China and Individuals of Foreign Countries and International Organizations* 1990 (PRC) (*Guojia Jiaowei Guowuyuan Zongjiaoju Gonganbu Waijiaobu Guanyu Chuli Mouxie Guojia He Guoji Zuzhi De Zhuhua Jigou Ji Geren Shanzi Zaihua Zaoshou Liuxuesheng Wenti De Tonhzhi*), promulgated by State Education Commission, State Council Bureau for Religions Affairs, the MPS and MFA on 26 December 1990.

[12] Department of Politics under the MPS, *Frontier Defence and Exit and Entry Administration,* the Series of Basic Textbook of People's Police Operation (*Bianfang Yu Churu Jing Guanli, Renmin Jingcha Gongan Yewu Jichu Jiaocai*), examined by Committee of Textbook Editing and Examination of the MPS, Internal Publication in Public Security Organs (*Gongan Jiguan Neibu Faxing*) (Beijing: the Publishing House of Qunzhong, 1999), 324.

[13] Article 1 and 2 of t*he Measures for the Implementation on Examination and Approval*

6. Government sponsored sports coaches, athletes, sports researchers, sports medical professionals and academic staff in sports education institutions exiting China,[14] and assistant coaches;[15]
7. Individuals temporarily exiting China who are employed by State-owned enterprises.[16]
8. Professionals, technical staff and managers of domestic enterprises, government sponsored institutions, the CPC and government departments, who are travelling for the purpose of further training;[17]
9. Individuals who are travelling for the purpose of undertaking training in accordance with a technology or enterprise contract, to perform a project, to give effect to a bilateral or multi-lateral economic treaty, to participate in a government-sponsored project which is to be performed in co-operation with a foreign party, or for the purpose of providing foreign aid;[18]

---

of Exit Abroad (Including Hong Kong and Macao) and Invitation Aliens to China of Employees of National Experimental Enterprises Group (for Trial Implementation) 1992 (PRC) (*Guangyu Guojia Shidian Qiye Jituan Renyuan Chuguo* (*Han Gangao*) *He Yaoqing Laihua Shixiang Shenpi De Shishi Banfa* (*Shixing*)), Promulgated by State Council Foreign Affairs office, State Planning Committee, State Commission for Restructuring the Economic System, State Council Production office on 31 March 1992.

[14] Article 2 of *the Provisional Measures on Administration of Government Sponsored Sports Technicians Exiting Abroad* 1992 (PRC) (*Guanyu Gongpai Chuguo (Jing) Tiyu Jishu Renyuan De Guanli Zaixing Banfa*), promulgated by State Sport Commission on 12 March 1990.

[15] Article 4 of *Provisional Rules on Some Issues of Government Sponsored Coaches Aid for Foreign Countries* 1990 (PRC) (*Guanyu Gongpai Yuanwai Jiaolian Renyuan Ruogan Wenti De Zaixing Guiding*), promulgated by State Sport Commission on 16 November 1990.

[16] Article 1 and 2 of *the Measures for the Implementation on Examination and Approval of Sending Employees to Temporally Exiting Abroad (Including Hong Kong and Macao) and Inviting Aliens to China by Industry Enterprises of the Ownership by the Whole People (for Trial Implementation)* 1993 (PRC) (*Quanmin Suoyouzhi Gongye Qiye Panqian Linshi Chuguo* (*Jing*) *Renyuan He Yaoqing Waiguo Jingmao Renyuan Laihua Shenpi De Shishi Banfa* (*Shixing*)), Promulgated by State Council Foreign Affairs office, the SHMO, State Commission of Economy and Trade and State Commission for Restructuring the Economic System on 29 June 1993.

[17] Article 2 of *the Provisional Detailed Rules of the Implementation of the Stipulations on Sending Term, Group and Individuals to be Trained Abroad* 1990 (PRC) (*Guanyu Paiqian Tuanzu He Renyuan Fu Guowai Peixun De Guanding De Zaixing Shishi Xize*), promulgated by State Council Introduction of Foreign Intellectuality Leading Panel office on 15 April 1990.

[18] Article 3 of *the Provisional Detailed Rules of the Implementation of the Stipulations on Sending Term, Group and Individuals to be Trained Abroad* 1990 (PRC) (*Guanyu Paiqian Tuanzu He Renyuan Fu Guowai Peixun De Guanding De Zaixing Shishi Xize*).

10. Individuals exiting China who have been selected by social mass Organisations;[19]
11. Contract workers who are sent abroad to execute agreements and arrangements concluded by the government with foreign countries;[20]
12. Contract workers selected by their work unit, which had entered into an agreement with a foreign party;[21]
13. Chinese citizens employed in foreign investment enterprises as the representatives of the foreign interest.[22]

This list details the extent to which elite members of Chinese society fall within the category of the public affairs passport. It means that, practically, most people who apply for passports must seek a public affairs passport. According to data from the State Bureau of Statistics (SBS), at the end of 2001, employees and staff in 72.41% of 'legal persons' (meaning organisations participating in civil activities on a legal basis) need to apply for a public affairs passport.[23] Of employed people 89.5% or 653.57 million are required to obtain a public affairs passport when applying to leave China in relation to travel associated with their work unit.[24] As

[19] Article 2 of *the Provisional Rules on Qualifications Recognition of Government Sponsored Institutions and Mass Organisations of Sending Group, Team and Individuals Abroad for Training* 1993 (PRC) (*Guanyu Shiye Danwei Shehui Tuanti Zuzhi Paiqian Tuanzu He Renyuan Fu Guo (Jing) Wai Peixun Gongzuo Zige Rending De Zaixing Guiding*).

[20] Article 8 Clause 1 Sub-clause 1 of *the Provisional Measures for the Procedures of Exiting Abroad Examination and Approval and Handling with Passport of Labours Sending Abroad* 1990 (PRC) (*Guanyu Waipai Laowu Renyuan Chuguo Shenpi Shouxu He Banli Huzhao De Zaixing Banfa*).

[21] Article 8 Clause 1 Sub-clause 2 of *the Provisional Measures for the Procedures of Exiting Abroad Examination and Approval and Handling with Passport of Labours Sending Abroad* 1990 (PRC) (*Guanyu Waipai Laowu Renyuan Chuguo Shenpi Shouxu He Banli Huzhao De Zaixing Banfa*).

[22] Article 4 of *the Reply of the Department of Consular under the MFA to Some Questions on Passport Affairs* 1993 (PRC).

[23] At the end of 2001, there were 5.1 million legal person units in China. 59.2% of these were enterprise legal person units, non-enterprises legal person unit account for 40.8%. Among enterprise legal person units, State-owned and collective-owned enterprise legal person units account for 53.4%. 40.8% + 59.2% × 53.4% = 72.41%. See State Bureau of the Statistics, "Gazette of Major Data of the Second Survey on National Basic Unit of Gazette of the Second Survey on National Basic Unit" (*Dierci Quanguo Jiben Danwei Pucha Gongbao: Dierci Quanguo Jiben Danwei Pucha Zhuyao Shuju Gongbao*) 17/01/2003, The Bureau of State Statistic, http://www.stats.gov.cn/tjgb/jbdwpcgb/qgjbdwpcgb/t20030117_61467.htm (accessed 12/09/2006).

[24] Calculated according to the date in State Bureau of the Statistics, 77.4% were employed by the governments, government-sponsored institutions, mass organizations, urban residents' committees, and village residents' committees. 11.1% were employed in

reported by *The China Daily* in 1996, 77.54% of individuals exiting China held a public affairs passport.[25] The percentage of people travelling on public affairs passports has gradually dropped to 39.4% of travellers in 2002.[26] Overall passport problems cannot be redressed, without resolving issues associated with the public affairs passport.

6.2.2 *Application procedures and examination criteria*

For most Chinese travelling on a public affairs passport, the prospect of complicated procedures and endless red tape, coupled with uncertain examination criteria, are an ordeal.[27] Article 2 of the *Circular of Organisation Department of the Central Committee of Chinese Communist Party on Strengthening Examination and Management on Individuals Exit China for Public Affairs (Extract)* 1989 (PRC) requires the various exit and entry examination authorities to seriously examine and strictly control applications for public affairs passports. For example, a fulltime student who is participating in a group exit, which was organised by a government department, must sit a national exam and satisfy various approval provisions set by the Department of International Cooperation and Exchange under the MOE and the Department of Consular Affairs under the MFA, prior to being granted permission to leave.[28] While these restrictions may prevent the

State-owned enterprises and collective-owned enterprises, "Gazette of Major Data of the Second Survey on National Basic Unit of Gazette of the Second Survey on National Basic Unit" (*Dierci Quanguo Jiben Danwei Pucha Gongbao: Dierci Quanguo Jiben Danwei Pucha Zhuyao Shuju Gongbao*) 17/01/2003, State Bureau of the Statistics, http://www.stats.gov.cn/tjgb/jbdwpcgb/qgjbdwpcgb/t20030117_61467.htm (accessed 12/09/2006); and the data from "Statistic Figures", http://www.china.org.cn/english/shuzi-en/en-shuzi/index.htm (accessed 09/05/2003), the number of employed people in China at the end of 2001 totalled 730.25 million.

[25] *The China Daily (Overseas version)*, 24 January 1997, Quoted in Huang, Ruilong, Bao, Sidun, Liu, Ling, "Overseas New Migrants over Last One Decade *(Jin Shinian Woguo Dalu Haiwai Xin Yimin)*", No. 1 [1998] *the Journal of Population & Economics (Renkou Yu Jingji*).

[26] State Bureau of the Statistics, *the Statistics Gazette of the People's Republic of China on 2002 National Economy and Social Development (Zhonghua Renmin Gongheguo 2002 Guomin Jingji he Shehui Tongji Gongbao)*, 28 February 2003, http://www.rctj.gov.cn/2003rctjnj/wzl.htm (accessed 16/09/2006).

[27] The ordeal imposed by the visa officers of some countries is a obstacle to enter into foreign countries.The further research is beyond the research scope of this book, and will be done in my future study.

[28] Article 5 of *the Circular of Ministries of Education, Public Security and Foreign Affairs on Some Affairs Regarding Fulltime Students Exit Abroad Short-term with Ordinary Passport for Private Affairs* 2002 (PRC) (*Jiaoyubu, Gonganbu, Waijiaobu Guanyu Zaixiao

expenditure of public funds on overseas travel, and serve to consolidate the communist regime, it is doubtful that such complicated procedures help protect RLR.

Ambiguous examination criteria create enormous scope for the examination authorities to exercise discretion. Vague criteria such as political reliability, loyalty, devotion to China, 'health in idea', 'decency in life style', and 'abidance of the rules' are applied.[29] They are non-legal terms but political propaganda terms (*Zhengzhi Shuyu*) in Chinese language. The examination and approval of public affairs passports is regarded as a task with high political sensitivity and the function of building and strengthening an honest and clean government.[30] Citizens who have not shown any sign of an improper political attitude will often find it easier to gain permission to exit. The time needed to obtain approval mainly depends on the contacts one has within the examination authorities, and bribery is not unknown because of the lack of precise processing period.

6.2.3 *Management of public affairs passports*

Since 1980, there has been unified management of public affairs passports. This management system was reinforced during the 1990s. Unified management means that relevant departments keep public affairs passports. The departments authorised to retain public affairs passports are prescribed by Articles 2 and 3 of the *Provisional Regulations on the Administration of ordinary passport for Public Affairs* 1993 (PRC). They include the foreign affairs departments of various ministries, enterprises and institutions under the direction of the State Council, national mass organisations, and provincial governments. These entities can delegate the power to retain passports to subordinate authorities. In addition, the work unit of the holder of a public affairs passport can also retain the passport.[31] In the case of re-use, individuals must present an introduction certificate issued by qualified employers unit to apply for permission.[32]

Xuesheng Duanqi Chuguo Chiyong Yinsi Huzhao Youguan Shixiang De Tongzhi), promulgated by the MOE, MPS and MFA on 25 January 2002.

[29] Article 2 of *the Circular of Organization Department of the Central Committee of Chinese Communist Party on Strengthening Examination and Management on Individuals Exit China for Public Affairs (Extract)* 1989 (PRC).

[30] Article 10 of *Related rules on Strengthening Examination and Approval of Exit China for Public Affairs (Extract)* (PRC) 1993 (*Guanyu Jiaqian Yingong Lingshi Chuguo (Jing) Shenpi He Guanli Gongzuo De Youguan Guiding (Zhaibian)*), promulgated by the General office of the Central Committee of the CPC and the General office of the State Council.

[31] Article 15 Clause 1 of the *Regulations on Passport and Visa* 1980 (PRC).

[32] Reuse of passport is prescribed in Article 6 Clause 4 of *the Circular of the Application for Passport and Visa for Individuals Temporally Exiting China in the Cause of their Duties* 1983 (PRC).

Individuals who breach the provisions for the management of public affairs passports receive serious punishment. Passports must be surrendered within a month of returning to China.[33] Failure to do so without reasonable excuse will result in a one- to three-year ban on being reissued with another. More seriously, the punishment may extend to the violators' leaders and colleagues; and the person who is responsible for collection of passports within work units will be punished if that person fails to collect a passport in a timely manner.[34] The practice of joint liability is viewed as outdated and widely criticised.[35] The denial of a colleagues' right to be granted a passport is an unsuitable penalty for the offence of failing to return a passport.

6.2.4 *Causes of the issues related to public affairs passports*

The existence of the public affairs passport can be seen as a consequence of the socialist system and public ownership of the economy. Based on this, all parties, mass organisations including trade unions, women's associations, academic associations, State-owned enterprises and institutions as well as various level governments, congresses, Courts and Procuratorates were under the leadership of the CPC. Their activities formed part of the State's activities. Their staffs were government officials or quasi-government officials; and travel in the course of their duties was carried out as much for their work unit as for the State. As such, they required a public affairs passport. However, according to international norms, public servants exit their national State in a private rather than public capacity, unless they are acting on behalf of the State in an official capacity, such as in foreign affairs or international relations. The function the person is to perform while overseas, rather than the character of the person's employment, determines the category of the passport.

---

[33] Article 10 of *the Provisional Regulations on the Administration of ordinary passport for Public Affairs* 1993 (PRC).

[34] Article 2 of *the Circular of the General office of the State Council on Transmission of the MFA and MPS on Some Issues of Timely Collection and Uniquely Keeping Passport of Individuals Exiting China in the Course of Their Duties and Strengthening Issuance Formality of the Certificate of Exiting China*, 1990 (PRC); the extension of the punishment of denying the colleagues of an individual who refused to return their passport is also prescribed by Article 10 of the *Provisional Regulations on the Administration of Ordinary Passport for Public Affairs* 1993 (PRC) and the Rules of State Council Administration for Affairs of State Organs on the Control of Passport 1990 (PRC).

[35] This practice of joint liability can be traced to the Xia Dynasty (2070 B.C. to 1600 B.C.), which is the first dynasty in China. See Yu, Shutong and Wen, Jia, Chief editors, *A New Chinese-English Law Dictionary (Xin Hanying Faxue Cidian)* (Beijing: Publishing House of Law, 1998), 513.

Until now, there has been no reform strategy to repeal the system in the near future. Maintaining the institution of public affairs passports will doubtlessly pose a great challenge to RLR in China. In May 2003, Luo Tianguang, the Director of the Department of Consular Affairs under the MFA, argued the reason to maintain the institution of public affairs passport:

> It is impossible to repeal the ordinary passport for public affairs in the present [because] the reform thinking of ordinary passport for public affairs is based on the careful consideration of China's actual situation and positive role of current ordinary passports for public affairs. The ordinary passport for public affairs could not be repealed unless it is very convenient for Chinese people exiting China to apply for visas within any [other passport] category.[36]

Yet the existence of public affairs passports does not equate with the ability to easily obtain a visa. The granting of a visa depends on a variety of conditions, of which the category of the relevant passport is only one, and it is not a decisive factor. The argument is unconvincing. Visas are also granted to holders of ordinary private passports. In 1984, the State Council recognised that foreign countries grant visas to Chinese nationals travelling on public affairs passports in light of their foreign policy towards China and the character of the functions of the applicant.[37] The balance between the positive and negative effects of the public affairs passport needs to be more carefully weighed.

6.3 Ordinary Passport for Private Affairs

Compared with public affairs passports, private passports are more popular in China. As of October 2002, more than 10,000 passports were issued daily by the MPS.[38] According to the Hainan Exit and Entry Administration in October 2003, the average national rate of private passport holders had increased to five in one thousand.[39] Nevertheless, the processing and management of private passports

---

[36] Quoted in Zhang, Jin "It is Impossible to Repeal Ordinary Passport for Public Affairs in the Present" (*Yingong Putong Huzhao Zaibu Quxiao*)", *Beijing Times*, 29 May 2003.

[37] Preface Par 2 of *the Circular of the State Council on Amending Article 6 of Regulations on Passport and Visa* (PRC) 1984 (*Guowuyuan Guanyu Xiuding Zhonghua Renmin Gongheguo Huzhao Qianzheng Tiaoli Diliutiao De Tonghzi*), promulgated by the State Council on 27 March 1984.

[38] Quoted in Wu, Inner, "Passport Gain Wider Currency in China", China Central Television, 15:10:23 17/10/2002, at English Channel http://www.cctv.com/news/China/FinanceABusiness/20021017/100400/html (accessed 18/04/2003).

[39] "Extension: Residents in Four Districts of Hainan Province May Apply for Passport Simpler" (*Fanwei Kuoda: Hainan Si Diqu Ke Jianhua Shenling Chuguo Huzhao Shouxu*), 21/10/2003, Xinhuanet, http://news.21cn.com/domestic/guoshi/2003/10/21/1309848.shtml (accessed 15/11/2003).

lags behind international standards. This section will discuss (i) the prohibition of non-registered resident area applications for private passports; (ii) application formalities for residents of small cities and rural areas; (iii) the retention of private passports by designated government departments; and (iv) the legality and effects of provisions regarding the revocation or invalidation of private passports.

6.3.1 *Prohibition of the application lodged in non-registered residential area*

According to Article 5 of the *Law on the Control Exit and Entry of Citizen* 1986 (PRC) and Article 3 Clause 1(1) of the *Detailed Rules for the Implementation of Law on the Control of Exit and Entry Citizens (Amendment)* 1994 (PRC), citizens must lodge an application for a private passport with the public security department in the place where they are a registered resident. It means that more than 120 million people are inconvenienced and forced to outlay considerable expense to apply for a private passport; and the efficiency of the exit and entry administration is reduced.[40] The Chinese government has noted this problem and adopted some measures, but has unfortunately failed to find a fundamental solution. As discussed in part 5.4, people from other provinces who work in Guangdong, Shanghai and Beijing may apply there for a private passport under some circumstances.

The household registration system introduced in 1958, and discussed in part 5.3 of this book, underlies the prohibition on applying for a passport outside an individual's registered residential area. In addition, there is no central database for issuing authorities in China. The prohibition ensures that a person may only hold one passport.

Cancelling the household registration will not resolve the issue, because the prohibition is not the corollary of the strict control of household registration, and citizens are unlikely to enjoy freedom of movement within the territory in the near future.[41] The establishment instead of a mutual information network that combines exit and entry information and household registration by 2005 will play a vital role in reducing the residential area limits on private passport applications.[42]

---

[40] There are more than 120 million migrant people in China. See "China at least 30 years away from zero population growth", http://english.peopledaily.com.cn/200312/30/eng20031230_131549.shtml (30/12/2003), *People's Daily*, (accessed 16/09/2006), and http://english.peopledaily.com.cn/200407/20/eng20040720_150248.html (20/06/2004), *People's Daily* (accessed 16/09/2006).

[41] Household registration system officials and experts have warned it takes a long time for crowded big cities in China to provide non-local residents with unrestricted access to residence. See "Residence System Reform Speeds up Human Resources Flow", 31 October 2001, *The People's Daily*, http://english.peopledaily.com.cn/200110/31/eng20011031_83627.html (accessed 30/12/2003).

[42] "State to Simplify Entry-exit Rules", 11/22/2002, *The China Daily*, http://www.chinadaily.com.cn/news/2001–11/22/content_94711.htm (accessed 16/09/2006).

6.3.2 *Over-elaborate formalities for residents in small cities and rural areas*

The reform strategy and measures simplifying over-elaborate formalities have been discussed in part 5.4 of this book. Its application has some costs. On the one hand, a simpler system will apply in medium and large cities. Local governments in these cities may lose some powers while their citizens will gain the right to a passport. At the very least, citizens will not need permission from their work unit or to pander to the person responsible for processing their private passport application.

On the other hand, the elaborate formalities will remain burdensome for citizens of small cities and rural areas. For example, a person in a small city may need to undertake a process whereby:

1. The applicant must obtain a private passport application form from the county exit and entry administration office upon presentation of their identity card.
2. The applicant may be required to ask their work unit head, or, if unemployed, the police from the town of registered residence, to comment on the application form; as well as requiring the applicant to ask the local Court or police to verify that they do not fall into any category by which they would be prohibited from exiting China.
3. The County exit and entry administration may accept the application after formally ensuring the form has been correctly filled in and all relevant authorities have commented on it.
4. The County level exit and entry administration then examine the application by verifying whether the relevant authorities comments are true, false or forged.
5. The County level exit and entry administration would make an initial decision about whether to approve the application.
6. If approved, the application would be transmitted to the municipal level exit and entry administration to make a fresh assessment.
7. The municipal level exit and entry administration would make a final decision whether to approve the application according to their processes of examination.
8. Finally, the passport may be issued by the municipal level exit and entry administration.

The time taken to process an application is also excessive. Under Article 5 Clause 1 of the *Detailed Rules for the Implementation of Law on the Control of Exit and Entry of Citizens* 1994 (PRC):

> The municipal or county public security bureau shall, within 30 days of receipt of the exit application, or within 60 days for rural areas or areas that are not easy to access, make a decision on approving of the exit application or not, and notify the applicant of the decision.

It actually takes much longer to fulfil the procedures because more time is needed to gain certificates from the relevant authorities and to transmit documents from county and municipal exit and entry administration offices.

The most often citied justification for the limits on application for private passports of residents in small cities and rural areas is their lower quality (*Wenhua Suzhi Bugou*). In the Chinese government's opinion the current quality of China's citizens means that citizens are not fit for more political rights. Premier Wen Jiabao has said, in an interview by Chief-editor of the *Washington Post* in November 2003, that the more positive political reform measures would not be adopted soon, due to the lower quality of Chinese nationals.[43] The right to be granted a passport that way becomes a political right – from the point of view of China's government, it is not a good time to endow all citizens with the right to be granted a passport.

In essence, maintaining the old system for residents in small cities and rural areas is a form of discrimination. As discussed in part 3.2.1 of this book, RLR is generally conceptualised as a right or freedom from the arbitrary interference of the State. The nature of RLR requires the State to accept citizens leaving and returning to the country, regardless of their place of residence. Although the State owes only minimum positive obligations to citizens, it does owe the citizens the obligation of furnishing them with a passport.

6.3.3 *Retention of passports by designated authorities*

Under the *Measures on Administration of Passport and Other Travel Abroad Documents of Officials Employed in Communist Party of China, Governments, Courts, Procuratorates, Justice Departments and Public Security Departments* 2003 (PRC), passports and other travel documents held by county level cadres (and above) are retained or withheld by the Personnel Department of the government or the Organization Department of a Committee of the CPC.[44] This means that this group of people cannot use their passport without approval from either of those two entities.[45] The primary reason for this requirement is to prevent corrupt officials from absconding from the territory with large sums of money.

---

[43] "The Premier of Wen, Jiabao Accepted the Interview of the Chief-editor of Washington Post" (*Wenjiabao Zongli Jieshou Huashendun Youbao Zhubian Caifang*), 23 November 2003, http://www.fmprc.gov.cn/chn/zxxx/t44934.htm (accessed 04/12/2003).

[44] Cadres in China means (1) officers of government institutions, military, or mass organizations; (2) personal who assume the office of leadership or management. See Dictionary Department, Institute of Linguistics, Chinese Academy of Social Sciences, *the Contemporary Chinese Dictionary (Chinese-English Edition)* (Beijing: Foreign Language Teaching and Research Press, 2002), 634.

[45] This system can be traced back to the *Regulations on Passport and Visa* 1980 (PRC)

According to Article 16 of the *Detailed Rule of the Implementation of Law on the Control of Exit and Entry of Citizens (Amendment)* 1994 (PRC):

> The Chinese passports and the Chinese travel permits, the major identification documents used by Chinese citizens for entering and leaving he country, shall be kept and used by the holders. No State departments, social Organizations, enterprises, government sponsored institutions or individuals shall withhold those certificates, other than the public security department and original issuing organ which shall have the power to revoke and retain the certificate according to law, and the Procuratorate and the Court which have the power to withhold the certificates according to law.

Yet the policy requiring the retention of private passports is invalid because CPC policy cannot prevail over relevant laws. Further, the retention of a passport based on the status of the holder is discriminatory and cannot be justified according to international norms. The practice restricts RLR of county (and above) level cadres.

The justification for retaining the passports of cadres on the grounds that they will abscond with large sums of money is anyway unconvincing. Not all will abscond with large sums of money. Those who do can be arrested and charged with criminal offences before leaving China. If it is acceptable to retain the passports of all regulated cadres, because some possibly abscond abroad. This begs the question of how the rights of innocent cadres are protected. The legitimacy and effectiveness of provisions, which safeguard the interests of the State by damaging the interests of innocent people, is obviously questionable.

6.3.4 *Revocation of passports or declaring passports invalid*

Revocation of a passport, or declaring it invalid, as a serious punishment for passport-related offences, is seldom exercised, as it deprives or limits RLR. By international norms, there are very few circumstances in which a passport can be revoked or invalidated. According to Article 22 of the *Detailed Rules for the Implementation of Law on the Control of Exit and Entry of Citizens (Amendment)* 1994 (PRC), passports can be revoked or declared invalid in China when:

(1) The holder has been sent back to China because he or she illegally entered, resided or stayed in the country of destination;
(2) The holder has used their passport or other overseas travel documents for the purpose of swindling and bluffing; or

Article 16 Clause 2 of which stipulates that individuals exiting China for private affairs shall return their passport to the public security department that issued the passport after they return to China. With the significant increase of individuals exiting China for private affairs, this practice has been practically repealed since 1987.

(3) The holder has engaged in activities prejudicial to the security, honour and the interests of the State.

The decision to revoke or invalidate passports or other overseas travel documents is made by the original issuing departments or its higher authorities.

These circumstances are detailed in Article 22 Clause 1 of the *Measures on the Administration of Chinese Citizens Tours Broad (Amendment)* 2002 (PRC). Specifically, Chinese "tourists are strictly prohibited from staying abroad and failing to return to China." Article 32 Clause 2 further provides "where a tourist stays abroad and fails to go back home, and is repatriated, their passport is revoked by the public security department".

It may be argued that the grounds for the first rule are justified. The illegal activities of entry, residence or continued presence in a foreign country violate the immigration laws of those States. Destination States can punish illegal immigrants by deportation, and prohibiting them from re-entering the territory for a set period. However, the principle of double jeopardy, whereby a person should not be punished twice for the same offence, means that the originating State should not punish its national for breaches of foreign laws for which they have already been punished by the foreign State. The provision is also incongruous with international norms. Article I (d) of the 1963 UN Draft Principles on RLR stipulates that

> The right of every national to leave one's country shall in no case be exercised contrary to the purposes and principles of the UN. This right shall be subject only to such limits as are determined by law solely for the purpose of securing due recognition and respect for the rights and freedoms of others and of meeting the just requirements of national security, public order, health or morals and the general welfare in a democratic society. Any limit that may be imposed shall not be aimed at destroying the right and shall be consistent with the purposes and principles of the UN.

It is uncertain whether the illegal activities of entering, residing or staying in a foreign country constitute a clear and present danger to the original State's national security, public order, health or morals, and general welfare. Consequently, it cannot be regarded as an acceptable reason to revoke or invalidate a passport.

Close attention must be paid to the second ground for revocation or invalidation. Where the use of one's passport or other overseas travel documents for the purpose of swindling and bluffing constitutes a crime according to *Criminal Law (Amendment)* 1997 (PRC), defendants are to be investigated for criminal responsibility; and prevented from exiting China on the ground that he or she is a suspect in a criminal matter as confirmed by a public security department, Procuratorate or a Court under Article 8 Clause 1(1) of the *Law on the Control of Exit and Entry of Citizens* 1985 (PRC). As such, this ground appears to be unnecessary.

Where an act does not warrant criminal punishment, it can be dealt with by way of administrative penalty by under Article 2 of the *Regulations on the Administrative Penalties for Public Security (Amendment)* 1994 (PRC), Article 14 of the *Law on the Control of Exit and Entry of Citizens* 1985 (PRC) and Article 24 of the *Detailed Rules for the Implementation of Law on the Control of Exit and Entry of Citizens (Amendment)* 1994 (PRC). An act that has minor adverse effects is not to be used as a basis for prohibiting exit and entry under Article 8 of the *Law on the Control of Exit and Entry of Citizens* 1985 (PRC). The weight of analysis suggests this provision is invalid. In practice, with the change in the status of the passport from a mark of privilege to a document of identity, the possibility of using a passport or other travel document for swindling and bluffing is extremely low, and as such, the provision should be repealed.

6.4 Conclusions

There are several bureaucratic barriers to RLR posed by the formalities of passport application and passport administration. The categories, scope and issuing authorities for passports in China are relatively unique in the world. Besides diplomatic passports and service passports, public affairs passport and private passports also exist. The scope of the first three categories has been intentionally broadened, and the scope of private passport narrowed. A variety of government authorities execute the power to issue passports. Different criteria adopted by passport processing authorities create a loophole in which a person can apply for a passport more than once.

Passport laws are inconsistent and outdated. The Chinese government has not amended passport laws or promulgated a new passport law for 25 years, within which time exit and entry administration has experienced the most significant change in China's history and a range new regulations and policies related to passports have been published. Public confidence in the dignity and integrity of passport laws is therefore undermined.

The issues surrounding public affairs passports attract more attention, not merely because of the category being special by world standards, but because 89.5% or 653.57 million employed people must obtain a public affairs passport when applying to leave China in relation to travel associated with their employers,[46] and 39.4% of all people going abroad held public affairs passports

[46] Calculated according to the State Bureau of the Statistics data, 77.4% were employed by the governments, government-sponsored institutions, mass organisations, urban residents' committees, and village residents' committees. 11.1% were employed in State-owned enterprises and collective-owned enterprises, "Gazette of Major Data of the Second Survey on National Basic Unit of Gazette of the Second Survey on National Basic Unit" (*Dierci Quanguo Jiben Danwei Pucha Gongbao: Dierci Quanguo Jiben Danwei Pucha Zhuyao Shuju Gongbao*) 17/01/2003, The Bureau of State Statistic, http://www.stats.gov.cn/tjgb/jbdwpcgb/qgjbdwpcgb/t20030117_61467.htm (accessed 12/09/2006); and the data from "Statistic Figures", http://www.china.org.cn/english/shuzi-en/en-shuzi/index.htm (accessed 09/05/2003), the number of employed people in China at the end of 2001 totalled 730.25 million.

in 2002.[47] Non-legal terms or political propaganda terms exist in the provisions of passport examination criteria. Ambiguous examination criteria alongside complicated application procedures, and a stress on strict political examination and unified management, make the exit of most Chinese on a public affairs passport an ordeal. Unfortunately, the reform of the public affairs passport regime is not yet on the Chinese government's agenda.

Despite planned reforms of over elaborate private passport application formalities for residents in large and medium sized cities, at least 120 million Chinese people have to spend unnecessary money and time on travelling between their living area and registered resident area when applying for a private passport, due to the prohibition on non-registered resident area applications. All county level cadres (and above) are unreasonably required to submit passports and other travel documents to designed authorities. Most of the grounds for the revocation or invalidation of passports have been proved to be gratuitous and might be dealt with instead under criminal law. There is a clearly long way to go before the Chinese authorities fully relax their control over the granting of passports to their citizens.

---

[47] The State Bureau of the Statistics "Gazette of the Statistics of Economic and Social Development of the People's Republic of China of 2002" (*Zhonghua Renmin Gongheguo 2002 Guomin Jingji He Shehui Tongji Gongbao*), 28 February 2003, http://www.rctj.gov.cn/2003rctjnj/wzl.htm (accessed 16/09/2006).

Chapter Seven
The Right to Leave of Chinese Citizens

INTRODUCTION

As indicated in Chapter five, since 1992 the Chinese government has adopted a series of reforms to simplify complex passport application procedures. Nevertheless, when compared to international norms analysed in part 3.3 of this book, several limits on the right to leave still exist.

7.1 GENERAL LIMITS ON THE RIGHT TO LEAVE OF CHINESE CITIZENS

The general provisions to be considered in this section form the legal basis for limiting the right to leave of citizens. The permissibility of those provisions will be discussed according to the appropriateness of the limits and the legal validity of interpretative provisions. The legitimacy of authorities providing prerequisite certificates will be discussed in part 7.3.3.

7.1.1 *Contents of general limits on the right to leave of Chinese citizens*

The foremost provision in this area is Article 8 of the *Law on the Control of Exit and Entry of Citizens* 1985 (PRC). It provides that:

> Approval to exit the country shall not be granted to persons belonging to any of the following categories:
>
> (1) Defendants in criminal cases or criminal suspects confirmed by a public security department, a People's Procuratorate or a People's Court;
> (2) Persons who, as notified by a People's Court, shall be denied exit owing to involvement in unresolved civil cases;
> (3) Convicted persons serving their sentences;
> (4) Persons undergoing rehabilitation through labour; and
> (5) Persons whose exit from the country will, in the opinion of the responsible department of the State Council, be harmful to State security or cause a major loss to national interests.

Article 6 clauses 3 of the *Explanation of the MPS on Some Issues on Implementation of Law on the Control of Exit and Entry of Citizens and Its Detailed Rules for the Implementation* 1987 (PRC) interprets that:

> (3) The reference to "approval to exit the country shall not be granted to persons whose exit from the country will, in the opinion (*Yijian*) of the responsible department of the State Council, be harmful to State security" in Sub-clause 5 shall be examined and approved by provincial public security departments or provincial national security departments. The reference to "persons whose exit from the country will cause a major loss to national interests" in Sub-clause 5 is to the persons who know important secrets of politics, military, technology and economy of the CPC and the governments, who, in the opinions of responsible departments of the Central Committee of the CPC, the State Council, the Central Military Commission and provincial level CPC commission, the governments and military departments, should not be granted approval to exit the country. Under this circumstance, public security departments or national security departments shall ask the approval from relevant departments before deciding whether to approve applications for leaving China. . . .
> (4) . . . known secrets expire, involve persons may be granted to exit China.

Another basic provision is to prevent defaulting taxpayers from leaving China.[1]

---

[1] Article 44 of *the Law on the Administration of Tax Collection (Amendment)* 2001 (PRC) regulates 'should a taxpayer who has not paid or has underpaid the amount of tax payer need to leave China, they shall settle the amount of tax payable with, or provide a guarantee to the tax authorities before leaving the country. If the taxpayer neither settles the amount of tax payable nor provides a guarantee, the tax authorities may notify the exit administration authorities to prevent the taxpayer from leaving the country." the Measures for *the Implementation on Preventing Defaulting Taxpayer from Exiting China* 1997 (PRC) detail the relevant procedures of preventing defaulting taxpayer leaving China. The Measures apply to all defaulting taxpayers, including Chinese citizens and aliens. According to the Measures, the formalities must be completed within 24 hours of the tax office learning of the taxpayer's intention to leave China and the tax office must send a member of its staff to the taxpayer's workplace.

7.1.2 *Appropriateness of the limits*

Compared to the recognised grounds for limiting the right to leave (discussed in part 3.4.2), the above prohibitions are appropriate in principle. However, there are no objective criteria against which 'harm to the State' or 'causing a major loss to national interests' can be judged. By international norms, knowing secrets cannot be an acceptable limit on the right to leave, especially when the persons have been discharged from active service.[2] It is also unclear as to what criteria are applied by administrative departments to make a decision, or what procedures are followed to create an opinion.

The absence of criteria leads to excessive administrative discretion. An example can be found in the limitations based on the outbreak of the SARS. The Chinese governments took measures to prohibit nationals from going abroad during the spring of 2003. Passengers could travel overseas after confirming they were free of the symptoms of the SARS, or were strongly urged to cancel their travel plans and seek medical treatment. It is generally accepted that the SARS was a risk to public health. However, it is uncertain what constitutes a 'risk' in the absence of detailed domestic interpretation.

7.1.3 *Legal validity of interpretative provisions*

According to Article 90 Clause 2 of the *Constitution of PRC (Amendment)* 2004, the *Explanation of the MPS on Some Issues on Implementation of Law on the Control of Exit and Entry of Citizens and Its Detailed Rules for the Implementation* 1987 (PRC) and the *Some Rules on the Issues of Prohibiting Aliens and Chinese Citizens from Exiting Chinas and Chinese Citizens* 1987 (PRC) are of questionable legitimacy.

The *Law on the Control of Exit and Entry of Citizens* 1985 (PRC) was promulgated by the Standing Committee of the National People's Congress (NPC). According to the hierarchy of Chinese laws, it prevails over laws of the State Council and its ministries.[3] The *Explanation of the MPS on Some Issues on Implementation of Law on the Control of Exit and Entry of Citizens and Its Detailed Rules for the Implementation* 1987 (PRC) was promulgated by the Ministry of Public Security (MPS). Article 6 clauses 3 and 4 of the explanation 1987 does not conform to Article 8 Clause 5 of the *Law on the Control of Exit and Entry of Citizens* 1985 (PRC). Thus, the decisions of the prohibition to exit are based on invalid legal basis. According to Article 88 Clause 1(3) of the *Law of Legislation* 2000 (PRC) the inconsistencies between the subordinate rules and

---

[2] For details, please see part 3.4.3 of this book.

[3] Article 67 Clause 1 (7), Article 89 Clause 1 (1) and Article 90 Clause 2 of *the Constitution of the PRC (Amendment)* 2004.

ministerial explanations with the primary laws can be also investigated and corrected by the State Council.

7.2 Special limits on the right to leave of Chinese citizens

7.2.1 *Overseas employment: skilled emigration*

Under Article 13 of the *Provisional Rules on the Administration of Sino-Foreign Joint Venture Skilled Personnel Intermediary Agency* 2003 (PRC), that:

> . . . Recruitment of the following personnel for employment abroad is not allowed:
>
> (1) Technical and management personnel undertaking State or provincial level key engineering or scientific research projects who have not obtained approval from the competent unit or department;
> (2) Serving government officials;
> (3) Personnel sent by the State to develop the western region whose term has not expired;
> (4) Secret service personnel still in service or no longer in service but are still bound by the confidentiality clause;
> (5) People under legal investigation;
> (6) People holding special posts who are temporarily prohibited by law from leaving the country or are subject to approval for leaving the country.

Additionally, under Article 3 of the *Provisional Rules on Attendance of Games or Competitions Abroad by Employment of Athletes* 1989 (PRC) retired athletes from national sports teams shall not be granted approval to be employed to attend games or competitions abroad, unless they are female athletes over 26 years old, or male athletes over 28 years old. In accordance with Article 3 Clause 1(1)(4) of the *Provisional Rules on Some Issues of State Dispatched Coaches Aid for Foreign Countries* 1990 (PRC) coaches and athletes cannot be employed abroad unless the coach is over the age of 50, and the athlete is over the age of 35, and they have a 'firm stand in politics' and 'live in an honest style'.

These provisions reflect concerns about the outflow of trained professional personnel. However, their aim is not achieved. Being discriminatory, they infringe on the right to leave, as per the principles outlined in part 3.3.1 of this book.

Social disruption and the attraction of a foreign country can spur skilled emigration. Social disruption caused by economic restructuring encourages people to look abroad for opportunities. The direct cause of most professional emigration is that suitable employment cannot be found in China.[4] The loss of an opportunity

---

[4] "The ability to find good jobs and earn much higher pay is the prime reason people are emigrating today." See "Globalization Affects Global Immigration", Book Review,

to work overseas may adversely affect a person's skills and knowledge, which is as much to the detriment of the individual as to the State that wants to retain them. Bill Gates has said that one of the strengths of the US economy is its ability to attract the best and the brightest from India, China and other countries.[5] Germany, France, Canada, Australia and South Korea adopt many programs aimed at attracting skilled immigrants to make up for local shortfalls.[6] From an international perspective, skilled emigration is a manifestation of human resource restructuring. It is an essential part of globalisation. The pattern of skilled emigration is not unique to China. The same issue faces all developing countries with an open economic policy. Therefore, if China intends to integrate into the world, and accept the consequences of modernisation and globalisation, the restructuring of human resource cannot be avoided.

The accepted legal solution to the 'brain drain' is to amend relevant laws to 'remove' (*Shu*) the barriers to keep potential skilled emigrants within the territory rather than to 'block' (*Du*) them to exit. In fact, the grounds for refusing to permit skilled nationals from leaving China will not stem the outflow. Recruitment through Sino-foreign joint venture personnel agencies is among a number of channels through which an overseas job can be sought. A person can resign from a job, which has placed them within one of the prohibited categories, and seek employment independently. 'Removing' creates an environment in which professionals are encouraged to remain in China and to attract people who are overseas to return or immigrate.

7.2.2 *Overseas pilgrimage*

The freedom of religious belief is acknowledged in China.[7] However there are three main limits on the right to leave China for the purpose of pilgrimage – which affect the freedom of religion and also RLR.

Workers Without Frontiers – the Impact of Globalization on International Migration, Stalker, Peter, International Labour Organization, 2000, http://www.blackwell-synergy.com/doi/abs/10.1111/1467-7660.00327?cookieSet=1&journalCode=dech (accessed 16/09/2006).

[5] "Economist: WTO entry changes much", 10/01/2000, *China Daily*, http://www.chinadaily.com.cn/chinagate/doc/2000-01/10/content_247755.htm (accessed 16/09/2006).

[6] "Talents Competition in New Century: Positive Measures in USA and Quick Reply in other Countries" (*Xinshiji Rencaizan: Meiguo Jiji Xina, Geguo Jinji Yingdui*), 09/12/2003, *Technology Daily*, http://www.hebei.com.cn/node2/node17/node1069/userobjectlai176518.html (accessed 16/09/2006).

[7] Article 36 of *the Constitution of the PRC (Amendment)* 2004 provides that "citizens of the People's Republic of China enjoy freedom of religious belief [and that] the State protects normal religious activities."

Firstly, individuals cannot freely go abroad for the purpose of pilgrimage. According to Article 4 of the *Circular of State Council Bureau for Religion Affairs, State Administration of Foreign Exchange, Ministry of Foreign Affairs, Ministry of Public Security, Bank of China, Customs General Administration and Civil Aviation Administration of China on Several Rules of Self-support Pilgrimage Abroad Administration (Amendment)* 1995 (PRC) (Circular of Pilgrimage Abroad 1995), individuals desiring to go on an overseas pilgrimage must start at Urumqi or Beijing. Secondly, the Chinese government has imposed a quota of 2,000 people per year who are permitted to take part in a pilgrimage.[8] Lastly, Article 3 of the Circular of Pilgrimage Abroad 1995 establishes that individuals who have made an overseas pilgrimage since 1979 shall not be granted permission to participate in an overseas pilgrimage again, and those who are likely to use the pilgrimage to do business or study abroad; or are over the age of 65, pregnant, senile, or seriously ill, are prohibited from travelling for this purpose.

The Chinese government has recognised that leaving China for the purpose of a pilgrimage is a normal religious activity.[9] Thus the obvious bias of restrictions is either in ignorance of international norms of the right to leave or the recognition serves purely as rhetorical propaganda.

7.2.3 *Overseas religious study*

Although the right of education has been accepted in Article 46 of the Constitution and thousands of students have studied abroad over the past two decades,[10] limits on overseas religious study remain, though in practice the limits are often ignored.

Chinese citizens are prohibited from receiving financial support from foreign missionaries (*Chuanjiao Jingfei*) to study abroad at religious institutions or to

---

[8] Article 1 (quota) and Article 3 (age) of t*he Circular of State Council Bureau for Religion Affairs, State Administration of Foreign Exchange, the MFA, MPS, Bank of China, Customs General Administration and Civil Aviation Administration of China on Several Rules of Self-support Pilgrimage Administration (Amendment)* 1995 (PRC).

[9] Preface of *the Circular of State Council Bureau for Religion Affairs, State Administration of Foreign Exchange, the MFA, MPS, Bank of China, Customs General Administration and Civil Aviation Administration of China on Several Rules of Self-support Pilgrimage Administration (Amendment)* 1995 (PRC) (*Guowuyuan Zongjiao Shiwuju Guojia Waihui Guanliju Waijiao Gonganbu Zhongguo Yinghang Haiguan Zongshu Mingyong Hangkong Zongju Guanyu Zifei Chaojing Ruogan Guiding De Tongzhi*).

[10] Official statistics show that in the past two decades, approximately 400,000 Chinese students have gone to 103 countries to study, making China the world's largest source of students studying overseas. See "China Sees Tide of Returning Talents", 29/06/2002, *The People's Daily*, http://service.china.org.cn/link/wcm/Show_Text?info_id=35844&p_qry=immigration (accessed 24/04/2003).

study religion at higher education institutions in foreign countries, under Article 3 of the *Circular of State Education Commission, State Council Bureau for Religions Affairs, Ministry of Public Affairs and Ministry of Foreign Affairs on Dealing with Some Issues of Recruiting Students Studying Abroad in China without Permission by Certain Departments and Individuals in China of Foreign Countries and International Organizations* 1990 (PRC). In accordance with the *Circular on Some Noteworthy Issues of Moslem Foreign Affairs* 1990 (PRC) the State Council Bureau for Religious Affairs is responsible for examination, approval and dispatch of Muslims students to study at foreign religious institutions, on the basis of a report from the Chinese Muslim Association. Where Chinese citizens lodge the application for self-funded study at religious educational institutions of Muslim countries, the public security departments will not accept their application unless they present an approval letter issued from provincial level religious authorities. The latter requirement was reiterated in 1996.[11]

The government's official position is that the restrictions on studying religion overseas are justified on the basis of avoiding interference to interior religious matters, avoiding religious infiltration, introducing new religions, and protecting China against hostile forces that may destroy the unity of Chinese nationality.[12] This essentially paranoid thinking can be traced to left-leaning policy, a poor economic environment, frequent political movements and hostility towards China by foreign countries prior to 1977.[13] Compared to the freedom to study in other disciplines, prohibitions on studying religious courses abroad are discriminatory. From the point of view of the right to leave, any discrimination on the grounds of studying is hardly justifiable.

7.2.4 *Limits on the right to leave based on the applicants' special status*

The right to leave can also be limited according to the applicant's kinship relationship, social status, health and gender – all unjustifiable grounds. Family members of wanted suspects and traitors are not permitted to leave China according to

---

[11] Article 3 Clause 3 (3) of *the Operational Norms of Application, Examination and Approval of Exiting China and Passport For Private Affairs of Citizens* 1996 (PRC).

[12] Preface Par. 1 of *the Circular of State Education Commission, State Council Bureau for Religions Affairs, the Ministry of Public Affairs and the MFA on Dealing with Some Issues of Recruiting Students Studying Abroad in China without Allowance by Certain Organizations in China and Individuals of Foreign Countries and International Organizations* 1990 (PRC) (*Guojia Jiaowei Guowuyuan Zongjiaoju Gonganbu Waijiaobu Guanyu Chuli Mouxie Guojia He Guoji Zuzhi De Zhuhua Jigou Ji Geren Shanzi Zaihua Zaoshou Liuxuesheng Wenti De Tonhzhi*).

[13] See part 6.3 of this book.

the *Circular of the MPS on Temporarily not Granting Permission to the Application for Exit of China of Domestic Family Members of Wanted Suspects and Traitors* 1991 (PRC).[14] Spouses and the adult children of staff of embassies and consulates in foreign countries may only visit relatives abroad once a year for no more than a month at a time, pursuant to *Provisional Measures for the Control of Self-funded Visiting Their Relatives who are the Staff of Embassies and Consulates General in Foreign Countries of Adult Children and Spouse* 1999 (PRC).

More limits are imposed on the individuals with the status of cadre and police. In the first place, cadres in active service at a departmental, bureau or municipality level or over are not permitted to exit China for private affairs on short trips. The principle of the management of the exit and entry of cadres is to handle sternly the application of leading cadres in active service, retired cadres and retired, veteran cadres respectively, to less sternly handle the application of leading cadres of the CPC and the government and non-CPC and the government respectively, and to handle leniently the application of cadres with and without the membership of the CPC.[15] The approval of the provincial level or ministerial level party Committees of the CPC must be received if cadres wish to permanently emigrate.[16] Cadres in active service at a divisional or county level, and their families, are not permitted to visit anyone outside the territory other than spouse, child or parent. This class of applicants is not permitted to take leave from their work in order to go abroad for personal overseas travel.[17] Senior retired cadres must gain approval from the party Committee of the CPC or a provisional or ministerial authority before leaving the territory.[18] The applications of police personnel to exit for

[14] *The Circular of the MPS on Temporal Prohibition on Exit China Application of Domestic Family Members of Wanted Suspects and Betrayal Criminals* 1991 (PRC), promulgated by the MPS in 1991 Gongtongzi No. (1991) 13.

[15] *The Circular on Some Matters of Examining and Management of Individuals Exiting and Entering for Private Affairs* 1999 (PRC).

[16] *The Circular of Department of Cadres under the Central Committee of Communist Party of China on Issues of Examination and Approval of Exiting China for Private Affairs of Senior Cadres* 1992 (PRC), "Cadres in active service of deputy provincial or ministerial level or over, including cadres in the processing of resign, shall not be granted to exit abroad for private affairs in principle. The Department of Cadres under Central Committee of CPA will examine and approval if special." Also see articles 3 and 7 of *the Circular on Some Matters of Examining and Management of Individuals Exiting and Entering for Private Affairs* 1999 (PRC).

[17] Article 4 Clauses 2 and 3 of the *Circular on Some Matters of Examining and Management of Individuals Exiting and Entering for Private Affairs* 1999 (PRC).

[18] Article 2 of *the Circular of Department of Cadres under the Central Committee of Communist Party of China on Issues of Examination and Approval of Leaving China for Private Affairs of Senior Cadres* 1992 (PRC) and the Department of Cadres under Central

private affairs or to marry aliens is not be approved unless they have been discharged from active service and the life of secrets know to them has expired.[19]

Applications to exit China can also be rejected on the grounds of ill health, senility or pregnancy.[20] If the health of the applicant poses a risk to public health, the prohibition may be permissible from an international perspective, but it is difficult to see how pregnancy, senility and normal sickness present such a risk. Young women are strictly forbidden to leave China in order to work as hairdressers, in dance halls, bars, entertainment venues or massage parlours under the *Reiteration of Strictly Forbidding of Sending Young Women to Abroad to Provide Erotic Services in the Name of Work* 1997 (PRC), the broad terms of which are very odd and insulting to women by any western perspective. However these women, once granted approval to leave China for some other purposes, can of course switch to a prohibited form of employment once in the foreign country. More importantly, the limits on the right to leave cannot be grounded on the assumption that women may go abroad for employment in an erotic service industry.

7.3 Prerequisite Certificates from the Departments in which the Applicants are Employed (*Gongzuo Danwei Yijian Qianzhi*)

Individuals are required to obtain the certificates of the department in which they are employed before lodging an application to leave China (the prerequisite certificates). This applies to normal applicants as well as those with a special identity. The prerequisite certificates for normal applicants[21] have been relaxed in

Committee of the CPA. The maximum period of exiting abroad is half year. Article 6 Clauses 1 and 3 of *the Circular on Some Matters of Examining and Management of Individuals Exiting and Entering for Private Affairs* 1999 (PRC).

[19] The period of secrets expiration is three years for top secret, two years for important secret and one year for secret under Article 3 of *the Circular of the Political Department of the Ministry of Public Security on Some Detailed Issues of Polices Leaving China for Private Affairs and Marry Aliens* 1992 (PRC).

[20] According to Article 5 Clause 4 of *Provisional Measures for the Administration of China National Tourism Administration on Departments of Tour to Thailand, Singapore and Malaysia* 1990 (PRC) those who are too senile to look after themselves, or are more than seven months pregnant are not permitted to travel to Thailand, Singapore or Malaya. Article 3 of the Circular of Pilgrimage Abroad 1995 regulate that the applicant must be evidenced healthy with the certificate of health examination issued by county level or over hospital.

[21] Article 1 Clause 2 of *the Explanation of Sixth Bureau of the MPS on Issues of Providing Comments of Employed the Organization Where the Applicant is Services of Citizens Exiting China,* 1989 (PRC) (*Gonganbu Liuju Guanyu Gongmin Shenqing Chuguo Tijiao Suozai Gongzuo Danwei Yijian Wenti De Shuoming*).

accordance with the reform strategy discussed in Chapter five, while the need of prerequisite certificates for applicants with a special identity remains. According to Su Qiang, an official of BEEA, "there are still some people, including government officials who cannot benefit from the new policy, considering national security and other interests."[22] The emphasis of the remainder of this section is on the prerequisite certificates imposed on applicants with a special identity, in particular, its' scope and questions.

7.3.1 *The scope of the prerequisite certificates*

The scope of the prerequisite certificates is very broad for applicants with a special identity. Under Article 2 of the *Suggestions of the MPS on Some Issues Concerning the Execution of Law of Exit and Entry of Citizens* 1985 (PRC) *and its Detailed Rules of the Implementation* 1987 (PRC):

1. Members of the CPC, military personnel (. . .) and public security personnel leaving China for private affairs shall firstly undergo interior examination and approval procedure of the CPC, military and public security departments in accordance with separated department system [. . .]
2. Key scientific and technical members of professional staff (. . .) who have applied to exit China in order to permanently reside abroad shall firstly ask for approval from the responsible departments of the Central Committee of the CPC, the State Council and provincial governments. The public security departments will then accept, examine and approve the application;
3. Ex-service army-personnel who have transferred to civilian work, and who possessed [. . .] important military secrets must ask for the certificates of their previous army service unit, and may not leave China within five years of ceasing their military duties;
4. Above provisions apply to exit to Hong Kong and Macao.

Persons with other special identities also meet the requirements for a prerequisite certificate under Article 4 of the *Detailed Rules for Implementing of the Law on the Control of Exit and Entry of Citizens (Amendment)* 1994 (PRC). Rather than being narrowed by the reforms, requirements were affirmed in 2002. The affirmation differed in its detail across regions, but was essentially similar. As relevant updated circulars of the MPS are not publicly available, the following evidence is based on a review of official reports and official online instructions for passport applications. For Shanghai, according to online instructions for ordinary passport applications from the Shanghai Exit and Entry Administration:

[22] Xiao, Xin, "Passport Application Simplified", 21/08/2003, *The China Daily*, http://www.chinadaily.com.cn/en/doc/2003–08/21/content_256754.htm (accessed 16/09/2006).

> Certificate from the departments where the applicant is in service is needed for applicants with the following identities:
>
> (1) Municipal level or over government cadres or retired cadres;
> (2) Government cadres at an intermediate level;
> (3) Personnel holding key positions in government departments and State-owned enterprises, working in the [key fields];
> (4) Staff in the Shanghai office of a central government department or Shanghai office of a provincial or metropolitan authority who holds one of the abovementioned positions.[23]

The Column of Comments of the Departments where the applicant is in service of Special Identity Applicants (*Teding Shenfen Shenqingren Zhi Danwei Yijianlan*) has been inserted into the Application Form for Ordinary Passport of the PRC (Shanghai Version) (*Zhonghua Renmin Gongheguo Putong Huzhao Shenlingbiao*) (Shanghai), which was produced by the BEEA in 2002.

In the case of Guangdong under the online instructions for ordinary passport application in Guangdong province, a broader interpretation is attributed to the term 'special identity applicants' than that attributed in Shanghai:

> Certificate from the departments where the applicant is in service is needed for applicants with the following identities:
>
> (1) Retired intermediate (department or county) level cadres;
> (2) Serving officials in State departments;
> (3) Members of the lading panel and Chief Financial Officer of State-owned enterprises;
> (4) Individuals with senior professional titles in higher education, research and medical institutions;
> (5) Individuals with special identities in the banking and insurance industries;
> (6) Military officers leaving China for private affairs.
>
> Certificate from the departments where the applicant is in service is needed for following affairs:
>
> (1) Members of a tour group;
> (2) Fulltime students in secondary schools and higher education institutions;
> (3) Self-funded individuals with associate college degrees studying abroad;
> (4) Individuals attending an overseas religious course;
> (5) Children adopted by aliens who leaving China permanently;
> (6) Individuals who have obtained overseas employment via an overseas employment intermediate agency;
> (7) Individuals who have obtained overseas employment via a labour service agency;
> (8) Individuals leaving China for cultural exchange.[24]

---

[23] "Applying for the Passport", http://gaj.sh.gov.cn/shpolice (accessed 06/01/2004).

[24] Exit and Entry Administration of Guangdong Public Security Department, "Exit of Chinese Citizens" (Zhongguo Gongmin Chuguo), http://www.gdcrj.com/zggmcg/CHINAGMISSS/index.htm (accessed 16/09/2006).

Given most applicants' special identities are government officials, Quanzhou in Fujian Province, has a specially designed Application Form for Leaving China for Private Affairs for Government Officials (*Guojia Gongzuo Renyuan Yinsi Chuguo (Jing) Shenqingbiao*).[25] This issue do not attract the attention of the authorities, as discussed in part 5.5 of this book.

7.3.2 *Questions on the prerequisite certificates*

The legal basis of the prerequisite certificates contained in the *Detailed Rules for Implementing of the Law on the Control of Exit and Entry of Citizens (Amendment)* 1994 (PRC) and recent reforms is questionable. Article 8 of the *Law on the Control of Exit and Entry of Citizens* 1985 (PRC) provides that exit approval shall only be withheld from five categories of applicants, and that all other applications are to be approved. However the description in part 7.3.1 above shows that public security departments shall not accept or approve exit applications unless the requirements of the prerequisite certificates are fulfilled. The requirements of prerequisite certificates thus contradict the *Law on the Control of Exit and Entry of Citizens* 1985 (PRC).

Secondly, the departments where the applicant is employed are not entitled to make certificates. According to Article 5 of the *Law on the Control of Exit and Entry of Citizens* 1985 (PRC), Chinese citizens who want to leave for private purposes need to apply to the public security department. The department is the sole agency responsible for making a determination. No reference is made to a requirement for additional certificates or consultation between the public security department and other government instrumentalities.

Article 1(5) of the *Law on the Control of Exit and Entry of Citizens* 1985 (PRC) expressly provides that a determination of whether the exit of an individual would be harmful to State security or cause a major loss to national interests, is to be made by the responsible departments of the State Council. The Central Committee of the CPC, the Central Military Commission and provincial CPC commission, the governments and military departments, are not the responsible departments of the State Council. Therefore, their opinions might not provide a legal basis of limiting individuals from leaving China.

Although the leadership of the CPC is entrenched in Preamble Par. 7 of *the Constitution of the PRC (Amendment)* 2004, and the Central Committee of the

[25] The reference to "government officials' in this context refers to national public servants. National public servants include: individuals engaged in public affairs in the State-owned companies and enterprises, and mass departments appointed by State-owned companies, enterprises and government sponsored institutions. Quoted in Xiao, Juan, "Quanzhou City Adopted Passport On Demand Policy" (*Woshi Shixing Anxu Shenling Huzhao*), 24 November 2003, *The Quanzhou Evening Daily*, http://www.dnzb.com.cn/gb/content/2003–11/24/content_1060483.htm (accessed 16/09/2006).

CPC, the Central Military Commission and provincial level CPC commissions, the governments and military departments, play conspicuous roles in national security and safeguarding national interests, these entities, according to Article 5 of the *Constitution of the PRC (Amendment)* 2004, must abide by the law and are not privileged to act beyond the law. Where they think that persons whose exit the country will be harmful to State security or cause a major loss to national interests, they only may make recommendations to the responsible departments of the State Council.

Lastly, the prevention of a person from leaving China on the grounds that he or she is unable to obtain a favourable certificate from their department is unfair. The status a person may have is multifarious and not subject to enumeration. The absence of a legal criterion for clarifying the categories for which a certificate is required, means that categories can be added and subtracted at will by local administrators. It makes for discrimination against applicants on the basis of status.

Therefore the requirements of prerequisite certificates impose an extra burden on passport application, making the procedure more complex and interfering with the right to leave. Yet more seriously, the prerequisite certificates could have long-term effects on the right to leave, as most of provisions were adopted during the period of reform and are regarded as positive and necessary measures.

7.4 Household Deregistration Prior to Leaving China

Household registration, the genesis of which has been discussed in part 5.3 of this book, is vital to Chinese daily life. It is not only a symbol of identity but also the basis of housing, medical, education and employment benefits. Under Article 7 of the *Detailed Rules for the Implementation of the Law on the Control of Exit and Entry of Citizens (Amendment)* 1994 (PRC):

> For anyone leaving to reside permanently in a foreign country, he or she shall go to the local police station or the residence registration office to deregister their household residence. For anyone leaving the country for a short period of time, he or she shall undergo the procedures of residence registration for a short-term absence from the country and, upon return to China, resume their regular household registration at the places of their original residence by presenting their passports.

Deregistration severs an individual's links with China. Unfortunately, the reforms do not change these provisions.[26] In fact, cancellation of household registration is

[26] "The Attempt to Eliminate the Distinctions Between Urban Residents and Rural Residents: New Reform of Residence System is Carrying out in China" (*Nuli Quxiao Shenfen Chabie, Zhongguo Zheng Tuixing Xin Yilun Hujizhi Gaige*), 25/07/2003, Xinhua News Net, http://news.xinhuanet.com/newscenter/2003–07/25/content_993575.htm (accessed 16/09/2006).

not effective, since border inspectors do not check if the individual has deregistered their household prior to letting them cross. Border inspector checks pertain only to passports, visas and exit registration cards.[27] The absence of collaboration between public security departments and border inspection departments, makes it possible for individuals to avoid deregistration.

The measures applied in other countries and regions are exemplary. In Taiwan, households are deregistered if the individual has been absent from the territory for more than two years. In that way, the actual exit has no direct bearing on later household deregistration.[28]

7.5 The Right to Access Foreign Exchange in China

China has been gradually relaxing restrictions on the right to access foreign exchange since 2002,[29] but current limits still hinder RLR. As discussed in part 3.2.4, foreign exchange restrictions imposed with a view to safeguarding the national economy should not be used to deny a national the right to leave.[30] Limits on the right to access foreign exchange can mean that nationals living abroad may lose financial support from home; and nationals at home may abandon the idea of travelling abroad. The restrictions on the right to access foreign exchange should be temporary and where possible avoided.

7.5.1 *Limits on the right to purchase foreign exchange*

Crucial to the right to access foreign exchange in China are the terms of the right to purchase foreign exchange. Under Article I (1) of the *Circular on Adjusting the Policies for Domestic Resident Individuals to Purchase Foreign exchange under Current Accounts* 2003 (PRC) which is promulgated by State Administration of Foreign Exchange (SAFE):

---

[27] Article 7 of *the Regulations of Inspection of Exit and Entry Border* 1995 (PRC) and Article 3 Clause 3 of *the Circular of the MPS on Handling Means of Some Issues on the Implementation of Checking, Monitoring and Prevention of Exit and Entry in Regulation of Inspection of Exit and Entry Border* 1995 (PRC).

[28] Articles 2 and 7 of *the Operation Points of Circular of Population of Nationals Who Exited Two Years Ago and Reentry* 2000 (Republic of China).

[29] *The Notice of Adjusting the Policy of Purchasing Foreign Exchange under Individual Regular Account by Residence within the Mainland (Guanyu Tiaozheng Jingnei Jumin Geren Jingchang Xiangmu Xia Gouhui Zhengce De Tongzhi)*, issued on 1 September 2003 by The SAFE, No. [2003] 104, http://www1.chinadaily.com.cn/en/doc/2003–11/11/content_281664.htm (accessed 26/11/2003)

[30] Article I (f) of the 1963 Ingles Draft Principles on RLR, adopted by the UN Sub-Commission on the Prevention of Discrimination and Protection of Minorities, Res. 2B (XV), UN Doc. E/CN. 41846 (1963).

> If a resident needs to purchase foreign exchange due to outbound travel, pilgrimage, to visit relatives, overseas hospitalisation, commercial investigation, employment, permanent emigration, international exchange, overseas training, overseas study, or to provide labour; and the period that he or she will remain outside the territory is less than six months, he or she may purchase foreign exchange to the equivalent value of US$3,000. If the period for which the person will remain outside the territory is over six months, he or she may purchase the equivalent of US$5,000.[31]

The preface of the *Circular* 2003 above further states that it means to satisfy the real foreign exchange demands of residents and to facilitate the purchase of foreign exchange from banks by individuals. It is almost impossible to limit the number of people exiting China by imposing restrictions on purchasing foreign exchange, based on the purpose for which the person is exiting. This then raises the related question as to whether a resident is prohibited from purchasing foreign exchange on the basis that they require it for other purposes other than those regulated, such as to pay an inheritance to a person who lives overseas, or to make a donation. Additionally, should the guiding limit of purchasing foreign exchange be calculated in accordance with the length of time that the person will remain outside the territory as indicated on their visa? The unanswerable questions challenge the aims of the *Circular* 2003.

With too few banks providing foreign exchange, procurement is neither convenient nor simple. Since October 2003, residents in all of Mainland China could buy foreign currency at a total of 2,831 branches of 16 banks.[32] In the context of a population of 1.3 billion, 460,000 people share each designated foreign exchange bank. Most of the designated banks are located in Beijing, Shanghai, Guangdong and coastal provinces, so the rate of 460,000:1 is actually much lower. Residents in rural areas or the mid-western regions have even less access to foreign exchange banks.

---

[31] Compared to Article 15 of *the Provisional Measures on the Administration of Domestic Resident Individuals Foreign Exchange* 1998 (PRC) (*Jingnei Jumin Geren Waihui Guanli Zaixing Banfa*), Huifa [1999] No. 305. Prior to the enactment of the 2003 Circular, residents could only purchase the equivalent of US$1,000 in order to travel to Hong Kong or Macao for the purpose of visiting relatives; US$2,000 to visit relatives in any other country; or a maximum of US$1,000 to travel abroad for any other purpose.

[32] "List of Nominated Bank with License of Selling Foreign Currencies to Individuals Going Abroad for Private Purposes", 27/10/2003, the State Administration of Foreign Currency, http://www.safe.gov.cn (accessed 26/11/2003); the monopoly of the Bank of China in selling foreign exchange was broken down in August 2002 with the help of a foreign exchange purchase information management system for individual buyers, developed by SAFE. See "Chinese Have Easier Access to Foreign Exchange Deals", *The People's Daily*, 2 August 2002, http://english.peopledaily.com.cn/200208/02/eng 20020802_100771.shtml (accessed 16/09/2006).

7.5.2 *Limits on the right to remit outward foreign exchange*

Personal outward remittances may financially support Chinese nationals who live overseas, and who travel abroad. Limits on the right to remit outward foreign exchange are mainly limits on remittance used as expenditure and as overseas investment. According to the Bank of China's[33] summary of the relevant provisions, individuals must follow complex formalities to remit foreign exchange within the guiding limits.[34] To avoid these formalities, which are costly and time-consuming, senders usually take advantage of a loophole in the regulations.[35] Because the provisions do not limit the annual remittance amount, the scheme does not affect the ability of the identity card-lenders to remit funds in the future. In any event, there is no national electronic database of remittance activity for banks to cross-reference. Further, banks are not entitled to prevent individuals from remitting at different branches during a short period, even on the same day. Therefore, the set limits do not achieve the goal of strictly controlling foreign exchange outflow. The current provisions also shed little light on personal overseas investment with foreign exchange,[36] which is one of conditions to apply for business skilled emigration.

---

[33] The Bank of China is only foreign exchange bank designated by the State Council of the PRC before August 2002.

[34] 1. If less than US$10,000 is remitted in a lump sum from an account of personal spot exchange deposit, or foreign banknotes less than US$2,000 are remitted in a lump sum from a foreign banknote holding or from an account of personal foreign banknote deposit, sender is only required to prove their identity and do not need to disclose the reason for the remittance; 2. If US$10,000 to US$50,000 is remitted in a lump sum from an account of personal spot exchange deposit, or foreign banknotes valued at US$2,000 to US$10,000 are remitted in a lump sum, an application must be made to the local SAFE. After the application is examined outward remittance procedures may be followed at a designated foreign exchange bank against the certificate of approval issued by local SAFE. 3. If US$50,000 or more is remitted in a lump sum from an account of personal spot exchange deposit, or foreign banknotes valued at US$10,000 US dollars are remitted outward in a lump sum, the local SAFE shall report it to the SAFE for examination and approval. Outward remittance procedures may be followed at the designated foreign exchange bank against the certificate of approval issued by the local SAFE. See the Bank of China, "International Remittance – Outward", http://www.boc.cn/cn/common/fourth.jsp?category=1098586663100 (accessed 16/09/2006).

[35] For example, if an individual plans to remit US$60,000 in cash in one day, the most expedient approach is to borrow ten or twenty identification cards from others, then remit the sum at several banks in US$2,000 lots.

[36] Resident individual may invest B-shares with an individual's own foreign exchange resources other than with purchased foreign exchange. See Article 1 Clause 2 of *the Supplementary Circular of the State Administration of Foreign Exchange on Relevant*

7.5.3 *Limits on the right to carry outward foreign currencies*

The formalities for applying for a *Permit for Carrying Outward Foreign Currency Across the Border* (*Xiedai Waibi Chujing Xukezheng*) over US$5,000 are petty and tedious. Under Article 8 of the *Provisional Measures for the Administration of Carrying Outward Foreign Currency Cash for Persons Entering or Exiting China* 2003 (PRC), it is likely to be time-consuming and costly. Chinese citizens and aliens cannot, in principle and by law, carry more than US$10,000 out of China.[37] If due to a particular circumstance, the individual may lodge the application according to Article 5 Clause 3 of the *Provisional Measures for the Administration of Carrying Outward Foreign Currency Cash for Persons Entering or Exiting China* 2003 (PRC), the branch or sub-branch of the SAFE at the locality of one's deposit bank or exchange-selling bank is supposed to apply a test of bona fide on the source and use of foreign exchange, in accordance with relevant regulations.[38]

In practice, it is almost impossible to legally carry foreign exchange in excess of US$10,000, as most residents exiting China do not fulfil exemption criteria, and have little chance of obtaining a Permit for Carrying Outward Foreign Currency across the Border. Article 2 Clause 2 of the *Circular of the SAFE and the General Administration of Customs on Printing and Distributing the Provisional Measures for the Administration of Carrying Outward Foreign Currency Cash for Persons Entering or Exiting China* 2003 (PRC) provides that under any of the following particular circumstances, a resident individual may apply for a Permit for an amount in excess of US$10,000, if he or she:

Matters about Investing in the B Stocks by the Domestic Residents 2001 (PRC), Huifa [2001] No. 31, 23 February 2001; B shares is a special share with a par value in Renminbi but subscribed and trade in US dollars in the Shanghai stock market, or in Hong Kong dollars in the Shenzhen stock market. See Dictionary Department, Institute of Linguistics, Chinese Academy of Social Sciences, *the Contemporary Chinese Dictionary (Chinese-English Edition)* (Beijing: Foreign Language Teaching and Research Press, 2002), page 2647.

37 Article C (c) of *the Circular on Relevant Issues Regarding the Introduction of New Version of "Certificate for Carrying Outward Foreign Currency Across the Border"* 1999, Article 2 Clause 2(3) of *the Circular of the SAFE and the General Administration of Customs on Printing and Distributing the Provisional Measures for the Administration of Carrying Outward Foreign currency cash for Persons Entering or Exiting China,* 2003 (PRC), and Article 7 Clause 2 of *Provisional Measures for the Administration of Carrying Outward Foreign Currency Cash for Persons Entering or Exiting China* 2003 (PRC).

38 Article C (B) of *the Circular on Relevant Issues Regarding the Introduction of New Version of "Certificate for Carrying Outward Foreign Currency Across the Border" Issued Jointly by State Administration of Foreign Exchange and General Administration of Customs* 1999.

(1) Is in a group exiting China composed of a large number of persons;
(2) Is in a scientific inspection group exiting China for a long time or for a long trip;
(3) Is a government leader visiting a foreign country;
(4) Is leaving for a country at war, a country with strict foreign exchange control policies, or a country with bad financial conditions or financial turmoil."

The phrases and terms 'a large number', 'a long time', 'a long trip', 'strict', 'bad' and 'turmoil' leave much scope for administrative discretion. Individuals seem unlikely to successfully apply for a Permit for an amount exceeding the prescribed limit. In order to avoid the guiding limits and overly elaborate formalities, some individuals purchase foreign exchange on the black market and risk smuggling the excessive foreign currency out of the country.[39]

7.5.4 *Laws governing foreign exchange*

Underdeveloped foreign exchange laws impose an indirect barrier on RLR. Strictly speaking, most of the current laws governing foreign exchange are internal policies because the SAFE is not entitled to promulgate national law. The SAFE promulgates most regulations governing foreign exchange for private purposes[40] and it is a bureau supervised by the People's Bank of China (the Central Bank), which is the Reserve Bank. The Central Bank has the same administrative level as Ministries and Commissions, which have legislative power.[41] The SAFE does not have legislative power [42] and needs to follow above hierarchy to formulate the rules governing foreign exchange. Therefore, the validity of SAFE's regulations is in dispute.

---

[39] "Black Market", http://www.chinaonline.com/features/currency (accessed 10/12/2003).

[40] For example *the Circular of the SAFE on Adjusting the Policies for Domestic Resident Individuals to Purchase Foreign exchange under Current Accounts* 2003 (PRC), *Detailed Rules of the Implementation on the Administration of Domestic Resident Individuals to Purchase Foreign Exchange (Amendment)* 2003 (PRC), *Provisional Measures on the Administration of Domestic Resident Individuals Foreign Exchange (Amendment)* 2003 (PRC) and *Provisional Measures for the Administration of Carrying Outward Foreign currency cash for Persons Entering or Exiting China*, 2003 (PRC).

[41] According to Article 71 (1) of *the Law of Legislation* 2000 (PRC): "the ministries and commissions under the State Council, the People's Bank of China and the Auditing office and other departments with administrative responsibilities directly under the State Council shall, according to the laws and administrative regulations, decisions and orders of the State Council, enact rules within their own authority."

[42] According to Article 9 (1) *the Regulations on the Procedure for Formulation of Rules* 2001 (PRC), "Where an internal agency established by a department under the State Council or any other agency deems it necessary to formulate departmental rules, an application shall be presented to the said department for establishment of the rules."

7.6 THE ADMINISTRATION OF INDIVIDUALS PROHIBITED FROM LEAVING CHINA (*XIANZHI CHUJING ZHIDU*)

The Chinese government has imposed the administration for individuals prohibited from leaving China. It places such people into one of the five categories discussed in part 7.1 above. Article 2 of the *Some Rules on the Issues of Prohibiting Aliens and Chinese Citizens from Exiting Chinas* 1987 (PRC) details the examination and approval authority in this system:

(1) Provincial level public security departments or national security departments are empowered to prohibit criminal suspects or violators from leaving China whose violation has not been punished and needs to be investigated the criminal responsibility;
(2) The People's Courts and People's Procuratorates are empowered to prohibit criminal suspects or violators from leaving China whose violation has not been punished and whose criminal responsibility needs to be run according to relevant laws, and notify the same level public security departments;
(3) National security departments are empowered to prohibit some aliens or Chinese citizens from leaving China, and notify the same level public security departments;
(4) The People's Court is empowered to prohibit the party of civil lawsuit, including an economic lawsuit, from leaving China, and notify the same level public security departments.

The means of the prohibition are prescribed as following by Article 3 of the *Some Rules on the Issues of Prohibiting Aliens and Chinese Citizens from Exiting Chinas* 1987 (PRC):

> The following means can be adopted separately when the People's Courts, People's Procuratorates, pubic security departments and national security department prohibits aliens and Chinese citizens from leaving China:
>
> (1) The affected person shall be informed orally or in writing that they are prohibited from leaving China unless the lawsuits or issues concerned has been resolved;
> (2) The affected person shall be convicted to live at home under surveillance, or post a bail pending trial with restricted liberty of movement; or they may be permitted to leave China after providing a property guarantee or a bond;
> (3) The affected person's passport or other valid travel documents shall be retained, however the relevant cases need to be resolved before the expiration of retained passport or other travel documents, the receipt of retaining also need to be issued . . .

The procedure of the prohibition must be followed under Article 4 of the *Some Rules on the Issues of Prohibiting Aliens and Chinese Citizens from Exiting China* 1987 (PRC):

> If the aliens and Chinese citizens need to be prohibited from leaving China at the border inspection port, the People's Courts, People's Procuratorates, pubic security departments and national security departments must fill in the *Notification of Limiting*

> *Individuals Exiting at the Border Inspection Port.* For the ports in this province, the notice shall be submitted to provincial public security departments who organize the prohibition activities; under really emergency circumstance, may ask for border inspection office to arrange the prohibition activities first, then complete missing prohibition procedures. For the ports outside of this province, relevant public security departments organise the prohibition activities together.

The administration of reporting and recording plays an important role in giving effect to the provisions prohibiting the exit of China. Nevertheless, its adverse effects cannot be ignored. Firstly, it is unacceptable to inform an individual that they have been prohibited from leaving the territory, orally or in writing without giving a reason for the decision. Secondly, there is no need to prohibit the person from leaving China under the exit and entry laws, because Article 51 of *the Law of Criminal Procedure (Amendment)* 1996 (PRC) contains provisions to the same effect. That is, there is already a body of law in place that ensures people who are due to stand trial in a criminal prosecution, or are a party to a civil case, remain in the territory.

Thirdly, only the People's Court, People's Procuratorates, and public security departments have the power to compel a person to live at home under surveillance (*Jianshi Juzhu*),[43] post bail pending trial (*Qubao Houshen*)[44] or retain passports and other travel documents.[45] After reviewing the *Law of National Security* 1993 (PRC) and the *Detailed Rules for the Implementation of Law of National Security* 1994 (PRC) and other laws regarding military units, it would seem, on balance, that, national security departments do not have the power or means to prohibit individuals from leaving China. Were any of these bodies to do so, they would unlawfully interfere with the individuals' right to leave. Fourthly, with respect to the calculation of a bond or security provision in Article 3(2), there is concern as to how that sum should be calculated in the absence of any guide.

Lastly, there are no provisions to limit the processing period. This greatly reduces the efficiency of controls over individuals prohibited from leaving China, especially those who want to abscond abroad and reside in areas where decision-makers have no jurisdiction.[46] It is not unusual for such individuals to have absconded before the national border inspection office has received notification from the MPS.

---

[43] Article 50 of *the Law of Criminal Procedures (Amendment)* 1996 (PRC).

[44] Article 51 of *the Law of Criminal Procedure (Amendment)* 1996 (PRC) stipulates "the People's Courts, the People's Procuratorates and the public security organs may, according to the circumstances of a case, issue a warrant to compel the appearance of the criminal suspect or defendant, order him to obtain a guarantor pending trial or subject him to residential surveillance."

[45] Article 16 of *the Detailed Rules for the Implementation of the Law on the Control of Exit and Entry of Citizens (Amendment)* 1994 (PRC).

[46] To illustrate the inefficiency of the system, the following hypothetical has been

7.7 CONCLUSIONS

There are numerous unacceptable limits on the right to leave of Chinese citizens. General limits on the right to leave are inappropriate and the legal validity of interpretative provisions are doubtful. Special limits on the right to leave are also questionable, based on their discrimination against overseas employment, overseas pilgrimage, overseas study, kinship relationships, social status, heath status and gender.

As 13 million Chinese citizens must follow the rule of prerequisite certification from the department in which they are employed, when applying to leave China, we could not accept that every Chinese exercise the right to leave at one's will. There is a lack of convincing argument to support the legal basis of the prerequisite certificates and the entitlement of the departments in which the applicant is employed. The rule of prerequisite certification discriminates as to the status of applicants. An extra layer of examination and approval are imposed upon application to leave, and the procedures become yet more complex.

The prospects of severing links with China caused by household deregistration prior to leaving China cannot be ignored. Household deregistration inhibits the right to leave and the right to return, the later will be discussed in next chapter. The right to access foreign exchange in China has been significantly limited. The foremost limits are focused on the right to purchase foreign exchange. Individuals are only entitled to purchase foreign exchange within guiding limits, allowing insufficient sums. Strict limits on the right to remit foreign exchange and carry foreign exchange outward exacerbate the effects of the limits on the right to purchase foreign exchange. The limits have discouraged many Chinese people from exiting China or have led them to illegally access foreign exchange on the black market. Laws governing foreign exchange in China lack legal validity. The legislative system of foreign exchange is inefficient. Problems can only be resolved by

---

constructed. 1. Gushi County People's Court of Henan Province is of the opinion that Jack Wang (JW), a party to a civil suit, who resides in Shanghai, should be prohibited from exiting China. 2. The Court official notifies JW that he is not to exit China. In order to prevent his absconding abroad, control measures must be put into place at the national border inspection offices. 3. The Court must report its decision to the Gushi County Public Security Bureau. 4. In turn, the Gushi County Public Security Bureau must report the Court's decision to Xinyang Municipality Public Security Bureau, its higher public security department. 5. The Xinyang Municipality Public Security Bureau must report the decision to the Henan Province Public Security Department. 6. As the Henan Province Public Security Department does not have the power to order border inspection offices in non-Henan provinces to prevent JW from exiting China, Henan Province Public Security Department may consult with responsible provincial public security department. 7. The responsible provincial public security department can then notify national border inspection officers not release JW from China.

improving legislative technique and by having overriding, or macro-level laws pertaining to the administration of foreign exchange.

In an era when information technology has greatly developed and illegal exit means are being emerged in an endless stream, it is difficult to argue that the impermissible limits could effectively prohibit individuals from leaving China. It may be possible for them to subvert the bad-knit formalities of applying to leave China. Meanwhile, the inefficient administration of individuals prohibited from leaving China, strengthens the point.

Chapter Eight
The Right to Return to China

Introduction

Limiting a citizen's ability to re-enter China may cause that person to become effectively stateless, force them to live illegally in a foreign country, in a place that he or she does not like, and prevent talented Chinese people from returning. In other words, the right to return is more absolute than the right to leave. However the issues surrounding the right to return to China have received much less attention than those associated with the right to leave.

Chinese citizens who were born in China and legally reside outside of China are referred to as *Huaqiao*.[1] At the end of the 20th Century there were 30 million *Huaqiao* in the world, 90% of them in Asia.[2] In China there are unfortunate and

---

[1] Article 2 Clause 1 of the *Law on Protection of the Rights and Interests of Returned Chinese Citizens who Legally Resided Outside of China and the Family Members of Chinese citizens who Legally Resided Outside of China (Amendment)* 2000 (PRC).

[2] Yang, Fajing, *the Introduction to Exit Abroad (Chuguo Zhishi Gailan)*, (Beijing: the Publishing House of Science Popularisation, 1990), 174. According to the statistics of Taiwan, Chinese people living overseas reached 36 million in 1993. See Chinese citizens who are legally residing outside of China Affairs Commission, the Republic of China, *The Republic of China, Chinese Citizens Who are Legally Residing Outside of China Affairs Statistics*, Taipei, Taiwan, 1994. According to *Hongkong Webwei Daily*, there are 50 million Chinese citizens who are legally residing outside of China and foreign citizens of

unacceptable limits placed on the right of these people to return to China. In addition, there are some 11 million Chinese migrants in the world, including those referred to as *Feifa Yimin*, and those who are dissidents, most of whom, although born in China are outside China illegally and cannot return because their passports have not been reissued, replaced or extended. Even leaving aside the human cost of exile, restrictions on the right to return in China encumber effective interchange and cooperation between China and the rest of the world.

The right of people to return to their country is universally accepted as a rule of law and it is guaranteed in the constitutions of many nations (even in principle by China, as a signatory to international instruments) – the instruments by which this is recognised place no restrictions on that right. The issue of the right to return in China is one that is crucial for China's future and for the development of the right to return in the world.

This chapter considers the issue firstly from the limits placed on the right of 16 million *Huaqiao* and *Feifa Yimin* and importantly, the limits on the right to return of Chinese citizens, including dissidents, are then considered, along with the process of merits review of administrative decisions regarding exit and entry in China. Finally, recommendations are canvassed for reform of the regulatory framework governing the right to return in China.

8.1 Limits on the Return of Chinese Citizens, Especially Dissidents

Human Rights Watch Asia has argued, from a political perspective, that the Chinese government's behaviour in imposing prohibitions on citizens, especially dissidents from returning to China, is unacceptable.[3]

Chinese descent up to 2005. According to the introduction of Lu Weixiong, the director of Chinese citizens who are legally residing outside of China Affairs of Guangdong Province, PRC, Chinese citizens who are legally residing outside of China stand for 10 percent. See *How Many Chinese Citizens Who are Legally Residing Outside of China? The Amount of Chinese citizens Who are legally Residing outside of China Double Every 10 Years (Haiwai Huaren You Duoshou? Quanqiu HUaqiao mei Shinian Fanyifan), 15/04/2005, Wenhui Daily*, http://www.torontoservice.com/readnews.asp?id=56713 (accessed 16/09/2006). This book prefers to the data originated from the PRC because this paper concentrates on the issues of the Mainland China, and the definition of "Chinese people living overseas" is not very clear.

[3] Human Rights Watch/Asia and Human Rights in China, *China: Enforced Exile of Dissidents: Government 'Re-entry Blacklist' Revealed*, Vol. 7 No. 1, January 1995, 6.

8.1.1 *The situation of limiting Chinese citizens, especially dissidents to return*

Citizens

Officially, the Chinese government does not recognise that the limits on return are designed for Chinese citizens.[4] But practically, the limits do mostly relate to citizens. One reason for this point of view is that the *Circular of Ministry of Public Security on Print and Delivery Measures of Examination, Approval and Circulation of a Circular of the Lists of Individuals Prohibited from Returning to China* 1992 (PRC) contains specialised provisions and is not exclusive of citizens. The other reason is that the *Law on the Control of Exit and Entry of Citizens* 1985 (PRC) and its detailed rules of implementation are cited as two of legislative foundations of above 1992 circular.[5] If the system of prohibiting certain individuals from returning to China did not cover Chinese citizens, it would be unnecessary to cite that law and its rules of implementation. Given the fact Hong Kong, Macao and Taiwan were not within the sovereignty of the PRC when above Circular 1992 was promulgated, citizens here imply residents in Mainland China.

Chinese dissidents who are outside of China

Prohibited citizens are generally dissidents. Article 1 (–5)) of above Circular 1992 prescribes:

> (2) Those engaged in the activities of terrorism, violence and subversion; or are suspected of undertaking these activities; or will return to China to undertake these activities ensured by efficient evidences;
> (3) Those who have engaged in activities of endangering Chinese national security, social and political stability, and social stability in minority areas; or will return to China to undertake these activities ensured by efficient evidences;
> (4) Those who have engaged in activities against the PRC abroad and do not have any act or other expressions of repentance;
> (5) Those who are wanted criminal suspects. . . . .

---

[4] See Section 6 of Chapter 4 of "the system of individuals prohibited from entering China", Department of Politics under the MPS, *Frontier Defence and Exit and Entry Administration, the Series of Basic Textbook of People's Police Operation:(Bianfang Yu Churu Jing Guanli, Renmin Jingcha Gongan Yewu Jichu Jiaochai)*, examined by Committee of Textbook Editing and Examination of the MPS, Internal Publication in Public Security Organs (*Gongan Jiguan Neibu Faxing*) (Beijing: the Publishing House of Qunzhong, 1999), 387 and 388.

[5] Preface of the *Circular of the MPS on Delivery Measures of Examination, Approval and Circulation of a Circular of the Lists of Individuals Prohibited from Entering China* 1992 (PRC) *(Gonganbu Guanyu Yinfa Buzhun Rujing Mingdan Shenpi Tongbao Banfa De Tongzhi).*

One would expect that if the prohibited citizens are convicted criminals or criminal suspects, the government would be most concerned with bringing them to justice in China as soon as possible, rather than banning them from entering the territory. The most realistic explanation as to why justice is not sought in China is that the prohibited citizens are Chinese dissidents who are outside of China. Further evidence to support this point is in Article 1 of the *Circular of the General Office of the State Council of Some Issues of Overseas Students* 1992 (PRC) which provides:

> Overseas students are welcome to return China for a job. [. . .] The Chinese government will not punish those who made wrong statements and wrong activities abroad (*Shuoguo Yixie Cuohua, Zuoguo Yixie Cuoshi*). Even if they have participated anti-government organizations and were engaged in activities of endangering the security, honour and interests of the State; so long as they can withdraw from such organizations and no longer be engaged in the anti-government activities which violate the Constitution and laws of our country.

In fact the dissidents dominate the re-entry blacklist of citizens. The text titled "A List of 49 Overseas Members of Reactionary Organizations Currently Subject to Major Control" was published by Human Rights Watch Asia and Human Rights in China.[6] The right to return, as expressly recognised in Article 13 (2) of the UDHR, Article 12 (4) of the ICCPR and other international and regional human rights instruments, cannot be discriminated against on the grounds of social status, occupation, age, gender, religion, ownership of property, race or colour, or political opinion.

Residents in Taiwan

Under Article 22 of the *Measures on the Control over Chinese Citizens Travelling to or from the Region of Taiwan* 1991 (PRC):

> Those within either of the following categories shall not be granted permission to enter the Mainland:
>
> (1) Those who are engaged in criminal activities;
> (2) Those who are likely to be engaged activities that undermine national security and national interests;
> (3) Those who have fabricated situations and presented forged certifications; and
> (4) Mental patients.
>
> Those who are for medical treatment and other special purposes may be exempted to grant permission.

---

[6] Human Rights Watch/Asia and Human Rights in China, *China: Enforced Exile of Dissidents: Government 'Re-entry Blacklist' Revealed*, Vol. 7 No. 1, January 1995, 1.

Taiwan has officially been a local administrative area of China since 1683, apart from a brief period of Japanese occupation between 1895 and 1945. The central government of the PRC has not exercised its sovereign powers over Taiwan, even though Taiwan is more and more lonely and marginal in the world.[7] On this basis, it is understandable that China would extend system of prohibiting individuals of Taiwan from returning to China.

Residents in the HKSAR and MSAR

Similarly, residents of the Hong Kong Special Administrative Region (HKSAR) and Macao Special Administrative Region (MSAR) are prohibited from returning to China under some circumstances, even after 1997 for the HKSAR and 1999 for the MSAR, when the territories returned to Chinese administration. Both regions are subject to Chinese sovereignty. Article 15 of *Interim Measures Concerning the Control over Chinese Citizens Travelling on Private Affairs to or from the Regions of Hong Kong or Macao* 1986 (PRC) provides:

> Those within either of the following categories shall not obtain the Home-Visiting Certificates for Compatriots from Hong Kong and Macao (*Gangao Tongbao Huixiangzheng*) or entry-exit passes:
>
> (1) Those who are likely to be engaged in such criminal activities as robbery, theft, and trafficking in narcotics;
> (2) Those who have fabricated situations and presented forged certifications; and
> (3) Mental patients.

After 1997 and 1999, the Home-Visiting Certificates for Compatriots from Hong Kong and Macao respectively was replaced with the Travel Permits, but the grounds for prohibition remain. The Ministry for Public Security (MPS) has argued that the prohibitions can be attributed to 'the special situation of China'[8] but have failed to identify what the special situation is. It is presumed that the special situation refers to the fact that China is one State with separate regimes in the HKSAR and MSAR.

---

[7] Wu, Wenxin, "Honestly Review the Functions and Significances of Chinese citizens who are legally residing outside of China Affairs Committee" (*Zhengshi Qiaoweihui De Zhineng Yu Jiazhi*), in *Microview Weekly*, Taiwan, Volume 493, at Domestic News Section, 5th May 2004; Also see "The Conference of Taiwan Affairs of Northern European Five Countries affirm the Democratic Contribution of Taiwan" (*Beiou Wuguo Taiwan Yiti Huiyi Kengding Taiwan Minzhu Chengjiu*), *Microview Weekly*, Taiwan, Volume 493, 5 May 2001.

[8] Department of Politics under the MPS, *Frontier Defence and Exit and Entry Administration, the Series of Basic Textbook of People's Police Operation: (Bianfang Yu Churu Jing Guanli, Renmin Jingcha Gongan Yewu Jichu Jiaochai)*, examined by Committee of Textbook Editing and Examination of the MPS, Internal Publication in Public Security Organs (*Gongan Jiguan Neibu Faxing*) (Beijing: the Publishing House of Qunzhong, 1999), 387.

8.1.2 *Practices of limiting Chinese citizens, especially dissidents to return*

Revocation and confiscation of passports

The revoking of passports is the most direct way to prevent a dissident from retuning to China. Article 4(1) of the *Measures of Examination, Approval and Notification of a Circular of the Lists of Individuals Prohibited from Returning to China* 1992 (PRC) provides:

> Where those with Chinese passports have been on the lists of individuals prohibited from returning to China, their passport shall be simultaneously revoked. If they are in the territory, the public security departments where the passport holders are located are responsible for declaring the revocation of passport, and arresting them. When they return to China with a revoked passport, border security check and administrative offices shall refuse their entry, confiscate the passport and send it to the original issuing department.

However the legal basis of revoking dissidents' passports is without substance. Article 22 Clause (1) (c) of *Detailed Rules for the Implementation of Law on the Control of the Entry and Exit of Citizens (Amendment)* 1994 (PRC) prescribes that where the passport holder has engaged in activities prejudicial to the security, honour and the interests of China, the original issuing department or its higher department has the power to revoke the passport and declare the passport invalid. As this provision actually limits the right to leave and return, according to international norms discussed in part 3.3.3 of this book, it must be strictly construed. This would mean that passport holders must be in China when the prejudicial activities occur, and it does not therefore apply to the activities of dissidents abroad.

It is also necessary to question if border security check and administrative offices have the power to confiscate passports and send them to the issuing department. Under Article 9 of the *Law on the Control of Exit and Entry of Citizens* 1985 (PRC), these government bodies only have the power to refuse a person to enter China. Pursuant to Article 16 of *Detailed Rules for the Implementation of Law on the Control of Entry and Exit of Aliens (Amendment)* 1994 (PRC), the power to confiscate passports is limited to the public security departments and the original issuing department.

Not replacing, reissuing or extending of passports

The policy of not replacing, re-issuing or extending dissidents' passports may indirectly prohibit dissidents from returning to China. According to Article 4(3) of the *Measures of Examination, Approval and Circulation of a Circular of the Lists of Individuals Prohibited from Returning to China* 1992 (PRC):

> Where those permanently residing in a foreign country with Chinese ordinary passports have been on the lists of individuals prohibited from returning to China, the prohibition on their returning to China might be exercised by not granting their

> application for passport replacement, re-issue and extension. For special circumstances, their passport might be revoked or declared invalid.

This is the main reason why "[no] dissident has ever been formally notified that they are no longer permitted to return to China; some only learned of the prohibition when they attempted to go back."[9]

As for not replacing, reissuing or extending of passports, there is a similarly inadequate legal foundation for the practice of revoking and confiscating passports. According to Article 17(1) of *Detailed Rules for the Implementation of Law on the Control of Exit and Entry of Citizens* 1985 (PRC), Chinese citizens who are legally residing outside of China may apply for an extension before the passport's term of validity expires. Under Article 21 of the just-mentioned detailed rules, where the passport will expire soon, or the attached pages for visas have been used up so that the terms of validity cannot be extended, or are damaged and can no longer be used, the holder may apply for a replacement or a re-issue of the passport.[10] Detailed rules for the implementation, which do not distinguish between applicants, suggest that dissidents are entitled to have their passport replaced, re-issued, or its term extended.

Flexible duration of the prohibition

The duration of prohibition on returning to China is flexible. According to Human Rights Watch Asia, the period of prohibition may be described by Chinese authorities as being "unlimited duration", "5 years duration" or "currently not subject to control".[11] Under Article 6 of the *Measures of Examination, Approval and Circulation of a Circular of the Lists of Individuals Prohibited from Returning to China* 1992 (PRC):

> The duration of prohibition on returning to China is generally 1 to 5 years. Those whose mental disease, leprosy, AIDS, venereal disease, active tuberculosis and other infectious diseases not treated, cannot enter China. . . . The responsible departments may extend the duration to over five years if they clarify the reasons for extension when reporting. They may conceal the list ahead of schedule or change other important items of the prohibitions if they timely notify the Bureau of Exit and Entry Administration.

The use of the term 'generally' is nebulous and elastic. The discretion of extending the period to over five years or concealing the ban ahead of schedule is too broad to keep a balance between the administration and citizens' interests. This

[9] Human Rights Watch Asia and Human Rights in China, *China: Enforced Exile of Dissidents: Government 'Re-entry Blacklist' Revealed*, Vol. 7 No. 1, January 1995, 10.2.

[10] Article 21 of *Detailed Rules for the Implementation of the Law on the Control of Exit and Entry of Citizens* 1985 (PRC).

[11] Human Rights Watch/Asia and Human Rights in China, *China: Enforced Exile of Dissidents: Government 'Re-entry Blacklist' Revealed*, Vol. 7 No. 1, January 1995, 10.

could be addressed by defining the terms more accurately, or by setting them against a criterion to aid the understanding of administrators and citizens alike.

8.1.3 *Effects of limiting Chinese citizens, especially dissidents to return*

The three practices of prohibition described above may have the effect of rendering a citizen practically stateless. Human Rights in China has criticised the central government's abusive interpretation of national security laws to restrict overseas dissidents from returning to China, and that in so doing, to have unilaterally denaturalised this group of overseas citizens. The group of effectively stateless dissidents is becoming larger.[12]

The effective deprivation of citizenship means that dissidents are not entitled to the rights prescribed by the constitution and law. Article 33 (1) and (3) of the *Constitution of the PRC (Amendment)* 2004 affirms "All persons holding the citizenship of the People's Republic of China are citizens of the People's Republic of China;" and "Every citizen is entitled to the rights [. . .] prescribed by the constitution and law." In effect, dissidents who are practically stateless are not Chinese citizens, so are no longer protected by the rights afforded to citizens under Chinese law.

From the perspective of law of nationality, it is possible to question the legal basis of depriving the citizenship of dissidents. Citizenship is usually lost when the citizens renounce it, and that renouncement is accepted by the State, or when the citizen has acquired another citizenship. This general rule has been accepted in Articles 9 to 11 of the *Law of Nationality* 1980 (PRC), which provide that:

> Article 9 Any Chinese citizens who legally resided outside of China and who has been naturalised as a foreign citizen or has acquired foreign citizenship of his or her own free will shall automatically lose Chinese citizenship.
>
> Article 10 Chinese citizens who meet the conditions may renounce Chinese citizenship upon approval of their applications . . .
>
> Article 11 any person who applies for renunciation of Chinese citizenship shall lose Chinese citizenship upon approval of the application.

[12] Wang, Dan, the student leader of the 1989 Beijing protests, and the coordinator of Chinese Justice Observation, commented in 20010.3 that "Lots of people have been refused to return to China, most of who did not like to publicise their rejection of a passport extension application for different reasons. It is said that a group of Chinese without Chinese nationality has came into being. See Human Rights in China, *Chinese Justice Observation Appeal to Amend Law on the Control of Exit and Entry of Citizens (Zhongguo Sifa Guancha Huyu Xiugai Churujing Guanlifa)*, Http://gb.hrchina.org/gate/gb/big5.hrchina.org/subsite/big5/article.adp?article_id=4224&subcategoryd=187 (accessed 10/05/2003).

Chinese dissidents who are outside of China do not fall into any of the above categories. Moreover, there are no provisions regarding deprivation of the citizenship in the *Law of Nationality* 1980 (PRC) or other relevant laws. That means that the Chinese government does not have a domestic legal basis to deprive any citizen of citizenship.

The indirect deprivation of citizenship is in violation of international law. According to Article 15(2) of the UDHR, "No one shall be arbitrarily deprived of his nationality, nor denied the right to change his nationality." Article 5 d (iii) of the *International Convention on the Elimination of All Forms of Racial Discrimination* 1966, provides that States Parties undertake to prohibit and to eliminate racial discrimination in all its forms and to guarantee the right to nationality of everyone, without distinction, to equality before the law. China has ratified both instruments and has a duty to respect their terms.

Presumably, the absence of a domestic or international legal basis for denying citizenship is the reason why the Chinese government does not directly deprive dissidents of citizenship. On humanitarian grounds, China should give sympathetic consideration to permitting the return of former residents, particularly those who are stateless and have maintained a strong link with China.

8.2 Limits on the return of *Huaqiao*

Members of the 5 million *Huaqiao,* who intend to return to China for permanent residence or employment must meet the requirements and undertake formalities contained in Chapter 3 of the *Law on the Control of Exit and Entry of Citizens* 1985 (PRC) and Chapter 3 of *Detailed Rules for Implementing of Law on the Control of Exit and Entry of Citizens (Amendment)* 1994 (PRC).

8.2.1 *Conditions of retuning to China for permanent residence or employment*

The purpose of returning should not define an accepted limit on the right to return. To protect the right to return to China means to protect the right to return permanently, temporarily, for employment, and so on – yet approval to return to China for permanent residence or for employment is conditional. Access to a system of household registration is the precondition of returning for permanent residence, as every Chinese citizen permanently residing in China must register one's residence. Thus the right of *Huaqiao* to return for permanent residence is conditional on their right to settle down in a particular city after returning.

Conditions imposed on applicants for permanent residence

In the absence of efficient original legislative texts related to the conditions of returning to China for permanent residence, official textbooks, academic texts, and government online application instructions have been used in order to explain how the conditions operate.[13] Generally, five categories of *Huaqiao* are eligible to return for permanent residence if they provide the required documentation:

(1) Chinese citizens' spouse, orphans and widows who are Chinese citizens legally residing outside of China and cannot resolve their living issue independently, and for whom a person in China will resolve the applicant's employment, housing and general needs after the applicant returns to China so that the assistance of the State is not required.
(2) Aged Chinese citizens who are legally residing outside of China who insist on returning to China due to being unaccustomed to the climate and customs of their host country, and cannot speak the language of that country, or who have bought property in China and have foreign exchange savings or pensions in China, and whose relatives in China can resolve their housing and general needs.
(3) Chinese citizens who are legally residing outside of China who cannot support themselves due to persecution, where the local Chinese embassy or consulate thinks that it is necessary for persecuted Chinese citizens who are legally residing outside of China to return to China, and the person accepts the arrangement proposed by the Chinese government.
(4) Chinese citizens who are legally residing outside of China who make an application to return to China for permanent residence within a short period of time after leaving China to reside permanently in a foreign country. The application needs to submit the approval of their former working unit and resolve their housing and general needs independently.
(5) High-quality Chinese citizens who are legally residing outside of China who are in high demanding in China.

[13] In regard to official textbooks, see Department of Politics under the Ministry of Public Security, *Frontier Defence and Exit and Entry Administration, the Series of Basic Textbook of People's Police Operation: (Bianfang Yu Churu Jing Guanli, Renmin Jingcha Gongan Yewu Jichu Jiaochai)*, examined by Committee of Textbook Editing and Examination of the MPS, Internal Publication in Public Security Organs (*Gongan Jiguan Neibu Faxing*) (Beijing: the Publishing House of Qunzhong, 1999), 382; and Wang, Guoliang and Zhu, Lin, *The Administration on Exit and Entry, One of Planning Textbooks of Higher Education of People's Police (Renmin Jingcha Gaodeng Jiaoyu Guihua Jiaocha: Churujing Guanlixue)*, Interior Published within Public Security Organs (*Gongan Jiguan Neibu Faxing*), (Beijing: the Publishing House of China University of People's Public Security, 2002), 101. For academic texts, see Xiang, Dang, *The Guide to the Law of Exit and Entry in China and Foreign Countries, (Zhongwai Churujing Falv Zhinan)* (Beijing: the Publishing House of China University of People's Public Security, 1998), 136. For government online application instructions, see "Returning to China for Permanent Residence of Chinese Citizens Who are Legally Residing Outside of China (*Huaqiao Huiguo Dingju*)" implemented by Exit and Entry Administration of Guangdong Public Security Department, http://www.gdcrj.com/zggmcg/hchgdj (accessed 19/06/2003).

With the exception of the fifth category (who are encouraged to return to China for permanent residence due to their potential financial and educational contribution to the development of China), applicants in other categories need to provide many documents to certify their own or their sponsor's ability to support their living and housing needs after returning to China. This can include titles to property, pension certificates, deposit statements and evidence of the relationship between the applicant and sponsor.

Specifically, for applicants in North Korea and Mongolia, under Article 2 of the *Circular of the State Council of Overseas Chinese Affairs Office, Ministry of Foreign Affairs, Ministry of Public Security, Ministry of Labour and Ministry of Finance on the Arrangement Measures for Returned Korean and Mongolian Chinese for Permanent Residence* (*Chaoqiao Mengqiao*) 1989:

> The application for returning to China *Huaqiao* legally residing in Korea and Mongolia will not be accepted unless the applicants provide the evidence that their housing and employment has been acquired and solved through their own efforts. . . .

It is accepted that the economies of North Korea and Mongolia are less developed than in China. Logically, Chinese citizens who are legally residing in Korea or Mongolia would like to return to China. But they must meet above cited conditions. According to the report of *Southern Municipality Daily, China* in 2004, the requirements of conditions imposed on applicants for permanent residence are increasingly strict. In addition to requirements to meet their own housing and employment needs, *Huaqiao* legal residing in Korea need to meet requirements including the requirements of the spouse separation duration[14] In short, China only permits Chinese citizens who are legally residing outside of China to resume permanent residence if they will not be a burden on the community.

Chinese citizens who are residing in Taiwan wishing to return to China for permanent residence

Chinese citizens who are residing in Taiwan also need to meet particular conditions to resume permanent residence. According to Article 1(1)(1) of the *Circular of Ministry of Public Security on Some Issues of Exit and Entry Mainland of Mainland Residents Granted Permanent Residence of Taiwan Regions* 1995 (PRC),

> The applications of Chinese citizens, who are residing in Taiwan, for returning to China for permanent residence shall be severely examined and approved. Where the applicant resided in Taiwan for more than five years, their applications should be

[14] "Korean Chinese is Discomfiture and Longing for Returning to China after the Explosion of the Train in North Korea" (*Longchuan Huoche Da Baozha Hou Chaoxian Huoqiao Chujing Ganga Pan Huiguo*), 29/04/2004, *Southern Municipality Daily* (*Nanfang Dushi Bao*), http://news.sina.com.cn/c/2004-04-29/10182432253s.shtml (accessed 16/09/2006).

> processed in accordance with the relevant provisions of No. [1990] 15 document of the Central Committee of the Communist Party of China (CPC). The Permit of Permanent Residence of Taiwan Compatriot (*Taiwan Tongbao Dingjuzheng*) shall be issued to approve applicants. Where [the applicant resided in Taiwan] for less than five years, they may undergo the procedure of regular household registration after returning and destroying their Taiwan travel documents and exit-entry documents.

Clearly, Chinese citizens who resided in Taiwan are not treated as Chinese citizens but as Taiwan residents. It is common sense that aliens need to abide by relevant conditions and undergo the procedures, if they wish to reside permanently in a foreign country and that citizens should be free to return to their State for any purpose, upon presentation of a passport. By contrast, the imposition of strict conditions on *Huaqiao* returning to China equates them with aliens or quasi-aliens rather than citizens.[15]

Returning to China for employment

Between 1949, the foundation of the PRC and 1978, with the exception of first several years after foundation, the Chinese government usually persuaded *Huaqiao* to withdraw applications for returning to China for employment, and to rather settle in host countries and integrate into local communities.[16] Since 1986, applications for returning to China for employment need to be supported by evidence that the applicant's qualifications meet the demands of the domestic employment market and that they have the ability to find a job in China.

8.2.2 *Formalities of returning to China for permanent residence or employment*

With the exception of returning to China for a short period of time,[17] return either for the purpose of assuming permanent residence or employment requires application to the responsible department in the light of complex formalities.

---

[15] Xiamen Government, *Entry and Exit Regulations*, http://www.xm.gov.cn/eng/investment%20guide/Investment%20Climate/200409/t20040921_24112.htm (accessed 16/09/2006).

[16] Mao, Qixiong, editor, *the Encyclopedia of Chinese Citizens Who are Legally Residing Outside of China and Foreigners with Chinese Decent: the Volume of Laws, Regulations and Policies (Huaqiao Huaren Baike Quanshu: Falv Tiaoli Zhengce Juan)* (Beijing: the Publishing House of *Huaqiao*, China), 2000, 494. Also see Xia, Chenghua, *On the Issues from the perspective of Southward Police of President Li Denghui (Cong Li Denghui Zongtong De Nanxiang Zhengce Kan Wenti)*, The Journal of Asia Study (*Yazhou Yanjiu*), 8th Issue, 1994, P183–188.

[17] Under Article 9 of *Detailed Rules for Implementing of the Law on the Control of Exit*

Returning for permanent residence

Article 10 of the *Law on the Control of Exit and Entry of Citizens* 1985 (PRC) provides that:

> Chinese citizens who are legally residing outside of China and want to return to China for permanent residence shall complete the relevant procedures at the diplomatic missions, consular offices or other agencies located abroad that are authorized by the Ministry of Foreign Affairs (MFA), or at public security departments of the relevant provinces, autonomous regions, or municipalities directly under the State Council.

Article 10 of *Detailed Rules for Implementing of Law on the Control of Exit and Entry of Citizens (Amendment)* 1994 (PRC) further provides that:

> . . . . They, through their relatives in China, may also make an application to the municipal or county public security bureau in the locality of their destination. Return residence permits shall be granted upon examination by the public security department or bureau of the provinces, autonomous regions or municipalities directly under the State Council.

The Sate Council for Overseas Chinese Affairs Office (OCAO) is responsible for the overall administration of *Huaqiao* who want to return for permanent residence. Provincial offices of OCAO examine and determine the applications in details. Under Article 5 (1) of the *Explanation of the Ministry of Public Security on Some Issues on the Implementation of Law on the Control of Exit and Entry of Citizens and Its Detailed Rules for Implementation* 1987 (PRC):

> The diplomatic [agencies] located abroad that are authorised by the MFA shall report the applications for returning to China for permanent residence of *Huaqiao* to the OCAO; Municipal or county public security departments shall refer the applications, which are lodged by Chinese citizens who are legally residing outside of China themselves or their domestic relatives on behalf of them, for returning to China for permanent residence of Chinese citizens who are legally residing outside of China to local office (OCAO). Provincial office (OCAO) shall grant the application upon consulting with relevant responsible departments, including the public security department. Provincial public security departments shall issue *Return Residence Permits of Huaqiao* (*Huaqiao Huiguo Dingju Zhengming*) pursuant to the approval letter from the OCAO.

---

and Entry of Citizens (Amendment) 1994 (PRC), "Chinese citizens who are legally residing outside of China and return to China to stay for a short period of time may enter the country by presenting their valid Chinese passport or valid Chinese travel permit or other valid entry-exit certificates."

Returning for employment

Article 11 of *Detailed Rules for Implementing of Law on the Control of Exit and Entry of Citizens (Amendment)* 1994 (PRC) stipulates:

> Chinese citizens who are permanent residents of a foreign country and request to return to China for employment shall make an application to China's labour and personnel department or to the host or employing organizations.

The application procedure was fully reviewed, as follows, in the *Explanation of Law and Regulations Governing Exit and Entry and the Collections of Related Regulations*:

> China's labour and personnel department, or the host or employing organization, shall make the decision according to the demand of the regional employment market. If granted, a Certificate of Engagement or Employment (*Pinqing Guyong Zhengming*), approved by labour and personnel department, is issued. Chinese citizens who are legally residing outside of China may then return to China for employment and register their household.[18]

The avoidance of complicated procedures

Obviously, the multi-staged approval process could take much time and energy, especially if relatives in China make the application on their behalf. Meanwhile, the absence of a maximum prescribed processing period could mean that the application takes even longer. To avoid complicated procedures, some *Huaqiao* might return to China without undergoing the required procedures of application and approval.

Under Article 7 of the *Regulation of Inspection of Exit and Entry Borders* 1995 (PRC) and Article 3(1) of the *Circular of the Ministry of Public Security on Handling Means of Some Issues on the Implementation of Checking, Monitoring and Prevention of Exit and Entry in Regulation of Inspection of Exit and Entry Borders* 1995 (PRC), border check and administration offices must release the individuals returning to China after checking their passport and other entry certificates. The purpose of returning to China is not checked. As such, it is possible that the OCAO and public security departments will not know who has re-entered the territory for the purpose of permanent residence or employment. The disconnection between the regulations regarding the inspection of exit and entry borders on the one hand, and the control of exit and entry on the other, provides an opportunity for *Huaqiao* to avoid the complex formalities.

---

[18] Mao, Fengping, editor, *The Explanation of the Law and Regulations Governing Exit and Entry and the Collections of Related Regulations* (*Chujing Rujing Falv Fagui Sijie Yu Xiangying Fagui Zhaibian)* (Changchun, China: the Publishing House of Jilin Renmin, 1994), 88.

8.2.3 *Household registration after returning to China*

The household registration system in China requires that all *Huaqiao* who wish to return must register upon return. The system, which in light of its historical background, is understandable, is also an important aspect of the limits imposed on the return of *Huaqiao*.

Article 11 of the *Law on the Control of Exit and Entry of Citizens* 1985 (PRC) provides that:

> After their entry into China, Chinese citizens who are legally residing outside of China and have come for permanent residence or employment shall register for regular residence in accordance with the provisions for the administration of residence. Those who have entered for a temporary stay shall register for temporary residence in accordance with the same provisions.

These provisions are detailed in the *Detailed Rules for Implementing of Law on the Control of Exit and Entry of Citizens (Amendment)* 1994 (PRC). In the case of returning for permanent residence or employment, Articles 12 of the Detailed Rules 1994 provided that returned Chinese citizens who legally resided outside of China for permanent residence or for employment are required to register their household:

> . . . . [W]ithin 30 days of arrival at their destination, undergo the procedures for regular residence registration at the local public security bureau by presenting their return residence permits or the certification of engagement of employment as approved by China's labor and personnel department.

This process creates a vital means of stopping *Huaqiao* from returning to China without undergoing the procedure of application and approval, because not to undergo the procedure means that the person will not hold the necessary residency permit or employment certificate, and will be unable to register their household.

For returning for temporary residency, Article 13 of the Detailed Rules 1994 provided that returned Chinese citizens who legally resided outside of China for a short period of time shall under go the registration procedures for temporary residence:[19]

> . . . . Anyone who lodges at such enterprises and institutions as guesthouses, hotels, inns, hostels or schools, or at State departments, social departments or other institutions, he or she shall fill in temporary lodging registration forms, whereas, for anyone

[19] A short period of time means less than one year, according to the Exit and Entry Administration and Bureau of Border Security Check and Administration in Jilin Province. See Exit and Entry Administration under Jilin Province Public Security Department and Bureau of Border Security Check and Administration under Jilin Province Public Security Department, editor, *The Kit of Exit, Entry and Frontier Defence (Shiyong Churu Jing Bianfang Zhishi Daquan)* (Changchun, China: the Publishing House of Jilin Wenshi, 1994), 37.

> who lodges at the homes of one's relatives or friends, one's relatives and friends, shall, within 24 hours, and 72 hours for those in rural areas, undergo temporary residence registration at the local police station or residence registration office.

Similar requirements of household registration can be found in Vietnamese law.[20]

8.2.4 *Reasons for the limits imposed on the return of* Huaqiao

The discussion so far demonstrates that the limits imposed on *Huaqiao* for permanent residence or for employment are not consonant with international norms and infringe on the right to return. Careful exploration of the reasons behind the limits being imposed is needed, before any ideas are advanced as to how to essentially relax government control over the return of this group.[21]

The first reason for the limits can be found in China's policy towards *Huaqiao* over time. Since the establishment of the PRC in 1949, the government has imposed a policy of supporting and encouraging that group to freely settle in host countries, assume the nationality of their host country, and to live in harmony with its people.[22] That implies, although it is not stated, that the Chinese government

---

[20] Chapter III Residence of *Ordinance on Entry, Exit and Residence of Foreigners in Vietnam 2000*, Standing Committee of National Assembly No. 24-2000-PL-UBTVQH10. Article 11 Clause 1 provides "Upon entry, foreigners must register the purpose and length of stay and their residential address in Vietnam, and their activities must comply strictly with the registered purposes."

[21] In 1990, the Consular-General of the PRC in New York submitted *Suggestions of Consulate-General of the PRC in New York on Relative Relaxation of Returning to China for Permanent Residence of Huaqiao to the OCAO, BEEA under MPS and the Department of Consular Affairs under the MFA* in which he expressed the hope that conditions could be relaxed and processing times shortened. These suggestions were rejected in *Opinions of State Council of Overseas Chinese Affairs Office, Exit and Entry Administration under MPS and Department of Consular Affairs under the MFA on Returning to China for Permanent Residence of Huaqiao* 1991 (PRC). The suggestion that processing of applications should take a maximum of three months was rejected on the grounds that such a proposal was unrealistic given the nature of the examination and approval process, and the time that it takes to post documents. The only suggestion that was accepted was that, in the case of overseas offices where applications are lodged, the application may be reported directly to a provincial office (OCAO). This removed the requirement of reporting the application to a county or municipal overseas office first.

[22] Yang, Fajing, *the Introduction to Exit Abroad (Chuguo Zhishi Gailan)* (Beijing: the Publishing House of Science Popularisation, 1990) pages 173–174; and Wang, Guoliang and Zhu, Lin, *The Administration on Exit and Entry, one of Planning Textbooks of Higher Education of People's Police (Renmin Jingcha Gaodeng Jiaoyu Guihua Jiaocha: Churujing Guanlixue)*, Interior Published within Public Security Organs *(Gongan Jiguan Neibu Faxing)* (Beijing: the Publishing House of China University of People's Public Security, 2002), 101.

has a passive policy towards or is uninterested in the return of *Huaqiao*, especially for permanent residence.

Such a policy may have once been a foil to the evident concern in many Southeast Asian countries that close connections between this group and the PRC could bring communist insurgency. With the improvement of the relations between China and other countries, such concerns in many Southeast Asian countries have passed their peak.[23] Another reason for such uninterest in the permanent return of *Huaqiao* can be found in concerns about China's huge population, now nearing 1.3 billion.[24] This huge number poses a challenge for economic development. In the context of strict national family planning policy and lack of employment opportunities, it is difficult for the government to welcome a large number of *Huaqiao* back to China.[25]

The official policy on *Huaqiao* in fact provides another significant reason to limit their return. This has been captured in Article 3 (2) of *Detailed Rules of the Implementation of Law on the Protection of the Rights and Interests of Returned Chinese Citizens Who Legally Resided Outside of China (Guiqiao) and the Family Members of Chinese Citizens who Legally Residing Outside of China (Qiaojuan) (Amendment)* 2000 (PRC):

> The State shall, in accordance with the practical conditions and the characteristics of returned Huaqiao (*Guiqiao*) and the family members of returned Huaqiao (*Qiaojuan*), give them appropriate preferential treatment, and the specific measures thereof shall be formulated by the State Council or the relevant competent departments under the State Council.

---

[23] President Hu Jintao and President Susilo of Indonesia signed the joint statement on establishing the strategic partnership between both countries. President Hu Jintao and President Arroyo of the Philippines decided to establish the strategic and cooperative relations committed to peace and development. These have pushed China's traditionally friendly relations with the three countries into a new development phase. During the visit of President Hu Jingtao in April 2005, both sides have reached wide consensus on further developing bilateral relations. President Hu Jintao and Sudan Bolkiah of Brunei unanimously agreed to continue China-Brunei friendly and cooperative relations of good neighbours. See *Li Zhaoxing Says That President Hu Jintao's Tour to Three Southeast Asian Countries Made Fruitful Achievements* (28/04/2005), http://www.fmprc.gov.cn/eng/zxxx/t193962.htm (accessed 16/09/2006).

[24] The population of China reached 1,286,975,468 in July 20010.3. CIA, *The World Factbook: China*, 18 December 2003, http://www.cia.gov/cia/publications/factbook/geos/ch.html (accessed 16/09/2006).

[25] The government has undertaken a range of comprehensive measures to control the quantity of population and improve the quality of population, such as "one child in one family policy." A strict national family planning policy has been in place since the 1970s for this purpose, which was given effect by Article 2 of the *Law on the Population and Family Planning* 2001 (PRC).

Based on this the government has promised to "make arrangements for Chinese citizens who are legally residing outside of China and have to return to the country and settle down here permanently."[26] The actual obligations of the government are contained in Article 4 of the *Law on the Protection of the Rights and Interests of Returned Chinese Citizens Who Legally Resided Outside of China and the family members of Chinese Citizens Who Legally Resided Outside of China (Amendment)* 2000 (PRC) which prescribes that:

> Local governments and departments concerned shall make arrangements for *Huaqiao* who have returned to reside permanently in the country pursuant to the relevant provisions of the State.

This obligation places a heavy financial burden on the State. Additionally, the arrangements may not satisfy *Huaqiao* on return, as much of the time, due to the developing nature of the economy in China, they are placed in jobs on farms, in forestry and factories.[27] Those who are dissatisfied may prefer to return to the foreign country from which they came.[28] This in turn escalates the financial cost of the arrangements made and damages China's reputation. Experience, from several waves of return from the 1950s to the 1970s, has proven the obligations costly. The current laws and regulations were promulgated to prevent the same series of events from occurring in future.

In summary, as Wang Guoliang has said in *Administration on Exit and Entry, one of Planning Textbooks of Higher Education of People's Police*:

---

[26] Article 5 the *Law on the Protection of the Rights and Interests of Returned Chinese Citizens who Legally Resided Outside of China and the Family Members of Chinese Citizens Who Legally Resided Outside of China (Amendment)* 2000 (PRC).

[27] See Article 9 Clause 1 of the *Law on the Protection of the Rights and Interests of Returned Chinese Citizens who Legally Resided Outside of China and the Family Members of Chinese Citizens Who Legally Resided Outside of China (Amendment)* 2000 (PRC), Article 6 to 8 of *Detailed Rules of the Implementation on Protection of the Rights and Interests of Chinese and Family Members of Chinese citizens who Legally Resided Outside of China 1993 (PRC)* and *Minute of National Working Meeting on Chinese citizens who are legally residing outside of China Farms and Factories (Quanguo Huaqiao Nongchang Gongchang Goongzuo Huiyi Jiyao)*. Also see Mao, Qixiong, Editor, *the Encyclopedia of Huaqiao and Foreign Chinese: the Volume of Laws, Regulations and Policies (Huaqiao Huaren Baike Quanshu: Falv Tiaoli Zhengce Juan)* (Beijing: the Publishing House of Huaqiao, 2000), 494.

[28] China experienced a lot of return migration during the 1950s and late 1970s. During this period, large numbers of Vietnam Chinese returned due to the anti-Chinese policy in South Vietnam. There was similarly a large wave of return migration from Indonesia during the 1960s. By the late 1970s, over 200,000 nationals had returned from Vietnam, Laos and Cambodia and Indonesia. Some of the nationals who had returned from Indonesia re-exited China illegally during the 1970s.

> The issues of *Huaqiao* who want to return to China for permanent residence [. . .] concentrate on the enforcement of the policy of arranging a job, housing and life of returned Chinese citizens who legally resided outside of China. Therefore, the application [of the policy] should be considered carefully and comprehensively.[29]

Hence, the right of *Huaqiao* to return is not the foundation upon which laws regarding their return are based – the laws instead reflect policy concerned with over-population and developing economic conditions.[30]

8.2.5 *Effects of the limits on the return of* Huaqiao

Effects of the limits on the return of *Huaqiao* can be analysed from both an international and domestic level. Internationally, the right to return is expressly recognised in many international and regional human rights instruments, as mentioned above. Hence, every individual *Huaqiao* is entitled to return to China. However, current policies towards this group and towards those of them who have returned, concentrate on encouraging either their integration into the host country or basic living arrangements in China, rather than the protection of their right to return. If they do not fit into one of the five prescribed categories, listed above, they may not be eligible to return to China freely. Similarly, if they cannot show that their qualifications will meet the needs of the employment market, they may also be prohibited from returning.

Clearly, the right of this group to return is seriously limited and domestically, the limits are unfair and arbitrary. China only approves the applications of *Huaqiao* to return for permanent residence if they will not burden the Chinese community and if they belong to one of the prescribed classes of eligible entrants. The universal right to return is abused for young *Huaqiao* and spouses who cannot support themselves, to name just two groups.

---

[29] Wang, Guoliang and Zhu, Lin, *The Administration on Exit and Entry, one of Planning Textbooks of Higher Education of People's Police* (*Renmin Jingcha Gaodeng Jiaoyu Guihua Jiaocha: Churujing Guanlixue*), Interior Published within Public Security Organs (*Gongan Jiguan Neibu Faxing*) (Beijing: the Publishing House of China University of People's Public Security, 2002), 101.

[30] MPS contend that even though Chinese citizens who are legally residing outside of China may return to China for permanent residence, they must lodge the application and be granted approval because of over population and developing economic situation. See Department of Politics under the MPS, *Frontier Defence and Exit and Entry Administration, the Series of Basic Textbook of People's Police Operation: (Bianfang Yu Churu Jing Guanli, Renmin Jingcha Gongan Yewu Jichu Jiaochai)*, examined by Committee of Textbook editing and Examination of the MPS, Internal Publication in Public Security Organs (*Gongan Jiguan Neibu Faxing*) (Beijing: the Publishing House of Qunzhong, 1999), 382.

In practice the limits on the right to return do not help solve China's underlying problems. Because the limits apply to all *Huaqiao*, it is very likely that the limits may simultaneously prohibit the return of those who are a potentially valuable asset to the country.[31] The prohibition may in fact only deepen underlying problems.

8.3 Limits on the Return of Chinese Illegal Migrants or *Feifa Yimin*

Chinese citizens who are illegally outside of China here refer to those who either illegally entered into a foreign country, or overstayed a legally acquired visa, namely Chinese illegal migrants (*Feifa Yimin*).[32] The definition is similar to that used in international legal parlance.[33] There are at least 11 million Chinese illegal migrants currently.[34] Chinese illegal migration is a trans-national issue and, as such, host countries of Chinese illegal migrants are also affected.[35]

---

[31] Then President Jiang, Zemin said in 1999 National Working Conference of Overseas Chinese that several millions Chinese citizens who are legally residing outside of China is Chinese unique and valuable resource. Quoted from Mao, Qixiong, *the Encyclopedia of Chinese citizens who are legally residing outside of China and Foreign Chinese: the Volume of Laws, Regulations and Policies (Huaqiao Huaren Baike Quanshu: Falv Tiaoli Zhengce Juan)* (Beijing: the Publishing House of Huaqiao, 2000), 493.

[32] Preface of the *Circular of the MFA and MPS on Replacing, Extending and Reissuing Passport for Irregular Emigrants* 1992 (PRC) *(Waijiaobu Gonganbu Guanyu Wei Feifa Yimin Bu Huan Fa Huzhao De Tongzhi).*

[33] The IOM usually called illegal migrants as irregular migrants. "Irregular migrants refers to migrants who have either entered without inspection, or entered with the use of an illegally acquired or falsified visa or passport or who overstayed a legally acquired visa. See definition made at the IOM, *Myths and Realities of Chinese Irregular Migration*, No. 1 of IOM Migration Research Series, Geneva, Switzerland: the IOM, 2000, 44 pages, 7.

[34] According to the figures released by the IOM in 2000, "conservative estimates gave around 10.2.7 million irregular migrants in late 1997 in East and South-East Asia alone, no small number in comparison to the estimated 5 million irregular migrants in the USA as of 1996 and 3 million in Europe." See IOM, *Myths and Realities of Chinese Irregular Migration*, No. 1 of IOM Migration Research Series, IOM, Geneva, Switzerland, 2000 44 pages, 12; Also James Chin argued in 2003, "to some extent, it could be said that China provides the largest number of East Asian irregular immigrants to Europe." See Chin, James K., "Reducing Irregular Migration from China". *International Migration*, Volume 41, Number 3 (September 01, 2003), pages 49–72, http://www12.georgetown.edu/sfs/isim/pages/IMJournal.html (accessed 16/09/2006), at 50.

[35] For example, in December 1994, "[t]he Chinese Government was effectively refusing to take back hundreds of people who have recently arrived by boat in Darwin, leaving Australia facing its worst refugee crisis in 15 years. Chinese officials are understood to have

Although Chinese can return to China with a valid Chinese passport, a practice widely accepted in law, by academic scholars and in government practice,[36] many Chinese illegal migrants cannot return because their passports have not been reissued, replaced or extended. This section concentrates on the conditions and formalities of passport re-issue, replacement and extension for Chinese illegal migrants, and its effects.

8.3.1 *Conditions of Passport Re-Issue, Replacement and Extension of Chinese Illegal Migrants*

Chinese overseas diplomatic missions, consular offices and other authorized agencies are responsible for handling applications for passport re-issue, replacement, and extension for citizens who are abroad, pursuant to Article 17(2) and Article 21 of *Detailed Rules for the Implementation of Law on the Control of Exit and Entry of Citizens* 1985 (PRC). Articles 1 to 7 of the *Circular of Ministry of Foreign Affairs and Ministry of Public Security on Passport Re-issue, Replacement and Extension of Irregular Migrants* 1992 (PRC) provide the conditions under which designated authorities process applications. This Detailed Rule is a unique internal policy in this regard and not accessible to the public. It is thus noteworthy to translate and quote most of the articles of it.

(1) Where the applicants left China with a legal passport and visa and overstayed without acquired visas, one's applications for passport re-issue or extension shall not be approved unless they have been granted or will be granted a permanent residence status of host country, or have been granted a work permit (the latter is only applied to the USA).

---

said they would not take any Vietnamese Chinese refugees – who make up the bulk of recent arrivals – unless they gave a written guarantee that they were going voluntarily – something they are considered unlikely to do . . . Australian officials were attempting to negotiate a more cooperative arrangement with China." See Middleton, Karen, "China "no" to boat people – Bolkus demands end to "racket", in *Age*, 29 December 1994; also the Australian Federal Government "has agreed to contributed to the cost of relocating nearly 800 Sino-Vietnamese boat people held in Australia, following the announcement today of a landmark deal under which detainees will be repatriated." See Hutcheon, Stephen, *Age*, 10 April 1995. Both are in Wright, Jillian, *Migration OZ Update*, June 1995, published by Bureau of Immigration, Multicultural and Population Research, Carlton South, Australia, 11.

36 Article 2 of the *Law on the Control of Exit and Entry of citizens* 1985 (PRC); Xiang, Dang, *The Guide to the Law of Exit and Entry in China and Foreign Countries (Zhongwai Churujing Falv Zhinan)* (Beijing: the Publishing House of China University of People's Public Security, 1998), 43; Xiamen Government, *Entry and Exit Regulations*, http://english.xm.gov.cn/investment%20guide/Investment%20Climate/200409/t20040921_24112.htm (accessed 16/09/2006).

(2) Where the applicants left China with [public affairs passports] or were smuggled from China without passports, then smuggled into a foreign country or enter a foreign country holding a false passport or travel documents, one's applications for passport replacement, re-issue or extension shall be strictly examined, not be granted unless they have been granted or will be granted a permanent residence status of host country, or been granted a work permit. The applicants also need to provide the detailed statement of smuggling and the detailed explanation of one's domestic situation.
(3) Where the applicants left China with [public affairs passport] in the name of a contract labour service, one's application for the replacement of an ordinary passport for private affairs shall not be granted unless they have provided the detailed written Statement of leaving China, have been or will be granted permanent residence status of host country, or been granted a permanent job. And host country might not make diplomatic negotiation with China if the application is granted.
(4) The situation of irregular migrants who gain the right of permanent residence in foreign countries due to the status of refugee is very complex. . . . Their applications for renunciation of Chinese nationality shall not be accepted. Their application for passport shall be strictly examined. Where they leave for a foreign country with [public affairs passport], the application for reissuing or replacing with [private passport] shall be respectively reported to the [designated authorities] . . .
(5) Where they applied for refugee status for only residing permanently, and agreed to honestly explain the purpose of their application for passport, give up refugee status, return old passports they originally held, overseas diplomatic missions and consular offices shall grant the application after criticizing and enlightening.
(6) Where the applicant left China with [private passport], legally entered other countries and overstayed without acquired visas, or illegally entered a foreign country with [private passport], the application for passport extension shall usually be acceptable. Overseas embassies and consulates may prolong the period of processing application according to the actual situation of different application. If the extension of passport might cause host country's to question or gather evidence against China, the application shall not be accepted.
(7) Where irregular migrants require to return to China due to being unable to support themselves, or are repatriated by the host country, overseas embassies and consulates may issue single-journey travel certificates and take prior passports back. . . .

As to irregular migrants who have been granted refugee status by the third country or areas, if host country insist in repatriating them, overseas embassy and consulates shall try the best to repatriate them to prior permanently residing country or areas.

With respect to irregular migrants who reject the repatriation of the host country, overseas embassy and consulates shall refuse the repatriation requirements by reason that the irregular migrants do not agree to return to China. Where the host country insists on requiring the Chinese government to accept the repatriated irregular migrants, overseas embassy and consulates shall uphold the principle of checking first and repatriating second.

It is extremely difficult to meet the requirements for permanent residence or work permission, because most Chinese illegal migrants do not have professional skills, business skills or immediate relatives legally present in the host country. If they did, it is likely that they would lawfully leave China and enter a foreign country. As such, the majority of applications from irregular migrants are not approved because they lack the required documentation.

The limits on the application of Chinese with refugee status in a foreign country for renunciation of Chinese citizenship are so serious that they violate the relevant provisions of China. Article 12 of the *Law of Nationality* 1980 (PRC) provides "State functionaries and military personnel on active service shall not renounce Chinese citizenship." Article 10 of the *Law of Nationality* 1980 (PRC) provides that Chinese citizens who have resided abroad may renounce their Chinese citizenship upon approval of their applications. Relevant Chinese laws do not clarify 'resided abroad'. According to the most authoritative dictionary in China, *The Contemporary Chinese Dictionary* (*Chinese and English*), it can be interpreted as either settling down in a certain foreign place with the status of foreign citizenship or with the status of foreign permanent resident.[37] Chinese citizens with refugee status in a foreign country do not fall in the categories of Article 12, but to the contrary, they meet the requirements of Article 8. So their application for renouncing Chinese citizenship should be granted. However, the circular stipulates that their applications shall not be accepted.

The requirement of firstly giving up refugee status in a foreign country, illustrates that China will not take back Chinese illegal migrants with refugee status in foreign countries. China argues that the system of political asylum in Western countries connives with the irregular migrant.[38] This places the issue of repatriated Chinese illegal migrants into the context of a disagreement over refugee systems between China and the West. The IOM has considered that China appears unwilling to accept asylum seekers whose applications have been denied.[39] Due to the big gap between China and other countries, especially Western countries, most refuges would like to return to China temporarily rather than permanently. Giving up refugee status in a foreign country implies that the refuges can't return to a foreign country. As a result, someone returning to China would not be giving up refugee status. According to Article 12 of the ICCPR, in no case may a person be arbitrarily deprived of the right to enter one's own country. The status of refugee in a foreign country may not be critical to an assessment of the right to return to

---

[37] Dictionary Department, Institute of Linguistics, Chinese Academy of Social Sciences, *The Contemporary Chinese Dictionary (Chinese-English edition)* (*Xiandai Hanyu Cidian*) (Beijing: Foreign Language Teaching and Research Press, 2002), 458

[38] Yang, Fajing, editor, *the Introduction to Exit Abroad (Chuguo Zhishi Gailan)* (Beijing: the Publishing House of Science Popularisation, 1990), 13.

[39] The IOM, *Myths and Realities of Chinese Irregular Migration*, No. 1 of IOM Migration Research Series, Geneva, Switzerland: the IOM, 2000, 44 pages, 30.

one's own country, yet the precondition of giving up refugee status before returning to China obviously interferes with the right of Chinese to return to China.

The legal criteria for accepting applications for passport extensions of Chinese who have legally left for a foreign country with a private passport and who have overstayed are inadequate. Under the provisions of the circular, approval does not rely upon the relevant provisions of Chinese law, but references the potential effects of granting the extension. Intergovernmental relations are placed ahead of a citizen's right to have their passport extended.

8.3.2 *Formalities of Passport Reissue, Replacement and Extension for Chinese Illegal Migrants*

The processing period of passport extension is normally four working days, and six working days for reissue and replacement in overseas diplomatic missions and general consular offices.[40] However, according to Article 8 (1)(3) of the *Circular of Ministry of Foreign Affairs and Ministry of Public Security on Passport Re-issue, Replacement and Extension of Chinese illegal migrants* 1992 (PRC):

> The processing period of passport re-issue and replacement is generally at least three months. Even though the applicant meets the requirements of the conditions, the period may be prolonged if the original passport was secretly altered, damaged, torn open or intentionally concealed, or destroyed by melting or burning. Overseas diplomatic missions and consular offices may decide the period, ranging from six months or over one year depending upon the nature of mistakes, attitude of acknowledgment and the reasons of application for re-issue and replacement.

Because the, similarly titled, *Circular of Ministry of Foreign Affairs and Ministry of Public Security on Passport Re-issue, Replacement and Extension of Irregular Migrants* 1992 (PRC) is an internal policy, the guidelines for protraction of the administrative process for passport extensions are not publicly accessible. The official explanations about the processing period are often very vague. In 2004, the Sydney Consulate General of the PRC website stated "the processing period for application for passport re-issue and replacement depends on the reply of domestic departments to Consulate General enquires."[41] Faced with an inaccessible policy and vague instruction, applicants are unable to predict how long the process will take or plan to take action to remedy an infringement of their rights.

---

[40] Consulate General of the People's Republic of China in Sydney, "the Chart of the Consular Affairs Fees and Urgent Fees" *(Banli Zhengjian Shouxu Shoufei Yilanbiao)*, October 2005, http://sydney.chineseconsulate.org/chn/hzqz/t217432.htm (accessed 16/09/2006).

[41] Consulate General of the People's Republic of China in Sydney, "the Chart of the Consular Affairs Fees and Urgent Fees" *(Banli Zhengjian Shouxu Shoufei Yilanbiao)*, October 2005, http://sydney.chineseconsulate.org/chn/hzqz/t217432.htm (accessed 16/09/2006).

It is argued that the protracted application process is regarded as a way of punishing and preventing irregular migration. An irregular migrant who violates laws may be punished in accordance with the relevant provisions of Chinese law, such as Article 22 of *Detailed Rules for the Implementation of Law on the Control of the Entry and Exit of Aliens (Amendment)* 1994 (PRC), Article 15 of the *Regulations of Inspection of Exit and Entry Borders* 1995 (PRC) and Article 322 of the *Law of Criminal* 1997 (PRC). It is unacceptable to punish a *Feifa Yimin* by drawing out administrative processes when laws exist to punish specific offences. The administrative strategy results in double punishment on Chinese illegal migrants, which could be seen as unfair or oppressive.

Administrative practices suggest that there is not necessarily a link between passport availability and illegal migration. In 2003, Zhang Fang and Ye Youse, the Deputy Director and Deputy Team Leader of the Exit and Entry Administration within the Fujian Province Public Security Department, stated "passports are possibly an important channel of increasing Chinese legal migrants and decreasing Chinese illegal migrants."[42] Protraction of the application process is thus not an effective way of decreasing illegal migrants. Clearly, the unacceptable procedural requirements further hamper qualified Chinese illegal migrants from returning to China.

8.4 The Abuse of the Right of Chinese Nationals Not to be Exiled

Under international norms, a State is under a duty to allow entry of a national and is prohibited from exiling that national, which has been analysed in part 3.5.4 of this book. Nevertheless, the situation of exiling nationals exists in China. The methodology adopted in this section draws on the case study of domestic dissident being exiled. The high profile attempts to expel dissidents, since the release of Tiananmen student leader Wang Dan from China for the purpose of obtaining medical treatment overseas in 1998, attracted much attention at the time. Under *China Country Report on Human Rights Practices for 1998* released by the US State Department:

> Tiananmen student leader Wang Dan was released from prison on medical parole in April [of 1997] on the condition that he leaves the country for medical treatment. Liu Nianchun was released under the same conditions in December [of 1997]. Both are now living abroad in exile.[43]

---

[42] Fujian Province is the largest source of illegal migrants of China. Zhang, Feng and Ye, Youshen, "Exit and Entry Administration According to Laws and Crackdown of Illegal Migration *(Shilun Yifa Guanli Churujing Xingwei Yu Daji Feifa Yimin Huodong)*", *Journal of Fujian Public Security College (Fujian Gongan Gaodeng Zhuanke Xuexiao Xuebao)*, No. 2 (2003), 36–39, 38.

[43] US Department of State, "China Country Report on Human Rights Practices for

The publication *China: Enforced Exile of Dissidents: Government "Re-entry Blacklist" Revealed* released by Human Rights Watch Asia, described that:

> [In] mid-1991, dissidents began to be asked by the police whether they would not prefer to leave China rather than face further detention or imprisonment. During several periods of detention during 1991, journalist Zhang Weiguo was apparently repeatedly asked this question. In his months of freedom between September 1993 and April 1994, Wei Jingsheng, China's most prominent dissident, was told that the passport could be issued quickly if he wanted to leave the country. In April–May 1994, China tried to send both of the "black hands' of the 1989 movement, Wang Juntao and Chen Ziming, out of the country. Both were serving thirteen-year prison terms. In late April, Wang was informed that his only chance of freedom was to leave the country, and he was immediately sent to the US. Chen was made the same offer, but refused exile.[44]

Both men have advocated the use of peaceful means for achieving greater democracy and human rights in China. Their alleged offences arose from the exercise of their internationally recognised rights to free speech and association during the protest movement of 1989. Neither is known to have committed any criminal act according to international law. Fortunately, the situation has improved. There have been no reports of exile in China in recent years.

Involuntary exile challenges the Chinese legal system. There are no provisions related to exile in current Chinese law including the Constitution, the *Law on the Control of Exit and Entry of Citizens* 1985 (PRC) and the *Law of Nationality* 1980 (PRC). Involuntary exile makes a mockery for "principle of the law as criterion" (*Yi Falv Wei Zhunshen*) and that "no organisation or individual is privileged to be beyond the Constitution or the law".[45] It is a typical example of "substituting one's word for legal provisions" (*Yiyan Daifa*).

It is almost impossible that Chinese authorities know nothing about the detriment to the rights of citizens and dignity of the legal system caused by involuntary exile. The discrepancy between recognition of rights and practices is political. As the IOM contended in *People's Republic of China: Migration in 1999*, "migration had political uses for dissidents and the State. For the former, exile provided an alternative to repression".[46] To appease human rights critics from the West, and to prevent them from engaging in "anti-revolutionary" activities, the authorities thus secretly pursued a policy of sending former political prisoners and other dissidents into involuntary exile abroad.

1998", http://www.State.gov/www/global/human_rights/1998_hrp_report/china.html (accessed 2/02/2004), 3.

[44] Human Rights Watch Asia and Human Rights in China, *China: Enforced Exile of Dissidents: Government "Re-entry Blacklist" Revealed"*, Vol. 7 No. 1, January 1995.

[45] Article 5 Clause 5 of the *Constitution of the PRC (Amendment)* 2004.

[46] The IOM, "the People's Republic of China – Migration in 1999", www.iom.org (accessed 18/06/2003).

8.5 Conclusions

The legal provisions prohibiting Chinese citizens from returning to China seriously breach the right to return to the State of nationality. Prohibitions intended to restrict the right to return of citizens, especially dissidents, such as the revocation and confiscation of passports, and not replacing, reissuing or extending of passports and arbitrarily prolonging the processing period, should be a second priority for reform in the limits on the return of Chinese citizens, especially dissidents. Chinese dissidents residing abroad are the most direct sufferers. The group of effectively stateless Chinese dissidents residing abroad is becoming larger.

Few among the 30 million *Huaqiao* lodge the applications to return to China for permanent residence or employment. This is not because they do not want to return but they hesitate at the prospect of the unattainable conditions and the complicated application procedures. The strict limits might first be attributed to the Chinese government's policies towards *Huaqiao*, based on overpopulation and economic development that aimed at supporting and encouraging their settlement in and assumption of the nationality of host countries. The costs of making arrangements for returned *Huaqiao*, born in several waves of return from the 1950s to the 1970s, also helps explain a policy of being uninterested in the return of *Huaqiao*.

The return of 11 million Chinese irregular migrants will pose financial burdens for China. However it is not acceptable to impose limits on their return based on that prospect. Chinese irregular migrants have difficulty meeting the impracticable requirements of passport re-issue, replacement and extension. More seriously, an applicant is unable to estimate how long an application will take, because of the overly flexible processing period. It seems convincing to presume that the government regards the protraction of the application process as a means of punishing and preventing illegal migration. This is a trans-national issue and host countries of Chinese irregular migrants are affected.

Even if the expulsion of Chinese nationals has passed it peak since the 1990s, the abuse of the right not to be expelled needs to be checked as an important issue, and is an important issue. If expulsion and exile are the same, Chinese nationals have the right not to be expelled or exiled from China. The expelled Chinese find it difficult to find a place to reside after being exiled, and are an effectively stateless group. Besides the challenges expulsion makes to the dignity of national legal system, it brings individual suffering and social instability. Given the clearly unpersuasive legal validity of involuntary expelling Chinese nationals, it can only be presumed that the foremost motive is political.

Chapter Nine

The Right of Travelling to or from the HKSAR, MSAR and Taiwan

INTRODUCTION

As a result of the advanced level of political and economic development in the HKSAR, MSAR and Taiwan, regulations for Chinese citizens travelling to or from those regions are similar to regulations governing their exit from and entry to foreign countries, with some distinct features. Statistics from the BEEA under the MPS in 2001–2002 revealed that 73.54% of people travelling to China came from the HKSAR and MSAR. Of people travelling abroad, 71.90% went to the HKSAR and MSAR. Travel to and from Taiwan is proportionately much less. In 2001, 3.77% of people travelling to China came from Taiwan, and 3.25% of people travelling abroad went to Taiwan. This extent of travel, and the principles underlying special arrangements for the regions, suggests that careful attention needs to be paid to the limits imposed on the right of travelling to or from the HKSAR, MSAR and Taiwan.

9.1 LIMITS ON MAINLAND CHINESE TRAVELLING TO OR FROM THE HKSAR OR MSAR

The *Provisional Measures on the Control over Chinese Citizens Travelling for Private Affairs to or from the Regions of Hong Kong or Macao* 1986 (PRC), which was promulgated in accordance with Article 17 of the *Law on the Control of Exit and Entry of Citizens* 1985 (PRC) by the MPS, is the key law governing the control of Mainland Chinese travelling to or from the HKSAR and MSAR. The MPS and the State Council Hong Kong and Macao Affairs office (SHMO) have also issued some interpretative regulations.[1]

These provisions have established the special system governing Mainland Chinese travelling to or from the HKSAR or MSAR. Although reforms discussed in Chapter five improved this system, some problems still need scrutiny. The focus of the special system has four administrative principles (i) unilateral examination and approval of the Mainland government (ii) the examination and approval of fixed quotas (iii) strict conditions of applying for travel to the HKSAR or MSAR, and (iv) different treatment of Mainland Chinese as opposed to the HKSAR and MSAR Chinese. This section will question these four principles, which have until now been uncritically accepted by the government and academics alike.

9.1.1 *Unilateral examination and approval of the Mainland government*

The Mainland government is unilaterally responsible for examining and approving the application of Mainland Chinese for travel to the HKSAR or MSAR. According to Article 3 of the *Provisional Measures on the Control over Chinese Citizens Travelling for Private Affairs to or from the Regions of Hong Kong or Macao* 1986 (PRC), Mainland Chinese travelling to the regions for private affairs must have the passes to Hong Kong and Macao or the passes to and from Hong Kong and Macao signed and issued by the public security departments of Mainland China. This special administration seems to stem from the sovereignty of China over the HKSAR and MSAR.

Unilateral examination and approval of the Mainland government existed after 1951.[2] After China resumed sovereignty over the HKSAR in 1997 and the MSAR

---

[1] Such as the *Explanation of Some Matters on Implementation of Provisional Measures on the Control over Chinese Citizens Travelling for Private Affairs to or from the Regions of Hong Kong or Macao* 1987 (PRC); the *Provisional Measures on the Control over Mainland Residents Travelling for Such Business, Training, Employment as Non-Public Affairs to or from Hong Kong Special Administration Regions* 1998 (PRC); and the *Interpretation by the Standing Committee of the National People's Congress Regarding Paragraph 4 in Article 22 and Category (3) of Paragraph 2 in Article 24 of the Basic Law of the Hong Kong Special Administrative Region of the People's Republic of China* 1999 (PRC).

[2] Prior to 1951, residents in Hong Kong, Macao and the Mainland China could travel between the three regions without passes or visas. The *Proclamation of the MPS, the Central People's Government on the control over Passengers Travelling to and from the Regions of Hong Kong or Macao* 1951 (PRC) established the current system, and a series

in 1999, the principle of unilateral examination and approval was not changed. The principle was accepted by the governments of the HKSAR and MSAR and extended to travel for public affairs.[3] The main exceptions cover those persons travelling to the HKSAR for employment, training and studying. In which case, applicants must obtain entry permission from the HKSAR Immigration Department in advance.[4]

At first glance, it may be argued that unilateral examination and approval may improve the protection of RLR of Mainland Chinese, because the Mainland governments seem to have the power to modify or cancel the conditions of leaving for the HKSAR or MSAR. In fact, the reverse occurs in practice.

Firstly, the unilateral nature is mainly a paper claim made by the HKSAR and MSAR governments, rather than a practical power exercised by the Mainland. The focus of the system is the setting of a fixed quota of Mainland Chinese. This fixed quota for settlement is determined by the competent authorities of the Mainland government after consulting with the regions. This has been legalised in Article 22 Clause 4 of the *Basic Law of the HKSAR Special Administrative Region* 1990 (PRC) and Article 22 Clause 4 of the *Basic Law of the MSAR Special Administrative Region* 1993 (PRC). In respect of the fixed quota for

---

of relevant measures were then adopted. Article 2 of the 1951 Proclamation stipulates "individuals travelling to or from the HKSAR or MSAR must file an application for Passes of Entry-exit (*Churu Tongxingzheng*) to the department in charge of public security under the people's government where the applicants are residing or leaving for." This was limited to mainland citizens travelling to or from the HKSAR or MSAR for private affairs. Mainland citizens travelling to or from the HKSAR or MSAR for public affairs, overseas Chinese and Taiwan residents travelling to or from the HKSAR or MSAR for private affairs were required to apply for visas from the British Hong Kong government and Portuguese Macao government. Under the preface of the Proclamation, the purpose of the Proclamation was to solidify social public security during the early establishment of the PRC by preventing counter-revolutionary saboteurs from engaging in undermining activities by secretly travelling to or from the HKSAR or MSAR.

[3] "Mainland officials and personnel who wish to enter Hong Kong for a visit are required to obtain an Exit-entry Permit for Travelling to or from Hong Kong and Macao for official purposes and an appropriate endorsement relating to the purpose of entry at the Hong Kong and Macao Affairs Office." See Paragraph 4 of "Arrangement for Entry to Hong Kong from the Mainland China", http://www.immd.gov.hk/ehtml/hkvisas_9.htm (accessed 19/09/2006).

[4] Article 3 Clause 1 (7) of the *Provisional Measures on the Control over Mainland Residents Travelling for Such Business, Training, Employment as Non-Public Affairs to or from Hong Kong Special Administration Regions* 1998 (PRC) promulgated by the MPS on 19 March 1998 and effective on 30 March 1998. And Su, Qiang and Li, Xu, "Detailed Measures of Beijing on Facilitating Mainland Talents Exiting SARS Work and Study", (*Beijing Fangbian Neidi Rencai Fu Gangao Gongzuo Jiuxue De Juti Cuoshi*), 11/06/2003, Xinhuanet, http://news.21cn.com/domestic/2003–07–11/1104534.html (accessed 23/07/2003).

visiting relatives resident in both regions, and travelling to the HKSAR, the MPS cannot decide without consulting with relevant departments of the HKSAR and MSAR.[5] Hence, the regions actually play a dominant role in determining the fixed quota of Mainland Chinese entrants.

Moreover, the vague status of the Mainland government seriously affects the unilateral exercise of power of examination and approval. According to the system, the Mainland government is responsible for applications to enter the HKSAR and MSAR, and applications to exit China. The Mainland government therefore has dual status when handling applications for travelling to the regions. It is well acknowledged that the rights and interests of Mainland Chinese must be carefully considered when their application for leaving China is examined and approved. Meanwhile, the rights and interests of HKSAR or MSAR Chinese must also be considered when applications for entering the HKSAR or MSAR are examined and approved. Disputes inevitably arise between the rights and interests of the two sides when one department is responsible for the examination of two applications.

This dual administrative role has confused the enactment, implementation and interpretation of the relevant provisions. It is sometimes difficult to distinguish if the term 'travelling to' in the *Provisional Measures on the Control over Chinese Citizens Travelling for Private Affairs to or from the Regions of Hong Kong or Macao* 1986 (PRC) refers to leaving China or entering the regions. This uncertainty may affect the protection of the right to leave of Mainland Chinese. Being the sole examination and approval power, the Mainland government needs to make a choice between the protection of the rights and interests of Mainland Chinese and HKSAR or MSAR Chinese. The Mainland government is in a dilemma because choosing the unilateral approach may jeopardize the rights and interests of one group over the other.

More precisely, the Mainland government, based on the requirements of restrictive conditions, multiple-level departmental approval and designated exit ports, seems to prefer to protect the rights and interests of HKSAR or MSAR Chinese. This preference jeopardizes the rights and interests of Mainland Chinese. This allegation can be substantiated under Article 5 of the *Provisional Measures on the Control over Chinese Citizens Travelling for Private Affairs to or from the Regions of Hong Kong or Macao* 1986 (PRC), which provides that the fixed quota for examination and approval is designed to safeguard and maintain the economic prosperity and social stability of the HKSAR and MSAR. The reason why the provisions are inclined to protect the rights and interests of the regions seems partially

[5] Department of Politics under the MPS, *Frontier Defence and Exit and Entry Administration, the Series of Basic Textbook of People's Police Operation:* (*Bianfang Yu Churu Jing Guanli, Renmin Jingcha Gongan Yewu Jichu Jiaocai*), examined by Committee of Textbook Editing and Examination of the MPS, Internal Publication in Public Security Organs (*Gongan Jiguan Neibu Faxing*) (Beijing: the Publishing House of Qunzhong, 1999), 342.

to stem from the high human rights consciousness, and the developed legal and political systems of the HKSAR and MSAR.

9.1.2 *Examination and approval of the fixed quotas*

The examination and approval of the fixed quotas has two facets or levels of application. For one, the number of persons of travelling to the HKSAR or MSAR cannot exceed the fixed quota. For the other, the MPS distributes different fixed quotas to various provincial regions on the Mainland in the light of the relationship between residents in those regions and the HKSAR and MSAR.[6] The initial motivation for fixed quotas was to reduce the number of returned overseas Chinese from inland areas who overstayed in the HKSAR or MSAR to await the results of visa applications to South-eastern Asian countries in the 1960s and 1970s.[7] These measures were eventually extended to all Mainland Chinese who wanted to enter the HKSAR or MSAR. The policy of controlling numbers (*Shidang Kongzhi Renshu*) entering the HKSAR or MSAR was officially adopted in 1973. In 1981, it was replaced by a policy of persuading people not to go to the HKSAR or MSAR any more. To further limit numbers, travel to or from the HKSAR or MSAR was divided into single travel or immigration (in 1982), and return travel or visiting (in 1984). The numbers of both types of travellers was limited according to different fixed quotas.

Examination and approval in accordance with fixed quotas was then legalised. Article 5 of the *Provisional Measures on the Control over Chinese Citizens Travelling for Private Affairs to or from the Regions of Hong Kong or Macao* 1986 (PRC) stipulates that Mainland Chinese travelling to the regions to settle shall be subjected to the measures of examination and approval of the fixed quota. The fixed quotas for travelling to the HKSAR for permanent residence increased from 75 persons per day in 1982 to 150 persons per day in 1999.[8] The Chinese

---

[6] Top five provincial level regions fixed quota are Guangdong, Jiangshu, Fujian, Shanghai and Beijing.

[7] In the 1960s and 1970s some South-East Asian Countries did not accept visa applications filed in the Mainland China. So, Mainland citizens mainly returned overseas Chinese and their family members who had been approved for exit abroad had to lodge visa applications and wait for the result in Hong Kong or Macao. Application processing usually took a long time, and some of the applications were finally rejected. This leads to many applicants overstaying in Hong Kong and Macao.

[8] Quoted in Department of Politics under the MPS, *Frontier Defence and Exit and Entry Administration, the Series of Basic Textbook of People's Police Operation:* (*Beanbag Yu Churl Jingo Gauntly, Rennin Gingham Gongan Yewu Jichu Jiaocai*), examined by Committee of Textbook Editing and Examination of the MPS, Internal Publication in Public Security Organs (*Gongan Jiguan Neibu Faxing*) (Beijing: the Publishing House of Qunzhong, 1999), 342.

government made some improvement to the system of the fixed quota of Mainland Chinese travelling to the HKSAR or MSAR for tourism. With the relaxation of the limits on RLR in recent years, the fixed quota for group tours through overseas travel agencies has been cancelled. Since 2003, the fixed quota for individual tourists has not applied to Guangdong, Shanghai and Beijing.[9] The history of examination and approval of fixed quotas shows that although control over Mainland Chinese travelling to or from the HKSAR or MSAR has been relaxed in recent years, it is still restrictive by world standards.

Different fixed quotas in various provincial regions leads to discrimination that is unjustified by international norms. Under the *Measures of Examination and Approval of Travelling to the HKSAR or MSAR for Permanent Residence of Mainland Chinese* 2004 (PRC) the pass marks for spousal migration for residents of Guangdong to the HKSAR are 255.7 (separation before 31 December 1997), and for residents of other parts of China 201.1 (separation before 30 June 1999). The pass marks of spousal migration to MSAR for residents of Guangdong and Fujian are 255.7 (separation before 31 December 1997), and for residents of other parts of China 182.7 (separation before 31 December 1999).[10] In order to exploit the preferential policy, and in a context of relaxed household registration, it is possible for the applicants to move to the regions where lower pass marks are required, so undermining the efficiency of fixed quota provisions.

9.1.3 *Strict conditions of applying for travel to the HKSAR or MSAR*

The requirements of applying for travel to the HKSAR or MSAR

The Chinese government has designed restrictive conditions on application for travel to the HKSAR or MSAR in order to maintain the fixed quota system and monitor the flow of traffic. According to Article 7 of the *Provisional Measures on the Control over Chinese Citizens Travelling for Private Affairs to or from the Regions of Hong Kong or Macao* 1986 (PRC):

> Persons may apply for approval to travel to and settle in the HKSAR or MSAR if the applicants conform to any of the following conditions:
>
> (1) Either spouse of a married couple settles down in Hong Kong or Macao, whereby separation between the couple has lasted many years;
> (2) A person's parents settling in Hong Kong or Macao are aged and in poor health, and must be taken care of by their son or daughter from an inland area;

[9] For more information on the improvement of the fixed quota, please see part 5.2 of this book.

[10] The *Measures of Examination and Approval of Travelling to Hong Kong or Macao for Permanent Residence of mainland Residents* 2004 (PRC) (*2004 Nian Neidi Jumin Fu Gangao Diqu Dingju Shenpi Banfa*).

(3) Helpless old people and children residing in inland areas, who have to seek support from their lineal relatives or close relatives who live in Hong Kong or Macao;
(4) In the event that lineal relatives settling in Hong Kong or Macao have nobody there to inherit their property, their son or daughter in inland areas may inherit the property in question, on condition that they settle in Hong Kong or Macao; and
(5) A person who is required to settle in Hong Kong or Macao in other special circumstances.

Various provincial governments may separately decide the minimum length of separation of spouses, in the light of the number of local applicants and the use of the local fixed quota. Special circumstances refer to applicants who have a HKSAR or MSAR birth certificate and have been granted an entrance permit. In these cases, the control over travel to Macao of Mainland Chinese is still strict.[11]

In order to redress the lack of applied criteria and supervisory measures, and to specify the processing criteria according to a points system, the MPS issued the *Operational Norms of Application, Examination and Approval of Exiting China and Passport For Private Affairs of Citizens* 1996 (PRC), and the *Operational Norms on the Control of Examination and Approval of Travelling to the HKSAR or MSAR for Permanent Residence of Mainland Chinese* 1997 (PRC). This provides for relatively open and fair processing. The pass mark for the points test has changed each year since 1997. The system has benefited the protection of RLR of Mainland Chinese travelling to or from the regions.

According to Article 8 of the *Provisional Measures on the Control over Chinese Citizens Travelling for Private Affairs to or from the Regions of Hong Kong or Macao* 1986 (PRC):

> Persons may apply for the approval to go to the HKSAR or MSAR for short-term visits if any of the following circumstances is conformed to:
>
> (1) The applicant has close relatives settled in the HKSAR or MSAR and needs to visit them;
> (2) The applicant's lineal or close relatives are compatriots of Taiwan and he or she needs to go to Hong Kong or Macao to meet them;
> (3) The applicant needs to travel to Hong Kong or Macao to visit a lineal relative or sibling of overseas Chinese returning to China or the lineal relatives of the family members of overseas Chinese who are unable to return to the Mainland China;
> (4) The applicant must go to Hong Kong or Macao so as to dispose of his or her property; and
> (5) The applicant, due to other special circumstances, must go to Hong Kong or Macao for a short term.

[11] Article 1 Clause 1 (1)(4)(5) of the *Explanations of Some Matters on Implementation of Provisional Measures on the Control over Chinese Citizens Travelling for Private Affairs to or from the Regions of Hong Kong or Macao* 1987 (PRC).

The various provincial governments separately decide the detailed conditions of allowing travel for short-term visits, in the light of the numbers of local applicants and the use of the local fixed quota.[12]

Prerequisite certificate from the department in which the applicants are employed

The prerequisite certificates from the department in which the applicants are employed, discussed in part 7.3 above, is also required in applying to travel to the HKSAR or MSAR. Serving and retired national public servants, who were county- or division-level cadres or above, need a certificate from the department where the applicant is or was in service, when applying to enter the regions for private affairs. Full-time students also need a certificate from their educational institution when applying to enter Honk Kong and Macao for private affairs.[13]

Visa exemptions for transitional travel

Compared to the immigration policies of the HKSAR to other countries, restrictions are tight and visa exemptions for inland Chinese are significantly limited. Material from the HKSAR Immigration Department demonstrates that, since 1993, the HKSAR exempted Mainland Chinese from carrying a visa when they are transiting through the region for up to seven days, provided that the usual immigration requirements are met, including possession of valid entry documents for the destination and confirmed onward bookings for an overseas journey. Passport holders of over 170 countries or regions such as Angola, Congo, Egypt, Ghana, India, Indonesia, Kenya, Mozambique, Philippines, Rwanda, Sri Lanka, Thailand and Zimbabwe, may visit or transit through the HKSAR for between 14 and 90 days without a visa or entry permit, in accordance with the type of travel documents held, provided the visitor has adequate funds to cover the duration of the stay without working and holds an onward or return ticket (unless in transit to Mainland China or the MSAR).[14]

---

[12] Article 2 of the *Explanation of Some Matters on Implementation of Provisional Measures on the Control over Chinese Citizens Travelling for Private Affairs to or from the Regions of Hong Kong or Macao* 1987 (PRC).

[13] Beijing Public Security Bureau, "Application for the Passes to and from Hong Kong and Macao" (*Shenban Wanglai Gangao Tongxingzheng*), http://www.bjanj.gov.cn (accessed 28/01/2004); and Guangdong Public Security Department, "Instructions to the Applications for the Passes to and from the HKSAR and MSAR on Line" (*Wangshang Shenban Wanglai Gangao Tongxingzheng Shuoming*), http://wwwgdcrj.com/wssq/index.htm (accessed 29/01/2003).

[14] "Visit Visa/Entry Permit Requirements for the Hong Kong Special Administration Region, and Holders of Foreign Passports in the Mainland", http://www.immd.gov.hk/ehtml/hkvisas.htm (accessed 19/09/2006).

Departure through designated ports

Mainland Chinese travelling to the regions for private affairs must depart through designated ports pursuant to Article 3 of the *Provisional Measures on the Control over Chinese Citizens Travelling for Private Affairs to or from the Regions of Hong Kong or Macao* 1986 (PRC). The requirement of travelling to the HKSAR or MSAR through a designated port only applies to Mainland Chinese. The designated ports are Shenzhen – for those bound for the HKSAR, and Gongbei – for those bound for the MSAR. Obviously, the designation of ports is convenient for the management of the authority, but results in inconvenience for the travel of Mainland Chinese.

Application conditions for Mainland Chinese travelling to the HKSAR or MSAR are stricter than for Mainland Chinese travelling to foreign countries, or for aliens travelling to the HKSAR or MSAR. The strict limits, especially the fixed quota on short-term visits is almost unrivalled anywhere in the world. The historical background and reality of Hong Kong or Macao does not provide an adequately persuasive basis for continuing restrictions and the consequent violations of RLR.

9.1.4 *Different treatments of Mainland Chinese as opposed to HKSAR and MSAR Chinese*

It is much simpler for HKSAR or MSAR Chinese to enter Mainland China, than it is for Mainland Chinese to enter the HKSAR and MSAR. Article 14 and 15 of the *Provisional Measures on the Control over Chinese Citizens Travelling for Private Affairs to or from the Regions of Hong Kong or Macao* 1986 (PRC) provides the circumstances under which application for travelling to Mainland China is approved or denied.

> Article 14 Compatriots from Hong Kong or Macao intending to enter the Mainland areas, [must submit] an application for the Home-Visiting Certificate for Compatriots from Hong Kong or Macao (*Gangao Tongbao Huixiangzhang*)[15] . . . The application for Home-Visiting Certificates shall be subject to the presentation of his or her residential status identification for examination and an application form. Compatriots from Hong Kong or Macao, who do not visit the Mainland areas frequently, may apply for an Entry-Exit Pass (*Ruchujing Tongxingzheng*) instead. The measures for obtaining the pass shall be the same as those for obtaining the Home-Visiting Certificates for Compatriots from Hong Kong or Macao.

[15] After 15 January 1999, the Home-visiting Certificate for Compatriots from Hong Kong and Macao was replaced with the Entry-exit Mainland Pass for Compatriots from Hong Kong and Macao (*Gangao Jumin Laiwang Neidi Tongxingzheng*).

> Article 15 A Home Visiting Certificate or Entry-Exit Pass may not be issued to:
>
> (1) Those who are likely to be engaging in such criminal activities as robbery, theft, and trafficking in narcotics;
> (2) Those who have fabricated situations and presented forged certificate; and
> (3) Mental patients.

Article 17 and 18 of the *Provisional Measures 1986* stimulate the application procedure of travelling to the Mainland China:

> Article 17 Compatriots from Hong Kong and Macao requesting return to the Mainland areas for a short stay shall, according to the provisions on the administration of residence registration, go through the procedures for the registration stay. . . . .
>
> Article 18 For compatriots from Hong Kong and Macao requesting return to the Mainland areas and settling there, an application shall be filed in advance to the public security of the municipality or county where the applicants intend to settle. Upon approval, they shall go through the procedures for permanent residence registration with the police station in the places of their destination by presenting the Home-Visiting Certificate for Compatriots from Hong Kong and Macao, with a signed statement justifying the intention of the certificate-holders to return to the Mainland areas and settle there.[16]

These provisions clearly demonstrate that HKSAR and MSAR Chinese are treated more favourably than aliens, and come close to enjoying freedom of movement within China. As Wang Guoliang has penetratingly said, in *The Administration on Exit and Entry, one of Planning Textbooks of Higher Education of People's Police*:

> HKSAR and MSAR Chinese with the valid Home Visiting Certificates or Entry-Exit Passes may enter China at any time from all open ports according to their will. They need not undergo the formalities of application any longer. There are no limits on travel times and affairs.[17]

Limited requirements are never applied. Mainland government regards the likelihood of applications for permanent residence of HKSAR and MSAR Chinese as very low: the responsible departments have not even designed a rele-

---

[16] Article 7 of the *Explanation of Some Matters on Implementation of Provisional Measures on the Control over Chinese Citizens Travelling for Private Affairs to or from the Regions of Hong Kong or Macao* 1987 (PRC) require that the public security bureau in Guandong process applications for residency in that region; whereas overseas Chinese affairs offices process applications for all other areas.

[17] Wang, Guoliang and Zhu, Lin, *The Administration on Exit and Entry, one of Planning Textbooks of Higher Education of People's Police* (*Renmin Jingcha Gaodeng Jiaoyu Guihua Jiaocha: Churujing Guanlixue*) Interior Published within Public Security Organs (*Gongan Jiguan Neibu Faxing*) (Beijing: the Publishing House of China University of People's Public Security, 2002), 110–111.

vant application form.[18] Due to the great economic and political differences between Mainland China and the HKSAR and MSAR these regions,[19] very few HKSAR and MSAR Chinese apply to resettle in Mainland China. The fact that HKSAR and MSAR Chinese enjoy almost the same freedom to enter the mainland as Mainland Chinese is at odds with the fact that the reciprocal liberties don't exist for the benefit of Mainland Chinese. At the very least, Mainland Chinese should enjoy the same treatment as aliens when entering the HKSAR and MSAR.

Given the high population density of the HKSAR and MSAR, it is understandable that Chinese authorities and some scholars contend that Mainland Chinese should not freely settle there.[20] However, it is difficult to support the argument that the citizens should be prohibited from travelling freely within the regions. Limits on entry into the HKSAR and MSAR for short-term visits could be significantly relaxed. The restrictive limits and different treatments may also discourage Chinese citizens from recognising the HKSAR and MSAR as parts of China.

9.2 Limits on Mainland Chinese travelling to or from Taiwan, and Taiwan Chinese travelling to Mainland China

Taiwan is part of the territory of China, and regulated under the Chinese Constitution.[21] As of December 2003, about 164 countries have recognised Taiwan's position within the territory of the PRC, including the USA, Japan,

---

[18] "The Download of Various Application Forms from the Net of Division of Exit and Entry Administration Department of Public Security of Guangdong Province", http://www.gdcrj.com/doc/index.htm (accessed 28/01/2004).

[19] Per capita GDP, in 2002, of the HKSAR was US$ 27,200. See "Missouri Economic Research and Information Centre, Missouri Department of Economic Development", Hong Kong, http://www.missourieconomy.org/indicators/international/cty5820.stm (accessed 19/09/2006); Per Capital GDP of the MSAR was US$ 18,500 in 2002. See "Missouri Economic Research and Information Center, Missouri Department of Economic Development, Macao", http://www.missourieconomy.org/indicators/international/cty5660.stm (accessed 19/09/2006); Per Capital GDP of the Mainland China was US$965. See State Bureau of Statistics, the PRC, "GDP Per Capital from 1952 to 2002", http://www.menet.com.cn/shuju/gmjj/gmjj-rjgdp.htm (accessed 15/04/2004).

[20] Exit and Entry Administration under Jilin Province Public Security Department and Bureau of Border Security Check and Administration under Jilin Province Public Security Department, editor, *The Kit of Exit, Entry and Frontier Defence* (*Shiyong Churu Jing Bianfang Zhishi Daquan*) (Changchun, China: the Publishing House of Jilin Wenshi, 1994), 57. And Xu, Jiali, editor, *The Guide to Going Abroad Consultation* (*Chuguo Zixun Daquan*) (Beijing: the Publishing House of Kexue Puji, 1992), 513–514.

[21] Para. 9 of Preamble of the *Constitution of the PRC (Amendment)* 2004.

Germany, the UK, France and Australia.[22] In theory, to travel to or from Taiwan and Mainland China is to travel within one territory. However, China does not have actual sovereignty over Taiwan.

The relationship between Taiwan and Mainland China has been hostile since the establishment of the People's Republic of China under a communist system in 1949. Prior to China's reform and opening up in 1978, Chinese from the Mainland and Taiwan could only meet in Hong Kong, Macao or other foreign countries. It has since become possible for Chinese in one state to visit and settle in the other. However, the Chinese government has imposed limits on Mainland Chinese travelling to or from Taiwan, which differ from those governing travel to or from the HKSAR, MSAR, foreign States, or within the territory.[23]

This section will explore (i) the context for limits imposed by Mainland China and Taiwan; (ii) the contents and effects of those limits, including the requirements of prerequisite certificates, invitation letters, and approval from Taiwanese authorities; and (iii) the pre-eminently political nature of the limits.

9.2.1 *Limits on travel to or from Taiwan of Mainland Chinese and the limits on travel to or from Mainland China of Taiwan Chinese*

Analysis of the limits of Mainland China on the travel of Mainland Chinese to or from Taiwan would be incomplete without first discussing Taiwan's limits on its own residents. Any relaxation in the approach by one side usually receives a positive reply from the other.

In July 1987, Taiwan ceased to operate under a system of martial law, which led to a relaxation of hostilities between the two sides. The *Circular of the General office of the State Council on the Measures for Receiving Compatriots from Taiwan Coming to the Mainland to Visit their Relatives or as Tourists* 1987 (PRC)

---

[22] "The Lists of the Countries having Diplomatic Relationship with the PRC" (*Yu Zhongguo Jianjiao Guojia Yilanbiao*), http://www.fmprc.gov.cn/chn/lbfw/jjbiao/t9650.htm (accessed 19/09/2006).

[23] Wang, Guoliang and Zhu, Lin, *The Administration on Exit and Entry, one of Planning Textbooks of Higher Education of People's Police* (*Renmin Jingcha Gaodeng Jiaoyu Guihua Jiaocha: Churujing Guanlixue*), Interior Published within Public Security Organs (*Gongan Jiguan Neibu Faxing*) (Beijing: the Publishing House of China University of People's Public Security, 2002), 112; Department of Politics under the MPS, *Frontier Defense and Exit and Entry Administration, the Series of Basic Textbook of People's Police Operation:* (*Bianfang Yu Churu Jing Guanli, Renmin Jingcha Gongan Yewu Jichu Jiaocai*), examined by Committee of Textbook Editing and Examination of the MPS, Interior Publication within Public Security Organs (*Gongan Jiguan Neibu Faxing*) (Beijing: the Publishing House of Qunzhong, 1999), 345; and Xiang, Dang, *The Guide to the Law of Exit and Entry in China and Foreign Countries* (*Zhongwai Churujing Falv Zhinan*) (Beijing: the Publishing House of China University of People's Public Security, 1998), 174.

was promulgated in October of that year. According to Article 1 of the *Circular*, Mainland China "warmly and sincerely welcomes compatriots from Taiwan to come to the Mainland to visit their relatives or as tourists, and guarantees that they have complete freedom of entry and exit."[24] Taiwan officially permitted ordinary people, other than national public servants and military or educational appointees, to travel to the Mainland China to visit relatives in November 1987.

The number of Taiwanese residents travelling to Mainland China steadily increased from 450,000 exits in 1988, to one million in 1991.[25] To meet this demand, Mainland China announced the *Measures on the Control over Chinese Citizens Travelling to or from the Region of Taiwan* in October 1991, effective as of May 1992. In 1992, the number of Taiwanese visitors to China jumped to 1.5 million. In response, Taiwan issued the *Regulations on the Entry Permission of Taiwan Permanent Residents to Inland Areas* in April 1993. These are still the foremost regulations governing this movement between Taiwan and China. In 1995, Taiwan promulgated the *Regulations on the Relationship between Taiwan residents Areas and inland Areas* to further relax travel restrictions, and permitted public servants below ninth level to visit relatives in Mainland China. In turn, China started to issue *Passes for Travelling to or from Taiwan for Mainland Chinese* (*Dalu Jumin Wanglai Taiwan Tongxingzheng*) to further simplify formalities.

Interaction between Mainland China and Taiwan in theory promotes the development of Chinese exit and entry laws. However, there are in practice many examples of the different treatment of Mainland and Taiwan Chinese. According to Article 13 of the *Measures on the Control over Chinese Citizens Travelling to or from the Region of Taiwan* 1991 (PRC), Taiwan residents may enter Mainland China either directly from Taiwan, or via the HKSAR, MSAR, or another foreign country. Conversely, Article 2 of the *Rules of Some Matters of the Application of Mainland Chinese Travelling to Taiwan for Visiting Relatives* 1988 (PRC), compels Chinese residents to enter Taiwan only through the HKSAR.

Additionally, the number of Chinese residents travelling to Taiwan is much lower than the number travelling to the HKSAR and MSAR. According to the MPS statistics,

> In the first half year of 2002, there are 77.58 million from Hong Kong and Macau special administrative regions (SARs), an 8.6–per cent rise; 3.51 million from Taiwan, a 2.95 per cent increase compared with 2001.[26]

---

[24] Article 1 of the *Circular of the General Office of the State Council on the Measures for Receiving Compatriots from Taiwan Coming to the Mainland to Visit their Relatives or as Tourists* 1987 (PRC).

[25] Quoted in Xiang, Dang, *The Guide to the Law of Exit and Entry in China and Foreign Countries* (*Zhongwai Churujing Falv Zhinan*) (Beijing: the Publishing House of China University of People's Public Security, 1998), 174.

[26] "China's Ports See Record Traffic", http://www.chinadaily.com.cn/en/doc/2002–07/16/content_128051.htm (accessed 08/07/2005).

9.2.2 *The contents and effects of the limits, including the requirements of prerequisite certificates, invitation letters, and approval from Taiwanese authorities*

Application requirements for travelling to Taiwan are stricter when compared with those for travelling to the HKSAR, MSAR and foreign countries. None of the 2001–2005 reforms in China related to travel to or from Taiwan. In effect, the main laws governing travel to or from Taiwan are those promulgated in 1992. The limits on travel to Taiwan mainly focus on three aspects: (i) prerequisite certificates from the department in which the applicants are employed; (ii) documentary evidence, especially an invitation letter from Taiwan, and (iii) the approval from the Taiwan authorities.

Prerequisite certificates from the departments in which the applicants are employed

According to Article 7(3) of the *Measures on the Control over Chinese Citizens Travelling to or from the Region of Taiwan* 1991 (PRC), Mainland Chinese applying for travel to Taiwan:

> Shall submit a certificate from the department or educational institution in which the applicant is employed or studying. An applicant who is not employed or studying shall submit a comment from the police station where the applicant's residence is registered in Mainland China.

These requirements are the same as those for travel to foreign countries before the recent overhaul of 2001 when they were partially abolished.[27] As argued in part 7.3 of this book, the prerequisite certificate from the department in which the applicant is employed is unfair, lacks legal foundation, and essentially limits the right to leave.

Documentary evidence, especially an invitation letter from Taiwan

Mainland Chinese must also provide documentary evidence, including an invitation letter from Taiwan, with their application to travel to Taiwan, pursuant to Article 7(4) of the *Measures on the Control over Chinese Citizens Travelling to or from the Region of Taiwan* 1991 (PRC). Article 8 prescribes documentation as including: an invitation to participate in economic, scientific, cultural, educational, sports or academic activities; certification of the applicant's relationship with a family member or friend in Taiwan; evidence that the applicant can be financially

[27] Only serving national public servants, individuals who are administratively referred to as national public servants, retired national public servants who are county/division level or over and full-time students are still required to provide certificates. For more information, see part 5.2 of this book.

self-supporting while travelling; marriage certificate; property title; and an approval letter from Taiwanese authorities. The Beijing and Shanghai authorities tend to focus on the letter of invitation accompanied by a statement of reasons for the journey.[28]

The tenuous grounds for justifying the need of an invitation from abroad have been incisively argued by Hurst Hannum:

> It might be argued that the requirement of an invitation from abroad before permission to leave is granted also is justifiable on the grounds of ensuring that an emigrant will be accepted by his or her country of destination and therefore will not become a burden on the rights of others. However, this argument confuses the right of an individual to leave with possibility that an individual may have to enter another country. The connection between being granted legal permission to leave and the speculative injury to others in a country of destination is simply too tenuous to be considered to fall within the 'rights and freedoms of others' exception.[29]

From this perspective, the requirement to provide documentary evidences, especially an invitation letter from Taiwan, is unacceptable.

Approval from the Taiwan authority

China does not permit Mainland Chinese to travel to Taiwan until Taiwan has granted permission for that person to enter by issuing a Travel Pass. Article 8 of the *Measures on the Control over Chinese Citizens Travelling to or from the Region of Taiwan* 1991 (PRC) stipulates that Mainland Chinese applying to travel to Taiwan for permanent residence must provide evidence that they will be granted permanent residence. Article 2(2) of the *Circular of Some Matters on Implementation of Measures on the Control over Chinese Citizens Travelling to or from the Region of Taiwan* 1991 (PRC) further provides that:

> In order to avoid overstaying due to being unable to enter Taiwan via HKSAR, Mainland Chinese shall not be granted permission to leave for Taiwan unless the public security department can ensure that they will be able to enter Taiwan without delay. The documents, which ensure that the applicant may enter Taiwan, include a photocopy of the exit and entry certificate, issued by the Taiwan authority, and a certificate issued by the China Travel Agency, Hong Kong.

In practice, public security departments in Mainland China clearly require Mainland Chinese to "submit a valid permit to enter Taiwan, and copy of a Travel

---

[28] "Mainland Residents Travelling to and from Taiwan" (*Dalu Jumin Wanglai Taiwan*), http://www.bjgaj.gov.cn/net_service/consultation/index.jsp?operation=personal&id=458 (accessed 19/09/2006); "Visiting Relatives in Taiwan or Settling Down in Taiwan", http://gaj.sh.gov.cn/shpolice (accessed 28/01/2004).

[29] Hannum, Hurst, *The Right to Leave and Return in International Law and Practice* (Dordrecht Netherlands: Martinus Nijhoff Publishers, 1987), 43.

Permit to Taiwan (*Taiwan Diqu Lvxingzheng*)."[30] The suitability of these provisions has been accepted by some Chinese academics.[31]

Although preconditions of the approval process are stated in relevant provisions and are recognised by some Chinese academics, no research has yet been undertaken as to the effect on those applying. The requirements affect applicants in two key ways. Firstly, the precondition of Taiwanese approval is more serious than the need of documentary evidence such as an invitation letter. It confuses the right of a Mainland Chinese person to leave with the ability of that individual to enter Taiwan. Secondly, applicants have to apply to the Taiwan authorities for entry when they do not yet possess the necessary travel documents. Only after being granted an entry permit from Taiwanese authorities, does the possibility of the right to leave China become a reality. Taiwan can refuse to grant a travel permit if the applicant does not have a passport to identify their status.

9.2.3 *Pre-eminently political nature of the limits*

Mainland China's enactment and enforcement of provisions to control travel to or from Taiwan, is in the first place an expression of political pressure. While some consideration of politics, based on hostilities between the two sides, might be accepted, ignoring RLR cannot. Chinese academics and officials are too accustomed to forms of control with an over-emphasis on politics, to call this in question and foreign academics are too unfamiliar with the situation to pay close attention to this matter. This sub-section aims to fill the gap.

Principles of control over travelling to or from Taiwan

The first principle of control is the aegis or political principle of 'one China' (*Yiguo*), of which Taiwan is an administrative region. Chinese law has never recognised and used the terms of 'Republic of China' and 'Taiwan'. Secondly, the Mainland government recognises the principle of two systems (*Liangzhi*), in which Taiwanese authorities control Taiwan. Thirdly, no Taiwan law is recognised

---

[30] "Mainland Residents Travelling to and from Taiwan" (*Dalu Jumin Wanglai Taiwan*), http://www.bjgaj.gov.cn/net_service/consultation/index.jsp?operation=personal&id=458 (accessed 19/09/2006); "Visiting Relatives in Taiwan or Settling Down in Taiwan", http://gaj.sh.gov.cn/shpolice (accessed 28/01/2004).

[31] Mo, Qibo editor, *The Administration of Citizen's Exit and Entry* (*Gongmin Churu Jing Guanli*) (Nanling, China the Publishing House of Giuangxi Minzu, 1997), 265 and Wang, Guoliang and Zhu, Lin, *The Administration on Exit and Entry, one of Planning Textbooks of Higher Education of People's Police* (*Renmin Jingcha Gaodeng Jiaoyu Guihua Jiaocha: Churujing Guanlixue*), Interior Published within Public Security Organs (*Gongan Jiguan Neibu Faxing*) (Beijing: the Publishing House of China University of People's Public Security, 2002), 111.

until it is favourable to Mainland China (*Yiwuo Weizhu Duiwuo Youli*). The three principles are deeply coloured politically and grant little importance to RLR.

The politics of responsible departments

According to Article 7 of the *Circular of Some Matters on Implementation of Measures on the Control over Chinese Citizens Travelling to or from the Region of Taiwan* 1991 (PRC), the Department of United Front Work of the Central Committee of the CPC and various local United Front Work departments[32] are responsible for the examination and approval of Taiwanese residents travelling to the Mainland for permanent residence. The responsibility for regulating travel to or from Taiwan is vested in party departments rather than administrative departments of government. Administrative decision-making is in this way politicised.

Policies of the CPC governing travel to or from Taiwan

The CPC has enacted some provisions in relation to China – Taiwan travel. These include the *Opinions on Properly Handling the Work of Taiwan Compatriots Travelling to Motherland to Visit the Relatives*, which was promulgated by the Leading Panel of Taiwan Affairs under the Central Committee of the CPC in 1987. The *Circular of the MPS on Some Issues of the Application for Travelling to or from Inland of Mainland Chinese who was Granted Permanent Residence of Taiwan Regions* (PRC) was promulgated by the MPS after consulting with the Department of United Front Work of the Central Committee of the CPC and Taiwan Affairs office of the State Council. In practice these policies are as effective as law.

Effects of the emphasis of political factors on individual rights and freedoms

Emphasis on political factors usually leads to limitation or deprivation of the rights and interests of both Mainland and Taiwan Chinese. The following are two

---

[32] The Department of the United Front Work is one of five departments under the Central Committee of the CPC that is responsible for united front work. The United Front has always been closely linked with the CPC. Deng, Xiaoping, the architect of China's reform and opening up, said that the most important issue for the United Front is the unification of the motherland. Quoted in "On United Front by Deng Xiaoping", (Deng Xioaping Lun Tongyi Zhanxian), http://www.zytzb.org.cn/zytzbwz/theory/lunshu/dengxiaoping/index.htm (accessed 19/09/2006); Also In 2000, Jiang, Zemin, the former General Secretary of the CPC, said at a national conference on United Front Work of the CPC, "the fundamental task of the United Front is to win people's hearts and mobilise all forces to reach the grand goal of the Party and the country." See "The Main Principles of The 19th Conference of National United Front Work" (*Di Shijiu Chi Quanguo Tongzhan Gongzuo Huiyi Jinsheng*), http://tltzb.tl.gov.cn/tdxc/new_page_264.htm (accessed 19/09/2006).

representative examples of this. The first concerns the Taiwan permanent resident status of Mainland Chinese. Article 2 of the *Circular of the MPS on Some Issues of the Application for Travelling to or from Inland of Mainland Chinese who have been Granted Permanent Residence of Taiwan Regions 1995 (PRC)* provides that:

> Inland China shall not recognise the status of Taiwan permanent residence of Mainland Chinese when they return to the Mainland with Exit and Entry Mainland Pass if they have been granted the status when approved only to temporarily remaining in Taiwan, but have not obtained approval from the relevant inland department responsible for Taiwan permanent residence. The Exit and Entry Mainland Passes of those Mainland Chinese are to be seized and they are to be treated as Mainland Chinese.

The inland authority has argued that a primary aim of these measures is to unify and regulate the issuance of travel documents and control over travel.[33] This argument is not persuasive because the same rule does not apply to Mainland Chinese who have acquired permanent resident status in foreign countries under similar circumstances. Conversely, the Chinese government not only recognises the foreign permanent residence status of persons with inland resident status acquired during a period of temporary travel, but also encourages them to return to China. This form of discrimination seems politically motivated. Whatever the reason, it limits the right of Mainland Chinese people to permanently reside in Taiwan.

The other example concerns Mainland permanent resident status of Taiwan Chinese. The Committee for the Assistance of Retired Veterans of the ROC promulgated the *Circular of the Operational Manual of the Application of Retired Veterans for Entering Inland Regions of to Permanently Reside* in 1992. Under the *Circular*, retired veterans who are permanent residents of the Mainland China may apply for an allowance from Taiwanese authorities. In order to do so, they must submit a certificate granting permanent residence, issued by the responsible inland department. Most retired veterans were born in the Mainland and left in 1949. This concession may be due to humanitarian considerations.

However, the Chinese government has indicated that Taiwan's payment of an allowance to veterans is aimed at:

> Buying popular support, reducing pressure, and abandoning the burden caused by retired veterans, by stimulating veterans without the ability to work to return to the Mainland China and remit an allowance to them.[34]

---

[33] Preface of the *Circular of the MPS on Some Issues of Exit and Entry Mainland of Mainland Residents Granted Permanent Residence of Taiwan Regions* 1995 (PRC) (*Gonganbu Guanyu Dalu Jumin Huozhun Dingju Taiwan Hou Shenqing Laiwang Dalu Youguan Wenti De Tongzhi*), promulgated by the MPS on 8 May 1995.

[34] Mo, Qibo and Zhu, Qiliang, *Zhongguo Gongmin Yinsi Chuguo Shouce* (*the Handbook of Chinese Citizens Going Abroad for Private Purpose*) (Nanling, China the Publishing House of Guangxi Renmin, 1997), 269.

The Department of Unified Front Work (*Tongzhan*) under the Central Committee of the CPC, and the MPS and the State Council of Taiwan Affairs office, jointly promulgated the *Circular on the Prohibition on Issuance of Notarial Certificate of Permanent Residence Certificate for Taiwan Compatriots* 1993 (PRC). The Ministry of Justice then issued the *Circular on the Prohibition on Issuance of Notarial Certificate of Permanent Residence Certificate for Taiwan Compatriots* 1993 (PRC), which prohibits the issuing of notarial certificates of permanent residence certificate to Taiwan residents, whether or not they have been granted permission to settle in China and have registered a household.

The view of the Chinese government regarding reasons for paying an allowance to veterans is questionable. The allowance to veterans is not big enough to be a great burden on Taiwan – it not hard to pay.[35] Furthermore, retired veterans may freely choose to stay in Taiwan or return to the Mainland, supported by superannuation and government allowances. More importantly, Taiwan residents with permanent residence status in Mainland China have the right to a certificate attesting to their status. Thus, the reasons for prohibiting the issuance of permanent residence certificates to retired veterans are unacceptable. The prohibition takes away the right to be issued with a notarial certificate, hinders the right to apply for an allowance, and limits their ability to reside permanently in Mainland China.

As a result, the gap between the number of Mainland Chinese travelling to Taiwan and of Taiwanese Chinese travelling to Mainland China is considerable. In 2001, the number of Mainland Chinese travelling to Taiwan was 105,400, or 0.00008% of the Mainland population;[36] compared with approximately 3.51 million Taiwan residents travelling to Mainland China, or 15.55% of the Taiwan population.[37] The figures illustrate that issues discussed in this section seriously limit the right to leave for Taiwan.

9.3 Conclusions

Given that 73.54% of people travelling to China came from the HKSAR and MSAR, and 71.90% of people travelling abroad went to those regions, it is imperative to analyse the limits on the right of travelling to or from the HKSAR or MSAR. This chapter has emphatically questioned and criticised the principles of processing applications, to which officials and other researchers have been too accustomed, to call into question.

---

[35] In 2002, Taiwan's per capita GDP was US$17,400. See *Networked Readiness Index Rank: Taiwan.tw*, Country Profiles, 264.

[36] "The People's Republic of China," http://www.dfat.gov.au/geo/china/index.html (accessed 19/09/2006).

[37] *The Numbers of Exits from and Entries into the Chinese Mainland Breakthrough 200 Million in 2001 (2001 Nian Woguo Churujing Renyuan Shouci Tupo 2 Yi Renci)*, the Bureau of Exit and Entry Administration under the MPS, 18/04/2003.

The principle of unilateral examination and approval by Mainland China does not improve the protection of RLR of Mainland Chinese. It is only a formal claim and the vague double status of the Mainland government in regard to its practice seriously affects the fair exercise of the power of examination and approval. The unilateral approach may jeopardize the rights and interests of one group over the other, to the detriment of Mainland Chinese.

Different fixed quotas in provincial regions are discriminatory. The practice of fixed quotas for temporary visits make for stricter limits on travelling to or from the HKSAR or MSAR. When permission is based on prerequisite certificates from the departments in which applicants are employed, on departure through designated ports, on limited visa exemptions for transit travel, and various provincial legislative limits, it is imperative to further ease these restrictive conditions. The discriminatory principles actually discourage Chinese citizens from recognising the HKSAR and MSAR as parts of China.

The 34-fold difference between the numbers of Taiwan Chinese travelling to the Mainland China and Mainland Chinese travelling to Taiwan clearly highlights the limits on the right to travel to or from Taiwan. The research for this Chapter reveals that an over-emphasis on politics, effected by the politicisation of administrative decision-making, as the foremost reason for this. The restrictive requirements, such as prerequisite certificates from the department in which the applicant is employed, a letter of invitation from Taiwan, and approval from the Taiwanese authorities underpin these issues. RLR is in turn ignored.

In fact, Mainland China controls travel to or from the HKSAR, MSAR or Taiwan of Mainland Chinese, on behalf of the authorities of the three regions. It may be recognised that the HKSAR and MSAR are part of China, so China does not see any thing unusual about asserting control. Presumably, the authorities of the three regions accept this as being a favourable arrangement. However, their acceptance does not mean that the arrangement conforms to international norms or improves the protection of the right to leave.

Chapter Ten
Chinese Emigration Intermediary Agency Laws

Introduction

A boom in exit and entry over last two decades triggered the emergence and development of Chinese emigration intermediary agencies (*Chujing Zhongjie Jigou*), which are unique to China and quite different, for instance, from overseas recruitment services in Vietnam, migration service organisations in Taiwan, registered migration agents in Australia and international travel agencies in China. 'Intermediary' (*Zhongjie*) in Chinese language means medium, intermedium, vehicle, and instrumentality (*Meijie*).[1] '*Meijie*' implies the persons, things, objects or realities that assist both parties to establish a relationship or conduct affairs,[2] for example to make contact or handle affairs on behalf of one party by appointment.

Emigration intermediary agencies in Mainland China provide legal services and information for citizens who go abroad for study, permanent residence, visiting family or friends, property inheritance, employment, travel, or training with a

---

[1] Dictionary Department, institute of Linguistics, Chinese Academy of Social Sciences, *The Contemporary Chinese Dictionary* (*Chinese-English edition*) (*Xiandai Hanyu Cidian*) (Beijing: Foreign Language Teaching and Research Press, 2002), 2482.

[2] Dictionary Department, institute of Linguistics, Chinese Academy of Social Sciences, *The Contemporary Chinese Dictionary* (*Chinese-English edition*) (*Xiandai Hanyu Cidian*) (Beijing: Foreign Language Teaching and Research Press, 2002), 1315, 1756 and 522.

license granted by the designated authority. They do this for example by applying for suitable foreign visas on behalf of their clients, as well as providing other relevant services for clients who need Chinese passports and notarial certificates, and providing reception services after arrival in the host country. There are seven types of Chinese emigration intermediary agencies in China that separately provide services for overseas study, exit and entry for private affairs, overseas employment, foreign labour trade and co-operation, overseas travel, overseas training at government expenses, and Sino-foreign joint venture skilled personnel.

The emigration intermediary agencies in China play an indispensable role in the realisation of RLR. The need of guidance in going abroad provided by intermediary agencies, especially given China's long period of being a closed country, is considerable. Knowledge, understanding and acceptance of foreign countries, as the basis of the desire and decision to go abroad, are cultivated by intermediary agencies. An intermediary agency can offer a wealth of information on foreign countries and emigration to clients.

Besides helping Chinese clients to apply for exiting China, including passport applications, the intermediary agencies also help the clients to choose and apply for the most suitable visa category. The assumption that applicants can lodge visa applications and maintain contacts with foreign immigration authorities rarely applies in China because of language barriers, complex immigration rules and an unfamiliar legal system. Nearly 70% of self-funded Chinese students, for instance, used an overseas study intermediary agency.[3] In 1998 to 1999, 52% of applications for foreign residency were lodged overseas for New Zealand,[4] and almost entirely through intermediary agencies in China. Emigration intermediary agencies also help clients on arrival in the host country, through reception services in-situ that ease concern about arrival and initial integration after successful application for a visa.

An advanced body of emigration intermediary agency law can enhance above-mentioned role of Chinese emigration agencies in realising RLR. This chapter will consider: (i) why the Chinese government regulates emigration intermediary agencies; (ii) the development of emigration intermediary agency laws; and (iii) the issues arising from emigration intermediary agency laws.

---

[3] "Ministry Website to Rate Intermediaries", 28 July 2003, *The China Daily,* http://www.chinadaily.com.cn/en/doc/2003–07/28/content_249602.htm (accessed 16/09/2006).

[4] Hon Lianne Dalziel the Minister of Immigration *Options for Setting Enforceable Standards for Immigration Consultants* Ministry of Immigration New Zealand Wellington 2001.

10.1 Why the Chinese Government Regulates Emigration Intermediary Agencies

There is a drive to have the Chinese government regulate emigration intermediary agencies. The very ineffectiveness of the agencies, in enhancing conditions for exit and entry, may in fact jeopardise the rights and interests of individuals intending to go abroad. Zheng Zhigeng, the Director of the Zejian Legislative Affairs Office, has said, "There will be a growing demand for intermediary services as governments at all levels step up administrative reforms."[5] In 2002, Zhu Rongji, the then Premier, reported that thoroughly standardising and restructuring the market economy was an inevitable choice for China, as a consequence of China's entry into the WTO and new steps taken to open China to the outside world. He further underlined that "it was necessary to regulate and standardise intermediary service organisations."[6]

In response to the problems created by chaos in the emigration intermediary agency market and to protect the rights and interests of individuals exiting China, the *Circular of the State Council on Strengthening the Management of the Activities of Emigration Intermediary Agencies* 2000 (PRC) was promulgated. The measures to regulate emigration intermediary agencies are one part of measures under Article 2 of the *Decision of the State Council Relating to Regulating and Regularising the Order of Market Economy* 2001 (PRC). These laws help protect the rights and interests of individuals exiting China, and reveal the causes of disorder within the emigration intermediary agency services market. Clearly, legal research on emigration intermediary agencies is needed.

10.2 The Development of Chinese Emigration Intermediary Agency Laws

The emigration intermediary agency industry has flourished in China since the 1990s. Illegal agencies rapidly grew in an inadequately regulated market. A series of statutes were then enacted to regulate various categories of intermediary agency. This subsection will review the recent legislative developments in each of the seven categories of agencies. This will then provide a basis for an analysis of the issues associated with the laws in the next section.

[5] "Eastern Province Enacts Rules to Regulate Intermediary Services", http://english.people.com.cn/20020/2/28/eng20020228_91101.shtml (accessed 19/09/2006).

[6] Zhu, Rongji, then Premier of the State Council, Par. 1 of Part V of "Report on the Work of the Government (16/03/2002)", http://www.english.gov.cn/official/2005–07/29/content_18337.htm (accessed 19/09/2006).

10.2.1 *Laws governing overseas study intermediary agencies*

The overseas study intermediary agencies (*Zifei Chuguo Liuxue Zhongjie*) are the agencies that are granted a 'Recognition Certificate of Operation Qualification of Self-funded Overseas Study Intermediary Agency Service' (*Zifei Chuguo Liuxue Zhongjie Fuwu Jigou Zige Rendingshu*), allowing them to offer information about foreign educational institutions, and assist prospective self-funded overseas students with applications for admission and passport and visa applications. In 2003, China had 270 authorised intermediary agencies, with nearly 10,000 staff.[7]

The *Circular of State Education Commission and Ministry of Public Security on Prohibiting Foreign and Domestic Departments and Individuals from Recruiting Students Studying Abroad Self-funded in China Without Allowance (PRC)* was promulgated in 1987 to protect self-funded students from being cheated by foreign and domestic agencies and individuals that were recruiting Chinese students to study abroad, and to protect Chinese "educational sovereignty" (*Jiaoyu Zhuquan*).[8] It concentrated on the prohibition of overseas study intermediary agencies for profit.[9] Before 1998, the Shanghai government had only approved one overseas study consultative centre to provide not-for-profit services.[10]

In 1999, the system of the Recognition Certificate of Operation Qualification of Self-funded Overseas Study Intermediary Agency Service was established to meet growing overseas study demands, and to protect the rights and interests of prospective overseas students under the *Rules on the Control of Intermediary Agency for Self-funded Overseas Study* 1999 (PRC). This Rule allowed any educational institutions with the status of legal person to operate an intermediary agency, thereby opening up more channels to facilitate overseas study. The Rule also provides for the management and supervision of legal overseas study agencies by the central government. Meanwhile, local governments enacted regional measures, such as the *Measures for the Control of Intermediary Agency for Self-funded Overseas Study (for trial Implementation)* 1999 (Beijing).

---

[7] "Ministry Website to Rate Intermediaries", 28 July 2003, *The China Daily,* http://www.chinadaily.com.cn/en/doc.2003–07/28/content_249602.htm (accessed 16/09/2006).

[8] Preface of the *Circular of State Education Commission on Prohibiting Foreign and Domestic Organs and Individuals from Recruiting Students Studying Abroad Self-funded in China without Allowance* 1987 (PRC) (*Guojia Jiaowei Gonganbu Guanyu Guoneiwai Zuzhi He Geren Bude Shanzi Zai Woguo Zaoshou Zifei Chuguo Liuxue Renyuan De Tongzhi*), jointly promulgated by State Education Commission and the MPS on 21 August 1987.

[9] Overseas study intermediary agency were regulated in the *Circular of State Education Commission and MPS on Prohibiting Foreign and Domestic Departments and Individuals from Recruiting Students Studying Abroad Self-funded in China Without Allowance* (PRC) 1987.

[10] Su, Huiyu and Li, Yiran, editor, *Yisi Churu Jing Bidu* (*The Guide to Exit and Entry for Private Purpose*), (Shanghai: The Publishing House of Wenhui, 1998), 3 and 4.

The enforcement of these laws is lax, and not all violations are prosecuted. Agency that are driven by profit have violated the laws by such acts as using a rented license, issuing misleading advertisements, forging documents, providing services in excess of their approved operational scope, and providing services without a license.[11] According to the news from Xinhua Network, in 2001, there were 309 overseas study intermediary agencies in Beijing, but only 46 held operational licenses.[12] The *Circular on Further Regulating Market Order of Self-funded Overseas Studying Intermediary Service* 2002 (PRC) was promulgated by the Ministry of Education (MOE) to address these activities. According to the *Circular*, each province was required to launch a campaign to crack down illegal overseas study agencies and report to the MOE. The MOE was then required to investigate agencies identified in the provincial reports.[13]

10.2.2 *Laws governing exit and entry intermediary agencies for private purposes*

Exit and entry intermediary agencies for private purposes (*Yisi Churujing Zhongjie Jigou*) are the agencies granted an 'Operation License of Exit and Entry Intermediary Agency for Private Purposes' (*Yisi Churujing Zhongjie Jigou Jingying Xukezheng*) to provide information and legal advice, make overseas travel arrangements, apply for passports, visas and notarial certificates on behalf of their clients, and other relevant services for citizens who are travelling abroad for permanent residence, to visit family or friends, or to inherit property. By April 2002, 658 exit and entry intermediary agencies for private affairs across approximately 28 provinces, autonomous regions and municipalities directly under the Central Government had been licensed.[14]

---

[11] In 2003, legal overseas study agencies charged a service fee of between C¥10, 000 to C¥30,000 (US$1,207 to US$3,623) per applicant. Many of these agencies are, in fact, acting as recruitment agencies for overseas educational institutions. See Chen, Tieyuan, *Overseas Study without Intermediary Agency: the Interview to Visa Officer of Foreign Countries in China* (*Piekai Zhongjie Qu Liuxue: Zhuhua Qianzheng Guan Fangtan*) (Beijing: the Publishing House of Writer, 2002), 3. Also see Preface of the *Circular on Further Regulating Market Order of Self-funded Overseas Studying Intermediary Service* 2002 (PRC), promulgated by the MOE in November 2002.

[12] "There are Many Traps in Overseas Study Intermediary Agency", (*Liuxue Zhongjie Jinshi Heiken*), http://learning.21cn.com/liuxue/dongtai/2001–04–11/354145.html (accessed 23/07/2003).

[13] Conclusions of the *Circular on Further Regulating Market Order of Self-funded Overseas Studying Intermediary Service* 2002 (PRC), promulgated by the MOE in November 2002.

[14] There were 108 agencies in Beijing, 33 agencies in Shanghai and 116 agencies in Guangdong.

Prior to 2001, all activities of these agencies that involved advertisement were prohibited by the *Circular of Ministry of Public Security on Strictly Prohibiting from Illegally Undertaking Activities of Soliciting Clients to Permanently Emigrate* 1995 (PRC). The prohibitions were aimed at preventing foreign collusion and profit-driven exploitation of applicants.[15] However, the demands for the agencies still exist, and with the development of economy, the demands are higher than ever.

To strengthen the administration of these agencies and to protect the legal rights and interests of citizens, the *Measures on the Administration of Emigration Intermediary Agency for Private Affairs* 2001 (PRC) were jointly promulgated by the MPS and State Administration of Industry and Commerce (SAIC) in July 2001. The *Measures* regulated the establishment and operation of agencies, and the management and use of reserve funds. From December 2000 to January 2001, various provincial-level public security departments inspected and closed down agencies that were operating illegally. Nationally, 361 unqualified agencies were closed down, and nearly 400 persons are arrested or detained.[16] Many provinces announced detailed rules of the implementation of above-mentioned *Measures*. For example, the *Some Rules on the Implementation of Measures on the Administration of Emigration Intermediary Agency for Private Affairs (for Trial Implementation)* 2002 (Beijing) was introduced in order to permit the investigation and detailed administration of agencies for private affairs in Beijing.

10.2.3 *Laws governing overseas employment intermediary agencies*

In 2000, there were more than 80,000 Chinese people working abroad.[17] The overseas employment intermediary agencies (*Jingwai Jiuye Zhongjie Jigou*) are those granted a "License of Overseas Employment Intermediary Agency" (*Jingwai Jiuye Zhongjie Xukezheng*) to offer services to individuals wanting to work overseas. Their functions include providing labour market information to Chinese workers, job recommendations and recruitment, execution of employment con-

---

[15] Preface of the *Circular of MPS on Strictly Prohibiting From Illegally Undertaking Activities of Soliciting Clients to Permanently Emigrate* 1995 (PRC) provides Over last few years, [. . .] some domestic units and individuals [. . .] in collusion with foreign "migration experts' or "migration services organisations', provide unauthorised "investment", "business' and 'skills' migration services to illegally attract and organize Chinese citizens to emigrate, and exploit others for the benefit of themselves. A few sneak ahead to take the chance of organising and sending illegal emigrants.

[16] Xinahua News Agency, *193 Exit and Entry Intermediary agency for Private Purposes were Qualified (193 Jia Yinsi Churujing Zhongjie Jigou Tongguo Zige Rending)*, 8 February 2002.

[17] Quoted in the *OECD, Migration and the Labour Market in Asia: Recent Trends and Policies*, the OECD Paris 2001, 130.

tracts, assisting applications for passports and visas, technology and language training, assistance with insurance, and protection of labour rights by mediation, arbitration and litigation.

Overseas employment from China began in the late 1970s. The *Regulations on the Administration for Overseas Employment Intermediary Agency* 1992 (PRC) prescribe that overseas employment intermediary agencies must be approved by the Ministry of Labour and Social Security (MLSS). This regulation ensures that overseas employment agencies operate lawfully and protect the basic rights and interests of labourers abroad. Some approved employment agencies engaged in illegal conduct, such as participating in illegal migration and sending young women abroad to provide erotic services. In response, the MLSS announced the *Circular of Ministry of Labour on Prohibition of Illegal Act of Overseas Employment* (PRC) in 1995. However the legal rights and interests, and sometimes even the life and safety of the labourers, were frequently infringed or put at risk as some agencies single-mindedly pursued profits. The MLSS then took measures to rectify and regulate overseas employment agencies in the *Circular on Management of Overseas Employment* (PRC) in 2000.[18]

In 2002, the *Regulations on the Administration for Overseas Employment Intermediary Agencies* (PRC) were enacted to further regulate overseas employment agencies. These regulations were based on prior legislative experiences and international norms. The regulations relate to procedures, management and scope of operations, obligations and duties of intermediary agencies, record keeping of overseas labour contracts and agency services contracts.[19] Agencies that did not comply with the new regulations were closed down following their introduction.[20] Agencies licensed prior to the introduction of the regulations needed to re-apply and re-register within 90 days of the date from which they became effective.[21]

[18] The measures include: (1) Ensuring that agencies are licensed to operate and closing down those that are not; (2) Using the mass media to inform citizens about the national overseas employment policy, conditions of legal employment, standards to which employment agencies must adhere, so that they can identify illegal agencies; (3) Opening a public hotline and encouraging people to report illegal overseas employment agency activities; (4) Investigation and resolution of reported problems.

[19] Article 2 of the *Circular on Some Matters of Implementation and Carrying Out Regulations on the Administration for Overseas Employment Intermediary agency (Amendment)* 2002, promulgated by the Ministry of Labour and Social Security on 24 June 2002 and effective at the same day.

[20] Article 3 of the *Circular on Some Matters of Implementation and Carrying Out Regulations on the Administration for Overseas Employment Intermediary agency (Amendment)* 2002, promulgated by the Ministry of Labour and Social Security on 24 June 2002 and effective at the same day.

[21] Article 39 of the *Regulations on the Administration for Overseas Employment Intermediary agency (Amendment) 2002 (PRC)*, jointly promulgated by the MLSS, MPS and SAIC on 14 May 2002.

10.2.4 *Laws governing the foreign labour trade and cooperation company*

The foreign labour trade and cooperation companies (*Duiwai Laowu Hezuo Jingying Gongsi*) are the agencies that operates under a '"Certificate of Operation Qualification of Foreign Economy Cooperation' (*Duiwai Jingji Heizuo Jingying Zige Zhengshu*) issued by the then Ministry of Foreign Trade and Economic Cooperation (MFTEC),[22] to undertake foreign projects, engineering, international labour cooperation and consulting services. They are licensed to organise and send workers in accordance with foreign contracts, and are responsible for the management of contract workers abroad. These activities are referred to as 'labour export' (*Laowu Chukou*). According to the SBS, by 1998 the total revenue of overseas projects exceeded US$11 billion.[23]

The *Provisional Measures on Procedures for Contract Workers Sent Abroad and Undergoing Passport Application* 1990 (PRC) established a series of very strict provisions related to sending contract workers abroad.[24] The *Provisional Measures on Procedures for Contract Worker Sent Abroad Leaving the Country* 1996 (PRC) emphasised the licensing system contained in the *Provisional Measures 1990*.[25] It also strengthened requirements for technical and personal training for workers.[26]

---

[22] The MFERT was renamed as the Ministry of Commerce in 2003.

[23] Statistical Communiqué of the People's Republic of China on the 1998 National Economic and Social Development, Quoted in Biao. Xiang, "Emigration from China: A Sending Country Perspective", in *International Migration*, Volume 41, Number 3 (September 01, 2003), 21–48. http://ejournals.ebsco.com/direct.asp?ArticleID=P8PYFR-BJLETKMYT3KQ4F (accessed 01–10–2003), 32.

[24] Article 3 of the *Provisional Measures on Procedures for Contract Workers Sent Abroad and Undergoing Passport Application* 1990 (PRC) provides that the sending unit means enterprises which, with approval of the MFERT and a business license issued by the administration of industry and commerce, are authorised to undertake foreign contracted project engineering and international labour cooperation. Article 4 provides that the sending unit cannot send contract workers abroad unless they are licensed to do so (*Waipai Laowu Renyuan Xukezheng*), and there is a concluded contract with a foreign party." Article 5 prescribes that no contract workers can be sent abroad unless approved by foreign trade and economic cooperation administration under vice-provincial governments or a relevant ministry.

[25] Article 4 of the *Provisional Measures on Procedures for Contract Worker Sent Abroad Leaving the Country* 1996 (PRC), jointly promulgated by the MFERT, MFA and MPS on 20 December 1996.

[26] Article 20 of *Provisional Measures on Procedures for Contract Worker Sent Abroad Leaving the Country* 1996 (PRC): "MOFTEC shall institute and perfect the adaptive training system prior to going abroad conducted for contract workers sent abroad. When issuing passports to contract workers abroad, the passport-issuing agency may examine their training qualification certificates when necessary."

The *Provisional Measures* 1990 and 1996 were significantly affected by a planned central economy, which could no longer meet the demands of reform and opening-up. The *Measures on Procedures for Contract Worker Sent Abroad Leaving the Country* 2002 (PRC) promulgated that the public security departments have unified responsibility for the examination and approval of contract workers sent abroad. The authority does not extend to examining the genuineness of overseas projects, and the limitations on trans-province designation of workers have been cancelled.

10.2.5 *Laws governing international travel agencies*

International travel agencies (*Guoji Lvxingshe*) are those granted an 'Operation License of Travel Agency' (*Lvxingshe Jingying Xukezheng*) for the purpose of handling exit, entry and visa applications on behalf of tourists, to solicit tourists for overseas travel, and to arrange overseas tourist accommodation in return for a fee. According to the World Tourism Organisation, China is among the top 10 nations for outbound tourism. From 1994 to 2003, the total number of outbound Chinese tourists reached nearly 100 million, at an annual growth rate of 10.87 percent.[27] This roaring tourist market has lured numerous travel agencies to share the outbound Chinese travellers' market. Only licensed international travel agencies can provide inbound and outbound travel services.[28]

The *Provisional Regulations on the Administration of Travel Agency* 1985 (PRC) and the *Regulations on the Administration of Travel Agency (Amendment)* 1996 (PRC) prescribe the payment of a quality-guarantee deposit, needed for an operational license, and a process of annual inspection. These were the earliest regulations regarding the compulsory standard of service, requirement of operational qualifications, and scope of the government supervision, in the area of emigration intermediary agencies. Similar systems have been incorporated into regulations dealing with other categories of emigration intermediary agencies.

---

[27] Also, Data from the Chinese National Tourism Administration indicates that there was a dramatic increase in the number of countries and regions that have signed agreements with China to accept Chinese tourists from 1988 (when there were only three such agreements), to September 2004 (when there were 73) China's outbound travellers reached 14.99 million in the first seven months of 2004, there was a 63.7 percent increase from the same period of 2003. "China's Outbound Travellers Reach 15.99 Million in the First Seven Months" (Jinian Tou Qigeyue You 1599 Wan Renci Chujing You), 17/09/2004, The State Bureau of Statistics, http://english.people.com.cn//200409/17/eng20040917_157376.html (accessed 19/09/2006).

[28] Article 5 Clause 2 of the *Regulations on the Administration for Travel Agencies (Amendment)* 2002 (PRC) amended pursuant to *Travel Agencies Administrative Measures* 1996 (PRC), promulgated by the State Council on 11 December 2001 and effective on 1 January 2002.

In 2001, the State Council promulgated the *Decision on Revising the Regulations on Administration of Travel Agency* to systematically regulate Sino-foreign international travel agency. This was a consolidation of the *Provisional Regulations of Trial Establishment of Sino-foreign Joint Equity Travel Agency* 1999 (PRC) and the *Regulations on Administration of Travel Agency (Amendment)* 2001 (PRC). Restrictions on foreign investment in international travel agencies were reformed again after China entered the WTO. According to the *Provisional Regulations of Administration of Foreign Holding and Foreign Self-funded Travel Agency* 2003 (PRC), foreign investors with an annual turnover of US$ 40 million may apply to establish foreign holdings and foreign self-funded travel agencies.[29]

The regulations mentioned so far have attempted to promote the order and development of the international travel agency industry. On the other hand, the *Provisional Measures on the Administration of Chinese Citizens Tour Abroad at Their Own Expenses* 1997 (PRC) and the *Measures on the Administration of Chinese Citizens' Tours Abroad* 2002 (PRC) emphasise the obligations and duties of international travel agencies with respect to safeguarding the rights and interests of tourists, and ensuring that they are able to make a timely return to China. The *Measures on the Administration of Chinese Citizens Tours Abroad* 2002 (PRC) strengthens the protection of tourists' rights and interests in the three respects of accessing information, economics and person and property.

10.2.6 *Laws governing overseas training at government expense intermediary agencies*

The overseas training at government expense intermediary agencies (*Chuguo Peixun Zhongjie Jigou*) are those issued with a 'License of Overseas Training Intermediary Agency' (*Chuguo Peixun Zhongjie Jigou Xukezheng*) to select and dispatch technical and managerial personnel to other countries and regions for training at government expense, and assist them with passport and visa applications. The State Administration of Foreign Experts Affairs (SAFEA) stresses that unauthorised agencies will be punished if they attempt to undertake these activities.[30] According to the SAFEA, about 40,000 people are currently sent abroad

---

[29] Article 3 and 4 of the *Provisional Regulations of Administration of Foreign Holding and Foreign Self-funded Travel Agency* 2003 (PRC), jointly promulgated by China National Tourism Administration and Ministry of Commerce on 12 June 2003 and effective on 11 July 2003.

[30] "20 Agencies Authorized to Send Personnel for Overseas Training", 1 January 2001, China Education and Research Network, www.edu.cn/20010101/21989.shtml (accessed 19/12/2003).

every year for training. Since 1978, there have been approximately 450,000 people sent for overseas training at government expense.[31]

The only relevant legislation, the *Provisional Rules on the Recognition of Overseas Training Qualification of Dispatching Groups and Personals to Other Countries for Training of the Institutions and the Mass Departments* was enacted in 1993, 15 years after the first group of trainees were sent abroad in 1978. Under Articles 5 and 6(3) of the *Provisional Rules*, overseas training agencies are classified as national or regional agencies. National agencies may select and dispatch personnel from anywhere in China, whereas regional agencies are limited to dealing with personnel from that region. The prohibition of agencies operating for profit restrains competition in the industry. The organising and dispatching of personnel overseas for profit is prohibited.[32]

Moreover, as the aim of the rules is to build an honest and accountable government, and to prohibit government employees from touring overseas at public expense,[33] it hardly protects individual trainees' rights to overseas training. Yang Hanyan, the Deputy Director of the SAFEA, observed that the granting of a License of Overseas Training Intermediary Agency is an important anti-corruption practice.[34] Finally, recognition of overseas training agencies has been slow. The SAFEA authorised the establishment of regional agencies in 1994 and 1995. The first 20 national agencies were established in 2000. Each is under the direct government control, which can have consequences both for the protection of the right to leave for training and the effective use of public money for training.

---

[31] "Overseas Training", http://www.safea.gov.cn/?menu=train&sub=cgpxgz (accessed 28/01/2004).

[32] According to Article 2 of *Circular on the Recognition of Qualification of Overseas Training of Dispatching Personals to Other Countries for Training of China Communication Centre of Science and Technology and other 19 Institutions and the Mass Departments* 2000 (PRC), Also see similar provisions at Article 4 Clause 5 of the *Provisional Rules on the Recognition of Overseas Training Qualification of Dispatching Groups and Personals to Other Countries for Training of the Institutions and the Mass Organs* 1993 (PRC) (*Guanyu Shiye Danwei Shehui Tuanti Zuzhi Panqian Tuanzu He Renyuan Fu Guo (Jing) Wai Peixun Gongzuo Zige Rending De Zaixing Guiding*).

[33] Preface of the *Provisional Measures on the Administration of Dispatching Groups and Personals to Other Countries for Training* 1993 (PRC) (*Guanyu Panqian Tuanzu He Renyuan Fu Guo (Jing) Wai Peixun De Zaixing Guanli Banfa*), jointly promulgated by the State Administration of Foreign Experts Affairs and the MFA on 20 October 1993.

[34] Quoted in "20 Agencies Authorized to Send Personnel for Overseas Training", 1 January 2001, China Education and Research Network, www.edu.cn/20010101/21989.shtml (accessed 19/12/2003).

10.2.7 *Laws governing Sino-foreign joint venture skilled personnel intermediary agencies*

The Sino-foreign joint venture skilled personnel intermediary agencies (*Zhongwai Hezi Rencai Zhongjie Jigou*) are those granted an 'Operation License of Skilled Personnel Intermediary Agency' (*Rencai Zhongjie Fuwu Xukezheng*). These are joint ventures between Chinese and foreign companies, both of which are engaged in skilled personnel agency services. These agencies may recruit skilled personnel for employment abroad. In relation to overseas recruitment, these agencies are permitted to recruit for any industry, other than the six prohibited categories of personnel (see part 9.2.1 of this book).[35] Sino-foreign skilled personnel agencies are the newest category among the emigration intermediary agencies, and have been actively developed in China over the past two years.

The limitations on foreign investment in the skilled personnel intermediary sector were relaxed after China joined the WTO in December 2001. The *Regulations on the Administration of Skilled Personnel Market 2001 (PRC)* allowed foreign investment in China's skilled personnel intermediary services in the form of joint ventures. Shanghai and Beijing respectively issued the *Circular of Shanghai Municipality of Sino-Foreign Equity or Cooperative Joint Venture Skilled Personnel Intermediary Agency in This Municipality* 2002 (Shanghai), and *Provisional Measures of the Beijing Municipality for Promotion the Establishment of Sino-Foreign Joint Venture Skilled Personnel Intermediary Agency* 2002 (Beijing).

The Ministry of Personnel (MOP), Ministry of Commerce (MOC) and SAIC then jointly promulgated the *Provisional Regulations of Administration of Foreign Holding and Foreign Self-funded Travel Agencies* 2003 (PRC). Under Article 11 of the *Provisional Regulations*, enterprises seeking to establish Sino-foreign joint venture skilled personnel intermediary agencies must submit a written application with the necessary documents to provincial personnel departments for approval.

10.3 THE ISSUES ARISING FROM CHINESE EMIGRATION INTERMEDIARY AGENCY LAWS

The rapid development of emigration intermediary agencies has played a conspicuous role in the realisation of RLR in China. However, due to a lack of legislative experience and the inveterate abuses of the separate management of different industries, there are many aspects of the laws greatly in need of improve-

[35] Article 13 of the *Provisional Regulations on the Administration of Sino-Foreign Joint Venture Personnel Intermediary Agency* 2003 (PRC) (*Zhongwai Hezi Rencai Zhongjie Jigou Guanli Zaixing Guiding*), jointly promulgated by the Ministry of Personnel, the MOC and SAIC on 4 September 2003.

ment. These issues currently impinge on the ability of the agencies to fully perform their role.

10.3.1 *Excessive demand for licenses and certificates*

In addition to a Business License of Industry and Commerce (*Gongshang Yingy Zhizhao*) issued by the administration of industry and commerce, each category of agency must have a specific license issued by the relevant department responsible for the agency. Most licenses or certificates have only provincial, as opposed to national, validity. Every agency is prohibited from providing services beyond the scope of their license in the guise of authorised services. One example of the prohibition is in Article 2 (2) of the *Measures on the Administration of Exit and Entry Intermediary Agencies for Private Affairs* 2001 (PRC) which underlines that, "These measures shall be neither applicable to agency service for Chinese citizens going abroad for studying, nor for employment, tourism or labour service".

It appears that the purpose of the separated license system is to protect the rights and interests of individuals exiting China, to foster the development of emigration intermediary agency market, and facilitate the management of agencies. Unfortunately, the system does not completely achieve these goals, on three key grounds.

Firstly, there is an insufficient base of practical experience or theoretical support for the separated license regime. In theory, it is difficult to distinguish between the precise scope of each category of agency, and there are cases when the same applicant needs to seek the services of two or more agents for one journey. For instance, an overseas student may additionally have the demand to become a permanent resident of the destination State. In practice, the authorities may not exactly understand this and therefore not enforce the permissible operational scope of each category of agency. For example, Chongqing Public Security Department responded to complaints made by a local international travel agency that some local exit and entry intermediary agencies for private affairs were providing international travel services. The Chongqing authority thought that the activities of the relevant exit and entry intermediary agencies for private purposes were legal, provided that the word "tour" was not used in advertisements, and no punishment was made.[36] Clearly, the terms of advertisement cannot really help distinguish if the operation of one emigration intermediary agency is beyond its permissible scope.

---

[36] Ding, Xiangle, *Snatch Customers Between Exit and Entry Intermediary Agency for Private Purposes and Overseas Travel Agencies* (*Chuguo Zhongjie Yu Lvxingshe Qiangke Zhuguan Bumen: Cantuan Bie Zoucuo Difang*), *Chongqing Evening Newspaper*, 21 March 2003.

The licensing system also limits the size of intermediary agencies and prevents them from offering comprehensive services. The complexity of being supervised by multiple government departments, coupled with the requirement of paying multiple quality guarantee deposits and reserve funds, discourages applications for multiple licenses. At the same time most agencies have no alternative but to operate regionally rather than nationally. Leaving aside the HKSAR and MSAR, there are 33 provincial administrative regions in China. If one intermediary agency wishes to develop a national business of one just kind of emigration intermediary service, it would have to apply for 33 licenses, and establish 33 reserve funds or quality-guarantee deposits. This represents a practically insurmountable obstacle.

A licensing system that restricts the opportunity for agencies to expand so to cut operational costs and increase their success rate, severely affects the development of the industry. Intermediary agencies may not become more popular and reliable, and so enhance public confidence with respect to individuals' right to leave, until they can.[37] The very survival of these businesses may be problematic in the sense that agencies must be able to meet the comprehensive demands of clients, if they are to remain viable.

In order to survive and develop in a competitive market, some agencies will either apply for more licenses and certificates to officially extend the scope of their business, or exploit vague provisions to secretly offer services that exceed the scope of their license. In the later case, the rights of individuals exiting China can be put at jeopardy by the illegal operation of businesses providing unlicensed services.[38]

10.3.2 *Overly strict admission criteria*

License applicants are required to meet the strict demands related to investors, human resources, finance and capital and business premises. The provisions related to admission criteria are set out in Appendix three of this book.

---

[37] Beijing Chuangxintian Investment Consultant Limited Company (*Beijing Chuangxintian Touzi Guowen Shiwusuo Youxian Gongsi*), "What Exit and Entry Intermediary agency for Private Purposes Can do" (*Yimin Zhongjie Gongsi Haiyou Zuowei Ma*), 13 August 2003, http://goabraod.sohu.com/53/30/article212083053.shtml (accessed 19/09/2006).

[38] For example, the Beijing Yingzhiye Cultural Exchange Company recruits students from Weihai in East China's Shandong Province. The Beijing Education Committee has suspended the company because Beijing is this company's legalised business area. See "Ministry Website to Rate Intermediaries", *The China Daily,* 28 July 2003, http://www.chinadaily.com.cn/en/doc.2003–07/28/content _249602.htm (accessed 19/09/2006).

Reserve funds or quality-guarantee deposits impose a significant financial burden on businesses. Their purpose is to provide compensation to clients whose rights have been infringed and to ensure the payment of fines and penalties. The funds must be deposited into a trust fund and held by a designated State-owned bank. The amount to be paid varies between provincial regions. For example, an emigration intermediary agency for private purposes shall have reserve funds of C¥2 million (US$ 241,546) in Beijing,[39] and C¥500, 000 (US$ 60,386) in Henan Province. And, an overseas study intermediary agency shall have reserve funds of C¥1 million (US$ 120,773) in Beijing,[40] and C¥500, 000 (US$ 60,386) in Anhui Province. Interests accrued from funds is paid to the agency according to the terms of the deposit. The interest rate at the Beijing Commercial Bank is 0.72% for a flexible term deposit, and 2.79% for a five-year fixed term deposit.[41] Such low rates of interest mean that Beijing agencies, unless they can obtain a return of at least 3% more, cannot maintain the same profit rate as other businesses.

This loss of revenue is particularly significant given that since 2003, countries such as Canada and Australia have successively increased their criteria for skilled immigration. According to a Beijing survey in 2003, the number of eligible Chinese skilled applicants will decrease by 78.3% for Canada and 38.4% for Australia.[42] Many agencies are finding it difficult to remain viable in the marketplace, and materials from the Beijing Administration of Exit and Entry indicate that 33 emigration intermediary agencies in Beijing have cancelled their licenses during 2002–2003.[43] To reduce the pressure of operations, Beijing Exit and Entry

---

[39] Article 27 of the *Some Rules on the Implementation of Measures on the Administration of Exit and Entry Intermediary agency for Private Affairs (for Trial Implementation)* 2002 (Beijing), promulgated by Beijing Municipality Public Security Bureau and Beijing Municipality Administration of Industry and Commerce on 1 January 2002 and effective on 1 January 2002. in 2004, the exchange rate between American dollars and Chinese yuan is 1:8.28.

[40] Article 7 of the *Measures for the Control of Intermediary agency for Self-funded Overseas Study (for Trial Implementation)* 1999 (Beijing), promulgated by Beijing Municipality Committee of Education, Beijing Municipality Public Security Bureau and Beijing Municipality Administration of Industry and Commerce on 2 November 1999 and effective at the same day.

[41] "The Interests Lists of Renminbi Deposit" (*Renminbi Cunkuan Lilv Biao*), Beijing City Commercial Bank, http://www.bccb.com.cn/cunkuablilv.asp (accessed 28/01/2004).

[42] Beijing Chuangxintian Investment Consultant Limited Company (*Beijing Chuangxintian Touzi Guowen Shiwusuo Youxian Gongsi*), "What Exit and Entry Intermediary agency for Private Purposes Can do" (*Yimin Zhongjie Gongsi Haiyou Zuowei Ma*), 13 August 2003, http://goabroad.sohu.com/53/30/article212083053.shtml (accessed 19/09/2006).

[43] "The List of The Third Round Recognized Exit and Entry Intermediary Agencies for Private Purpose" (*Disanpi Yinsi Churujing Zhongjie Jigou Tongguo Zige Rending Mingdan*), Beijing Administration of Exit and Entry, http://minyi.beijing.gov.cn/fwdh/

Administration Department refunded C¥1 million (US$ 120,000) to the agencies in 2003 as required.

Secondly, the requirement that agency employ at least five qualified staff also imposes a financial burden on the industry, particularly if the workload reduces to the extent that it is no longer necessary for businesses to maintain a full compliment of staff. The workload may reduce below viable levels as a result of deregistration or changes of market. By comparison, many registered Australian migration agencies not only provide various migration services, but also employ only one or two qualified staff.

Finally, applications for most licenses and certificates filed by foreign investors are not accepted. Law firms are not automatically entitled to the qualification of providing intermediary services in China, as in respect of being qualified in other countries. They must instead submit new applications.[44] Investors hesitate at the prospect of overly strict admission criteria. As a consequence, the limitations on the investor affect the development of emigration intermediary agencies.

10.3.3 *Irregular examination and approval*

Applications to establish emigration agencies are often examined and approved in an irregular manner. They are processed in batches rather than in accordance with the order in which they are lodged. Batches of licenses for exit and entry intermediary agency for private affairs were issued in February 2002 (219), March 2002 (193), April 2002 (250) and September 2003 (14 license issued). Overseas education agency licenses were issued by the MOE in 2000 (246) and again in 2003 (242).

Irregular examination and approval of applications creates a bureaucratic barrier to entry into the industry. While the purpose of the agencies is to grasp business opportunities and generate profit, these opportunities are lost if the application process is protracted and unpredictable. This may mean that potential agents lose interest.

The main reason for the irregular examination and approval of applications is to regulate the market and reduce the workload of responsible departments. However, the facts demonstrate that this administrative method fails. The solution to reducing administrative workloads is to create more efficient systems, rather than processing in batches.

---

sm/crj/crjggzjsgylb/t20050119_202502.htm (accessed 16/09/2006), and "The List of Exit and Entry Intermediary Agencies for Private Purpose" (*Yinsi Churujing Zhongjie Jigou* Mingdan) http://www.bjgaj.gov.cn/net_service/consultation/index.jsp?operation=personal &id=446 (accessed 16/09/2006).

[44] Zhao, Yufei, "Question Why the Application Filed by Law-firm for Exit and Entry Intermediary Agency Shall not be Accepted" (*Ziyi Yisi Churujing Zhongjie Huodong Guanli Banfa: Yimin Yewu Zenneng Dui Lvshi Shiwusuo Guanshang Damen*), *Chinese Lawyer* (*Zhongguo Lvshi)* No. 2 [2002], 71–72.

10.3.4 *Non-recognition of Chinese emigration intermediary agencies by foreign countries*

Even though Chinese emigration intermediary agencies have established relationships with relevant counterpart services overseas, and have directly signed valid cooperative agreements with them, foreign countries do not necessarily recognise licensed Chinese emigration agencies. This weakens the credibility of the Chinese system.

Chen Tieyuan has found that 16 countries, including the USA, Australia, Canada, France and Japan, do not recognise Chinese-licensed overseas study intermediary agencies.[45] Traditional immigration countries do not recognise Chinese-licensed agencies for private affairs. Australia only recognises licensed agencies for private affairs that hold an Australian migration agent's certificate. With respect to group tourism, destination countries only recognise travel agencies approved by their own State.

In the absence of bilateral agreements with destination countries and common standards of regulation and protection for migrants between countries, policymakers have difficulty in developing a coherent strategy. Bilateral initiatives are important because migration is a dynamic process that involves both the country of origin, or sending country, and the country of destination. These agreements have mainly evolved as a product of the initiatives of destination countries to improve supervision over emigration agencies. They reflect the weaknesses of the Chinese regime governing emigration intermediary agencies, which is both internally problematic and at one remove from the international community.

10.3.5 *Joint liability of intermediary agencies*

The joint liability of emigration intermediary agencies, whose clients violate the provisions regarding exit and entry, is inappropriately emphasised by the legislation. Article 22(2) of the *Measures on the Administration of Chinese Citizens Tours Abroad (Amendment)* 2002 (PRC) sets out that:

> When a tourist stays abroad and fails to return to China, the tour guides shall make reports to the tour organiser and China's embassy or consulate in that country. The tour organiser shall make reports to the administration department in charge of tourism and the public security organ in time. When the relevant authorities deal with the affairs concerned, the tour organiser shall give assistance.

---

[45] Sixteen countries are the USA, the UK, Australia, Canada, Germany, France, Japan, New Zealand, Singapore, South Africa, South Korea, Sweden, Spain, Brazil and Mexico. Chen, Tieyuan, *Overseas Study without Intermediary Agency: the Interview to Visa Officer of Foreign Countries in China* (*Piekai Zhongjie Qu Liuxue: Zhuhua Qianzheng Guan Fangtan*) (Beijing: the Publishing House of Writer, 2002), 2–6.

The relevant punishment is provided in Article 32 Clause 1 of the *Measures on the Administration of Chinese Citizens Tours Abroad (Amendment)* 2002 (PRC) which provides that:

> Where a tourist stays abroad and fails to return to China, and the tour group guide fails to duly make a report to the tour organiser and China's embassy or consulate in the country of destination, or the tour organiser fails to make a timely report to the relevant authorities in violation of the provisions of Article 22, the tour organiser shall be warned and suspended from operating the business for organising tours abroad, and the tour group guide shall have its Tour Group Guide Certificate suspended by the administrative department in charge of tourism.

The aim is to minimise the number of people who stay abroad illegally, by imposing responsibilities on the tour organiser and guide. Similar punishment has been undertaken, as discussed in part 8.3.3 of this book, of individuals who breach provisions for the management of public affairs passports. This rule might be traced to practices of Xia Dynasty (2070 B.C. –1600 B.C.) in which individual was punished for being related to or friendly with somebody who had been convicted of an offence.[46] It is fair to assert that it is inappropriate to punish tour organisers and guides when tourists fail to return to China.

10.3.6 *Inadequate supervision of the operations of emigration intermediary agencies*

A lack of suitable supervision of the operations of emigration agencies seriously affects the maintenance and improvement of service quality and professionalism. The issues in this regard mainly focus on the overseas experience, qualifications, and continuing education of professional staff, and the enforcement of service standards.

It is common sense that all professional emigration agency staff should not only to meet the strict admission standards, but must undergo compulsory continuing education. For example, in Australia, registered migration agents cannot renew their annual registration unless they have received 10 'continuing education points' and maintain access to current reference materials. There are no compulsory requirements related to continuing education, overseas experience or qualifications for professional staff in China. With respect to enforcement of professional service standards, agencies may manage their finances, clients' records and staff as they think fit. The most important form of supervision over the oper-

---

[46] Dictionary Department, Institute of Linguistics, Chinese Academy of Social Sciences, *The Contemporary Chinese Dictionary (Chinese-English edition)* (Beijing: Foreign Language Teaching and Research Press, 2002), 513.

ation of intermediary agencies is the annual inspection. Agencies can pass their annual inspection so long as seriously illegal activities have not occurred.

In order to crack down the illegal activities of emigration agencies, the MPS, MOE, MLSS, and SAIC have jointly acted on a national scale. However, only advanced legal measures, rather than ad hoc or erratic reform measures, can maintain an orderly market. The current approach risks undermining public confidence in the existing legal system. The formulation of suitable rules for supervision of the emigration industry is an urgent task.

10.3.7 *The administration of emigration intermediary agencies*

There are some advantages to administering the industry on a regional or agency-type basis. However, supervision of such a broad range of activities places pressure on the bureaucracy, limiting their ability to respond quickly and flexibly to changed circumstances. Administrators tread a fine line between ensuring that they have sufficient power to regulate the emigration industry and not creating incentives for irregular migration. Administrators must be careful to avoid using their licensing powers to create a monopoly in an industry sector. A tightly controlled market may increase the price of services to potential migrants, whereas a liberal system may open the market to fraudulent operators. The State needs to decide whether or not to use the free market to regulate the industry. Use of the market in this way could improve the flow of information and create competition within the industry. Equally, protection of migrants' rights cannot be used to justify the creation of additional bureaucratic hurdles. The regulatory system should form a dependable mechanism to prevent unscrupulous emigration consultants from breaching their fiduciary responsibilities for profit, or mismanaging their clients' affairs.

10.4 Conclusions

Emigration intermediary agencies are unique to China and pertinent to any analysis of RLR in China. An increased rate of exit and entry over the last two decades has triggered their emergence. Due to the lack of legislative experiences and correct legislative aims, many issues exist in the laws for the emigration intermediary agencies established since the 1990s and especially 2000s.

Investors are discouraged by the prospect of overly strict industry admission criteria, and the excessive demands of licenses and certificates limit the size of agencies and prevent them from offering comprehensive services. Irregular examination and approval of applications further creates a bureaucratic barrier to entry into the industry. Non-recognition of foreign countries further reflects the weaknesses of the Chinese regime governing emigration intermediary agencies, which is problematic internally and at one remove from the international community.

It is fair to assert that the laws for joint liability of emigration intermediary agencies, whose clients violate provisions regarding exit and entry, are inappropriate. The lack of suitable supervision of the operation of emigration agencies seriously affects the maintenance and improvement of service quality and professionalism. Formulation of suitable rules regarding supervision of the industry is an urgent task. These issues combined, while unresolved, mean that the administration of emigration intermediary agencies cannot respond quickly and flexibly to reform.

Chapter Eleven
Chinese Exit and Entry Administrative System

Introduction

This chapter will build on and recount earlier work, to conduct a systematic analysis of the administration of exit and entry in China and related issues and implications for RLR. The chapter examines (i) the functions of exit and entry administrative authorities; (ii) the discretions of those authorities;[1] and (iii) the merits review of administrative decisions regarding exit and entry.

11.1 Functions of Exit and Entry Administrative Authorities

As is clear from the book so far, a wide range of authorities administer the control of exit, entry, transit, residence and travel of Chinese citizens and aliens and supervise the establishment and supervision of emigration intermediary agencies. Exit and entry administrative functions are distributed across 15 ministerial-level authorities – for immigration, emigration, nationality, border inspection, criminal

[1] As for general administrative system in the Chinese government, please refer to *Appendix 1 of The Structure of the Chinese State Organisations*.

investigation, household registration, foreign exchange control, and emigration agencies, and further divided into various levels between central and local governments. The complexity is far from conforming to the needs of a massively growing number of international travellers. The need of an objective examination of the current system and issues germane to the protection of RLR is vital.

11.1.1 *The division of the functions of exit and entry administrative authorities*

The division of functions between the central and local governments

China's administrative units are currently based on a five-level system dividing the nation into central government, provinces and autonomous regions and municipalities under the central government, municipalities and cities with districts, counties and cities without districts, and townships.

The overall administrative authority for exit and entry is a matter of Chinese foreign affairs.[2] Under Article 89 Clause 1(4) (9) of the *Constitution of the PRC (Amendment)* 2004, the State Council conducts foreign affairs. However, this division is sometimes flexible. For example, the expense of expelling aliens, in theory a cost for central authorities, is in practice afforded by local financial authorities.[3] The flexibility of the division of functions has the potential to jeopardize the overall effectiveness of the system. This division between the central and local governments has an historical basis in the period between 1949 and 1958, discussed previously in part 5.3.1.

More recent reform has empowered local authorities, devolving functions to them, and allowing for only selective intervention by central government. Local programs have effectively improved administration, and have more importantly, in some circumstances, engaged and included local communities in their design. In the light of their expanded functions, local governments have enacted numerous rules and regulations to control and improve exit and entry administration within their administrative areas, as discussed in parts 5.4 and 5.5. Local rules can

---

[2] "The PRC Department of Public Safety Police Specific Setup", http://www.chinesecop.com/CNP01.html (accessed 19/12/2003).

[3] Under Article 3 Clause 5 of the *Rules of the Supreme People's Court, the Supreme People's Procuratorate, the Ministry of Public Security, the Ministry of Foreign Affairs, the Ministry of Justice and the Ministry of Finance on Implementation Measures of Forced Expelling Aliens* 1992 (PRC), if a foreign embassy or general consulate in China cannot afford or refuses to afford the expense caused by the forced expulsion of an alien, the Chinese government shall afford the expense. Based on parity principle of power and responsibility, the "Chinese government" in this context means the Central government. However, Article 7 of the Rules stipulates the opposite: the local financial department that forced the expulsion of an alien shall incur the expense.

then tend to usurp central government duties and obligations, such as the license of emigration intermediary agencies at the provincial rather than national level, discussed in part 10.3.1 above.

The division of functions among various departments of the central government

The Ministry for Public Security (MPS) is the principal, yet not the sole ministry responsible for exit and entry administration. There are then two authorities under the MPS. One is the Bureau of Exit and Entry Administration (BEEA), which is responsible for the acceptance and processing of passport and visa applications. Local exit and entry administrators mainly do this, although the MPS has an overriding power. The other is the Bureau of Border Security Check and Administration (BBSCA), which is responsible for border inspection. In addition, another 14 ministries, State Council offices and departments affiliated to the State Council are responsible for different parts of exit and entry administration.[4]

The division of functions of various departments of central government might be accounted for by the structure of the State Council. The ministries and committees under the State Council are responsible for the exit and entry administration in detail. Under Article 8 of the *Law of the Organisation of the State Council* 1982 (PRC):

> The establishment, dissolution or merger of ministries and committees of the State Council shall be proposed by the Premier and decided by the NPC or, when the NPC is not in session, by its Standing Committee.

The Premier may actually decide the establishment, dissolution or merger of ministries and committees of the State Council. Because both the State Council and National People's Congress (NPC) are under the leadership of the CPC, legislative and executive powers are combined in China. The decision of the NPC or the Standing Committee of the NPC is usually a mere formality. The People's Congress can pass all initiatives of the State Council. Nevertheless, adherence to the formality can demand a great deal of time and energy. To strengthen direct control over some special affairs, the State Council at times directs departments affiliated to it and its offices to share the functions of the ministries and committees.[5] As for exit and entry administration, seven of the 15 competent departments

---

[4] Fourteen State Council offices and departments affiliated to the State Council of the State Council are Ministry of Foreign Affairs, Ministry of State Security, Ministry of Communication, the MOC, MOE, MLSS, MOP, CNTA, the Central Bank, SAFEA, State Council Bureau for Religious Affairs, STO, SHMO and SOCO.

[5] According to Article 11 of the *Law of the Organization of the State Council* 1982 (PRC), the State Council may establish a certain number of directly affiliated agencies to take charge of various specialized work and a certain number of administrative offices to assist the Premier in handling specialised affairs.

under the State Council are departments affiliated in this way, and when compared to ministries and committees, those affiliated departments are more dependent on the State Council.

Formulating tasks and responsibilities of the ministries and committees, according to Article 89 of the *Constitution of the PRC (Amendment)* 2004, falls within the jurisdiction of the State Council. Unfortunately, delays in formulation and timely adjustment of tasks are often the case.[6] The inertia of a near 40 year-old system, the complication of joint administration of 15 departments under the State Council, and the foreign or international character of exit and entry administration hinder the Central government from complete reform. It is understandable why current reforms progress cautiously, and why almost every aspect of issues discussed from chapters eight to fourteen, relate to public security and other departments.

The detailed divisions of the functions of exit and entry administration

The detailed divisions of the functions of exit and entry administration in China are more complex than in other countries in the world. The functions of exit and entry administrative authority are organised in the light of the categories of administrative authority in Appendices four to ten of this book. Each appendix lists the functions of different levels of administrative authority. In summary:

1. The MPS and its local authorised public security departments administer:
   - Exit and entry for private affairs of Chinese citizens;
   - Entry, travel and residence of aliens lodged in China.
2. The MFA and its local foreign affairs departments administer:
   - Exit and entry for public affairs of Chinese citizens;
   - Entry, transit, travel and residence of aliens, lodged outside China.
3. Chinese diplomatic missions, consular offices or other agencies abroad authorised by the MFA issue, cancel, revoke and retain, or declare invalid Chinese passports and alien's visas.

---

[6] Delay can be contributed to three causes. The first is that China is in transition. There are not enough experiences or time to reform the administrative tasks and responsibilities. The second relates to powers and interests. It is difficult to separate vested powers and functions of the departments under the State Council into other departments. The third factor is social stability. Owing to concern about social instability caused by administrative reform, the State Council seldom adjusts the sensitive powers and functions of the departments. As Jiang Zemin, the former President of China underlined in the report at the 16th CPC Congress in November 2002, "ensur[ing] stability is a principle of overriding importance and balance reform, development and stability." See Jiang, Zemin, the President of the PRC, "Build a Well-off Society in an All-Round Way and Create a New Situation in Building Socialism with Chinese Characteristics: Report at 16th China Communist Party Congress (8/11/2002)", http://russian.china.org.cn/english/features/49007.html (accessed 19/09/2006).

4. The Bureau of Harbour Superintendence or its authorised harbour superintendent departments issue, cancel, revoke and retain, or declare invalid seafarer's passports.
5. The Bureau of Borders Security Check and Administration under the MPS and Border Inspection Stations administer exit and entry border inspection.
6. The Sate Council of Hong Kong and Macao Affairs office (SHMO) and State Council of Taiwan Affairs office (STO) are responsible for the provisional examination and approval of travel to or from the HKSAR, MSAR and Taiwan for public affairs.
7. Overseas Chinese Affairs departments examine and approve applications of overseas Chinese and Chinese in the HKSAR, MSAR and Taiwan for returning to and settling in Mainland China in consultation with provincial public security departments.
8. Six ministries and their authorised local departments are jointly responsible for the administration of emigration intermediary agencies.
9. The CPC and other departments and units are responsible for:
   - the provisional examination and approval of exit and entry for public affairs, and
   - exit and entry of individuals with special status for private affairs.

11.1.2 *Issues and implications of functions of exit and entry administrative authorities*

The complex system of exit and entry administration seriously affects the efficiency of exit and entry administration and the realisation of RLR in the following three principal respects.

Fragmented and incoherent administration

The fragmentation of administrative authority across 15 ministerial-level departments results in a pattern of inefficient communication and inconsistent or incoherent decision-making. No single department can complete an entire process. Six separate ministerial-level departments, for instance, administer emigration intermediary agencies. This can easily lead to delays in processing applications and reduce the quality of administration. Poor intra-governmental communication, as outlined earlier in the book, can also undermine the identification and control of individuals prohibited from entering or exiting China.

Overlapping functions may lead to administrative oversight and inefficiency

The tables in Appendices four to ten of this book also show how functions can overlap between departments or sections within departments. The fact that Chinese migration authorities may examine and punish persons who violate migration laws, is a typical example; according to international norms, migration and police authorities should exercise separate powers. This can adversely affect communication and co-operation between China and other nations, and among administrative authorities.

The overlapping functions of various government departments may also cause individual departments to ignore their main responsibilities and focus on disputes arising from trivial matters, or to shift responsibility onto others when confronted with a problem. Duplication of administrative functions limits the extent to which the services can be improved or functions performed in a fulsome way.

Concentration of functions on the ministerial and provincial levels of administration

The functions of the exit and entry administrative authorities are overly concentrated on the ministerial and provincial level administration. Local offices have limited access to processing, which undermines local exit and entry administration. Applicants must spend time and money travelling to the provincial or national capital to lodge applications.

11.2 Discretions of Exit and Entry Administrative Authorities

The greater the discretion of exit and entry administrative authorities over decisions made, the more easily RLR is infringed. Generally, administrative discretion is too broad in China, and has obstructed RLR.

11.2.1 *The scope of discretion*

The scope for discretion in decision-making for responsible departments, especially public security departments, in regard to exit and entry is broad. Departments are empowered to decide how and if to approve applications in certain situations and within certain bounds. Although the relevant laws generally prescribe the conditions that must be satisfied before a decision is made, the interpretation of those provisions is discretionary.

The exit and entry administrative authorities are entitled to enact interpretative legislation regarding the laws promulgated by the Standing Committee of the NPC and the State Council. Article 19 of the *Law on the Control of Exit and Entry of Citizens* 1985 (PRC) provides that, "The Ministry of Public Security, the Ministry of Foreign Affairs, and the Ministry of Communications shall, pursuant to this law, formulate rules". Article 30 of the *Provisional Measures on the Control over Chinese Citizens Travelling for Private Affairs to or from the Regions of Hong Kong or Macao* 1986 (PRC) stipulates that, "The Ministry of Public Security shall be responsible for organising the implementation of these Measures and for the interpretation hereof". Article 43 of the *Measures on the Control over Chinese Citizens Travelling to or from the Region of Taiwan* 1992 (PRC) prescribes that, "The Ministry of Public Security shall be responsible for the interpretation of these Measures". By international norms, the Congress or Courts usually exercise the power of interpreting statutes in accordance with the doctrinal separation of legislative, executive and judicial powers. Allowing the administrative authority to interpret the scope of their own power, limits the extent to which the Courts can fetter the discretion of the administrative arms of government.

The proliferation of departmental or ministerial rulings further supports the argument that administrative discretion is too broad. The exit and entry administrative authorities are entitled to enact internal policies to give further detail to legislation. Most of these are internal policies and not open to the public.[7] This book has mentioned over 300 rules, measures, circulars, explanations, opinions, decisions, rules and regulations relating to exit and entry laws, which are promulgated by approximately 40 ministerial level departments. The circulars and notices cited in this book account for approximately one third of that. The bureaucratic barrier to RLR resulting from unpublished official documents was discussed in part 6.5.

If there are no relevant laws to be applied, the understanding of the exit and entry administrative authority will be implemented. Article 9 of the *Measures on the Control over Chinese Citizens travelling to or from the Region of Taiwan* 1992 (PRC), for instance, provides that:

> The public security department shall, within 30 days of receipt of the application for travelling to Taiwan, or within 60 days for the applicants who reside at remote areas with poor transportation facilities (*Dichu Pianpi Jiaotong Bubian*), make a decision on approving of the application or not, and notify the applicant of the decision. The urgent (*Jinji*) application shall be processed at any time.

Public security departments may interpret the terms 'a remote areas with poor transportation facilities' and 'urgent' according to their understanding, which can differ in each case.

---

[7] The Bureau of Party, Government Foreign Affairs Cadre under Department of Personal of Central Committee of Chinese Communist Party, the Introduction of the editor in *The Collection of Popular Official Documents and Letters, Regulations and Laws Governing Examination and Administration of Exiting Abroad* (*Chuguojing Shenpi Ji Guanli Gongzuo Changyong Wenjian Fagui Xuanbian*), Internal Publication (*Neibu Faxing*) (Beijing: the Publishing House of Dangjian Duwu, 1994).

11.2.2 *Issues and implications of discretionary scope*

The nature of exit and entry discretion can be classified as the power to (i) decide whether to approve an application; (ii) choose a form of administrative punishment; and (iii) choose an enforcement measure.

Discretion to approve applications

Appendices four to ten of this book provide many examples of this form of discretion. One example is in the granting of return residence permits for overseas Chinese. Chinese diplomatic missions, consular offices or other agencies located abroad and authorised by the MFA, and provincial public security departments have this power under Article 10 of the *Detailed Rules for the Implementation of the Law on the Control of Exit and Entry of Citizens (Amendment)* 1994 (PRC), yet its provisions are too vague to be implemented. In practice, these entities examine and approve applications according to their internal policies, as discussed in part 7.1.2. Another example is Article 7 of *Law of Nationality* 1980 (PRC), under which:

> Foreign nationals or stateless persons who are willing to abide by China's Constitution and laws and who meet one of the following conditions may be naturalised upon approval of their applications: . . . (3) they have other legitimate reasons.

The MPS has broad discretion in their interpretation of "other legitimate reasons".

Discretion to punish

Discretion in the choice of administrative punishment is another significant aspect of the broad and uncertain powers conferred on administrative authorities. Under Article 23 of the *Detailed Rules for the Implementation of the Law on the Control of Exit and Entry of Citizens* 1985 (PRC):

> If any persons have used or altered certificates or other person's certificates for entering or leaving the country, they shall, in addition to having the forged certificates confiscated, be subject to a warning, or held in detention for up to five days. . . .

The form of the punishment and the period of possible detention are left to the discretion of public security departments. Similarly, the description of a 'minor' offence, contained in Article 28 of the *Provisional Measures on the Control over Chinese Citizens Travelling for Private Affairs to or from the Regions of Hong Kong or Macao* 1986 (PRC) is so nebulous that the public security departments have enough discretion to reach opposite conclusions on the same facts.

Additionally, the public security department has the discretion to determine the nature of the penalty imposed, namely to make a choice between a fine or period of detention, and can even decide the length of an illegal alien's detention under Article 40 of the *Detailed Rules for the Implementation of the Law on the Control of Exit and Entry of Aliens 1985* (PRC), by which detention is limited to a minimum of three and maximum of 10 days. According to Zhan Weiguang in "Features, Causes and Solutions of Crimes Against Control of Exit and Entry", in the *Collection of Papers on the Control of Exit and Entry (III)*;

> Officials in charge of exit and entry administration who do not have a strong sense of legality and know little about the laws and rules related to exit and entry administration; do not know how to deal with violations of the exit and entry administration. The violators are often only fined. The majority of people therefore fail to understand that all violations of the exit and entry administration are criminal in character, not merely administrative; and the deterrent function of criminal law is markedly reduced.[8]

This lack of understanding on the part of officials in charge of exit and entry administration as to the penalties for violation of exit and entry laws, while it hampers the efforts of public security departments to investigate and prosecute unlawful acts, may also exaggerate the possibilities of violating an individual's RLR.

Discretion in regard to enforcement measures

If the discretion in regard to law enforcement measures is not properly exercised, it may interfere with RLR because violators or suspected violators may be subjected to unfair punishment. Article 3 of the *Some Rules on the Issues of Exit Abroad Prohibiting Aliens and Chinese Citizens Exiting Abroad* 1987 (PRC) provides that:

> [The] Following means can be adopted separately when the People's Court, People's Procuratorate, Pubic Security organs and national security organs prohibit aliens and Chinese citizens from exiting China;
> (1) The affected party shall be informed orally or in writing that they are prohibited from exiting China unless the lawsuits or relevant issues have been resolved;
> (2) The affected party may [either] be ordered to live at home under surveillance, post bail pending trial with restricted freedom of movement, or permitted to travel abroad after providing property guarantee or payment of a bond;
> (3) The affected party's passport or other valid travel documents can be retained.

The Courts, Procuratorates, pubic security departments and national security departments have broad discretion in choosing any of the enforcement measures.

In the interest of administrative efficiency, infringements of rights caused by abuses of discretion are not subject to administrative review and do not attract criminal liability. Judicial review of administrative decisions generally focuses on

---

[8] Zhan, Weiguan, *the Features, Causes and Solutions of Crimes Against Control of Exit and Entry* in Committee of Exit and Entry Administration under Chinese Association of Police (ed), *The Collection of Papers on The Control of Exit and Entry (III)* (*Churujing Guanli Lunwenxuan (san)*), Interior Published within Public Security Organs (*Gongan Jiguan Neibu Faxing*), the Publishing House of Qunzhong, Beijing China, 2001, page 276.

legitimising the discretion. An administrative decision can be set aside if there has been an illegal use of discretion, but this generally only occurs when there has been a manifestly unfair decision, allowing many minor breaches to go unchecked. The implications of the broad administrative discretion are serious. It provides many opportunities for government department and officers to generally profit and abuse their power.

11.3 Merits Review of Administrative Decisions Regrading Exit and Entry

The development of international migration law has led to some important developments in regard to exit and entry administration in national legal systems, by which States have increasingly limited governmental immunities and have developed innovative responses to RLR violations. The scope of exit and entry administrative decision-making needs to be explained before investigating the current issues of merits review in China. For the purposes of this analysis, a decision includes an approval or refusal of an application, as well as the formulation of administrative recommendations or comments. Appendices 2, 11 and 12 of this book summarise the merits review of administrative decisions in regard to penalties, processing of applications and law. The three appendices show that there are many serious issues in regard to merits review of administrative decisions and limits on RLR, associated with the current remedies.

11.3.1 *The mechanism for merits review of administrative decisions*

Contrary to the list given, Appendix 11 indicates that there is only one decision upon which the merits of an administrative decision can be reviewed, namely refusal to permit a citizen's exit of China or refusal to issue a passport for citizens. Additionally, applicants exiting China for public affairs are not entitled the same review rights as those exiting for private affairs. Under Article 16 (b) of the 1972 Uppsala Declaration on RLR, an individual should be informed in writing of the reasons for revoking or invalidating an earlier decision. Appendices 2, 11 and 12 show that no such mechanism exists.

Merits review of migration decisions can offer expedient, efficient and relatively inexpensive oversight of primary decisions and allow individuals to seek a fresh decision. To achieve the goals of regularity and fairness, the exit and entry administration must provide individuals with a means of redress when a decision has been made. With the exception of a few circumstances, such as an application lodged by aliens outside the country, it is almost commonplace that an individual be entitled to seek a review of the merits of the decision. Undoubtedly, the lack of a mechanism for merits review of administrative decisions severely limits the protection of RLR.

11.3.2 *Treatment to applicants of the Mainland, HKSAR, MSAR and Taiwan Chinese*

The second issue is the discrimination between nationality and place of residences in Mainland China, the HKSAR, MSAR and Taiwan, and for aliens, in terms of their rights of appeal against penalties. In effect, the range of available remedies does not correspond with the scope of the penalties that can be imposed.

This inconsistency is illustrated when the *Measures on the Control over Chinese Citizens Travelling to or from the Region of Taiwan* 1992 (PRC) is compared with the *Law on the Control of Exit and Entry of Citizens* 1985 (PRC), the *Provisional Measures on the Control over Chinese Citizens Travelling for Private Affairs to or from the Regions of Hong Kong or Macao* 1986 (PRC), and the *Law on the Control of Exit and Entry of Aliens* 1985 (PRC). These laws create penalties for illegal entry or exit activities, but only *Measures on the Control over Chinese Citizens Travelling to or from the Region of Taiwan* 1992 (PRC) provide remedies for all penalties. There is no review for penalties in the *Provisional Measures on the Control over Chinese Citizens Travelling for Private Affairs to or from the Regions of Hong Kong or Macao* 1986 (PRC). The same issues arise in relation to the *Law on the Control of Exit and Entry of Citizens (Amendment)* 1994 (PRC) and its detailed rules of the implementation, in which there are reviews only for of the penalties of a fine, a disciplinary warning and confiscation of forged certificates. Accordingly, the availability of some reviews depends on the status, nationality or purpose of travel of individuals.

11.3.3 *Relationship between the merits review and external remedies*

The third issue relates to the choice of an avenue of review to appeal against a decision. Articles 15 of the *Law on the Control of Exit and Entry of Citizens* 1985 (PRC), Article 50 of the *Detailed Rules for the Law on the Control of Exit and Entry of Aliens (Amendment)* 1994 (PRC) and Article 39 of the *Measures on the Control over Chinese Citizens Travelling to or from the Region of Taiwan* 1992 (PRC) permit a citizen against whom a penalty has been imposed to appeal to the public security departments at the next highest level for a final decision; or to institute proceedings in Court. This implies that the choice of one avenue or review forecloses the opportunity to use the other.

Because there is no substantial independent review tribunal in China, if an individual opts for an administrative review, the fairness of the review may not be questioned. Under Articles 3 and 12(1) of the *Law of Administrative Review* 1999 (PRC), a legal affairs department within the administrative authority reviews the decision. The legal affairs department is also required to perform various other functions and as such, is not independent of the authority. In complex cases, reviews are conducted in consultation with the next most senior department, which seldom overturns an original decision. In developed countries, such as Australia, there are external independent review tribunals, which can re-examine the evidence used to reach the decision and substitute its own findings for that of the original decision-maker.

If the affected individual chooses to institute proceedings in Court, cost and delay in reaching a final decision are issues. According to Article 5 of the *Law of Administrative Procedure* 1990 (PRC), a Court finding only results in a review of the legality of the decision, rather than its merits.

11.4 Conclusions

The system of administration of exit and entry in China faces serious issues. Its functions are diffusely allocated, sometimes overlap, and are also concentrated on power at the ministerial and provincial levels. The system cannot support administrative authorities in effective decision making. There is potential in this for the evasion of responsibility, unprincipled practice and a focus on trivial issues ahead of substantive matters of administration.

As to discretionary powers, authorities are not only entitled to enact interpretative laws, but may enact internal policies to further detail legislation. If there are not relevant laws to be applied, the understanding of the authorities can prevail. This discretion is far too broad; authorities can arbitrarily decide applications for exit and entry. In each case, RLR is undermined in China.

The mechanism of merits review of administrative decisions is almost non-existent. There is only one decision upon which the merits of an administrative decision might be reviewed, namely refusal to permit an individual's exit of China or refusal to issue a passport for citizens. There are no remedies for violations of the right to leave for public affairs. The right of appeal against penalties is discriminatory and for Chinese citizens, exists in terms of their residence in the Mainland, HKSAR, MSAR and Taiwan. The choice of internal remedies forecloses the opportunity to use the external remedies and vice versa.

Chapter Twelve

The Need to Protect RLR in China, the Factors in Favour, and Resolving Practical Concerns against it

INTRODUCTION

The issues analysed from Chapters six to eleven do not indicate that protecting RLR in China is prevented in the current political, economic, cultural and legal circumstances. On the contrary, the foundations of RLR, discussed in Chapter two, and its development in China, discussed in Chapter five, demonstrate that the protection of RLR is consistent with principles of legal philosophy, the trend of the development of RLR, international norms and globalisation. The worldwide development of RLR alongside considerable changes in China, have laid a solid foundation to reform the regulatory framework governing RLR in China. This Chapter will examine why it is necessary to protect RLR in China, discuss the factors that favour its protection, and suggest the means of resolving some practical concerns that militate against reform.

12.1 THE NEED TO PROTECT RLR IN CHINA

The issues analysed from Chapters six to eleven evinced that the outdated regime of exit and entry administration, established and developed over last 50 years, has hampered China's economic and social development. Since the introduction of reform and opening up policies in 1978, the need to protect RLR in China has gradually increased. In particular, protection of RLR is needed to (i) protect the human rights of Chinese citizens (ii) meet the demands of a socialist market economy and of further opening up to the world; (iii) respond to changing patterns of migration; and (iv) fulfil China's international obligations.

12.1.1 *Protecting the human rights of Chinese citizens*

Without the protection of RLR in China, it is hard to say human rights have been safeguarded in China. The conception of human rights is accepted *per se* in China, even though the Chinese government rejects the Western conception of human rights and opposes human rights being made a political issue, as will be discussed below. Article 33 Clause 4 of the *Constitution of the PRC (Amendment)* 2004 stipulates "the State respects and safeguards human rights". In 1999 and 2001, the spokesperson of the Ministry of Foreign Affairs (MFA) affirmed that, "The Chinese government has all along respected the universal principle of human rights".[1]

The then President Jiang Zemin thought in 2002 that to develop socialist democracy China should ensure that the people exercise their rights as the masters of the country.[2] Premier Wen Jiabao argued that the tremendous wealth created by China in the past quarter of a century is due to "the policy of reform and opening-up, [and] in the final analysis, to the freedom-inspired creativity of the Chinese people".[3] The Chinese Foreign Minister, during a meeting with a Russian Human Rights representative, stated that the Chinese government would like to resolve the differences on the issue of human rights through equal dialogue and on the basis of mutual respect.[4]

Based on its recognition of human rights and acknowledgement of their importance, the Chinese government has committed itself to effectively protect human rights, and supports the development of the international human rights movement.

---

[1] "Spokesperson on the 1999 Human Rights Report Issued by the US State Department", 15/11/2000, Ministry of Foreign Affairs of the PRC, http://www.fmprc.gov.cn/eng/xwfw/2510/2535/t15110.htm (accessed 20/09/2006); and "Spokesperson On Us Annual Human Rights Report (20/02/2001)", Ministry of Foreign Affairs of the PRC, http://www.fmprc.gov.cn/eng/xwfw/2510/2535/t22772.html (accessed 20/09/2006)

[2] Jiang, Zemin, the President of the PRC, "Build a Well-off Society in an All-Round Way and Create a New Situation in Building Socialism with Chinese Characteristics: Report at 16th China Communist Party Congress (8/11/2002)", http://www.china.org.cn/english/features/49007.htm (accessed 20/09/2006) Paragraph 19.

[3] Wen, Jiaobao, the Premier of the State Council, "Turning Yours Eyes to China", Speech at Harvard University on 11 December 2003, http://www.fmprc.gov.cn/eng/zxxx/t56076.htm (accessed 19/12/2003).

[4] "Chinese FM Meets Russian Human Rights Representative", (16/03/2000), http://www.fmprc.gov.cn/eng/wjb/wjbz/2467/t14261.htm (accessed 20/09/2006).

In *Fifty Years of Progress in China's Human Rights*, the government affirmed that full realisation of human rights is "a basic goal of China's cross century development."[5] In the words of State Councillor Tang Jiaxuan, it is the sacred duty of the Chinese government to promote and protect human rights.[6] In February 2004, a spokesperson for the MFA stressed that; "[the] Chinese Government has always committed itself to protecting human rights of the Chinese people."[7]

From the perspective of the universal principle of human rights, as discussed in Chapter three, the recognition and protection of human rights implies the right to leave and return to one's country. Chinese authorities and scholars also directly acknowledge RLR and its protection. In *The Administration on Exit and Entry*, which is used by the MPS in the education of police, Zhu Lin has contended that "RLR is not only recognised by all States in the world but also by international conventions".[8] Wong Li has claimed, in *International Immigration Law and the Practice*, that "RLR is widely recognised as one of fundamental human rights by all States in the world [and] should be adopted and detailed in international migration law".[9] Significantly, Premier Wen Jiabao has said:

> The essence of reform is to [. . .] respect and protect the freedom of the Chinese people to pursue happiness. There has been gradual lifting of the former improper restrictions, visible and invisible, on people's freedom in choice of mobility, travel [. . .] and lifestyle.[10]

Certain Chinese scholars accept that the protection and promotion of RLR should be regarded as one of leading principles guiding the research of migration law or the reform of laws governing the exit and entry administration.[11]

---

[5] "Information Office of the State Council of the PRC, "Fifty Years of Progress in China's Human Rights", June 2000, http://www.fmprc.gov.cn/eng/topics/3711/t18992.htm (accessed 20/09/2006) at Part VI.

[6] Tang, Jiaxuan, "Foreign Minister Tang Jiaxuan at the 54th Session of the UN General Assembly", 20/11/2000, http://www.fmprc.gov.cn/eng/ziliao/3602/3604/t18058.htm (accessed 20/09/2006).

[7] "Spokesperson Zhang Qiyue's Remarks on the Country Report on Human Rights Issued by the US (26/02/2004)", http://www.fmprc.gov.cn/eng/xwfw/2510/t69782.htm (accessed 02/03/2004).

[8] Wang, Guoliang and Zhu, Lin, *The Administration on Exit and Entry*, *one of Planning Textbooks of Higher Education of People's Police* (*Renmin Jingcha Gaodeng Jiaoyu Guihua Jiaocha: Churujing Guanlixue*) Interior Published within Public Security Organs (*Gongan Jiguan Neibu Faxing*) (Beijing: the Publishing House of China University of People's Public Security, 2002), 44.

[9] Wong, Li, *International Immigration Law and the Practices* (*Guoji Yiminfa Lilun Yu Shijian*) (Beijing: the Publishing House of Law, 2001), 26.

[10] Wen, Jiaobao, the Premier of the State Council, "Turning Yours Eyes to China", Speech at Harvard University on 11 December 2003, http://www.fmprc.gov.cn/eng/zxxx/t56076.htm (accessed 19/12/2003).

[11] For the research of migration law, see Wong, Li, *International Immigration Law and*

Major discrepancies still exist between the polices as written and those implemented, even though the government has reformed its enforcement policies and procedures to better align them with international human rights ethics. The UN High Commissioner for Human Rights, Mary Robinson, observed in August 2002 that Chinese law and practice still falls short of international human rights ethics.[12] RLR needs to be protected to realise effective protection of human rights, to so maintain the Chinese faith in human dignity and in the universal observance of human rights.

12.1.2 *Meeting the demands of a socialist market economy and further opening China to the world community*

In essence, China's economic reform represents a shift from a centralised planned economy to a more market-oriented system, and a decision to open China to the effects of globalisation. Doing a better job in opening up by 'bringing in' and 'going out' has been established as a goal of economic development and restructuring in the first two decades of the 21st century.[13] Jiang Zemin has explained that,

> By both 'bringing in' and 'going out', [China] should actively participate in international economic and technological cooperation and competition and open wider to the outside world.[14]

Zhu Rongji has emphasised the increase of labour export.[15]

---

the Practices (*Guoji Yiminfa Lilun Yu Shijian*) (Beijing: the Publishing House of Law, 2001), 26. For the reform of laws governing the exit and entry administration, see Lin, Yicong, "On the Principle of the Amending of Current laws Governing the Exit and Entry Administration", in Committee of Exit and Entry Administration under Chinese Association of Police, editor, *The Collection of Papers on The Control of Exit and Entry (III)* (*Churujing Guanli Lunwenxuan (san)*), Interior Published within Public Security Organs (*Gongan Jiguan Neibu Faxing*) (Beijing:the Publishing House of Qunzhong, 2001), 15.

[12] "Human Rights Watch World Report 2003: Asia: China and Tibet", http://hrw.org/wr2k3/asia4.html (accessed 20/09/2006).

[13] Jiang, Zemin, the President of the PRC, "Build a Well-off Society in an All-Round Way and Create a New Situation in Building Socialism with Chinese Characteristics: Report at 16th China Communist Party Congress (8/11/2002)", http://www.china.org.cn/english/features/49007.htm (accessed 20/09/2006) at Part IV.

[14] Jiang, Zemin, the President of the PRC, Par. 17 of Part I of "Build a Well-off Society in an All-Round Way and Create a New Situation in Building Socialism with Chinese Characteristics: Report at 16th China Communist Party Congress (8/11/2002)", http://www.china.org.cn/english/features/49007.htm (accessed 20/09/2006).

[15] Zhu, Rongji, Premier of the State Council, Par 3 of Part IV of "Report on the Work of the Government 2002", (16/03/2002), http://english.gov.cn/official/2005-07/29/content_18337.htm (accessed 16/09/2006).

To fully master the economic opportunities offered by reform, international exchange and cooperation, China needs to accelerate the steps of integration into the world economy. China and the ASEAN agreed, in 2000, to gradually establish a China-ASEAN free trade zone over the next 10 years. New Zealand has agreed, in 2004, to launch negotiations with China for a free trade agreement as soon as possible.[16] Exchanges and cooperation between the Mainland and Hong Kong and Macao also need to be strengthened.[17]

The current system of exit and entry administration in China has evolved from a centralised planning system, quasi-agricultural society, and a society and culture closed or quasi-closed to the outside world. China once adopted an 'iron curtain' approach to maintaining social stability, by consolidating its agrarian base and ensuring its security in the international arena. With the improvement of the socialist market economy, increased industrialisation, and membership of the WTO, the current system of exit and entry administration cannot meet the requirements of China's economic development, and lags behind in the protection of RLR.

It is hard to imagine that China's economic goals can be reached, and international exchange and cooperation between China and the rest of the world significantly improved, without the realisation of RLR. According to goals of the CPC, by 2020 China will have, in the main, achieved industrialisation and established a fully-fledged socialist market economy and a more open and viable economic system.[18] Transnational movement of Chinese people is an indefeasible requirement of opening wider. The high rate of migration workers' movement is beneficial for the realisation of free trade and a common currency area. Chinese economic development and the protection of RLR are mutually dependent and reinforcing. Economic development creates conditions for the protection of RLR; and RLR assists in economic development.

12.1.3 *Responding to changing patterns of migration*

Patterns of Chinese exit and entry have greatly changed over past 25 years. In 2001, 21.34% of the Chinese population exited and re-entered for the purpose of

---

[16] *China, New Zealand to Launch FTA Talks*, 22/11/2004, *China Daily*, http://www.china.org.cn/english/BAT/112773.htm (accessed 20/09/2006).

[17] Zhu, Rongji, Premier of the State Council, Par 9 of Part VII of "Report on the Work of the Government 2002" (16/03/2002), http://english.gov.cn/official2005-07/29/content_18337.htm (accessed 16/09/2006).

[18] Jiang, Zemin, the President of the PRC, "Build a Well-off Society in an All-Round Way and Create a New Situation in Building Socialism with Chinese Characteristics: Report at 16th China Communist Party Congress (8/11/2002)", http://www.china.org.cn/english/features/49007.htm (accessed 20/09/2006) at Part III paragraph 5.

overseas tourism, 2.92 % as students and 1.74% as permanent emigrants.[19] By contrast, the number of citizens who undertook these forms of travel in 1979 was negligible. In the years 1990 to 2003 Chinese migration grew by an average of 12 percent each year. In 2003, 39.7 million Chinese were registered to leave and re-enter the territory.[20] Illegal migrants, discussed in part 8.2 of this book, had increased to 11 million in number at the end of 1990s.

Chinese migration, however, and as discussed with the aid of dramatic graphs in part 7.3, is still much lower than other countries. With the further development of Chinese society, a huge migration stock may emerge, and the changing pattern of entry and exit will be yet more significant. The director of exit and entry administration under the MPS, Ren Yingchao, has reflected that;

> In the early years of the foundation of the PRC, a resident card was all that the people needed to carry because people hardly left their birthplace. After the opening-up, the growing need for mobility gave rise to citizen ID cards. Now in an increasingly international world, even national ID will not do. Passports will be the new substitute in the near future.[21]

Without facing and solving the challenges of RLR caused by changing patterns of migration, it is very difficult in practice to make passports the new form of ID. The principle challenges are forms of discrimination with respect to RLR of Chinese citizens in Mainland China in regard to (ii) the places of household registration; (ii) status of CPC membership and cadre (iii) the purposes of entry or exit; (iv) residence in the Mainland China, HKSAR, MSAR and Taiwan. Other challenges include the need to:

(1) Improve foreign investment by facilitating investors' exit, entry and residency;
(2) Resolve the issues of Chinese Illegal migrants in other countries and foreign Illegal migrants in China;
(3) Remove obstacles to the transfer of foreign exchange into and out of China;
(4) Rectify and standardise emigration intermediary services to safeguard not only the interests of the applicants wishing to exit but the interests of intermediary agencies in improving services;

---

19 "The Numbers of Exits from and Entries into the Chinese Mainland Breakthrough 200 Million in 2001" *(2001 Nian Woguo Churujing Renyuan Shouci Tupo 2 Yi Renci)*, the Bureau of Exit and Entry Administration under the Ministry of Public Security, 18/04/2003.

20 "China Sees Unusual Fall in Exit-entry Numbers in 2003", 12/01/2004, *People's Daily Online*, http://english.people.com.cn/200401/12/print20040112_132362.html (accessed 20/09/2006).

21 Quoted in Wang, Chuyan, "Passport Gain Wider Currency in China", CCTV, 18 October 2002, http://www.cctv.com/english/news/TVNews/MorningNews/20021018/100241/html (accessed 1/10/2003).

(5) Reform the institutional aspects of exit and entry administration;
(6) Provide efficient remedies for violations of RLR;
(7) Solve the conflicts between Chinese laws for exit and entry, and between ratified international instruments and Chinese law.

Great importance should be attached to these challenges, and effective measures should be found to meet them. The core of solving these challenges is to protect RLR. RLR is a fundamental right of Chinese, which has a direct bearing on their vital interests. Unlike riots, strikes and mass demonstrations designed to dramatise popular grievances against the government, emigration poses no direct threat to the existing political order. To be effective, RLR policy needs to be fine-tuned to take account of this none-too-subtle distinction. As the most populous country in the world, the need to resolve these issues is more urgent in China than in other countries.

12.1.4 *Fulfilling China's international obligations*

Even China has its own methods and reasons, but one thing is for sure: from the perspective of both international law and domestic law, there is no excuse for an open China to refuse to fulfil its international obligations to protect RLR. The Chinese government has accepted citizens' RLR in the light of Article 1 of the *Law on the Control of Exit and Entry of Citizens* 1985 (PRC) the general provisions of which lay the way to protect RLR in principle.

The Chinese government has ratified the UDHR, CERD, CSR and its Protocol of 1967, The *Charter of the UN*, the CRC and ICESCR. These conventions contain the provisions related to RLR discussed in part 2.2.2 of this book.[22] Estoppel by international treaties and agreements of the parties is the basic principle of international law. Under Article 142 *General Principles of the Civil Law* 1986 (PRC), Article 238 of the *Law of Civil Procedure* 1991 (PRC), Article 72 of the *Law of Administrative Procedure* 1990 (PRC) and Article 178 of the *Rules on the Procedure of Handling with Administrative Cases of Public Security Organs* 2003 (PRC), ratified international conventions prevail over domestic law to the extent of any inconsistency. Thus the Chinese government is bound to perform legal obligations to protect RLR.

Additionally, China is also obliged to ensure that its practices in relation to RLR conform to customary international law, which was discussed in Chapter three of

[22] Article 1 Clause 3 of the *Charter of the United Nations* 1945 provides that one of purposes of the UN is "to achieve international co-operation in…promoting and encouraging respect for human rights and for fundamental freedoms for all without distinctions as to race, sex, language, or religion." The right to work regulated in ICESCR is closely related to RLR. Another 4 conventions' provisions have been mentioned in part 2.2.2.4 of this book.

this book. For China, customary international law is mainly based on the UDHR and ICCPR. Initially, the UDHR was not legally binding upon China since the UDHR only encourages States parties to achieve human rights through moral aspirations. However, the UDHR is gradually becoming acknowledged as part of customary international law. Meanwhile, the Chinese government does not deny the status in customary international human rights law of the ICCPR to non-Party States. The ICCPR, as a foremost international human rights instrument is undoubtedly universal in its statement of principle in relation to RLR.[23] In *Human Rights in China 2000: White Paper of Human Rights*, the Chinese government acknowledged that being ratification to the ICCPR[24] implied that the Chinese government attached great importance to the positive role of the ICCPR in promoting and protecting human rights.[25]

As discussed in Chapter three, RLR has become one of the human rights recognised in the UDHR and ICCPR. As a consequence of the development of the UDHR and the acknowledgement of the ICCPR, it is necessary for the Chinese government to promote and protect RLR in China according to both instruments and bring their practices of human rights into conformity.

More significantly, the Chinese government officially recognises customary international law as one of its legal sources. The former Vice Foreign Minister Wang Guangya stated in 2002 that, "human rights can get nowhere without international law and basic norms governing international relations".[26] In his 2002 Report, Zeng Peiyan, the then Minster in charge of the State Development Planning Commission said that in order to fully exploit the basic role of the market, "international practices will be taken into consideration".[27]

---

[23] 152 States ratified the ICCPR up to June 2004. 156 States ratified it in May 2006. See http://www.ohchr.org/english/countries/ratification/4.htm, May 2006, the Office of the United Nations High Commissioner for Human Rights, http://www.ohchr.org/english/countries/ratification/4.htm (accessed 20/09/2006).

[24] The Chinese government signed the ICCPR in October 1998. See "Laogai: Reform Through Labor in China" by Ramin Pejan, the *Human Rights Brief* Volume 7, Issue 2, beginning at page 22, see http://www.wcl.american.edu/hrbrief/07/21aogai.cfm (accessed 20/09/2006).

[25] Information Office of the State Council of the PRC, *Human Rights in China 2000, White Paper of Human Rights*, Beijing: 2000, at Part 7.

[26] Wang, Guangya, "Statement by H. E. Vice Foreign Minister Wang Guangya at the 58th Session of the United Nations Commission on Human Rights, Geneva, 2 April 2002, United Nations High Commissioner For Human Rights", http://www.china-un.ch/eng/gjhyfy/hy2002/t85149.htm (accessed 20/09/2006).

[27] Zeng, Peiyan, Par. 1 of Part III of "Report on the Implementation of the 2001 Plan for National Economic and Social Development and on the Draft Plan for National Economic and Social Development", 20/03/2002, http://www.fmprc.gov.cn/eng/topics/3701/3702/t18932.htm 02/t85149.htm (accessed 20/09/2006).

In practice, the Chinese government made a reference to customary international law when amending the regulations governing RLR. In January 2002, the government introduced measures to reform the use of a passport by overseas students. The Preface of the *Circular of Ministries of Education, Public Security and Foreign Affairs on Some Affairs Regarding Fulltime Students Exit Abroad Short-term with Ordinary Passport for Private Affairs* 2002 (PRC) stipulates that international norms are to be consulted and followed in relation to fulltime students travelling abroad at the expense of the government. China's domestic legislative practice, ratified international conventions, and official attitude towards the inclusion of the UDHR and ICCPR in customary international law, altogether underscore the need to perform its legal obligations to protect RLR in China.

12.2 Factors Favouring Protection of RLR in China

Economic reform over the past 25 years is the primary factor in support of RLR protection in China. This has been followed by process of democratisation and constitutional reform, growing awareness of RLR among Chinese people and the emergence of the international environment favouring protection of RLR in China.

12.2.1 *Economic reform*

Twenty-five years of economic reform, bringing democratisation and the "opening up" of China has provided the State with a considerable material foundation for protecting RLR. China's macro-economic achievements have been very impressive. According to official statistics, by the end of 2005, Chinese GDP reached C¥ 18.23 trillion (equal to US$ 2.4 trillion), placing China fourth in the world in terms of economic aggregate. China chalked up a trade volume of US$ 1.4221 trillion and rank it the third in the world, practically used the gross direct foreign investment of US$60.3 billion which placing China the No.1 destination of foreign investment, by the end of 2003, China's foreign currency pool totalled US$ 818.9 billion, and the country had the world's the largest foreign exchange reserves.[28] In 2001, China became a member of the WTO and Beijing won its bid to host the 2008 Olympic Games. These events have exerted a far-reaching influence on the future development of the economy. In 2002, Jiang

---

[28] Li, Deshui, The Minister of State Statistics Bureau, "2005 GDP Reached 18.23.21 Trillion" (*2005 Nian Guonei Shengchan Zongzhi Da 182321Yiyuan*), 25/01/2006, http://www.china.com.cn/chinese/jingji/1104702.htm (accessed 06/08/2006).

Zemin observed that, "on the whole, the people made a historic leap from having only adequate food and clothing to leading a well-off life."[29]

The considerable material foundation has stimulated overseas travel by Chinese, described in part 102.2 of this book, and produces many spaces for reforming the exit and entry administration. The limits on foreign exchange and household registration will be lifted. Guo Shouqing, the then director of the SAFE, said in 2003 that China would continue easing restrictions on foreign currency purchases by domestic enterprises and individuals.[30] Chinese legislators will make the breakthrough reform of the household registration system. A proposal for reform of household registration on the basis that it is no longer appropriate in the light of the transition to a market economy and increased rates of migration, was submitted to the NPC in 2001. The proposal aimed to put an end to the practice of separating rural and urban household registration in order to facilitate the transfer of excessive rural labour to urban areas.[31] Further reform of entry and exit administration is also possible.

12.2.2 *Democratisation and constitutional reform*

China's process of democratisation and constitutional reform to protect human rights, provide China with a political and legal foundation to protect RLR. China's political reform lags behind the reforms of the economic system, however the trend of democratisation is an inevitable consequence of a move towards a market economy. Jiang Ping, a prominent Chinese jurist, has predicted that the government's stronghold on power will be limited by a market economy, because the free market enterprise system requires a suitably modern State. Democracy is the basic characteristic of such a State. Thus, the orientation and pace of the democratisation will continue in accordance with the development of China's market economy.[32]

China officially adheres to a policy of developing democracy. Hu Jingtao, the President of the PRC stressed in 2004 that citizens' orderly political participation

---

[29] Jiang, Zemin, the President of the PRC, Par 13 of Part I of "Build a Well-off Society in an All-Round Way and Create a New Situation in Building Socialism with Chinese Characteristics: Report at 16th China Communist Party Congress (8/11/2002)", http://www.china.org.cn/english/features/49007.htm (accessed 20/09/2006).

[30] *The Notice of Adjusting the Policy of Purchasing Foreign Exchange under Individual Regular Account by Residence within the Mainland (Guanyu Tiaozheng Jingnei Jumin Geren Jingchang Xiangmu Xia Gouhui Zhengce De Tongzhi)*, issued on 1 September 2003 by The SAFE, No. [2003] 104.

[31] "2001: Call for New Residence System, 14.03/2001", http://www.cctv.com/1m/980/721/82533.html (accessed 20/09/2006).

[32] Jiang, Ping, *Comments on Chinese Democracy and constitutional Development*, in Itoh, Fumio (ed), *China in the Twenty-first Century: Politics, Economy, and Society*, United Nations University Press, Tokyo, Japan, 1997, 219.

should be expanded and people's democratic election, democratic decision-making, democratic management and democratic supervision in line with laws should be guaranteed.[33] Jiang Zemin underlined in 2002 that China must respect and guarantee the political, economic and cultural rights and interests of the people.[34]

The development of democracy and the protection of human rights has been the subject of constitutional reform in China. Article 7 of *The Amendment of Constitution of the PRC 2004* imposes a duty on the State to respect and safeguard human rights. Article 1 of the Amendment recognises that the development of a socialist market economy, socialist democracy, improved socialist legal system, and coordinated development of the socialist material, political and spiritual civilisation, are important means of achieving reform in the primary stages.

Although the conception of human rights and the relationship between human rights and RLR are at odds, as earlier analysed – incorporating human rights into the Constitution is of epoch-making significance.[35] At the least it has clarified, as Professor Xu Xianming has said, that "China accepts the moral standards of human rights, [and] under that principle the public power that respects and guarantees human rights will be supported, while the disdaining and trampling on human rights should be corrected".[36] It is more possible to protect RLR in China than ever before. Democratic reform and incorporating human rights into the Constitution will drive the enactment of laws related to further protecting RLR.

12.2.3 *Growing awareness of RLR and growing Chinese communities abroad*

Since the reforms of 1978, Chinese society has gradually equalised, international communication has become more extensive, and Chinese people have developed an awareness of human rights, social equality and participation in civil society. The development of democracy and increasing importance placed on developing a human rights record will challenge traditional attitudes towards emigration. Global economic integration will demand increased population movement to and

---

[33] "President Hu Urges People's Democratic Participation", http://english.peopledaily.com.cn/200404/28/eng20040428_141732.shtml (accessed 29/04/2004).

[34] Jiang, Zemin, the President of the PRC, Par 7 of Part III of "Build a Well-off Society in an All-Round Way and Create a New Situation in Building Socialism with Chinese Characteristics: Report at 16th China Communist Party Congress (8/11/2002)", http://www.china.org.cn/english/features/49007.htm (accessed 20/09/2006).

[35] "55 New Economic Terms Since Founding of the PRC – Part Two", http://english.people.com.cn//200411/15/eng20041115_163932.html (accessed 29/11/2004).

[36] "Top Legislators Consider Amending Constitution Again", *The People's Daily*, 9 March 2004, http://english.peopledaily.com.cn/200403/09/eng20040309_136921.shtml (accessed 11/03/2004).

from China. Leaving China has begun to be regarded as a normal activity.[37] The Chinese desire for equal opportunities in standards of living and freedom of movement, as Lu Jing has suggested, is more important than ever.[38] The desire among Chinese people to pursue human rights, and create wealth provides an inexhaustible reservoir of motivation to fully implement RLR.

The migration of Chinese from China, over the past 25 years, is a growing phenomenon. Overseas students increased from 3,000 in 1978 to 146,000 of 2001.[39] Based on the theory of Doris Meissner,[40] Chinese emigration is likely to increase over the next 10 to 15 years. According to Ronald Skeldon:

> The 33 million estimate at the end of the 20th century for the number of Chinese overseas had increased from around 22 million in 1985, and from 12.7 million in the early 1960s. Given the generally low fertility of overseas populations, this suggests a significant role for migration from China (include Hong Kong and Taiwan) over the second half of the 20th century.[41]

The increase of the migration of Chinese from China has resulted in the formation of large and effective Chinese communities abroad. These communities remit knowledge and understanding to their friends and family members in China about other countries, and produce social, cultural, political and economic links between the destination countries and China. These situations not only help Chinese people in going abroad but also facilitate a more rapid adjustment and orientation on arriving in destination countries. Overseas returnees usually have an overseas educational background and the newest way of thinking.[42] They contribute to an increasing awareness of migration and people's capacity to go abroad.

---

[37] Going abroad was only dream for most Chinese before the middle of the 1980s. See "China's Outbound Travellers Reach 15.99 Million in the First Seven Months" (Jinian Tou Qigeyue You 1599 Wan Renci Chujing You), 17/09/2004, The State Bureau of Statistics, http://english.people.com.cn//200409/17/eng20040917_157376.html (accessed 19/09/2006).

[38] Lu, Jing, *On the Freedom of the Movement* (*Lun Qianxi Ziyou*), the thesis of LLM, Chinese People's University, Beijing: 2000, 19.

[39] Biao. Xiang, "Emigration from China: A Sending Country Perspective", *International Migration*, Volume 41, Number 3 (September 01, 2003), at 21–48, http://ejournals.ebsco.com/direct.asp?ArticleID=P8PYFRBJLETKMYT3KQ4F (accessed 01–10–2003), 28–29.

[40] Sustaining economic development can simulate emigration over next ten to fifteen years. See Meissner, Doris, "Rapporteur's Conclusions of the Second Session" at the OECD, *Migration and Development: New Partnerships for Co-operation,* Head of Publications Service, OECD, Paris Cedex, France 1994, at 299.

[41] Skeldon, Ronald, "China: From Exceptional Case to Global Participant", April 2004, http://www.migrationinformaiton.org/Profiles/display.cfm?ID=219 (accessed 19/09/2006).

[42] The Chinese government reports that more than 20,000 Chinese students studying abroad returned last year, while the number was 18,000 in 2000 and 12,000 in 2001. The number of returned students is expected to hit a new record in 2004. See "China Encourage More Students Studying Overseas to Serve Motherland", http://english.people.com.cn//200411/15/eng20041115_163905.html (accessed 29/11/2004).

12.2.4 *The international environment favouring protection of RLR in China*

Economic and technological factors bind States in such a way that no country can exist in isolation. In a shrinking world, States must prepare to take responsibility for each other, to achieve global cooperation, and to find mutually acceptable ground rules for developing a co-operative spirit, despite immense differences of culture, history, politics and standards of living. It is impossible to ignore human rights in China in view of the threat that Chinese communism has posed to world peace, the economic relationship that other States want to pursue with China, and the influence that Chinese culture has had on human development. If the world needs China, then presumably a common ground must be found between China and the world to facilitate co-operation.

The concerns on China's human rights records are of interest to the international community and foreign countries and integral to their ability to trade with China and access its markets. Australia's interest in the development and reform of China, and protection of China's human rights, can be understood as an extension of its own interest in China.[43] US policy to protect human rights springs from American ideals and its sense of national interest.[44]

The concerns of Western countries on RLR in China can also be attributed to the important role of Chinese people living overseas and Chinese skilled and professional workers. Chinese people abroad play a significant role in the economy of Southeast Asia, Europe and America.[45] China exports skilled and professional workers to all regions of the world, notably the USA, Canada, Australia and New Zealand.

The above conditions create a favourable environment in which the international community, particularly the West, might propose ways of reaching an acceptable common ground for laws governing RLR in China. The US is actively engaged in taking steps to decrease the number and severity of human rights abuses in China. In the US Committee or Refugees publication, *China: The Country Reports on Human Rights Practices*, the terms 'exile' and 'foreign travel, emigration and repatriation' always appear in connection with the expressions "respect for human rights" and 'respect for civil liberties'.[46] With the development of China, such concerns will accordingly increase.

---

[43] Kent, Ann, *Human Rights in PRC*, Discussion Paper No. 3, 1989–90, Legislative Research Service, the Parliamentary of the Commonwealth of Australia, 6.

[44] Colin L. Powell, "Preface", at "Supporting Human Rights and Democracy: The US Record 2002–2003", the Bureau of Democracy, Human Rights, and Labour, 2003 http://www.State.gov/g/drl/rls/shrd/2002/21763.htm (accessed 05–07–2033).

[45] Sowell, Thomas, *Migrations and Cultures: A World View*, Basic Books, A member of the Perseus Books Group, 1996, page176.

[46] US Committee for Refugees, *Worldwide Refugee Information Country Reports: China (including Tibet)* 1998 to 2003.

Even if the extent to which international pressure has been effective remains open to question, it at least provides another criteria by which Chinese people and Chinese authorities can appraise RLR in China. China is no longer indifferent to international criticism of RLR, especially when made by developed and powerful countries. China has regularly entered into dialogue on human rights with the European Union (EU), Australia, Canada, and Norway[47] and also published *Human Rights Record of the United States* in March 2003, in response to publication of *Country Reports on Human Rights Practices for 2003* by the US in February 2003.[48] Any efforts to improve RLR in China will find support in the international community and foreign countries. Foreign concern and Chinese responses may exert a subtly positive influence on the thinking of Chinese people and authorities regrading RLR.

12.3 Practical Concerns about Protecting RLR in China

Despite being both necessary and feasible to protect RLR in China, there are concerns as to whether the protection of RLR might give rise to social issues. Some of these concerns have been discussed in parts 79.2.3, 8.1.5, and 10.3.3 of this book. The purpose of this section is to explode representative myths that form the justification for opposing reform of the regulatory framework governing RLR in China.

12.3.1 *It would make no practical difference to many Chinese people*

The absence of any practical difference for the many Chinese people is often cited as a main reason for not granting RLR in China; that even if RLR was conferred, few people could or would ever take advantage of it. In *Some Thoughts on Democracy*, Judge Zhu Muzhi suggested that democracy that fails to take into account the demands of the people or the national interest blurs the essential difference between true democracy and pseudo democracy. He argued that advocates of such ideas either harbour ulterior motives or are muddle-headed.[49] Zhang

[47] Information Office of the State Council of the PRC, *Human Rights in China 2000, White Paper of Human Rights*, Beijing: 2000, at Part 7.

[48] "Spokesperson Zhang Qiyue's Remarks on the Country Report on Human Rights Issued by the US (26/02/2004)", http://www.fmprc.gov.cn/eng/xwfw/2510/t69782.htm (accessed 02/03/2004).

[49] Zhu, Muzhi, "Some Thoughts on Democracy", No. 4 [2002] *Human Rights Magazine*, http://www.humanrights-china.org/zt/03111201/200312003129103621.htm (accessed 26/02/2004).

Youyu, a constitutional jurist and one of its framers, explained that the reason freedom of movement is not constitutionally guaranteed is that there were too many practical issues associated with its enforcement to prevent the chaos that it was expected to generate.[50]

The notion of practical indifference is based on the false premise that the ability to exploit a right is a precondition to its necessity. Mexico-US migration, for example, illustrates this argument. Of 109 million Mexican people, less than 9 million have emigrated to the USA, illegally or legally.[51] Mexicans enjoy RLR, even though 90% will never take advantage of the right. The majority of people never exercise some rights, such as the right to freedom of peaceful assembly and association, the right not to be enslaved, and the right to form and join trade union. This does not justify their denial or detract from their importance.

Many low-income families in China are not in a position to send family members overseas. The costs of travel, foreign language difficulties, cultural differences, and lack of support mechanisms in the foreign countries, represent formidable barriers to international mobility. However, the deprivation of RLR to all Chinese people cannot be justified on the grounds that some people will be unable to exercise the right. There are increasing numbers of Chinese people who can.

12.3.2 *It would not benefit Chinese personal development when used for a special purpose*

Other critics of RLR reform argue that exiting China for a 'special purpose' such as for religious pilgrimage, or middle school study, is unbeneficial to that person's development. Such limits are inconsistent with RLR, as well as other rights such as freedom of religion and right to an education. Maurice Cranston has argued that a State is only justified in detaining a national within the territory to the extent necessary for the discharge of a duty. Detaining a person within the territory for the purpose of forbidding recreational or any other activity is unjustified.[52]

---

[50] Zhang, Youyu, Quoted in Yin, Xiaohu and Lin, Yan, "The Change of the Chinese Legal Stipulations Regarding to the Freedom of Movement and the Thoughts on the Change" (*Woguo Falv Guanyu Qianxi Ziyou Guiding De Bianhua Jiqi Sikao*), No. 6 [2001] *The Journal of Jurisprudence* (*Faxue*), pages 10–14, 11.

[51] Martin, Philip and Widgren, Jonas, *International Migration: Facing the Challenge* (Washington, the USA: Population Reference Bureau, 2002), 39 pages, 5.

[52] Cranston, Maurice, "The political and Philosophy Aspects of the Right to Leave and Return" in Vasak, Karel and Liskofsky, Sidney (ed), *the Right to Leave and Return: Papers and Recommendations of the International Colloquium Held in Uppsala, Sweden, 19–21 June 1972*, The American Jewish Committee, Arbor, the USA, 1976.

Whether exiting China is beneficial or not to an individual's development depends on a value judgment. Article 1 Clause 1 of the ICCPR provides that "All people have the right of self-determination [. . .] they freely pursue their economic, social and cultural development". As such, the Chinese government is neither qualified nor at liberty to impose a uniform system of values on its citizens.

12.3.3 *It would cause the loss of talented Chinese and internal instability*

RLR is limited for members of the CPC, government officials, employees of State-owned enterprises and institutions, and professionals, in order to prevent the loss of talented Chinese and the onset of internal instability, which was analysed in part 7.2.1 of this book. This justification is without legal or practical foundation. From a legal perspective, limiting RLR in relation to these groups does no more than give effect to the policies of the CPC, State-owned enterprises and public institutions, because they are not lawgivers. Their 'laws' are only internal policies in effect. The affected individual cannot be detained inside China for the purpose of fulfilling an illegal obligation.

Practically, the loss of talented Chinese to developed States is unacceptable grounds for refusing to grant RLR. In any event, it is unclear whether China would actually suffer a significant loss of its professional class. Emigration might assist the economy of an originating State. According to 2002 global data, US$ 65 billion was remitted by emigrants to their State of origin. This sum exceeded the foreign aid that these countries received in the same year.[53] Additionally, it is difficult to see how emigration is a threat to internal stability, unless relaxing emigration restrictions would lead to a mass exodus, which anyway requires other States welcoming the exodus.

If this elite group in China are detained for the benefit of the whole population, the justification reflects the outdated concept of "the greatest good for the greatest number", discussed in part 2.1.3 of this book. The effect of the justification is that RLR is granted in a discriminatory manner by permitting poorly skilled people to leave China, but not highly qualified people. This discrimination in terms of personal skills is incompatible with RLR.

12.3.4 *It would encourage people to illegally exit China and settle overseas*

The relaxation of RLR may encourage people to illegally exit China and settle overseas, thus creating more opportunities to abscond abroad with dirty money,

[53] Martin, Philip and Widgren, Jonas, *International Migration: Facing the Challenge*, (Washington, the USA: Population Reference Bureau, 2002), 39 pages, 35.

and be free from worry about returning to China. Thus, the argument goes, with restricted RLR a passport will not be issued to possible corrupt officials absconding abroad, extended or reissued for a person who has illegally exited China and settled overseas, the later of which has been discussed in part 8.2.1 of this book. Actually, the number of people who illegally exit China, approximately 50,000 per annum in the 1990s,[54] compared to the lawful cohort, 1.13 million people who exited China for private affairs per year during the period between 1986 and 2001,[55] is very small. As analysed in part 8.2.2 of this book, there is no direct relationship between illegal migrants and passport issuance. Moreover, RLR cannot be denied merely because the possibility that a very small proportion of Chinese people might illegally leave for other countries.

Over 4,000 Chinese corrupt officials with more than US$5 billion absconded abroad in the past two decades.[56] The situation is worsening.[57] One of the most important measures adopted to stop this, is the retention of passports. Under the *Measures on Administration of Passport and Other Travel Abroad Documents of officials Employed CPC, governments, Courts, Procurator Courts, Justice Departments and Public Security Departments* 2003 (PRC), passports and other travel documents of intermediate cadres and above are retained by designated departments. The issues of passport retention have been considered in part 6.2.3 and 6.3.3 of this book to argue that the retention of passports does not reduce the frequency of corrupt officials absconding.

It is difficult to argue the retention of passport alone or at all can effectively prohibit individuals, including corrupt officials with large sums of dirty money, from leaving China. It may be possible for corrupt officials to subvert the badly knit formalities of applying for leaving China. Xiang Biao's opinion that "not all the institutions and staff involved [passport administration] can be tightly regulated" is worth keeping in mind.[58] Meanwhile, there are no laws to regulate how

---

[54] The IOM, *Myths and Realities of Chinese Irregular Migration*, No. 1 of IOM Migration Research Series, the IOM, Geneva, Switzerland, 2000, 44 pages, 13.

[55] Wang, Leiming, Xinhua News Agency, "Citizens May Exit Abroad for Private Purpose Easier and Faster" (*Woguo Gongmin Yinsi Chuguo Gengjia Bianjie*) (19/09/2002), http://news.xinhuanet.com/newscenter/2002-08/29/content_543014.htm (accessed 16/09/2006).

[56] Conference about the pursuit of corrupt officials' absconding abroad, held by the Supreme People's Procuratorate 2001.

[57] In September 2003, a director of the Provincial Bureau of Anti-Embezzlement and Bribery under the Provincial People's Procuratorates said "up to now, the exact number is impossible to determine. Based on foreign news, during the period of outbreak of SARS in April and May 2003, 180 intermediate (current and retired) cadres disappeared, absconded or remained overseas without an intention of returning to China. See Sun, Yafei and Liu, Jianqiang, "Bowstring of Corrupt Officials Absconding Abroad" (Zhongguo Waitao Tanguan De Jiaosuo), 09/09/2003, *Southern Weekend* (*Nanfang Zhoumo*), http://www.people.com.cn/GB/shiz/heng/1026/2110972.html (accessed 16/09/2006).

[58] Biao. Xiang, "Emigration from China: A Sending Country Perspective". *International*

departments in which the applicants are in service, or the responsible departments, issue the certificates. This results in loopholes in the examination and approval of applicants with special identities. As such, under the current system, corrupt officials have the opportunity to gain genuine passports to abscond abroad.

Corrupt officials may bribe police who are responsible for border inspection. The success rate of bribery is very high.[59] Retention of passports by the designated departments, despite containing the name and photograph of the holder, does not appear to interrupt the flow of corrupt officials, who can obtain a second false passport under another name. Lastly, the co-existence of public affairs passports and private passports enables many officials to hold two passports simultaneously. It has been reported that some corrupt officials who had absconded had obtained a public affairs passport and travelled abroad as part of an official delegation.[60]

From an international perspective, as Zhang Yesui, China's Vice Foreign Minister said in December 2003, "corruption can only be effectively contained and punished through adequate and comprehensive international cooperation".[61] Retention of passports as a measure to stem corruption is rather like giving up eating for fear of choking. It runs contrary to the objective of reducing the rate of absconding, and violates the right to leave. Unless the legislative loopholes are closed, the problem will persist.

12.3.5 *It will damage other States' interests*

The argument against granting RLR to all Chinese people is that China's massive population would damage the interests of other States to whom the population

---

Migration, Volume 41, Number 3 (2003), 21–48, http://ejournals.ebsco.com/direct.asp?ArticleID=P8PYFRBJLETKMYT3KQ4F (accessed 01–10–2003), 26.

[59] According to *Collection of Violation and Crime Cases of Exit and Entry Border inspection Departments 2000*, assisting or secretly releasing persons past border control points whose without an appropriate passport or visa to pass accounted for approximately 80% of the offences committed by border control police.

See Zhang, Yong, *the Establishment of Education and Prevention Regime on Professional Violation and Crime of Frontier Inspection Polices* in Committee of Exit and Entry Administration, Chinese Association of Police, editor, *The Collection of Papers on The Control of Exit and Entry (III) Interior Published within Public Security Organs* (*Churujing Guanli Lunwenxuan (san)*), Interior Publication within Public Security Organs (*Gongan Jiguan Neibu Faxing*) (Beijing: the Publishing House of Qunzhong, 2001), 82.

[60] Biao. Xiang, "Emigration from China: A Sending Country Perspective". *International Migration*, Volume 41, Number 3 (September 01, 2003), 21–48. http://ejournals.ebsco.com/direct.asp?ArticleID=P8PYFRBJLETKMYT3KQ4F (accessed 01–10–2003), 26.

[61] H.E. Zhang Yesui, "Statement by Vice Foreign Minister of the People's Republic of China Said at High-Level Political Conference for the Purpose Of Signing the Unite Nations Convention Against Corruption", Merida, 10 December 2003, http://www.fmprc.gov.cn/eng/zxxx/t56955.htm (accessed 30/12/2003).

would move. For example, one concern in developed countries – particularly, perhaps, in Europe – is that with a base population of 1.3 billion, China could come to dominate the global migration system and change the character of destination societies.[62]

In fact, granting RLR to all Chinese will not dramatically alter migration patterns. In 2002, RLR was protected in relation to approximately 75% of the world's population. International migration accounted for 3% of that population.[63] The Mexican example drawn earlier demonstrates that the freedom to leave a country does not cause people to emigrate as to be separated from their social and cultural environment.

Additionally, the eventual realisation of RLR depends on the receiving States' immigration policy. Foreign States may be expected to adjust their immigration policy in response to any reform of Chinese migration law, to protect their national interests. Australia, New Zealand and Canada successfully control their immigration stock by setting an annual quota. As such, foreign States would determine the actual influence that liberalisation of the Chinese RLR would have.

Moreover, improving economic conditions in China can reduce the effect of a liberalised RLR on immigration States. This will remove a motivating factor behind emigration, namely the chance of better employment prospects abroad, and would answer the concerns raised by critics of RLR reform. A vibrant economy exists to which migrants and students can return. China may progress through the migration 'hump' or transition from emigration to immigration.

12.3.6 *It would be irrelevant to other countries*

Opponents of reform argue that the expansion of RLR in China is irrelevant to other countries, so therefore unnecessary. However, RLR in China is inextricably related with other countries, especially the countries having great economic, political and cultural interests with China, such as Australia. In 2003, the Australian Prime Minister John Howard affirmed, the importance that Australia attaches to its trading, economic and social ties with China.[64] China is Australia's third largest trading partner. Australia is China's twelfth largest trading partner.[65]

---

[62] Skeldon, Ronald, "China: From Exceptional Case to Global Participant", April 2004, http://www.migrationinformation.org/Profiles/display.cfm?ID=219 (accessed 19/09/2006).

[63] The IOM, *International Migration Report 2002*, ST/ESA/SER.A/220 (Geneva, Switzerland: IOM, 2002), 64 pages, 2.

[64] "Premier Wen Jiabao Holds Talks with Visiting Australian Prime Minister John Howard (18/08/2003)", http://www.fmprc.gov.cn/eng/zxxx/t25065.htm (accessed 26/09/2003).

[65] "People's Republic of China, China: Relative Importance to Australia" http://en.chinabroadcast.cn/ce_critoday/archives/2006/03/31/news/Fact%20Sheet.htm (accessed 20/09/2006).

Further, Australia issues about 100,000 students visas each year, of which one in eight is made available to a Chinese student.

Liberalisation of RLR in China will create more trading, tourism and educational opportunities both for China and the States with whom it deals. The total value of foreign trade for China has passed 1 trillion US dollars. The development of China's foreign trade is shared with other countries in the world.[66] The economic achievement is not divorced from the movement of people into and out of China. The issue of RLR in China is crucial both for the future of China, and for the part China will play in the future of RLR in the world.

12.4 Conclusions

The protection of RLR in China is not only a result of logical legal analysis but also of practical social demands. The protection of human rights in China cannot be divorced from the protection of RLR. The trends market economics, industrialisation and global integration within China define the need for China to open wider to the world, allowing much more free movement across its borders. A migration program focussed on the protection of RLR needs to be well designed to accommodate greatly changing patterns of migration that have emerged since reform and opening up policies implemented in 1978. The Chinese government also needs to fulfil legal obligations of protecting RLR, if only to improve its image in the world, but more meaningfully, to substantiate its own expression of a Chinese belief in the dignity of human rights.

Today, there are impressive economic achievements, sound political and legal development, and growing awareness of RLR and migration in China, which together lays a solid foundation to improve the protection of RLR. Going abroad is becoming a part of normal life for Chinese people. The trend of democratisation will be an inevitable consequence of market economics. Democratic reform and incorporating human rights into the Constitution will drive the enactment of laws related to RLR. The desire among Chinese people to pursue RLR may provide an inexhaustible reservoir of motivation to protect RLR. Meanwhile, foreign attempts to improve RLR will remain of consequence because such concerns originate from the consideration of their national self-interest. Such attempts and Chinese responses may exert a subtly positive influence on the thinking of Chinese people and authorities regarding RLR.

Impractical concerns about adverse effects arising from the protection of RLR in China risk losing the chance of successful reform. The notion that it makes no

[66] "How to Look at the Breakthrough of Trillion US Dollars in China's Foreign Trade?", *The People's Daily*, http://english.people.com.cn/200412/11/eng20041211_166937.html (accessed 20/12/2004).

practical difference to the majority of Chinese people, in particular, is based on the false premise that the ability to exploit a right is a precondition to its necessity. The deprivation of RLR to all Chinese people cannot be justified on the grounds that some people will be unable to exercise the right. Chinese people have the right of self-determination and to freely pursue their economic, social and cultural development. The same principle applies to a fear that protection of RLR is unbeneficial to a person's development, when used for a special purpose. Such limits are inconsistent with other rights such as freedom of religion and right to an education.

If an elite group are detained for the benefit of the whole population, as is the case with limits on RLR for public affairs passports, RLR is effectively granted in a discriminatory manner by permitting poorly skilled people to leave China, but not highly qualified people. Illegal exit is not a justification for denying RLR of all people, because the number of people who illegally exit China is very small compared to the lawful cohort. Moreover, the protection of RLR in China will not damage other States' interests, because the eventual realisation of RLR depends on the receiving States' immigration policies. There appears to be little evidence to indicate that expansion of RLR in China is of no relevance to other countries, because opportunities created by its expansion are beneficial both for China and the States with which it deals.

Chapter Thirteen
Recommendations and Conclusions

Introduction

In the Introduction to this book, the overall research objective was to explore the Chinese regulatory framework governing RLR to determine its consistency by reference to international human rights ethics. This approach has demonstrated that the development of Chinese society demands a re-examination of the regulatory framework governing RLR, and a greater awareness of the need to protect RLR. Increased priority given to the protection of RLR, may improve the likelihood that an effective legal resolution of issues associated with its protection, is found. This chapter, in drawing together the conclusion of this book, recommends the means by which the Chinese regulatory framework governing RLR might be improved. Six recommendations focused on the design of a new unified migration law are explained separately.

The existing regulatory framework governing RLR is incapable of delivering adequate protection for people who exit and enter China. The recommendations in this chapter are based on the premise that the regulatory structure crushes the possibility of exiting and entering China for part of Chinese population; especially *huaqiao*, irregular Chinese migrants; and all Chinese dissidents who want to return. It has also been argued that these issues undermine the protection of human rights, stifle political and economic reform, and discourage the spirit of creativity and the promotion of international exchange.

The protection of RLR needs a coherent and malleable regulatory system. The existing regulatory framework governing RLR cannot achieve that. A four-year reform strategy published in 2001 supported reforming the exit and entry administration, including the existing laws. Reform is also supported by the newest amendment of the Constitution in March 2004, under which the State is obliged to respect and protect human rights. Although the need for reform of law governing RLR is becoming urgent, the measures that need be taken by the Chinese government remain uncertain.

13.1 Factors that Help Determine the Extent of the Reform

Before providing recommendations for regulatory framework reform, it is important to analyse the factors that help determine the extent of the reform. They consist of six aspects.

The reform of the regulatory framework governing RLR should be part of a systematic process that simultaneously addresses a number of issues currently facing contemporary Chinese society. Along with migration law reform, protection of RLR requires reform of laws governing households, foreign exchange, emigration intermediary agencies, administrative law, administrative procedural law, labour exports, border inspection, the political structure, as well as the content of legal education. In addition to this multifaceted approach to reform, China, as the President of the Supreme People's Court of the PRC, Xiao Yang has accepted:

> May learn from the experiences and lessons of safeguarding human rights in the world, collate the universal standard of human rights in concluded or acceded to international human rights conventions, systematically summarise past work of safeguarding human rights, and make a comprehensive plan to guide future work of safeguarding human rights.[1]

The reform of the regulatory framework governing RLR needs to be a gradual process. In March 2004, *The People's Daily* reported that "Just 20 years ago, human rights were still regarded as a so-called 'capitalist notion' in China".[2] Relevant research and publicity were prohibited. China's history of complete gov-

---

[1] Journalist of *The Journal of Human Rights, Correct Appliance of the Law and Impartial Trial under the Law: Strengthen the Safeguard of Human Rights in the Realm of Justice in a Down-to-earth Way: the Interview of the Comrade Xiao, Yang, the President of Supreme People's Court* (*Zunque Shiyong Falv Yifa Gongzheng Caipan Qieshi Jiaqiang Sifa Lingyu De Renquan Baozhang: Fang Zuigao Renmin Fayuan Yuanzhang Shouxi Dafaguan Xiao Yang Tongzhi*), *The Journal of Human Right* No. 6 (2002), 3–8, at 8.

[2] "Human Rights to Be Enshrined in Constitution", 9 March 2004, *The People's Daily*, http://english.peopledaily.com.cn/200403/09/eng20040309_136924.shtml (accessed 11/03/2004)

ernmental control of exit and entry will make it difficult for comprehensive reform of the regulatory framework governing RLR to occur quickly. Hasty reform measures may result in a deadlocked process and social disruption, which could have an adverse effect. Hence, the reform process needs be staged.

It can be expected that any reform process will endure some transitional problems. Indeed, the more extensive the changes are, the greater the adjustment is. Initially, there may be an increase in personnel costs as the responsible departments undergo training to become familiar with new requirements. There may also be a risk that some personnel experience difficulty in understanding or complying with the changed rules. The reform strategy and its measures need to ensure that these initial problems are managed so that the regulatory objective can be achieved.

If the scope of administrative discretion is too wide, the application of reformed laws may result in inconsistent decision making. Yet the administrative authority cannot comprehensively implement legislation if their discretion is too narrow. Uncertainty arising from wide administrative discretion may cause individuals to anticipate how the government might apply new laws, and given the fact, argued already, that the discretionary powers of exit and entry administration in China are too broad, reforms need to narrow the scope for discretion.

Reforms modelled on Western human rights notions may not be entirely suitable in China. Human rights theory is useful in analysing the foundations and efficiency of existing law, insofar as the analysis was premised on the full recognition of human rights of the Chinese government. In fact, "China has its own understanding of human rights which differs from that of Western developed countries."[3] Reformers need to move beyond human rights theory to adopt a holistic approach in framing new regulations for the protection of RLR in China.

Finally, both temporary and permanent solutions are sought here while focusing on the permanent solution. The recommendations provide a strategic direction for the resolution of the issues discussed from Chapters eight to thirteen, rather than detailed plans with respect to each issue. Effective reform will arise from tackling the issues at root, rather than by addressing the issues that flow as their consequence.

13.2 Recommendations for Improving the Regulatory Framework Governing RLR

Six recommendations have been formulated to assist in reforming the regulatory framework governing RLR in China so that the protection of RLR can be realised.

---

[3] "Human Rights to Be Enshrined in Constitution", *The People's Daily*, 9 March 2004, http://english.peopledaily.com.cn/200403/09/eng20040309_136924.shtml (accessed 11/03/2004).

These are (i) incorporating RLR into the Constitution; (ii) enactment of a uniform Chinese migration law; (iii) establishment of an effective administrative system; (iv) reform of relevant laws and regulations; (v) enhancement of public awareness of RLR; and (vi) the use of information technology in exit and entry administration.

13.2.1 *Incorporating RLR into the Constitution*

The highest priority of reform of RLR is constitutional protection. This might be achieved even if China's capacity to give full effect to the right has not matured, because RLR can be stated in abstract terms in the preamble. Dr. Du Chengming has observed that China's constitutional rights are both practical rights, which people can enjoy in life, but also ideal rights, which the Chinese government will spare no effort to develop.[4] The current Constitution, which was amended in 1982, clarifies the basic rights of Chinese citizens without referring to RLR. RLR is a basic human right that is constitutionally guaranteed, with some permissible limits, in most Constitutions all over the world, and in most international human rights conventions. Economic and political reforms demand that RLR be constitutionally guaranteed in China, as in other countries. China needs to incorporate RLR into the constitutional norms for the protection of fundamental human rights or citizens' rights, as well as including a clause to bring international migration law into domestic law.

Although it is hoped that RLR will be constitutionally guaranteed as soon as possible, it is predicted that this is unlikely to occur until 2010. The cycle of constitutional amendment under the procedures contained in Article 64 of the Constitution[5] has historically been approximately five years.[6]

Incorporating RLR into the Constitution is not enough for its protection. Constitutional amendment only provides a legal basis for broader RLR reform under the theory of the Chinese constitutionalism – a constitutional provision cannot compel legislative implementation. Further to parts 4.4 of this book, incorporating RLR into the Constitution does not invalidate inconsistent laws. For this

---

[4] Dr. Du, Chengming, "On Migration Freedom"(*Lun Qianxi Ziyou Quan*), Vol. 54 No. 4 July 2001 *Wuhan University Journal (Social Sciences)* (*Wuhan Daxue Xuebao (Shehui Kexue Xuebao)*), 406–410, at 410.

[5] Article 64 Clause 1 of the *Constitution of the PRC (Amendment)* 2004 "amendments to the Constitution are to be proposed by the Standing Committee of the National People's Congress or by more than one-fifth of the deputies of the National People's Congress and adopted by a vote of more than two-thirds of all the deputies to the Congress."

[6] Amendments to the *Constitution of the PRC* 1982 were made in 1988, 1993, 1999 and 2004.

reason, the importance of the application of a constitutional provision regarding RLR in judicial practice and by legislators must be stressed.

13.2.2 *The enactment of a uniform Chinese migration law*

Prior to constitutional reform, it is recommended that a uniform migration law be enacted along the following seven lines.

13.2.2.1 Benefits of and favourable conditions for a uniform migration law

Even though Article 5 Clause 2 of the *Constitution of the PRC (Amendment)* 2004 expressly prescribes that "no laws or administrative and local regulations need contravene the Constitution", there is no effective mechanism for constitutional review of the validity of legislation. Conflicts of laws governing exit and entry with the Constitution have influenced judicial decisions, resulting in localism and sabotage of the integrity of the national legal system. Reform of the current regulatory framework is concerned with constitutional amendment and legislative practice. As neither constitutional reform, nor changes to legislative practice are expected to occur quickly, enactment of a uniform scheme of migration law may provide a more realistic means of protecting RLR.

Reform of passport law has laid a useful foundation for enacting a uniform migration law. Passport law reform has emphasised the right to leave, which is only part of the overall RLR. However, other aspects of RLR, including the right to return, the right of nationals not to be exiled, the right against expulsion, the administration of emigration intermediary agencies, and the remedies to violations of RLR, need to be closely considered. These are becoming more important as China develops. In recent years, especially since China's entry into the WTO in December 2001, some work has been done to review the regulatory framework governing RLR. According to the *Legislative Program of the Standing Committee of the Tenth National People's Congress*, the Bill of the Law of Passport will be deliberated by the Tenth NPC (2003 to 2007).[7] The legislature needs resolve to change the Bill of the Law of Passport into the Bill of the Law of Migration, and pass a uniform code before the approximate date of 2007.

[7] Zhang, Shuo, "Five Years Legislative Program was Published, Including 76 Bills" (*Zhongguo Gongbu Wunian Lifa Guihua, 76 Jian Falv An Bangshang Youmin*), 18/12/2003, China News Agency, http:/news.china.com/zh_cn/domestic/945/20031217/11588970.html (accessed 20/09/2006).

13.2.2.2 Legislative purpose of Chinese migration law

The purpose of the existing regulatory framework governing RLR is to promote international exchange, safeguard State sovereignty, and maintain the security and public order of China. The purpose of a uniform migration law would be to protect RLR by unifying entry and exit control, safeguarding national security and public order, regulating migration matters, and implementing migration guidance. To achieve this, the principles of non-discrimination, openness and transparency would need to be adhered to. Policies would need to be formulated through a process that is inclusive of the stakeholders in the migration process, especially emigrants. Policies should reflect the activities and interests of the poor. This might mean decentralising migrant support services, and locating government services, such as 'One-stop shops' for counselling and information services in rural areas.

13.2.2.3 The complete regulation of exiting China

The current Chinese exit and entry administration laws do not comprehensively deal with exiting China. The laws do not cover exiting China for the purpose of public affairs, or to travel to the HKSAR, MSAR and Taiwan for the purpose of public affairs, even though such travel is indispensable. At present, rules governing public affairs related exits are regulated by unpublished departmental and CPC policies. The issues associated with public affairs passports were discussed in part 6.2 of this book.

Applications for travel documents, in particular passports for private travel, are based on a complex range of criteria that discriminates between applicants on the grounds of residential area, occupation, education and social status. There are five major criteria for overseas travel documents. These are (i) residents in rural and small city areas; (ii) residents in medium and large sized city areas; (iii) residents who are public servants and managerial staff in State-owned enterprises and public institutions; (iv) residents in Mainland China who want to travel to the HKSAR and MSAR; and (v) residents in Mainland China who want to travel to Taiwan. Other minor criteria for private passport applications, such as religious pilgrimage, also apply.

On the one hand, a uniform application criterion for travel documents when going abroad for private and public affairs needs be established. Impermissible limitations on exiting China to foreign countries, or to the HKSAR, MSAR and Taiwan need to be further relaxed or abolished. A uniform application criterion might eliminate the discrimination that is caused by different criteria. On the other hand, the scope of restrictions on public affairs passports needs to be dramatically curtailed. This might enable more citizens to gain permission to leave for private affairs. Moreover, to improve administrative efficiency a national database of people who are prohibited from exiting China needs be established. The enactment of a comprehensive exit rules may improve the system of examination and approval of exit applications so as to make them suitable for domestic conditions and international norms, and to guarantee fair and efficient law enforcement.

13.2.2.4 The complete regulation of returning to China

Relaxation or abolition of the limits on the rights of Chinese nationals returning to China from overseas is more urgent than the relaxation or abolition of limits on exit. Limiting the right to leave deprives the person of a recognised freedom, limiting a national's ability to re-enter China may cause that person to become effectively stateless, force them to live illegally in a foreign country, in a place that he or she does not like, and prevent talented Chinese people from returning. In other words, the right to return is more absolute than the right to leave. However the issues surrounding the right to return to China have received less attention than those associated with the right to leave. As discussed in Chapter five, the current reform strategy does not deal with the prohibition and limits on returning to China.

Beyond the general recommendation that the right to return to China needs to be carefully considered, four detailed suggestions can be added.

1) Limits on the return of Chinese citizens residing abroad and irregular Chinese migrants needs to be abolished. These groups need an absolute right to return to China.
2) Prohibitions imposed on the return of overseas Chinese dissidents and residents in the HKSAR, MSAR and Taiwan needs to be relaxed. The grounds upon which permission to return is refused need to be clarified, as the refusal of permission becomes increasingly confused with related policies on national security, public health and martial law. A database of people who are prohibited from entering China needs to be established and the procedure for prohibiting entry needs to be transparent and simplified.
3) Talented overseas Chinese need the right of return as Mainland Chinese residents. Foreign citizens who were originally from China must be given assistance in obtaining permanent residence or Chinese citizenship before other aliens.
4) Administrative procedures associated with the movement and residence of overseas returnees and foreigners needs to be simplified. Management of this group of potential immigrants may extend beyond the policy of attracting them to settle in China via migration law. Simplification of the procedures related to movement and residence within China may help their economic and social reintegration.

13.2.2.5 The reform of administration of emigration intermediary agencies

The laws governing emigration intermediary agencies need to be addressed as part of an overall legislative scheme of migration law. The following recommendations relate to the content of Chinese migration law.

1) The various agencies need be consolidated and placed under one umbrella of an administrative authority.[8] The MPS is the most appropriate authority for this function. Further, the licensing system needs to be simplified.
2) In order to reduce the cost of managing emigration intermediary agencies and make them more effective, restrictions and barriers to trans-regional emigration intermediary agencies marketing and investment could be abolished. Administrative powers that do not separate the functions of government from the management of enterprises, and which divest institutions of their administrative functions, in addition to powers that hamper market development and fair competition, need be repealed.
3) The control of agencies needs be changed from direct regulation by the responsible government departments to direct supervision by an industry-based association. This will promote administrative efficiency within the agency. The MPS needs to retain an indirect supervisory role over agencies by formulating policy guidelines. Further, the internal disciplinary measures adopted by agencies needs be improved by reference to the standards of the industry-based association.
4) The conditions for establishing an agency need to focus on the qualifications of the agent, in addition to the current capital requirements. As noted in part 10.3.2 of this book, the magnitude of reserve funds that are required to establish an agency, while aimed at reducing the frequency of illegal conduct on the part of individual agents, are prohibitive. The reserve fund concept needs to be replaced by compulsory insurance. A model for the regulation of compulsory insurance in this industry can be found in relation to laws governing overseas travel agencies.[9]

---

[8] In accordance with the statement by Xiang Huaicheng, the Finance Minister in 2000 in *China to Further Rectify Intermediary Organs, The People's Daily*, 24 August 2000, http://english.people.com.cn/english/200008/24/eng20000824_48942.html (accessed 20/09/2006).

[9] Article 2 of the *Measures of Purchasing Travel Agency Responsibility Insurance of Travel Agencies* 2001 (PRC), "travel agencies engaging travel service may purchasing travel agency responsibility insurance (*Lvxingshe Zeren Baoxian*). Article 10 of the *Measures of Purchasing Travel Agency Responsibility Insurance of Travel Agencies* 2001 (PRC), the limit of compensation for overseas tourist is 160,000 RMB yuan (equal to 19,350 US dollars). The limit of accumulated compensation for international travel agencies is 4 million RMB yuan (equal to 483,700 US dollars).

5) Migration agents need to be familiar with the migration law of China and receiving countries. A license should not be granted to establish an agency unless a minimum legal training requirement has been completed. This will improve the quality of newly established agencies.
6) The limits imposed on agents' access to foreign investment need to be abolished. Under the WTO agreement, China is obliged to expand the services available to foreign businesses with respect to the promotion of Chinese industry. Migration agents are well placed to attract reputable foreign enterprises into China. Foreign investors need to be afforded the same opportunities as their Chinese counterparts. Services need to be improved by making government practices more efficient and predictable, and by fostering competition between agencies.
7) The requirement that five staff members with tertiary qualifications must be employed by each agency needs to be relinquished on the grounds that it is unreasonable to regulate the minimum number of qualified staff in a market economy. The employment of staff, whether qualified or unqualified, is a commercial decision for each agency depending on the size of the agency and the nature of the services they provide.
8) The annual re-examination of qualified agencies and the possibility that the agent can lose their capacity to practice if the examinations are failed twice is too lenient. Loss of a practicing certificate is currently limited to agents who have engaged in unlawful conduct. Agents need to be required to attend ongoing education courses as part of their annual re-certification. To further maintain the standards of agents' practice, the MPS website, or that of an industry-based association, needs to publicise the way in which agents are disciplined.
9) The requirements for extension of the duration of agencies' licenses need to be simplified.

13.2.2.6 The improvement of remedies for violations of RLR

Procedural fairness needs to be applied to administrative decisions that affect RLR, along with other aspects of administrative procedure, and laws concerning administrative penalties and licensing. The following recommendations are aimed at resolving issues related to remedies for violations of RLR.

The conception of a remedy of administrative review needs to be established. A remedial framework would correct the improper use of the term 'appeal' (*shensu*) that appears in Article 15 of the *Law on the Control of Exit and Entry of Citizens* 1985 (PRC), Article 29 Clause 2 of the *Law on the Control of Exit and Entry of Aliens* 1985 (PRC); and Article 50 of the *Detailed Rules for the Law on the Control of Exit and Entry of Aliens (Amendment)* 1994 (PRC). These provisions allow a citizen to 'appeal' against an administrative penalty imposed by a public security department. The term 'administrative review' (*Xingzheng fuyi*) is more appropriate than 'appeal'. A conception of a remedial framework would lay a solid foundation from which to further regulate administrative review in migration law.

The remedy of administrative review should apply to all administrative penalties and decisions with respect to exit and entry in China. Extending the scope of administrative review may remove the discrimination caused by the imposition of penalties and by administrative decisions generally, such as the discriminatory grounds upon which a person may be permitted to enter or leave, based on the purpose of their travel.

The separate principles of merits review and external remedies, which were discussed in part 11.3.3 of this book, need be merged to form a doctrine of administrative review. It is recommended that the existing merits review structure be changed so that if a person is aggrieved by an initial decision, he or she may apply for review to an administrative review tribunal within a certain period after receiving the notice of the decision. The administrative review tribunal would be required to review the decision within certain period after the receipt of the application. If the applicant is still dissatisfied with the decision, proceedings could be instituted in a Court within a certain period of receiving the tribunal's decision.

13.2.3 *The establishment of an effective exit and entry administrative system*

Without an effective administrative system for exit and entry, these recommendations will be ineffective. Reform of the administrative system will be difficult because it entails partial reform of government departments. Nevertheless, the challenge must be faced in order to comprehensively reform the regulatory framework and protect RLR.

A new uniform exit and entry administration responsible for private affairs and border security

The entities that administer exit and entry, and border security checks and administration need to be merged. Existing functions related to the police need to be vested in the criminal investigation and public security departments. The authorities dealing with aliens' residence registration need be incorporated into the household administration department. This restructuring would be relatively simple because it would fall under the existing MPS system. The new exit and entry administration department would remain subordinate to the public security department, which uniformly exercises the functions of assessing passport applications, issuing passports, granting visas and checking passports and visas at the border.

A new uniform exit and entry administration for all private affairs

Exit and entry authorities for private affairs administration need to be devolved to the new exit and entry administration under the MPS, thereby establishing a uniform private affairs system. The Overseas Chinese Affairs Offices, under this change, would no longer be responsible for the exit and entry administration of *huaqiao*.

A combined uniform exit and entry administration for all private affairs and public affairs

Exit and entry administration for public affairs needs to be clearly defined and made transparent and open. Currently, the MFA and its authorised branches are responsible for the administration of public affairs travel to and from foreign countries. The SHMO and STO are responsible for the administration of public affairs travel to the respective regions. The administration of exit and entry for public affairs need to be merged into the new exit and entry administration for all private affairs, to build an effective, systematic and comprehensive system.

Avenues of review: establishment of an administrative review tribunal and judicial reform

An independent administrative review tribunal needs to be established, and judicial proceedings needs to be improved to provide effective remedies to violations of RLR. The experiences of the Australian Appeals Tribunal could be a possible modle for China. The relevant detailed analysis and research need to be further done in the future study. It is necessary to reform the working mechanisms of judicial bodies and the management system of their human, financial and material resources; and to gradually separate their judicial and administrative functions.

Further reforms: placing limits of on administrative discretion and decentralisation of authority

Additionally, the discretion of the exit and entry administration needs to be limited. This can be achieved by enacting more specific rules and regulations, which will overcome existing ambiguity and flexibility. The inclusion of detailed criteria and procedures can be a priority when drafting the new laws. Secondly, local exit and entry authorities may be vested with more power. This would be achieved by transferring functions from the ministerial and provincial level of administration to the municipal and county levels. This revised structure would allow ministerial and provincial administration to focus on policy formulation, while permitting local administrative bodies to implement policies at 'grass roots'. Decentralisation would eliminate unnecessary red tape; create an efficient and transparent system and curb corruption. All authorities would be required to obey the law when carrying out their administrative duties and perform their functions strictly within their jurisdiction.

13.2.4 *The reform of related laws and regulations*

RLR policies may be integrated with the laws of nationality, foreign exchange, household registration, tourism, education, labour administration, freedom of information and national security, in order to reap the full benefit of emigration, not only for China but for those States to which Chinese people are sent.[10] As such, the reform of related laws and regulations needs to be part of a package of regulatory framework reforms. This subsection addresses the two most important areas related areas for reform: nationality law and foreign exchange law. Recommendations for the other relevant areas are beyond the scope of this research.

Nationality law

Existing nationality laws need to be reformed in two principle respects: the recognition of dual nationality; and relaxation of the conditions of naturalization.

The current policy of not recognizing dual nationality need to be reformed to maintain a much more close relationship with Chinese citizens residing abroad and to encourage more talented citizenss who live overseas to return. Given China's low level of economic development, most people prefer to acquire or retain foreign nationality, even under the premise of renounceing the nationality of China. The recognition of dual nationality may reduce this phenomenon. Additionally, integration of an immigrant in a host country facilitates access to the immigrant's country, enriching the culture of the host country, and does not equate to the breaking of cultural ties with the home country. There are few convincing arguments to support the view that the recognition of dual nationality will cause disputes between the countries of nationalities.

A country's system of naturalization plays a key role in the retention of permanent residents and the attraction of aliens. Even though Article 7 of the *Law of Nationality* 1980 (PRC) stipulates that people who have settled in China may be naturalized upon approval of their applications, there are no related laws speci-

[10] According to the *Legislative Program of the Standing Committee of Tenth National People's Congress*, the *Law of Passport, Law of the Freedom of Government Information* will be formulated and promulgated in the period between 2003 and 2008. See Zhang, Shuo, "Five Years Legislative Program was Published, Including 76 Bills" (*Zhongguo Gongbu Wunian Lifa Guihua, 76 Jian Falv An Bangshang Youmin*), 18/12/2003, China News Agency, http://news.china.com/zh_cn/domestic/945/20031217/11588970.html (accessed 20/09/2006).

fying who is eligible, when and where an application can be lodge, or how much may be paid. This means that the process of naturalization is almost impossible in practice. It is recommended that an applicant may be eligible for Chinese nationality if the person is:

- A permanent resident of China for three of the preceding five years, including a total of eighteen months in the preceding two and a half years;
- Can speak, listen, read and write Chinese;
- Is of good character;
- Understands the nature of the application;
- Understands the nature of the responsibilities and privileges of Chinese nationality;
- Will be present in China for at least one year of the two years following naturalization.

Under the new migration system, an eligible person could lodge an application at any county and municipality level exit and entry administration office.

Foreign exchange law

The reform of foreign exchange law will be beneficial for Chinese people's going abroad. Amendments to existing foreign exchange laws need to be made in following respects.

Effective measures are needed to allow domestic residents to purchase, remit and carry larger sums of foreign exchange when they travel overseas. The complex process of access to foreign exchange should be simplified. A streamlined approval process is needed. The criterion for a maximum amount of foreign exchange needs to be refined. This book, in the absence of the relevant expertise, does not attempt to recommend what the maximum sum may be. In any event, such a calculation is not necessary for the argument raised here.

Moreover, when funds are from a legitimate source, license requirements for individual investors need to be varied to suit registration requirements with a provincial foreign exchange authority. The boldest measure would be to allow domestic institutions and individuals to invest in overseas capital markets or other financial markets. More banks needs to be entitled to provide foreign exchange services. Close attention need be paid to upgrading the quality and uniformity of foreign exchange laws.

13.2.5 *The enhancement of public awareness of RLR*

Implementation of the system so far described is of less value and effect if there is a lack of public awareness of RLR. To date, broad public education of individual liberties has been minimal. Awareness of RLR needs to be promoted in order to give effect to the reforms. Public education can be achieved by (i) publication and distribution in Chinese and other ethnic dialects of the various UN conventions regarding RLR to which China has ratified or acceded; (ii) an increase in the amount of university-based training in relation to RLR; and (iii) using the mass media to broadcast special programmes to convey information on matters of RLR protection.

The major obstacle in providing administrative redress for grievances, or implementing public education programmes, is found in the structurally inadequate, poorly funded Chinese institutions, whose purpose it is to fulfil those obligations. Rectifying this requires a concerted and coordinated effort over time. This would heighten public and political responsiveness to the role of human rights in daily living.

13.2.6 *The acceleration of the use of information technology in exit and entry administration*

Acceleration of the use of information technology in exit and entry administration, and the promotion of electronic administration to improve government working efficiency and exercise more effective supervision, is vital. Information networks need to be established by the exit and entry and border check administrations. Then, information networks between the exit and entry administration, household administration, public security, criminal investigation services, and the nationality administration need to be linked. Finally, the scope information networks needs to be extended to the foreign affairs authority, foreign exchange administrative authority, Customs, overseas embassies and consulates, the Courts and Procurators.

13.3 Conclusions

This book has identified numerous regulatory gaps and deficiencies, which if left unattended, could seriously undermine the objective of maintaining the confidence of the people of China in RLR, encapsulated in Article 33 Clause 3 of the *Constitution of the PRC (Amendment)* 2004 and Article 12 Clause 2 of the UDHR. Current regulations have failed by not providing people who want to leave and return to China with statutory safeguards, and not guiding migratory flows in an orderly manner.

The intention of this research is not only to criticise and expose the deficiencies of RLR in China, but to investigate the possibility, necessity and solution of adequately addressing these problems. Measures, such as those recommended above, may be devised to address the deficiencies in the regulatory framework governing RLR, especially that governing exit and entry administration. In adopting the recommendations made in this book, the legislature will not only level the playing field for everyone wanting to enter and exit China, but will help to reduce systemic risks and technical barriers imposed by the current system which adversely affect RLR. The legislature may acknowledge that migration policy will need to develop on a day-by-day basis until it becomes an integral part of overall economic and social policy at the regional, national and international levels. This may be closely combined with technological and economic development.

There is still a long way to go before the Chinese authorities protect RLR. A strategy designed to increase public awareness of RLR and secure further governmental protection offers the most promising chance of success. Given continuing resistance to change, however, the process is likely to be tortuous and frustrating. Liberty, like all great, unfinished projects, requires constancy as well as conviction. With concerted and sustained efforts by the Chinese people and the international community, I dare to hope for the day when we will see China recognise and share RLR values adopted by the rest of the world.

Appendix One
The Structure of the Chinese State Organisations

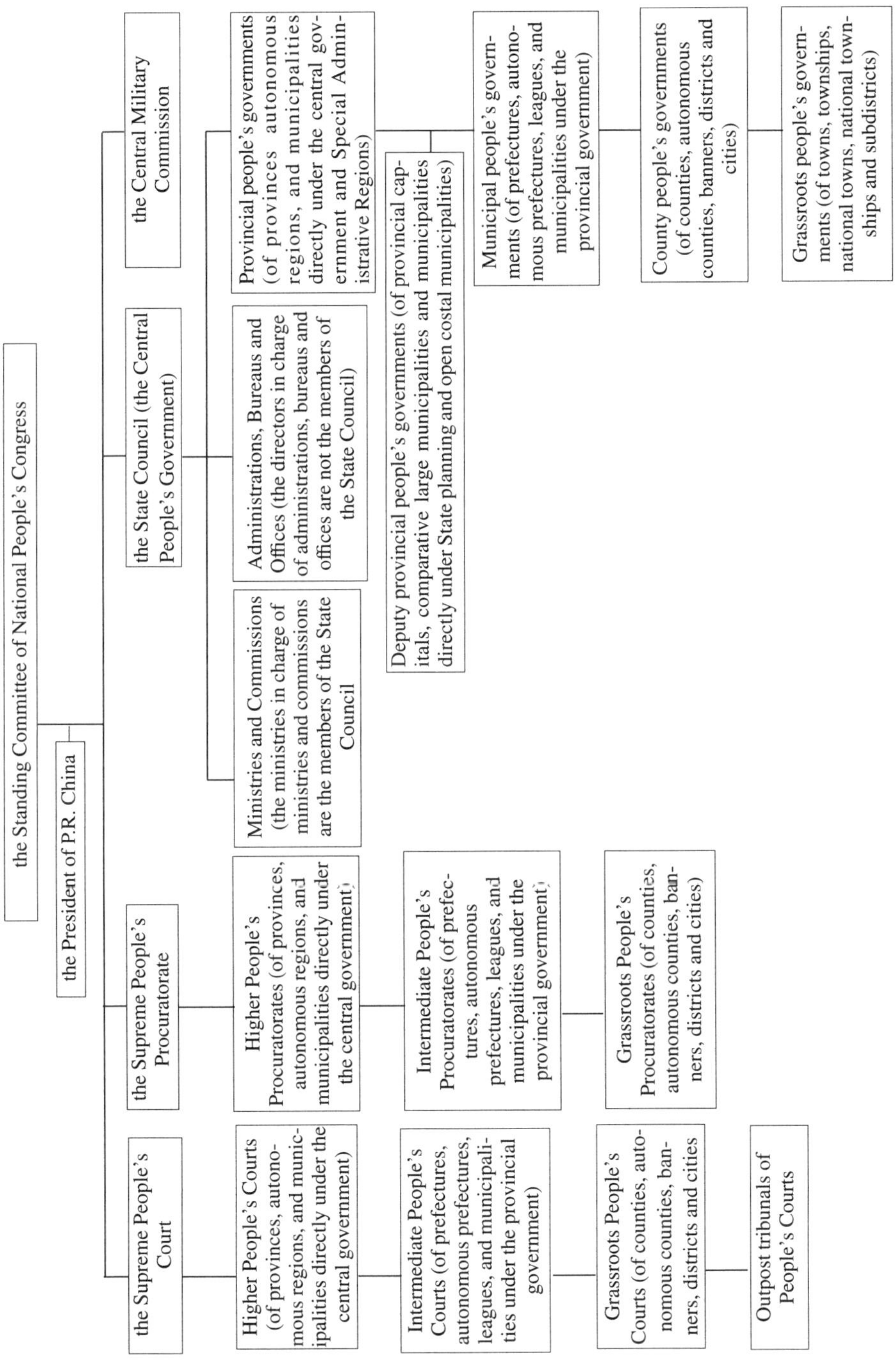

Appendix Two

Merits Review of Administrative Decisions under Chinese Administrative Laws and Administrative Procedure Laws

No.	Remedies	Scope	Sources
1	Administrative procedure	The People's Court shall accept suits brought by citizens . . . against any of the following specific administrative acts: (1) an administrative sanction, such as detention, fine, rescission of license or permit, order to suspend production of business or confiscation of property, which one refuses to accept; . . . (4) refusal by an administrative organ to issue a permit or license, which one considers oneself legally qualified to apply for, or its failure to respond to the application.	Article 11 Clause 1 (1) and (4) of the *Law on Administrative Procedure* 1989 (PRC).
2	Administrative review	A citizens "can apply to administrative departments for review if he or she (1) does not accept a disciplinary warning, fine, the forfeiture of illegally obtained items, the forfeiture of illegal treasures, an order suspending business operations, a temporary suspension or seizure of permits, or a temporary suspension or seizure of licenses; . . . . (3) does not accept the alteration, termination, or rescission of a permit, license, certificate of intelligence, or certificates; . . . . (11) there is of the opinion that the administrative department has infringed their legal rights and interests.	Article 6 Clause 1 (1), (3) and (11) of the *Law on Administrative Review* 1989 (PRC).
3	Complaint	Article 2 Complaints can be made against government departments of county level or above in relation to: . . . Article 8 the following matters may be inquired by a complainant. . . . (2) accuse or expose violations of law or negligence by the staff of administrative authorities; (3) infringements of the rights or interests of the complainant; and (4) other matters.	Articles 2 and Article 8 Clause 1 (2), (3) and (4) of the *Rules on Compliant Reporting* 1995 (PRC).

4	State compensation	Article 3 The victim have the right to compensation if an administrative departments or its functionaries, in exercising their administrative functions and powers, commit any of the following acts violating the right of a citizen: (1) detaining a citizen in violation of the law or unlawfully taking compulsory administrative measures in restraint of their personal freedom;. . . . Article 4 . . . [or] commit any of the following acts violating upon property right: (1) illegally imposing administrative sanctions such as fines, revocation of certificates and licenses, ordering suspension of production and business, or confiscation of property. . . .	Article 3 Clause 1(1), and Article 4 Clause 1 (1) of the *Law of State Compensation* 1994 PRC
5	Administrative penalty	Citizens. . . . against whom a penalty is imposed by administrative departments shall have the right to state their case and the right to defend themselves; those who refuse to accept administrative penalty shall have the right to apply for administrative review or bring an administrative lawsuit in accordance with law.	Article 6 (1) of the *Law of Administrative Penalty* 1996 (PRC).
		The types of administrative penalty shall include: (1) disciplinary warning; (2) fine; (3) confiscation of illegal gains or confiscation of unlawful property or things of value; (4) ordering for suspension of production or business; (5) temporary suspension or rescission of permit or license; (6) administrative detention; and others as prescribed by laws and administrative rules and regulations. (7) others as prescribed by laws and administrative rules and regulations.	Article 8 of the *Law of Administrative Penalty* 1996 (PRC).
		An administrative organ, before deciding on an administrative penalty that involves ordering for suspension of production or business, rescission of business permit or license or imposition of a comparatively large amount of fine, shall notify the party that he or she has the right to request a hearing. . . .	Article 42 (1) of the *Law of Administrative Penalty* 1996 (PRC).
6	Administrative license	Article 7 Citizens, legal persons or other organizations shall enjoy the right of making statement and defence in respect of the implementation of administrative license by administrative authority and have the right to apply for administrative review or bring administrative action according to law. If their lawful rights and interests are damaged due to the illegal implement of administrative license by administrative authority, they shall have the right to claim compensation according to law.	Article 7 of the *Law on Administrative License* 2003 (PRC)

Appendix Three

Admission Criteria of Chinese Emigration Intermediary Agencies

Overseas study intermediary agencies

Overseas study intermediary agencies shall not be set up unless the following conditions are satisfied.

(1) It shall be an education institution or education service institution offering service for Chinese citizens with status of legal person;
(2) Its legal representative shall be a Chinese citizen with domestic registered permanent residence;
(3) It shall have staff who are familiar with laws, regulations and policies of this country and other relevant countries on self-funded overseas study intermediary agencies, and possess an educational background of at least junior college. At least 5 personnel with qualifications in foreign languages, law, finance, or secretarial skills must be employed;
(4) It shall have established stable relations with overseas education institutions, and have directly signed valid cooperative agreements with them;
(5) It shall have reserve funds of at least C¥ 500,000 (US$60,386).[1]

[1] Article 3 of the *Rules on the Control of Intermediary Agencies for Self-funded Overseas Study* 1999 (PRC), promulgated by the Ministry of Education, the Ministry of Public Security and State Administration of Industry and Commerce on 17 June 1999 and effective

Exit and entry intermediary agencies for private purposes

Emigration intermediary agencies for private purpose shall comply with following conditions.

(1) It shall comply with conditions for the establishment of an enterprise with status of legal person;
(2) Its legal representative shall be a Chinese citizen with domestic registered permanent residence and full civil capacity, comply with the relevant provisions on registration and administration of enterprise's legal representatives, have not been subject to criminal punishment for the crime of impairing control of the border (or boundary with a region);
(3) It shall have at least 5 staffs who are familiar with laws, regulations and policies of this country and other relevant countries on entry and exit. The main staff shall possess educational background of junior college or above, and have not been subject to criminal punishment for the crime of impairing control of the border (or the boundary with a region). Personnel in foreign languages, law, and finance with professional qualifications must be employed;
(4) It shall have established regulations and systems that guarantee the normal operation of agency service, and
(5) It shall have established relations with overseas entry and exit service agencies, and have directly signed valid cooperative agreements with them.[2]
(6) It shall have reserve funds of at least reserve funds of C¥ 500,000 (US$60,386).[3]

Overseas employment intermediary agencies

An overseas employment intermediary agency shall fulfil the following conditions:

(1) It shall meet requirements for the establishment of an incorporated enterprise;
(2) It shall have full-time staff with professional qualifications in law, foreign language, and accounting; and sound working systems for the regulation of staff;
(3) It shall have a reserve fund at least C¥ 500,000 (US$60,386).[4]

at the same day; and Article 2-5 of the *Detailed Rules for the Implementation of Rules on the Control of Intermediary Agencies for Self-funded Overseas Study* 1999 (PRC).

[2] Article 6 of the *Measures on the Administration of Exit and Entry Intermediary Agencies for Private Affairs* 2001 (PRC).

[3] Article 25 of the *Measures on the Administration of Exit and Entry Intermediary Agencies for Private Affairs* 2001 (PRC).

[4] Article 5 Clause 1 (1) (2) (3) of the *Regulations on the Administration for Overseas Employment Intermediary Agencies (Amendment)* 2002 (PRC).

Foreign labour and co-operation company

Foreign labour and co-operation companies must comply with Article 7 of the *Provisional Measures on the Administration of Foreign Labour and Cooperation* 1993 (PRC), which requires that the applicant be State-owned large industrial enterprise, and have made a significant contribution to foreign labour and cooperation. A foreign labour cooperation company needs reserve C¥ 1 million (US$ 120,000) for sending general labourers, and C¥ 200,000 (US$240 000) for sending special kinds of labours.[5]

International travel agencies

International travel agencies shall not be set up unless the following conditions are satisfied:

(1) There is a sufficient fixed business premises;
(2) It has necessary business facilities;
(3) It has employed at least 4 managers who have been trained and issued qualification certificates by Chinese National Tourism Administration (CNTA), and one certified accountant;
(4) The registered capital and quality-guarantee deposit are not less than C¥ 1.5 million (US$181,159) and C¥ 1 million (US$120,773). The minimum registered capital required for the Sino-foreign equity joint venture agencies is C¥ 4 million (US$483,092).[6]

Overseas training at government expense intermediary agencies

To establish an overseas training intermediary agency or foreign labour and cooperation company, applicants need to meet the similarly strict conditions, especially with respect to the nature and ownership of the applicants. Overseas training agencies must comply with Article 4 of the *Provisional Rules on the Recognition of Overseas Training Qualification of Dispatching Groups and Personals to Other Countries for Training of the Institutions and the Mass Departments* 1993 (PRC), which requires that the applicant be an institution, and had been operating as an overseas training agency for at least 3 years.

---

[5] Article 6 Clause 2 of *Provisional Measures of the Reserve Funds of Foreign Labour Cooperation* 2003 (PRC) *(Duiwai Laowu Hezuo Beiyongjing Zaixing Banfa)*.

[6] Article 6, 7, 8 and 27 of the *Regulations on the Administrative of Travel Agencies (Amendment)* 2001 (PRC) amended pursuant to *Travel Agencies Administrative Measures 1996 (PRC)*; and Article 9, 10, 13 of the *Detailed Rules of the Implementation of Regulations on the Administration of Travel Agencies* 2003 (PRC) *(Lvxingshe Guanli Tiaoli Shishi Xize)*, promulgated by the CNTA on 10 June 2003.

Sino-foreign joint venture for skilled personnel intermediary agencies

An Operation License of Skilled Personnel Intermediary agency for Sino-foreign joint-venture skilled personnel intermediary agencies will be issued provided that:

(1) The Chinese and foreign parties must have independently operated as skilled personnel agencies for at least three years and be of good reputation.
(2) There is a sound management structure and proficient human resources management specialists, including at least 5 professionals with junior college qualifications and skilled personnel agencies service certificates;
(3) There is a fixed business venue, sufficient capital and office facilities; There is registered capital of not less than US$300,000; The share of foreign party is not lower than 25%, and the share of Chinese party is not lower than 51%;
(4) The business has sound articles of association, management system,, operational rules and a clearly defined business scope;
(5) The business is entitled to independent civil rights and capable of assuming civil liabilities.[7]

Reason for overly strict admission criteria

The overly strict admission criteria can be accounted for on the basis of standardising and rectifying the emigration intermediary agencies service market. In 2002, Premier Zhu, Rongji reported "the qualifications of all kinds of market entities need to be carefully examined to properly control market access."[8] The control of market access was regarded as a way of achieving this objective.

Impacts of overly strict admission criteria

On balance, strict admission criteria, especially in relation to the requirement of minimum reserve funds and staff qualifications, have played a positive role in controlling market access. However, the disadvantages are also obvious.

---

[7] Article 6 Clause 1 (1) to (5) of the *Provisional Regulations on the Administration of Sino-Foreign Joint Venture Personnel Intermediary Agency* 2003 (PRC) *(Zhongwai Hezi Rencai Zhongjie Jigou Guanli Zaixing Guiding).*

[8] Zhu, Rongji, Premier of the State Council, Par 3 of Part V of "Report on the Work of the Government 2002" (16/03/2002), http://english.gov.cn/official/2005-07/29/content_18337.htm (accessed 16/09/2006).

Appendix Four

Functions of Public Security Departments in Relation to Exit and Entry Administration

No.	Responsible departments	Functions	Sources
1	Ministry of Public Security (MPS)	Examine and approve applications for naturalization and for renunciation or restoration of Chinese nationality lo\dged in China; issue a certificate to any person whose application has been approved.	Article 17 the *Law of Nationality* 1980 (PRC).
		Order alien who have committed serious offences to leave China within a time limit or make an order of deportation.	Article 30 of the *Law on the Control of Exit and Entry of Citizens* 1985 (PRC).
		Grant Operation Licenses for Exit and Entry Intermediary Agency for Private Affairs.	Article 5(2) of the *Measures on the Administrative of Emigration Intermediary Agency for Private Affairs* 2001 (PRC).
		Record License of Overseas Study Intermediary Agency with MOE.	Article 4 the *Rules on the Control of Intermediary Agency for Self-funded Overseas Study* 1999 (PRC).
		Examine and approve the applications for permanent residence of aliens in China.	Article 5 of the *Regulations on Examination and Approval of Permanent Residence of Aliens in China* 2004 (PRC).

		Change the visa decisions made by its authorized departments if necessary.	Articles 26 (2) of the *Law on the Control of Exit and Entry of Aliens* 1985 (PRC).
2	the MPS and its authorized local public security departments	Handle applications for refugee status lodged in China.	Articles 15 and 25 of the *Law on the Control of Exit and Entry of Aliens* 1985 (PRC).
		Issue or cancel private passports, or declare such passports invalid.	Articles 12(1) and 13 of the *Law on the Control of Exit and Entry of Citizens* 1985 (PRC).
3	Agency in the HKSAR or MSAR of the BEEA under the MPS	Handle applications of Taiwan Chinese for travel documents who want to travel to inland China via HKSAR or MSAR.	Article 13(2) the *Measures on the Control over Chinese Citizens Travelling to or from the Region of Taiwan* 1992 (PRC).
4	Agency of the BEEA under the MPS	Handle applications from Taiwan Chinese for travel documents who want to travel directly to inland China.	Article 13(1) the *Measures on the Control over Chinese Citizens Travelling to or from the Region of Taiwan* 1992 (PRC).
5	Public security department in ports designed by the MPS	Handle applications from Taiwanese residents for travel documents to travel directly to inland China for special affairs.	Article 13(1) of the *Measures on the Control over Chinese Citizens Travelling to or from the Region of Taiwan* 1992 (PRC).
		Handle applications from aliens for visas.	Article 6 of the *Law on the Control of Exit and Entry of Aliens* 1985 (PRC).
6	Provincial public security departments	Certify the qualifications of exit and entry intermediary agency for private affairs.	Article 5(1) of the *Measures on the Administrative of Exit and Entry Intermediary Agency for Private Affairs* 2001 (PRC).

Appendix Four (*cont.*)

No.	Responsible departments	Functions	Sources
		Examine and approve applications of Chinese citizens residing abroad for returning to China for permanence residence.	Article 10 of the *Law on the Control of Exit and Entry of Citizens* 1985 (PRC).
		Grant return residence permits for Chinese citizens residing abroad	Article 10 of the *Detailed Rules for the Implementation of the Law on the Control of Exit and Entry of Citizens (Amendment)* 1994 (PRC).
		Grant return residence permits for Taiwan residents.	Article 7 the *Circular of Some Matters on Implementation of Measures on the Control over Chinese Citizens Travelling to or from the Region of Taiwan* 1992 (PRC).
		Not grant Chinese citizens to exit China.	Article 6 (1) and (3) of the *Explanation of Ministry of Public Security on Some Issues on Implementation of Law on the Control of Exit and Entry of Citizens and Its Detailed Rules for the Implementation* 1987 (PRC).
		Prohibit criminal suspects and (Chinese citizens and aliens) from exiting China.	Article 2(1) of the *Some Rules on the Issues of Exit Abroad Prohibition of Aliens and Chinese Citizens* 1987 (PRC).
		Verify application of aliens in China for permanent residence.	Article 5 of the *Regulations on Examination and Approval of Permanent Residence of Aliens in China* 2004 (PRC).

7	Provincial public security departments, or its authorized public security departments	Process applications for passport extensions lodged by Chinese citizens in China.	Article 17(2) of the *Detailed Rules for the Implementation of the Law on the Control of Exit and Entry of Citizens (Amendment)* 1994 (PRC).
		Replace or reissue passports and exit and entry certificates	Article 21 of the *Detailed Rules for the Implementation of the Law on the Control of Exit and Entry of Citizens (Amendment)* 1994 (PRC).
		Issue Chinese exit and entry passes.	Article 19 of the *Detailed Rules for the Implementation of the Law on the Control of Exit and Entry of Citizens (Amendment)* 1994 (PRC).
8	Guangdong Province Public Security Department	Sign and issue Home Visiting Passes and Exit and Entry Passes for Hong Kong or Macao compatriots.	Article 14 of the *Provisional Measures on the Control over Chinese Citizens Travelling for Private Affairs to or from the Regions of Hong Kong or Macao* 1986 (PRC).
		Handle applications for permits to drive motor vehicles from and to Hong Kong or Macao.	Article 16 of the *Provisional Measures on the Control over Chinese Citizens Travelling for Private Affairs to or from the Regions of Hong Kong or Macao* 1986 (PRC).
9	Prefecture or municipal public security departments	Accept applications for an Operation License of Exit and Entry Intermediary Agency for Private Affairs	Article 5(1) of the *Measures on the Administrative of Exit and Entry Intermediary Agency for Private Affairs* 2001 (PRC).

Appendix Four (*cont.*)

No.	Responsible departments	Functions	Sources
		Accept applications for permanent residence of aliens in China	Article 5 of the *Regulations on Examination and Approval of Permanent Residence of Aliens in China* 2004 (PRC)
10	County or above public security departments	Detain aliens who have illegally entered or are residing in China for the purposes of investigation, supervision of their residence, or deportation.	Article 27 of the *Law on the Control of Exit and Entry of Aliens* 1985 (PRC).
		Warn, fine or detain illegal aliens for a maximum of ten days.	Article 29(1) the *Law on the Control of Exit and Entry of Aliens* 1985 (PRC).
11	County or municipal public security departments	Accept applications from Chinese citizens residing abroad to return to China for permanence residence	Article 10 the *Detailed Rules for the Implementation of the Law on the Control of Exit and Entry of Citizens (Amendment)* 1994 (PRC).
		Handle applications for passport alteration or remarks lodged in China	Article 20 of the *Detailed Rules for the Implementation of the Law on the Control of Exit and Entry of Citizens (Amendment)* 1994 (PRC).
		Handle applications from the HKSAR and MSAR residents to return and resettle in inland areas.	Article 18 of the *Provisional Measures on the Control over Chinese Citizens Travelling for Private Affairs to or from the Regions of Hong Kong or Macao* 1986 (PRC).

		Handle applications for travelling to the HKSAR and MSAR for private affairs	Article 6 of the *Provisional Measures on the Control over Chinese Citizens Travelling for Private Affairs to or from the Regions of Hong Kong or Macao* 1986 (PRC).
		Handle applications for travelling to Taiwan for private affairs	Article 6 of the *Measures on the Control over Chinese Citizens Travelling to or from the Region of Taiwan* 1992 (PRC).
		Accept applications for Chinese nationality lodged in China	Article 15 of the *Law of Nationality* 1980 (PRC).
12	Police station or Residence Registration Office in which they are registered	Temporary residence registration of Chinese citizens who are permanent residents of a foreign country and who have returned to China for a short time	Article 13 of the *Detailed Rules for theImplementation of the Law on the Control of Exit and Entry of Citizens (Amendment)* 1994 (PRC).
		Deregistration of the applicants' household registration before leaving the country to reside permanently in a foreign country	Article 13 of the *Detailed Rules for the Implementation of the Law on the Control of Exit and Entry of Citizens (Amendment)* 1994 (PRC).
		Handle the registration of temporary residents in the HKSAR or MSAR	Article 17 of the *Provisional Measures on the Control over Chinese Citizens Travelling for Private Affairs to or from the Regions of Hong Kong or Macao* 1986 (PRC).
13	Police station or Residence Registration Office of the applicants' original residence	Residential deregistration for a short-term absence from the country and,upon return to China, resumption of applicants' regular household registration	Article 7 of the *Detailed Rules for the Implementation of the Law on the Control of Exit and Entry of Citizens (Amendment)* 1994 (PRC).

Appendix Four (*cont.*)

No.	Responsible departments	Functions	Sources
14	A public security department	Give a warning to any person who, in violation of the provisions of *Law on the Control of Exit and Entry of Citizens* 1985 (PRC), leaves or enters the country illegally, forges or alters an exit and entry certificate, uses another person's certificate as one's own or transfers one's certificate or placed them in detention for not more than 10 days.	Article 14 of the *Law on the Control of Exit and Entry of Citizens* 1985 (PRC).
		Sign and issue travel documents for travel to Taiwan.	Article 10 of the *Measures on the Control over Chinese Citizens Travelling to or from the Region of Taiwan* 1992 (PRC).
		Examine and approve applications of serving police to exit.	Article 2(1) of the *Explanation of Ministry of Public Security on Some Issues on Implementation of Law on the Control of Exit and Entry of Citizens and Its Detailed Rules for the Implementation* 1987 (PRC).
15	Public security departments – either the original issuing department or department in which they are registered	Process applications of Chinese citizens residing in China for passport extension.	Article 17(2) of the *Detailed Rules for the Implementation of the Law on the Control of Exit and Entry of Citizens (Amendment)* 1994 (PRC).

16	Public security departments – either the original issuing department or higher department	Revoke or declare invalid passports and other exit and entry certificates.	Article 22 of the *Detailed Rules for the Implementation of the Law on the Control of Exit and Entry of Citizens (Amendment)* 1994 (PRC).
		Revoke Home-Visiting Passes and Exit and Entry Passes for Hong Kong or Macao Compatriots.	Article 25 of the *Provisional Measures on the Control over Chinese Citizens Travelling for Private Affairs to or from the Regions of Hong Kong or Macao* 1986 (PRC).
17	Local public security departments	Residential registration for Chinese citizens who are permanent residents of a foreign country and have returned to China for permanent residence or employment.	Article 12 of the *Detailed Rules for the Implementation of the Law on the Control of Exit and Entry of Citizens (Amendment)* 1994 (PRC).
18	Higher level public security departments	Make the final appellate decision in relation to detention of citizens by a public security department	Article 15 of the *Law on the Control of Exit and Entry of Citizens* 1985 (PRC).
		Make the final appellate decision in relation to a fine or detention of aliens by a public security department-Article 29(2) of the *Law on the Control of Exit and Entry of Citizens* 1985 (PRC).	

Appendix Five
Functions of Foreign Affairs Departments in Relation to Exit and Entry Administration

No.	Responsible departments	Functions	Sources
1	Ministry of Foreign Affairs	Change the visa decisions made by its authorized departments if necessary.	Articles 26 (2) of the *Law on t he Control of Exit and Entry of Aliens* 1985 (PRC).
2	MFA and authorized local foreign affairs departments in China	Issue, cancel, revoke and retain public affairs passports, or declare such passport invalid.	Articles 12(1) and 13 of the *Law on the Control of Exit and Entry of Citizens* 1985 (PRC); Article 16 of the *Detailed Rules for the Implementation of the Law on the Control of Exit and Entry of Citizens (Amendment)* 1994 (PRC).
3	Chinese diplomatic missions and consular offices	Accept applications for Chinese nationality lodged abroad.	Article 15 the *Law of Nationality* 1980 (PRC).
4	Chinese diplomatic missions, consular offices or other agencies located abroad authorized by MFA	Issue, cancel, revoke, retain and extend passports and travel documents, or declare such documents invalid.	Article 12(2) of the *Law on the Control of Exit and Entry of Citizens* 1985 (PRC); Article 16 and 17(2) of the *Detailed Rules for the Implementation of the Law on the Control of Exit and Entry of Citizens (Amendment)* 1994 (PRC).

Examine and approve applications lodged abroad from Chinese citizens residing abroad for returning to China for permanence residence.	Article 10 of the *Law on the Control of Exit and Entry of Citizens* 1985 (PRC).
Issue Chinese travel permits.	Article 18 of the *Detailed Rules for the Implementation of the Law on the Control of Exit and Entry of Citizens (Amendment)* 1994 (PRC).
Handle applications lodged abroad for passport alterations or remarks.	Article 20 of the *Detailed Rules for the Implementation of the Law on the Control of Exit and Entry of Citizens (Amendment) 1994 (PRC)*.
Replace or reissue passports or the exit and entry certificates.	Article 21 of the *Detailed Rules for the Implementation of the Law on the Control of Exit and Entry of Citizens (Amendment)* 1994 (PRC).
Handle applications of Taiwanese residents for travel documents for inland China travel via a third State.	Article 13(3) of the *Measures on the Control over Chinese Citizens Travelling to or from the Region of Taiwan* 1992 (PRC).

(Appendix Five) (*cont.*)

No.	Responsible departments	Functions	Sources
		Accept applications lodged abroad from Taiwanese residents for permanent residence in the inland China.	Article 7 of the *Circular of Some Matters on Implementation of Measures on the Control over Chinese Citizens Travelling to or from the Region of Taiwan* 1992 (PRC).
		Handle applications for refugee status lodged by aliens abroad	Articles 15 and 25 of the *Law on the Control of Exit and Entry of Aliens* 1985 (PRC).
		Issue, cancel, revoke and retain visas to aliens, or declare such visas invalid	Article 6 of the *Law on the Control of Exit and Entry of Aliens* 1985 (PRC).
5	Provincial foreign affairs administration	Examine and approve the application for License of Overseas Training Intermediary Agency in consultation with provincial education administration and public security department	Article 3 (3) of the *Provisional Rules on the Recognition of Overseas Training Qualification of Dispatching Groups and Personals to Other Countries for Training of the Institutions and the Mass Departments* 1993 (PRC).

Appendix Six

Functions of Border Security Check and Administration

No.	Responsible departments	Functions	Sources
1	Bureau of Border Security Check and Administration under the MPS	Administer exit and entry border inspection	Article 2 of the *Regulations of Exit and Entry Border Inspection* 1995 (PRC).
2	Border inspection stations	Take necessary measures to limit the area of the activities of aliens who are denied entry, and are ordered them to leave China on the next available means of transportation.	Article 15 of the *Detailed Rules for the Implementation of the Law on the Control of Exit and Entry of Aliens (Amendment)* 1994 (PRC).
		Exclusive authority to impose penalties for any violation of the *Regulation of Inspection of Exit and Entry Borders Inspection* 1995 (PRC).	Article 31 of the *Regulations of Exit and Entry Border Inspection* 1995 (PRC).
		Refuse Chinese citizens and aliens entry into or departure from the country.	Article 8 of the *Regulations of Exit and Entry Border Inspection* 1995 (PRC); Article 15 of the *Detailed Rules for the Implementation of the Law on the Control of Exit and Entry of Citizens (Amendment)* 1994 (PRC); Article 12 of the *Detailed Rules for the Implementation of the Law on the Control of Exit and Entry of Aliens (Amendment)* 1994 (PRC).

Appendix Six (*cont.*)

No.	Responsible departments	Functions	Sources
		Carry out border inspection on persons leaving or entering the country and their luggage and other personal belongings;	Article 14 of the *Detailed Rules for the Implementation of the Law on the Control of Exit and Entry of*
			Article 10 of the *Detailed Rules for the Implementation of the Law on the Control of Exit and Entry of Aliens (Amendment)* 1994 (PRC).
		Supervise transportation leaving or entering the country; Guard restricted areas in ports and terrestrial borders.	Article 4 of the *Regulations of Inspection of Exit and Entry Borders* 1995 (PRC).

Appendix Seven

Functions of Hong Kong and Macao Affairs Offices, Taiwan Affairs Offices and Overseas Chinese Affairs Offices in Relation to Exit and Entry Administration

No.	Responsible departments	Functions	Sources
1	State Council Hong Kong and Macao Affairs Office	Provisionally examine and approve applications of inland residents for travelling to Hong Kong and Macao for public affairs	Article 4 of the *Measures of Examination and Approval of Sending Individuals to be Employed in Hong Kong and Macao for a Long Term* 1991 (PRC)
2	State Council Taiwan Affairs Office	Provisionally examine and approve applications of inland residents for travelling to Taiwan for public affairs	Article 1 the *Circular of Some Matters on Implementation of Measures on the Control over Chinese Citizens Travelling to or from the Region of Taiwan* 1992 (PRC).
3	Provincial Taiwan Affairs Offices or United Front Work Departments	Provisionally examine and approve applications lodged in China by Taiwanese residents to enter China for permanent residence.	Article 7 the *Circular of Some Matters on Implementation of Measures on the Control over Chinese Citizens Travelling to or from the Region of Taiwan* 1992 (PRC).
4	Provincial Overseas Chinese Affairs Offices	Examine and approve applications of the HKSAR and MSAR Chinese for returning and settling in inland China consultation with other departments	Article 7 of the *Explanation of Some Matters on Implementation of Provisional Measures on the* in *Control over Chinese Citizens Travelling for Private Affairs to or from he Regions of Hong Kong or Macao* 1987 (PRC).

Appendix Seven (*cont.*)

No.	Responsible departments	Functions	Sources
		Examine and approve applications from overseas Chinese for returning and resettling in China in consultation with provincial public security departments	Article 5 of the *Explanation of Ministry of Public Security on Some Issues on Implementation of Law on the Control of Exit and Entry of Citizens and Its Detailed Rules for the Implementation* 1987 (PRC).

Appendix Eight

Functions of Departments Responsible for Emigration Intermediary Agencies

No.	Responsible departments	Functions	Sources
1	Chinese National Tourism Administration	Supervision and administration of international travel agency	Article 4 of the *Regulations on the Administrative of Travel Agencies (Amendment)* 2001 (PRC); Article 6 of the *Detailed Rules of the Implementation of Regulations on the Administrative of Travel Agencies* 2003 (PRC).
2	Ministry of Commerce (prior MFTEC)	Examine and approve applications to engage in foreign labour and cooperation	Article 8 of the *Provisional Measures on the Administrative of Foreign Labour and Cooperation* 1993 (PRC).
3	Ministry of Education	Recognize the operation qualification of self-funded overseas study intermediary agency service in consultation with the MPS	Article 4 the *Rules on the Control of Intermediary Agencies for Self-funded Overseas Study* 1999 (PRC).
4	Ministry of Labour and Social Security	Recognize the qualification of overseas employment intermediary agency.	Article 6 of the *Regulations on the Administrative for Overseas Employment Intermediary Agencies (Amendment)* 2002 (PRC).

Appendix Eight (*cont.*)

No.	Responsible departments	Functions	Sources
5	Ministry of Personnel	Record Operation License of Skilled Personnel Intermediary agency.	Article 8 of the *Provisional Regulations on the Administrative of Sino-Foreign Joint Venture Personnel Intermediary Agencies* 2003 (PRC).
6	Provincial commerce administrations	Manage reserve funds of foreign labour and cooperation company.	Article 4 of the *Provisional Measures of the Reserve Funds of Foreign Labour Cooperation* 2001 (PRC).
7	Provincial education administrations	Accept applications for the Recognition Certificate of Operation Qualification of Self-funded Overseas Study Intermediary Agency Service.	Article 4 the *Rules on the Control of Intermediary Agencies for Self-funded Overseas Study* 1999 (PRC).
8	Provincial labour and social security administrations	Provisionally examine and approve the applications for the License of Overseas Employment Intermediary Agency, after being approved by the Public Security Department	Article 6 of the *Regulations on the Administrative for Overseas Employment Intermediary Agencies (Amendment)* 2002 (PRC).
9	Provincial personnel administrations	Examine and approve applications for the Operation License of Skilled Personnel Intermediary agency.	Article 8 of the *Provisional Regulations on the Administrative of Sino-*

			Foreign Joint Venture Personnel Intermediary Agencies 2003 (PRC).
10	State Administration of Foreign Experts Affairs	Examine, approve and grant the License of Overseas Training Intermediary agency (National level)	Article 5(1)(a) of the *Provisional Rules on the Recognition of Overseas Training Qualification of Dispatching Groups and Personals to Other Countries for Training of the Institutions and the Mass Departments* 1993 (PRC).

Appendix Nine

Functions of Other Responsible Governmental Departments in Relation to Exit and Entry Administration

No.	Responsible departments	Functions	Sources
1	Bureau of Harbour Superintendence or its authorized harbour superintendent departments	Issue, cancel, revoke and retain seafarer's passport or declare such passports invalid	Articles 12(1) and 13 of the *Law on the Control of Exit and Entry of Citizens* 1985 (PRC); Article 16 of the *Detailed Rules for the Implementation of the Law on the Control of Exit and Entry of Citizens (Amendment)* 1994 (PRC).
2	Labour and personnel departments	Accept applications of Chinese citizens who are permanent residents of foreign countries who want to return to China for employment.	Article 11 of the *Detailed Rules for the Implementation of the Law on the Control of Exit and Entry of Citizens (Amendment)* 1994 (PRC).
3	Ministry of State Security	Undertake measures to prevent certain Chinese citizens and foreign citizens from exiting China	Article 2(3) of the *Some Rules on the Issues of Exit Abroad Prohibition of Aliens and Chinese Citizens* 1987 (PRC).
4	Provincial security departments	Prohibit criminal suspects from exiting China	Article 2(1) of the *Some Rules on the Issues of Exit Abroad*

			Prohibition of Aliens and Chinese Citizens 1987 (PRC).
5	State Council Bureau for Religious Affairs	Provisionally examine and approve application for exiting China for pilgrimage	Article 1(1) of the *Circular of State Council Bureau for Religion Affairs, State Administrative of Foreign Exchange, Ministry of Foreign Affairs, Ministry of Public Security, Bank of China, Customs General Administrative and Civil Aviation Administrative of China on Several Rules of Self-support Pilgrimage Administrative (Amendment)* 1995 (PRC).
6.	State Administrative of Foreign Exchange	Control the purchase, remittance and carrying of foreign exchange for the purposes of exiting China for private and public affairs	Article 6 of the *Provisional Measures on the Administrative of Foreign Exchange of Individual Residents in Inland* 1998 (PRC); Article 1 of the *Circular of State Administrative of Foreign Exchange on Some Matters of Improving the Administrative of Selling Foreign Exchange for Public Affairs* 2002 (PRC).

Appendix Ten

Functions of Other Departments and Units in Relation to Exit and Entry Administration

No.	Responsible departments	Functions	Sources
1	The Committee of Chinese Communist Party	Provisionally examine and approve applications for exiting China from Party members.	Article 2(1) of the *Explanation of Ministry of Public Security on Some Issues on Implementation of Law on the Control of Exit and Entry of Citizens and Its Detailed Rules for the Implementation* 1987 (PRC).
2	Responsible departments under the Central Committee of CPC, the State Council and provincial administration.	Provisionally examine and approve the application of various professional groups for exiting China	Article 2(2) of the *Explanation of Ministry of Public Security on Some Issues on Implementation of Law on the Control of Exit and Entry of Citizens and Its Detailed Rules for the Implementation* 1987 (PRC).
3	Deputy provincial level or provincial level governments	Examine, approve and grant a License of Overseas Training Intermediary Agency (Regional level)	Article 5 (1) (a) of the *Provisional Rules on Qualifications Recognizance of Government Sponsored Institutions and Mass Organizations of Sending Group, Team and Individuals Abroad for Training* 1993 (PRC).

4	Guangdong province government	Provisionally examine and approve applications from Guangdong residents for travelling to Hong Kong or Macao for public affairs	Article 4 of the *Measures of Examination and Approval of Sending Individuals to be Employed in Hong Kong and Macao for the Long Term* 1991 (PRC).
5	Military unit with which applicant originally served.	Provisionally examine and approve applications for exiting China of demobilized military personnel who know confidential information and were discharged from active military services within 5 years	Article 2(3) of the *Explanation of Ministry of Public Security on Some Issues on Implementation of Law on the Control of Exit and Entry of Citizens and Its Detailed Rules for the Implementation* 1987 (PRC).
6	The CPC Committee of Peoples' Liberation Army	Provisionally examine and approve applications for exiting China from serving Army personnel	Article 2(1) of the *Explanation of Ministry of Public Security on Some Issues on Implementation of Law on the Control of Exit and Entry of Citizens and Its Detailed Rules for the Implementation* 1987 (PRC).
7	Courts and the Procuratorates	Withhold passports	Article 16 of the *Detailed Rules for the Implementation of the Law on the Control of Exit and Entry of Citizens (Amendment)* 1994 (PRC).
8	The host or employing organization	Accept applications of Chinese citizens who are permanent residents of a foreign country from returning to China for employment	Article 11 of the *Detailed Rules for he Implementation of the Law on the Control of Exit and Entry of Citizens (Amendment)* 1994 (PRC).
9	Working units sending Chinese citizens abroad for public affairs	Power to apply to the MPS or the local foreign affairs department for an exit certificate on behalf of their employees	Article 6 of the *Law on the Control of Exit and Entry of Citizens* 1985 (PRC).

Appendix Ten (*cont.*)

No.	Responsible departments	Functions	Sources
10	United Front Work Department under the Central Committee of the PRC.	Provisionally examine and approve applications lodged abroad by Taiwanese residents for travelling to China for permanent residence	Article 7 the *Circular of Some Matters on Implementation of Measures on the Control over Chinese Citizens Travelling to or from the Region of Taiwan* 1992 (PRC).

Appendix Eleven

Merits Review of Administrative Decisions Concerned the Imposition of Penalties on Exit and Entry

No.	Administrative penalties	Sources of administrative penalties	Remedies	Sources of remedies
1	Detention	Article 29(1) of the *Law on the Control of Exit and Entry of Aliens* 1985 (PRC). Article 40, 41, 42 and 48 of the *Detailed Rules of the Implementation o Law on the Control of Exit and Entry of Aliens (Amendment)* 1994 (PRC).	An affected individual may, within 15 days of receiving the notification, appeal to the - public security department at the next highest level, which shall make the final decision; or institute proceedings in the local Court.	Article 29(2) of the *Law on the Control of Exit and Entry of Aliens* 1985 (PRC). Article 50 of the *Detailed Rules of the Implementation of Law on the Control of Exit and Entry of Aliens* 1985 (PRC).
		Article 14 the *Law on the Control of Exit and Entry of Citizens* 1985 (PRC). Article 23, 24 and 25 of the *Detailed Rules of the Implementation o Law on the Control of Exit and Entry of Citizens (Amendment)* 1994 (PRC).	As above	Article 15 of the *Law on the Control of Exit and Entry of Citizens* 1985 (PRC).
		Articles 33 to 36 of the *Measures on the Control over Chinese Citizens Travelling to or from the Region of Taiwan* 1992 (PRC).	As above	Article 39 of the *Measures on the Control over Chinese Citizens Travelling to*

Appendix Eleven (*cont.*)

No.	Administrative penalties	Sources of administrative penalties	Remedies	Sources of remedies
				or from the Region of Taiwan 1992 (PRC).
		Articles 26, 27 and 28 of the *Provisional Measures on the Control over Chinese Citizens Travelling for Private Affairs to or from the Regions of Hong Kong or Macao 1986 (PRC).*	N/A	N/A
2	Fine	Article 29 of the *Law on the Control of Exit and Entry of Aliens* 1985 (PRC). Article 40 to 47 of the *Detailed Rules of the Implementation o Law on the Control of Exit and Entry of Aliens (Amendment)* 1994 (PRC).	An affected individual may within 15 days of receiving the notification, appeal to the public security department at the next highest level, which shall make the final decision; or institute proceedings in the Local Court.	Article 29(2) of the *Law on the Control of Exit and Entry of Aliens* 1985 (PRC). Article 50 of the *Detailed Rules of the Implementation of Law on the Control of Exit and Entry of Aliens* 1985 (PRC).
		Articles 33 to 38 of the *Measures on the Control over Chinese Citizens Travelling to or from the Region of Taiwan* 1992 (PRC).	As above	Article 39 of the *Measures on the Control over Chinese Citizens Travelling to or from the Region of Taiwan* 1992 (PRC).

3	Order to leave the country within a specified time, or deportation.	Article 30 of the *Law on the Control of Exit and Entry of Aliens* 1985 (PRC). Article 40, 42, 43, 44, 46 to 47 of the *Detailed Rules of the Implementation o Law on the Control of Exit and Entry of Aliens (Amendment)* 1994 (PRC).	N/A	N/A
		Article 40 of the *Measures on the Control over Chinese Citizens Travelling to or from the Region of Taiwan* 1992 (PRC).	N/A	N/A
4	Shorten period of residence.	As above	As above	As above
5	Disciplinary warning	Articles 37 and 38 the *Measures on the Control over Chinese Citizens Travelling to or from the Region of Taiwan* 1992 (PRC).	An affected individual may, within 15 days of receiving the notification, appeal to the public security department at the next highest level, which shall make the final decision; or institute proceedings in the local Court.	Article 39 of the *Measures on the Control over Chinese Citizens Travelling to or from the Region of Taiwan* 1992 (PRC).
		Article 14 the *Law on the Control of Exit and Entry of Citizens* 1985 (PRC). Article 23 and 25 of the *Detailed Rules of the Implementation of Law on the Control of Exit and Entry of Citizens (Amendment)* 1994 (PRC).	N/A	N/A
		Article 29 of the *Law on the Control of Exit and Entry of Aliens* 1985 (PRC).		

Appendix Eleven (*cont.*)

No.	Administrative penalties	Sources of administrative penalties	Remedies	Sources of remedies
		Article 42, 43, 45 and 46 of the *Detailed Rules of the Implementation o Law on the Control of Exit and Entry of Aliens (Amendment)* 1994 (PRC).	N/A	N/A
		Articles 26 and 28 *Provisional Measures on the Control over Chinese Citizens Travelling for Private Affairs to or from the Regions of Hong Kong or Macao* 1986 (PRC).	N/A	N/A
6	Confiscation of forged certificates	Article 23 of the *Detailed* the *Rules for the Implementation of Law on the Control of Exit and Entry of Citizens (Amendment)* 1994 (PRC).	N/A	N/A
		Article 47 of the *Detailed* the *Rules for the Implementation of Law on the Control of Exit and Entry of Aliens (Amendment)* 1994 (PRC).	N/A	N/A
		Article 26 of the *Provisional Measures on the Control over Chinese Citizens Travelling for Private Affairs to or from the Regions of Hong Kong or Macao* 1986 (PRC).	N/A	N/A

Appendix Twelve
Merits Review of Administrative Decisions Concerned the Processing of Applications for Exit and Entry

No.	Administrative decisions	Sources of administrative authority	Remedies	Sources of remedies
1	Refusal to permit exit China or refusal to issue a passport	Article 23 of the *Law on the Control of Exit and Entry of Aliens* 1985 (PRC).	N/A	N/A
		Article 8 of the *Law on the Control of Exit and Entry of Citizens* 1985 (PRC).	N/A	N/A
		Article 12 the *Measures on the Control over Chinese Citizens Travelling to or from the Region of Taiwan* 1992 (PRC).	N/A	N/A
		Article 13 of the *Provisional Measures on the Control over Chinese Citizens Travelling for Private Affairs to or from the Regions of Hong Kong or Macao* 1986 (PRC).	N/A	N/A
		Article 6(1) of the *Operational Norms of Application, Examination and Approval of Exiting Abroad and Passport For Private Affairs of Citizens* 1996 (PRC).	Affected individuals have the right to query the decision, and the relevant department must respond.	Article 6(2) of the *Operational Norms of Application, Examination and Approval of Exiting Abroad and Passport For Private Affairs of Citizens* 1996 (PRC).

Appendix Twelve (*cont.*)

No.	Administrative decisions	Sources of administrative authority	Remedies	Sources of remedies
2	Failure to determine an application within prescribed time	Article 6(1) of the *Operational Norms of Application, Examination and Approval of Exiting Abroad and Passport For Private Affairs of Citizens* 1996 (PRC).	As above	As above
3	Withhold exiting China	Article 24 of the *Law on the Control of Exit and Entry of Aliens* 1985 (PRC).	N/A	N/A
		Article 9 the *Law on the Control of Exit and Entry of Citizens* 1985 (PRC).	N/A	N/A
		Article 24 the *Measures on the Control over Chinese Citizens Travelling to or from the Region of Taiwan* 1992 (PRC).	N/A	N/A
		Article 20 of the *Provisional Measures on the Control over Chinese Citizens Travelling for Private Affairs to or from the Regions of Hong Kong or Macao* 1986 (PRC).	N/A	N/A
4	Refusal to permit exit to the HKSAR, MSAR or Taiwan, or refusal to issue travel	Articles 6, 7, 10 and 12 of the *Measures on the Control over Chinese Citizens Travelling to or from the Region of Taiwan* 1992 (PRC). destinations documents for those	N/A	N/A

		Articles 11 and 13 of the *Provisional Measures on the Control over Chinese Citizens Travelling for Private Affairs to or from the Regions of Hong Kong or Macao* 1986 (PRC).	N/A	N/A
5	Refusal to permit Chinese nationals to return for permanent residence	Article 10 the *Law on the Control of Exit and Entry of Citizens* 1985 (PRC).	N/A	N/A
		Article 10 the *Detailed Rules of the Implementation o Law on the Control of Exit and Entry of Citizens (Amendment)* 1994 (PRC).		
		Article 20 the *Measures on the Control over Chinese Citizens Travelling to or from the Region of Taiwan* 1992 (PRC).	N/A	N/A
		Article 18 the *Provisional Measures on the Control over Chinese Citizens Travelling for Private Affairs to or from the Regions of Hong Kong or Macao 1986 (PRC).*	N/A	N/A
6	Refusal to permit overseas Chinese to return for employment	Article 11 of the *Detailed Rules for the Implementation of Law on the Control of Exit and Entry of Citizens (Amendment)* 1994 (PRC).	N/A	N/A
7	Refusal to register a permanent household	Article 11 of the *Law on the Control of Exit and Entry of Citizens* 1985 (PRC).	N/A	N/A

Appendix Twelve (*cont.*)

No.	Administrative decisions	Sources of administrative authority	Remedies	Sources of remedies
		Article 12 of the *Detailed Rules for the Implementation of Law on the Control of Exit and Entry of Citizens (Amendment)* 1994 (PRC).		
		Article 20 the *Measures on the Control over Chinese Citizens Travelling to or from the Region of Taiwan* 1992 (PRC).	N/A	N/A
		Article 18 the *Provisional Measures on the Control over Chinese Citizens Travelling for Private Affairs to or from the Regions of Hong Kong or Macao* 1986 (PRC).	N/A	N/A
8	Refusal to extend the term of a passport or other travel documents	Article 17 of the *Detailed Rules for the Implementation of Law on the Control of Exit and Entry of Citizens (Amendment)* 1994 (PRC).	N/A	N/A
		Article 22 the *Provisional Measures on the Control over Chinese Citizens Travelling for Private Affairs to or from the Regions of Hong Kong or Macao* 1986 (PRC).	N/A	N/A
9	Refusal to re-issue/ replace a passport or other travel documents	Article 29 the *Measures on the Control over Chinese Citizens Travelling to or from the Region of Taiwan* 1992 (PRC).	N/A	N/A

		Article 24 the *Provisional Measures on the Control over Chinese Citizens Travelling for Private Affairs to or from the Regions of Hong Kong or Macao* 1986 (PRC).	N/A	N/A
		Article 21 of the *Detailed Rules for the Implementation of Law on the Control of Exit and Entry of Citizens (Amendment)* 1994 (PRC).	N/A	N/A
10	Revocation /invalidation of passports	Articles 16 and 22 of the *Detailed Rules for the Implementation of Law on the Control of Exit and Entry of Citizens (Amendment)* 1994 (PRC).	N/A	N/A
		Articles 31 and 32 the *Measures on the Control over Chinese Citizens Travelling to or from the Region of Taiwan* 1992 (PRC).	N/A	N/A
		Article 25 the *Provisional Measures on the Control over Chinese Citizens Travelling for Private Affairs to or from the Regions of Hong Kong or Macao* 1986 (PRC).	N/A	N/A

Bibliography One
Bibliography in Chinese

1. "The Pros and Cons of Young Children Studying Abroad" (*Zhaoning Liuxuesheng Xianxiang Toushi*), *Chinese Scholars Abroad* (*Shengzhou Xueren*) No. 6 (2001), www.chisa.edu.cn (April 2003), 166
2. Bao, Dazhang, *The Explanation of Regulations and Proced.ures Governing Exit and Entry in Taiwan* (*Taiwan Diqu Chujing Rujing Faling Shouxu Xiangjie*) (Taibei, China: 1957)
3. Bureau of Exit and Entry Administration, the Ministry of Public Security, *The Collection of Laws and Regulations Governing Exit and Entry of the PRC* (*Zhonghua Renmin Gongheguo Churu Jing Guanli Fagui Huibian*) (Beijing: the Publishing House of Qunzhong, 1987)
4. Bureau of Party, Government Foreign Affairs Carders under Department of Personal of Central Committee of Chinese Communist Party, *The Collection of Popular Official Documents and Letters, Regulations and Laws Governing Examination and Administration of Exiting Abroad* (*Chuguo(jing) Shenpi Ji Guanli Gongzuo Changyong Wenjian Fagui Xuanbian*), *Internal Publication* (*Neibu Faxing*) (Beijing: the Publishing House of Dangjian Duwu, 1994)
5. Cao, Dejin and Xu, Qun, "The Reasons of Overstay of Overseas Students and Its Countermeasures (*Chuguo Liuxue Renyuan Zhiwai Bugui De Yuanyin Ji Duice*)", *Journal of the Administration of Hospital of People's Liberation Army* (*Jiefangjun Yiyuan Guanli Zazhi*), No. 8 (3) (1998), 256–258
6. Cao, Shuji, *The History of Chinese Migration: the Period of the Qing Dynasty and the Public of China* (*Zhongguo Yimin Shi: Qing Minguo Shiqi*) (Fuzhou, China: the Publishing House of Fujian Renmin, 1997)
7. Cen, Dejian, *Research on Problems of Illegal Immigration* (*Feifa Yimin Xianxiang de Falv Sikao*), the Book of LLM, The University of People, China, Beijing: 2002

8. Chen, Haoshen editor, *The Collection of Historical Materials on Overseas Labour Exiting Abroad* (*Huagong Chuguo Siliao Hvbian*), The Publishing House of China, Beijing: 1985
9. Chen, Tieyuan, *Overseas Study without intermediary Agencies: the interview to Visa Officer of Foreign Countries in China* (*Piekai Zhongjie Qu Liuxue: Zhuhua Qianzheng Guan Fangtan*), the Publishing House of Writer, Beijing: 2002
10. Chen, Yuetao, *The Writing on the Documents of the Exit and Entry Administration of Public Security Organs* (*Gongan Churujing Guanli Wenshu Xiezuo*), *Series of the Applicable Writing of Public Security Organs* (*Gongan Yingyong Xiezuo Congshu*), Interior Published within Public Security Organs (*Gongan Jiguan Neibu Faxing*) (Beijing: the Publishing House of China University of People's Public Security, 1999)
11. Committee of Exit and Entry Administration under Chinese Association of Police, editor, *The Collection of Papers on the Control of Exit and Entry* (*III*) (*Churujing Guanli Lunwenxuan* (*san*)), Interior Published within Public Security Organs (*Gongan Jiguan Neibu Faxing*) (Beijing: the Publishing House of Qunzhong, 2001)
12. Committee of Exit and Entry Administration under Chinese Association of Police, editor, *The Collection of Papers on the Control of Exit and Entry* (*II*), (*Churujing Guanli Lunwenxuan* (*er*)), Interior Published within Public Security Organs (Gongan Jiguan Neibu Faxing) (Beijing: the Publishing House of Qunzhong, 1999)
13. Dai, Chaowu, *Immigration Policy in the USA and Emigration in Asia* (*Meiguo Yimin Zhengce Yu Yazhou Yimin*) (Beijing: the Publishing House of Zhongguo Social Science, 1999)
14. Department of Exit and Entry Administration, Beijing Public Security Bureau, *the Kit of Eixt and Entry* (*Churujing Xuzhi*) (Beijing: the Publishing House of Renshi, 2000)
15. Department of Exit and Entry Administration, Jilin Public Security Bureau, editor, *The Handbook of Exit and Entry Administration* (*Churu Jing Guanli Zhishi Shouce*) (Changchun: the Publishing House of Jilin Renmin, 1988)
16. Department of Exit and Entry under Ministry of Public Security & Department of Border Security Checking and Administration, "Great Change Over Last 50 years: the Analysis of the Data of Exit and Entry of Individuals (*Fenyun Bianhuan Wushi Nian: Cong Churujing Renyuan Tongji Shuju Kan Jianguo Yilai De Jubian*)", *People's Public Security* (*Renmin Gongan*), No. 22 (1999)
17. Department of Legal and Policy Research of the Ministry of Public Security, China, *The Collection of Laws and Regulations regarding Public Security: 1950–1979* (*Gongan Fagun Huibian:1950–1979*) (Beijing: Qunzhong Publishing House, 1980)
18. Department of Politics under the Ministry of Public Security, *Frontier Defence and Exit and Entry Administration, the Series of Basic Textbook of People's Police Operation*: (*Bianfang Yu Churu Jing Guanli, Renmin Jingcha Gongan Yewu Jichu Jiaochai*), examined by Committee of Textbook Editing and Examination of the Ministry of Public Security, Internal Publication within Public Security Organs (*Gongan Jiguan Neibu Faxing*) (Beijing: the Publishing House of Qunzhong, 1999)
19. Dictionary Department, institute of Linguistics, Chinese Academy of Social Sciences, *The Contemporary Chinese Dictionary* (*Chinese-English edition*) (*Xiandai Hanyu Cidian*) (Beijing: Foreign Language Teaching and Research Press, 2002)
20. Division of Human Resource, the Ministry of Agriculture, China, *The Outline of Examination and Administration of Going Abroad* (*Chuguojing Renyuan Shencha Guanli Dagang*), Internal Publication (*Neibu Faxing*) (Beijing: the Publishing House of Chinese Agriculture, 1999)

21. Dong, Lihua and Ma, Yong, *The Legal Guide of Studying Abroad at One's Own Expense* (*Zifei Chuguo Liuxue Falv Zhinan*) (Beijing: Zhishi Publishing House, 2000)
22. Du, Chengming, "On Migration Freedom (*Lun Qianxi Ziyou Quan*)", *Wuhan University Journal* (*Social Sciences Edition*) Vol. 54 No. 4 July 2001, pages 406–410
23. Du, Minmin, editor, *The Returning of Overseas Chinese: the Series of Youth Patriotism Education* (*Qingnian Aiguo Zhuyi Jiaoyu Congshu: Wode Zhongguo Xin: Ji Zuwai He Guiguo Huaqiao*) (Changchun, China: the Publishing House of Jilin Technology and Science, 1985)
24. Duan, Chenrong, *The Study on Population Migration* (*Renkou Qianyi Yanjiu: Yuanli Yu Fangfa*) (Chongqing, China: Chongqing Publishing House, 1998)
25. Duan, Kuang, Translator, *The Living and Legal Guide to Aliens in Japan* (*Waiguoren Zai Reben de Shenghuo Yu Falv Zhinan*) (Shanghai: the Publishing House of Shanghai Kexue Puji, 1992)
26. Exit and Entry Administration under Jilin Province Public Security Department and Bureau of Border Security Check and Administration under Jilin Province Public Security Department, editor, *The Kit of Exit, Entry and Frontier Defense* (*Shiyong Churu Jing Bianfang Zhishi Daquan*) (Changchun, China: the Publishing House of Jilin Wenshi, 1994)
27. Fan, Qiangwei, *Human Rights Battle between China and the USA/EU* (*Lun Woguo Yu Meigou de Renquan Douzheng*) (Beijing: the Book of Doctor of Science Socialism, 2001)
28. Fu, Qing, *The Guide to Chinese Citizen Exit and Entry* (*Zhongguo Gongmin Churu Jing Quanshu*) (Beijing: The Publishing House of Qunzhong, 2000)
29. Hao, Jinmin, *international Human Rights Law* (*Guoji Renquan Fa*) (Jinan, China: the Publishing House of Shandong University, 1993)
30. Hao, Zaijing, *The Migration, Exit and Entry of Hong Kong* (*Yingxiong Mowen Chuchu: Xianggang De Yimin Yu Churu Jing*) (Beijing: the Publishing House of Renmin Wenxue, 1997)
31. Hong, Wanping, Dong, Lishan and Yu, Hang, *The Guide to Go Abroad for Private Purpose* (*Yinsi Chujing Zhinan*) (Changchun, China: the Publishing House of Jilin Renmin, 1992)
32. Hornby, A. S., *Oxford Advanced Learner's English-Chinese Dictionary* (*Niujin Gaoji Yinghan Shuangjie Cidian*), 4th edion (Hong Kong and Beijing: The Commercial Press and Oxford University Press, 1997)
33. Information Office of the State Council of The People's Republic of China, *Human Rights in China: 1991, White Paper of Human Rights* (*English Versions*) (Beijing: 1991)
34. Information Office of the State Council of The People's Republic of China, *Human Rights in China, 2000, White Paper of Human Rights* (*English Versions*) (Beijing: 2000)
35. Information Office of the State Council of The People's Republic of China, "Fifty Years of Progress in China's Human Rights (June 2000) (English Versions)", http://www.fmprc.gov.cn/eng/32282.html (accessed 20/05/2003)
36. Jiang, Zemin, the President of the People's Republic of China, "Build a Well-off Society in an All-Round Way and Create a New Situation in Building Socialism with Chinese Characteristics: Report page 16th China Communist Party Congress (8/11/2002) (English Versions)", http://www.fmprc.gov.cn/eng/37815.html (accessed 19/07/2003)

37. Jin, Liangjun, editor, *The Guide to Visa, Exit and Entry in the World* (*Shijie Geguo Qianzheng Yu Churu Jing Zhinan*) (Beijing: the Publishing House of Chinese Gongshang Lianhe, 1999)
38. Journalist of *the Journal of Human Rights*, "Correct Appliance of the Law and Impartial Trial under the Law: Strengthen the Safeguard of Human Rights in the Realm of Justice in a Down-to-earth Way: the Interview of the Comrade Xiao, Yang, the President of Supreme People's Court (Zunque Shiyong Falv Yifa Gongzheng Caipan Qieshi Jiaqiang Sifa Lingyu De Renquan Baozhang: Fang Zuigao Renming Fayuan Yuanzhang Shouxi Dafaguan Xiao Yang Tongzhi)", *the Journal of Human Right*, No. 6 [2002], 3–8
39. Lan, Bo, *The Questions and Answers to Exit and Entry Administration in China, the Series of Popularizing Legal Knowledge in Minor Nationality Area* (*Minzu Diqu Puji Falv Zhishi Congshu: Woguo Churu Jing Guanli Wenda*) (Beijing: the Publishing House of Minzu, 1987)
40. Legal System Working Committee, the National People's Congress Standing Committee, China, *The Volume of Administration Law, Compilation of Laws, Regulations, Rules and Judicatory Explanation of the PRC* (*Zhonghua Renmin Gongheguo Falv Xingzhengfagui Guizhang Sifa Jiesi Feilei Huibian Xingzhengfajuan*) (Beijing: the Publishing House of Beijing University, 1998)
41. Li, Changfu, *The History of Chinese Colonization* (*Zhongguo Zhimin Shi*) (Shanghai: The Publishing House of Shangwu, 1937)
42. Li, Changfu, *The History of Overseas Chinese in South East Asia* (*Nanyang Huaqiao Shi*) (Shanghai: The Publishing House of Shangwu, 1937)
43. Li, Debing, *The History of Modern Chinese Emigration* (*Jindai Zhongguo Yimin Shiyao*) (Harbing, China, the Publishing House of Harbing, 1994)
44. Li, Hengmei, editor, *The Collection of the Papers Regarding Migration History* (*Yimin Shi Lunji*) (Jinan, China: Qilu Publishing House (*Qilu Shushe*), 1998)
45. Li, Qirong, *Migrants and Modern USA* (*Yimin Yu Jindai Meiguo*) (Beijing: the Publishing House of Chinese Huaqiao, 1991)
46. Li, Shaozhong, *Research of Modern Chinese Human Rights Issues* (*Dangdai Zhongguo Renquan Wenti Yanjiu*), the thesis of Doctor of the History, Hunan Normal University, Changsha, China: 1999
47. Li, Wenhui, *Review of the Control of the Exit and Entry: the Collection of Papers on the Control of Exit and Entry of Shanghai Public Security Organs* (*Churujing Guanli Zongheng: Shanghai Gongan Churujing Guanli Lunwenji*), internal publication (*Neibu Faxing*) (Beijing: the Publishing House of Police education, 1998)
48. Liang, Maoxin, *The Research on Immigration Policy in the USA* (*Meguo Yimin Zhengce Yanjiu*) (Changchun, China: The Publishing House of Dongbei Normal University, 1996)
49. Liu, Jixuan and Su, Shi, *The History of Chinese Cololizaiton in South East Asia* (*Zhonghua Minzu Tuozhi Nanyang Shi*) (Shanghai: Shanghai Shudian, 1937, reprint in 1990)
50. Liu, Shengping, Xia, Yong, editor, *Human Rights and the World* (*Renquan Yu Shijie*) (Beijing: the Publishing House of People's Courts, 1996)
51. Lu, Jing, *The Study on the Freedom of Migration* (*Lun Qianxi Ziyou*), the thesis of LLM (Beijing: The University of People, China, 2002)
52. Mao, Fengping, editor, *The Explanation of the Law and Regulations Governing Exit and Entry and the Collections of Related Regulations* (*Chujing Rujing Falv Fagui Sijie*

Yu Xiangying Fagui Zhaibian) (Changchun, China: the Publishing House of Jilin Renmin, 1994)
53. Mao, Qixiong, *The Encyclopedia of Overseas Chinese and Foreign Chinese: the Volume of Laws, Regulations and Policies* (*Huaqiao Huaren Baike Quanshu: Falv Tiaoli Zhengce Juan*) (Beijing: the Publishing House of Overseas Chinese of China, 2000)
54. Meng, Peiyuan, "Relationship Between Man and Nature in Traditional Human Rights Concepts of China and West", *the Journal of Human Rights*, No. 1 [2003] http://www.humanrights-china.org/zt/03111201/200312003129103111.htm (accessed 26/02/2004)
55. Mo, Qibo and Zhu, Qiliang, *the Handbook of Chinese Citizen's Going Abroad for Private Purpose* (*Zhongguo Gongmin Yinsi Chuguo Shouce*) (Nanling, China: the Publishing House of Guangxi Renmin, 1997)
56. Mo, Qibo, editor, *The Administration of Citizen's Exit and Entry* (*Gongmin Churu Jing Guanli*) (Nanling, China: the Publishing House of Giuangxi Minzu, 1997)
57. Overseas Chinese Affairs Commission, the Republic of China, *The Republic of China, Overseas Chinese Affairs Statistics* (Taipei, Taiwan: 1994)
58. Pan, Ling, *The History of Chinese Migration* (*Yanhuang Zisun – Huaren Yimin Shi*) (Shanghai: The Publishing House of Sanlian Book Store, Shanghai Branch, 1993)
59. Shen, Chen, "Language and Culture: Two Goals of Foreign Language Teaching in China, Lessons from History and Perspectives for the future", *Australia Review of Applied Linguistic* 12 / 2, 1989, 51.
60. Su, Huiyu and Li, Yiran, editor, *The Guide to Exit and Entry for Private Purpose* (*Yisi Churu Jing Bidu*) (Shanghai: The Publishing House of Wenhui, 1998)
61. Sun, Longji, *The Deep Structure of Chinese Culture* (Guiling, China: The Publishing House of Guangxi Normal University, 2004)
62. the Ministry of Public Security of the the PRC, *The Control of Country Board and Administration of Exit and Entry* (*Bianfang Yu Churujing Guanli*) (Beijing: the Publishing House of the University of People's Public Security, 1999)
63. Wan, Zhenshan, editor, *The General Updated Guide of the Exit and Entry of individuals* (*Zuixin Renyuan Churu Jing Quanshu*) (Beijing: the Publishing House of Renshi, 2002)
64. Wang, Guoliang and Zhu, Lin, *The Administration on Exit and Entry, one of Planning Textbooks of Higher education of People's Police* (*Renmin Jingcha Gaodeng Jiaoyu Guihua Jiaocha: Churujing Guanlixue*), Interior Published within Public Security Organs (*Gongan Jiguan Neibu Faxing*) (Beijing: the Publishing House of China University of People's Public Security, 2002)
65. Wen, Xongfei, *The History of Overseas Chinese in South East Asia* (*Nanyang Huaqiao Tongshi*) (Shnaghai, the Publishing House of Shangwu, 1943)
66. Wong, Li, "Chinese Migration Legislation and International Norms (*Zhongguo Yiming Lifa Yu Guoji Guanli*)", *Journal of Hangzhou University*, Vol. 26 No. 2 June 1996, 25–29
67. Wong, Li, *International Immigration Law and the Practices* (*Guoji Yiminfa Lilun Yu Shijian*) (Beijing: the Publishing House of Law, 2001)
68. Xiang, Dang, *The Guide to the Law of Exit and Entry in China and Foreign Countries,* (*Zhongwai Churujing Falv Zhinan*) (Beijing: the Publishing House of China University of People's Public Security, 1998)
69. Xie, Xiuying, "Economic Analysis on the Upsurge of Studying Abroad at One's Own

Expense and its Younger Trend" (*Zifei Chuguo Liuxue Re Jiqi Dilinghua Qushi De Jingjixue Fenxi*), *Journal of Shanxi Youth Managerial Cadres Institution* (Shanxi Qingnian Guanli Ganbu Xueyuan Xuebao), Vol. 16 No. 1 of 2003, 24–26.

70. Xu, Jiali, editor, *The Guide to Going Abroad Consultation* (*Chuguo Zixun Daquan*) (Beijing: the Publishing House of Kexue Puji, 1992)
71. Xu, Jongqi, *The Comparative Study between China and South Korean regarding Aliens Exit and Entry and Legal Status* (*Waiguoren Churu Jing Jiqi Falv Diwei De Hanzhong Falv Falv Bijiao*), the thesis of LLM, Beijing: China Institute of Foreign Relationship, 2001
72. Yan, Bei, *The Migration of Chinese Population in the New Period* (*Xin Shiqi Zhongguo Renkou Qianyi*) (Changsha, China: the Publishing House of Hunan Education, 1999)
73. Yang, Fajing, editor, *The Introduction to Exit Abroad* (*Chuguo Zhishi Gailan*) (Beijing: the Publishing House of Science Popularization, 1990)
74. Yang, Guozhen, *the China's Coastal Society and Emigration Overseas in Ming Dynasty and Qing Dynasty* (*Mingqing Zhongguo Yanhai Shehui Yu Haiwai Yimin*) (Beijing: the Publishing House of Higher Education, 1997)
75. Yang, Yuguan, *United Nations Human Rights Treaty Bodies and the Their Comments (Lianheguo Renquan Gongyue Jigou Yu Jingdian Yaoyi)* (Beijing: the Publishing House of China University of People's Public Security, 2004)
76. Yang, Yuguan, *Human Rights Law: Internatonal Convenant on Civil and Political Eights* (Beijing: the Publishing House of China University of People's Public Security, 2003)
77. Yi, Songgong, "Why the Student in Middles Schools and Higher Educational Institutions Would Like to Go Abroad (*Dazhong Xuesheng Weihe Yao Chuguo*)", *Society* (*Shehui*), No. 6 of 1999, 9–11
78. Yin, Xiaohu and Lin, Yan, "The Change of the Chinese Legal Stipulations Regarding to the Freedom of Movement and the Thoughts on the Change (*Wuoguo Falv Guanyu Qianxi Ziyou Guiding De Bianhua Jiqi Sikao*)", *The Journal of Jurisprudence*, No. 6 [2001], 10–14
79. Yu, Huaying and Gong, Yu, *The Legal Study on Exit, Entry and international Trade* (*Churu Jing Yu Guoji Jingmao Falv Wenti Yanjiu*) (Chongqing, China: the Publishing House of Xinan Normal University, 1997)
80. Yu, Shutong and Wen, Jia editor, *A New Chinese-English Law Dictionary* (*Xin Hanying Faxue Cidian*) (Beijing: the Publishing House of Law, 1998)
81. Zeng, peiyan, the Commission of Planning and Reform, China, *Report on the Implementation of the 2001 Plan for National Economic and Social Development and on the Draft Plan for National Economic and Social Development* (12/03/2002) (*English Versions*)
82. Zeng, Shaocong, *Migration in South East Asia: Migration to Taiwan and Filliping by Sea in Ming Dynasty and Qing Dynasty, the Series of Sea and China* (*Dongyang Hanglu Yimin: Mingqing Haiyang Yimin Taiwan Yu Feilvbing De Bijiao Yanjiu, Haiyang Yu Zhongguo Congshu*) (Nanchang, China: the Publishing House of Jiangxi Gaoxiao, 1998)
83. Zhang, Fan, editor, *The Update Guide to the People Going Abroad* (*Zuixin Chuguo Renyuan Zhinan*) (Hangzhou, China: the Publishing House of Zejiang Wenyi, 1991)
84. Zhang, Feng and Ye, Youshen, "Exit and Entry Administration According to Laws and

Crackdown of Illegal Migration (Shilun Yifa Guanli *Churujing Xingwei Yu Daji Feifa Yimin Huodong*)", *Journal of Fujian Public Security College* (*Fujian Gongan Gaodeng Zhuanke Xuexiao Xuebao*), No. 2 (2003), 36–39 (38)

85. Zhang, Xiuming, "The Return of Overseas Students Since Reform and Opening-up and Their Place: the Analysis of the Questionnaire Survey of Returned Overseas Students (*Gaige Kaifang Yilai Liuxuesheng De Huigui Ji Chujing: Genju Guiguo Liuxusheng Wenjuan DiaoCha De Fenxi*)", *Journal of Research of the History of Overseas Chinese and Foreign Chinese* (Huaqiao Huaren Lishi Ynajiu), No.2 (1999), 50–62
86. Zhang, Yonghe, *Origin of Rights: a Research Report on the Freedom of Human's Migration* (*Quanli de Youlai: Renlei Qianyi Ziyou de Yanjiu Baogao*) (Beijing: the Publishing House of Jiancha, 2001)
87. Zhang, Youxue, "An analysis of the Phoenomeon of Carving out of the Chinese Students Who Have Returned from Overseas Study" (Chinese version), *Chinese Scholars Abroad*, No. 4 (2001), 134, www.chisa.edu.cn (accessed 26/04/2003)
88. Zhao, Yufei, Question Why the Application Filed by Law-firm for Exit and Entry Intermediary Agency Shall not be Accepted (*Ziyi Yisi Churujing Zhongjie Huodong Guanli Banfa: Yimin Yewu Zenneng Dui Lvshi Shiwusuo Guanshang Damen*), *Chinese Lawer* (*Zhongguo Lvshi*), No. 2 [2002], 71–72
89. Zhu, Guohong, *Overseas Chinese: a History Research on international Migration* (*Zhongguo De Haiwai Yimin – Yixiang Guoji Qianyi De Lishi Yanjiu*) (Shanghai: the Publishing House of Fudan University, 1994)
90. Zou, Ruihan, *The Guide of Exit and Entry* (*Churu Jing Xuzhi*) (Xiamen, China: the Publishing House of Lujiang, 1990)

Bibliography Two

Bibliography in English

1. "America Retreats from Human Rights Motion against China", *The Times*, 16 March 1998, 13
2. "Bottom line for U.S. and China: no Kowtows on Human Rights" , *The New York Times,* 27 March 1994
3. "Clinton U-turn as He Defends links with China", *The Daily Telegraphy*, New York: 25 October 1997,11
4. "Cook takes on global 'evil'", *The Guardian,* 18 July 1997, London, 5
5. "Facts and Figures on International Migration", *Migration Policy Issues,* No. 2, March 2003, International Organization for Migration, Geneva, Switzerland, 1
6. "Human Rights Watch World Report 2003: Asia: China and Tibet", http://nadaily.com/cgi-bin/nph-proxyb.cgi/010000A/http/hrw.org/wr2 (accessed 5/07/2003)
7. "Manual of Service of the Immigration Office National Police Agency of the Ministry of Interior of the Republic of China 2002", http://www.immigration.gov.tw (accessed 26/11/2003)
8. "Report of Improving Service Quality of The Immigration Office National Police Agency of the Ministry of Interior of the Republic of China 2001", http://www.immigration.gov.tw (accessed 26/11/2003)
9. Akehurst, Michael, *A Modern Introduction to International Law*, 6th edition (London: Harper Collins Academic, 1987)
10. Amerasinghe, C. F., *Local Remed.ies in International Law* (Cambridge, the UK: Grotius Publication Ltd., 1990)
11. Andreassen, Bard-anders and Swinchart editor, Theresa, *Human Rights in Developing Countries Yearbook 1992* (Oslo, Norway: Nordic Human Rights Publications and the Norwegian Institute of Human Rights, 1993)

12. Andreassen, Bard-anders and Swinehart, Theresa editor, Human Rights institutes in Norway, Denmark, the Netherlands, Finland and Swed.en (Compile), *Human Right in Developing Countries Yearbook 1990*, (Kehl, Strasbourg and Arlington: N. P. Engel Publisher, 1991)
13. Aristide Zolberg R., "International Migration in Political Perspective," in Mary M. Kritz, Charles B. Keely, and Silvano M. Tomasi, editor., *Global Trends in Migration: Theory and Research in International Population Movements* (New York: Centre for Migration Studies, 1980)
14. Australian Foreign Affairs and Foreign Trade Ministry, "People's Republic of China: Australia-China Bilateral Relationship", http://www.dfat.gov.au/geo/china/cb_bilateral.html (accessed 22/10/2003)
15. Australian Foreign Affairs and Foreign Trade Ministry, *People's Republic of China: Country Information*, http://www.dfat.gov.au/geo/china/cb_background.html (accessed 22/10/2003)
16. Australian Human Rights Center, "Human Rights in Taiwan: Issues for the 21st Century," http://www.ahrcentre.org/reports/Human_Rights_in_Taiwan.htm (accessed 04/09/2003)
17. Baehr, Peter R. et al. editor, *Human Rights: Chinese and Dutch Perspectives* (the Hague, the Netherlands: Kluwer Law international, 1996)
18. Baehr, Peter, Hey, Hilde, Smith Jacqueline and Swinehart, Theresa editor, *Human Right in Developing Countries 1994 Yearbook* (Kehl, Strasbourg and Arlington: N. P. Engel Publisher, 1995)
19. Baehr, Peter, Sadiwa, Lalaine and Smith Jacqueline editor, *Human Right in Developing Countries 1996 Yearbook* (the Hague, the Netherlands: Kluwer Law international, 1996)
20. Baubock, Rainer, *Transnational Citizenship: Membership and Rights in International Migration,* (Cheltenham, the UK and Northampton, the USA: Edward Elgar, 1994)
21. *Bellagio IV Population Conference Ulvshale Denmark: Working Papers of the Rockefeller Foundation* (New York: The Rockefeller Foundation, 1977)
22. Bentham, Jeremy, *Anarchical Fallacies*, Blackstone, *Volume 1,* 369–370
23. Beresford, Melanie and Phong, Dang, *Economic Transition in Vietnam: Trade and Aid in the Demise of a Centrally Planned. Economy* (Cheltenham, the UK and Northampton, the USA: Edward Elgar Publishing Ltd., 2000)
24. Bevan, Vaughan, *The Development of British Immigration Law* (Beckenham, the UK: Croom Helm, 1986)
25. Bhagwati, Jagdish N. and Wilson editor, John Douglas, *Income Taxation and International Mobility* (Massachusetts, the USA: the Massachusetts institute of Technology, 1989)
26. Biao. Xiang, "Emigration from China: A Sending Country Perspective", *International Migration*, Volume 41, No. 3 (2003), 21–48, http://ejournals.ebsco.com/direct.asp?ArticleID=P8PYFRBJLETKMYT3KQ4F (accessed 01/10/2003)
27. Blischenko, I. P., vice-president of the Association of Soviet Lawyers, *Right to Leave and to Return to one's Country*, 1988, 1/21
28. BØ, Bente, Puntervold, *Immigration Control, Law and Morality: Visa Policies towards Visitors and Asylum Seekers, an Evaluation of the Norwegian Visa Policies within a Legal and Moral Frame of Reference* (Oslo: Unipub Forlag og Forfatterren, 2002)
29. Bobbio, N. *The Age of Rights* (Cambridge, the UK: Political Press, 1995)

30. Bossuyt, Marc J., *Guide to the "Travaux Preparatoires" of the international Covenant on Civil and Political Rights* (Dordrecht, the Netherlands: Martinus Nijhoff Publishers, 1987)
31. Bradley, Catherine, *What Do We Mean by Human Rights: Freed.om of Movement* (London, Franklin Watts, 2002)
32. Briggs, Vernon M., Jr., *Mass Immigration and the National interest*, 2nd (New York, the USA: M. E. Sharpe, inc., 1996)
33. Brohmer, Jurgen, *State Immunity and the Violation of Human Rights* (the Hague, the Netherlands: Martinus Nijhoff Publishers, 1997)
34. Brown, Judith M. & Foot, Rosemary *Migration: The Asian Experience* (London: The Macmillan Press Ltd., 1994)
35. Brownlie, Ian and Goodwin-Gill, Guy S. editor, *Basic Documents on Human Rights*, 4th edition (Oxford, the UK: Oxford University Press, 2002)
36. Brownlie, Ian, *Principles of Public international Law*, 4th edition (Oxford, the UK: Oxford University Press, 1990)
37. Buckland, W. W. and Mcnair, Arnold D., 2nd ed.ion revised. by Lawson, F. H., *Roman Law and Common Law: A Comparison in Outline* (Cambridge, Cambridge University Press, 1952)
38. Buggy, T. P., *Chinese Immigration and the Emergence of an Australian Image of China, 1848–1861*, the thesis of M.A., Macquarie University, Australia,1978
39. Bureau of Democracy, Human Rights and Labor, U.S. Department of State, *Vietnam Country Reportss on Human Rights Practices: 2002*, Washington D.C., 2003, 26 pages
40. Butler, W. E., *Soviet Law* (*2nd edition*) (London: Butterworth & Co. (Publishers) Ltd., 1988)
41. Caenegem, R. C. Van, *Legal History: A European Perspective* (London: the Hambledon Press, 1991)
42. Campbell, E., & Whitmore, H., *Freedom in Australia,* Sydney, 1966
43. Campbell, Persia Crawford, *Chinese Coolie Emigration to Countries within the British Empire China* (London: Frank Cass and Company Ltd., 1923)
44. Campbell, Tom D. editor, *The international Library of Essays in Law and Legal Theory Second Series: Legal Positivism*, Dartmouth Publishing Company Ltd. (Aldershot Hants England and Brookfield Vermont, the USA: Ashgate Publishing Limited., 1999)
45. Cantor, Norman F. and Werthman, Michaels editor, *The History of Popular Culture to 1815* (New York: the Macmillan Company and London: Collier-Macmillan Ltd. 1968)
46. Cardozo, Benjamin N., *The Growth of the Law*, Yale University Press, New Haven, the USA: 1966
47. Castles, Stephen. and Miller, Mark, *The Age of Migration*, 3rd edition (Basingstoke and New York, the USA, Palgarave Macmillan, 2003)
48. Chalidze, Valery, *To Defend These Rights* (New York: Random House, 1974, 98–99)
49. Charlesworth, Hilary, McCorquodale, Robert etc., editor, *The Australian Year Book of international Law* 2001 Volume 21, the Centre of International and Public Law, Faculty of Law, Australian National University, 2001
50. Chaturved.i, R. G., *Philosophy of Law* (Jaipur, India: the Institute for Research and Advanced. Studies, 1984)
51. Chen, Lifu, *The Confucian Way: A New and Systematic Study of 'the Four Books'*, translated. from the Chinese by Liu, Shih Shun (London: KPI Limited.), 1986

52. Chin, James K., "Reducing Irregular Migration from China". *International Migration*, Volume 41, No. 3 2003, 49–72, http://ejournals.ebsco.com/direct.asp?ArticleID=445TEX0XG8PNYXEQH1X5 (accessed 01/10/2003)
53. Choi, C. Y., *Chinese Migration and Settlement in Australia* (Sydney: Sydney University Press, 1975)
54. Coenelius, Wayne A., Philip L. Martine, and James F. Hollifield, editor, *Controlling Immigration: a Global Perspective* (Stanford, Calif.: Stanford University Press, 1994)
55. Commonwealth of Australia, *Australia's Third Report under the international Covenant on Civil and Political Rights: March 1987 – December 1995* (Barton, ACT, Australia: the Attorney-General's Department Robert Garran Office, 1998)
56. Congressional – Executive-Commission on China, "The People's Republic of China", http://www.cecc.gov/pages/virtualAcad/his/prc.php (accessed 04/01/2005)
57. Craig, P.P., *Administrative Law*, (fourth ed.ion) (London: Sweet & Maxwell Ltd., 1999)
58. Cranston, Maurice, *What are Human Rights?* (New York: Taplinger Publishing Co., Inc., 1973)
59. Crock, Mary and Saul, Ben, *Future Seekers: Refugees and the Law in Australia* (Sydney: The Federation Press, 2002)
60. D'amato, Anthony, *Jurisprudence: a Descriptive and Normative Analysis of Law* (Dordrecht, the Netherlands: Martinus Nijhoff Publishers, 1984)
61. Dalziel, Lianne, Minister of Immigration, New Zealand, *Options for Setting Enforceable Standards for Immigration Consultants*, 2001
62. David, Rene and Brierley, John E. C., *Major Legal System in the World Today: An Introduction to the Comparative Study of Law,* 3rd edtion (London: Stevens & Sons, 1985)
63. Davidson, Alastair, "Globalization and Citizenship", *ARENA Journal* No. 12 1998, 83/105
64. Davis, Michael C. editor, *Human Rights and Chinese Values: Legal, Philosophical, and Political Perspectives* (New York: Oxford University Press, 1995)
65. De, Sous La Direction editor, *The Limit of Human Rights in Comparative Constitutional Law* (Cowansville, Canada: Les edition Yvon Blais inc. 1986)
66. "Defining Migration Priorities in an Interdependent World", *Migration Policy Issues* No. 1, March 2003, Migration Policy and Research Programme, International Organization of Migration
67. Delmas-Marty, Mireille editor, *the European Convention for the Protection of Human Rights: internaitonal Protection Versus National Restrictions* (Dordrecht, the Netherlands: Martinus Nijhoff Publishers, 1992)
68. Democratic People's Republic of Korea, *Second Periodic Report of the Democratic People's Republic of Korea on its Implementation of the International Covenant on Civil and Political Rights 25th December 1999*, Human Rights Committee, CCPR/CPRK/2000/2 4 May 2000
69. Dennery, Etienne *Asia's Teemin Millions: and Its Problems for the West* (Port Washington: Kennikat Press, 1931)
70. Department of Justice, Equality and Law Reform, *International Comparative Study of Migration Legislation and Practice* (Dublin, Ireland, The Stationary Office, 2002), 128 pages
71. Department of Public Information, the United Nations, "The Universal Declaration of Human Rights: A Magna Carta for All Humanity", DPI/1937/A—December 1997, http:www.unhchr.ch/udhr/miscinfo/carta.htm (accessed 18–05–2003)

72. Dijk, P. van and Hoof, G. J. H. van, *Theory and Practice of the European Convention on Human Rights* (Deventer/Netherlands: Kluwer Law and Taxation Publishers), 1984
73. Dixon, Martin, *Textbook on international Law* (London: Blackstone Press Ltd., 1990)
74. Drake, Michael editor, *Population in indusfor Trial Implementationization* (London: Methuen & Co. Ltd., 1969)
75. Dukelow, Daphne A. *The Dictionary of Canadian Law* (Barrie, Ontario, Canada,A Carswell Publication, 1991)
76. Edwards, R. Randle, Henkin, Louis and Nathan, Andrew J., *Human Rights in Contemporary China* (New York: Columbia University Press, 1986)
77. Eide, Asbjorn and Mubanga-Chipoya, Chama, *Conscientious Objection to Military Service: Report prepared. in pursuance of resolutions 14 (XXIV) and 1982/30 of the Sub-Commission on Prevention of Discrimination and Protection of Minorities* (New York: the United Nations, 1985)
78. Eide, Asbjorn and Mubanga-Chipoya, Chama, *Conscientious Objection to Military Service*, report prepared in pursuance of resolutions 14 (XXXIV) and 1982/30 of the Sub-Commission on Prevention of Discrimination and Protection of Minorities, E.85.XIV.1 (New York: United Nations, 1985)
79. Ermacora, Felix, Nowak, Manfred. and Tretter, Hannes editor, *international Human Rights: Documents and introductory Notes* (Vienna, Austria: Law Books in Europe, 1993)
80. ESC Res. 1503, 48 UN ESCOR Supp. (No. 1A) at 89, UN Doc. E/4832/Add.1 (1970)
81. Feinberg, Joel and Gross, Hyman, editor, *Philosophy of Law*, 3rd (Belmont, the USA: Wadsworth Publishing Company, 1986)
82. Fitzgerald, C. P., *The Chinese View of their Place in the World* (Amen House, London: Oxford University Press, 1964)
83. Flemin, John G., *The Law of Torts,* 6th edition (Sydney: the Law Book Co., 1983)
84. Foldesi, Tamas, "The Right to Move and Its Achilles" Hell, The Right to Asylum", *Connell Journal of International Law*, Spring 1993, 289
85. Freedman, Warren, *The Right to Travel: A Right or A Privilege? Work Paper of Sao Paulo Conference on the Law of the World* (Washington, the USA: the World Peace Through Law Centre, 1981)
86. Freeman, M. D. A., *Lloyd's Introduction to Jurisprudence,* 7th edition (London: Sweet & Maxwell Ltd., 2001)
87. Friborg, Coran editor, *Brain Drain Statistics: Empirical Evidence and Guidelines, Report on international Expert Meeting in Stockholm 1973 and Guidelines for Future Studies* (Stockholm: Offsetoriginals i Sundt offset, 1975)
88. Friedman, Lawrence M., *A History of American Law* (New York: Simon and Schuster, 1973)
89. Friedmann, Daniel and Barak-Erez, Daphne editor, *Human Rights in Private Law* (Oregon, the USA: Hart Publishing Co, 2001)
90. Friedmann, W., *Legal Theory* (London: Law Publishers, 1944)
91. Friedberg, Rachel M. and Hunt, Jennifer, "The Impact of Immigrants on Host Country Wages, Employment and Growth", *Journal of Economical Perspectives*, Volume 9, No. 2, Spring 1995, 23–44
92. Gao, M. C. F. and Liu. X. "From Student to Citizen: A Survey of Students from the People"s Republic of China (PRC) in Australia". *International Migration*, Volume 36,

No. 1 (March 1998), 27–48, http://ejournals.ebsco.com/direct.asp?ArticleID=ND9C6QUN9G11LWTAQXN0 (accessed 01/10/2003)

93. Garcia-Amador, F. V., Sohm, Louis B. and Baxter, R.R., *Recent Codification of the Law of State Responsibility for injuries to Aliens* (New York: Oceana Publications, inc., 1974)
94. Garner, Bryan A., (ed. in Chief), *Black's Law Dictionary,* 7th edition, West Group, St. Paul, Minn., 1999
95. George, Robert P., *in Defense of Natural Law* (London: Clarendon Press, 1999)
96. Ghandhi, P. R., "The Human Rights Committee and Derogation in Public Emergencies", *German Yearbook of International Law* 1989, 326
97. Giese. Karsten, "New Chinese Migration to Germany: Historical Consistencies and New Patterns of Diversification within a Globalized Migration Regime". *International Migration*, Volume 41, No.3 2003, 155/185, http://ejournals.ebsco.com/direct.asp?ArticleID=KGDYHW2NFRNQFNHXH7A7 (accessed 01/10/2003)
98. Glaser, William A., *The Brain Drain: Emigration and Return, Findings of a UNITAR Multinational Comparative Survey of Professional Personnel of Developing Countries who Study Abroad* (London: Pergamon Press, 1978)
99. *Globalization Affects Global Immigration*, Review of *Workers Without Frontiers – the Impact of Globalization on International Migration* by Stalker, Peter, International Labour Organization, 2000, http://search.chinadaily.com.cn/isearch/ I_textinfo.exe?bdname=cndy_printedition&listid=10291&selectword=MIGRATION <18/06/2003>
100. Goodwin-gill, Guy S., *International Law and the Movement of Persons Between States* (Oxford: Oxford University Press, 1978)
101. Guerassimoff. Carine, "The New Chinese Migrants in France". *International Migration*, Volume 41, No. 3 2003, 135–154, http://ejournals.ebsco.com/direct.asp?ArticleID=NCLK1QYBQX3W8A7MPW8G (accessed 01/10/2003)
102. Guild, Elspeth and Minderhoud, Paul editor, *Security of Residence and Expulsion: Protection of Aliens in Europe* (the Hague, the Netherlands: Kluwar Law Internaitonal, 2000)
103. Haines, Robin F., *Emigration and the Labouring Poor: Australian Recruitment in Britain and Ireland, 1836* (London: Macmillan Press Ltd., 1997)
104. Hall, Davis L. and Ames, Roger T., *Thinking Through Confucius* (Albany, the USA: State University of New York Press, 1987)
105. Hannum, Hurst, *The Right to Leave and Return in international Law and Practice* (Dordrecht, the Netherlands: Martinus Nijhoff Publishers, 1987)
106. Harding, Alan, *A Social History of English Law* (London: Penguin Books Ltd., 1966)
107. Hart, H. L. A., *Essays in Jurisprudence and Philosophy* (Oxford: Clarendon Press, 1983)
108. Hart, H. L. A., *The Concept of Law* (London: Oxford University Press, 1961)
109. Hastie, W., *Outlines of the Science of Jurisprudence: an introduction to the Systematic Study of Law* (Holmes Beach, the USA: Gaunt Inc., 2000)
110. Healey, Justin editor, *Human Rights and Civil Riights, Issues in Society, Volume 139*, The Spinney Press, independent ed.ucational Publisher, Balmain, Australia, 2000
111. Healey, Kaye, editor, *Global Migration: Issues for the Nineties, Volume 47* (Balmain, Australia, The Spinney Press, 1995)
112. Hedwig Rudolph & Mirijana Morokvasic, *Bridging States and Markets: International Migrations in the early 1990s*, Berlin, 1993

113. Hegarty, Angela and Leonard, Siobhan editor, *A Human Rights: An Agenda for the 21st Century* (London: Cavendish Publishing Limited, 1999)
114. Held, D., McGrew, A., Goldblatt, D., and Perraton, J., *Global Transformations: Politics, Economics, and Culture* (Cambridge: Polity Press, 1999)
115. Held, D., *Political Theory and the Modern State* (Oxford: Basil Blackwell, 1989)
116. Henkin, Louis, editor, *The international Bill of Rights: the Covenant on Civil and Political Rights* (New York: Columbia University Press, 1981)
117. Henriques, H. S. Q., *The Law of Aliens and Naturalization including the Text of the Aliens Act, 1905* (London: Butterworth & Co., 1906)
118. Hogg, Quintin, *The Brain Drain*, CPC Outline Series No. 1 (London: the Conservative Political Centre, 1967)
119. Hosack, John, *on the Rise and Growth of the Law of Nations, as Established. by General Usage and by Treaties, From the Earliest Time to the Treaty of Utrecht* (Covent Garden, the UK: Jas. Wade, 1882)
120. Hugo, Graeme, Rudd, Dianne and Harris, Kevin, *Emigration from Australia: Economic Implications*, Second report on an ARC SPIRT grant CEDA information Paper No. 77, Adelaide University Australia, 2001
121. Hui, One Jin, *Chinese indentured. Labour: Coolies and Colonies in Robin Cohen, The Cambridge Survey of World Migration* (Cambridge: Cambridge University Press, 1995)
122. Human Rights Committee, *Equality of Rights Between Men and Women: General Comment 28: 29/03/2000*, ICCPR General comment 28, http://www.unhchr.ch/tbs/doc.nsf/(symbol)/CCPR.C.21.Rev.1.Add.9.+CCPR+comment+28.En?OpenDocument (accessed 30–05–2003)
123. Human Rights Committee, *Freedom of Movement (Art. 12): 02/11/99.* CCPR/C/21/Rev.1/Add.9, CCPR General comment 27. (General Comment), http://www.unhchr.ch/tbs/doc.nsf/(symbol)/CCPR.C.21.Rev.1.Add.9.+CCPR+comment+27.En?OpenDocument (accessed 30–05–2003)
124. Human Rights Committee, *Position of Aliens*, General Comment 15/27, 22/07/1986
125. Human Rights in China, *Custody and Repatriation Not Welcome at the Party: Behind the "Clean-up" of China's Cities – A Report on Administrative Detention under "Custody and Repatriation,* HRIC Arbitrary Detention Series, No. 2, New York: 1999, 63 pages http://iso.hrichina.org:8151/download_repositiory/a/c&r%2099.doc (accessed 1–06–2003)
126. Human Rights Watch, "Human Rights Watch Report 2001: Vietnam: Human Rights Developments," www.hrw.org/wr2k1/asia/vietnam.html (4/12/2003)
127. Human Rights Watch, "Human Rights Watch World Report 2001: A Human Rights Framework (Introduction)", http://www.hrw.org/wr2k1/intro/intro01.html (accessed 25/07/2003)
128. Human Rights Watch, *Human Rights Watch World Report 2001: Asia*, http://www.hrw.org/wr2k1/asia/index.html (accessed 25/07/2003)
129. Human Rights Watch, *Human Rights Watch World Report 2002: Asia: China and Tibet*, http://nadaily.com/cgi-bin/nph-proxyb.cgi/010000A/http/hrw.org/wr2 (accessed 5/07/2003)
130. Human Rights Watch/Asia and Human Rights in China, *China: Enforced Exile of Dissidents: Government "Re-entry Blacklist" Revealed"*, Vol. 7 No. 1, January 1995
131. Humphrey, John P., *Human Rights & the United. Nations a Great Adventure* (New York: Transnational Publishers, Inc, 1984)

132. Hunter, Ian, and Saunders David editor, *Natural Law and Civil Sovereignty: Moral Right and State Authority in Early Modern Political Thought* (New York: Palgrave Macmillan, 2002)
133. Ian Brownlie, CBE, QC and Guy S., Goodwin-Gill, *Basic Documents on Human Rights*, 4th edtion (Oxford, the UK: Oxford University Press, 2000)
134. Immigration Office National Police Agency of the Ministry of Interior of Republic of China, "the Manual of Service for the People, Immigration Office" (*Ruchujing Guanliju Weiming Fuwu Shouce*), September 2002, www.immigraiton.gov.tw (accessed 28/11/2003)
135. Immigration Office National Police Agency of the Ministry of Interior of Republic of China, "the Enforcement Plan of Upgrading Service Quality all the Round in 2002" (*Neizhengbu Jingzhengshu Ruushujing Guanliju Jiushiyi Niandu Quanmian Tisheng Fuwu Pingzhi Zhixing Jihuashu*), www.immigraiton.gov.tw (accessed 28/11/2003)
136. Ingles, Jose D, *Study of Discrimination in Respect of The Right of Everyone to Leave any Country,Iincluding His Own, and to Return to His Country: Special Repporteur of the Sub-commission on Prevention of Discrimination and Protection of Minorities,* United Nations Publication Sales No.: 64. XIV. 2 New York 1963
137. Inter-American Commission on Human Rights, "Sixth Report on the Situation of Political Prisoners in Cuba", 1979, O.A.S Doc. No. OEA/Ser. L/V/II 48; doc. 7 at 9 *International Migration Review,* New York: 24
138. International Organization for Migration, "the People's Republic of China – Migration in 1999", www.iom.org (accessed 18/06/2003)
139. International Organization for Migration, *International Migration Report 2002*, ST/ESA/SER.A/220 (Geneva, Switzerland: International Organization for Migration, 2002)
140. International Organization for Migration, *International Respect for Migrations' Rights,* 2002 (Geneva, Switzerland: International Organization for Migration, 2002)
141. International Organization for Migration, *Myths and Realities of Chinese Irregular Migration*, No. 1 of IOM Migration Research Series (Geneva, Switzerland: International Organization for Migration, 2000)
142. International Organization for Migration, *The Link between Migration and Development in the Least Developed Countries* (Geneva, Switzerland: International Organization for Migration, 2001)
143. International Organization for Migration, *The State of Migration Management in Central America: an Applied Research, Final Report* (Geneva, Switzerland, International Organization for Migration, 2002)
144. Ired.ale, Robyn, Hawksley, Charles and Castles, Stephen editor, *Migration in the Asia Pacific: Population, Settlement and Citizenship Issues* (Cheltenham, the UK and Northampton, the USA, Edward Elgar Publishing Limited) 2003
145. Iredale, Robyn, "The need to Import Skilled Personnel: Factors Favoring and Hindering its International Mobility", *International Migration* Vol. 37(1) 1999, 89–114 http://ejournals.ebsco.com/direct.asp?ArticleID=TW74D522315K6-EVM8G0K (accessed 01/10/2003)
146. Irick, Robert L., *Ch'ing Policy Toward the Coolie Trade 1847 – 1878*, Chinese Materials Centre, Asian Library Series No. 18, 1982
147. Isin, Engin F. and Turner, Bryan S. editor, *Handbook of Citizenship Studies* (London: Sage Publications, 2002)

148. Professor Young-bum Park, Korea Labour Institute, Seoul, "Issues Paper from the Republic of South Korea", Asia Pacific Migration Research Network, *Migration Issues in the Asia Pacific* compiled by compiled by Patrick Brownlee and Colleen Mitchell, http://www.unesco.org/most/apmrnw12.htm (accessed 24/07/2006)
149. Itoh, Fumio, editor, *China in the Twenty-first Century: Politics, Economy, and Society* (Tokyo, Japan: United. Nations University Press, 1997)
150. Jagerskiold, S., "Freed.om of Movement" Henkin, L. editor, *The international Bill of Rights: The Covenant on Civil and Political Rights* (New York: Columbia University Press, 1981)
151. James F. Hollifield, *Migration Theory*, Routled.ge, New York: 2000
152. Joseph, Sarah and Sehultz, Jenny et al, *The international Covenant on Civil and Political Rights: Cases, Materials, and Commentary* (New York: Oxford University Press, 2000)
153. Judith M. Brown & Rosemary Foot, *Migration: The Asian Experience* (London: The Macmillan Press Ltd. 1994)
154. Kao, Charles H. C. (Gao, Xijun), *Brain Drain: a Case Study of China* (Taipei, the Republic of China: Mei Ya Publications Inc., 1971)
155. Keely, Charles B., *Globalization Transforms, Trade-Migration Equation* (Oxford: Blackwell Publishing Ltd. 2003)
156. Keith, Ronald C. and Lin, Zhiqiu, *Law and Justice in China's New Marketplace* (New York: Palgrave, 2001)
157. Kelsen, Hans, *The Communist Theory of Law* (New York: Frederick A. Praeger, Inc. 1955)
158. Kent, Ann, *Human Rights in the People's Republic of China*, Discussion Paper No. 3, 1989–90, Legislative Research Service, the Parliamentary of the Commonwealth of Australia, 1990
159. Kibreab, Gaim, "Citizenship Rights and Repatriation of Refugees", Volume 37, International Migration Review, vol. 37, No. 1, 24–73
160. Kim, Hyung I, *Fundamental Legal Concepts of China and the West: A Comparative Study* (Port Washington, the USA: Kennikat Press Corp. 1981)
161. Kirkbride, Paul, editor, *Globalization: The External Pressures,* (West Sussex, the UK: John Wiley & Sons, Ltd., 2001)
162. Koessler, "Subject, Citizen, National and Permanent Allegiance", 56 *Yale Law Journal* 58. (1946)
163. Kofman, Eleonore and Youngs, Gillian, editor, *Globalization: Theory and Practice* (New York: Pinter, 1996)
164. Kokko, Ari and Sjoholm, Fredrik, *The Internationalization of Vietnamese*, The European Institute of Japanese Studies in its series EIJS Working Paper Series with No. 193.
165. Koser, *The Return and Reintegration of Rejected Asylum Seekers and Illegal migrants*, No. 4 IOM Migration Research Series (Geneva, Switzerland: International Organization for Migration, 2001)
166. Kramer, Matthew H., *in Defense of Legal Positivism: Law without Trimmins* (New York: Oxford University Press, 1999)
167. Krieger, Silke and Trauzettel, Rolf, editor, *Confucianism and the Modernization of China* (Mainz, Eschwege, Germany: V. Hase & Koehler Verlag, 1991)
168. Kuttner, S., *Gratian and Plato,* in Church and Government in the Middle Ages, Essay presented to C. R. Cheney, Cambridge, 1976

169. Laczko. Frank, "Introduction: Understanding Migration between China and Europe". *International Migration*, Volume 41, No. 3 (2003), http://ejournals.ebsco.com/direct.asp?ArticleID=DKET6U2Y1B0DEAWEA2QK (accessed 01/10/2003)
170. Laroque, Pierre, *The Future of Migration*, the OECD, 1990
171. Lechner, Frank J. and Boli John, editor, *Globalization Reader* (Malden, the USA, Blackwell Publishers, 2000)
172. Lee, Tahirih V., editor, *Foreigners in Chinese Law* (New York and London: Garland Publishing, Inc., 1997)
173. Lee, Tahirih V., editor, *Law, the State and Society in China* (New York: Garland Publishing inc., 1997)
174. Lester, Lord of Herne Hill QC and Joseph, S., "Obligations of Non-Discrimination" in Harris, D. and Joseph S. editor, *The international Covenant on Civil and Political Rights and United. Kingdom Law* (Oxford: Clarendon Press, 1995)
175. Liechtenstein v. Guatemala (Nottebohm Case) Second Phase, Judgement, *International Court Journal* reports 1955, Rep 4
176. Lockwood, B. Jr., Finn, J. and Jubinsky, G., *Working Paper for the Committee of Experts on Limitation Provisions,* 7 HRQ 35, 1985.
177. Lowell, B. Lindsay, *Skilled Migration abroad or Human Capital Flight?*, http://www.migrationinformation.org/Feature/display.cfm?ID=135 (accessed 05/06/2003)
178. Lumpur, Kuala, *Reality of Labour Migration of Vietnam and Her Policies*, Paper presented at a Meeting on the Implications of Changing Patterns of Asian Labour Migration, 1991
179. Macdonald, Ian A. & Black, Nicholas J, *Immigration Law and Practice in the United. Kingdom*, 3rd ed. (London: Butterworths, 1991)
180. Mackerras, Colin, Taneja, Pradeep and Young, Graham, *China Since 1978 (2nd edition)* (South Melbourne, Australia: Addison Wesley Longman Australia Pty Ltd., 1998)
181. MacNair, Francesco Hayez, *Their Chinese Abroad: Their Position and Protection A Study in International Law and Relations* (Shanghai: Commercial Press, 1926)
182. Mark Wooden, Robert Holton, Graeme Hugo and Judith Sloan, *Australia Immigration: a Survey of the Issues,* New York: the Bureau of Immigration Research, 1990
183. Market Information and Analysis Section, Department of Foreign Affairs and Trade, Australia, *China: the Fact Sheet*, using the latest data from the ABS, the IMF and various international sources, October 2003
184. Marr, David G. and White, Christine P., editor, *Postwar Vietnam: Dilemmas in Socialist Development*, Cornell Southeast Asia Program, New York, 1988
185. Martin, David A., *The New Asylum Seekers: Refugee Law in the 1980s: the Ninth Sokol Colloquium on international Law, international Studies in Human Rights Volume 10* (Dordrecht, the Netherlands: Martinus Nijhoff Publishers, 1988)
186. Martin, Francisco Forrest, Schnably, Stephen J., Slye, Ronald C. etc., *international Human Rights Law & Practice: Cases, Treaties and Materials* (the Hague, the Netherlands: Kluwer Law International, 1997)
187. Martin, Philip and Widgren, Jonas, "International Migration: Facing the Challenge", in *Population Bulletin*, March 2002 issue (Population Reference Bureau, Washington, the USA: 2002)

188. McGrew, T., "A Global Society", *Modernity and Its Future* edited by Hall, S., Held D. and McGrew T., (Cambridge: Polity Press, 1992)
189. McWilliams, P. K., *Canadian Criminal Evidence*, 3rd edition (Aurora: Canada Law Book, 1988)
190. Meron, Theodor, editor, *Human Rights in international Law: Legal and Policy Issues, Volume I* (Oxford, the UK: Clarendon Press, 1984)
191. Meron, Theodor, *Human Rights and Humanitarian Norms as Customary Law* (New York: Oxford University Press, 1989)
192. Meron, Theodor, *Human Rights Law-Making in the United. Nations: a Critique of instruments and Process* (New York: Clarendon Press, 1986)
193. Molony, John, *History of Australia* (Ringwood, Australia: Penguin Books Australia Ltd., 1987)
194. Mozaffari, Mehdi, *Globalisation and Civilizations* (London: Routledge Taylor & Francis Group, 2002)
195. Ness, Peter Van, *Human Rights and Democracy in China: Four Theories on Why the World Should Care*, working paper No. 167, Peace Research Centre, Research School of Pacific Studies, Canberra: The Australian National University, 1996
196. Neumann, Franz, *The Rule of Law: Political Theory and the Legal System in Modern Society* (Warwickshire, the UK: Berg Publishers Ltd., 1986)
197. Nguyen, D. T. and Bandara, J. S., *Emigration Pressure and Structural Change: Vietnam*, A report prepared under UNDP Technical Support Services 1, ILO East Asia Multidisciplinary Advisory Team (ILO/EASMAT) and ILO Regional Office for Asia and the Pacific, Unpublished document issued without formal editing by ILO, Bangkok 1996
198. Nicolet, Alan, *The World of the Citizen in Republican Rome* (Berkeley, the USA: University of California Press, 1988)
199. Nieto. Gladys, "The Chinese in Spain". *International Migration*, Volume 41, No. 3 (2003), 215–237, http://ejournals.ebsco.com/direct.asp?ArticleID=DMFMH0U-6K7D2Y85AYQXF (accessed 01/10/2003)
200. Noll. Gregor. "Rejected Asylum Seekers: The Problem of Return". *International Migration*, Volume 37, No. 1 (1999), 267 -288, http://ejournals.ebsco.com/direct.asp?ArticleID=TCM1DEBBV1G3C1TRHU0G (accessed 01/10/2003)
201. Nowak, Manfred., *U.N. Covenant on Civil and Political Rights: CCPR Commentary* (Kehl am Rhein · Strasbourg · Arlington: N. P. Engel, Publisher, 1993)
202. Nygh, Peter E. and Butt, Peter, General ed., *Butterworths Australian Legal Dictionary* (Sydney: Butterworths)
203. Nyíri. Pál, Chinese Migration to Eastern Europe. *International Migration*, Volume 41, No. 3 (2003), 239–265, http://ejournals.ebsco.com/direct.asp?ArticleID=F9TLFXE966B5175UB932 (accessed 01/10/2003)
204. Orfield, Lester B. and Re, Edward D., *Cases and Materials on International Law*, Revised Edition (Indianapolis, Kansas City and New York: The Bobbs-Merrill Inc., 1965)
205. O'Meara, Patrick, Mehlinger, Howard D. and Krain, Mattew, *Globalization and the Challenges of a New Century* (Bloominton, the USA: Indiana University Press, 2000)
206. Panhuys, P. Van, *The Roles of Nationality in international Law: An Outline* (Leyden, Netherlands: A. W. Sythoff, 1959)

207. Papademetrious, Demetrios, G., *Reflections on International Migration and its Future* (Geneva, Switzerland, International Organization for Migration, 2002)
208. Perry, Elizabeth J. and Selden, Mark, editor, *Chinese Society: Change, Conflict and Resistance* (London, Routledge, 2000)
209. Plender, Richard, *International Migration Law*, Revised. 2nd ed., (Dordrecht, the Netherlands: Martinus Nijhoff Publishers, 1988)
210. Pohlenz, Max, *Freed.om in Greek Life and Thought* (Reidel: Dordecht, 1966)
211. Population Division, Department of Economic and Social Affairs, *International Migration Report 2002,* United Nations Secretariat, *2002*, ST/ESA/SER.A/220, New York: United Nations, 2002
212. Population Division, Department of Economic and Social Affairs, United Nations Secretariat, *International Migration: Explicit Policies, Uncertain Consequences,* UN/POP/MIG/2002/BP/2, New York: United Nations, 2002, 15 pages
213. Population Division, Department of Economic and Social Affairs, United Nations Secretariat, *Measuring International Migration: Many Questions, Few Answers,* UN/POP/MIG/2002/BP/1, New York: United Nations, 2002
214. Population Division, Department of Economic and Social Affairs, United Nations Secretariat, *International Migration from Countries with Economies in Transition: 1980–1999*, ESA/P/WP.176 , New York: United Nations, 2002
215. Potter, David, Goldblatt, David, Kiloh, Margaret and Lewis, Paul, editor, *Democratization* (Malden MA, the USA: Blackwell Publishers Inc., 1997)
216. Potter, Pitman B., *The Chinese Legal System: Globalization and Local Legal Culture* (London and New York: Routledge, 2001)
217. Powell, Colin L. Preface to *Supporting Human Rights and Democracy: The U.S. Record 2002–2003* by the Bureau of Democracy, Human Rights, and Labour, the State Council, the USA, http://www.state.gov/g/drl/rls/shrd/2002/21763.htm (accessed 05–07–2033)
218. Provost, Rene, *State Responsibility in international Law,* editor (Burlington, the USA: Ashgate Publishing Company, 2002)
219. Purcell, Victor, *The Chinese in South East Asia* (London: Oxford University Press, 1965)
220. Ramcharan, B. G., *The Concept and Present Status of the international Protection of Human Rights: Forty Years After the Universal Declaration* (Dordrecht, the Netherlands: Martinus Nijhoff Publishers, 1989)
221. Read, William, *Legal Thinking: Its Limits and Tensions* (Philadelphia, the USA: University of Pennsylvania Press, 1986)
222. Reid, Karen, *A Practitioner's Guide to the European Convention on Human Rights* (London: Sweet & Maxwell, 1998)
223. Robertson, A. H., *Human Rights in the World: an introduction to the Study of the international Protection of Human Rights*, 2nd edition (Manchester, the UK: Manchester University Press, 1982)
224. Robin, Cohen, *The Cambridge Survey of World Migration* (Cambridge: Combridge University Press, 1995)
225. Robinson, Nehemiah, *The Universal Declaration of Human Rights: Its Origin, Significance, Application, and interpretation*, New York: Institute of Jewish Affairs, World Jewish Congress, 1958
226. Robinson, Vaughan, *Migration and Public Policy* (Cheltenham, the UK: Edward Elgar Publishing Limited, 1999)

227. Roche, Peter, *Citizenship in the Western Tradition* (Chapel Hill, the USA: University if North Carolina Press, 1992)
228. Rosenblum, Victor G., *Law as a Political instrument* (New York: Random House, Inc., 1955)
229. Rousseau, Jean-Jacques, *The Social Contract*, Translated and introduced. by Cranston, Maurice (Harmondsworth, Middlesex, England: Penguin Books Ltd, 1968)
230. Rubenstein, Kim, *Australian Citizenship Law in Context* (Pyrmont, Australia, Lawbook Co., 2002)
231. Ryan. Jan, "Chinese Women as Transnational Migrants: Gender and Class in Global Migration Narratives". *International Migration*, Volume 40, No. 2 (2002), 93–116, http://ejournals.ebsco.com/direct.asp?ArticleID=Y68W70EMXGPAGE 1NVEM-5DF7 (accessed 01/10/2003)
232. Seidman, Ann, Seidman, Robert B. and Payne, Janice editor, *Legislative Drafting for Market Reform: Some Lessons from China* (London: Macmillan Press Ltd., 1997 and New York: St. Martin's Press, Inc., 1997)
233. Shelton, Dinah, *Remedies in International Human Rights Law* (New York: Oxford University Press, 1999)
234. Sherwin-White, A. N. *Roman Citizenship* (Oxford: Clarendon Press, 1939)
235. Shih, Chih-yu, *Collective Democracy Political and Legal Reform in China* (Hong Kong: The Chinese University Press, 1999)
236. Sibley, N. W., "The Passport System", *Journal of the Society of Comparative Legislation*, new series Volume vii (1906), 26–33
237. Skeldon, Ronald, "Migration from China (Contemporary China: The Consequences of Change)", *Journal of International Affairs,* Winter 1996 Volume 49 No. 2, 434–455 http://web6.infotrac.galegroup.com/itw/infomark/740/651/3737-4829w6/purl=rc1_EAI (accessed 25/07/2003)
238. Sieghart, Paul, *The international Law of Human Rights* (New York: Oxford University Press, 1983)
239. Sik, Ko Swan and Sang, Chang Hyo editor, *Nationality and international Law in Asian Perspective* (Dordrecht, the Netherlands: Martinus Nijhoff Publishers, 1990)
240. Simon Fisher, *Agency Law* (Sydney: Butterworths, 2000)
241. Simon, Denis Fred. and Kau, Michael, Y. M., *Taiwan: Beyond the Economic Miracle* (New York: M. E. Sharpe Inc., 1992)
242. Skeldon, Ronald, editor, *Emigration from Hong Kong: Tendencies and Impacts* (Hong Kong: The Chinese University Press, 1995)
243. Sowell, Thomas, *Migrations and Cultures: A World View* (New York: Basic Books, A member of the Perseus Books Group, 1996)
244. Stahl, Charles, Ball, Rochelle, Inglis, Christine and Gutman, Pamela, *Global Population Movements and Their Implications for Australia* (Canberra, Australia: Australian Government Publishing Service, 1993)
245. Stalker, Peter, *The No-Nonsense Guild to International Migration* (Oxford, the UK: New Internationalist Publications Ltd, 2001)
246. Stein, Peter, *Legal Evolution: The Story of an Idea* (Cambridge, the UK: Cambridge University Press, 1980)
247. Steiner, Henry J. and Alston, Philip editor, *international Human Rights in Context: Law, Politics, Morals: Text and Materials*, 2nd edition (New York: Oxford University Press, 2000)

248. Stipp, John L., Dirrim, Allen, W. and Hollister, C. Warren, *The Rise and Development of Western Civilization: 1660 to the Present* (New York, London and Sydney, John Wiley & Sons, Inc., 1967)
249. Stockman, Norman, *Understanding Chinese Society* (Malden, the USA: Polity Press in association with Blackwell Publishers Ltd., 2000)
250. Stokke, Hugo, Suhrke, Astri and Todtersen, Arne editor, *Human Rights in Developing Countries Yearbook 1997* (the Hague, the Netherlands: Kluwer Law International, Nordic Human Rights Publications, 1998)
251. *Submission on Immigration Consulting Industry*, The National Citizenship and Immigration Law Section of the Canadian Bar Association, 2002
252. Sun, Wangning, *Leaving China: Media, Migration, and Transnational Imagination* (Maryland, the USA, Rowman & Littlefield Publishers, Inc., 2001)
253. Swales, John M. & Feak, Christine B., *Academic Writing for Graduate Students Essential Tasks and Skills: A Course for Bonnative Speakers of English* (Michigan, the USA: The University of Michigan Press, 1994)
254. Swinburne University, editor, *The Collection of Conference Papers, Globalization and Citizenship: An international Conference*, Melbourne, 1997
255. Tan, zhimin, "The Discuss on Current Permission System of Entry into Mainland Area of Residents in Taiwan Area" (*Taiwan Diqu Renming Jingru Dalu Diqu Xianxing Xukezhi Zhi Tantao*) (12 October 1998), www.immigraiton.gov.tw (accessed 28/11/2003)
256. Teather, David C. B. and Yee, Herbert S. editor, *China in Transition* (London: Macmillan Press Ltd. and New York: St. Martin's Press, Inc., 1999)
257. Thayer, Carlyle A. and Marr David G. editor, *Vietnam and the Rule of Law*, Department of Political and Social Change, Research School of Pacific Studies, Canberra: Australian National University, 1993
258. The Central Intelligence Agency, "The World Fact book: China", 18 December 2003, http://www.cia.gov/cia/publications/factbook/geos/ch.html (accessed 2/02/2004)
259. The OECD, *Migration and Development: New Partnerships for Co-operation* (Paris Cedex, France: France Head of Publications Service, the OECD, 1994)
260. The OECD, *Migration and the Labour Market in Asia: Recent Trends and Policies*, Paris: the OECD, 2001
261. The OECD, *The Changing Course of international Migration,* (Paris Cedex, France: Head of Publications Service, the OECD, 1993)
262. The OECD, *the Future of Migration*, The secretary-general of the OECD, 1986
263. The UNHCR, *The Haitian Interdiction Case 1993 Brief Amicus Curiae,* 6 IJRL 86 (1994)
264. The United Nations doc. ICCPR/C/79/Add. 55 (1995), para. 16.
265. The United Nations General Assembly, "Report of the World Conferences on Human Rights Vienna, 14–25 June 1993 Report of the Secretary-General", Distr. General A/CONF.157/24 (Part I), 13 October 1993
266. The United Nations, *International Migration Policies and Programs: A World Survey*. Sales No. E.82 XIII.4
267. The United Nations, *Recommendations on Statistics of International Migration. Revision 1*, Sales No. E.98.XVII.14, 1998
268. The World Bank, "Vietnam – Poverty Assessment and Strategy", Report No. 13442–VN, World Bank, Washington, D.C. USA, 1995

269. Thunø. Mette, "Channels of Entry and Preferred Destinations: The Circumvention of Denmark by Chinese Immigrants". *International Migration*, Volume 41, No. 3 (2003), 99/133, http://ejournals.ebsco.com/direct.asp?ArticleID=3V5R8-BJXFJKHYAKM4VRL (accessed 01/10/2003)
270. Tomlinson, John, *Globalization Culture* (Cambridge, the UK: Polity Press in association with Blackwell Publishers Ltd., 1999)
271. Torpey, John, *The invention of The Passport: Surveillance, Citizenship and the State* (Cambridge, the UK: Cambridge University Press, 2000)
272. Turack, Daniel C., *The Passport in international Law*, Lexington Books, D.C. Health and Company, Toronto, Canada, 1972
273. Twining, William, *Globalisation and Legal Theory* (Evanston, the USA: Northwestern University Press, 2000)
274. US Committee for Refugees, "China: World Refugee Survey 2003 Country Reports", http://refugees.org/world/countrypt/easia_pacific/2003/china.cfm (accessed 2/02/2004)
275. US Department of State, "China (Including Hong Kong and Macao): Country Reports on Human Rights Practices 2000", http://www.state.gov/g/frl/rls/hrrpt/2000/eap/684.htm (accessed 2/02/2004)
276. US Department of State, "China (Including Hong Kong and Macao): Country Reports on Human Rights Practices 2001", http://www.state.gov/g/frl/rls/hrrpt/2001/eap/8289.htm (accessed 2/02/2004)
277. US Department of State, "China (Including Hong Kong and Macao): Country Reports on Human Rights Practices 1999", http://www.state.gov/g/frl/rls/hrrpt/1999/eap/684.htm (accessed 2/02/2004)
278. US Department of State, "China (Including Hong Kong and Macao): Country Reports on Human Rights Practices 2002", http://www.statc.gov/g/frl/rls/hrrpt/2002/eap/684.htm (accessed 2/02/2004)
279. US Department of State, "China: Country Reports on Human Rights Practices 1998", http://www.state.gov/www/global/human_rights/1998_hrp_report/china.html (accessed 2/02/2004)
280. Vasak, Karel and Liskofsky, Sidney, editor, *the Right to Leave and Return: Papers and Recommendations of the international Colloquium Held in Uppsala, Sweden, 19–21 June 1972*, The American Jewish Committee, Arbor, the USA: 1976
281. Vaughan Robinson, *Migration and Public Policy* (London: Edward Elgar Publishing Limited., 1999)
282. Vietnam Business Forum, *Sub-Working Group on Administrative Reform Review of Licenses/Permits and Related Issues*, 2002, http://vibforum.vcci.com.vn (accessed 2/02/2004)
283. Vietnam, "Ninth Period Report on the Implementation of the International Convention on the Elimination of All Forms of Racial Discrimination", Distr. General CERD/C/357/Add.2, 17 October 2000, http://www.hri.ca.fortherecord2001/documentation/tbodies/cerd-c-357–ad (accessed 04/12/2003)
284. Vietnam, *Second Period Report on the Implementation of the International Convention on Civil and Political Rights*, Distr. General CCPR/C/VNM/2001/2, 14 May 2001
285. Vinogradoff, Paul, *Outlines of Historical Jurisprudence, Volume Two, The Jurisprudence of the Greek City* (Oxford, the UK: Oxford University Press, 1922)

286. Waddington, Clare, "International Migration Policies in Asia: A Synbook of ILO and other Literature on Policies Seeking to Manage the Recruitment and Protection of Migrants, and Facilitate Remittances and Their Investment", Paper presented at Regional Conference on Migration, Development and Pro-Poor Policy Choices in Asia 2003, www.livelihoods.org, (accessed 05/12/2003)
287. Walters, R. P., *A History of the League of Nations, Volume II* (London: Oxford University Press, 1952)
288. Wang, Gungwu, *Don't Leave Home: Migration and The Chinese* (Singapore: Times Academic Press, 2001)
289. Wang, Sing-wu *The Organization of Chinese Emigration 1848–1888 with Special Reference to Chinese Emigration to Australia*, San Francisco: Chinese Materials Centre Inc. 1978
290. Wang, Singwu, "the Attitude of the Ch'ing Court Towards Chinese Emigration", *Chinese Culture*, Vol. IX, No. 4, 1968, 62–63
291. Washington: Government Printing Office, *Senate Hearings on Soviet Pentecostals Residing in the U.S. Embassy in Moscow*, 19 November 1981, ser. J-97–82, at 125
292. Weis, P., *Nationality and statelessness in international Law,* 2nd revised. Editions (Alphen aan den Rijn, The Netherlands: Sijthoff & Noordhodd International Publishers B. V., 1979)
293. Weis, P., *Nationality and statelessness in international Law* (London: Stevens & Sons Limited., 1956)
294. Wellman, Carl, *A Theory of Rights: Persons Under Laws, institutions, and Morals* (Totowa, New Jersey, the USA: Rowman & Allanheld Publishers, 1985)
295. Wichberg, Wdgar, "The Chinese as Overseas Migrants in Brown", in Brown, Judith M. & Foot, Rosemary, editor, *Migration: The Asian Experience* (London: The Macmillan Press Ltd., 1994)
296. Williams, Paul editor, *The international Bill of Human Rights* (Glen Ellen, the USA: Entwhistle Books, 1981)
297. Willis, F. Roy, *Western Civilization an Urban Perspective: Volume II from the 17th Century to the Contemporary Age*, D. C. (Lexington, the USA: Heath and Company, 1973)
298. Wolfgang Weidlich and Sonis Michael, "Interregional Migration: Dynamic Theory and Comparative Analysis", *Regional Science: Retrospect and Prospect* by Nijkamp P., Boyce D. E. and Shefer Daniel, Springer, Berlin, Germany 1988, 359–400
299. Wong, Alan, *Hong Kong: Stronger than Ever* at dinner talks at Four Seasons Hotel, Sydney, 10 July 2003
300. *World Population Monitoring 1997: Issues of International Migration and Development,* United Nations publication, Sales No. E. 98. XIII. 4
301. Wu, Yuanli et al., *Human Rights in the People's Republic of China* (Boulder, Colorado, the USA: Westview Press, 1988)
302. Xian, Lixian, "The Discussion on Application Procedure of Entry into Mainland Area of Residents in Taiwan Area" (*Taiwan Diqu Jingru Dalu Diqu Shengqing Chengxu Zhi Taitao*) (14 March 2000), www.immigraiton.gov.tw (accessed 28/11/2003)
303. *Year Book of International Law Commission 1977* (pt. 2) at 31, UN Doc. A/CN.4/SER.A/1977/Add.1 (Part 2) (1978)
304. Young, Song Ji, "The Invisible Refugees: North Korean Asylum Seekers in China", http://iso.hrichina.org/iso/article.adp?article_id=4248&subcategory_id=287 (accessed 18/05/2003)

305. Zayonchkovskaya, Zhanna, The Russian Federation. In *International Migration in Central and Eastern Europe and the Commonwealth of Independent States*, UNECE Economic Studies No. 8, UNECE and UNFPA Sales No. GV.E.96.0.22, Geneva and New York
306. Zhang. Guochu, "Migration of Highly Skilled Chinese to Europe: Trends and Perspective". *International Migration*, Volume 41, No. 3 (2003), 73–97, http://ejournals.ebsco.com/direct.asp?ArticleID=CTM27M34E7REQMFE2J8M (accessed 01/10/2003)
307. Zhao, Suisheng, *China and Democracy: the Prospect for a Democratic China* (New York and London: Routledge 2000)
308. Zhu, Muzhi, "Some Thoughts on Democracy", *The Journal of Human Rights*, No. 4 (2002), http://www.humanrights-china.org/zt/03111201/20031200312910362 1.htm (accessed 26/02/2004)

Table of Cases

Aptheker v. Secretary of State (1964) 378 the USA 500
Arrowsmith v. the UK (1978) 3 EUCT 218
Canon Garcia v. Ecuador (1988) Comm. 319/1988 UN Doc. CCPR/C/43/D/319/1988. 891
Celepli v. Sweden (1994) Communication No. 456/1991, UN Doc. CCPR/C/51/D/456/1991
Chahal v. United Kingdom (1996) 23 EUCT 413
De Wilde, Ooms and Versyp v. Belgium (1971) 2832/66; 2835/66;2899/66 EUCT 1
Giry v. the Dominican Republic (1990) Comm.No. 193/1985, UN Doc. CPR/C/39/D/193/1985
Golder v. the UK (1975) 1 EUCT 524 EUCT
Gonzalez del Rio v. Peru (1987) Comm. No. 263/1987, UN Doc. CCPR/C/46/D/263/19
Hammel v. Madagascar (1990) Comm. No. 155/1983 (2 April 1986), UN Doc. CCPR/C/OP/2
Handyside v. the UK, (1976) 1 EUCT 737, App. no. 5493/72, Ser A vol. 24
Hertzberg et al. v. Finland (1985) Comm. No. 61/1979, UN Doc. CCPR/C/OP/1 at 124
James, Young and Webster v. the UK (1981) 4 EUCT 38
Kent v. Dulles (1958) 357 the USA 116
Koremastu v. United States (1944) 323 US 214, 65 S. Ct. 193, 89 L. Ed. 194
Liechtenstein v. Guatemala (Nottebohm Case) (1955) ICJ Reports 4, 22
Malone v. the UK (1984) EUCT App. No. 8691/79, Ser. A Vol. 82
Maneka Gandhi v. Union of India and another (1978) 1 SCC 248, 293–294: AIR 1978 SC 597
Marcos v. Manglapus (1989) 178 SCRA 760
Maroufidou v. Sweden (1979) Comm. No. 58/1979, HRC. 1981 Report, Annex XVII. 471, 472
Minor v. Happersett (1874) 21 Wall, 88 US 162

Peltonen v. Finland (1994) Comm. No. 492/1992, U.N. Doc. CCPR/C/51/D/492/1992
Pinkney v. Canada (1984) Comm. No. 27/1978 (2 April 1980), U.N. Doc. CCPR/C/OP/1 at 12
Rex v. *Brailsford* [1905] KB 730
Satwant Singh Sawhney v. Ramarthnam et al. (1967) 2 SCR 525. 12
Silver et al. v. the UK (1983) EUCT, App. No. 5947/72, Ser. A No. 61
State v. Manuel (1838) Dev. & Bat. 20, 24–26
Stewart v. Canada (1996) Comm. No. 538/1993, UN Doc. CCPR/C/58/D/538/1993
Sunday Times v. the UK (1979) EUCT 1, 6538/74
V.M.R.B v. Canada (1987) Comm. No. 236/1987, CCPR/C/33/D/236/1987
Van Duyn v. Home office (1974) ECR 1337 or (1975)1 CMLR 1
Vidal Martins v. Uruguay (1982) Comm. No. R.13/57, UN Doc. Supp. No. 40 (A/37/40)
X. v. Switzerland (1997) Comm. No. 38/1995, UN Doc. CAT/C/18/D/38/1995
Zemel v. Rusk 381 the USA 1 (1965)

List of Chinese Statutes[1]

1. *Amendment of Article 6 of Regulations on Passport and Visa* 1984 (PRC) (*Zhonghua Renmin Gongheguo Huzhao Qianzheng Tiaoli Diliutiao Xiuding*), promulgated by the State Council on 27 March 1984
2. *Application Procedure and Some Notable Matters of Travelling for Public Affairs to the Regions of Taiwan* 1994 (PRC) *(Yingong Futai Shenbao Chenxu He Ruogan Zhuyi Shixiang)*, promulgated by Taiwan Affairs Office under the Ministry of Agriculture on 16 March 1994, Nongtaiban [1994] 1
3. *Basic Law of Hong Kong Special Administrative Region* 1990 (PRC) (*Xianggang Tebie Xingzhengqu Jibenfa*), promulgated by the National People's Congress on 4 April 1990
4. *Circular for Exit-Entry Procedures for Deputies of the National People's Congress and Commissaries of the National People's Political Consultative Conference Who Reside in the Regions of Hong Kong or Macao and Other Relevant Matters When They Return to the Inland* 1982 (PRC) (*Guanyu Xianggang Aomen Diqu Renda He Zhengxie Daibiao Churujing Chengxu He Fanhui Neidi Qita Shiyi De Tonghzi*), promulgated by the State Council
5. *Circular for Extending and Re-issuance of Passport of Illegal Migrants* 1992 (PRC) (*Guanyu Wei Feifa Yimin Bu Huanfa Huzhao De Tongzhi*), promulgated by the Ministry of Foreign Affairs and the Ministry of Public Security
6. *Circular of Application for Passport and Visa for Individuals Exiting Abroad Temporarily for Public Affairs* 1983 (PRC) *(Linshi Yingong Chuguo Renyuan Shenban Huzhao Qianzheng Xuzhi)*, promulgated by the Consular Affairs Division under the Ministry of Foreign Affairs on 19 July 1983

[1] The promulgation date and effective date of statutes in this appendix are the same day unless the effective date is specially noted.

7. *Circular of Establishment of Exit and Entry Intermediary Agencies for Private Affairs* 2001 (Beijing) (*Sheli Yinsi Churujing Zhongjie Jigou De Tongzhi*), promulgated by Beijing Municipality Public Security Bureau and Beijing Municipality Administration of Industry and Commerce on 19 December 2001
8. *Circular of Formalities Concerning Ratification and Approval of International Treaties and Agreements* 1992 (PRC) (*Guanyu Canjia He Pizhu Guoji Tiaoyue He Xieding Chengxu De Tongzhi*), promulgated by the General Office of the State Council
9. *Circular of Handling with Aliens Who Illegally Entering China and Illegally Residing In China in Accordance with the Laws* 1992 (PRC) (*Guanyu Yifa Chuli Feifa Rujing He Feifa Juliu Waiguoren De Tongzhi*), promulgated by the Ministry of Public Security on 6 April 1992
10. *Circular of the Ministries of Education, Public Security and Foreign Affairs on Some Affairs Regarding Fulltime Students Exit Abroad Short-term with Ordinary Passport for Private Affairs* 2002 (PRC) *(Jiaoyubu, Gonganbu, Waijiaobu Guanyu Zaixiao Xuesheng Duanqi Chuguo Chiyong Yinsi Huzhao Youguan Shixiang De Tongzhi)*, promulgated by the Ministry of Education, the Ministry of Public Security and the Ministry of Foreign Affairs on 25 January 2002
11. *Circular of the Ministry of Education, the Ministry of Public Security on Delegating Examination and Approval Power of Primary School and Secondary School Students Exit Abroad for Summer or Winter Study Tour* 1999 (PRC) *(Jiaoyubu Gonganbu Guanyu Xiafang Zhongxiao Xuesheng Fu Jingwai Xia (Dong) Lingying Deng Huodong Shenpi Quanxian De Tongzhi)*, Jiaowaizhong No. [1999] 31
12. *Circular of the Ministry of Finance on Strengthening Administration of Purchasing Foreign Exchange with Renminbi under Non-trading and Non-operation Activities* 1999 (PRC), (*Guanyu Jinyibu Jiaqiang Feimaoyi Feijingying Xing Gouhui Renminbi Xiane Guanli De Tongzhi*), Caiwaizi [1999] No. 439, 8 August 1999
13. *Circular of the Ministry of Foreign Affairs and the Ministry of Public Security on Passport Re-issue, Replacement and Extension of Irregular Migrants* 1992 (PRC) *(Waijiaobu Gonganbu Guanyu Wei Feifa Yimin Bu Huan Fa Huzhao De Tongzhi)*, jointly promulgated by the Ministry of Foreign Affairs and the Ministry of Public Security on 30 October 1992
14. *Circular of the Ministry of Labour on Prohibition of Illegal Acts of Overseas Employment* 1995 (PRC) (*Laodongbu Guanyu Jingzhi Feifa Chuguo Laowu Huodong De Tongzhi*), promulgated by the Ministry of Labour on 28 April 1995
15. *Circular of the Ministry of Public Security on Delivery Measures of Examination, Approval and Circulation of a Circular of the Lists of Individuals Prohibited from Entering China* 1992 (PRC) *(Gonganbu Guanyu Yingfa Buzhun Rujing Mindan Shenpi Tongbao Banfa De Tongzhi)*, promulgated by the Ministry of Public Security on 17 February 1992
16. *Circular of the Ministry of Public Security on Handling Means of Some Issues on the Implementation of Checking, Monitoring and Prevention of Exit and Entry in Regulation of Inspection of Exit and Entry Borders* 1995 (PRC) (*Gonganbu Guanyu Shishi Chujing Rujing Bianfang Jiancha Tiaoli Zhong Jiancha Jianhu He Zuzhi Churujing Deng Wenti Chuli Banfa De Tongzhi*), promulgated by the Ministry of Public Security on 13 October 1995
17. *Circular of the Ministry of Public Security on Printing and Delivery Internal Regulations and Explanations of Implementation of Two Detailed Rules of*

Implementation of Law on the Control of Exit and Entry of Citizens and Citizens 1987 (PRC) *(Gonganbu Yinfa Guanyu Zhixing Liangge Churujing Guanlifa Shishi Xize De Neibu Guiding Shuoming De Tongzhi)*, promulgated by the Ministry of Public Security on 19 February 1987

18. *Circular of the Ministry of Public Security on Repealing Some Regulative Documentation* 2001 (PRC) *(Gonganbu Guanyu Feizhi Bufeng Guifanxing Wenjian De Tongzhi)*, promulgated by the Ministry of Public Security on 5 April 2001, Gongtongzi [2001] 16
19. *Circular of the Ministry of Public Security on Simplifying the Formality of Citizens Exiting Abroad again for Private Affairs* 1992 (PRC) *(Gonganbu Guanyu Jianhua Woguo Gongmin Yinsishi Chujing Zaichujing Shouxu De Tongzhi)*, Promulgated by the Sixth Bureau of the Ministry of Public Security on 10 June 1992
20. *Circular of the Ministry of Public Security on Simplifying the Formalities of Mainlanders Short-term Exiting and Entry the Areas of Hong Kong or Macao* 2002 (PRC) (*Gonganbu Guanyu Jianhua Neidi Jumin Duanqi Wanglai Gangao Diqu De Tongzhi*), promulgated by the Ministry of Public Security in June 2002
21. *Circular of the Ministry of Public Security on Simplifying the Formality of Intermediate and Senior Science and Technology Personals Exiting Abroad for Private Affairs* 1992 (PRC) *(Gonganbu Guanyu Jianhua Zhongji Gaoji Keji Renyuan Yinsi Chujing Shouxu De Tongzhi)*, promulgated by the Ministry of Public Security on 27 August 1992
22. *Circular of the Ministry of Public Security on Some Issues of the Application for Traveling to and from Mainland of Mainland Residents who was Granted Permanent Residence of Taiwan Regions* 1995 (PRC) (*Gonganbu Guanyu Dalu Jumin Huozhun Dingju Taiwan Hou Shenqing Laiwang Dalu Youguan Wenti De Tongzhi*), promulgated by the Ministry of Public Security on 8 May 1995
23. *Circular of the Ministry of Public Security on Strictly Prohibiting From Illegally Undertaking Activities of Soliciting Clients to Permanently Emigrate* 1995 (PRC) (*Gonganbu Guanyu Jianjue Zhizhi Feifa Congshi Zhaolai Yimin Huodong De Tongzhi*), promulgated by the Ministry of Public Security on 9 August 1995
24. *Circular of the MPS on Temporally not Grant Permission to the Application for Exit China of Domestic Family Members of Wanted Suspects and Traitors* 1991 (PRC) (*Gonganbu Guanyu Zhanshi Bu Pizhun Tongji Xianyifa He Panguo Zuifan Guonei Jiasu Chuguo Shenqing De Tongzhi*), promulgated by the Ministry of Public Security in 1991 Gongtongzi No. (1991) 13
25. *Circular of Organization Department of the Central Committee of Chinese Communist Party on Strengthening Examination and Management on Individuals Exit Abroad for Public Affairs (Extract)* 1989 (PRC) *(Zhonggong Zhongyang Zuzhibu Guanyu Jiaqiang Dui Yingong Chuguo Renyuan Shencha He Guanli Gongzuo De Tongzhi (Zhailu))*
26. *Circular of Recognition of 108 Exit and Entry Intermediary Agencies for Private Affairs* 2002 (Beijing) (*Guanyu Rending 108 Jia Yinsi Churujing Zhongjie Jigou De Tongzhi*), promulgated by Beijing Municipality Public Security Bureau on 10 April 2002
27. *Circular of Regulating the Administration of the Passport and Visa Application and Exiting Abroad of Seamen Sending Abroad* 1995 (PRC) *(Guanyu Waipai Haiyuan Banzheng Chujing Guanli Gongzuo De Tonghzi)*, jointly promulgated by the Ministry

of Foreign Trade and Economic Cooperation, the Ministry of Public Security and the Ministry of Communication on 30 March 1995

28. *Circular of Some Matters on Implementation of Measures on the Control over Chinese Citizens Travelling to or from the Region of Taiwan* 1992 (PRC) *(Guanyu Zhixing Zhongguo Gongmin Wanglai Taiwan Diqu Guanli Banfa Ruogan Wenti De Tongzhi)*, promulgated by the Ministry of Public Security on 9 May 1992
29. *Circular of State Administration of Foreign Exchange and General Administration of Customs on Relevant Issues Regarding the Introduction of New Version of "Certificate for Carrying Outward Foreign Exchange Across the Border*1999 (PRC) (*Guojia Waihui Guanli Ju Haiguan Zongshu Guanyu Faxing Xinban Xiedai Waihui Chujing Xukezheng De Tongzhi*)
30. *Circular of State Administration of Foreign Exchange on Issues on Regulating Policies of Sales and Payment of Foreign exchange to Domestic Chinese Citizens for Studying Abroad or in Hong Kong, Macao and Taiwan at their Own Expenses* 2001 (*Guojia Waihui Guanli Ju Guanyu Xiang Jingnei Jumin Chuguo Huozhe Zai Xianggang Aomen He Taiwai Zifei Liuxue Xiaoshou Waihui Guanli Zhengce De Ruogan Wenti De Tongzhi*), promulgated by the State Administration of Foreign Exchange on 5 November 201 and effective on 1 December 2001
31. *Circular of State Administration of Foreign Exchange on Prepayment of Cash Deposits in RMB to Purchase and Pay Foreign Exchange by Personnel Who Study Abroad or in Hong Kong, Macao, and Taiwan at Their Own Expenses* 2000 (*Guanyu Zifei Chujing Liuxue Renyuan Yujiao Renminbi Baozhengjin Goufuhui De Tongzhi*), Hui Fa [2000] No.82
32. *Circular of State Administration of Foreign Exchange on Some Matters of Improving the Administration of Selling Foreign Exchange for Public Affairs* 2002 (PRC) (*Guojia Waihui Guanli Ju Guanyu Zuohao Yingong Chuguo Shouhui Guanli Gongzuo Youguan Wenti De Tongzhi*), promulgated by State Administration of Foreign Exchange on 20st November 2002, Huifa [2002] 118
33. *Circular of State Administration of Industry and Commerce on Strengthening the Control of Advertisement of Intermediary Agencies for Self-funded Overseas Study* 1999 (PRC) (*Guojia Gongshang Xingzheng Guali Ju Guanyu Jiaqiang Zifei Chuguo Liuxue Zhongjie Fuwu Guanggao Guanli De Tongzhi*), promulgated by State Administration of Industry and Commerce on 17 July 1999
34. *Circular of State Administration of Industry and Commerce on the Control of Advertisement of Intermediary Agencies for Exit and Entry for Private Affairs* 2001 (PRC) (*Guojia Gongshang Xingzheng Guanli Ju Guanyu Yishi Churujing Zhongjie Jigou Guanggao Guanli De Tongzhi*), promulgated by the State Administration of Industry and Commerce in September 2001
35. *Circular of State Administration of Industry and Commerce on the Prohibition of Release of Emigration Advertisement* 1995 (PRC), promulgated by State Administration of Industry and Commerce in 1995, Gongshang Guangzi [1995] No. 184.
36. *Circular of State Council Bureau for Religion Affairs, State Administration of Foreign Exchange, the Ministry of Foreign Affairs, the Ministry of Public Security, the Bank of China, Customs General Administration and Civil Aviation Administration of China on Several Rules of Self-support Pilgrimage Abroad Administration (Amendment)* 1995 (PRC) *(Guowuyuan Zongjiao Shiwu Ju Guojia Waihui Guanli Ju*

Waijiaobu Gonganbu Zhongguo Yinghang Haiguan Zongshu Minyong Hangkong Zongju Guanyu Zifei Chaojing Ruogan Guiding De Tongzhi), jointly promulgated according to *Some Rules on Self-funded Pilgrimage Abroad* 1990 (PRC) on 28 January 1995

37. *Circular of State Education Commission and the Ministry of Public Security on Prohibiting Foreign and Domestic Organs and Individuals from Recruiting Students Studying Abroad Self-funded in China without Allowance* 1987 (PRC) (*Guojia Jiaowei Gonganbu Guanyu Guoneiwai Zuzhi He Geren Bude Shanzi Zai Woguo Zaoshou Zifei Chuguo Liuxue Renyuan De Tongzhi*), jointly promulgated by the State Education Commission and the Ministry of Public Security on 21 August 1987
38. *Circular of the State Education Commission, the Ministry of Public Security and the Ministry of Foreign Affairs on Holding Ordinary Passport for Private Passport of Citizens Studying Abroad* 1993 (PRC) *(Guojia Jiaoyu Weiyuanhui Gonganbu Waijiaobu Guanyu Gongmin Chuguo Liuxue Chiyong Yinsi Putong Huzhao De Tongzhi)*, Promulgated by the State Education Commission, the Ministry of Public Security and the Ministry of Foreign Affairs on 8 July 1993
39. *Circular of the State Education Commission, State Council Bureau for Religions Affairs, the Ministry of Public Affairs and the Ministry of Foreign Affairs on Dealing with Some Issues of Recruiting Students Studying Abroad in China without Permission by Certain Departments and Individuals in China of Foreign Countries and International Organizations* 1990 (PRC) *(Guojia Jiaowei Guowuyuan Zongjiaoju Gonganbu Waijiaobu Guanyu Chuli Mouxie Guojia He Guoji Zuzhi De Zhuhua Jigou Ji Geren Shanzi Zaihua Zaoshou Liuxuesheng Wenti De Tongzhi)*, promulgated by the State Education Commission, State Council Bureau for Religions Affairs, the Ministry of Public Affairs and the Ministry of Foreign Affairs on 26 December 1990
40. *Circular of the Application for Passport and Visa for Individuals Temporally Exiting Abroad in the Cause of their Duties* 1983 (PRC) *(Linshi Yingong Chuguo Renyuan Shenban Huzhao Qianzheng Xuzhi)*, promulgated by the Department of Consular Affairs under the Ministry of Foreign Affairs on 19 July 1983
41. *Circular of the Beijing Musicality People's Government on the Implementation of the Law On Administrative License* 2003 (PRC) (*Beijingshi Renmin Zhengfu Guanyu Shishi Xingzheng Xukefa De Tongzhi*), promulgated by the State Council in 2003, Jingzhengfa [2003] 28
42. *Circular of the General Office of the Central Committee of Chinese Communist Party and the General Office of the State Council on Transmission of the Measures on the Assigning Administration of National Foreign Culture Exchange Affairs to the Ministry of Culture* 1993 (PRC) (*Zhonggong Zhongyang Bangongting Guowuyuan Bangongting Guanyu Zhuanfa Wenhuabu Guanyu Quanguo Duiwai Wenhua Jiaoliu Guikou Guanli Guanli Banfa De Tongzhi*), Tingzi No. [1993] 30
43. *Circular of the General Office of the Central Committee of Chinese Communist Party and the General Office of the State Council on Refraining of Excessively Sending Group, Team and Individuals Exit Abroad* 1986 (PRC) (*Zhonggong Zhongyang Bangongting Guowuyuan Bangongting Guanyu Zhizhi Lanpai Tuanzu He Renyuan Chuguo De Tongzhi*), promulgated on 23 January 1986
44. *Circular of the General Office of the State Council of Some Issues of Overseas Students* 1992 (*Guowuyuan Bangongting Guanyu Zaiwai Liuxue Renyuan Youguan Wenti De Tongzhi)*, promulgated by the General Office under the State Council on 12 August 1992

45. *Circular of the General Office of the State Council on the Approval and Transmission of a Report Submitted by the National Tourism Administration Concerning the Strengthening of Tourist Work* 1988 (PRC) (*Guowuyuan Bangongting Guanyu Pizhun He Zhuanfa Guojia Lvyou Guanli Ju Guanyu Jiaqiang Lvyou Gongzuo De Baogao De Tongzhi*), promulgated by the General Office of the State Council on 21 December 1988
46. *Circular of the General Office of the State Council on the Measures for Receiving Compatriots from Taiwan Coming to the Mainland to Visit their Relatives or as Tourists* 1987 (PRC) (*Guowuyuan Bangongting Guanyu Taiwan Tongbao Lai Zuguo Dalu Tiaqing Lvyou Jiedai Banfa De Tongzhi*), promulgated by the General Office of the State Council on 16 October 1987
47. *Circular of the General Office of the State Council on Transmission of the Ministry of Foreign Affairs and the Ministry of Public Security on Some Issues of Timely Collection and Uniquely Keeping Passport of Individuals Exiting Abroad in the Course of Their Duties and Strengthening Issuance Formality of the Certificate of Exiting Abroad* 1990 (PRC) *(Guowuyuan Bangongting Zhuanfa Waijiaobu Gonganbu Guanyu Jishi Shoujiao Bing Jizhong Baoguan Yingong Chuguo Renyuan Huzhao He Jinyibu Yange Chuguo (Jing) Zhengmin Hefa Shouxu Wenti De Tonghzi)*, promulgated by the Ministry of Foreign Affairs and the Ministry of Public Security on 19 July 1990
48. *Circular of the Ministry of Public Security on Seriously Carrying out the File of Gongfa(Jing) [84] 59 and Further Relaxing Exiting Abroad for Private Affairs (Abstract)* 1984 (PRC) (*Gonganbu Guanyu Renzhen Guance Zhixing Gongfa (Jing) 59 Hao Wenjian Jinyibu Fangkuang Yisi Chuguo De Tongzhi (Zaiyao)*), promulgated by the Ministry of Public Security on 22 November 1984
49. *Circular of the Ministry of Public Security, the Ministry of Education, the Ministry of Labour and Social Insurance, the State Administration of Industry and Commerce for Rectifying and Regulating Exit and Entry Intermediary Agencie* 2000 (PRC) (*Gonganbu Jiaoyubu Laodong He Shehui Baozhangbu Guojia Gongshang Xingzheng Guanli Ju Guanyu Qingli Zhengdun Churujing Zhongjie Jigou De Tongzh*i), promulgated and as effective as 27 November 2000
50. *Circular of the Organization Department under the Central Committee of Communist Party of China on Issues of Examination and Approval of Exiting Abroad for Private Affairs of Senior Cadres* 1992 (PRC) (*Zhonggong Zhongyang Zuzhibu Guanyu Shenpi Gaoji Ganbu Yisi Chuguo (Chujing) Wenti De Tongzhi*), promulgated by the Organization Department under the Central Committee of Communist Party of China on 20 August 1992
51. *Circular of the People's Bank of China on Issuing the Regulation on the Administration of Domestic Foreign Exchange Account* 1997 (PRC) (*Zhongguo Renmin Yihang Guanyu Xiafa Guanli Jingnei Waihui Zhanghu Guiding De Tongzhi*), Yinfa [1997] No. 416
52. *Circular of the Political Department of the Ministry of Public Security on Some Detailed Issues of Polices Exiting China for Private Affairs and Marrying Aliens* 1992 (PRC) (*Gonganbu Zhengzhibu Guanyu Gongan Ganjing Yinsi Chuguo(jing) He Tong Waiguoren Jiehun Deng Youguan Jige Juti Wenti De Tongzhi*), promulgated on 11 May 1992
53. *Circular of the State Administration of Foreign Exchange and the General Administration of Customs on Printing and Distributing the Provisional Measures for the Administration of Carrying Foreign Currency Cash for Persons Entering or Exiting the Territory* 2003 (PRC) (*Guuojia Waihui Guanli Ju Haiguan Zongshu*

Guanyu Ying Fa Xiedai Waibi Xianchao Chujing Zanxing Banfa De Tongzhi), Huifa [2003] No. 102

54. *Circular of the State Administration of Foreign Exchange on Adjusting the Policies for Domestic Resident Individuals to Purchase Foreign Exchange under Current Accounts* 2003 (PRC), (*Guojia Waihui Guanli Ju Guanyu Tiaozheng Jingnei Jumin Jingchang Xiangmu Xia Gouhui Zhengce De Tongzhi*), HuiFa [2003] No.104, 1 September 2003
55. *Circular of the State Administration of Foreign Exchange on Adjusting Policies on Chinese Citizens' Purchase of Foreign Exchange for Tour Abroad* 2002 (PRC) (*Guojia Waihui Guanli Ju Guanyu Tiaozheng Zhongguo Gongmin Chuguo Lvyou Gouhui Zhengce De Tongzhi*), Hui Fa [2002] No. 55
56. *Circular of the State Administration of Foreign Exchange on Relevant Issues Regarding Well Selling Foreign Exchange to Persons who Exit from the Territory for Public Affairs* 2002 (PRC) (*Guojia Waihui Guanli Ju Guanyu Zuohao Yingong Chuguo Shouhui Gongzuo Youguan Wenti De Tongzhi*), Huifa [2002] No. 118. 20 October 2003
57. *Circular of the State Administration of Foreign Exchange on Relevant Issues Regarding Further Deepen the Reform of Foreign Exchange Administration on Overseas Investment* 2003 (PRC) (*Guojia Waihui Guanli Ju Guanyu Jinyibu Shenhua Jingwai Touzi Waihui Guanli Youguan Wenti De Tongzhi*), Huifa No. [2003] 120
58. *Circular of the State Council of Overseas Chinese Affairs Office, the Ministry of Foreign Affairs, the Ministry of Public Security, the Ministry of Labour and the Ministry of Finance on the Arrangement Measures for Returned Korean and Mogonian Chinese for Permanent Residence* 1989 (PRC) (*Guowuyuan Qiaowu Bangongshi Waijiaobu Gonganbu Laodongbu Caizhengbu Guanyu Chaoxian Menggu Huaqiao Guiguo Anzhi Banfa De Tongzhi*), promulgated by of the State Council of Overseas Chinese Affairs Office, the Ministry of Foreign Affairs, the Ministry of Public Security, the Ministry of Labour and the Ministry of Finance on 9 November 1989, [89] Qiaoneihui Zi No. 019
59. *Circular of the State Council on Amending Article 6 of Regulations on Passport and Visa* (PRC) 1984 (*Guowuyuan Guanyu Xiuding Zhonghua Renmin Gongheguo Huzhao Qianzheng Tiaoli Diliutiao De Tonghzi*), promulgated by the State Council on 27 March 1984
60. *Circular of the State Council on Strengthening the Management of Activities of Intermediary Agencies of Exit and Entry for Private Affairs* 2000 (PRC) (*Guowuyuan Guanyu Jiaqiang Yinsi Churujign Zhongjie Huodong Guanli De Tongzhi*), promulgated by the State Council in 2000, Guofa [2000] No. 25
61. *Circular of the State Council on the Implementation of the Law on Administrative Sanctions* 1994 (PRC) (*Guowuyuan Guanyu Shishi Xingzheng Chufa Fa De Tongzhi*), promulgated by the State Council on 9 October 1994
62. *Circular of the State Council on the Unified Responsibility of the Ministry of Public Security Regarding the Administration of the Exit and Entry for Private Purpose of Citizens* 1956 (PRC) (*Guowuyuan Guanyu Woguo Gongmin Yinsi Chuguo De Guanli Gongzuo You Gonganbu Tongyi Zhangwo De Tongzhi*), promulgated by the State Council on 14 November 1956
63. *Circular of the State Council on Transmitting the Opinions of the Ministry of Public Security Concerning Expediting Small Town Registered Residence Management System Reform* 2001 (PRC) (*Guowuyuan Guanyu Zhuanfa Gonganbu Jiashu Xiachengzhen Huji Guanli Tizhi Gaige De Tongzhi*), promulgated by the State Council in March 2001

64. *Circular on 2002 Annual Examination for Exit and Entry Intermediary Agencies for Private Affair* 2002 (Beijing) (*Guanyu 2002 Yinsi Churujing Zhongjie Jigou Nianjian De Tongzhi*), issued by Exit and Entry Administration under Beijing Municipality Public Security Bureau on 17 December 2002
65. *Circular on Encouraging Returned Personnel to Establish Business in Beijing* 2001 (Beijing) (*Guanyu Guli Huiguo Renyuan Zai Jing Chuangli Qiye De Tongzi*), made pursuant to *Measure for the Implementation of Encouraging Returned Personnel to Establish Business In Beijing* 2001 (Beijing), promulgated by Personnel Bureau of Beijing Municipality
66. *Circular on Further Regulating Market Order of Self-funded Overseas Studying Intermediary Service* 2002 (PRC) (*Guanyu Jinyibu Guifa Zifei Chuguo Liuxue Zhongjie Jigou De Tongzhi*), promulgated by the Ministry of Education in November 2002
67. *Circular on Relevant Issues on Regularizing Banks' Settlement of Massive Foreign Exchange Holdings of Individual Residents* 2004 (PRC) (*Guanyu Guifan Jumin Geren Waihui Jiehui Guanli Youguan Wenti De Tongzhi*), promulgated by State Administration of Foreign Exchange, take into effect on 1 April 2004
68. *Circular on Simplifying the Approval of Sending Abroad Personnel Managing Overseas Enterprises of Processing and Assembling with Materials* 2002 (PRC) (*Jianhua Waipai Renyuan Guanli Haiwai Chuli Wuzi Qiye De Tongzhi*), promulgated by the Ministry of Foreign Trade and Economic Cooperation and the Ministry of Foreign Affairs
69. *Circular on Simplifying the Formality of Undergoing Temporary Residence Registration in the Mainland of Taiwan Residents* 1992 (PRC) (*Guanyu Jianhua Banli Taiwan Jumin Zai Dalu Zanzhu Shouxu De Tongzhi*), promulgated by the Ministry of Public Security on 17 June 1992
70. *Circular on Some Matters of Examination and Management of Individuals Exiting and Entering for Private Affairs* 1999 (PRC) (*Guanyu Yinsi Chujing Renyuan Shencha Guanli Youguan Wenti De Tongzhi*), promulgated by the Branch of the Ministry of Agriculture of Communist Party of China of on 24 March 1999, Nongdangzufa [1999] 10
71. *Circular on Some Matters of Implementation and Carrying Out Regulations on the Administration for Overseas Employment Intermediary Agencies (Amendment)* 2002 (*Guanyu Guance Shishi Jingwai Jiuye Zhongjie Guanli Guiding Youguan Wenti De Tonghzi (Xiuding)*), promulgated by the Ministry of Labour and Social Security on 24 June 2002
72. *Circular on Some Noteworthy Issues of Moslem Foreign Affairs* 1990 (PRC) (*Guanyu Yishilanjiao Shewai Gongzuo Zhong Ying Zhuyi De Jige Wenti De Tongzhi*), promulgated by the State Council Bureau for Religious Affairs in 1990
73. *Circular on the Amendment of Provisional Regulations of Trial Implementation Establishment of Sino-Foreign Joint Equity Travel Agencies* 1999 (PRC) (*Guanyu Xiuding Shiban Zhongwai Hezi Lvxingshe Zanxing Banfa De Tongzhi*), promulgated by China National Tourism Administration and the Ministry of Foreign Trade and Economic Cooperation on 19 April 1999
74. *Circular on the Prohibition on Handling with Notarial Certificate of Permanent Residence Certificate for Taiwan Compatriots* 1993 (PRC) (*Guanyu Bude Banli Taibao Dingjuzheng Gongzheng De Tongzhi*), promulgated by the Ministry of Justice on 20 October 1993, Sifatong [1993] 113
75. *Circular on the Prohibition on Issuance of Notarial Certificate of Permanent*

Residence Certificate for Taiwan Compatriots 1993 (PRC) (*Guanyu Bude Chuju Taibao Dingjuzheng Gongzheng De Tongzhi*), jointly promulgated by the Department of Unified Front under the Central Committee of CPC, the Ministry of Public Security and the Ministry of Justice in 1993, Tongfa [1993] 14

76. *Circular on the Recognition of Qualification of Overseas Training of Dispatching Personals to Other Countries for Training of China Communication Center of Science and Technology and other 19 Institutions and the Mass Organs* 2000 (PRC) (*Guanyu Rending Zhongguo Kexue Jishu Jiaoliu Zhongxin Deng Shijue Jia Shiye Danwei He Shehui Tuanti Juyou Zuzhi Panqian Tuanzu He Renyuan Chuguo (Jing) Peixun Gongzuo Zige De Tongzhi*), promulgated by the State Administration of Foreign Experts Affairs on 1 December 2000
77. *Constitution of the PRC* 1999 (*Zhonghua Renmin Gongheguo Xianfa*), as amended by *Constitution of the PRC* 1982 promulgated by the National People's Congress on 15 March 1999
78. *Decision of the State Council Relating to Regulating and Regularizing the Order of Market Economy* 2001 (PRC) (*Guowuyuan Guanyu Zhengdun He Guifan Shichang Jingji Zhixu De Jueding*), promulgated by the State Council on 8 May 2001
79. *Decision on Encouraging Students Overseas to Serve the Motherland in Various Forms* 2001 (PRC) (*Guanyu Guli Haiwai Liuxue Renyuan Yi Duozhong Xingshi Weiguo Fuwu De Ruogan Yijian*), promulgated by Ministries of Personnel, Education, Science and Technology, Public Security and Finance
80. *Detailed Rules for Implementing of the Law on the Control of Exit and Entry of Citizens (Amendment)* 1994 (PRC) (*Gongmin Churujing Guanli Fa Shishi Xize Xiuding*), made pursuant to the *Law on the Control of Exit and Entry of Citizens* 1985 (PRC), promulgated by the Ministry of Public Security, the Ministry of Foreign Affairs and the Ministry of Communications, and approved by the State Council on 15 July 1994.
81. *Detailed Rules for the Implementation of Law of National Security* 1994 (PRC) (*Guojia Anquan Fa Shishi Xize*), promulgated by the State Council on 4 June 1994
82. *Detailed Rules for the Implementation of Measures for the Administration on Agency Services for Self-funded Studying Abroad (for Trial Implementation)* 1999 (Beijing) (*Beijingshi Zifei Chuguo Liuxue Zhongjie Fuwu Guanli Banfa (Shixing)*) made pursuant to *Measures for the Administration on Agency Services for Self-funded Studying Abroad* 1999 (PRC), promulgated by the Bureau of Education (Beijng), the Bureau of Public Security (Beijing) and the Administration of Industry and Commerce (Beijing)
83. *Detailed Rules for the Implementation of National Security* 1994 (PRC) (*Guojia Anquanfa Shishi Xize*), made pursuant to *National Security Law* 1993 (PRC), promulgated by the State Council
84. *Detailed Rules for the Implementation of Provisional Regulations of Quality Guarantee Deposit for Travel Agencies* 1995 (PRC) (*Lvxingshe Zhiliang Baozhengjin Zanxing Guiding Shishi Xize*), promulgated by China National Tourism Administration on 1 January 1995
85. *Detailed Rules for the Implementation of Rules on the Control of Intermediary Agencies for Self-funded Overseas Study (for Trial Implementation)* 1999 (PRC) (*Zifei Chuguo Liuxue Zhongjie Fuwu Guanli Guiding Shishi Xize (Shxing)*), promulgated by the Ministry of Education, the Ministry of Public Security and State Administration of Industry and Commerce on 24 August 1999
86. *Detailed Rules for the Implementation of the Law on the Control of Entry and Exit of*

Aliens 1986 (PRC) (*Waiguoren Rujing Chujing Guanlifa Shishi Xize*), made pursuant to the *Law on the Control of Exit and Entry of Aliens* 1985 (PRC), promulgated by the Ministry of Public Security and the Ministry of Foreign Affairs, and approved by the State Council on 27 December 1994

87. *Detailed Rules for the Implementation of the Law on the Control of Entry and Exit of Aliens (Amendment)* 1994 (PRC) (*Waiguoren Rujing Chujing Guanlifa Shishi Xize Xiuding*), made pursuant to the *Law on the Control of Exit and Entry of Aliens* 1985 (PRC) promulgated by the Ministry of Public Security and the Ministry of Foreign Affairs on 15 July 1994, and approved by the State Council on 13 July 1994
88. *Detailed Rules for the Implementation of the Law on the Control of Entry and Exit of Citizens* (Amendment) 1994 (PRC) (*Gongmin Chujing Rujing Guanlifa Shishi Xize*), made pursuant to *Law on the Control of Exit and Entry of Citizens* 1986 (PRC), promulgated by the Ministry of Public Security and the Ministry of Foreign Affairs on 15 July 1994, and approved by the State Council on 13 July 1994
89. *Detailed Rules for the Implementation of the Laws on the Administration of Tax Collection* 1993 (PRC) (*Suishou Zhengguan Fa Shishi Xize*), promulgated by the State Council on 4 August 1993
90. *Detailed Rules of the Implementation of the Ministry of Foreign Affairs on Carrying out Some Rules of the General Office of the Central Committee of Chinese Communist Party and the General Office of the State Council on Serious Restriction Cadres in the Organs of Party Committees and Governments Exit China* 1987 (PRC) (*Waijiaobu Guanche Zhixing Zhonggong Zhongyang Bangongting Guowuyuan Bangongting Guanyu Yange Kongzhi Dangzheng Jiguan Ganbu Chuguo Wenti De Ruogan Guiding De Shishi Xize*), promulgated on 7 October 1987
91. *Detailed Rules of the Implementation of Regulations on the Administration of Travel Agencies* 2003 (PRC) (*Lvxingshe Guanli Tiaoli Shishi Xize*), promulgated by China National Tourism Administration on 10 June 2003
92. *Detailed Rules of the Implementation on Protection of the Rights and Interests of Chinese and Family Members of Overseas Chinese* 1993 (PRC) (*Guiqiao Qiaojuan Quanyi Baohufa Shishi Xize*), made pursuant to *Law on Protection of the Rights and Interests of Returned Overseas Chinese and Family Members of Overseas Chinese Law* 1990 (PRC), promulgated by the State Council on 19 July 1993
93. *Detailed Rules of the Implementation on the Administration of Domestic Resident Individuals to Purchase Foreign Exchange for Private Purpose* 2002 (PRC) (*Jingnei Jumin Geren Yinsi Gouhui Guanli Shishi Xize*)
94. *Directive of the State Council on Establishing Regular Household Registration System* 1955 (*Guowuyuan Guanyu Jianli Jingchang Hukou Dengji Zhidu De Zhishi*), promulgated by the State Council of the PRC on 22 June 1955
95. *Explanation of the Ministry of Public Security on Some Issues on Implementation of Law on the Control of Exit and Entry of Citizens and Its Detailed Rules for the Implementation* 1987 (PRC) (*Gonganbu Guanyu Zhixing Zhongguo Gongmin Chujing Rujing Guanli Fa Ji Shishi Xize Ruogan Wenti De Shuoming*), promulgated by the Ministry of Public Security on 19 February 1987
96. *Explanation of Some Matters on the Implementation of Chapter Six of Measures on the Control over Chinese Citizens Travelling to or from the Region of Taiwan* 1992 (PRC) (*Guanyu Zhixing Zhongguo Gongmin Wanglai Taiwan Diqu Guanli Banfa Diliuzhang Youguan Wenti De Tongzhi*), promulgated by the Ministry of Public Security on 20 June 1992

97. *Explanation of Some Matters on Implementation of Measures on the Control over Chinese Citizens Travelling to or from the Region of Taiwan* 1992 (PRC) (*Guanyu Zhixing Zhongguo Gongmin Wanglai Taiwan Diqu Guanli Banfa Ruogan Wenti De Tongzhi*), promulgated by the Ministry of Public Security on 9 May 1992
98. *Explanation of Some Matters on Implementation of Provisional Measures on the Control over Chinese Citizens Travelling for Private Affairs to or from the Regions of Hong Kong or Macao* 1986 (PRC) (*Guanyu Zhixing Zhongguo Gongmin Wanglai Gangao Diqu Zanxing Guanli Banfa Ruogan Wenti De Shuoming*), promulgated by the Ministry of Public Security on 19 February 1987
99. *Explanation of the Enforcement of the Amendment of Two Detailed Rules of the Implementation* 1995 (PRC) (*Zhixing Liangge Shishi Xize Xiuding Neirong De Shuoming*), promulgated by the Ministry of Public Security on 13 February 1995
100. *Explanation of the Law on Administrative License (Draft)* 2003 (PRC) (*Guanyu Xingzheng Xukefa (Caoan) De Shuoming*), promulgated by the Standing Committee of the National People's Congress on 23 August 2003
101. *Explanations of the Sixth Bureau of the Ministry of Public Security on Issues of Providing Comments of Employed The organization Where the Applicant is Services of Citizens Exiting Abroad* 1989 (PRC) (*Gonganbu Liuju Guanyu Gongmin Shenqing Chuguo Tijiao Suozai Gongzuo Danwei Yijian Wenti De Shuomin*), promulgated by the Sixth Bureau of the Ministry of Public Security on 11 March 1989
102. *General Principles of the Civil Law* 1986 (PRC) (*Minfa Tongze*), promulgated by the National People's Congress on 12 April 1986 and effective on 1 January 1987
103. *Implementation Opinion of Shanghai Municipality on Provisional Regulations of the Establishment and Administration of Sino-Foreign Equity or Cooperative Joint Venture Employment Agencies* 2002 (Shanghai) (*Shanghaishi Guanyu Jianli He Guanli Zhongwai Hezi Hezuo Rencai Zhongjie Jigou Guanli Zanxing Guiding De Shishi Yijian*), promulgated pursuant to *Provisional Regulations of the Establishment and Administration of Sino-Foreign Equity or Cooperative Joint Venture Employment Agencies* 2002 (PRC) on 23 April 2002
104. *Implementing Measures on Protection of the Rights and Interests of Returned Overseas Chinese and Family Members of Overseas Chinese* 2002 (Guangdong) (*Guangdongsheng Guanyu Guiqiao Qiaojuan Quanyi Baohufa Shishi Banfa*), made pursuant to *Law on Protection of the Rights and Interests of Returned Overseas Chinese and Members of Overseas Chinese* 2000 (PRC), promulgated by the People's Congress of Guangdong Province
105. *Instruction to Application for the License for a Overseas Employment Intermediary Agencies* 2003 (Beijing) (*Beijingshi Guanyu Shenqing Jingwai Jiuye Zhongjie Jigou Xukezheng De Shuoming*), issued by Beijing Municipality Labour and Social Security Bureau in 2003
106. *Interpretation by the Standing Committee of the National People's Congress Regarding Clause 4 Article 22 and Category (3) of Clause 2 Article 24 of the Basic Law of the Hong Kong Special Administrative Region of the People's Republic of China* 1999 (PRC) (*Quanguo Renda Changweihui Guanyu Xianggang Tebie Xingzheng Qu Jiben Fa Di 22 Tiao Di 4 Kuan He Di 24 Tiao Di 2 Kuan Di 3 Xiang De Jieshi*), promulgated by the Standing Committee of the National People's Congress on 26 June 1999
107. *Law of Administration Penalty* 1996 (PRC) (*Xingzheng Chufa Fa*), made pursuant

to the *Constitution of the PRC* 1993, promulgated by the Standing Committee of the National People's Congress

108. *Law of Civil Procedure* 1991 (PRC) (*Minshi Shusong Fa*), promulgated by the National People's Congress on 9 April 1991
109. *Law of Criminal (Amendment)* 1997 (PRC) (*Xing Fa (Xiuding)*), promulgated by the National People Congress on 14 March 1997
110. *Law of Criminal Procedure (Amendment)* 1996 (PRC) (*Xingshi Shusong Fa (Xiuding)*), promulgated by the National People's Congress in accordance with the *Law of Criminal Procedure* 1979 on 17 March 1996
111. *Law of National Security* 1993 (PRC) (*Guojia Anquan Fa*), promulgated by the Standing Committee of the National People's Congress on 22 February 1993
112. *Law of Nationality* 1980 (PRC) promulgated by the National People's Congress on 10 September 1980
113. *Law of the Legislation* 2000 (PRC) (*Lifa Fa*), promulgated by the National People's Congress on 15 March 2000 and effective on 1 July 2000
114. *Law of the Organ of the State Council* 1982 (PRC) (*Guowuyuan Zuzhi Fa*), promulgated by National People's Congress on 10 December 1982
115. *Law on Administrative License* 2003 (PRC) (*Xingzheng Xuke Fa*), promulgated by the Standing Committee of the National People's Congress on 27 August 2003 and effective on 1 July 2004
116. *Law on Administrative Procedure* 1989 (PRC) (*Xingzheng Shusong Fa*), promulgated by the Standing Committee of the National People's Congress on 4 April 1989 and effective on 1 October 1990
117. *Law on Administrative Review* 1999 (PRC) (*Xingzheng Fuyi Fa*), promulgated by the Standing Committee of the National People's Congress on 29 April 1999 and effective on 1 October 1999
118. *Law on Administrative Supervision* 1997 (PRC) (*Xingzheng Jiancha Fa*), promulgated by the Standing Committee of the National People's Congress on 9 May 1997
119. *Law on Protection of the Rights and Interests of Returned Overseas Chinese and Family Members of Overseas Chinese* 1990 (PRC) (*Guiqiao Qiaojuan Quanyi Baohu Fa*), promulgated by the Standing Committee of the National People's Congress on 7 September 1990
120. *Law on Protection of the Rights and Interests of Returned Overseas Chinese and the Family Members of Overseas Chinese (Amendment)* 2000 (PRC) (*Guiqiao Qiaojuan Quanyi Baohu Fa (Xiuding)*), promulgated by the Standing Committee of the National People's Congress according to *Law on the Protection of the Rights and Interests of Returned Overseas Chinese and the Family Members of Overseas Chinese* 1990 (PRC) on 31 October 2000
121. *Law on State Compensation* 1994 (PRC) (*Guojia Peichang Fa*), promulgated by the Standing Committee of the National People's Congress on 12 May 1994 and effective on 1 January 1995
122. *Law on the Administration of Tax Collection (Amendment)* 2001 (PRC) (*Suishou Zhengguan Fa (Xiuding)*), promulgated by the Standing Committee of National People's Congress on 28 April 2001 pursuant to the *Law on the Administration of Tax Collection* 1992 (PRC)
123. *Law on the Control of the Entry and Exit of Aliens* 1985 (PRC) (*Waiguoren Rujing Chujing Guanli Fa*), promulgated by the Standing Committee of National People's Congress on 22 November 1985 and effective on 1 February 1986

124. *Law on the Control of Exit and Entry of Citizens* 1985 (PRC) (*Gongmin Chujing Rujing Guanli Fa*), promulgated by the Standing Committee of National People's Congress on 22 November 1985 and effective on 1 February 1986
125. *Legal Rights and Interests of Overseas Labours* 2002 (PRC) (*Haiwai Laogong Hefa Quanyi De Tongzhi*), promulgated by the Ministry of Foreign Trade and Economy Cooperation in January 2002
126. *Measures for the Administration on Exit and Entry Agency Service for Private Affairs (for Trial Implementation)* 2001 (PRC) (*Yinsi Churujing Zhongjie Huodong Gunali Banfa Ruogan Guiding (Shixing)*), promulgated by the Ministry of Public Security and the State Administration of Industry and Commerce
127. *Measures for the Administration of the Use of Foreign Exchange on Temporally Exiting the Territory for Public Affairs* 2002 (PRC) (*Yingong Linshi Chuguo Yonghui Guanli Banfa*), No. [2003] 314, the Ministry of Finance
128. *Measures for the Control of Exit and Entry Taiwai Regions of Chinese Citizens* 1992 (PRC) (*Zhongguo Gongmin Wanglai Taiwan Diqu Guanli Banfa*), jointly promulgated by the Ministry of Public Security, the Ministry of Foreign Affairs and the Ministry of Communication on 1 May 1992
129. *Measures for the Control of Intermediary Agencies for Self-funded Overseas Study (for Trial Implementation)* 1999 (Beijing) (*Beijingshi Zifei Chuguo Liuxue Zhongjie Fuwu Guanli Banfa (Shixing)*), promulgated by Beijing Municipality Committee of Education, Beijing Municipality Public Security Bureau and Beijing Municipality Administration of Industry and Commerce on 2 November 1999
130. *Measures for the Implementation on Examination and Approval of Exit Abroad (Including Hong Kong or Macao) and Invitation Aliens to China of Employees of National Pilot Enterprises Group (for Trial Implementation Implementation)* 1992 (PRC) *(Guangyu Guojia Shidian Qiye Jituan Renyuan Chuguo (Han Gangao) He Yaoqing Laihua Shixiang Shenpi De Shishi Banfa (Shixing))*, Promulgated by the State Council Foreign Affairs Office, State Planning Committee, State Commission for Restructuring the Economy System, State Council Production Office on 31 March 1992
131. *Measures for the Implementation on Examination and Approval of Sending Employees to Temporally Exiting Abroad (Including Hong Kong or Macao) and Inviting Aliens to China by Industry Enterprises of the Ownership by the Whole People (For Trial Implementation)* 1993 (PRC) (*Quanmin Suoyouzhi Gongye Qiye Panqian Linshi Chuguo (jing) Renyuan He Yaoqing Waiguo Jingmao Renyuan Laihua Shenpi De Shishi Banfa (Shixing)*), Promulgated by State Council Foreign Affairs Office, State Council Hong Kong or Macao Affairs Office, State Commission of Economy and Trade and State Commission for Restructuring the Economy System on 29 June 1993
132. *Measures for the Implementation on Preventing Defaulting Taxpayer from Exiting Abroad* 1997 (PRC) (*Jingzhi Weifushuizhe Chujing Shishi Banfa*), promulgated by the Ministry of Public Security and State Tax Administration on 20 February 1997
133. *Measures of Administration on Citizens Tours Abroad* 2002 (PRC) (*Zhongguo Gongmin Chuguo Lvyou Guanli Banfa*), promulgated by the State Council
134. *Measures of Beijing Municipal People's Government on Formulation of Rules and Regulations* 2002 (Beijing) (*Beijingshi Renmin Zhengfu Guizhang Zhiding Banfa*), promulgated by Beijing Municipal People's Government on 21 May 2002 and effective on 1 June 2002

135. *Measures of Examination and Approval of Intermediary Agencies of Introducing Foreign Professional Talents to Work in China* 1996 (PRC) *(Waiguo Zhuanye Rencai Laihua Gongzuo Zhongjie Jigou Shenpi Banfa)*, promulgated by the State Administration of Foreign Experts Affairs on 30 May 1996
136. *Measures of Examination and Approval of Sending Individuals to be Employed in Hong Kong and Macao for a Long Term* 1991 (PRC) (*Guanyu Paiwang Gangao Diqu Changzhu Renyuan De Shenpi Baifa*), promulgated by the State Council Hong Kong and Macao Office on 10 August 1991
137. *Measures of Examination and Approval of Traveling to Hong Kong or Macao for Permanent Residence of Inland Residents* 2004 (PRC) (*2004 Nian Neidi Jumin Fu Gangao Diqu Dingju Shenpi Banfa*), promulgated by the Ministry of Public Security in December 2003
138. *Measures of Examination, Approval and Circulation of a Circular of the Lists of Individuals Prohibited from Entering China* 1992 (PRC) (*Buzhun Rujing Mindan Shenpi Tongbao Banfa De Tongzhi*), promulgated by the Ministry of Public Security on 17 February 1992
139. *Measures of Purchasing Travel Agencies Responsibility Insurance of Travel Agencies* 2001 (PRC) (*Lvxingshe Toubao Lvxingshe Zeren Baoxian Guiding)*, promulgated by State National Administration of Tourism on 15 May 2001
140. *Measures of Taiyuan Municipal Peopls's Government on Legislation* 2002 (Taiyuan) (*Taiyuanshi Lifa Tiaoli*), promulgated by Taiyuan Munipal People's Congress on 24 May 2002
141. *Measures of the General Office of the Central Committee of Chinese Communist Party and the General Office of the State Council on Adjusting Examination and Approval Power of Sending Individuals Exit Abroad Temporarily and Inviting Aliens to Visit China* 1993 (PRC) (*Zhonggong Zhongyang Bangongting Guowuyuan Bangongting Guanyu Tiaozheng Paiqian Linshi Chuguo Renyuan He Yaoqing Waiguo Renyuan Laihua Shenpi Quanxian De Banfa*)
142. *Measures on Administration of Passport and Other Travel Abroad Documents of Officials Employed by the CPC, governments, Courts, Procuratorial Courts, Justice Departments and Public Security Departments* 2003 (PRC) (*Dangzheng Sifa Gongan Anquan Ganbu Huzhao Ji Qita Chuguo Zhengjian Guanli Banfa*), promulgated by the Central Committee of Communist Party of China in August 2003
143. *Measures on Encouraging Personnel Who Study Abroad to Service Sichun Province* 2003 (Sichun) (*Sichuanshen Guli Haiwai Liuxue Renyuan Laichuan Fuwu Banfa*), promulgated by Sichun People's Government of China in 2003
144. *Measures on Procedures for Contract Workers Sent Abroad Leaving the Country (Amendment)* 2002 (PRC) (*Waipai Laowu Renyuan Chengxu Banfa*), amended pursuant to *Provisional Measures on Procedures for Contract Workers Sent Abroad Leaving the Country* 1996 (PRC), promulgated by the Ministry of Foreign Trade and Economy Cooperation on 1 April 2002
145. *Measures on Prohibition of Exit and Entry of National Currency* 1951 (PRC) (*Jingzhi Guojia Huobi Churu Guojing Banfa*), promulgated by the Government Administration Council, Central People's Government
146. *Measures on the Administration of Chinese Citizens' Tours Abroad at Their Own Expense (Amendment)* 2002 (PRC) (*Zhongguo Gongmin Zifei Chuguo Lvyou Guanli Banfa*), promulgated by the State Council on 1 July 2002

147. *Measures on the Administration of Exit and Entry Intermediary Agencies for Private Affairs* 2001 (PRC) (*Yinsi Churujing Zhongjie Huodong Guanli Banfa Ruogan Guiding*), jointly promulgated by the Ministry of Public Security and State Administration of Industry and Commerce on 17 July 2001 and effective 17 July 2002
148. *Measures on the Administration of Opening Employment Cooperation with Hong Kong Region* 1996 (PRC) *(Dui Xianggang Diqu Kanzhan Laowu Hezuo Guanli Banfa)*, promulgated by the Ministry of Foreign Trade and Economic Cooperation on 5 September 1996, Waijingmao Hefa [1996] 605
149. *Measures on the Administration of Opening Normal Employment Cooperation with Macao Region* 1998 (PRC) *(Dui Aomen Diqu Kanzhan Putong Laowu Hezuo Guanli Banfa)*, jointly promulgated by the Ministry of Foreign Trade and Economic Cooperation and the State Council Hong Kong and Macao Affairs Office, Waijingmao Hefa [1998] 430
150. *Operational Manual of the Processing of Aliens Visas* 1995 (PRC) (*Shenli Waiguoren Qianzheng Chaozuo Shouce*), promulgated by the Ministry of Public Security in 1995
151. *Operational Norms of Application, Examination and Approval of Exiting Abroad and Passport For Private Affairs of Citizens* 1996 (PRC) *(Gongmin Yinsishi Chuguo Huzhao Shenqing Shenpi Guanli Gongzuo Guifan)*, promulgated by the Ministry of Public Security on 3rd December 1996
152. *Operational Norms on the Control of Examination and Approval of Traveling to Hong Kong or Macao for Permanent Residence of Inland Residents* 1997 (PRC) *(Neidi Gongmin Fu Gangao Diqu Dingju Shenpi Guanli Gongzuo Guifan)*, promulgated by the Ministry of Public Security in May 1997
153. *Opinions for Encouraging Enterprises to Develop Business Overseas* 1999 (PRC) (*Guli Qiye Fazhan Haiwai Yewu De Jianyi*), promulgated by the General Office of the State Council
154. *Opinions of the State Council Overseas Chinese Affairs Office, Exit and Entry Administration under the Ministry of Public Security and Department of Consular Affairs under the Ministry of Foreign Affairs on Returning to China for Permanent Residence of Overseas Chinese* 1991 (PRC) (*Guowuyuan Qiaoban Gonganbu Liuju Waijiaobu Lingshisi Guanyu Lvju Guowai Zhongguo Gongmin Shenqing Huiguo Dingju De Yijian*), jointly promulgated by State Council Overseas Chinese Affairs Office, the Bureau of Exit and Entry Administration under the Ministry of Public Security and Department of Consular Affairs under the Ministry of Foreign Affairs on 27 February 1991
155. *Opinions on Well Handling with the Work of Taiwan Compatriots Traveling to Motherland to Visit the Relatives* 1987 (PRC) (*Guanyu Zuohao Taibao Lai Zuguo Dalu Tanqin Gongzuo De Yijian*), promulgated by the Leading Panel of Taiwan Affairs under the Central Committee of Communist Party of China in 1987, Zhongbanfa [1987] 14
156. *Part Seven of Overseas Talents of Outline of Program of National Talents Forster from 2002 to 2005* (*2002–2005 Nian Quanguo Rencai Duiwu Jianshe Guihua Gangyao*), promulgated by the General Office of the Central Committee of the CPC and the General Office of the State Council in 2002
157. *Proclamation of the Ministry of Public Security, the Central People's Government on the Control over Passengers Traveling to and from the Regions of Hong Kong or Macao* 1951 (PRC) (*Zhongyang Renmin Zhengfu Gonganbu Guanyu Wanglai*

Xianggang Aomen Lvke Guanli De Bugao), promulgated by the Ministry of Public Security on 2 August 1951 and effective on 1 September 1951

158. *Provisional Detailed Rules of the Implementation of the Stipulations on Sending Term, Group and Individuals to be Trained Abroad* 1990 (PRC) *(Guanyu Paiqian Tuanzu He Renyuan Fu Guowai Peixun De Guanding De Zanxing Shishi Xize)*, promulgated by the State Council Introduction of Foreign Intellectuality Leading Panel Office on 15 April 1990
159. *Provisional Measures for Citizens Travelling on Private Affairs to or from the Regions of Hong Kong or Macao* 1986 (PRC) (*Zhongguo Gongmin Yin Sishi Wanglai Xianggang Diqu Huozhe Aomeng Diqu De Zanxing Guanli Banfa*), promulgated by the Ministry of Public Security and Approved by the State Council on 25 December 1986
160. *Provisional Measures for the Administration of Carrying Foreign Exchange Cash for Persons Entering or Exiting the Territory* 2003 (PRC) (*Xiedai Waibi Xiaoshao Churujing Guanli Zanxing Banfa*) No. [2003] 102 of the State Administration of Foreign Currency
161. *Provisional Measures for the Administration of China National Tourism Administration on Organization of Tour to Thailand, Singapore and Malaysia 1990* (PRC) (*Guojia Lvyouju Guanyu Zuzhi Woguo Gongmin Fu Dongnanya Sanguo Lvyou De Zaoxing Guanli Banfa*), promulgated by China National Tourism Administration on 5 December 1990
162. *Provisional Measures for the Procedures of Exiting Abroad Examination and Approval and Handling with Passport of Labours Sending Abroad* 1990 (PRC) *(Guanyu Waipai Laowu Renyuan Chuguo Shenpi Shouxu He Banli Huzhao De Zanxing Banfa)*, Promulgated by the Ministry of Foreign Economic Cooperation and Trade, the Ministry of Labour, the Ministry of Foreign Affairs and the Ministry of Public Security on 14 December 1990
163. *Provisional Measures of the Administration of Intermediary Agencies of Introducing Foreign Professional Talents to Work in China* 1995 (PRC) (*Waiguo Zhuanye Rencai Laihua Gongzuo Zhongjie Jigou Zanxing Guanli Banfa*), jointly promulgated by State Administration of Foreign Experts Affairs and State Administration of Industry and Commerce on 25 August 1995
164. *Provisional Measures of the Beijing Municipality for Promotion the Establishment of Sino-Foreign Joint Venture Skilled Personnel Intermediary Agencies* 2002 (Beijing) (*Beijingshi Guli Sheli Zhongwai Heying Rencai Zhongjie Fuwu Jigou Zanxing Banfa*), jointly promulgated by Beijing Municipal Bureau of Personnel, Beijing Administration of Industry and Commerce, Beijing Committee of Foreign Trade and Economic Cooperation on 14 June 2002
165. *Provisional Measures of the Reserve Funds of Foreign Labour Cooperation* 2001 (PRC) (*Duiwai Laowu Hezuo Beiyongjing Zanxing Banfa*), promulgated by the Ministry of Foreign Trade and Economic Cooperation on 27 November 2001
166. *Provisional Measures of the Reserve Funds of Foreign Labour Cooperation (Amendment)* 2003 (PRC) (*Duiwai Laowu Hezuo Beiyongjing Zanxing Banfa) (Xiuding)*, promulgated by the Ministry of Commerce on 21 August 2003
167. *Provisional Measures on Administration of State Dispatched Sports Technicians Exiting Abroad* 1992 (PRC) (*Guanyu Gongpai Chuguo (jing) Tiyu Jishu Renyuan De Guanli Zanxing Banfa*), promulgated by the State Sport Commission on 12 March 1990

168. *Provisional Measures on Exit of Aliens in China 1954 (PRC) (Waiguo Qiaomin Chujing Zanxing Banfa),* promulgated by the Ministry of Public Security on 10 August 1954
169. *Provisional Measures on Procedures for Contract Workers Sent Abroad Leaving the Country and Undergoing Passport Application* 1990 (PRC) (*Guanyu Paiqian Laowu Chujing He Banli Huzhao Chengxu De Zanxing Banfa*), jointly promulgated by the Ministry of Foreign Trade and Economic Cooperation, the Ministry of Labour, the Ministry of Foreign Affairs and the Ministry of Public Security, approved by the State Council on 14 December 1990
170. *Provisional Measures on Procedures for Contract Workers Sent Abroad Leaving the Country* 1996 (PRC) (*Guanyu Banli Waipai Laowu Renyuan Chuguo Shouxu De Zanxing Guiding*), jointly promulgated by the Ministry of Foreign Trade and Economy Cooperation, the Ministry of Foreign Affairs and the Ministry of Public Security approved by the State Council on 20 December 1996
171. *Provisional Measures on Residence Registration and the Issuance of Residence Certificate of Aliens in China* 1954 (PRC) (*Waiguo Qiaomin Juliu Dengji Ji Juliuzheng Qianfa Zanxing Banfa*), promulgated by the Ministry of Public Security on 10 August 1954
172. *Provisional Measures on the Administration of Chinese Citizens' Tours Abroad at Their Own Expense* 1997 (PRC) (*Zhongguo Gongmin Zifei Chugu Lvyou Guanli Zanxing Banfa*), promulgated by China National Tourism Administration and the Ministry of Public Security and approved by the State Council on 1 July 1997
173. *Provisional Measures on the Administration of Dispatching Groups and Personals to Other Countries for Training* 1993 (PRC) *(Guanyu Panqian Tuanzu He Renyuan Fu Guo(Jing)Wai Peixun De Zanxing Guanli Banfa)*, jointly promulgated by the State Administration of Foreign Experts Affairs and the Ministry of Foreign Affairs on 20 October 1993
174. *Provisional Measures on the Administration of Domestic Resident Individuals Foreign Exchange (Amendment)* 2003 (PRC) (*Jingnei Jumin Geren Waihui Guanli Zanxing Banfa*), Huifa [1999] No. 305
175. *Provisional Measures on the Administration of Foreign Currency Exchange Agencies* 2003 (PRC) (*Waibi Duihuai Jigou Guanli Zhaixing Banfa*), The People's Bank of China No. [2003] 6
176. *Provisional Measures on the Administration of Foreign Exchange of Individual Residents in Inland* 1998 (PRC) (*Jingnei Jumin Geren Waihui Guanli Zanxing Banfa*), promulgated by State Administration of Foreign Exchange on 1 September 1998, Huifa [1998]11
177. *Provisional Measures on the Administration of Foreign labour and cooperation* 1993 (PRC) (*Duiwai Laowu Hezuo Guanli Zanxing Banfa*), promulgated by the Ministry of Foreign Trade and Economic Cooperation on 5 November 1993
178. *Provisional Measures on the Administration of Foreign Organs and Domestic Intermediary Agencies of Introducing Foreign Experts Culture and Education* 1993 (PRC) (*Guanyu Dui Jieshao Waiguo Wenjiao Zhuanjia Laihua Gongzuo De Jingwai Zuzhi He Jingnei Zhongjie Jigou Guanli De Zanxing Banfa*), promulgated by State Administration of Foreign Experts Affairs on 15 June 1993
179. *Provisional Measures on the Administration of the Ministry of Agriculture on Agricultural Interchange and Communication with the Regions of Taiwan* 1998

(PRC) *(Nongyebu Duitai Nongye Jiaoliu Huodong Guanli Zanxing Banfa)*, promulgated by the Ministry of Agriculture on 9 September 1998, Nongbanfa [1998] 14

180. *Provisional Measures on the Administration of Opening Senior Employment Cooperation with Hong Kong Special Administration Regions* 2000 (PRC) (*Dui Xianggang Tebie Xingzhengqu Kanzhan Gaoji Laowu Hezuo Guanli Zanxing Banfa*), jointly promulgated by the Ministry of Foreign Trade and Economic Cooperation on 25 December 2000, Waijingmao Hefa [2000] 660
181. *Provisional Measures on the Control over Inland Residents Traveling for Such Business, Training, Employment as Non-Public Affairs to or from Hong Kong Special Administration Regions* 1998 (PRC) *(Neidi Jumin Congshi Shangwu Peixun Jiuye Deng Feigongwu Huodong Wanglai Xianggang Tebie Xingzhengqu De Zanxing Guanli Banfa)*, promulgated by the Ministry of Public Security on 19March 1998 and effective on 30 March 1998
182. *Provisional Measures on the Exit and Entry National Border of Overseas Chinese,* 1951 (PRC) (*Huaqiao Churu Guojing Zanxing Banfa*), promulgated by the Ministry of Public Security on 2 August 1951
183. *Provisional Measures on the Experiments of China-foreign Equity Joint Venture Travel Agencies* 1998 (PRC) (*Shiban Zhongwai Hezi Lvxingshe Zanxing Banfa*), jointly promulgated by China National Tourism Administration and the Ministry of Foreign Trade and Economic Cooperation on 2 December 1998
184. *Provisional Measures on Travel of Aliens in China* 1954 (PRC) (*Waiguo Qiaomin Lvxing Zanxing Banfa*), promulgated by the Ministry of Public Security on 10 August 1954
185. *Provisional Provisions of the Special Economic Zones in Guangdong Province for the Control of Personnel Entering and Leaving China* 1981 (Guangdong) (*Guangdong Sheng Jingji Tequ Renyuan Churujing Zanxing Banfa*), adopted by the 13th Session of the Standing Committee of the Fifth People's Congress of Guangdong Province on November 17, 1981 and promulgated on 24 December 1981
186. *Provisional Regulations of Administration of Foreign Holding and Foreign Self-funded Travel Agencies* 2003 (PRC) (*Waiguo Konggu Waishang Duzi Lvxingshe Zanxing Guiding*), jointly promulgated by China National Tourism Administration and the Ministry of Commerce on 12 June 2003 and effective on 11 July 2003
187. *Provisional Regulations of Quality Guarantee Deposit* 1995 (PRC) (*Lvxingshe Zhiliang Baozhengjin Zanxing Guiding*), promulgated by China National Tourism Administration on 1 January 1995
188. *Provisional Regulations of the Establishment and Administration of Sino-Foreign Equity or Cooperative Joint Venture Employment Agencies* 2001 (PRC) (*Sheli He Guanli Zhongwai Hezi Hezuo Jingwai Jiuye Zhongjie Jigou Zanxing Guiding*), promulgated by the Ministry of Labour and Social Security and the State Administration for Industry and Commerce on 9 October and effective on 1 December 2001
189. *Provisional Regulations on the Administration of Ordinary Passport for Public Affairs* 1993 (PRC) (*Guanyu Yingong Huzhao Guanli De Zanxing Guiding*), promulgated by the Ministry of Public Affairs in December 1993
190. *Provisional Regulations on the Administration of Sino-Foreign Joint Venture Personnel Intermediary Agencies* 2003 (PRC) (*Zhongwai Hezi Rencai Zhongjie Jigou Guanli Zanxing Guiding*), jointly promulgated by the Ministry of Personnel, the Ministry of Commerce and State Administration of Industry and Commerce on 4 September 2003

191. *Provisional Regulations on the Administration of Travel Agencies 1985 (PRC)* (*Lvxingshe Guanli Zanxing Tiaoli*), promulgated by the State Council on 11 May 1985
192. *Provisional Regulations on the Administration of Urban Household* 1951 (PRC) (*Chengshi Hukou Guanli Zanxing Tiaoli*), promulgated by the Ministry of Public of Security on 16 July 1951
193. *Provisional Rules on Attendance of Games or Competitions Abroad by Employment of Athletes* 1989 (PRC) (*Yundongyuan Shoupin Dao Guo(Jing)wai Cansai De Ruogan Guiding*), promulgated by State Commission for Physical Culture and Sports on 31 May 1989
194. *Provisional Rules on Some Issues of State Dispatched Coaches Aid for Foreign Countries* 1990 (PRC) *(Guanyu Gongpai Yuanwai Jiaolian Renyuan Ruogan Wenti De Zanxing Guiding)*, promulgated by State Sport Commission on 16 November 1990
195. *Provisional Rules on the Administration of the Establishment of Sino-Foreign Equity Joint and Sino-Foreign Cooperation Job Intermediary Institutions* 2001 (PRC) (*Zhongwai Hezi Zhongwai Hezuo Zhiye Jieshao Jigou Sheli Guanli Zanxing Guiding*), jointly promulgated by the Ministry of Labour and Social Security and State Administration of Industry and Commerce on 9 October 2001
196. *Provisional Rules on the Exit, Entry and Stay of Aliens in China* 1951 (PRC) (*Waiguo Qiaomin Churu Ji Juliu Zanxing Guize*), promulgated by Government Administration Council on 28 November 1951
197. *Provisional Rules on the Recognition of Overseas Training Qualification of Dispatching Groups and Personals to Other Countries for Training of the Institutions and the Mass Organs* 1993 (PRC) (*Guanyu Shiye Danwei Shehui Tuanti Zuzhi Panqian Tuanzu He Renyuan Fu Guo (Jing) Wai Peixun Gongzuo Zige Rending De Zanxing Guiding*), promulgated by State Administration of Foreign Experts Affairs in June 1993, Waizhuanfa [1993] 204
198. *Provisions on Registration of Marriages Between Chinese Citizens and Foreigners* 1983 (PRC) (*Zhongguo Gongmin Yu Waiguoren Hunyin Dengji Banfa*), promulgated by the Ministry of Civil Affairs and approved by the State Council
199. *Provisions on the Introduction of High Quality Talents Abroad 1997(Shanghai)* (*Yinjin Guowai Gaokeji Rencai Banfa*), promulgated by Shanghai People's Government on 10 April 1997
200. *Public Circular on Issues Concerning Compatriots in the Region of Hong Kong or Macao Traveling to and from with Compatriots in the Region of Hong Kong or Macao Returning Certificate* 1979 (Guangdong) (*Guangdongshen Guanyu Qianfa Gangao Tongbao Huixiangzheng Ruogan Wenti De Gonggao*), promulgated by the Guangdong Bureau of Public Security in 1979
201. *Regulation of Inspection of Exit and Entry Borders 1995 (PRC)* (*Chujing Rujing Bianfang Jiancha Tiaoli*), promulgated by the State Council on 1 September 1995
202. *Regulations for Encouragement of Investment by Overseas Chinese and Compatriots from Hong Kong or Macao* 1990 (PRC) (*Guli Huaqiao Gangao Tongbao Touzi De Guiding*), promulgated by the State Council
203. *Regulations for Labour Cooperation with Hong Kong Region* 1996 (PRC) (*Yu Xianggang Diqu Laowu Hezuo De Guanding*), promulgated by the State Council on 5 September 1996
204. *Regulations for the Administration on Agency Services for Self-funded Studying*

Abroad 1999 (PRC) (*Zifei Chuguo Liuxue Zhongjie Fuwu Guanli Guiding*), promulgated by the Ministry of Education and the Ministry of Public Security, and the State Administration of Industry and Commerce on 24 August 1999

205. *Regulations of Overseas Chinese Contributions or Donations* 1997 (Shanghai) (*Shanghaishi Huaqiao Juanzheng Tiaoli*), promulgated by Shanghai Municipality People's Government
206. *Regulations on Border Inspection* 1965 (PRC) (*Bianfang Jiancha Tiaoli*), promulgated by the State Council on 30 April 1965
207. *Regulations on Examination and Approval of Permanent Residence of Aliens in China 2004* (*Waiguoren Zai Zhongguo Yongjiu Juliu Shenpi Guanli Banfa*), promulgated by the Ministry of Public Security, and effective as of 15 August 2004.
208. *Regulations on Passport and Visa* 1980 (PRC) *(Zhonghua Renmin Gongheguo Huzhao Qianzheng Tiaoli)*, promulgated by the State Council 13 May 1980
209. *Regulations on the Record-keeping for Regulations and Rules* 2001 (PRC) (*Fagui Guizhang Beian Tiaoli*), promulgated by the State Council on 14 December 2001 and effective on 1 January 2002
210. *Regulations on Simplifying the Procedure of Examination and Approval of the Chinese Staff Employed in Foreign Investment Enterprises Going Abroad (or to Hong Kong or Macao)* 1993 (PRC) (*Jianhua Waishang Touzi Qiye Zhong Fang Renyuan Chuguo (Huozhe Gangao) Shouxu De Guiding*), promulgated by the Special Economic Zones Office of the State Council, and approved by the State Council
211. *Regulations on the Administration for Overseas Employment Intermediary Agencies (Amendment)* 2002 (PRC) (*Jingwai Jiueye Zhongjie Guanli Guiding (Xiuding)*), jointly promulgated by the Ministry of Labour and Social Security, the Ministry of Public Security and the State Administration of Industry and Commerce on 14 May 2002 and effective on 1 July 2002
212. *Regulations on the Administration for Overseas Employment Intermediary Agencies* 1992 (PRC) (*Jingwai Jiuye Zhongjie Guanli Guiding*), promulagted by the Ministry of Labour.
213. *Regulations on the Administration of Entry, Exit, Transit, Residence and Travel of Aliens in China* 1964 (PRC) (*Waiguoren Rujing Chujing Guojing Juliu Lvxing Guanli Tiaoli*), promulgated by the State Council on 13 April 1964
214. *Regulations on the Administration of Labour Marke*t 2000 (PRC) (*Laodong Shichang Guanli Guiding*), effective on 8 December 2000
215. *Regulations on the Administration of Skilled Personnel Market* 2001 (PRC) (*Rencai Shichang Guanli Guiding*), effective on 1 October 2001
216. *Regulations on the Administration of Travel Agencies (Amendment)* 1996 (PRC) (*Lvxingshe Guanli Tiaoli*), promulgated by the State Council on 15 October 1996
217. *Regulations on the Administrative Legislation Procedure* 1989 (PRC), promulgated by the Standing Committee of the National People's Congress on 4 April 1989, and effective as of 1 October 1990
218. *Regulations on the Administrative of Travel Agencies (Amendment)* 2001 (PRC) (*Lvxingshe Guanli Tiaoli*), amended pursuant to *Travel Agencies Administrative Measures* 1996 (PRC), promulgated by the State Council on 11 December 2001 and effective on 1 January 2002
219. *Regulations on the Procedure for Formulation of Rules* 2001 (PRC) (*Guizhang Zhiding Chengxu Tiaoli*), promulgated by the State Council on 16 November 2001 and effective on 1 January 2002.

220. *Regulations on the Procedure for the Formulation of Administative Regulations* 2001 (PRC) (*Xingzheng Fagui Zhiding Chengxu Tiaoli*), promulgated by the State Council on 16 Novermber 2001 and effective on 1 Juanuary 2002
221. *Reiteration of Strictly Forbidding of Sending Young Women to Abroad to Do Erotic Service by the Name of Working* 1997 (PRC) (*Guanyu Congshen Yanjing Yi Waipai Laowu Deng Minyi Xiang Jingwai Paiqian Nv Qingnian Congshi Seqing Fuwu De Tongzhi*), promulgated by the Ministry of Foreign Trade and Economy Cooperation. No. [1997] 803
222. *Related rules on Strengthening Examination and Approval of Exit China for Public Affairs (Extract)* (PRC) 1993 (*Guanyu Jiaqian Yingong Lingshi Chuguo(jing) Shenpi He Guanli Gongzuo De Youguan Guiding (Zhaibian)*), promulgated by the General Office of the Central Committee of Communist Party of China and the General Office of the State Council
223. *Reply of the Department of Consular under the Ministry of Foreign Affairs to Some Questions on Passport Affairs (Excepts)* 1993 (PRC) (*Waijiaobu Lingshisi Guanyu Huzhao Gongzuo De Jige Wenti De Dafu (Jiexuan)*), promulgated by the Department of Consular Affairs under the Ministry Foreign Affairs
224. *Rules Governing the Implementation of the Measures for the Administration on Agency Services for Exit and Entry for Private Affairs* 2002 (Beijing) (*Beijingshi Guanyu Shishi Yinsi Churujing Zhongjie Huodong Guanli Banfa Ruogan Guiding (Shixing)*), made pursuant to the *Measures for the Administration on Agency Services for Exit and Entry for Private Affairs* 2001 (PRC), promulgated by the Bureau of Public Security (Beijing) and the Administration of Industry and Commerce (Beijing) on 1 January 2002
225. *Rules of Providing Convenience of Enter and Residence with Senior Talents and Investors of Foreign Nationalities* 2003 (PRC) (*Guanyu Wei Waiguoji Gaochenci Rencai He Touzizhe Tigong Rujing Ji Bianli De Guiding*), jointly promulgated by the Ministry of Public Security, the Ministry of Foreign Affairs, the Ministry of Education, the Ministry of Technology and Science, the Ministry of Personnel, the Ministry of Labour and Social Insurance, the Ministry of Foreign Economic Relations and Trade, State Council Overseas Affairs Office and State Bureau for Foreign Experts in April 2003
226. *Rules of Some Matters of the Application of Inland Residents Traveling to Taiwan for Visiting Relatives* 1988 (PRC) (*Guanyu Neidi Gongmin Shenqing Qu Taiwan Diqu Tanqing Deng Wenti De Guiding*), promulgated by the Ministry of Public Security on 16 November 1988
227. *Rules of the Supreme People's Court, the Supreme People's Procuratorate, the Ministry of Public Security, the Ministry of Foreign Affairs, the Ministry of Justice and the Ministry of Finance on Implementation Measures of Forced Expelling Aliens* 1992 (PRC) (*Zuigao Renmin Fayuan Zuigao Renmin Jianchayuan Gonganbu Waijiaobu Sifabu Caizhengbu Guanyu Qiangzhi Waiguoren Chujing De Zhixing Banfa De Guiding*), promulgated by Supreme People's Court, Supreme People's Procuratorate, the Ministry of Public Security, the Ministry of Foreign Affairs, the Ministry of Justice and the Ministry of Finance on 31 July 1992
228. *Rules of the Organization Department under the Central Committee of Communist Party of China on Some Issues of Exiting Abroad or to Hong Kong or Macao of Party Member* 1981 (PRC) (*Zhonggong Zhongyang Zuzhibu Guanyu Gongchandangyuan Yinsishi Chuguo Huo Qu Gangao Diqu De Ruogang Wenti De Guiding*), promulgated

by the The Organization Department under the Central Committee of Communist Party of China on 11 September 1981

229. *Rules of the Organization Department under the Central Committee of Communist Youth League of China on Some Issues of Exiting Abroad or to Hong Kong or Macao of League Member* 1981 (PRC) (*Gongqingtuan Zhongyang Zuzhibu Guanyu Gongqingtuanyuan Yinsishi Chuguo Huo Qu Gangao Diqu De Ruogang Wenti De Guiding*), promulgated by the the Organization Department under the Central Committee of Communist Youth League of China on 21 September 1981
230. *Rules on Complaint Reporting* 1995 (PRC) (*Xingfa Tiaoli*), promulgated by the State Council on 28 October 1995 and effective on 1 January 1996
231. *Rules on Examination and Appraisal of Public Security Organs' Law Enforcement Quality* 2001 (PRC) (*Gongan Jiguan Zhifa Zhiliang Kaohe Pingyi Banfa*), promulgated by the Ministry of Public Security on 10 October 2001
232. *Rules on the Control of Intermediary Agencies for Self-funded Overseas Study* 1999 (PRC) (*Zifei Chuguo Liuxue Zhongjie Fuwu Guanli Guiding*), promulgated by the Ministry of Education, the Ministry of Public Security and State Administration of Industry and Commerce on 17 June 1999
233. *Rules on the Procedure of Handling with Administrative Cases of Public Security Organs* 2003 (PRC) *(Gongan Jiguan Banli Xingzheng Anjian Chengxu Guiding)*, promulgated by the Ministry of Public Security on 26 August 2003 and effective on 1 January 2004
234. *Some Regulations on the Reform of Current Administration of Exit and Entry* 1984 (PRC) *(Guanyu Gaige Xianxing Ruchujing Guanli Banfa De Ruogan Guiding)*, promulgated by the Ministry of Public Security on 28 November 1984, Gongfa (Jing) [84] 189
235. *Some Rules of the General Office of the Central Committee of Chinese Communist Party and the General Office of the State Council on Serious Restriction Cadres in the Departments of Party Committees and Governments Exit China* 1987 (PRC) (*Zhonggong Zhongyang Bangongting Guowuyuan Bangongting Guanyu Yange Kongzhi Dangzheng Jiguan Ganbu Chuguo Wenti De Ruogan Guiding*)
236. *Some Rules on the Implementation of Measures on the Administration of Exit and Entry Intermediary Agencies for Private Affairs (for Trial Implementation)* 2002 (Beijing) (*Guanyu Shishi Yinsi Churujing Zhongjie Huodong Guanli Banfa Ruogan Guiding (Shixing)*), promulgated by Beijing Municipality Public Security Bureau and Beijing Municipality Administration of Industry and Commerce on 1 January 2002 and effective on 1 January 2002
237. *Some Rules on the Issues of Prohibiting Aliens and Chinese Citizens from Exiting China* 1987 (PRC) (*Guanyu Yifa Xianzhi Waiguoren He Zhongguo Gongmin Chujing Wenti De Ruogan Jiuding*), promulgated by the Supreme People's Court, the People's Procuratorates, the Ministry of Public Security and the Ministry of National Security on 10 March 1987
238. *Suggestions of the Ministry of Public Security on Some Issues Concerning the Execution of Law on the Control of Exit and Entry of Citizens 1985 (PRC) and its Detailed Rules of the Implementation* 1987 (PRC) (*Gonganbu Guanyu Zhixing Zhongguo Gongmin Churujing Guanlifa Ji Shishi Xize Ruogan Wenti De Shuoming*), promulgated by the Ministry of Public Security on 19 February 1997
239. *Suggestions of National Tourism Administration Concerning the Further Checking-*

up and Rectification of Tourist Agencies 1990 (PRC) (*Guojia Lvyou Guanli Ju Guanyu Jinyibu Zhengdun He Guifan Lvxingshe De Jianyi*), promulgated by China National Tourism Administration in 1990

240. *Suggestions of the Ministry of Public Security on Relaxing the Conditions of Examination and Approval of Exiting Abroad for Private Affairs* 1984 (PRC) (*Gonganbu Guanyu Fangkuang Yinsi Chuguo Shenpi Tiaojian De Qingshi*), promulgated by the Ministry of Public Security on 11 April 1984
241. *Supplementary Circular of the State Administration of Foreign Exchange on Relevant Matters about Investing in the B Stocks by the Domestic Residents* 2001 (PRC) (*Guojia Waihui Guanli Ju Guanyu Jingnei Jumin Touzi B Gu Youguan Wenti De Bucong Tongzhi*), Huifa [2001] No. 31, 23 February 2001
242. *Supplementary Opinions of State Education Commission, the Ministry of Foreign Affairs and the Ministry of Public Security on Issuing Ordinary Passport for Private Passport for Citizens Studying Abroad Sent by the State* 1993 (PRC) (*Guojia Jiaoyu Weiyuanhui Waijiaobu Gonganbu Guanyu Wei Gongpai Liuxue Renyuan Huanling Yinsi Putong Huzhao De Buchong Yijian*), promulgated by State Education Commission, the Ministry of Foreign Affairs and the Ministry of Public Security in March 1993
243. *Urgent Announcement of Several Conspicuous Problems About Labour Export to Gulf Countries* 2002 (PRC) (*Guanyu Xiang Haiwan Guojia Paiqian Laowu Ying Zhuyi De Jige Wenti De Jinji Tongzhi*), promulgated by the Ministry of Foreign Trade and Economy Cooperation in January 2002

List of Other States and Region's Statutes

Australia

1. *Australian Citizenship Act* 1948 (Cth)
2. *Australian Migration Act* 1958 (Cth)
3. *Australian Migration Series Instruction*

Taiwan, China

4. *Enforcement Regulations of the Immigration Law* 1999 (ROC) (*Ruchuguo Ji Yimin Fa Shixing Xize*)
5. *Enforcement Regulations of the Nationality Law* 2001 (ROC) (*Guoji Fa Shixing Xize*)
6. *Enforcement Rules of the Implementation of Regulations on Passport Abroad* 1952 (ROC) (*Chuguo Huzhao Tiaoli Shixing Xize*)
7. *Enforcement Rules of the Implementation of Regulations on Passport (Amendment)* 2002 (ROC) (*Huzhao Tiaoli Shixing Xize*)
8. *Immigration Law 1999 (ROC)* (*Ruchuguo Ji Yimin Fa*)
9. *Key Points of Establishment of Review Committee of Non-permission and Banning from Exit and Entry, the Ministry of Interior (Amendment)* 2000 (ROC) (*Neizhengbu Buyu Xuke Ji Jingzhi Ruchuguo Anjian Shencha Weiyuanhui Shezhi Yaodian*)
10. *Law of Nationality* 2000 (ROC) (*Guoji fa*)
11. *Martial Act of* 1934 (ROC) (*Jieyan Fa*)
12. *Measures of Ministry of Education of Sending Overseas Students* 1943 (ROC) (*Jiaoyubu Xuanpai Liuxuesheng Banfa*)
13. *Measures of Visas of Foreign Passport* 1951 (ROC) (*Waiguo Huzhao Qianzheng Banfa*)
14. *Measures on the Administration of Exit of Military Service Person and Reservists in*

the Region of Taiwan 1957 (ROC) (*Taiwan Diqu Yinan Ji Houbei Junren Chujing Chuli Banfa*)

15. *Measures on the Administration of Seafarers in the Period of Suppression* 1954 (ROC) (*Kanluan Shiqi Haiyuan Guanli Banfa*)
16. *Operation Points of Circular of Population of Nationals Who Exited Two Years Ago and Reentry* 2000 (ROC) (*Guoren Chujing Man Liangnian Weirujing Ji Zairujing Renkou Tongbao Zuoye Yaodian*)
17. *Provisional Measures of Issuing Passport Exiting Abroad* 1929 (ROC) (*Chuguo Huzhao Zanxing Banfa*)
18. *Regulations Governing Visiting, Residence and Permanent Residence of Aliens* (ROC) 1999 (*Waiguoren Tingliu Juliu Ji Yongjiu Juliu Banfa*)
19. *Regulations of the Taiwan Province on the Registration of the Exit of the Servicemen, Government Employees, Teachers and Travelers of the Taiwan Province* 1949 (ROC) (*Taiwan Sheng Chujing Jun Gong Jiao Renyuan Ji Lvke Dengji Banfa*)
20. *Regulations on Guidance and Management on Migration Service Organizations and Their Employees* 1999 (ROC) (*Yimin Yewu Jigou Jiqi Congye Renyuan Fudao Guanli Banfa*)
21. *Regulations on Passport 2002 (ROC) (Huzhao Tiaoli*)
22. *Regulations on Permission of Exit and Entry of Nationals (Amendment)* 2003 (ROC) (*Guomin Ruchuguo Xuke Banfa (Xiuding)*)
23. *Regulations on Permission of Hong Kong Permanent Residents Enter into and Permanently Resident in Taiwan Areas (Amendment)* 2002 (ROC) (*Xianggang Aomen Jumin Jinru Taiwan Diqu Ji Juliu Dingju Xuke Banfa (Xiuding)*)
24. *Regulations on the Certificate of Overseas Chinese Identity* 2002 (ROC) (*Huaqiao Shenfen Zhengmin Tiaoli*)
25. *Regulations on the Entry and Exit in Taiwan during the Rebellion Suppression Period* 1957 (ROC) (*Kanluan Shiqi Taiwan Diqu Rujing Chujing Guanli Banfa*)
26. *Regulations on the Entry Permission of Mainland Permanent Residents to Taiwan Areas (Amendment)* 2002 (ROC) (*Dalu Diqu Renmin Jinru Taiwan Diqu Xuke Banfa (Xiuding)*)
27. *Regulations on the Entry Permission of Taiwan Permanent Residents to Mainland Areas* 1993 (ROC) (*Taiwan Diqu Renmin Jinru Dalu Diqu Xuke Banfa*)
28. *Regulations on the Entry Permission of Taiwan Permanent Residents to Mainland Areas (Amendment)* 2002 (ROC) (*Taiwan Diqu Renmin Jinru Dalu Diqu Xuke Banfa (Xiuding)*)
29. *Regulations on the Exit and Entry Means of Nationals with Registered Permanent Residence and Hong Kong or Macau Permanent Residence* 2001 (ROC) (*Jianjuyou Huji Guomin Ji Xianggang Huo Aomen Jumin Shenfenzhe Ruchu Guo Fangshi*)
30. *Regulations on the Relationship between Residents in Taiwan Areas and Mainland Areas* 1992 (ROC) (*Taiwan Diqu Yu Dalu Diqu Renmin Guanxi Tiaoli*)
31. *Regulations on the Relationship between Residents in Taiwan Areas and Mainland Areas (Amendment)* 1995 (ROC) (*Taiwan Diqu Yu Dalu Diqu Renmin Guanxi Tiaoli (Xiuding)*)
32. *Regulations on the Relationship between Residents in Taiwan Areas and Mainland*

Areas (Amendment) 2002 (ROC) (*Taiwan Diqu Yu Dalu Diqu Renmin Guanxi Tiaoli (Xiuding)*)

The USA

33. *Act of Cuban Liberal and Democratic Solidarity* 1996 (USA)
34. *Passport Act of* 1926 (USA)
35. *U.S. Code of Federal Regulations Title 22 – Foreign Relations*

Vietnam

36. *Circular of the Ministry of Interior Providing Guidance on the Implementation of Government Decree No. 24/CP dated March 23, 1995 on Entry and Exit Proceedings* 1995 (Vietnam)
37. *Circular of the Ministry of Labour, War Invalids and Social Affairs Providing Guidance on the Implementation of Decree No.07/CP dated 20 January 1995 of the Government, on Sending Vietnamese Labourers Abroad to Work for a Limited Period of Time* 1995 (Vietnam)
38. *Circular of the State Bank of Vietnam Guiding the Implementation of the Prime Minister's Decision No.61/2001/QD-TTg of April 25, 2001 on the Organization-Resident's Obligation to Sell and Right to Buy Foreign Currencies* 2001 (Vietnam)
39. *Circular of the State Bank of Vietnam Providing Guidelines on the Implementation of Governmental Decree No.63/ND-CP Dated August 17, 1998, on Foreign Exchange Management* 1999 (Vietnam)
40. *Circular on Entry, Exit, Residence and Travel Providing Guidelines on the Implementation of Decree No. 04/CP of the Government dated 18 January 1993 Stipulating in Detail the Implementation of the Ordinance on Entry, Exit, Residence and Travel of Foreigners in Vietnam 1993* and *Circular on Entry, Exit, Residence and Travel of Foreigners in Vietnam* 1993 (Vietnam)
41. *Circular on Guiding the Granting of Non-Vietnamese Nationality Certificates 1999*
42. *Circular on Prescribing the Regime of Collection, Remittance and Use Management of Fees for Granting Passports, Visas and Papers on Entry, Exit, Transit and Residence in Vietnam* 2003 (Vietnam)
43. *Civil Code of Socialist Republic of Vietnam* 1995
44. *Constitution of Socialist Republic of Vietnam* 1992
45. *Decision No. 210/QD-TTg of 27 October 1999 on the Policy Towards Vietnamese Living Abroad* (Vietnam)
46. *Decision of the Government of Vietnam on Encouraging Money Transfer of Overseas Vietnamese* 1999 (Vietnam)
47. *Decision on Carrying Cash in Foreign Exchanges and Vietnamese Dong Through Border Gates* 1999 (Vietnam)
48. *Decree of the Government of Vietnam Guiding the Execution of Expulsion Penalty* 2001 (Vietnam)
49. *Decree of the Government of Vietnam on Exit and Entry of Vietnamese Citizens* 2000 (Vietnam)

50. *Decree of the Government of Vietnam on Foreign Exchange Management* 1998 (Vietnam)
51. *Decree of the Government of Vietnam on the People's Identity Card* 1999 (Vietnam)
52. *Decree of the Government of Vietnam Prescribing the Functions, Tasks, Powers and Organizational Structure of Vietnam National Administration of Tourism* 2003 (Vietnam)
53. *Joint Circular Guiding the Granting of General Passports and Laissez-Passers to Vietnamese Nationals Overseas According to the Government's Decree No. 05/2000ND-CP of March 3, 2000 on Exit and Entry of Vietnamese Citizens* 2002 (Vietnam)
54. *Joint Circular of the Ministry of Finance and the Ministry of Labour, War Invalids and Social Affairs Guiding the Amendments and Supplements to Joint Circular No. 16/2000/ttlt-btc-bldtbxh of February 28, 2000 on Financial Regime for Vietnamese Labourers and Specialists Sent Abroad to Work for Definite Periods of Time* 2001 (Vietnam)
55. *Joint Circular of the Ministry of Finance, the Ministry of Justice and the Ministry of Foreign Affairs Guiding the Collection, Payment, Management and Use of Fees for Granting, Restoration or Relinquishment of Vietnamese Nationality and for Granting of Vietnamese Nationality Certificates or Vietnamese Nationality Loss Certificates* 1998 (Vietnam)
56. *Key Points of Establishment of Review Committee of Non-permission and Banning from Exit and Entry, the Ministry of Interior (Amendment)* 2000 (Vietnam)
57. *Law of Nationality* 1988 (Vietnam)
58. *Ordinance of Standing Committee of National Assembly on Entry, Exit and Residence of Foreigners in Vietnam* 2000 (Vietnam)
59. *Ordinance on Entry, Exit, Residence and Travel of Foreigners in Vietnam* 1992 (Vietnam)
60. *Regulation of the Ministry of Education and Training on Administration of Overseas Students in Vietnam* 1999 (Vietnam)
61. *Vietnam Provisionally Stipulating a Number of Measures to Prevent and Handle Violations in the Field of Sending Labourers and Experts to Work Abroad* 1999 (Vietnam)

List of International Instruments

1. *African Charter on Human and Peoples' Rights* 1981, enter into force on 21 October 1986, 1520 UNTS No.26, 363 OAU doc. CAB/LEG/67/3/rev.5; 21 ILM 58 (1982), AFR
2. *American Convention on Human Rights* 1969, enter into force on 18 July 1978, OAS Treaty Series, No. 36 (1969), AMR
3. *American Declaration of the Rights and Duties of Man* 1948, AMDRM
4. *Arab Charter on Human Rights* 1994, 2 month after 7 ratification or accession, 8 *Human Rights Law Journal 151 (1997)*
5. *Charter of United Nations*, entered into force on 24 October 1945, Charter of UN
6. *Concluding Document of the Vienna Meeting of January 15, 1989 CSCE*
7. *Convention on the Reduction of Stateless* 1961, enter into force on 13/12/1975, 989 UNTS 175, CRS
8. *Convention on the Rights of the Child* 1989, enter into force on 02 September 1990, 1577 UNTS 3, CRC
9. *Convention Relating to the Status Refugees* 1951, 28 July 1951, enter into force on 22 April 1954,189 UNTS 137, CSR
10. *Declaration on the Right to Leave and the Right to Return,* adopted by the Uppsala Colloquium, Uppsala, Sweden, on 21 June 1972, 1972 Uppsala Declaration on RLR
11. *Draft Declaration on Freedom and Non-Discrimination in Respect of the Rights of Everyone to Leave Any Country, including His Own, and to Return to His Country*, by Mubanga-Chipoya, E/CN.4/Sub.2/1987/10, 10 ff
12. *Draft Principles on Freedom and Non-Discrimination in Respect of the Rights of Everyone to Leave Any Country, including His Own, and to Return to His Country*, prepared by Judge Jose Ingles, UN Sales No. 64. XIV.2, UN Doc. E/CN.4/Sub.2/220/Rev.1 (1963), 1963 Ingles Draft Principles on RLR

13. *Draft Principles on Freedom and Non-Discrimination in respect of the Rights of Everyone to Leave Any Country, including His Own, and to* Return *to His Country,* adopted by the UN Sub-Commission on the Prevention of Discrimination and Protection of Minorities, Res. 2B (XV), UN Doc. E/CN. 41846 (1963), 1963 UN Draft Principles on RLR
14. *European Convention for the Protection of Human Rights and Fundamental Freedoms 1950,* enter into force on 03 September 1953, ETS No. 5, EHR
15. *European Convention on the Legal Status of Migrant Workers* 1977, enter into force on 01 May 1993, ETS No. 93
16. *European Social Charter (Revised)* 1996, enter into force on 01 July 1999, ETS No.163
17. *European Social Charter 1961,* enter into force on 26 Febuary 1965, ETS No. 35
18. *Final Act of the Helsinki Conference on Security and Cooperation in Europe* 1975, adopted on 1 August 1975
19. *General Comment No. 27 of the HRC on Freedom of movement (Art. 12):* 02/11/99., adopted on 2 November 1999 by Human Rights Committee, CCPR/C/21/Rev.1/Add.9, General Comment No. 27 of HRC on Freedom of Movement (Article 12)
20. *General Comment No.31 [80] of HRC: the Nature of the General Legal Obligation Imposed on States parties to the Covenant*, adopted on 29 March 2004 (2187 meeting) by Human Rights Committee, CCPR/C/21/Rev.1/Add.13, General Comment No. 31 of HRC on Freedom of Movement (Article 12)
21. General Conclusions No. 15 (XXX) "Refugees without an Asylum Country" in *Conclusions on the International Protection of Refugees adopted by the Executive Committee of the UNHCR Programme* (Geneva: Office of UNHCR, 1990), General Comment No. 15 of the HRC on Position of Aliens
21. *International Convention on the Elimination of All Forms of Racial Discrimination* 1966, enter into force on 04 January 1969, *660 UNTS 195,* CERD
22. *International Convention on the Protection of the Rights of All Migrant Workers and Their Families 1990,* 3 month after 20 ratification, UNGA Res. 45/158
23. *International Covenant on Civil and Political Rights 1966*, 16 December 1966, enter into force on 23 March 1976, 999 UNTS 171, ICCPR
24. *International Covenant on Economic, Social and Cultural Rights* 1966, enter into force on 3 January 1976, 993 UNTS 3, ICESCR
25. *Protocol No. 4 of European Convention for the Protection of Human Rights and Fundamental Freedom*, ETS No. 46, EHR P4
26. *Protocol Relating to Status of Refugees 1967*, 31 January 1967, enter into force on 04 October 1967, 660 UNTS 267, Protocol relating to the CSR
27. *Statute of the International Court of Justice*, ICJ
28. *Strasbourg Declaration on the Right to Leave and Return 1986*, adopted by Experts on the Right to Leave and Return on 26 November 1986, 1986 Strasbourg Declaration on RLR
29. *The Bangkok Declaration 1993*, adopted by the Asian Preparations Conference of the Second Conference on Human Rights
30. *Universal Declaration of Human Rights* 1948, UDHR, G.A. res.217 A(III), UN Doc.A/810, UDHR
31. *Vienna Convention on the Law of Treaties* 1960, adopted 22 May 1960, entered into force 27 January 1980, UN Doc. A/CONF. 39/27

Index